G000126362

The *LADY MARY'S*
Pilgrimage to
SOUTH WEST BRITAIN

– Caroline Harris –

An environmentally friendly book printed and bound in England
by www.printondemand-worldwide.com

Mixed Sources
Product group from well-managed
forests, and other controlled sources
www.fsc.org Cert no. TT-COC-002641
FSC © 1996 Forest Stewardship Council

PEFC Certified
This product is
from sustainably
managed forests
and controlled
sources
PEFC www.pefc.org
PEFC/16-33-415

This book is made entirely of chain-of-custody materials

i

www.fast-print.net/store.php

The Lady Mary's Pilgrimage to South West Britain
Copyright © Caroline Harris 2011

All rights reserved

No part of this book may be reproduced in any form by photocopying
or any electronic or mechanical means, including information storage
or retrieval systems, without permission in writing from both the
copyright owner and the publisher of the book

ISBN 978-178035-046-2

First published 2011 by
FASTPRINT PUBLISHING
Peterborough, England.

Contents

Dedication

This book is dedicated to the wise teacher WHITE EAGLE who has been my guide and mentor through this lifetime and in previous incarnations. For me, White Eagle is a trusted Master and beloved Brother of the Light. I honour him. I honour his wisdom. I honour and try to follow his pathway of Divine Love.

I have been told that White Eagle is a great Being of Light, an Initiate, one of those at the right hand of God. He has returned in more recent years in the guise of an American Indian through the mediumship of Grace Cooke, for the purpose of establishing the White Eagle Lodge and to bring to humanity something of the Mysteries of the Cosmos. He has come in on the Ray of Love to show us 'The Way' - to show us how we can ALL travel that pathway of purity and truth and love which can be manifested through our own 'Heart Rose'.

WHITE EAGLE's RESPONSE

"Dear Peace Rose it is with joy that I offer you some words now. I acknowledge with the deepest honour that you dedicate your book of wisdom to me. You and I have met in many incarnations and the one you are remembering at present is an Egyptian one. I was then a Priest, the father figure to you during your life and brought you to your initiation. The bond of those and other years never dies. So blessed one, I too honour you, for all your endeavours in this lifetime and past incarnations. I am blessing this book - these words which I know you write from the heart. May the Light of Divine perfection fill your heart with the purist love and may your life continue to become one of spiritual fulfillment. I salute you dear Peace Rose. I honour you. I bless you. And you know what I'm going to say - 'keep on keeping on' "

Acknowledgements

I first offer my blessed thanks to those from the WORLD BEYOND. To the Lady Mary, for honouring me with this sacred Mission and for being my constant loving guide during my Pilgrimage. To all the Great Beings of Light - the Masters and those from the Angelic Realms - who have formulated my Mission with Our Lady, and been my companions and protectors along the way. To my personal guides, helpers and family from the Land of Light, who have shared my Pilgrimage and made themselves known at pertinent times.

I offer a heartfelt thanks to those from THIS WORLD. To my precious family and dear friends, who have considerately curtailed their curiosity and not asked too many questions! Also, for allowing me the time and space to work, and on occasions when voicing their thoughts, have unwittingly come up with spot-on snippets of intuitive information which have turned out to be appropriate for the moment.

And FINALLY I wish to thank those good folk who towards the end of my writing have been of assistance, each in their own way. First to Nick, of AVA Images Photographers, Kingsteignton, Devon, www.avaimages.co.uk for transposing my chosen photographs to CD for computor access, and who has kindly taken my portrait for '*About the Author*'. To Barrie, of Gomango Creative, Chudleigh, Devon, www.barrie@gomangocreative.co.uk for providing computor reproductions of my hand-composed maps. To the publishers Fast Print Publishing, who have been most helpful to a novice like me, and who in publishing my book have been instrumental in bringing this sacred work into the public domain.

Preface

THIS IS MARY'S STORY - the Lady Mary - Mother of the great Initiate the Master Jesus, who was illumined by the Christ Light. She is Beloved Mary - the *'Rose in the Heart'* who represents that Divine element within every human heart. This is an account of MARY'S pilgrimage to the mystic South West of the British Isles 2,000 years ago at the beginning of the Piscean Age. She had a special Mission to fulfil.

THIS IS ALSO MY STORY - I discovered that I too, had an associated Mission to fulfil in this present day at the start of the Aquarian Age. This is the story of MY pilgrimage through the South West, as I follow in Mary's footsteps, either in the physical or on the inner planes. This is my own journey of self-discovery to the Heart of the Rose. For this short and most sacred time of my life, Beloved Mary has been an integral part of my consciousness - our lives have become so entwined.

For some while I had been told by my spirit messengers that I would write a book and my thoughts lately had turned in that direction. The work I thought would have been linked to pilgrimage, as for many years I have explored sacred sites and visited ancient churches. However, somewhere along the line, my initial plan was 'hi-jacked' by Our Lady - Mary!

WALES - ST MICHAEL'S CHURCH, TREFENTY.

It all begin in the spring of 2008, when Mary made herself known to me in Wales at the ruined St Michael Church, Trefenty, in Carmarthenshire. While travelling in the area and having looked at the map, I just KNEW I had to go in search of this ancient church. My first impression on arriving was *'I know this place.'*

After exploring the derelict church and the pilgrim graves, I sat down for a short attunement to the Light. I was astounded, as from the inner planes the **LADY MARY** spoke to me. She told me that following her escape from the Holy Land after the crucifixion, she and others were guided to Britain and landed on these ancient shores. She then said: *"BUT YOU KNOW - YOU WERE HERE - YOU WERE WITH US DEAREST SISTER."* Well that threw me. I realized then why I had the urge to journey to this sacred place. My Cosmic memory was being opened up and I was being shown a glimpse of a past life. I had picked up on Mary's presence, but was not prepared for such a revelation. The significance of her words hit me - this was so profound. I felt very blessed to have this beautiful Being of Light make this special Cosmic link. Even more disclosures were to come on a subsequent occasion in Wales, when I was informed that in that lifetime my name was **NAOMI** and that I was Mary's daughter!

Initially Mary told me that I was to keep all this close to my heart. However, as time passed I received more insights wherein Mary made it clear that I was to write this book, as she wished her story to be out in the public domain.

I was very reluctant to do so for two reasons. The FIRST - I was not sure how my intuitively received messages from Mary, or as I was to discover from other Beings of Light, would be received, due to their subjective expression which cannot be verified. The SECOND reason is that I quickly became aware that because of the personal nature of some of the words, they could appear to be feeding the personal ego, when the exact opposite is the truth. I am humbled and feel very blessed at being afforded this treasured opportunity to serve the Brethren of Light in this way. Further - I was told in no uncertain terms by the sixth century British monk and historian **GILDAS,** that I had an obligation to do so - his words: *"DO IT DEAR ONE - DO IT - IT IS YOUR DUTY. DO NOT LET WORDS BE WASTED AND KEPT TO YOURSELF - SEND THEM OUT."* Well - what could I do but obey!

These initial encounters with our gracious Lady are documented in full in the PROLOGUE.

THE SOUTH WEST OF ENGLAND

So how do my trysts with the Lady Mary in Wales connect her to the South West of Britain? It was by way of a 'chance' remark. I had returned to Wales in August 2008 in order to revisit Trefenty and to undertake my own pilgrimage to follow the *'Pathway of the Beloved'* as revealed by Megan Wingfield in her book *'The Grail Journey through Wales'*. I was staying at The Black Lion Inn in Pontrhydfendigaid as I wished to take a look at the nearby Strata Florida Abbey. Two dear people, members of the White Eagle Lodge to which I belong, had travelled quite a distance to meet with me. We were sharing a little about my present pilgrimage, when one of these lovely ladies, having read of Mary's arrival in Carmarthenshire with her family after the crucifixion (identified in the above book) said: *"I wonder what became of Mary's daughters - there must be descendents all over Wales."* I kept my counsel at Mary's request, but remembered that just a few days previously at Red Roses in Carmarthenshire, I had been told by Mary that I was one of those daughters! Then the next eye-opener. We continued chatting and I was telling them of my explorations to ancient sites such as the Merrivale Ceremonial Complex on Dartmoor in Devon, my home county, when one of the ladies suddenly came out with: *"Merrivale - Mary's Vale."* Of course - it clicked - this place name was not by chance. I then knew intuitively that Beloved Mary had been there. This opened up a raft of questions. When did she go there? Where else did Mary travel in the South West of England? Why did she visit these sacred Isles? With whom did she travel? She had already told me of her arrival in Wales after the crucifixion, thus confirming Megan Wingfield's discoveries, but I had no idea that she might have journeyed to Britain before that time.

Merrivale was to be my first visit when time allowed on my return from Wales. THIS was the connection - THIS was my start point. Gradually more and more was revealed. I was to understand that Mary DID come to the Westcountry with her daughter Naomi and the boy Jesus under the protection of Joseph of Arimathea. They landed on the south coast of Cornwall in the Roseland Peninsula and travelled around Cornwall, then on through Devon, completing their pilgrimage at Glastonbury in Somerset, staying in Druidic settlements along the way. Joseph of Arimathea an uncle of Jesus, and a tin merchant with mining interests in the South West especially throughout Cornwall, would have had intimate knowledge of the conditions and terrain of the area and therefore was the ideal guide.

THE MISSION

Mary's Mission in these sacred British Isles at the beginning of the Piscean Age was threefold. FIRST - to reactivate the ancient ATLANTIAN Temples at certain of the Druidic sites, which had been lifted into the Etheric at the time of the catastrophies eons ago. It was disclosed to me that these ancient Isles were the last remnants of the lost continent of Atlantis. SECONDLY - at other ancient Druidic sites, she was to perform a special DRUIDIC Ceremony to invoke the Light of the Cosmos in order to heal and revitalize the land. In the THIRD instance, at those Druidic Temple sites dedicated to THE GODDESS, Mary's role as High Priestess in the Egyptian Temple of Isis, was to bring a special blessing for the Sacred Feminine.

My Mission now at the beginning of the Aquarian Age as identified by Mary, was also threefold. At those sites with an Atlantean Temple in the Etheric, I was to earth this ancient Temple. Secondly, I was to re-enforce that powerful Cosmic Light at specific Druidic sites. Then - at those places dedicated to the Goddess, I was to strengthen the beautiful energies of the Sacred Feminine and bring these energies into balance with the masculine. Not much then!

THE CEREMONIES

To undertake these sacred 'tasks' I soon realized that special Ceremonies of Light would be required. This being the case, using my intuition and under Divine guidance, I prepared one Ceremony for the Atlantean Temple sites, another for the Druidic Temple sites, and a third for those holding an association with the Goddess. Some sites had two dedications so I adjusted the wording accordingly (see end of Preface for full details of the Ceremonies). It was also made clear to me that in order to enact these Ceremonial 'duties' some sites I was to visit in person whilst for others I could perform a home Ceremony.

SOME DEFINITIONS

THE ROSE IN THE HEART

Why do I refer to the Lady Mary as the *'Rose in the Heart'?* The ancient symbol of *'The Rose'* embodies the Sacred Feminine. The Lady Mary is the archetype of that Goddess energy. She is Divine Mother, the perfect wisdom and love aspect represented within the Ancient Mysteries by the Rose. The Rose is the Chalice of the Heart, which comes to full expression through personal sacrifice and attainment - what the Rosicrucian's call *'the Rose on the Cross of Matter'.* So through Earthly experience, our heart receives the love of the gentle Divine Mother which fills our whole being with deep compassion.Thus the petals of the Sacred Rose at our heart centre, open fully to absorb the Rays of the Golden Sun, and we can receive and work with the Christ Light.

WHITE EAGLE

Who is White Eagle? White Eagle is the spirit guide channelled through the mediumship of Grace Cooke. With her husband Ivan, Grace Cooke began the White Eagle Lodge in London in 1936. To this day White Eagle, whose name is symbolic of a wise spiritual teacher, guides the work of The Lodge, which is now a worldwide organization. It promotes a pathway of gentle spiritual unfoldment through meditation, service and healing. Also offered are teachings such as; the Seven Rays, the Spiritual Laws, Sacred Geometry, Pythagorean Principles, Astrology, Creativity and Sacred Sound thus adhering to the philosophies of the ancient Mystery Schools. White Eagle's incarnation as an American Indian Chief is but one of many. My association with him spans innumerable years in this life and goes back into past lifetimes. The incarnation referred to in this book is as Is-Ra, High Priest in the Temples of ancient Egypt, where he was my mentor. In contacts throughout this book White Eagle refers to me as Peace Rose, his spiritual name for me.

THE STAR

Reference is made on occasions to *'the Star'* or *'the Sun-Star'.* This is the ancient symbol of the Christ Star with which the White Eagle Lodge identifies. It is the perfect symmetry of two equilateral triangles blended as one to give the balanced Six Pointed Star, which is representative of an Initiate who has attained balance and harmony in all aspects of his/her life - *'man made perfect'* - the perfection to which we are all striving as we seek communion with God. The downward triangle indicates the Heavenly Light being directed to Planet Earth, while the upward triangle equates to us as human beings, feet firmly planted on the ground, aspiring to that higher spiritual life. Visualising the Star with the Cosmic Christ Light can be a powerful focus for healing, whether on an individual level, for World healing or healing of Mother Earth.

THE CHRIST

When this word is mentioned in the text it refers to the universal Christ Light - the Spirit of Love. It is recognized that one of the most notable vehicles for this Divine principle is the Master Jesus. When the Christ Light entered into his being, he was illumined and it was then he performed his miracles and spoke with words of the spirit. The Lady Mary when in incarnation was equally illumined at times, as were other saints and wise ones. In the Bible this Christ Light is referred to as the Holy Ghost and you will find many references of someone being *'filled with the Holy Ghost'*.

INTUITIVE INSIGHT

The words and inspirations in the text from Mary and other Higher Beings I receive intuitively. I do not consider it to be automatic writing wherein a spirit helper takes control. I am in a state of deep attunement yet conscious of my surroundings, and words just roll off my pen. It is important to say, that all the messages recounted in my composition, some which express ancient esoteric wisdom, others which simply offer confirmation, are EXACTLY as I received them except where identified otherwise. As such they are sometimes very personal, but to remove this aspect would be to destroy the very essence of their beauty and content. My replies often in the form of a blessing are similarly expressed. I make no apologies for the format adopted here, as this book is not an erudite treatise but is a work of the heart. Alongside this, some of my expressed thoughts come out of a certain knowingness - a form of inner cognizance which I cannot explain, except to acknowledge and accept that they are inspirationally received. Further and interestingly, there are times when intuitive knowledge from the Light Beings is kept from me until a future occasion - which does not always arise! You will also find within these pages anomalies with traditional thinking and perhaps with some New Age wisdom BUT it is my truth as I am witness to it.

GENDER

Words used in this work such as God, Brethren, Masters, Man etc. are not intended to be purely masculine but are inclusive of the feminine aspect. When they are communicated in this general terminology, it is because the language appears to be more in keeping with tradition or the flow of the wording seems to call for it

RESEARCH

Before beginning my journey with the Lady Mary I chose not to do any pre-reading, in order that I would not be influenced and that no preconceived ideas would colour my inspirations. Any past knowledge was I believe, deliberately withheld - hidden in the deep recesses of my mind. Any research I undertook came out of a subject being brought up during my pilgrimage.

PILGRIMAGE

For me, pilgrimage is undertaking a journey of the heart - the act of walking in purposeful fashion across the land, perhaps along an ancient trackway or to a sacred Druidic settlement. It may be strolling through a quiet woodland, across a deserted beach, alongside a slow flowing river or climbing a mountain. Each footstep is a footstep of love feeling the earth beneath my feet. As I walk, I walk with respect, fully conscious that I am moving through a living breathing landscape, the same today as it has always been. I offer a blessing to the little people who nurture the land with such dedication and joy. At Druidic sites I tune in to the magical mystical world of our ancestors. I always ask permission of the guardian to enter therein and acknowledge as I leave. A prayer, an invocation for the Light, a blessing and a small offering seal my pilgrimage.

FINALLY

This book is a precious testament to my faith and belief in the Divine Beings - the Angels and Masters - who have presented themselves to me and 'walked' at my side for the duration of my Mission. Please enjoy the journey with the Lady Mary precious Pilgrims of Light. Let it be YOUR journey of self- discovery as it has been mine. Before beginning our pilgrimage I offer you a Rose Meditation followed by a message from our beloved Lady - Mary, which I feel fully prepares me for my journey.

'TEMPLE OF THE ROSE' MEDITATION

I am sitting in my own sacred space before my little home altar, which is graced with a pink rose. I light my candle and watch as the flame flickers and stills. My 'Ohm' CD *'Ultimate Om' by Jonathan Goldman'* is playing quietly. I am in my peaceful space. I focus on the rose - this most beautiful flower of perfection - I now bring that vision into my heart centre. Gently I am being drawn up into the Temple of the Rose on the inner planes. The Temple is exquisite - rose petals of delicate pink cover the walls and the dome. My inner vision shows me an altar on which is a Golden Chalice and a translucent pink rose. The Divine essence emanating from the Rose Temple is now filling my senses. I am bathed in a rosy-pink glow and enfolded in the purist love. Mary's sacred words:

MARY

"No-one is denied access to this Temple of the Rose - to this sanctuary of the heart - it is for everyone. All that is required is pure intent and an open loving heart. As you become aware of the beautiful pink rose at your heart centre it gradually becomes ethereal and its beauty and delicacy will bring you dear ones into the Rose Temple. With your inner

vision, see the Temple walls covered with pink petals of the Rose (I was already there). *The beauty and magic of such a Temple enfolds you and encompasses you in its loving embrace. Smell the perfume of the Rose. As its essence begins to fill your nostrils and enters deep within your being, you find that you are becoming completely at-one with the Rose. It is filling your heart centre. It is encompassing your whole being, enabling you to touch the heights of perfection. The Rose IS perfection. It is the flower of the heart. It is your own Heart Rose which enables you to dwell in its purist essence - its perfect form. It IS perfection.*

The Rose as a symbol of the heart has ever been. It has been an integral part of our ancient civilizations. It was so in Lemuria, Hyperboria and Atlantis. All these civilizations have come and gone but have left their mark on this precious Planet of yours. The knowledge from the last continent to go below the seas has not been lost. It was passed on through your Egyptian and American Indian civilizations. It filtered through to ancient Greece, to Tibet, to The Andes and to many other points of power on your Earth Plane. In your sacred Isles of Britain the Light has always been there - the knowledge has always been there - BUT for a long time has been hidden. Gradually these sacred Isles are being awakened. The sleeping dragon is being roused. The knowledge and awareness is returning. You dearest one and many other Light Workers are preparing the way - 'THE WAY' and it SHALL be known. The Light WILL return to these Isles. The joy of worship, nurturing the soil, blessing and healing the land has begun. Yes - it HAS begun. This is the time for the Light to return. We welcome this dear one.

We recognize and welcome the dedication and love with which you and others of like mind open their hearts to the loving influence of the Sacred Feminine aspect of the Godhead. All must be brought into balance. The Lost Goddess is to be returned to her rightful place alongside her male counterpart. Not separate, not on a higher level as once was, BUT sharing equally the mastership as in the ancient world.

There is such a blessing pouring down to this precious Planet Earth. I see it now - the little Stars of Light - sparkling, shining out around your Planet. They are above - they are within - they are below. The Light is becoming brighter dear workers for the Light. We in the Land of Light see this Golden Age approaching. Not within the next few years or even few hundred years BUT it has begun. The turning around has begun. Your beautiful Planet WILL survive. There is much disaster talk around in the human race, but whatever actually happens, your Planet WILL SURVIVE. Know that dear ones. It is destined to once again BE that Golden World of past times. This is so important to know dear ones, because we are wishing you to constantly hold this precious Planet in the Light of His countenance. We would wish you to harbour no thoughts of disaster, which is very prevalent in your media. We would wish you only to see good and a positive future - a World of perfection filled with the purest Light energies.

The vibrations are gradually being lifted to come into line with what is needed for the New Age - the Age of Enlightenment - the Age of YOUR Enlightenment. It has begun. The minds and hearts of many visionaries and scientists are opening to new knowledge. Soon the two will become conjoined in wisdom - in their understanding of Universal Law. This will happen sooner than you think. This is beginning now. Great visionaries are coming into incarnation. Great scientists are being born. What a combination.

Scientific understanding combined with spiritual values will coalesce. This WILL happen for this is The Law. The Law of Harmony and Perfect Understanding will prevail.

Dear ones it is your right - it is your legacy - it WILL be. This is TRUTH. Bless you dear Sister of Light. Once again we offer you our most beautiful pure love essence - this essence which will fill your heart centre as that perfect rose. The 'Rose in the Heart' is there for you all dear ones. God Bless you all."

The Ceremonies

ATLANTEAN TEMPLE CEREMONY

I lay down my small white cloth. On it I put; my CANDLE, a SILVER SIX POINTED STAR and a piece of WHITE QUARTZ CRYSTAL.

I light the CANDLE and as it jumps into life I am aware of the Eternal Flame of Truth.

I visualize that great SUN-STAR symbolic of the Cosmic Christ in the Heaven World, shining its rays of Golden Light down to enfold me and this sacred place.

My WHITE QUARTZ CRYSTAL is for the Druids and is the link between ancient times and this present day.

I speak the words of: 'The Great Invocation' (source unknown).

THE GREAT INVOCATION

From the point of Light within the Mind of God
Let Light stream forth into the minds of men.
Let Light descend on Earth.

From the point of Love within the Heart of God
Let love stream forth into the hearts of men.
May Christ return to Earth.

From the Centre where the Will of God is known
Let purpose guide the little wills of men.
The purpose which the Masters know and serve.

From the Centre which we call the race of men
Let the Plan of Love and Light work out.
And may it seal the door where evil dwells.

Let Light and Love and Power restore the Plan on Earth.

I am saying: *"Blessed ones, most powerful and gracious Cosmic Beings of Light - the Angels and Archangels - our Beloved Masters. I am calling on your presence this sacred day for the work I am being asked to do. I am calling on Archangel Michael for your protection this day. I am calling in the energies of that great continent of Atlantis and the Priests and Priestess of ancient times."*

On the cloth I lay down my MERLINITE CRYSTAL with the words:

"I am calling on Merlin the great alchemist to be present and work his magic this day.'"

On the cloth I lay down my TURQUOISE CRYSTAL with the words:

"I am calling in the energies of ancient Egypt - especially I call on Is-Ra, High Priest of the old times in Egypt for your presence this day."

On the cloth I lay down my ROSE QUARTZ CRYSTAL with the words:

"I am calling in the energies of the Divine Sacred Feminine - especially I call on Beloved Mary, the Rose in the Heart to be present this day."

"I AM CALLING IN ALL THESE POWERFUL ENERGIES - NOW"

I am saying:

"Great Beings of Light - I ask that I be used as a Channel for the Light and for Healing.

Let the ancient Temple of Atlantis be brought down from the Etheric Realm where it now resides and be securely grounded on Mother Earth.

Let this Temple act as a powerful energy link between the Cosmos, our Earth Plane and the Great Crystal at the Centre of the Earth.

Let this Temple be prepared for the new vibrational energies of the Aquarian Age leading Planet Earth into the new Golden Age.

Let this Temple restore Light and Healing to this ancient site. From here let the Rays of Light shine out across these mystic British Isles making preparation for the New Jerusalem.

Let the Light from this place beam its Ray of Healing out into the World and to all Humanity."

"LET THE LIGHT SHINE...........LET IT BE DONE "

My Ceremony is complete.

I am saying: *"Oh Great Beings of Light I honour you all and I thank you for your presence this sacred day."*

I sit quietly in attunement for a short while. I now close my Physic Centres with the Equal Sided Cross of Light within a Circle of Light. I visualize this ancient symbol of protection and place it on; the crown of my head, my third eye, my throat centre, my heart, my solar plexus, my sacral centre and at the base of my spine. I visualize myself enfolded in a beautiful sphere of Golden Light. To ensure that I am well grounded I again visualize Golden Light, this time at my left foot, and spiral that Light around my body in a clockwise direction seven times to the crown of my head, then bring the Light down through my spine, through my feet and right into the Earth.

Finally I rise and take the White Quartz Crystal and the Rose Quartz Crystal and bury them at an appropriate place in this sacred site.

DRUIDIC TEMPLE CEREMONY

The wording for this sacred Ceremony is identical, except that I take out any reference to the Temple of Atlantis and insert the following in the appropriate places in the text:

1.   *"I am calling in the energies of the Priests and Elders of this ancient Druidic Temple."*
2.   *"Let this ancient Druidic Temple in this sacred place be reactivated this day."*

CEREMONY for the TEMPLE of the GODDESS

The wording for this sacred Ceremony is identical, except that I take out any reference to the Temple of Atlantis and the Druidic Temple and insert the following in the appropriate places in the text:

1.   *"I am calling in the energies of the ancient Temple of the Goddess."*
2.   *"Let this ancient Temple dedicated to the Divine Sacred Feminine be reactivated this day. Let the Love Wisdom energies of the Blessed Mother be balanced and brought into alignment with the Will and Power energies of the Beloved Father."*

PROLOGUE
Wales – First Contact

WALES - MY EARLY ENCOUNTERS WITH THE LADY MARY

My initial contact with Beloved Mary took place at the ruined ST MICHAEL CHURCH just south of Trefenty in Carmarthenshire. It was early May 2008 and I was on holiday with a Welsh friend staying in a caravan near Amroth, South Pembrokeshire. We had had an amazing week visiting ancient sites, old churches and holy wells, walking the bye-ways and pilgrim routes through the Welsh countryside. It was not until our final day that the true nature of my trip came to light. My notes of that time take up the story.

ST MICHAEL'S CHURCH, TREFENTY.

We certainly make full use of our valued time together as this is Saturday, going home day, yet we have more places on our agenda. The St Michael Church at Trefenty with its pilgrim graves is the main focus.

The ancient church is situated on one bank of the upper reaches of the River Taf in Carmarthenshire. We park up at Trefenty Farm, ask permission to leave the car, walk through the farm buildings, across a field and are standing looking down towards the estuary. I see a clump of trees and realize this little copse enfolds the church - excitement is mounting.

On reaching the gated entrance to the churchyard, which is today covered with two foot high grass, there tucked away amongst magnificent trees, is St Michael's Church. What a very special place - I am enveloped in its serene atmosphere. I feel at home and am aware of the most wonderful energies. First my friend and I look round the ruins of the church. The grey stone walls are in tact, displaying Gothic-arched stone doorways and trefoil design window frames. An old piscine and stoop are still in evidence. Small trees are growing in its midst and bright green ivy entwines around the whole, adding a mystical quality to this ancient ruin which seems still to be very much alive. The rather crumbling bell-tower accessed from the outside by a creaky old door, is home to a colony of rooks.

The Pilgrim Graves, St Michael's Church, Trefenty

Detail of a carving on a Pilgrim Grave, St Michael's Church, Trefenty

Close to the church on its south side underneath a gigantic yew tree are the pilgrim graves - how old I cannot say, yet have the impression they are well over a thousand years. There are three graves identified by ancient worked stone, fashioned to give the impression of the human body, each having a rounded head and oblong body with defined legs and feet. The headpieces have engraved on them the ancient symbol of the Equal Sided Cross of Light within the Circle of Everlasting Life. The body sections have either a Jesus cross or a rather strange depiction of a human figure with a Celtic cross. My thoughts impinge on them being Templar graves. Whooshing our way now through the long grass we reach the estuary and look out over the mud flats. There is a high wind blowing which adds to the atmosphere of this hallowed place. On the river bank we discover more ancient graves. The most poignant are those enclosed within low stone-wall edging which encompass three graves, the central one being quite tiny - obviously that of a child. Was this a family grave? Perhaps they died together as a result of an accident or plague - who knows? I leave a small offering for the departed ones.

Now I am feeling that I just have to be alone. I go back to the ruined church and sit on an ancient granite stone verbalizing the words: *"most sacred place - you most beautiful church - thank you for guiding me here Angels."* I am picking up the gentle energies of a Light Being whom I 'know' to be the Lady Mary. She has this message for me:

THE LADY MARY

"My dear pilgrim - fellow Sister of the Light - we welcome you to our sanctuary. When we arrived on these ancient shores it was here in this very spot we settled to build our little community. We had had a tumultuous journey and arrived in this safe haven. There were a few of us - a small band of seafarers - of travellers who escaped our own land to find sanctuary in this ancient Isle (I know Mary is talking of Joseph of Arimathea and others from the Holy Land). *As we trod on the earth we knelt in thankfullness at our safe arrival. Here was our settlement for some while.*

We were guided to this perfect spot by the use of The Crystal in the Bay of Carmarthen which we know dear sister you have heard about. But you know, YOU WERE HERE - YOU WERE WITH US dearest sister. More can be revealed at a later date. Dearest sister we honour you - we bless you - we thank you for your pilgrimage. You do not know yet why you were meant to be here, but you will know when it is right for you. We would like you to return to your own little sanctuary and take some time to assimilate the experiences. Yes, you will return here to this spot sooner than you think. We will travel with you - we will be waiting for you. Blessed sister go on your way now. We offer you our blessing and deepest heart love. May the love of the Divine always rest in your heart. You are our beloved sister - our fellow traveller - go in peace."

Mary draws in the air as a benediction, the Cross within the Circle and I am conscious of a quite exquisite pink rose. I am filled with emotion - tears of joy whelm up. My heart aches as I feel the sweetest love. I have come home. I am on my knees saying: *"Thank you blessed one for your welcoming words which fill me with such joy."*

As I sit here receiving these sacred words from Beloved Mary, I hear the most beautiful lilting sing-song sound - a voice seems to be calling - which I put down to perhaps two branches of a tree rubbing together in the high wind. However, when my friend who has been off doing her own thing finds me, she asks if I had been calling her because she had heard a voice! Isn't this wonderful: *"Blessed Mary I thank you for this sacred contact."* I leave a small pink quartz crystal as an offering for Mary. My dear friend realizes how emotionally affected I am with this place. I tell her nothing except that I felt I had a link with a past life. Finally to say that, St Michael was the Angelic protector of these voyagers from a far-off land. With his influence still holding in this sacred landscape, it would seem somehow appropriate that this church is dedicated in his name.

It is so difficult to tear myself away. Yet, as we retrace our steps across the field to the car in the farmyard, I know I shall be back.

RETURN TO ST MICHAEL'S CHURCH

And return I do. It is in the summer of this same year. I have booked into a B & B at Llansteffan for a couple of days at the start of my pilgrimage to follow the *'Pathway of the Beloved'*. On route to Trefenty Farm I find myself taking the little road leading towards a village called RED ROSES. Just to the south-west of the village is an ancient burial mound marked on the map as *'Tumulus'*. My friend and I discovered this earlier in the year and once again I am here. This is one of the places it is alleged the Lady Mary died and was initially buried. However, as this is a subject with no clear conclusion AND not relevant to this story, I do not propose adding to the speculation with my own personal findings. What IS pertinent is what Mary shares with me.

Today is very hot and sunny as I climb over the fence into the freshly cut cornfield. After spending some while wandering around the tumulus with my dowsing rods, I retreat to the top of the field and sit in the shade of a tree. I have questions for Mary which come from my insights and I wish for confirmation. I speak with her: *"Blessed Mary I am here - I have returned to Wales"* and the conversation goes like this:

MARY: *"Dearest one you are one of my special children of my heart. Peace be with you."*

ME: *"Was I one of your female children Mary?"*

MARY: *"Yes dearest one - your name was Naomi* (the name Naomi had come to me when I was in meditation at St Anthony's Well, Llansteffan yesterday evening) *and you were the Light of my life. I loved ALL my children but as the first female child to be born, you were especially blessed."*

ME: *"I feel my heart is overflowing beloved mother of mine."*

MARY: *"You are following the pathway which you and I and others took a long time ago and it is good that you at this time, are drawn to this experience. You will return* to your little sanctuary refreshed, revitalized and full of abounding love and peace. We shall commune with each other at a future time, but for now accept this blessing which I have shared with you, ponder on it and keep it close to your heart. I bless you dearest child of mine. Go forth now in joy, in peace and in awareness. For this is a joyful day for you my child."

ME: "I thank you beloved one. I bless you. Know that you will always be a part of my heart as we are all a part of that great heart. How blest am I. Let me open my heart to receive all that there is for me to receive."

So, a little more of this story is revealed. I am quite overwhelmed with the information. I leave an offering of a small posy of wild flowers for Mary.

Very close to Red Roses in the hamlet of Eglwys Gwmyn is the ancient CHURCH of ST MARGARET MARLOES. In the springtime my friend and I paid a visit here and it is enticing me once again. One sign of the antiquity of this church is that it dwells within a round churchyard. It has much of historical interest and many treasures, but due to limited space I will tell you of just one of those treasures. There is an age-old Ogham Stone which is kept locked away in a large box at the back of the church. A key is needed to open it which can be collected from a house opposite the church. The stone is inscribed in Latin '*Avitoria Filia Cunigni*' (Avitoria daughter of Cynin), with a similar inscription in Ogham, the ancient Irish Celtic language. Cynin a local saint to whom the church was originally dedicated, was the son or grandson of Brychan and his daughter was buried here about AD 450/500.

TREFENTY here I come - at last. On arrival at the farm I knock on the door to enquire if I may leave my car while I visit the ruined St Michael Church. The farmer has become rather puzzled as to why so many people are interested in the church and surrounding landscape. He holds me in at least a half-hour conversation, during which time I find myself walking over his land dowsing.

Energy moves in spirals and through the power of the intuitive mind, one can 'tune-in' to the ancient energies held in the landscape and receive. I help him by confirming that in his field was a Celtic village with a burial ground and that there is a cellar in an old building on his land, plus I give him an approximate date for the foundations of his house!

But, I am eager to be on my way - the little church is calling me. However, before I can leave, my farmer acquaintance has two things to disclose. One - this very morning the last Sunday of July, an annual service was held at the derelict St Michael Church. Two - someone had told him that by dowsing they had discovered St Steffan (of nearby Llansteffan) is buried under the old yew tree in the graveyard. It is good to be visiting on their annual service day but I am glad to hear the service is over and folk have gone. I shall find out about St Steffan.

From the hill the view of the copse of trees which enfolds the church is before me and my heart sings with joy once more. Steadfastly I walk the little pathway across the field and down to the Church of St Michael. Stepping into the ancient ruins, I stand within its sacred walls for some while listening to the silence of the ages. On a stone shelf are flowers left from the morning service. I am completely alone. I hear the words: *"Beloved child - welcome."* I now prepare a little altar on a large oblong stone therein, laying down a pure white cloth, a candle and a six pointed silver star. For my offerings I have a small bunch of wild flowers picked locally, a stone from Dartmoor and a beautiful shell from Llansteffan beach. Having first lit my candle, I sit in attunement, soaking up the peace and stillness. I speak with Mary: *"Beloved Mary, Joseph of Arimathea and all travellers on that voyage, I bring you blessings and the purest love. Beloved Mary, thank you for guiding me on this pilgrimage."*

MARY

"Dear dear child - once again you are welcome to our sacred place - our safe haven after our long sea voyage. I have told you much on your last visit and at Red Roses. Now you KNOW why you are on this pilgrimage. You are following the 'Pathway of the Beloved' as it is written but YOU dear child are following your heart. You are being guided to places which will help you link with your Cosmic memory - and it is good. You will learn a little more of your past at each place you travel too. For now I would wish you be still and tune in to past memories."

My inner vision shows me the Lady Mary dressed in a long brown kind of dress/habit helping to pull in a boat at the estuary edge. I now become aware of a tall Druid standing very still close to me - he holds a staff on which are Celtic symbols. It is impressed upon me that here is Joseph of Arimathea. I close my little Ceremony and blow out the candle with the words: *"Let the Light of the Christ Star bring revitalization, pure love and deep peace to this sacred place."*

Leaving the sanctuary of the church I am now standing before the pilgrim graves next to the yew tree. I offer a blessing: *"I honour you pilgrims of the past. Your physical bodies are at rest in this peaceful spot - your souls soar."* I dowse and there are approximately three hundred and fifty burials in this graveyard. The great yew is surrounded by an old stone wall originally about three foot in height, but now in a ruinous state. Confirmation is given me that St Steffan is indeed buried here. After his burial the wall was built, then the sacred yew tree was planted as a memorial and indicator of the position of his body, which I understand for some reason had to be kept secret. Finally I take a saunter round the graveyard. The long grasses and high winds of the spring have given way to well cropped grass and stillness on this beautiful summer's day. For a short while I sit on a seat looking through the trees at the estuary reflecting on events of my day. I know I will have to leave soon and am reluctant to do so, but the sacred memories will remain within my heart.

Back at the farm my farmer 'friend' is hovering, so I tell him that I did dowse and could confirm that St Steffan IS buried under the yew. He tried prodding me for more information still very puzzled at the popularity of this little derelict church on his land. All I said was that people nowadays were interested in our ancient heritage and perhaps felt inclined to seek out the quiet sacred places.

LLANSTEFFAN, THE CHURCH AND HOLY WELL

Yesterday I arrived at Llansteffan. Megan Wingfield in her book '*The Grail Journey Through Wales*' (Page 157) tells us: '*I believe that Joseph of Arimathea and Mary, Jesus's mother, reached land on the sands near what is now Llansteffan in Carmarthen Bay. I had previously 'seen' their ship in my meditation, entering the bay.*' It is my assertion that from this initial landing place, they travelled up-river in small row boats to the site of the now St Michael Church. Here the little party '*settled to build our little community*' - Mary's words. In time they journeyed on through Wales to eventually make a home in Anglesey. I am to learn later that as Naomi, Mary's daughter, I travelled throughout Wales with a Druidic Priestess called Mair teaching the Celtic Christian message of devotion, love and service. I ponder on Mary and her family's journey which took them to Britain after the crucifixion. First, the escape from the Holy Land into Egypt with constant fear of discovery, followed by a hazardous sea voyage. They had protection on all levels but their anxiety must have been very real. As Mary herself told me at the St Michael Church on my first visit: '*As we trod on the earth we knelt in thankfullness at our safe arrival.*'

The 'Thanksgiving Window' at Llansteffan Church

I am at the CHURCH OF ST YSTYFFAN in Llansteffan. I have been here before but this time it has a more profound meaning. There has been a church on this site since the sixth century, the original rough structure probably built by St Steffan himself. From the heat of the day and busyness of the little village, I step into the cool stillness of this delightful little church. Once again as at the Eglwys Gwmyn church, there is much of historical interest, but I shall stick to the key features which are relevant to my story. The modern stained glass *'Thanksgiving Window'* over the altar designed and made by John Petts, is most striking and for me a welcome tribute to Our Lady. The overall vision is of rose-pink luminosity. Each tiny section of glass depicts ancient symbology or images of the natural world, of which the rose predominates. At the apex are three large inter-woven circles representing The Trinity from which flow the other beautiful stained glass work. The delicate beauty of this window renders me quite speechless. Another gem is a full length statue of the Madonna and Child set on a plinth. It is sculptured from a single yew tree by John Talbot and its mellow tones are so appealing. It is a beautiful expression of Beloved Mary. In the quiet sanctuary of the little church I receive a blessed welcome from St Steffan which ends: *"………this is hallowed ground - this is sacred to The Beloved."* His precious words are followed by a compassionate acknowledgment of my presence from the Lady Mary, whom I 'see' wearing a blue robe.

On this most lovely of summer evenings I begin my walk to ST ANTHONY'S HOLY WELL. I have undertaken this pilgrimage on two previous occasions, but none so special as today. Leaving the village of Llansteffan, the narrow road leads into woodland, where a little pathway eventually runs down to Scots Bay on the River Towy, which is an extension of Llansteffan beach. The large expanse of fine white sand laid out before me brings to mind a picture of the voyagers coming in to land on these shores 2,000 years ago. Shoes and socks come off and I delight in the feel of the soft warm sand between my toes as I run down to the waters edge. The sea rippling on the shoreline is sparkling in the early evening sunshine. I splash my way across the beach collecting some beautiful seashells as I go. Now at the top of the bay, with my footwear back on, from St Anthony Cottage just below Lord's Park hill, I walk up the lane until I reach an old narrow door in a high stone wall, which indicates the entrance to St Anthony's Well. Pushing the door open with difficulty I realize that all is very overgrown, indicating to me that it has been a while since anyone has been here.

I step into a little secluded haven, words issuing from my mouth: *"As I enter your sanctuary I come in peace and love."* The sun has left this little shrine by this time in the day and my eyes need to adjust to the semi-darkness. Immediately in my view-line set in a triangular stone frame is a small statue of St Anthony, his head haloed with a Celtic cross. At his feet are a hare, an otter and a squirrel no doubt representative of his hermit status. With a blessing I place a few wild flowers within the folds of his tunic. A stone wall plaque tells me that *'St Anthony of Egypt (c.251-256) the first Christian hermit, had a powerful influence in the Celtic church in South Wales. According to tradition, a Welsh hermit Antwyn (Anthony), who had taken the name of his great Egyptian predecessor, settled near this spot probably in the sixth century. It is probable that he used water from the well to baptize converts to Christianity.'*

Statuette at St Anthony's Well, Llansteffan

St Anthony's Well today is dried up - a rather sad reflection of its past glory when its refreshing waters would have quenched the thirst of many a pilgrim. I pour some water from Lustleigh Cleave at the edge of Dartmoor in Devon, which I have brought with me, onto the dry earth saying: *"Blessed St Anthony I offer you this sacred water from the spring in Lustleigh Cleave. May this help the waters to flow freely and pure here once more."* I lay down my offerings of a beautiful leaf and some purple heather from Dartmoor. I light a candle and voice *'The Great Invocation'* then sit in quiet attunement. I hear:

ST ANTHONY

"Blessed pilgrim you are most welcome to my Holy Well. It was here that the purist of water was drunk in my time. It was here that the blessing of healing was offered. Many a pilgrim passed this way. Enjoy dear pilgrim. I thank you for your offerings especially for the water from your precious Dartmoor. It is recognized and it is accepted with special thanks - bless you. (I am feeling the presence of Mary) *- yes, the beloved Mary was here before my time. She brought the Light into Britain here after the crucifixion and shared her visions of 'The Way' with all with whom she came into contact. She is truly a blessed Lady."*

I also receive from St Anthony, confirmation of Mary's landing on these shores and that she will be my guide on my forthcoming pilgrimage through Wales. I am saying: *"I humbly offer myself in service to all humanity. I rededicate myself to the Light.*" As I blow out my candle I see the Holy Light radiating from this place out unto the mystic Isles of Britain. I also receive a few special words from Beloved Mary.

It is the following day and I just have to return to this Holy Well before leaving for Trefenty. I am sitting quietly in the little sanctuary when I sense another presence - this time it is Gildas. I wonder what he has to say:

GILDAS

"*Christianity is but one thread of a Universal Religion. The Celtic form of Christianity is the pathway you are following at this time. BUT don't forget dear one - IT IS JUST ONE PATH on the road to ultimate enlightenment. And - what is enlightenment? It is when the soul - the spirit - is so attuned to the finer ethers that it has no need for the coarseness of a physical body. Of course there are occasions when an Enlightened One chooses to return to the Earth Plane and inhabit a physical body for the purpose of the future enhancement of humanity. Such a one was our dear and beloved Master Jesus who touched the Earth for a very short precious time in order to bring in the Light and BE that Love, and perform what are now called miracles. But do not forget that miracles are happening all the time. Miracles are a part of everyday life. You dear pilgrim have witnessed miracles in YOUR everyday life - and you know this! Miracles do not have to be powerful expansive happenings. Miracles can be little events and experiences which can touch the heart and heal the heart and mind - indeed heal all the subtle bodies. You understand this dear one but we would wish that you pass this message on.*"

Gildas continues with a lot of personal stuff which is not appropriate here but which include the rather firm words reported in 'The Preface' that I must do my duty and write my book! He closes with: "*May God's blessing be with you at all times. May the blessings of the Saints of Old and the Masters of Light guide and protect you on your pilgrimage - Amen.*"

I thank Gildas for his welcome message.

Before I leave South Wales, I must make mention of the plethora of place names associated with Mary and the Holy Land evidenced in the landscape, which could add substance to her being in this area all those years ago. Looking at the Ordnance Survey map I count over thirty, some of which I now make note. Going north and west from Trefenty we have Red Roses, West Rose, Rhos (Rose) Goch, Hebron, Rhos-Fawr, Hermon and Rhos Hill. Around Llansteffan there is Ffynnon Fair (St Mary's Well), Lord's Park and St Anthony's Well. In the town of Carmarthen is St Mary's Church and Heol Santes Fair (St Mary's Street) where a rather ugly modern building stands on the site of the original St Mary Church. Finally the east of Carmarthen offers up Rosamon, Bethlehem, Salem and another Hermon.

Now we are up to date, I can address Mary's sacred Mission in the South West of Britain some twenty odd years earlier.

Introduction to the South West

MY PLAN OF ACTION

I begin my pilgrimage with the Lady Mary through the South West of England, with the premise that 2,000 years ago, she DID come to the mystic Isles of Great Britain with her blessed son Jesus and her daughter Naomi, under the protection of Joseph of Arimathea, her brother. For Mary and her family, the journey through ancient Dummonia (Cornwall, Devon and Somerset), was undertaken either on horseback along ancient trackways, or by boat via the river network and at sea around the coastline. At this, the start of my Mission with Beloved Mary, I know of no written evidence of Our Lady having visited the South West, though visits by Jesus are widely documented. Having said that, as I proceeded, I did come across a tradition handed down verbally through the tin mining fraternity, which tells of Joseph of Arimathea bringing Mary and the boy Jesus to Cornwall - perhaps this pilgrimage. I have also been given to understand that Anna, Mary's mother, was a Celtic princess from Cornwall. If this was so, it is quite feasible that excursions from the Holy Land might have been made over the years to meet with family. Plus, when I arrived in Glastonbury at the end of my Mission, I did hear rumour that the Mother of Jesus had been to this sacred place.

We already know the reason for Mary's pilgrimage to the South West of Britain - to revive the Cosmic Light at ancient sites. But what of Jesus and Naomi. For Jesus, this journey held significance for any pilgrimages which were to come in the future with Joseph and later with Mary Magdalene. For Naomi, her destiny was to tread the ancient soil of Britain and make contact with Mair her future travelling companion in Wales after the crucifixion.

For ease of comprehension, I have chosen to divide Mary's pilgrimage into three main sections; Part I CORNWALL, Part II DEVON, Part III SOMERSET. At the beginning of each county I will give an INTRODUCTION plus detail of MARY'S JOURNEY with a MAP.

I shall embark on a series of pilgrimages which turn out to be between one and four days. As living pilgrimages, the written word reflects my thoughts and insights of the moment, and combine with inspirational words from Mary and other Beings of Light. My intention is to visit in person each of the ancient Temple sites on Mary's pilgrimage wherever possible - where this is not, I shall make the link through attunement. My only regret come the end, is that I could not walk each footstep of Mary's journey in actuality - this would have been an undertaking of many years, which time I do not have. As far as I can I shall travel in a logical order, first making pilgrimage to Cornwall, then on through Devon and finally into Somerset. However, on my return from Wales, before beginning my journeying with Mary in Cornwall, I was impressed to visit some local sites in Devon; Merrivale Ceremonial Complex, Hembury Castle and Buckfast Abbey. Then a stay with family in Somerset took me to its north coast where I explored Kilve, Holford and the surrounding area. Except for a brief insight as to a connection with Merrivale discovered in Wales, I did not know in advance that Mary had visited any of these places. In retrospect I realize that even at this early stage in my journeying with Beloved Mary, she was beginning to influence my decisions and guide my actions. My experiences and the intuitive messages received at these locations, opened up for me many insights and much information as to Mary's Mission, some of which was quite puzzling at the time but which became clearer as I progressed. Any such discoveries are documented in their rightful place in Mary's travelling therefore kept in context. Subsequent findings which are linked, will be referenced accordingly throughout the narrative.

CHARTING MARY'S JOURNEY

The exercise of charting Mary's route proved to be challenging and at times somewhat daunting! In the first instance I opened up a map of South West Britain and my eye was drawn to the Roseland Peninsula in Cornwall. I stared at this area intently when suddenly my intuition told me - of course - the ROSELAND PENINSULA - 'ROSE-LAND' - THIS is where 'Mary the Rose' landed. Further, I 'KNOW' it was at PLACE in St Anthony-in-Roseland on the Peninsula. This revelation - this eureka moment - was to be one of many similar experiences on my journeying with Mary: *"Thank you Mary beloved one - bless you."*

Following this initial discovery and after my first pilgrimage to Cornwall which was taken on trust one step at a time, I was in no doubt that before I continued with my activities, I had to accurately chart Mary's journey through Cornwall. My 'equipment' for this fascinating task was to be a map, my precious pink quartz dowsing crystal, my intuition and a 'fine tooth-comb'! I had put aside a 'Map Day' which turned out to be a 'Map Week'! To begin, I lit my candle and sat quietly, tuning into the energies of Mary, asking for her guidance, and received a beautiful response.

The day ran away with me. It was spent pouring over $1\frac{1}{4}$ inch to the mile Ordnance Survey maps of Cornwall laid out on the floor of my sitting room. I plotted a little of Mary's journeying on the Roseland Peninsula, into its Hinterland and the east coast of the Lizard Peninsula. By 3.00 pm I was becoming 'goggled-eyed'. The sun was shining, so I headed out for a short walk through my local woods to the estuary close to where I live on the south coast of Devon. There is nothing like a bit of fresh air and change of scene to blow the cobwebs away. On my return, cup of tea in hand, I continued.

The following day and for the rest of the week I 'carried on charting' by the end of which I became overwhelmed with the sheer enormity of my Mission with Mary, especially as more details of the pilgrimage were coming to light. Hopefully I am old enough (that's a yes), and wise enough (not sure about that one), to view this from a higher perspective and NOT PANIC! I decided to put aside time for an attunement and make the link with the Higher Beings. I knew that this connection would bring me back to my still centre and clear my mind. I lit a candle and sat before my little home altar. Beloved Mary came in very close and had obviously 'picked up' on my inner thoughts and was aware of my dilemma:

MARY

"Dearest child we KNOW. We UNDERSTAND. We are so happy dearest one with your insights and how you are going about your 'work'. As you are now realizing there is much to do and not perhaps quite as you at first thought. HOWEVER it is good. The way forward is planned by the Cosmic Beings. I am their instrument dearest sister as much as you are. We are ALL working to bring that sacred Light back to re-energize these British Isles. We each have a role to play. Just carry on using your intuitive recollection and all will be well. We do know that you have much to do dear sister, but you WILL do it. It is decreed from the highest levels of Universal Memory. This story - MY story - WILL be told and you will be that instrument to take the knowledge and insight into the public domain. We bless you dear Sister of Light. As your dear White Eagle might say 'keep on keeping on' and all will be well. My heart of the sacred rose is within your being. Let its pure vibrations and peaceful energies fill your every sense. Smell its perfume - bathe in its very essence - be aware of its pure energies. For it is a glorious expression of the purist love. Thank you for making contact in this way. You will feel revived and at peace. God bless you my child."

What can I say? Once again I am receiving uplifting and wise words from Mary. I thank her: *"Oh Mary my beloved one, I thank you for this opportunity to serve and to realize the joy and wonder of it all. Let me always remember that place of perfect peace - the Rose in the Heart - where all things are possible."*

Eventually I did succeed in charting Mary's pilgrimage through Cornwall, and discovered which of the ancient sites housed a Druidic Temple, which were dedicated to the Goddess and which had an Atlantean Temple in the Etheric. I embarked on the same exercise at the beginning of my pilgrimage through Devonshire and then Somerset, where I also learnt of a Hyperborean Temple in the Etheric at Glastonbury. Putting together all my findings, I could see clearly that Mary had done quite a lot of weaving about in Cornwall yet had taken a more direct route through Devon and Somerset. Why was this I queried? The answer came, that by following the path she did, it enabled her to visit the key sacred centres in the South West where the Cosmic Light could be directed to the Earth and to the Great Crystal at its core, thus impregnating our precious Planet with renewed vibrational energies.

Full details of Mary's pilgrimage through the mystic South West of Britain is documented in *'MARY'S JOURNEY'* for each county. In that text I have highlighted the Druidic settlements where Mary stayed and identified the nature of the specific sites where a sacred Ceremony was enacted.

A BRIEF SYNOPSIS OF MARY'S JOURNEY THROUGH THE SOUTH WEST

Mary landed in the Roseland Peninsula in the south of CORNWALL and her travelling in that area included a sea crossing to the Lizard Peninsula. After taking a boat over the River Fal she journeyed overland through West Cornwall until she reached its furthermost tip - Cape Cornwall. On arrival she first took a trip to the Isles of Scilly, followed by a comprehensive pilgrimage around The Cape. Her journeying then took her along the coast of North Cornwall, with an excursion inland to Castle-an-Dinas, before returning to the coast at the Camel Estuary. From there Mary went east across the county to eventually climb to Bodmin Moor. She rode north over open moorland to the coast once again, this time for a sea trip to Hartland. Now in DEVON, Mary travelled south through West Devon to Brent Tor before turning east to traverse the wild expanse of Dartmoor. The final leg of Mary's pilgrimage through Devon, was directly north through Mid Devon. Crossing the border into SOMERSET, Mary reached the heights of Exmoor and on to the North Somerset coast at Porlock for the next stage of her journey. From here she went by both sea and land to reach The Quantock Hills. Finally her pilgrimage took her across the Quantock ridge, through the Somerset Levels to Glastonbury.

CEREMONIAL TEMPLE SITES

CORNWALL

1.	Place Sacred Hill	Atlantean
2.	Cow-y-Jack	The Goddess/Atlantean
3.	Veryan Castle	Atlantean
4.	Golden Fort	Druidic
5.	Cowlands	The Goddess/Atlantean
6.	Carn Brea	Atlantean
7.	Tolcarne Wartha	Druidic
8.	St Michael's Mount	Druidic
9.	Men-an-Tol	Atlantean
10.	Portreath	Druidic
11.	Castle-an-Dinas	Atlantean
12.	The Hurlers	Druidic
13.	Dozmary Pool	Atlantean

DEVON

1.	Brent Tor	Druidic
2.	Merrivale	Atlantean
3.	Hembury Castle	Atlantean
4.	Hound Tor	Druidic

SOMERSET

1.	Cow Castle	The Goddess
2.	Culbone Hill	Atlantean
3.	Glastonbury Tor	Hyperborean

PLACE NAMES

While I was undertaking the exercise of plotting Mary's journey through the South West, I became conscious of a predominance of place names in the landscape with association to her. These would either be as **MARY** in the form of 'Mary', 'Merry', 'Mara', 'Maer' (possibly a derivation of Mair, Welsh for Mary) etc. A few examples are; Marazion, Mary Tavey, Merryfield and Maer itself. Further expression of Mary would be in the word **ROSE** incorporated in place names as 'Rose' or 'Ros'. Again some examples; Roscassa, Roseudgeon and Rose Hill. Then there is **HEART** as in; Hartland, and Hart Tor and **HOLY** as in; Holwell Lawn and Holyford. A second interesting discovery were the sheer numbers of names with a **BIBLICAL** connotation for instance; Port Isaac, Temple, Paradise and Goonzion. Alongside these, were many names with **DRUIDIC** connections; Oke(Oak)hampton, Drew(Druid)steignton and Ash(Ash)burton. Then there were those related to **THE GODDESS** and the Sacred Feminine such as; Cowlands, Cow-y-Jack and Harepath. Finally, even links with ancient **EGYPT** came to light with places such as; Lion Rock and Tye (mother of Akhnaton).

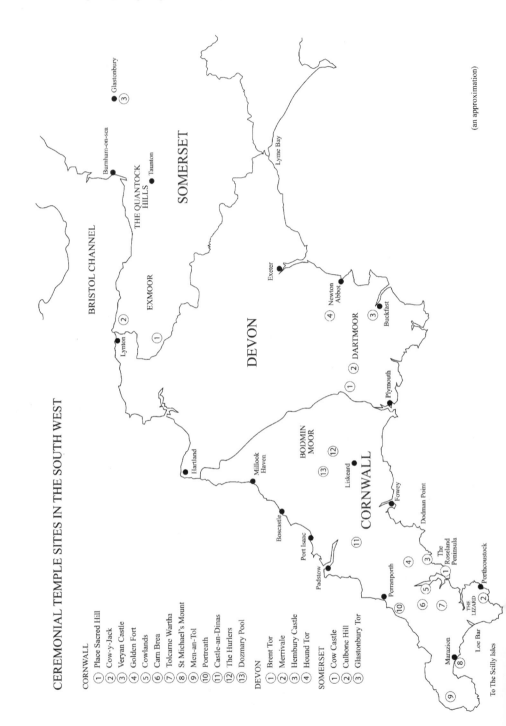

CEREMONIAL TEMPLE SITES IN THE SOUTH WEST

CORNWALL
1. Place Sacred Hill
2. Cow-y-Jack
3. Veryan Castle
4. Golden Fort
5. Cowlands
6. Carn Brea
7. Tolcarne Wartha
8. St Michael's Mount
9. Men-an-Tol
10. Portreath
11. Castle-an-Dinas
12. The Hurlers
13. Dozmary Pool

DEVON
1. Brent Tor
2. Merrivale
3. Hembury Castle
4. Hound Tor

SOMERSET
1. Cow Castle
2. Culbone Hill
3. Glastonbury Tor

(an approximation)

Part I – Cornwall

Introduction to Cornwall

The Lady Mary with Naomi, Jesus and Joseph of Arimathea landed on Cornish soil in the Roseland Peninsula after their long sea voyage from the Holy Land. They travelled extensively in Cornwall and during their pilgrimage they stayed at many Druidic settlements. A full resume of their journey is detailed in *'MARY'S JOURNEY - CORNWALL'*. As a reminder, Mary had a sacred Mission to fulfil. She was to revitalize any Atlantean Temple in the Etheric Realm and re-energize the Cosmic Light at Druidic Temple sites and those dedicated to the Goddess. A point of interest is that there were occasions when she and Naomi travelled separately from Jesus and Joseph. Joseph as the owner of tin mines in Cornwall wished to inspect his mining operations and would sometimes take the boy Jesus with him. I shall identify these instances when we reach them.

In order to follow Our Lady's journey through Cornwall and engage in her sacred Mission I undertook four pilgrimages. One in the Autumn of 2008, the other three between January and April of the following year. As mentioned, on return from my first pilgrimage I was able to chart Mary's journeying around Cornwall, gradually building up a picture of the Temple sites where she and her family stayed. Alongside this I learnt of those places where she wished me to reactivate the Cosmic Light or earth an ancient Atlantean Temple. I was also made aware of the sites where I was to pay personal homage and those where I could enact a Ceremony from my home sanctuary. In addition to this, in the privacy and comfort of my own home, I could type up my notes, research any topic which had arisen, prepare my Ceremonies and do my attunements, which often gave way to insights from Mary and other Light Beings. So those early weeks were exceedingly busy, brought much insight and were a foretaste of what was to come.

My initial pilgrimage to Cornwall began at Place in St Anthony-in-Roseland after which I headed down to Cape Cornwall. I booked my accommodation - two nights at Boswinger Youth Hostel which is about ten miles east of the Roseland Peninsula and two nights at Penzance Youth Hostel in The Cape. Before I left Devon apart from starting in the Roseland Peninsula, I had no preconception of where I would be asked to go but my trust in Mary's guidance was sacrosanct. On my short pilgrimage much to my surprise, or was it so surprising, I was to find myself in some of the significant places of her journeying all those years ago. It was while I was in Penzance that I received direct communication from Mary with a specific request to visit Men-an-Tol Druidic settlement, where she wished me to earth an ancient Atlantean Temple. By the time of my second trip to Cornwall I knew in advance that I was to earth a Temple from Atlantis at Carn Brea near Redruth. With this in mind I booked into a B & B at the little village of Rosgroggan close-by. During my next excursion to Cornwall my criteria was to enact another Atlantean Ceremony this time at Castle-an-Dinas, which is located approximately twelve miles east of Newquay. I performed the sacred Ceremony on the first day of my pilgrimage. After this I drove to Treyarnon Bay Youth Hostel on Cornwall's north coast, where I had organized a stay for a couple of nights. This proved to be the perfect place from which to explore the Camel Estuary. For my final pilgrimage I was to base in Boscastle, where the youth hostel is situated right on the harbour. On this occasion I was asked to conduct two Ceremonies on Bodmin Moor, one for the Druidic Temple of The Hurlers and the other for Dozmary Pool which held an Atlantean Temple in the Etheric. These sacred acts accomplished I then took the opportunity to visit some special places in the area.

In my 'INTRODUCTION TO THE SOUTH WEST' I scanned out a few place names I discovered which were relevant to Mary and linked subjects. Since then I have studied the map even more closely, and have found over one hundred names of similar significance in Cornwall alone - far too many to list. However, you may wish to seek them out for yourselves. To get you started I will give you a few names in the approximate order of Mary's journey; St Just-in-Roseland, Mount Hermon, Rosevallon, Cowlands, Salem (Jeru-salem) Marazion, Roskear Croft, Merry Maidens, Sancreed, Jericho Farm, Rosevidney, Lady Downs, Rejerrah, Camelford, St Merryn, Jesus Well, Port Isaac, Rosecraddock, Bethany, St Annes, Herod's Foot, Mount Ararat, Holwood, Lord's Park and Maer.

Evidence of Celtic living and Druidic worship are to be found right across this county with an abundance in Cape Cornwall. There are ancient monuments of all descriptions; settlements, cromlechs, standing stones, quoits, chambered tombs, fogous, villages, stone circles and so forth, which stand majestically within the present day landscape, giving indication of Cornwall's antiquity and sacred heritage.

The past will come alive for the dedicated pilgrim of today, who may wish to travel the old paths through this ancient land. My own pilgrimages to Cornwall with Beloved Mary, allowed me to visit some of those sacred sites of my past life as Naomi, and to revisit places of my youth in this incarnation. Each mystical place - each sacred encounter - contributed to the gradual unfoldment of my Mission with Mary and brought for me increasing feelings of gratitude and humbleness.

Mary's Journey - Cornwall

CHAPTER 1 THE ROSELAND PENINSULA

PLACE SACRED HILL - ATLANTEAN Home Ceremony

The beginning for Mary, Jesus, Naomi and Joseph of Arimathea was their arrival in Cornwall at Place in St Anthony-in-Roseland where they stayed at a Druidic settlement. On **PLACE SACRED HILL** was a Druidic Tree Temple with an Atlantean Temple in the Etheric. After the Atlantean Light Ceremony enacted by Mary, Joseph with Jesus left Mary and Naomi as Joseph wished to attend to his mining interests further west and north. These two journeyed by boat via Carrick Roads, up Restonguet Creek and the Carnon River, to eventually arrive at the settlement of Carn Brea, where Mary and Naomi joined them at a later date. During this time of separation, Mary and her daughter had the support and guidance of their Druid companions. Still in the Roseland Peninsula, they left Place and embarked on a journey up the Percuil River to St Just-in-Roseland, then on to a settlement a little to the east of **ROSCASSA**. From here they went overland through Rosevine leaving by sea from Porthcurno across Gerrans Bay to land at Carne Beach.

CHAPTER 2 THE LIZARD PENINSULA.

COW-Y-JACK - ATLANTEAN & THE GODDESS Home Ceremony

While Mary and Naomi were staying at Place they were to visit the Lizard Peninsula on a separate pilgrimage. They took a boat across Falmouth Bay to land at Swanpool beach on the east coast, and went across country through Penrose Farm and Rosemerry Farm to a settlement south of **MAWNAN SMITH**. They then travelled south to Durgan on the Helford River, followed by a short boat trip around Dennis Head and into the mouth of a little estuary, where they made land at Gillan Harbour. They continued their journey in a southerly direction over Roskridge Beacon to a Druidic Atlantean Temple site dedicated to the Goddess at **COW-Y-JACK**. Here Mary's role was twofold. One was to reactivate the ancient Atlantean Temple in the Etheric, and two, as the archetype of the Sacred Feminine, she was to bring the Goddess energies into focus through a special blessing. Subsequent to this, both Mary and Naomi made their return journey to the Roseland Peninsula. They passed through Rosnithon to the coast at Porthcoustock then across the water to Place.

CHAPTER 3 INTO THE HINTERLAND

VERYAN CASTLE - ATLANTEAN Home Ceremony
GOLDEN FORT - DRUIDIC Home Ceremony

Reconnecting to Carne beach, Mary and her daughter made a brief overland journey to **VERYAN CASTLE.** Once again a sacred Ceremony was enacted to revitalize an Atlantean Temple. After this they returned to the coast and took a short sea trip around Nare Head, across Veryan Bay, to reach a settlement high up on **DODMAN POINT,** which is identified as a fort on the map. After a short stay here, Mary and Naomi left by sea for Porthluney Cove near Caerhays, and thence up river to Tubbs Mill. Then followed a journey to the settlement of **ROSEVALLON**. From here they travelled north through Tregony and by river to Golden Mill, before climbing up to **GOLDEN FORT** Druidic settlement. At this ancient site Mary was instrumental in invoking the Cosmic Light. Finally in this area, their travelling returned them to Golden Mill and down-river past Tregony to a settlement a little to the south of what is now **BORLASE WOOD**.

CHAPTER 4 ACROSS THE FAL

COWLANDS - ATLANTEAN & THE GODDESS Home Ceremony
CARN BREA - ATLANTEAN Ceremony on site
TOLCARNE WARTHA - DRUIDIC Home Ceremony

After Borlase Wood, Mary and Naomi left the Roseland Peninsula and its Hinterland. They crossed the River Fal close to the now King Harry Ferry to **COWLANDS** settlement on the opposite bank. Cowlands had a Temple dedicated to the Goddess and an Atlantean Temple in the Etheric. The ancient site was situated at the head of a creek about a mile inland. Mary reactivated the Atlantean Temple and offered a sacred blessing for the Goddess. After the Ceremony she and Naomi went up the River Fal, into the Truro River, to link with the Kenwyn River at Truro. This river took them north-west to a settlement south of **ROSEWORTHY**. They then travelled west through Salem to **CARN BREA**. It is here they met with Joseph and Jesus after much travelling by both parties. They all participated in a Cosmic Light Ceremony for the ancient Atlantean Temple. Once again their ways parted. Mary and Naomi headed south, across Nine Maidens Down to stay at **TOLCARNE WARTHA** settlement. At this site they made contact with Anna, Mary's mother, whom I learnt lived close-by, having returned to her homeland from the Holy Land. Following a Druidic Ceremony farewells were said, after which Mary with Naomi continued south to Hendra and on via Trewennack to Helston. Their journey took them through Loe Valley, down-river to land at Penrose, then to a settlement west of **ST ELVAN,** where once more they caught up with Joseph and Jesus.

CHAPTER 5 WEST TO THE CAPE

MARAZION (ST MICHAEL'S MOUNT) - DRUIDIC Home Ceremony

MEN-AN-TOL - ATLANEAN Ceremony on site.

Leaving **ST ELVAN** the journey which Mary, Naomi, Jesus and Joseph undertook led them further into West Cornwall. They made their way back to Penrose for Loe Bar, where the river flowed out onto open land, as in Mary's time there was no bar. Also in those days the sea was further out at this point. therefore their journey to Pra Sands was over land. From here they went inland to the settlement at **MEMI.** After a short stay Mary and her family journeyed via Rosudgeon to a Druidic settlement at **MARAZION.** Opposite Marazion is **ST MICHAEL'S MOUNT** which housed a Druidic Temple of Light. I am told Mary did visit St Michael's Mount riding through the then forested terrain, where she carried out a sacred Ceremony of Light. Leaving Marazion the little party travelled west across land (now sea) into Cape Cornwall arriving at what is now Lamorna Cove, but which in Mary's day was the outlet of a huge river. They travelled up-river to the Druidic settlement of **MERRY MAIDENS.** This time it was Joseph alone who left the group for his business ventures.

Now it gets interesting. Mary, Jesus and Naomi, went back to the coast to take a journey first on horseback, then by boat across to The Scilly Isle which was one island 2,000 years ago and was the last remnants of the ancient fabled land of Lyonesse. They stayed on St Mary's now the main island, at the settlement of **ST MARY'S POOL,** now submerged.

Returning to the mainland Mary and her children retraced their steps to Lamorna Cove for **MERRY MAIDENS**. It is from here they began their travelling in earnest around Cape Cornwall. First they went north and west to **CARN BREA** settlement (a second one). Then they headed east overland through Carn Euny and Sancreed to a settlement at **ROSEHILL**, which is now on the northern outskirts of Penzance. Leaving Rosehill they journeyed north through Madron to reach the ancient Atlantean Temple site of **MEN-AN-TOL** with the Nine Maidens circle about a mile away. They stayed at a settlement in the valley immediately below this circle, therefore I shall call it **NINE MAIDENS**. At Men-an-Tol Mary conducted a Ceremony to reactivate the Atlantean Temple. To complete their journeying round The Cape, Mary, Jesus and Naomi went east to **CHYSAUSTER,** then north for a settlement at **ROSEWALL HILL**, finally leaving Cape Cornwall by travelling south over Trink Hill and Trencron Fort.

CHAPTER 6 TRAVELLING THE NORTH COAST

PORTREATH - DRUDIC Home Ceremony

From Cape Cornwall Mary and her children soon reached the Druidic community of **ST ERTH**. They then travelled through Geal just below

Rosewarne to stay at a settlement south of **MERRY MEETING,** where Joseph rejoined the group. They journeyed on together through Roscroggan and Merrose Farm to an ancient Druidic Temple site on the hill above **PORTREATH**. It is here Mary took part in a further Ceremony of Light. This area was the heart of tin mining territory for many centuries. Indications on the map give us; Wheal Bassett, Wheal Plenty, Wheal Rose and Wheal Kitty, so perhaps an important area for Joseph in his day. From Portreath, Mary and her companions made their way to the coast, and took a short sea voyage around St Agnes Head to land at Perranporth beach. They then went on to **CUBERT** settlement inland from Penhale Sands.

CHAPTER 7 CAMEL CORNER

CASTLE-AN-DINAS - ATLANTEAN Ceremony on site

Mary and her little party left Cubert going over Quintrel Downs to a settlement at **PORTH,** set just below Porth Reservoir. From there they went east via Rosewastis to reach the Atlantean Temple site of **CASTLE-AN-DINAS**, where Mary was once again called upon to perform a sacred Ceremony for an Atlantean Temple residing in the Etheric Realm. At the close of the Ceremony, Joseph and Jesus left the others and headed back to the coast at Flory Island, in order to take a sea voyage. I haven't a clue as to where they went, but the next time I hear of them is at Port Isaac. While Mary and Naomi were staying at Castle-an-Dinas, they both travelled quite a way east to a settlement at **ROSEHILL** north of Lanivet, in order to meet with their Celtic family, then returned to their base at Castle-an-Dinas. On finally leaving this site, they headed north through Rosenannon, over St Breock Downs to the River Camel close to Bodellick, from where they crossed to Cant Hill. They journeyed on through Rock and Jesus Well to the Druidic settlement of **BREA HILL**. After a brief stay, Mary and Naomi left for Port Isaac to meet with Joseph and Jesus who had arrived by boat. The little group of travellers together once more, then went south through Central Cornwall, via St Endellion, to reach **CASTLE KILLIBURY** the last settlement in Camel Corner.

CHAPTER 8 TO BODMIN MOOR

THE HURLERS - DRUIDIC Ceremony on site
DOZMARY POOL - ATLANTEAN Ceremony on site

From Castle Killibury Mary and her family set off in an easterly direction through St Mabyn, crossing the River Camel near Merry Meeting and on through Blissland to a settlement at Temple. From here their journey took them south via the Warleggan River and on over Warleggan Downs to reach **GOONZION DOWNS** settlement. Going east once more, they crossed the St Neot River, then the River Fowey at Ashford Bridge, to a settlement in what is now the centre of **LISKEARD**. They then travelled north through Merrymeet and Minions, to reach Bodmin Moor for an ancient settlement called **THE CHEESEWRING.** Just below The Cheesewring is **THE HURLERS** with its ancient Druidic Temple, where Mary enacted a sacred Light Ceremony. This Cosmic act completed, Mary with Jesus, Naomi and Joseph travelled west across Bodmin Moor to **DOZMARY POOL**, in order that she might revitalize a Temple of ancient Atlantis. The settlement itself is situated just to the north of Higher Langdon. Having accomplished her sacred 'duty', Mary returned to the high moor, going east to King Arthur's Bed, then across the moor to **NINE STONES** settlement and over Foxtor to a site at **BRAYDOWN.**

The last stage of Mary's pilgrimage through Cornwall, saw her and her family going directly north over Wilsey Down to **WARBSTOWE BURY** settlement, then north, north-west to Rosecare, and north to Trengayor. From this point, they went down-river to the coast at Millook Haven and by boat to Bude Haven for a settlement at **MAER.** They embarked on a final sea voyage in Cornwall, which took them to the entrance of the Abbey River by Dyers Lookout, for Hartland in Devon. This completed the Cornish part of Mary's pilgrimage in the South West.

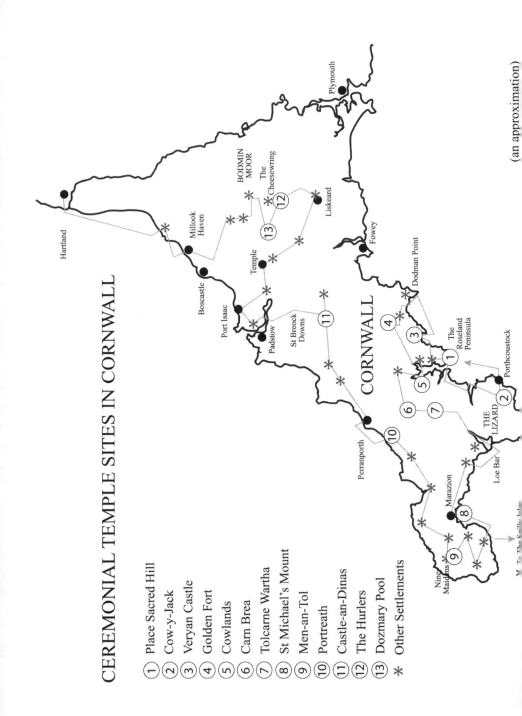

CEREMONIAL TEMPLE SITES IN CORNWALL

1. Place Sacred Hill
2. Cow-y-Jack
3. Veryan Castle
4. Golden Fort
5. Cowlands
6. Carn Brea
7. Tolcarne Wartha
8. St Michael's Mount
9. Men-an-Tol
10. Portreath
11. Castle-an-Dinas
12. The Hurlers
13. Dozmary Pool

* Other Settlements

(an approximation)

CHAPTER 1
THE ROSELAND PENINSULA
The Secret of Place

I am in Cornwall, standing on the little stone quay at PLACE in St Anthony-in-Roseland on the Roseland Peninsula, where the Lady Mary, Naomi, Jesus and Joseph of Arimathea came ashore in the South West of Britain. The water of the inlet gently laps against the quay wall. The sun is moving in and out of white fluffy clouds. I watch fascinated as each time it emerges, its rays strike the surface of the water, sending out great swathes of light - myriad little sparkling stars shoot out in all directions. I am looking across the Percule Estuary to St Maws with its whitewashed houses shining in the sunlight. I turn and face Place Manor, set in woodland with its beautiful gardens protected from the sea by a high stone wall. This locale has strong associations for me. Memories of a past visit in this lifetime come to mind, for it was here over forty years ago, that my husband and I came on honeymoon to stay at Place Manor. Now, Cosmic memories of a long distance past come floating into my consciousness and I am again embodying my past life as Naomi, as she steps ashore in this foreign land.

THE BEGINNING

I return to the start of my Cornish pilgrimage. It is September 2008 when my Mission with the Lady Mary in the South West begins. I am back in Devon after my journeying in Wales following the '*Pathway of the Beloved*'. My first 'task' is very special. I am to have an attunement with Mary, for her guidance and insights on my Welsh pilgrimage need to be acknowledged. In the sacred space of my own home I put on some soft music and light the candle on my little altar. Beloved Mary is very close - her presence is almost tangible and I am overwhelmed with the deepest love. For Mary: "*Oh Mary - how blest am I beloved one. Your Divine essence has always filled my heart but now it is more potent and the depth of my devotion so profound. I thank you for your guidance on my pilgrimage to Wales and all the insights received.*"

MARY

"Beloved child. Welcome home. There is so much more. I will speak with you again very soon. God Bless you dear one."

I thank Mary for her contact. Eventually all is up to date with my notes and photographs, so Wales can be safely put aside for the moment.

There are the usual chores to be undertaken on returning from a journey. It is during this time that I am able to visit several places in Devon and Somerset as mentioned in the 'INTRODUCTION TO THE SOUTH WEST'. It is also during this time I am to discover Mary's landing place in Cornwall on the Roseland Peninsula and decide that this will be my starting point on my forthcoming pilgrimage. However, where do I go after that? While looking at the map I am getting more and more confused until I retire to bed without making a decision. Well - it is the middle of the night and I am woken up. My beloved Mary has seen fit to interrupt my sleep pattern! This waking in the wee small hours will become a habit, as I am to discover. I know I am being asked to 'tune-in' so I gather about me a wrap, collect my notepad and pen, light my candle and wait quietly in the stillness of the night. I ask for her guidance but she knows of my quandary:

MARY

"Beloved one, follow your intuition. I will guide you. Do not get 'bogged down' as you would say with detail at this stage. Look at the wider picture. You have intuitively chosen your start point where we landed, at what is called the Roseland Peninsula. Make that your first port of call in Cornwall and you will be guided from there. I will be with you all the way dear one. You will intuitively know the right pathway. Bless you and may the Light of all Eternity ever be with you. May you be enfolded in the loving arms of Jesus, my son, the Saviour and your Master - our Master - the Blessed One - the One who taught us 'The Way' - the way of purity and truth. He is all Love. He is all Light. He is my beloved Son. Bless you my child."

I thank Beloved Mary and am once again, totally filled with love for this beautiful Being of Light. A decision has been made and all is well - I can sleep easy.

MY PILGRIMAGE - DAY 1

So it begins - my pilgrimage to Cornwall with the Lady Mary. It is now early October. Before I set out I am to have a special attunement. I prepare my sacred altar. First I lay out a white cloth which is edged with purple iris in dedication to White Eagle. On it I put a pure white candle with a pink rose for Mary - the *'Rose in the Heart'*. I lay down a silver cutout of a six pointed star as personification of the great Cosmic Sun. I have before me pictures of the Lady Mary and of the Master Jesus. In the background my Ohm CD is playing softly. I light the candle and leave the room, closing the door quietly behind me, in order to allow the energies to build. Some ten minutes later I re-enter, sit in my chair and gently rest a beautiful pink and mauve scarf over my head. My hands automatically rise in prayer fashion. This ritual which becomes regular practice, immediately brings me into the presence of Beloved Mary. As I allow my breathing to slow to a gentle rhythm, my outer mind stills, and I find that I am moving into my inner being. I have entered that secret place where spirit abides and visions come to pass. I am ready. As I speak with Our Lady and the great Beings of Light, my prayer reflects the sacredness of my forthcoming Mission: *"Beloved Ones. Let me come into your presence with thanksgiving. My pilgrimage begins this very day. Beloved Mary be my guide and helpmate - let me follow in your footsteps on this pilgrimage to Cornwall. May those ancient Masters, the Brethren of Light walk with me. I ask the protection of Archangel Michael and the presence of All Angels. I offer myself in service to Thee, in love and all humility and pray that I be worthy of the task ahead. Let Mary's Mission be my Mission. Let me make good representation of my insights. Let those insights be pure and always from a place of love - from within the sacred heart. Let all that takes place be to Thy honour and glory. Amen."* I receive the following words from Mary addressed to me as the past embodiment of Naomi:

MARY

"Dearest daughter of mine. I will be with you every step of the way. I will be your guide and your comforter. You will KNOW that I walk with you. There will be times when I shall be able to talk with you. There will be other times when I will wish you to be still. You will know dearest one - you will know. Go forth this day in the wonder of future experiences. Let the Rose of Divine Love ever bloom in your heart - for it is so. We welcome your enthusiasm. We welcome this opportunity to share with you our pilgrimage through Cornwall. As you already know, we landed at the Roseland Peninsula. I shall tell you more when you are there. I wish you a blessed journey. You will be quite safe in all that you do. There will be times when we will wish you to reactivate ancient Light Centres. You will be protected by the beloved Archangel Michael BUT your heart of love is also your protection. Always dwell in that pure heart-love dearest one. For it is your Divine essence shining through The Rose. Bless you dear Sister of Light. Let your pilgrimage begin."

I acknowledge Mary's words, blessing and honouring her presence. I am soon to realize on my amazing journey, that I am never to be shown the whole picture - that would make it far too easy! Information is filtered through to me little by little when it is necessary for me to receive it. The key to my inner strength on this sacred pilgrimage lies in great dollops of Divine Trust!

MY JOURNEY BEGINS

Following my attunement I am ready to begin my Mission. There is no rush so I quietly load the car and eventually leave about 10.00 am. As I set off for Cornwall the sun is shining - what a good omen. This is very welcome after weeks of miserable weather. I am feeling as if the sun is shining in my heart. I am full of love, peace and joy all mixed with eager anticipation. I have made my sleeping arrangements in youth hostels at Boswinger for the Roseland Peninsula and Penzance for Cape Cornwall, another area which is drawing me. The mileage from my home town in Devon to the Roseland Peninsula I reckon to be approximately a hundred miles.

I am keen to return to Place Manor with its ancient church of St Anthony attached to it, quite literally via a door from the kitchen. As far as I know, this is the only church in the country which has such an intriguing set-up. As I am driving, my thoughts turn to St Anthony, an Egyptian saint whom we have already come across at the Holy Well at Llansteffan in Carmarthenshire. St Anthony would I believe, have forged a strong link between Britain and Egypt in ancient times. On arrival in the Roseland Peninsula, my intention is to call in at the hotel which is Place Manor and perhaps have a pot of tea.

I am driving along the main A38 heading west to Cornwall, passing now the high land of the Dartmoor National Park to my right. There are monuments of the past spread all over the moor, from Bronze Age and Iron Age settlements, to the more recent Industrial Age. It must have been a crowded place to live in past times! For me, Dartmoor holds a mystical quality and I have spent many happy days exploring the ancient landscape. Mary comes to mind, as I am now passing south of Hembury Fort and then Merrivale Ceremonial Complex, both Atlantean sites which I have discovered she visited. You will read of my insights in this regard later in the book. For now - onward to Cornwall. Crossing the River Tamar at Plymouth via the road bridge, I am in Celtic Cornwall - hurrah - I feel as if I have come home! Very soon the heights of Bodmin Moor come into view - another area where evidence of ancient settlements flourish. The moors are high-lighted by the sun and look very inviting, but not for today. I have a Mission - the Roseland Peninsula is calling me and Mary is waiting.

PLACE, ST ANTHONY-IN-ROSELAND

I am so close yet so far away. My car journey has been rather long and tedious as I have managed to take a few wrong turns in the Cornish country lanes. I have become as we say in walkers 'speake' *'Temporarily Misplaced'*. However, I am now in the Roseland Peninsula and eventually find myself on the little road to Place. I drive through deep sunken lanes with high stone walls from which great trees emerge, their roots melding into the old stone as one. Their height and density almost block out the sunlight, making the lanes appear even deeper. The little sun there is struggling through the tree canopy, is dappling on the ground in front of me - it is quite magical. I am here at last in this ancient landscape, as Cosmic memories are about to be played out. I am already beginning to feel the essence of past times hereabouts. My little road is running almost parallel to the Percuil River, then crosses Froe Creek one of many little creeks in this part of Cornwall. Through the trees I see a sailing boat moored up on the mud waiting for high tide lift-off. The whole little scene has a touch of the *'Daphne du Mauriers'* about it!

A no-through road leads me to Place Manor where a sign tells me it is now Place House - the first indication of change. I turn into the long drive which leads to the front of the property as I did forty years ago. Today it appears to be a private estate and I feel as if I am trespassing. But in spite of this I continue to the front entrance feeling very brave. I don't know what I shall do if the dogs come out! From the distance Place House looks a rather impressive mansion, yet as I get closer I realize that it is very dilapidated and appears forlorn and neglected. The front door is locked. I peer through a window. It is obviously not an hotel any more, so my idea of afternoon tea has gone. I have even put on tidy clothes for my journey, in order that I would look respectable when I called in to what I thought might be a posh hotel! I know three friends who would have been sorely disappointed at such a result - no freshly made real leaf tea to be imbibed out of elegant china and perhaps sugar lumps with tongs! Ah well. There is obviously no-one about. I take a few photographs of the house and the estuary before leaving. I am not set upon by dogs or arrested!

I drive a hundred or so yards down a narrow lane and park up on the small jetty from where the little motor boat ferries passengers between Place and St Maws in the summer months. From here I have a front view of Place House and the grounds. This tiny harbour certainly is a safe mooring for boats. I can well understand the party of voyagers from the Holy Land feeling greatly relieved on reaching this little haven and being welcomed by their Celtic family, at the end of what could have been a risky sea voyage. Today, the water of the inlet is very very still, shimmering in the sunlight. There are a few little sail boats bobbing about gently on the surface. There is an air of tranquility about this quintessentially South Cornish coastal scene.

I am sitting on the quay wall reflecting on past times. Visions come in. I am Naomi, Mary's daughter, stepping off a small sailing craft onto the shores of this land of my ancestors, of which I have heard so much. What an adventure for a young person. What an adventure for the boy Jesus also, for I suspect it was the first of many visits to these ancient Isles. As Naomi, I am feeling the excitement and anticipation in spite of being quite exhausted after the voyage.

ST ANTHONY'S CHURCH - HISTORY AND INSIGHTS

Returning to the present day, I ask a couple sitting on the quay if they know anything of the history of Place House and who is living there now. The history fails them, but I am told that an elderly lady, one of the Sprys, a family who have owned the property for generations, lives there by herself, and that her husband is buried in the churchyard. I then ask directions to the church as I cannot recall a way to reach it other than through the property. I follow their instructions and walk back up the narrow lane, soon to reach a granite-stone stile on my right, with a signpost for the St Anthony Church. As I climb over the stile I ask the guardian of this ancient woodland for permission to enter saying that, I come in love. I receive:

The Norman-Saxon Arch at St Anthony's Church, Place

Detail of the Arch at St Anthony's Church, Place

GUARDIAN

"You are most welcome pilgrim. Please enjoy our beautiful woodland We are very happy for you to be here. This is a special and sacred place and we know that you will respect this. The little people are always busy you know - they work very hard in order to bring about the loveliness you see before you. Enjoy your day."

This is a delightful welcome and I feel like curtseying and saying: *"Well thank you kind sir"* - so I do - well I don't actually curtsey you understand - that would have been a bit over the top! On entering the stillness of the woods, I follow the little path through the trees as if in a walking meditation. It is leading me behind Place House. This really is 'A Place of Peace' within 'The Peace of Place'. I pass what looks like an old stone trough, but which is described on its plaque as a medieval coffin. I now see the spire of the St Anthony Church just peeping through the trees.

Standing at the main entrance to the church I look up at the arch. I am remembering, that when my husband and I stayed at Place Manor, our host was Edward Harte, who informed us he had been researching the legend of Joseph of Arimathea and the boy Jesus having arrived on these shores at what is now called Place, an adaptation of Palace, and that the ancient story is depicted in the symbology of the arch between the dog teeth. Harte had written a small booklet about his findings entitled '*The Story of PLACE - St Anthony-in-Roseland*' which we bought and which I still have in my possession. On my return from Cornwall I was able to access it and can give you a little of the history of Place which shows a substantial connection between the Mediterranean, the Holy Family and this part of the South West. So a brief resume.

1. First of course, we have the patron saint St Anthony of Egypt born in AD 251 who came to Britain to preach the Christian message.

2. Regarding the arch, Harte tells us (Page 11) that it is: '*A very beautiful combination of two different forms of Architecture - Norman and Saxon. It has two rows of dog teeth after the Norman fashion; a Saxon Arch inside with the Saxon Sign - The Lamb and the Cross - on it.*' Then (Page 12): '*Our Lord visited here himself with St Joseph of Arimathea. It is the only ancient record there is to support the Legend of Glastonbury. It tells you that he came with his Uncle to Cornwall for tin; their boat got into trouble off St Anthony Head, where there is a lighthouse today.*' Apparently Jesus and Joseph sheltered at Place while their boat was being made seaworthy and left behind a shrine over which the present day church is built.

3. Further, Harte's research indicates that the attached Place Manor which was originally a Celtic monastery, is said to have been built where an ancient Phoenician settlement once stood. According to old records, the Phoenicians traded with Cornwall 2,000 years before the birth of Christ.

4. Another snippet of information which strengthens the link, is that the Church Bell is made of wrought bronze which is said to be the hardest metal in existence, and the tools which were used to shape it are the same as were used to cut the stone for the pyramids of Egypt. Page 22 of his booklet tells us: '*The last people who knew the secret of making it were the early High Priests of the Temple of Ammon in Egypt, Amon Ra.*' and over the

page: *'The Bell could have been brought to Cornwall in one way only - by the Phoenicians for those Celtic Monks when they built the first Monastery.'*

5.   Finally, my up-to-date discovery that the Lady Mary visited Place with her family 2,000 years ago.

Returning to the legend of Jesus and Joseph, if this holds water, I am curious as to why the Lady Mary, Jesus mother, does not feature in any ancient myths, yet my insights tell me quite clearly that she did come here. What is the evidence in the landscape which points to her presence? I myself would suggest three connections which have possibly escaped notice. One - the name itself - Rose-land. A second - the St Anthony Church which was originally dedicated to - yes you've guessed it - St Mary, or to be perfectly accurate, St Mary de Valle (St Mary in the Valley). Also, at St Anthony's Head in ancient times, there was a chapel dedicated to St Anne, Mary's mother and our Lord's grandmother.

I enter the dark interior of St Anthony's Church. Two people are just leaving and I have this sacred sanctuary to myself. The church is built in the old style before the tenth century, in the shape of a cross with a tower at the centre. Today it is rather austere, yet in Tudor times the interior would have been magnificent, its walls adorned with paintings, Italian mosaic flooring and carvings, all in brilliant colours. At one time it contained many treasures, among them a three foot tall black ebony cross and a figure of Our Lord carved in white marble. It is said that one day Father Ambrose saw Henry VIII's fleet enter Falmouth, and fearing that the church would be ransacked, quickly secreted the treasures away. He never disclosed where he hid them and the secret died with him. As I walk down the aisle I see at the base of the tower the coat of arms of Henry VIII - the three leopards for England. There is another for Ann Boleyn - five white falcons in flight. These both in commemoration of their visit while on honeymoon. Harte in his booklet tells of a naval victory over the French by Admirable Henry Thomas Spry. As a reward Henry gave Place Manor and its church, plus the whole of the Roseland Peninsula to Admiral Spry. It is registered that St Anthony's Church is the only church Henry VIII restored rather than destroyed.

I have with me for Beloved Mary a beautiful pink rose which I now place gently on the stone slab before the altar. I am saying: *"Mary my beloved one, I offer you this rose in honour of my deepest love and in dedication of my pilgrimage."* I sit in one of the old oak pews with my mauve and pink scarf around my shoulders and breathe myself into that heart-place until it fills with the essence of this pink rose of love. The silence and sacredness of this ancient building enfolds me. Mary is here:

MARY

"My dearest daughter I welcome you to Place. This was the place where our little group made land. The terrain in front of what is now Place House was different in those days. There was no harbour wall, the water just lapped gently onto a foreshore. This was

a very safe haven. As we landed we were welcomed by our Druid family. It was 'written' above (an ancient prophecy or received wisdom?) *of our pending visit and we were made very welcome. We had had an arduous sea voyage. There were times when I wondered if we would make it to these shores in safety. However, I never lost my trust in Divine providence. I KNEW the Angels were protecting our little party. Of course for the young people - for Jesus my beloved son and for you my dearest daughter Naomi, it was just an adventure. Another one was about to begin. We stayed here for some little while in this safe haven recovering from our ordeal. We were offered a little hut with bedding of straw where we could rest our weary bones. After we were all well and strong again then we were able to share in the Ceremonies of these our Druid friends. It was agreed that we should ALL participate in the Ceremony at the next full moon.* ('ALL' I knew included Jesus and Naomi. I was not aware that children in Druidic society took part in such Ceremonies. However, perhaps because of their Temple training, which would have been known, this was acceptable).

Not far from here dearest one there is a SACRED HILL. It was here where we were to gather and perambulate in spiral fashion to the top, where there was a Druid Temple of Light. This was a Temple of Trees - great oak trees - within which the Light could pour down and manifest on the Earth. Our leader, the Arch Druid, indicated that I should be the one to invoke the Light on this occasion. This was indeed a privilege but it was known that this would be my role. I stepped forward. I was dressed in a white robe as were all the Druids. My arms held high I tuned into the very highest, the purist, the most powerful Light - the Christ Light had entered my being and I was totally filled with Divine Light. I was aware of little except being immersed in a very powerful Light and vibrational energy. It would seem that the Earth itself vibrated to the power of the Cosmic Rays. I brought the Light from the Cosmos to seal it in the Earth for all times. Find this 'Hill of Power' dearest one. I will guide you. I will speak with you again dearest daughter. God Bless you."

I have a vision of what I can only describe as a huge Globe of Light way up in the Heavens, shining down rays of Golden Light to the Earth. The Light focuses its firey energy right into the centre of the Druidic Tree Temple. Mary herself is illumined within this Light - what a joy to receive such insights. I thank her for her sacred words and blessings.

She has gone. Suddenly the temperature seems to have dropped and I am feeling quite cold. As I turn to leave, I spy a small door to my right set into the church wall. Of course, this was the door leading to the kitchen of Place Manor which was the old refectory of the ancient monastery. Through this door many years ago was my first introduction to St Anthony's Church.

I step out into the sunshine. A robin is singing and bees are buzzing in the warm air. I see a bench seat which I failed to notice on the way in. On it is a plaque which reads: *'In memory of Edward Harte from his friends'* - what a lovely tribute. It is good to know that he has not been forgotten. Sitting on the seat I reflect on Mary's words. It was obvious that the Druid Elders knew of their coming and made provision for them. It would also seem that they were aware of the special powers and status of this precious lady, as she was granted the honour of acting as a Druid Elder for the Full Moon Ceremony. As a High Priestess in the Egyptian Temples, she was in tune with Cosmic forces and 'more than qualified' for this sacred role.

I now go in search of the 'Hill of Power' of which Mary talks. I see some old stone steps leading upward through the woodland. Uphill is good - perhaps this is where I shall find the ancient Tree Temple? I pass an old ruined cottage, its ivy-clad walls forming a beautiful shiny green Gothic arch. At the top of the steps I look up and there above me is a field on a rise. I search around for an entrance, but with no luck. There is absolutely no way I can climb up the high wall, over the barbed wire fence and fight my way through the thick undergrowth - unusual for me, but there you are! I have come unstuck on a few occasions in the past attempting such exploits - this time I refrain from trying. It is getting rather late in the day so I will regroup on the morrow.

I retrace my steps to the St Anthony Church, on through the woods and out into the lane. I once again acknowledge the guardian of this sacred woodland. Everything seems so quiet as I walk back to the harbour, when all of a sudden I am startled by a flurry of about thirty pheasant taking off from a field alongside the lane. I reach the little jetty and just for a moment stand in silence, focusing on the calm clear water of the inlet, still graced with the sun. I start talking with a gentleman whom I can only call an 'old salt' with his white beard and blue seaman's hat. True to form he was a sailor. He tells me that thirty years ago he and his family used to sail across from St Maws to visit Place Manor Hotel for cream teas - all gone now sadly.

OFF TO BOSWINGER

I am due at Boswinger Youth Hostel and reluctantly have to go. On leaving the Roseland Peninsula, I drive in an easterly direction and soon reach the hostel, which is bang in the middle of the little hamlet of Boswinger just above Hemmick beach. I sign in and after a cup of tea, start out on a walk downhill to the cove about half a mile away. The views opening up are of a magnificent sandy beach. Its far cliffs are golden - lit up by the dying sun which is now beginning its drop behind the horizon of the sea, producing the most stunning red and orange visual display. I am able to take some marvellous photographs. Wandering over the sands, across the seaweed to the edge of the water, the ozone reaches my nostrils and I inhale deeply.

I am now walking back uphill to Boswinger. In a field next to the road is a beautiful dusky cow with big brown eyes. Her mates are doing what cows do - chewing the cud. But this one was watching me - very curious at this human person walking past her field. I walk a few steps and she rushes off in a 'panic' - I stand still and she returns to look over the hedge. This happens on several occasions. Good game - good game. She is very lovely and we have a sort of inner communication! I continue my slow uphill stroll. Hearing heavy breathing behind me, I turn around and this young guy, barefoot and in a wet suit, with a surf board tucked under one arm, comes striding past me. Oh to be young again. I comment that it is a bit of a struggle going uphill, to which he charitably agrees!

As a final tribute to this incredible day, after my supper, I step outside to view the night sky. In this part of Cornwall there are few distracting lights. The silvery moon is up and twinkling stars shine out brilliantly against the backdrop of a soft velvety-black sky. The Planet Venus is clearly visible at this time of the year. This beautiful Planet of Beauty and Harmony, the embodiment of Divine Love, brings Mary to mind once more: *"Thank you beloved one for your presence and insights this day.'*

RETURN TO ST ANTHONY-IN-ROSELAND

It is the second day of my Cornish pilgrimage and I am to return to Place in order to search for the Druidic Hill Temple. First, an attunement with Mary to make that spiritual link as a precursor to my journey. As I leave the hostel two chough fly overhead, a sign that from here in direct chough flight-path, is the Lizard Peninsula, where these magnificent birds are making a comeback. Quite striking in appearance, their shiny black plumage has a bluish gloss to it and they have a bright orange bill. In the air they can perform skilful aerobatics. Certainly a success story for the Royal Society for the Protection of Birds who have a preservation strategy in place.

My route takes me through St Michael Caerhays and Veryan, both places on Mary's journey after she leaves the Roseland Peninsula (see Chapter 3). Driving through Rosevine I stop to take a peek at the St Gerrans Parish Church. In the sixth century, Gerrans II was the last King of Germania - this part of Cornwall. He was a very holy man, who upon his death was canonized and later a church was dedicated to him. The ancient church is a delight having kept its ancient character in spite of a Millennium modernization project. In the churchyard is a tenth century Cornish wheel cross nearly seven foot in height. As I wander among the gravestones, the most beautiful tortoiseshell cat comes to greet me and definitely deserves a stroke and tickle under the chin.

Onward to Place. I like these old fashioned road signs with a hand and finger pointing the direction, as in this case to *'St Anthony'*. Soon I am dropping down through the narrow tree-lined lane to the harbour of Place. As the inlet comes into view I voice: *"I am back dearest Mary. I have returned."*

I am sitting on the quay wall. The ethereal blue of the sky is reflected in the clear still water before me. Deep in contemplation, I have temporarily forgotten why I was meant to be here. Mary's words are now coming back to me. She has asked that I look for the 'Hill of Power'. Yesterday at the hill behind St Anthony's Church, I was not picking up any strong energies, but put this down to being tired at the end of a long day.

PLACE SACRED HILL

Suddenly up I get. My expedition is on once more. I know where I am to go. - I have to walk in another direction away from Place House. Setting off from the harbour, I pass through a kissing gate, take a right, and start along a little field-path. Looking to my left I see a grassy hill. THIS IS IT. THIS is the 'Hill of Power'. This is the Hill Temple of the Druids where Mary, Jesus, Naomi and Joseph joined in their Moon Ceremony. Mary has got me here - I offer my heartfelt thanks. Now - what is the best route to the top? I spy a huge ash tree which is calling to me and set off up the hill. On reaching the tree I put my hands on its bark feeling the energies saying: *"Oh sacred tree. I honour you. I bless you."* I lay at its base a few bright yellow flowers like miniature suns, which I have picked for the deva. Sitting with my back to its trunk I hear:

Place Sacred Hill indicating centralized hay bale

DEVA OF THE ASH

"Welcome person of Light. This is a surprise. Thank you. Thank you. I have the BEST position on the hill, full view of beloved Place and the estuary beach where Mary and her little band of pilgrims landed. I have seen much - not that visitation you understand. I am not THAT old! But I have been here a very long time and I have seen much. Thank you for recognizing my presence human person. (I certainly felt the surprise the deva was expressing at my recognition and I could feel its energies lifting). *I thank you for your gift. I accept graciously for they are offered in love. Thank you human person. I AM the guardian of this sacred hill. The older trees have long gone but I am still here, and yes dear pilgrim person* (in answer to my unspoken question), *this IS the hill that Mary has talked about. It is here that the ancient Druids*

perambulated for their worship. I am so blessed at growing on this hill and standing sentinel in this position."

From me: "*Bless you and thank you precious tree deva.*" I have a vision of the ancient Druids dressed in white robes, walking from Place settlement in the valley, spiralling up in a clockwise direction to the summit of the hill. This place is FOREVER. I am in no rush to leave. From the estuary below I hear the oystercatcher's loud cry - the sun is warm on my face - the wind is rustling the leaves of my handsome ash tree. Everywhere is all so full of life and energy and yet there is a stillness in the air - this is a moment of enchantment.

Because I decide to try and spiral up the hill as in days gone by, I get myself into all sorts of trouble stumbling around in long wet grass, brambles and ditches. The higher I climb, so the wind which was a gentle breeze by the ash tree, becomes stronger. My hair is blowing about. Now - I am Naomi with long brown hair flying loose, precessing my way up the hillside in times past. I pick up a sort of a path winding round the hill and come to my first oak tree - a fine specimen. I offer a blessing and am rewarded with a few words of acknowledgement. I ask permission to take a small piece of twig from this tree sacred to the Druids. At the top of the field, on reaching a rather dilapidated and broken five-barred gate, I look ahead of me and see a cut hay field. Over the gate I go, through the brambles and nettles, over a second ramshackle gate and into the hay field. Obviously these gate entrances have not been in use for many years.

In the far distance is a mound which looks to be a bale of hay. As I get closer I see that it IS a bale of hay. Why has just one bale of hay been left in the middle of this huge field? It would seem to be marking the central point of the field. I keep on saying: "*How odd - how very odd - how very very odd*" as I walk around it. Then I KNOW. THIS is the centre of the ancient Temple of the Druids. I am amazed at my insight, for there is nothing in the landscape to indicate its past heritage. I lay down my oak twig offering with a small piece of pure white quartz for the Druids. Mary speaks with me:

MARY

"*My dearest one. You have reached the goal. This is the EXACT centre of this ancient Druidic Temple. The hay bale is left because IT IS KNOWN, if not with the Earthly mind, within the deep inner being, this ancient knowledge which is hidden deep within us all. Bless you my child. Enjoy the rest of your day.*"

I say: "*Beloved Mary. This is wonderful. I thank you for this confirmation. Bless you.*"

I stand next to the bale of hay and begin to feel the vibrational energy emanating from the earth beneath my feet. These are the vibrations of all life. This is the unbroken thread which moves us from one incarnation to another, sometimes offering us a chance to relive past experiences. As of now at this Druidic Temple, I am in another space and time - I am reconnecting to my past life as Naomi - this is a home coming. I have the feeling that this sacred hill holds a deeper mystery and that anything more there is to learn here, will unfold for me at the right time. It is some while later I discover Place Sacred Hill has an Atlantean Temple in the Etheric and I am to earth it from the sanctuary of my own home.

THE CEREMONIES OF LIGHT

It is on my return from this first pilgrimage to Cornwall, that I planned and prepared my three sacred Light Ceremonies. One, to earth any Atlantean Temple in the Etheric, a second for Druidic Temple sites and a third for those sites with a dedication to the Goddess. Following this sacred task, I was ready to undertake the Mission to earth the Atlantean Temple here at Place Sacred Hill. By now, I was aware of two other places in the area where I was to perform a Ceremony; at Veryan Castle Atlantean site and at Golden Fort Druidic settlement (see Chapter 3). All were to be activated from my home sanctuary. My plan was to set aside a whole day for my three Light Ceremonies. I chose a Sunday which I felt would enable me to work in a quieter space. At first I thought I might initiate one Ceremony, take a break and type up my notes, before I moved on. However, as I was having an early morning attunement, it became clear to me that I was to stay within my bubble of sacred Light for the duration. An idea formulated in my mind therefore, to perform my first Ceremony at 9.00 am for Place Sacred Hill, 12.00 noon for Veryan Castle and finally 3.00 pm for Golden Fort. This way I could close each one down, take a little break and prepare for the next, all the time remaining quite still and secluded in my haven of peace. I discovered that in practice my plan worked well and this became the most sacred of days.

PLACE SACRED HILL ATLANTEAN TEMPLE CEREMONY

It is 9.00 am. I prepare for my Ceremony. The telephone is turned off as I do wish not to be disturbed as I dedicate myself to Mary's Mission. I cleanse my sacred space by smudging with sage. The curtains are partly closed blocking out a little of the bright sunlight, which beautiful energy seems to be shining a blessing on this special day. I gently rest my mauve and pink scarf over my head as I settle down. Before me I have a picture of Our Lady. On my altar are a candle, a white quartz crystal and a silver star. I light my candle and the flame leaps into action. I visualize that great Sun-Star in the Heavens pouring its Light down to enfold me and my little sanctuary in its Cosmic Ray. I place myself in the Merkaba that protective and sacred Body of Light. I am aware of my little room being filled with a vast company of Beings from the Land of Light. My dedication: *"Beloved Masters - Great Beings of the ancient times - I honour you ALL. I offer myself in service to humanity. I ask for your guidance and your protection. Let good work be done this day. Amen."*

MARY

"Beloved one you have chosen your day well. I am with you. I bless you."

In my imagination I picture myself standing on the stone quay at Place in St Anthony-in-Roseland. As before, the clear still water is lit up by the morning sun and there are little stars of sunlight dancing on its surface. I now see myself walking to the base of the sacred hill. As I perambulate up the hillside I acknowledge my tall elegant ash tree, then spiral around in a clockwise direction, passing the great oak, to its top. I am dressed in a white robe. I reach the one bale of hay left standing in the middle of the cut field, the very centre of the ancient Druidic Tree Temple, which I subsequently learnt was of Atlantean descent. To my inner vision the hay field is full of Light - the rays shining down, right from the heart of the Cosmos - from the 'Sun behind the Sun' - that all encompassing Light which shines on Universes beyond our imagination.

I begin my Ceremony to earth the ancient Atlantean Temple. First *'The Great Invocation'* then following the format laid out in my Preface, the three crystals are placed on my altar; the merlinite for Merlin, the turquoise.for Is-Ra and the rose-pink quartz for Beloved Mary. As I voice the words: *'Let the ancient Temple of Atlantis be brought down from the Etheric Realm where it now resides and be securely grounded on Mother Earth'*, I am aware of a great Ray of Light striking the ground in the centre of this ancient Druidic site, like a lightening bolt. The powerful beam goes through the Earth, right into its central core, to the heart of the great Earth Star Crystal. I can feel its tremendous vibrational energy, which seems now to be coming right through my physical body. I focus on staying still and upright in my chair, while consciously and deliberately ensuring that I am well grounded Before me now is an inner picture of a Temple with pure white columns, resting on the hilltop at Place Sacred Hill. the Atlantean Temple is earthed. It is done.

As I am completing the last words, I am aware of a strong presence drawing close. These words are offered to me from one of the ancient Brethren:

PRIEST OF ATLANTIS

"Sister of Light. We the Elders and Priests of the community who were in this area of Atlantis - at this sacred place - on this hallowed ground - thank you for your work this day. Our beautiful healing Temple is once more grounded on the very sod of Mother Earth. All OUR Brethren - all YOUR Brothers and Sisters are filled with great joy that you beloved sister have returned to us. We thank you. We bless you. You are one of us and ever shall be. Many many dear souls in incarnation at this time were our Brethren in past times.

This is a profound and VERY important era for Earth people, as preparations are being made for the New Age. As this Aquarian Age advances, so will the minds and hearts of all humanity be cleansed and balanced in order to prepare each individual for the new World of Gentleness and Light. The very purist energies of the 5th Dimension must abide with the Earth people. The changes are gradually being made and the link with the 5th Dimension is being grounded with Earth people. Let this New Age begin. Let the changes happen. Let hearts be filled with the purist love energies. Let the outer minds of humanity be integrated with their inner being in order to produce pure wisdom. The wisdom of the heart is the Rose within the Heart and it is from this sacred space that everything that is done - is done. THIS dearest Sister of Light is The Key. Your beloved White Eagle of this incarnation is teaching you that inner wisdom of the heart, which comes from deep within the Cosmos. This is profound truth.

The Rays of the Great Light are pouring down on this precious Planet in order to bring about the Perfected Being. We are watching your progress on the Earth Plane with great interest. We KNOW at the present time it is very difficult for the human mind to comprehend, with all the woes and tragedies in your World, that a time will come when all will be at peace. Dear Brethren - and we speak to ALL our dear Brothers and Sisters of the Earth Plane - dear Brethren, I can assure you - IT WILL BE SO. The time WILL come when the lion will lie down with the lamb. Each Brother and Sister regardless of the seemingly present separation of colour, creed and race, will unite and be as one. There is NO doubt of this my Brethren. THIS is what we are ALL working towards - to perfect the human being in all aspects. This perfection is part of a long long process which began at the beginning of time.

When the World was young - when the World was in its infancy - God brought forth THE LIGHT - and it was so. God brought into being THE WORD and this has manifested itself in all Planets of the Universe. Dear Brethren - IT IS SO. We want you ALL now to go through your Earthly life in full awareness of this spiritual truth held within The Mysteries and being offered to our Brethren on Earth. YOU dear ones, are so blessed to be part of these profound changes which are to come to pass on your Planet.

Rest assured dear ones, there is nothing to fear - NOTHING - for you are all held in the loving arms of your Father-Mother God - your Creator, who brought you forth from the heart of all Creation. Please dear Earth family - NO FEAR. Just feel the joy of the new Creation which is all part of the pathway of Light ever moving upwards to your own individual enlightenment. SERVICE - dear ones - always give of your best for the up-liftment of your beloved Planet. Seek for your own fulfillment in the offering of yourselves in complete and perfect service. For in THAT dear ones is YOUR salvation. THAT is the way to eternal peace and perfect understanding. Let the Light always shine in your hearts. Let the purity of that Light go out to heal the sick. Always, see the Light from the Cosmos shining pure and clear to bring upliftment and Light into the dark recesses of your Planet. For they only appear to be dark because the Light is not recognized and activated. ALL IS LIGHT. Always know this. Always believe this. FOR IT IS SO. This ancient Temple from Atlantean days will be a part of the New Jerusalem in these sacred British Isles. It will be a Beacon of Light to ALL. God bless you my Brethren. God Bless you."

I thank this beautiful Master from the ancient continent of Atlantis for his presence and sacred words. As he leaves me, I feel the energies dropping and I become a little shivery - it is time to close my first Ceremony of today. I speak the words: *"Blessed Archangel Michael I thank you for your protection this day. Great Beings of Light - ALL those who have been instrumental in bringing forth this ancient Temple from the Etheric Realm to Earth, I honour you and I thank you for your presence."* Finally - in my imagination, I rise and take the white quartz crystal and the pink quartz crystal and bury them close to the centre of this ancient Atlantean site on Place Sacred Hill.

I sit quietly in reflection for a long while. I close this remarkable spiritual connection by following my normal closing-down procedure, sealing my chakra centres, enfolding myself in Light and ensuring that I am well grounded. I blow my candle out, offering the Light as healing for the World and leave my sacred altar space quiet and still. It is now time for a short break and a hot drink before I proceed with my second Ceremony.

Meanwhile, back to the reality of my physical pilgrimage to Place Sacred Hill. I am standing taking in the views, which from this spot are far reaching. Below, looking very diminutive, are Place House and the St Anthony Church, almost hidden amongst the tall trees. In the distance I see the blue waters of the Fal Estuary and St Maws, with its little whitewashed houses, looking for all like a scene from Greece. When I was at the quay earlier I was thinking that I did not wish to leave - I would have liked to spend my days exploring this magical area. BUT, now I know I can go. My Mission - Mary's Mission - is complete for now. I knew at the time that there was more work to be done here, which culminated in my Light Ceremony for the ancient Temple of Atlantis. I am feeling so elated and full of joy that after leaving the hayfield I run down the field shouting out: *"thank you - thank you"* to all the blessed ones!

Driving the winding lanes back to Boswinger, I have a panorama of the coastline. In the evening sunshine, two small white-sailed boats are whisking along on the crest of the waves. My thoughts are once more returning to Place Sacred Hill where my beloved Mary has indeed guided me. I respect and value her insights. I am immersed in the wonder of it all and filled with the deepest love. The *'Rose in the Heart'* is a reality.

ST JUST-IN-ROSELAND

After the Moon Ceremony at Place Sacred Hill, it is now that Joseph takes the boy Jesus off on their own travelling, to inspect his Cornish tin mines. Meanwhile, Mary and Naomi make their pilgrimage to the Lizard Peninsula (see Chapter 2). They are not to meet again until Carn Brea settlement some weeks later. On leaving The Lizard, Mary and Naomi returned to the settlement at Place, from where with their guides, they set forth by boat up the Percuil River to St Just-in-Roseland.

It is Day 3 of my pilgrimage - where shall I go today? Where does Mary go after Place? At this early stage in my journeying with the Lady Mary, I have not the wisdom to ASK her! I am still floundering around hoping my intuition works for me. With the map before me St Just-in-Roseland seems to be catching my eye, so I will start there. If I remember correctly from a visit many years back, the setting for the church is rather special. Before leaving I ask a blessing on my day. Having breakfasted I set off for the twelve mile drive to St Just-in-Roseland, which is on the west side of the Roseland Peninsula, set on a little creek leading from the stretch of water called Carrick Roads. As I drive along, I am already aware of Mary's presence. Her essence is somehow imbued in this sacred landscape - at its intrinsic heart. In this regard, she is the archetype of the Earth Mother. I soon arrive at the pretty village of St Just-in-Roseland and turn off for the church down a no-through road. Well - what a surprise, at the Church of St Just, there are no parking spaces left. At a guess there must be about thirty cars in the car park and spilling out on to the road. A black-suited gentleman is walking towards me. I stop the car and he informs me that there is a funeral at 11.00 am which will last for at least an hour. It is now 10.55 am. I am a little disappointed because, I know I have much to fit into this day before I leave the area for Penzance. Never mind, perhaps there is a reason for this.

With an hour to fill, I drive on down a very narrow road and park up opposite a small boat building yard on St Just Pool creek. Little sailing craft are moored up on the sandy foreshore and others are floating on the still water. This is such a peaceful scene and I welcome this moment of tranquility - a gift from Spirit certainly. I cannot help thinking: *"God works in mysterious ways His wonders to perform!"* It has obviously been registered in the Land of Light that I wished for a little quiet time.

After a relaxing drink in the car, I walk down the stone steps to the beach and wander along contentedly, collecting some nice seashells as I go. I pick my way carefully over the slippery dark-brown seaweed covered rocks. Then, a further gift from the Gods is presented to me. I see many small pieces of white quartz on the rocks and in the rock pools. This is wonderful - my little supply has almost run out: *"Thank you so much Mary - thank you."* After asking the Universe for permission, I fill the pockets of my fleece with these treasured objects. I am a very happy person and very thrilled at my find - sorry - the offering from the Angels! I look at the low cliffs to see veins of white quartz within the strata of the grey rock. On my return home, I wash and cleanse all my precious pieces of quartz and remove the green seaweed stains. I almost feel that they do not need cleansing because they are washed twice daily by the salty sea, and the energies in the creek are so pure. However, they are now 'spruced up' and ready for any future placements.

Following this bit of excitement, I spend a congenial half an hour sitting in the lee of the rocks on the shingle beach in the most idyllic conditions. The sun is warming my face and lighting up the waters of the estuary before me. The tide is creeping closer and the seaweed which was once clinging to the rocks, is now being lifted off ever so gently and floating gracefully on the surface of the water in long wavy fronds, happy in its natural element. On the far side of the creek is a large old pink painted house, seeming to be precariously hanging over the cliff, the sunlight giving it a rosy glow. What views it must have up and down the creek. What tales it could tell of past times. Now another offering! I notice some apples on the beach where I am sitting. Looking up I see that there is an apple tree growing right on the cliff edge above me. Into my bag go a few choice windfalls. It is now 12.00 noon and I have a short attunement for World healing. It is so peaceful here that I could stay for a good while longer, but I do feel it is time to move on. I have been granted this little respite - I must not be greedy. Back in the car, I have a sandwich before driving the half mile or so back to the church.

THE CHURCH OF ST JUST

I am now parked in the freed-up car park high above the St Just Church. From the lych gate I look down on the ancient church nestling within a steep wooded combe on the edge of the creek above St Just Pool. The magnificent churchyard garden with its large ancient granite stones, is filled with subtropical plants, which have been collected by that well travelled Cornishman John Treseder. The scene before me is quite delightful - a veritable 'Garden of Eden'. Walking down the gently stepped path lined with carved slate monuments, I am blessing all the trees and shrubs and thanking the nature spirits who care for this special garden with such tenderness.

I am standing now on the edge of the creek by the church before a huge ancient granite Celtic cross. This is a reminder that the Celtic Church flourished in Cornwall and St Just was one of the many Christian missionaries who preached the Gospel of Love, as professed by the Master Jesus, in this ancient land. Visits of Jesus to the mystic British Isles have been recorded in many ways, but I have recently come across a most profound poem which registers Jesus landing at St Just Pool. It is in a small booklet written by A.E. Coulbeck, Rector of St Just-in-Roseland Church, entitled '*Granite Stones in St Just-in-Roseland Churchyard*'. He offers no indication as to its source but just adds at the end of the poem *(with acknowledgement)*.

Here, by the quiet bay our Lord once stood, they say:
A story or a dream? Or half-glimpsed vision that must always seem - Incredible?
So deep - the long past centuries sleep. The generations share the silence.
Nothing shows a legend's drift, or where a seed may fall from unrecorded memory,
Gone with all the leaves that every autumn blew away,
And sunlight lost with every close of day.
Here in the churchyard by the little bay we feel the legend's loveliness,
Nor sift truth from evasion, knowing poetry may lift an unsuspected truth,
and make legend and dream into reality.
I do not know if long ago the Arimathean came…..
I know that Christ has been here, all the same!

Stepping into the quiet interior of St Just Church, I find myself within a large spacious building - a rather grand arched colonnade of white Gothic stonework runs its length. Sadly, Victorian restoration has removed much of its medieval splendour. For me the most striking features today are the beautiful stained glass windows. Over the altar, one depicts the Virgin Mary and Mary Magdalene with the Christ figure. Another illustrates the Tree of

Life with Solomon and Abraham. Many saints are portrayed, including St Anthony, St Francis, St David, St Peter and of course St Just. I sit for an attunement and St Just is making his presence known very forcefully:

ST JUST

"Dear pilgrim you are SO welcome to this little church dedicated to me. We are ALL pilgrims through life. In my day if one was imbued with the Living Christ it was quite normal to give up all to follow our Master. I was blessed with this awareness and found myself here on the Roseland Peninsula for the best part of my ministry. You will dear pilgrim, discover my Holy Well and close-by I had my cell. In my early days there was virtually nothing along this foreshore - it was wild and barren land. Gradually though, even in my lifetime, a small community was set up. Pilgrims travelled through to sites of special worship. Travellers arrived, and voyagers from across the seas landed. We lived a very simple life. The seas hereabouts abounded with fish and shellfish of all sorts. There were hedgerows full of berries and fields of mushrooms. As I say our way of life was quite simple. Our needs were fully met. We wanted for nothing. This was because our needs were small indeed.

In my day there were still the remnants of Druidic worship. Although the Romans had almost wiped out this form of worship, little did they realize that it was our way also. We called it as it is still known today, Celtic Christianity, which had its roots in 'The Way' the perfect way to live - in simplicity, in truth, loving all, condemning none, (where have I heard these words before - White Eagle?), always on hand to bless those in need, to heal the sick, to offer a helping hand. Not for us the trappings of the Roman Church. We understood their principles, their creed and we delivered what was desired by them - the Holy Powers, BUT we lived in a simple way, expressing the simple adage of our beloved Master Jesus, the Christ, to 'Love your neighbour as yourself. Do good to those who harm you. Bless and heal with no thought of self, for all is provided.' The Light cometh. The Light lighteth up the land. The Light filters through into all the recesses of the heart till it is filled with that Redeeming Love.

We knew of Joseph of Arimathea bringing Jesus to this ancient land. The legend was still very strong in the landscape and THIS was the reason why we, the saints of old, came to these precious Isles following in the footsteps of our Master. We came to spread the Gospel, which we did. We were prepared to suffer if needs be, go without sustenance if this was to be the case, BECAUSE our Lord died for us and we were His Servants of Light. Beloved Mary, our Virgin Mother - we KNEW of her visit here with the Master Jesus as a boy.

Thank you dear pilgrim for visiting our church. We know you will leave your offerings where you think appropriate. We bless you. We thank you. We wish you well on your journey with Beloved Mary, our blessed and gracious Lady. Amen."

I rejoice at receiving these words from St Just himself: *"Thank you blessed St Just for your words of wisdom and your blessings - thank you."* All that he has expressed I need to reflect on. One key point is that in his day it was known that the Lady Mary came to these shores with the boy Jesus. Why is it hidden today?

WHO WAS ST JUST?

It seems to be generally accepted that he was Prince Iestyn one of the sons of the fifth century Cornish King Geraint I, ruler of the ancient Celtic Kingdom of Dumnonia. According to a church leaflet written by J. Vavasor Hammond: *'As far back as AD 550, the church was founded in honour of St Just, apparently one of the many Celtic missionaries who preached the Gospel in these islands and whose Churchmanship of pure, primitive order was ruled, first and foremost, by steadfast appeal to Scriptural standards. To these Celtic Christians we owe a great debt, not only for their missionary labours, but also for their sturdy testimony to the independent origins and status of our ancient British Christianity.'* These comments tie in very much with St Just's own words and the overall picture is of a devotional, contented holy man of good faith, dedicated to his missionary work

CELTIC CHRISTIANITY

Shall we take a brief look at the above. Celtic Christianity had its roots in ancient Celtic culture which expressed its belief system through everyday worship. This was a celebration of the great Earth Mother and respect for all living things. It recognized and worked with the natural rhythm of life through the regular cycle of the four seasons - winter, spring, summer and autumn - brought into being by the Earth's annual orbit around the sun. Within this natural cycle, each season had a purpose. Winter was a time of rest and renewal, when the seeds lay dormant in the ground. Springtime brought the great awakening, as new shoots broke forth into the light from deep within the dark earth, and buds appeared on the trees. Throughout the summertime was the flowering and leafing, wherein nature was seen in all its glory. Autumn - this was for the fruiting, the harvest and planting for next year's growth. The Celts celebrated each season with Fire or Solar Festivals. Midwinter and midsummer were marked by the solstices and the mid point of spring and autumn by the equinoxes. Their Fire Festivals brought into play the great Cosmic Light, which was invoked by their leaders, the Druid Priests. This Light and the vibrational energies generated, were used to heal the land, help with crop growth and bring balance and harmony to the natural world. Over time, as the Roman Church took a firmer grip, the ancient Celtic festivals were converted into Christian seasonal celebrations. For your interest I list the Celtic seasonal cycle and alongside, their Christian counterparts. The dates put forward apply to the Northern Hemisphere and can vary slightly.

December 21st - 25th	Winter Solstice	Christmas
February 2nd	Imbolc	Candlemas
March 21st	Spring Equinox	Easter
May 1st	Beltane	May Day
June 21st - 24th	Summer Solstice	Midsummer
August 1st	Lammas	First Harvest
September 23rd - 24th	Autumn Equinox	Harvest Festival
October 31st - November 2nd	Samhain	Halloween.

So how does Celtic Christianity compare to Roman Christianity of its day? There are some key differences.

First and foremost is in their belief system. For the Celtic tradition, the fifth century British Celt Pelagius, preached that essential goodness was inherent in man and that he had freewill, thereby was responsible for his own actions. However, the argument set out by Augustine of Hippo for the Roman Church in the same era, was that man was inherently evil and that life was pre-ordained by God. With this argument the door was opened to relinquish personal responsibility and introduce the concept of repentance and forgiveness of sins by an all powerful God, which could only be accessed through the priest. The Roman Church was very much a male dominated, authoritarian organization, whereas the Celtic Church, which revered the Sacred Feminine, was more egalitarian, thus allowing for woman to share in the ministry. Further, the religion professed by the Roman Church was centred round the parish and its priest. The Celtic way was based in the monastery, from where missionary monks went forth to preach the Gospel as did Christ's disciples. In AD 664, the Synod of Whitby was set up in order to try and solve the many differences. Judgment fell on the authority of St Peter for the Roman Church to whom Jesus said: *'you are Peter, on this rock I shall build my church.'* The result of this decision was that the doctrines of the Roman Church were enforced in strict adherence to Rome. One of the outcomes of this new dictate was that the Celtic Cistercian monastic communities were gradually replaced by the Benediction order.

ST JUST'S HOLY WELL

The church clock strikes its mellow tone as I exit the St Just Church. I feel inspired to leave my offerings - a beautiful shell from Llansteffan beach in Carmarthenshire and a trine-shaped stone from Kilve on the North Somerset coast, close to the Celtic cross by the creek. Leaving the churchyard I follow a sign for *'St Just's Well'*. As I turn into the little path leading to the Holy Well, a sense of great reverence comes over me, as I realize that St Just himself would have walked this way. The well has a beautifully preserved stone entrance and sunlight is playing on luxuriant green ferns surrounding this little sanctuary. There is an abundance of lovely clear water within, which seems to be seeping through the vegetation from the hillside above. This is a joy to behold because so many of our ancient wells are very muddied or dried up, as for example the St Anthony Holy Well in Llansteffan. I am completely alone. I leave a shiny piece of white quartz on the edge of the stone entrance saying: *"I offer this small token from a heart filled with love and in respect for the sacredness of this place of yours St Just."* My impression is that the waters of this Holy Well are imbued with healing properties and I dab a little of the precious water on my third eye and heart centre.

St Just's Holy Well

I am sorry I have not brought with me an exchange gift of water. In the boot of my car I keep a bag containing offerings and small phials of water collected from sacred places - holy wells, rivers and lakes. So I decide on the 'big trek'. First of all, it's up the steep path from the well, then over the little stone stile, up the many steps climbing back through the churchyard gardens, out onto the road and then down the road to the car! I collect a bottle which holds water from Holy Brook below Hembury Fort on Dartmoor and return the same route. Once again I am lucky as I have the ancient well to myself. I pour the water from Holy Brook into the St Just Well with a blessing, thus transferring the energies from Devon to Cornwall Before I leave, I ask permission to collect a little of the fresh clear water. At the end of my time here, once again I climb back up the many steps to the top road - am I dedicated or what! It is at this point I go in search of St Just's cell and believe I have discovered its position in some woodland above the well.

Back at the car, I sip a little coffee from my flask, quietly mulling over events. A Shearing's coach arrives - about thirty people alight and file past, heading for the St Just-in-Roseland Church. I am so glad I visited earlier, when all was peaceful, being magically divested of humans. I have had such a inspirational time here, for which I once again utter my heartfelt thanks.

At the close of my day I am to go to Golden Fort in Roseland's hinterland (see Chapter 3) and then drive west to Penzance for Cape Cornwall (see Chapter 5). Although Beloved Mary has not featured in my travelling today, I have been aware of her presence as the ever loving guide. On leaving St Just-in-Roseland, she and Naomi journeyed overland to the settlement of Roscassa, at which site Mary enacted a Cosmic Light Ceremony. They then went east through Rosevine to the coast near Porthcurno, from where they took a boat across Gerrans Bay to Carne Beach. This was the start point for the next stage of Mary's pilgrimage which took her and Naomi through The Hinterland.

CHAPTER 2
THE LIZARD PENINSULA
The Goddess Awakens

The Lady Mary, while staying at Place in St Anthony-in-Roseland, took a pilgrimage to the Lizard Peninsula, where I understand her destination was to be Cow-y-Jack Druidic settlement. While looking at the map of The Lizard I am struck by two things. First, the sheer number of '*Roses*' in the east of the peninsula, a possible indication of Mary having been there. Secondly, the place name '*Cow-y-Jack*' - a link with Hathor the Cow Goddess of ancient Egypt, seemed too obvious to be random and could not be ignored. I asked Mary and was told, that this was indeed a Temple dedicated to the Goddess and that there was also an ancient Atlantean Temple in the Etheric.

Excellent - but my puzzle was, how did Mary get there on her journeying through Cornwall? I was trying to bring her south to the Lizard Peninsula from central Cornwall as part of her pilgrimage west. I failed miserably until suddenly the light dawneth! Of course, she would have made a separate journey from the Roseland Peninsula. Obvious really, but not so when crawling on the floor immersed in the map. I had to make a conscious link with Mary, put myself in her shoes and the answer came. Both Mary and Naomi undertook this pilgrimage to Cow-y-Jack with their Druid companions. They first crossed Falmouth Bay to Swanpool beach on the east coast of The Lizard, where they initially stayed at a settlement south of Mawnan Smith. From there they went south overland to Durgan, followed by a short sea journey around the coastline to Gillan Harbour, then on across land over Roskridge Beacon to the settlement of Cow-y-Jack. Whilst there Mary took part in a sacred Ceremony to reactivate the ancient Atlantean Temple and I shall perform a Ceremony of Light to earth it.

The busy Christmas season is upon us. For a short while I was feeling a little frustrated at not being able to continue with my Mission with Beloved Mary and just a bit separate from her essence. However, after receiving the following inspirational words, I realized that this was all part of my journey. My feelings were obviously registered above, because as has happened on numerous occasions, I was woken in the middle of the night and knew I was to go into the silence. I lit my candle and with my Ohm CD playing very quietly in the background, I settled down. This is what I received:

MARY

"Child, we are with you. We never leave you. You are just not aware of our presence when involved so fully with normal life in the physical. We will never leave you and you will ALWAYS return to us. For you and I have a job to do. Our Mission is not complete. We have much to do. All is well you know dearest child - all is well."

From Mary I was aware of great tenderness. For myself I was feeling deep emotion. The quintessence of the soft pink rose of Divine Mother, starting at my heart centre, gradually encompassed my whole being. I was saying: *"Blessed Mary. I am overwhelmed with feelings of the deepest love. I am back in this place of joy. Why can I not always be here Beloved One?"* From Mary:

MARY

"Dear child it is not possible when living this Earthly life to be totally at-one with all life all the time. Or to be at-one with the Divine essence all the time. Because of the existence of free will which offers you - your soul - choice, how one uses that element of choice, determines if one feels fulfilled and at peace within oneself.

Even in ones darkest hour and I am not suggesting this has been for you at this time, but even in ones darkest hour, you are NEVER left alone. There is always an Angel of Light, watching over you, guiding your pathway - so full of compassion. This beautiful Being is unable to interfere with your choices, but as your Guardian Angel, is your compassionate protector at all times - ALL LOVE. Once each soul in incarnation realizes the significance of this, then the unbearable becomes the bearable. So never forget your Angel of Light is on hand at all times. You have a Divine friend who will never leave you. I hear you saying beloved child 'yes I do know this - I do understand this.' It is so, but do we forget at difficult times? Do we forget to make that contact? Do we forget to ask for help? I think so. This beloved one is not an admonishment. It is a compassionate recognition of a normal part of Earthly existence which we have ALL felt at times of darkness.

Rest assured, that each one of you dear children is so blessed, for each is a part of that great heart of compassion and pure love which is for all time. The Angels of Light and Love protect you ALL. The Masters of Light guide and guard you. All the Beings of Light are yours for the calling. You remember what our beloved son Jesus taught 'Ask and it shall be given unto you. Seek and ye shall find.' The Beloved Ones are SO close dear children of the Earth Plane - so close. Talk with them - walk with them - and peace will your yours - for ever more."

I offer a special blessing to Mary for her wise words. A gentle reprimand perhaps but one filled with compassion. This experience is a little lesson for me which I am happy to share with you as it might be of value. I am sure there are times when we ALL forget the loving presence of our Guardian Angel or beloved Master or Guide. These Beings of Light - these beautiful companions of our innermost, are always on hand to help us. Dear White Eagle will often remind us that we must ASK for help, as it is in hearing our call, that the Wise Ones are able to draw close. But in times of need we so often forget. I thought I had got this one 'sussed' by now!

I am now going much deeper into meditation. I am bringing in an Egyptian link. Into my inner awareness are coming Nefertiti, Horus and Hathor so I am firmly placed in ancient Egypt. It is bringing to mind that Mary and Joseph her husband, were Essene Brethren, who underwent training for the priesthood in the Temples of Egypt. I have also learnt that Jesus and Naomi were 'released' from their Temple training in order to undertake this spiritual pilgrimage to the mystic Isles of Britain.

As these thoughts are whirling around, I am being 'taken over' by a very powerful entity which I 'know' is from ancient Dynastic times in Egypt, long before these happenings 2,000 years ago. Sitting to full stature in what I can only describe as a throne, with my arms resting on its arms, I am feeling totally empowered and very strong. Then the Sun God of The Aton speaks with me - AKHNATON. I am astonished. I am to write down his words. While Akhnaton is with me I have a total change of personality - I have become Akhnaton. I am aware, that although seated firmly on my throne, there is an awkwardness of stance. I am also conscious of my having a slightly mis-shapen physical body and elongated head.

After he had left me and I returned to normal consciousness, I closed down my attunement and went to my bookcase. I have a very old book, which has sat there for years gathering dust, which is called *'The Secret Place of the Lion'* by George Hunt Williamson. Williamson gives a description of Akhnaton (Page 54): *'He was a small man, not over five feet five inches tall, and displayed feminine characteristics. He had a swollen belly and an elongated skull poised on an unusually long neck.'* This is EXACTLY how I was feeling and visualizing myself while sitting on that throne. The aspect of the description which talks of him displaying feminine characteristics, was obviously apparent to the people, because according to Williamson: *'behind his back he was called 'Sister of Egypt'* (Page 54). Akhnaton speaks:

AKHNATON

"I am Akhnaton of the One God. The Sun is King. I represent the male-female aspect of the Godhead. I am THE ONE - the chosen one who later incarnated as THE CHRIST- Jesus of the Holy Land. I am He who is ALL LIGHT. I live in the Sun's essence. I am the King who reigneth over ALL. But, I am also Compassion and Love. I am Purity and Truth. I am you. You are me. We are one. YOU and I are ONE. It is so. It is decreed. You are one with the Sun of Life. All Creation is yours Earth people. KNOW THIS. You are not alone. You are not separate. You are ONE with ALL Creation - with ALL Life. You are the Sun. You are the Heart of the Sun. The Sun of all Creation shines in you - shines through you. You manifest Light. You ARE Light.

You and I are ONE. I am the Light of the World. I am this Light I am your Light. You are my Light."

These last three short sentences I am speaking. Gradually the powerful masculine aspect of this Great Being recedes and I become imbued with the gentle feminine side of Akhnaton. I find that I am smiling. The energies are softer now and I become encompassed in a warm pink glow. The Divine Mother principle is taking over from the Father principle. The following words are now received from the feminine Akhnaton:

AKHNATON

"I am the Heart. I am the Love. I am you and you are me. We are one. We are one Heart of Divine essence. I am the Sacred Feminine essence of all time. I am the embodiment of that perfect and pure Rose. I am SHE who is all Compassion - all Love. I am the embodiment of Divine Will, Wisdom and Power and Love. I am Truth. I am Purity. I am the Sun. I am the Moon. I am YOU. You are ME. I am in you. You are in me. We are ONE."

As the Spirit Being who is Akhnaton leaves me, I am saying: *"Divine Being - I thank you. Master of Light - I thank you. Great Akhnaton - I thank you."* I am totally overwhelmed. The beauty and power of this Master of the One Light has filled me completely. I am honoured and privileged. This great entity has gone - the energies have shifted and I am shivering. If I needed any proof that THEY - the beautiful Beings of Light had not left me - this was it! A simple message of the Law of Non-Separation was it seems, manifested from the highest level of perfect understanding - from deep within Cosmic Life. I do not profess to have full comprehension of what is expressed here. However, it would seem that the dual aspects of the Godhead - the male and the female - was epitomized in the incarnated being of Akhnaton and as such, were in part an expression of the Ancient Mysteries.

Questions are now arising. It would seem that Mary has brought Akhnation into our story - why? Does he have a part to play in Mary's Mission with me today? Was Mary in incarnation at the same time as Akhnaton? No answers as yet, but I am sure they will be given me.

The night is moving on a pace. As I sit here quietly mulling over these happenings, I am remembering, that when I was at Nine Maidens in Cape Cornwall on the last day of my Cornish pilgrimage, some weeks before this encounter, I was picking up a strong Egyptian link and names from the dynastic era were being given to me, including Akhnaton (see Chapter 5). Also, when looking at the map of the Lizard Peninsula, certain place names of apparent Egyptian descent stood out. One was *'Tye Rocks'* (Queen Tiyi was the name of Akhnaton's mother). Then there was *'Lion Rock'* and *'Lion's Den'* close to a Biblical name *'Enoch.'* The Lion or Sphinx of ancient Egypt in The Mysteries, is said to represent one who seeks Divine Truth. Also representative of Egypt we have St Anthony in the Roseland Peninsula across from The Lizard. At this stage I am realizing, that the link with Egypt is strong and well identified in this particular area of Cornwall.

THE CHRIST MASS

It is the 1st of December 2008. A most remarkable and spectacular happening in the night sky was made manifest this night. It was a triple conjunction of the new crescent Moon with the Planets, Venus and Jupiter. This magical event was witnessed by myself and a few friends around 6.00 pm. The night was cold - the sky was clear and in the unfathomable blackness amidst myriad stars, this mystical sight was revealed. Out came the binoculars, as we were eager to get an even clearer picture. The physical sight was awe-inspiring as the two Planets looking like one huge Star of Light, lined up at the lower right hand edge of the slither of the silver crescent Moon. It is hard to describe the enchantment and magnetism. The event itself seemed to be heralding in the sacredness of Christmas - the CHRIST MASS. The inner meaning of the beautiful Venus brings a harmonious aspect to the season of love and goodwill, and offers to the World its outpouring of peace. Jupiter extends to us all, new opportunities to expand our own spiritual awareness and connection to the Cosmos as we enter this sacred time of year.

It is the following day and I know Beloved Mary has been waiting for me as I come before my altar. Remembering her words of wisdom a day or so ago, the busyness of the season has evaporated and I am in a different space. I am quite calm. There is a stillness in the air. It is as though the Angels are preparing the way once again for the celebration of the birth of our Saviour - Jesus the Christ, who came to Earth in human form a little over 2000 years ago. The magic of Christmas has never left me. Each year throughout my life, I feel the excitement and am responsive to its holiness. This year is no exception. I wait quietly in contemplation:

MARY

"Dear child - be still now. Reflect on the significance of this CHRIST MASS. In the stillness and silence of your own heart you will remember much. Soul memories will return to you and this Christ Mass will be a profound experience for you dear one. Nearer the day put aside time for remembering the birth of our beloved Jesus. I will speak with you again. For now we would wish only that you go forth in joy and reverence for this special time of your calendar year. You will know that the date which is celebrated as the birth of our Saviour is not the ACTUAL birth date. However, it is good that this time has been chosen and been set aside for worship in this way.

New beginnings and expansion of consciousness is especially efficacious with the magnificent Jupiter in such a significant position in your sky at this time. My beloved Planet Venus is helping to prepare the way for the stillness to enter every human heart at this time, to harmonize conditions and bring peace on all levels - peace to the human heart and peace to all humanity. Peace be with you my child. I will speak with you again."

As the Holy Mother leaves me, I am aware of a very strong but gentle energy entering my being - it is Joseph of Arimathea. This is the first contact he has made with me on my pilgrimage with Mary in Cornwall and yet he had a key role to play as her protector during her travelling in the South West of Britain. As you will see, he also undertook this role to safeguard Mary in the Holy Land. His words refer to the well-known Christmas story - the journey Mary and Joseph made to Bethlehem at the time of Jesus' birth. Following a ruling from Caesar Augustus that all were to be taxed according to their own city, Joseph as a descendent of David, was obliged to leave Galilee and travel to Bethlehem in Judea, which was the city of David. Joseph of Arimathea:

JOSEPH OF ARIMATHEA

"I was in the Holy Land at the time of the birth of Jesus. I travelled with my sister Mary and Joseph her husband to Bethlehem where she gave birth. They had need of a protector and helper on that journey and I was one of the many who travelled with them. The journey was long and arduous and very tiring for Mary in the advanced stages of her pregnancy. (I find myself mentally asking the question: *"Where was I at that time?"* meaning - where was Naomi, Mary's two year old daughter, which age disclosure was given me by Mary at Buckfast Abbey - see Chapter 11). *You dear Naomi were safe in the arms of Elizabeth your aunt and cared for by her for the duration of the time when Mary and Joseph were away.*

THE BABE WAS BORN - our beloved Jesus came into incarnation and there was much rejoicing in the Heavenly Spheres. The Saviour of all mankind, who had prepared himself during many incarnations, returned to the Earth in his new physical body. The tidings had come to pass. The Star - the most beautiful Planet of Venus - prepared the soul for its reincarnation and its Light guided many to worship and behold the new born incarnated Christ Being. The Light shone all about - the Heavens were ablaze with the magnificence and the wonder of this Cosmic Act. IT WAS DONE. A New Age had begun and our beloved Master of Light had come to Earth. As I say, there was much rejoicing.

For you now dear Naomi, this event will take on new meaning and you will be greatly blessed. There is a blessing for the whole of humanity at this time. For many many people, their hearts will stir with an incoming Cosmic Love of which they are not always aware. But, the beauty of this Christ Mass season WILL reach the hearts of ALL men and women. Amen Amen Amen."

My response to these sacred words from Beloved Mary and Joseph of Arimathea: *"Blessed Beings of Light I thank you for your beautiful insights this day. Amen."*

At this point I am a little curious as to Mary's children, so after this attunement, I collect my Holy Bible which belonged to my mother and is over one hundred years old. I see it is printed in 1906 and cost 'Ten-pence' (10d), and was produced by The British and Foreign Bible Society. I also notice on the front page that it is: *'Appointed to be read in CHURCHES'* which my dear mother has altered to *'ANYWHERE'*! In *Luke Chapter 2 Verse 7* the words:

'And she brought forth her first born son......' This does not exclude the possibility of a daughter having been born earlier. We will discuss the Virgin birth further into the book. Something else: *Matthew Chapter 13 Verse 55* talks of the brothers of Jesus as being James, Joses, Simon and Judas. Sisters are mentioned but not named.

SOME CHRIST MASS REFLECTIONS

The birth of our Saviour in the stable in Bethlehem does hold a profound significance for me this year, as my path of service is interlaced with the Lady Mary's Mission. As the Christ Mass draws nearer, I feel that I am embracing at an even deeper level, that Cosmic connection with the Christ Light and our beloved Master Jesus. The celebrations with my own family at Christmas-time will I know be treasured. Before then in the sanctuary of my own home, I settle for a period of stillness. I am aware of the presence of Angels. My prayer: *"Beloved Mary - the 'Rose in the Heart'. At this sacred time of the year - the time of the Christ Mass - I tune in to the energies of the loving heart. I tune in to the Light from the great Sun-Star - that Star which guided the Shepherds and the Wise Men to worship at the stable - to worship at the cave in the heart - to worship the reborn Light - the Sun/Son - the Babe - at this Christ Mass. My blessed Mary, I am with you now in the stable where the Light shineth all around. Teach me of the inner mysteries of the birth of the Christ Child."* Mary:

MARY

"Dearest daughter - my Sister of Light. I acknowledge your presence and your words. I in turn offer a blessing from the purist sacred heart. The Light from the Heaven World is all about - it shineth within your heart as it shineth in the heart of ALL humanity."

Mary has brought in the energies of White Eagle and these are his words:

WHITE EAGLE

"Christmas - the CHRIST MASS - what is in a name? The celebration of the Christ Mass is not just for those of you living in the western world. You alone do not have a monopoly of the birth of this great Being - this great Light - this pure essence right from the heart of the Logos. This Christ essence is of all times - it has always been and always will be. It is the love - the perfection - the joy - the trust - within every human heart. It is the secret of Universal Light - it is the essence of pure intent. The Christ Light is the love in every human heart. The Christ Light is the joy which we can all encounter when we offer ourselves to be channels for that Light. The Christ Light is the vibration of the magical Flame of the Cosmos - the Eternal Flame of Truth. The Christ Light is manifested in and through the Being - the great Initiate - known to you as JESUS, THE CHRIST.

Jesus - born as a babe, came into manifestation in human form. His beloved mother Mary the blest one, offered herself for this task of the greatest, profound and sacred joy - Beloved Mary with whom you now dearest sister, walk your life for a short time. But you know, she is always with you as the Divine essence of love in your heart, as she is within each human heart. This blest and blessed Lady is the epitome of purist love and perfection. She came to Earth with a role to play. She suffered greatly but she also received great joy. Her suffering at the loss of her beloved child Jesus, was always with her throughout her life (see Chapter 7). It was she also, who took on the pain of the World. She is to be revered and blessed by all people - all souls now on Earth - not just those who call themselves Christians. She is a Being of Divine Light. She is the love in every human heart. Welcome this gentle but profound Being of Light into YOUR heart this Christ Mass time my children. The Beloved Mary and her Son Jesu the great and gentle Initiate, are always there for you to call on - always there in each human heart. I leave you now dear Peace Rose.

With these thoughts I offer the blessing of the eternal Father and Mother God and Christ the Son at this Christ Mass time. Amen. Mary wishes to speak with you now."

As White Eagle offers this benediction he stands before me robed in white. At his heart centre is a Golden Star which is radiating brilliant luminous Heavenly Light. He draws the ancient sacred symbol of the Cross within the Circle in the air. Now a personal message from Mary:

MARY

"My dear little Pillar of Light - for indeed you are just that. For this special time in your life you are MY Pillar of Light, who has offered herself in service to bring in that ancient Light to feed the hearts of all humanity, and to bring the Light back to the sacred Isles of Britain. At this time of year we would all in the Land of Light, bless you dear Sister for your endeavours, and your heart filled with love. Be at peace now. Walk with your hand in the hand of our Beloved Son Jesus, through whom the Christ Light flowed. Enjoy the peace and beauty and love of this season of joy. Bless you dear one. Bless you. Go forth with joy in your heart and all will be well."

I thank Mary and White Eagle for their presence and blessing at this sacred time of the year. I am now ready for the Christ Mass celebrations with great happiness and a peaceful heart.

White Eagle has given us many beautiful words pertaining to the Christ Mass. This extract is taken from *The White Eagle Lodge Journal - Stella Polaris - December/January 2005/6.* On Page 18 White Eagle says: *'Many question the truth of this old, old story of the birth of Jesus, of the visitation of the Shepherds and the Wise Men. Nevertheless this old Christian story contains a universal truth which you can accept in all its simplicity. It presents a profound Cosmic truth, a truth which has been again and again demonstrated to humanity from the beginning - if there ever was a beginning! It always has been and always will be, this truth of Divine birth in matter.*

Don't let the little lower mind analyse and doubt this when you all enjoy the story of the birth in the stable. It means of course that Jesus Christ is born in a very humble, lowly state. The gentle Christ is worshipped by the Shepherds and the Magi. The simple and the wise all worship the Christ. The Shepherds signify those who have a little knowledge, who, through meditation and contemplation, behold the Light in the Heavens. They are the young Initiates. They follow the Star to the birthplace. The Wise Men are those who have occult knowledge of a more advanced type, but they too have learnt the lesson of humility. *They come as messengers to every human soul entering upon physical life. They bring gifts of Gold, Frankincense and Myrrh to that soul. Students of astrology know well that every soul that incarnates does so with certain opportunities or gifts. Every soul has to learn the value of Gold, both physical and spiritual. Every soul is sprinkled with the incense of Wisdom. Every soul is sent into the world with potentialities, but must also taste the Myrrh or bitterness, as well as the joy in life. Think of the significance of this story; and remember also at Christmas time the adoration of the Divine Mother and the Christ Child in her arms.'*

Now from me a short poem.

CHILD OF THE STAR

*Let the **Star of Light** shine bright and strong over our beloved Planet.*
Let it be a Beacon for the searcher of truth.
May Deep Peace fill the hearts of each and everyone this Christmas-tide.
*The message of Peace and Joy on Earth is for **all** humanity.*
Let that sweet song go forth to touch each soul with Love.
*Night is falling - there is a hush in the air - the Child is born - the **Child of the Star of Light** is born.*
Born to help humanity to rise as if on wings of light to that Heavenly Sphere.
*Let the **Star of Light** shine bright and strong over the whole earth…*
*Let the **Star of Light** manifest in perfect love within each human heart….*
*The **Christ Child** is the Bearer of that Light.*
***We** are the Custodians of that Light.*
Let us be worthy of this privilege
Let us take the Star into our own hearts,
*That we may be filled with Peace, Love and Joy this **Christ Mass**.*
*Let the **Christ Child** be within us all for we are so blessed.*
*Let the **Light** from the great **Star** shine in each precious heart.*
*Let us be as that little child, for we are each a **Child of the Star**…*

HATHOR THE EGYPTION COW GODDESS

After celebrating the Christ Mass, I am ready to proceed with Mary's Mission I return in thought to the Cow-y-Jack settlement on the Lizard Peninsula - the Temple site dedicated to Hathor. First, who was Hathor? What do we know of her? Hathor was a very ancient Egyptian cow-deity going back beyond Dynastic times. She was associated with the great Temple of Kom Ombo situated on the River Nile. There are many inconsistencies with identification, but the most popular myth is that she was the wife of Horus, the Sun God - Ra - the Divine King. Here one of her titles was Mistress of the Universe and the Skies - the Heavenly or Celestial cow. In this respect Hathor was the great Mother Goddess and as a fertility deity, was represented in the Milky Way She was also recognized as the Goddess of Love, very much synonymous with Isis. In fact, different cultures claimed her for their own in this respect. For the Hebrews, she was Astarte and the Greeks embraced her as

Aphrodite. Later in the Christianized version she became embodied in the Virgin Mary. Other titles she holds are Goddess of Joy and Mistress of Jubilation due to her association with dance and music - her musical instrument being the sistrum. There are many interpretations of the Goddess Hathor in sculptures. In one beautiful portrayal she is wearing a long red dress, wearing her turquoise musical neckless, holding her staff and an ankh, one of her symbols. On her head is the Sun-disc cupped by cow's horns, which image is representative of the crescent Moon - the feminine aspect encompassing the great Sun God - Ra.

CEREMONY FOR THE ATLANTEAN TEMPLE OF THE GODDESS AT COW-Y-JACK.

As this site is not only dedicated to the Goddess but also one which houses an ancient Atlantean Temple in the Etheric Realm, I propose performing my Ceremony to earth the Atlantean Temple with one or two additions relating to the Goddess. Before I begin my sacred Ceremony, Mary wishes to say a few words:

MARY

"Dear Child thank you for your contact today. Yes, we are ready now for you to proceed with the next stage of your journey in the South West. First, as you know, we would wish you to reactivate the ancient Temple of the Goddess at Cow-y-Jack in the Lizard Peninsula. When I was at Place I did a special pilgrimage there (ah confirmation), *in order to reactivate the ancient Atlantean Temple in the Etheric and to bring a blessing and Light to the land from the Cosmos. It is for you now dear one to reaffirm this ancient Cosmic Light and bring the Atlantean Temple to be earthed for its further use in the coming Age. We would ask that you put aside a special time for this sacred task. Once more we thank you for your dedication to this work designated by the ancient Brotherhood, to bring that Light back to these sacred Isles Thank you dear child and bless all your endeavours."*

It is 12.00 noon New Years Eve 2008. Is this a fortuitous day to enact my sacred Ceremony according to the planetary alignments, I ask myself? I am very much a novice when it comes to Astrology, but will attempt to interpret the position of the Planets at this time. If there are any professional Astrologers among you - bear with me! According to *'Raphael's Astronomical Ephemeris of the Planets' Places for 2008'* on this day I see that transiting Mercury the Planet of Communication and transiting Jupiter the Planet of Expansion, are conjunct (both at 28.49 degrees) in the sign of Capricorn. In this position Mercury and Jupiter together will bring a pure strong link with the higher realms of consciousness. Both Planets moving through the earth sign of Capricorn would deem this to be a perfect time to reactivate and earth the ancient energies. Finally, both Planets are conjunct Venus in my own birth chart, which aspect brings a harmonious blessing of Divine Love. Over all, 31st December would appear to be a favourable day to actualize my Ceremony.

As before I meticulously cleanse my sacred space with sage. I set up my altar with a silver star, a candle and a piece of white quartz crystal for the ancient Druids. Today I also have a beautiful pink rose for Mary and the Sacred Feminine. My prayer: *" Beloved Mary - great Beings of Light - Blessed Ones - I enter this sacred space with pure intent and the deepest love. Let me be a pure channel for the Light as I activate your Divine will this day. Amen."*

As each beautiful crystal is presented - the merlinite, the turquoise and rose-pink, my inner vision shows me the Lizard Peninsula and the ancient Atlantean Temple at Cow-y-Jack. I am seeing this on a mountain top and realize that I have returned to Atlantean times. As I watch I see a Ceremony taking place in the Etheric. A vast number of Elders in white robes are standing in a circle chanting. Then all is still and I know it is my turn! This is the moment to enact my Ceremony to bring the Atlantean Temple into physical form. As I intone the sacred words and reach the point where I invoke the ancient Temple of Atlantis to be grounded on Mother Earth, a Priest of the old times strikes the Sacred Earth with his staff, thus sealing the deed. I hear the sound loudly and quite distinctly. I am conscious that the Cosmic Light has shot through Planet Earth to its central core. Following this, I add a special blessing for the Sacred Feminine and bring into perfect balance the male/female vibrational energies at this hallowed place. In my imagination, I place beneath the ground close to the Temple altar at Cow-y-Jack, both white and pink quartz crystals.

Now images of ancient Egypt come in. There is a Temple with the Winged Disc on a huge lintel set above its gleaming white entrance pillars. I see the Sphinx and the Eye of Horus. The smell of the sea assails my nostrils which I think is a bit odd. I am taken below ground to the Inner Sanctum of the Temple within the Sphinx. This is the place of the hidden Mysteries. The smell I am experiencing could well be a 'below the earth' smell. I am going deeper into my meditation now. From somewhere Mary is talking with me:

MARY

"Bless you dear child bless you. We - all the Masters of that Universal Christ Light - bless you."

She is gone. Within this vast Temple of Light and Sound, the great Ohm resounds throughout the sacred space. The Temple is filled with white robed Brethren. There is an altar on which resides a Chalice and pure white flame. A beautiful Master dressed in a white robe with a gold braid tie is standing behind the altar. His arms are raised up offering a benediction. It is Is-Ra (White Eagle in his Egyptian incarnation) and he wishes to speak with me:

IS-RA

"My dear Sister of Light. We welcome you to this Temple below the Sphinx in the ancient world. In time your memory of such times will return to an even greater degree. For now, we welcome your presence within this ancient Brotherhood. We wish you to feel

the vibrations of the powerful energies within this Temple. You have already been aware of what you thought was the smell of the sea. It is indeed similar, because here under the Sphinx, we are touching a lower level of land - we are below the surface of the Earth. Thus - there is a certain smell which permeates through this sacred place.

In this lifetime you have not had the opportunity of visiting this ancient land. In time dear one - in time..... Now, we would wish that you go deeper into the silence of all Eternity, and with your inner vision and awareness look to the stars - reach for the Flame of Eternal Truth which you will find in the Cosmos - that flame which is within your own heart.

This Temple of the Sphinx has indeed a direct ley line link with the Temple of Cow-y-Jack, as it has with ALL the ancient Temples in Britain. You yourself know through a meditative vision, of a direct link with the ancient Sun Temple of Stonehenge. In the Golden Age of past it is known that one could be transported - teleported if you wish - from place to place on your Planet. This indeed happened to you beloved one. In an experience you witnessed through an inner vision, you were part of an ancient Ceremony at Stonehenge. You were allowed to experience the actual concept of spiritual death, in order that you be reborn into the Light. Yes - indeed the experience WAS real. In those ancient days, you were transported in the sarcophagus to the Temple in Egypt I was your guide. Here you were initiated into the ancient Brotherhood of old and became a Priestess. This knowledge you then took back with you to ancient Britain, where you shared much with your Druid companions.

You have indeed had more than one physical incarnation in ancient Egypt, but this I am talking about is a time of accomplishment on an Etheric level through physical transportation from Stonehenge. By this I mean, that you allowed yourself to raise your physical vibrations to such a high degree, that your Etheric counterpart guided and protected your physical body as you went forth to re-emerge in the physical sense in Egypt."

These last words answer an earlier query I had regarding Etheric transportation and the re-emergence of a temporary physical body at the destination (see Chapter 3) - thank you Is-Ra.

At this juncture I will share with you the meditative experience at Stonehenge to which Is-Ra is referring. It was in the Spring of 2003 and I was sitting quietly listening to soft music with a very special friend. Suddenly we felt drawn to do a meditation. As I went into the silence I was immediately lifted into the Light and overshadowed by Spirit. These are my insights confirmed by my mediumistic friend and written down at the time. As you will read, it was a very physical experience.

MEDITATION AT STONEHENGE

'The first thing I was conscious of was a huge eye in front of me. Then, I was 'taken' to the ancient Sun Temple of Stonehenge in Wiltshire, which appeared to be very much as it is today, open to the skies, but more complete - the huge grey Sarsen uprights capped with the smaller Blue-stones. As I watched, the whole circle became totally infused with Light and I was aware of Druid Elders in white robes. I found myself kneeling before the

Rose Altar and one of the Elders, whom I can only describe as a Master, came forward and drew the ancient sign of the Equal Sided Cross within the Circle on my third eye centre. I realized this was a ritual opening of the third eye. I was dressed in some kind of long light robe. I had long dark curly hair braided in thick plaits which hung down in front of me over each shoulder. My hair almost immediately changed to straight and jet black in colour with a fringe and hanging to shoulder level. Obviously a reflection of the different cultures within ancient Britain and Egypt. I was being led forward and gently laid in a tomb - a sarcophagus. I felt myself crossing my hands on my chest - right hand over left (I was aware that I was physically doing this). The top of the sarcophagus closed over me and I was conscious that I must breathe very lightly to preserve the air. I felt no fear - just complete trust that all would be well. I went into some kind of state of suspended animation.

I 'awoke' to find myself in Egypt. The lid was lifted - I put my arms up and was very tenderly helped out of the 'coffin' by a person on either side of me. Then I was guided down a long cubed shaped corridor of Light and led into a deep underground chamber which I thought was below a pyramid. However, my physic friend told me afterwards that I was under the Sphinx. I could not tell the size of the chamber - it seemed both finite and infinite at the same time. The whole area was pulsating with Light, Colour and Sound - the most indescribably beautiful place I have ever been in. The very walls seemed to emanate the magic of the colours and sounds. I was taken before an altar of shimmering Light on which was a Chalice with a flame. As I stood there, a great shaft of pure White Light came down from the Cosmos and struck right into the heart of the little flame (I could actually hear a sort of rushing sound). As it did so, the whole area was filled with this Heavenly Light and a lesser Light shot from the flame right into my heart centre. I was given SEVEN BLESSINGS; Love, Power, Light, Protection, Peace, Wisdom and Joy.

My Egyptian guide NHAMI who identified herself a while back, was by my right side. She led me from this beautiful place until we both stood in front of the largest doors I have ever seen. We were like little ants - miniscule in comparison. I hear the words 'IT IS NOW TIME'. The huge doors silently opened forward as if by some magical power. I was then aware of my dear friend - my soul sister - with whom I was meditating, standing with me. (As I relive this I am picking up that she was Nhami of that past life). A man dressed in a simple white robe led me forward, to once again stand before an altar - it was IS-RA - our dear White Eagle. On the altar was a Golden Grail Cup, which as I focused on it, fluctuated between the Grail Cup and the most beautiful open-petalled White Lotus. I was handed the cup which was very heavy (I was conscious that I was physically taking the cup - I could feel its weight). I raised the Grail Cup to my lips, sipped the nectar and handed it back. I was then offered a little solid gold Six Pointed Star - my hands formed the shape of a heart as I brought the Star very gently right to my heart centre. I heard the words 'INFINITE JOY' and it was at this point that I realized, the whole had been an initiation in this life and a re-enactment of a past life initiation.'

That is the end of my Meditation and I then write: '*Slowly I opened my eyes and gradually returned to physical awareness. I asked my friend if I may share my* experiences with her. It is after this that she confirmed many things which linked to a heart awakening for her also. It is hard to describe how I was feeling - perhaps the words given 'Infinite Joy' best sums it up. The emotion of the whole experience suddenly struck us. We sat quietly together holding each others hands, then dissolved into tears of joy! For me the tears seem to whelm up from deep deep within at the wonder of such a profound shared soul experience. I can only say how amazed I am and how very very blessed and privileged I feel.'

My prayer: "I bless you dear White Eagle and beloved Minesta (Grace Cooke) and all those in the Land of Light who have made this possible. I thank you for guiding me forward along my Earthly journey. I thank you for your ever gentle, loving and wise presence. I give my life to the service of the Great White Light."

Back in the now - in my little room before my altar, I return to my Ceremony at Cow-y-Jack. Is-Ra is talking with me, when suddenly there is a change and a very commanding entity comes in which I know to be Akhnaton once more:

AKHNATON

"I am the Sun King. I am the Light. I reign supreme. There is but one God and I am the representative of that one Cosmic Light.

We have met before Sister. Now I wish to share with you a little more insight into our world. I built a great Temple. I built a great City near the Nile in ancient Egypt. Many followed me. It was the beginning of the acknowledgement of the one true Light - THE SUN.

We and by that I mean my wife Nefertiti and myself, ruled over this City of the Sun and it was good for a very long time. But there was jealousy abroad. There were those who wished to return to the old ways. The Priests of old had to a certain extent lost their power. Hidden conflict was rife, which eventually spilled out into concealed warfare - it was very subtle. The Temple of the Sun - the Flame of Eternal Truth and Light was doomed. It was time to retreat. My work was done. No more could I do this incarnation, but it was a beginning - the beginning of reintroduction of the 'One-God' concept to the people of the Earth Plane.

I was to reincarnate much much later as your beloved Jesus, whom the Christ Light shone through, as representative of the one true God. Once again it would appear that the darker elements of the Universe had won when the Master Initiate Jesus was crucified. But NO - his life - my incarnation as Jesus 2,000 years ago in your time scale, ignited The Flame - sealed the Flame of Cosmic Truth in the very soil of your Earth Plan. As his spilled blood seeped into the Earth, so a great awakening to Cosmic Life was activated. It was sealed in the sod for all times and a new Age of Enlightenment had begun with the Piscean Age.

Now, we are on the cusp of the Aquarian Age and what was formulated 2,000 years ago, is ready to be reactivated. The Light will shine once more and THIS TIME will bring your beautiful Planet ever nearer to the Golden Age. You and many many beloved Light Workers will be instrumental in bringing in that new Golden Age - the Age of the Temple of the Sun/Son - that one true God. We would wish that this message go out to the masses - to those who will listen - for they will be the salvation of your beautiful Planet. There is nothing to fear. All is in the hands of our Father-Mother God - that one true and pure energy of perfect Light - THE SUN - the Light behind everything that IS.

I leave you now. Go forth Pilgrim of Light and with your fellow Light Workers secure the future for your Planet, through knowledge, wisdom and love. Amen."

Akhnaton has withdrawn and the temperature has cooled considerably. I sit very still for a long time. Finally, I offer a blessing to this great Being of Light. My Ceremony at Cow-y-Jack is complete. I close my physic centres and ensure I am well grounded following such profound experiences. I offer myself in 'humble adoration' to the Light and to the Wise Beings who manifest the Ancient Wisdom. My beloved Mary, the Heart-Rose of Love, has directed so much into my life and my gratitude really is eternal.

NEW YEAR'S EVE

It is midnight on this New Year's Eve and I am hearing the bells ring out from our local St Michael Church. Reflecting on my past year, the many wondrous experiences and insights are coming to mind.

What does a New Year mean for you? Is it a time to review the year gone as I am doing, aware of the blessings received and challenges overcome? Perhaps you will be looking forward to the year ahead and wondering what the future holds. For many of us it is time for resolutions. We may wish to improve our physical well-being through exercise, diet, giving up smoking etc. For some, maybe it will be an opportunity to release old hurts and move forward with renewed hope. There are those who could be considering big life changes in one respect or another. Whatever our resolutions - perhaps our dreams - big or small, the majority of us will make them and the majority of us will let them drop! How can we ensure that they stick and don't get put away on Twelfth Night with the Christmas decorations, or at the very least forgotten by the end of January? How can we keep our plans and hopes alive? In brief, I would say; by careful planning, writing down our desires, putting into place a good dose of positive thinking and asking for Divine assistance.

What does White Eagle offer us on this subject? Over the years he has given us many beautiful, deeply spiritual New Year messages, but I have chosen to offer a very practical one. On Pages 9/10 of 'The Way of the Sun' he talks about looking forward positively and the use of visualization techniques: 'In your own lives always look forward, anticipate good. By anticipating good, by anticipating blessings and happiness, you are actually drawing these to you; you are creating through your imagination. Imagination is part of the psychic gift implanted in man's soul. Therefore, we say to you from spirit, use your heavenly imagination, imagine yourself in a state of perfect health, imagine yourself in a state of harmony. If your conditions are inharmonious, see them becoming smoother, better. Disciplined imagination is the key to creation. Perhaps you are unaware that whenever you think negatively you are actually creating negative conditions for yourselves. To create positive good, you must always think positively. If you do this habitually you will clear the mists which gather *round you - mists in your own soul, mists in your mind.....We cannot impress upon you too strongly to think always in terms of progress, of happiness and of achievement; and you will become healthy and happy. This is our special message for you as you stand at the beginning of a new year. For as you **image** your conditions, so you are setting into operation the machinery which will bring about the very picture you hold in your mind. As you **think** light, as you **think** good, you will become a creator, with God, of a beautiful world, a beautiful humanity.'*

I do hope that you find these wise words helpful and that perhaps you can use the action of positive imagery as a support mechanism to enable you to discover and maintain fulfillment within your own lives.

THE COSMIC WHEEL

It is some days after my sacred Ceremony. I am sitting looking out of my window at what is a beautiful winter's day, clear blue skies and thick frost on the grass. I am nibbling at some fruit for my breakfast and giving much thought to this subject, which has been brought up in different guises. There seems to be a Thread of Life - a Cosmic Wheel - constantly revolving, linking groups of people through the ages. A link has already been established between Akhnaton, the Sun King of ancient Egypt and Jesus, the Cosmic Christ of the Holy Land. Is it possible that the same group of people, perhaps the Elders and Priests from Atlantean days, reincarnated during Egyptian Dynastic times, through to initiating a presence in the Holy Land 2,000 years ago, leading to the present day Light Workers, all their lives being interwoven? Obviously a very generalized hypothesis, but I believe this could be so.

While mulling these things over, it suddenly becomes imperative that I have an attunement. My third eye is tantalizingly vibrating - it can not wait until my 12.00 noon link - I am being called NOW. As always I reverently prepare my sacred space. In the silence I am immediately enveloped in the soft loving energies of the Rose. I am saying: *"I enter into your presence Blessed Ones in love and with a pure heart."* My inner vision takes me along a pathway of shining Light, right into the heart of the Sun - right into the Sun Temple. Before me is an altar cloaked in white, on which is a Grail Cup holding the Eternal Flame. Very quickly an extremely imposing Being enters my aura. The robes of this Angelic Being are golden like the Sun - in fact he is all gold from head to toe - he is total dazzling Golden Light. These are the words I receive:

GOLDEN ANGEL

"My Child. Welcome to OUR World. The World of Light and everlasting truth - the World where mysteries unfold and knowledge of the innermost kind can be given. You dearest child have many questions, the overall pattern of which is accurate. BUT there is more - much more.

If you look to what you have already surmised on your pilgrimage with our blessed Lady, you will remember your comprehension and realization that the South West of the British Isles are the last remnants of that once great continent of Atlantis. Does not this indicate to you the most powerful link with the Ancient Mysteries and the great plan from deep within the Cosmos. Now add to this the great Sun God Akhnaton who came into incarnation in Dynastic times in Egypt and you have the link with the Great SUN - the one God - that powerful entity of Divine love and joy and power which we ALL worship and adore. Each incarnation of our beloved Master Jesus, the Infinite Sun/Son, is indicative of once more bringing the great Light to the Earth. This in itself is a miracle - the Light from the Cosmic manifesting itself through human form. Think on this child.

I am aware you wish to know more precise details of Group Incarnation in the different ages that have passed. But for now these words will have to be your answer. YOU KNOW. We don't have to spell out the detail dear one -YOU KNOW - and that is enough. We are aware you wish to pass esoteric knowledge on to others. We are aware that the curious mind works overtime. We know of your desires, BUT for now these words I offer you will suffice. My child it is not always necessary to know the whole truth from an outer perspective. Truth lies in the heart - in that pure gentle energy of the Divine Rose of Love. It is here that you will discover your own truth dear child.

It is not necessary to know my name (in answer to my unspoken question), just to say that I am from the Angelic Realm. I watch over and care for Earthlings. I am your Angel of the purist Light and love and mystical knowledge. I am he through which all life is activated. I am the Light of the World. I am the Love of the World. I am Cosmic Truth. I am the Shining Angel vibrating at a very high frequency. I am the Guardian of your Planet Earth. My name is not important. I bring to you ALL Earthlings a great blessing. I bring you Hope - I bring you Light - I bring you Joy. The New Age as it is dawning will manifest in your loving tender hearts and then and only then, will your Planet rise once again to the higher vibrations and into the higher dimensions you know of. We wish you ALL a new beginning as your New Year begins. For this is the time for new beginnings. Open your hearts to love Earthlings - to pure unconditional love, and truth and wisdom will be yours. Amen."

As this beautiful commanding Being of Golden Light from the Angelic Realm is leaving me, I am becoming aware of the gentle, softer energies of the feminine essence coming through and Beloved Mary is with me. She is wearing a robe of the most heavenly blue. She says nothing but smiles graciously. She is just making her presence known: *"Beloved Mary - the Heart Rose - I acknowledge your blessed presence. I acknowledge the great Angelic Being who spoke with me. I acknowledge all the Beings of Light. I bless you ALL."* Following this profound Angelic encounter I am once more humbled and feel so very blessed. More and more I am to realize that precise details of events on Earth are not always to be bestowed on us. The answer lies in the loving heart. Through this, truth will manifest when we are ready to receive - there are no short cuts. We are all to be tried and tested to the enth degree, before we have a clear understanding and are ready to enter that perfect state of being.

It is the following day - well early morning - 1.00 am. It is White Eagle's turn to assist me to an early morning rise - but what the heck! He wishes to offer some insight on this topic:

WHITE EAGLE

"My dear child Peace Rose, we meet again. You will have by now realized the link - the thread of time - which runs through all life. It is indeed the ANCIENT MYSTERIES. Each New Age produces an opportunity to reinvent the Ancient Wisdom in order that it might be 'fit' for the age in question. As each new era dawns then new ways of interpreting ancient truths are offered, BUT it is the same truth - that Cosmic truth which WAS at the beginning of time. That great firey energy of Power and Light which you call God, is manifest in human form at the beginning of each new age - the cycle is continuous, like a great Cosmic Wheel and ever shall be. Each age gradually merging into the next. As each age comes into being, so the process which helps it to manifest, produces new vibrations on your Earth Plane, which can cause great upheavals. It is often a time of wars and great sacrifice, which unfortunately is sometimes necessary in order to bring in the Light and ultimately bring peace to your World. We wish you to understand this Sister of Light in order that the message can go forth, that through the turmoils of change, WILL come the peace and security which you all crave.

You can be secure in the knowledge that the Cosmic journey from one incarnation to another, will bring to each soul a deeper understanding of the way to truth and eternal life through the Rose in the Heart. The Rose from which all the thorns have been removed by the diligent outworking of The Law. As each soul earns the right to further knowledge of the Ancient Wisdom, so the Rose becomes the epitome of perfection to which we all aspire. As each age moves on, so humanity moves ever close to the Godhead - ever closer to the realization of Cosmic truth. Each incarnation adds to the inner wisdom and esoteric knowledge of the whole. So - there IS a thread - a Golden Thread of Truth - a continuous Thread of Life, which flows effortlessly from one life to the next.

After a period of 'rest' in the higher dimensions of the Land of Light, so the soul is made ready for its next journey into incarnation. The soul realizes that in order to progress on its Cosmic journey of understanding The Mysteries, it has to once more experience Earthly life and so an opportunity is opened up for that soul. A life is chosen which will offer progression. If accepted, then preparation is made for the incarnation to take place and an Angel is immediately 'attached' to the incarnating soul, who will stay for the duration of the incarnation. This Angel is different to the Guardian Angel. The Guardian Angel is a Being of Light permanently attached to the soul. An Angel of Birth is one who travels with that soul through its incarnation on Earth. Bless you dear Peace Rose."

Once again I thank dear White Eagle for his precious words. So the Golden Thread - the Cosmic Wheel - just different ways of phrasing the same truth.

Before leaving this subject, I give you a communication I received recently from Confucius the ancient Chinese philosopher, wherein another aspect of the Cosmic Wheel is explored. It was during a Meditation group that I was aware of being overshadowed by an entity, who intimated his name was Confucius. I was unable to write words down at the time, but was conscious of the subject - the Wheel of Life. On returning home I tuned in once again. The main tenet of Confucian philosophy I know to be the attainment of goodness for its own sake, but what does Confucius have to impart on this subject? Confucius:

CONFUCIUS

"Confucius he say....that the Wheel of Life is the Centre of Life. The Wheel is everlasting - its arch is continuous it has no beginning and it has no end - it is alpha and omega. The Wheel of Life becomes the spiral of pure energy which vibrational frequency transmits pure energy in order to support the Universal Light and Life. The Light you see is the Light which has always been - the Light of all times. It has always been and always will be. It is the vibrational energy of the Spiral of Light which hones the perfection of life on your Planet. I speak this.

I say to you, look Sister of Light to comprehend this spiral of vibrational energy which is the foundation of each individual's DNA. There is much we would share with you in time Sister of Light. Open your eyes and your mind to EVERY possibility. Nothing is by chance in this Universal Perpetual Light. The frequency of each aspect of Universal Light is the energy needed to produce the flow of the life force of the Planet. I say this to you, study these things child. I wish you to learn of the Universality of ALL things that are. The great I AM is the WORD - the beginning of all there is. In the beginning was the Word and the Word was with God and the Word was God. God is the Light of the Universe. God is the Cosmic Energy - the field of many proportions.

Confusius say....seek for truth - seek for the understanding of the workings of the Cosmos. For each individual atom holds the life-force of the whole Universe. Each individual atom is a complete macrocosm of the whole. The molecule and the atom they make up the nucleus of what is the centre of the Universe - the whole aspect of life is here - within one atom. The DNA spiral is the building block of life. It is the building block of individual life of each person. It is the building block of the Universe. There are three Systems and many Universes. There is no beginning - there is no end. Life is eternal - the Cosmos is for ever. Confucius say these things to you - it is truth. Learn of these things child. This is just the beginning of your understanding of LIFE.

Confucius say...There is more. I will speak with you again Sister of Light. Amen."

What a great joy to have this contact with Confucius and to receive a little more insight into Cosmic Life. I thank this wise soul for his message.

REINCARNATION

These words of wisdom offering different aspects of the Cosmic Wheel, bring into focus the much debated subject of Reincarnation, which is not always easy to understand. If we believe it to be true, then we each have our own concept of how it transpires. I will throw into the melting pot my own elementary offering. Obviously our great Cosmic journeying is rather more involved!

So in simplistic terms I will take an analogy and liken the Soul to an Orange. When the Soul is ready for a new experience of life on Earth (or another Planet, but don't let's go there), then one segment of that Orange - one part of the Whole Soul - breaks away and awakens to a new life on the

Earth Plane. This part of the soul, now in human incarnation, travels its Earthly journey, experiencing much, learning its lessons and overcoming challenges. At the end of its life-span it returns to be connected to its whole self. Here it can be nurtured, refreshed and revitalized within the bosom of the Whole Soul. After a period of time, the need for further Earthly experience in order to accomplish soul growth, is recognized by the Soul. It is then that another part of the Whole Soul - another segment of the Orange - is released and travels to the Earth in physical incarnation.

If this concept holds water, then it is quite feasible to comprehend how two sections of the Whole Soul can incarnate on the Earth Plane at the same time, thus bringing into being the notion of Twin Souls, because they would be from the one source. Okay so far.

Now if this premise is acceptable, then the same parallel could apply to Group Incarnation, wherein multiple parts of the Whole Soul can be in incarnation at the same time - giving the idea of a soul family. Thus we could have a large - perhaps vast - group of people, choosing to be born into circumstances wherein their lives interweave, giving boundless opportunity for soul growth through their relationships, and which could perhaps offer a chance to clear Karmic debt. A second precept here is that they may have chosen to be drawn together in a specific lifetime for a Divine purpose - in order to advance humanity through service to the great Cosmic Light, working in cooperation with the Masters of Light and those from the Angelic Realms. This interconnectedness would account for the strong ties many of us feel to those with whom we come into contact throughout our lives.

In my analogy, each incarnated individual soul is therefore a part of the discarnate Whole Soul - ALL IS ONE. It is thus, that the Law of Oneness and Non-Separation comes into play, wherein the actions of each individual, affects the whole. What a responsibility we have!

Can my elementary deliberations on Reincarnation give us just a little more insight into the manifestations of the Cosmic Wheel in action? - Possibly.

CHAPTER 3
INTO THE HINTERLAND
Exploring the Heartland

During this section of her pilgrimage through the mystic South West of Britain, the Lady Mary and her daughter Naomi, travelled an area east and north of the Roseland Peninsula taking in; Veryan Castle, Dodman Point, Caerhays and Tregony, to eventually arrive at Golden Hill Fort. On landing at Carne Bay they first journeyed to Veryan Castle, where Mary reactivated the Atlantean Temple in the Etheric Realm. I follow this up with a home Ceremony to earth it.

On Day 2 of my Cornish pilgrimage, my journey back to the Roseland Peninsula from Boswinger took me through Veryan village, yet I didn't actually seek out Veryan Castle. Why not? In the first instance, my main focus was to return to Place to look for the 'Hill of Power' of which Mary spoke. Secondly, its significance didn't register at the time, probably because my thoughts were elsewhere. Looking at the map of this area, there are again quite a few 'Rose' names, alongside interestingly, a 'Creed' to the east of Golden Fort.

To pick up on my narrative of the time. Leaving Boswinger Youth Hostel I am now heading back to Place. It would seem that I am going through 'pheasant country'. My first experience of them is as I pass the main entrance to Caerhays Castle. Along the road and surrounding verges, there are masses of these large game birds, flying and stumbling every which way. They nearly get under my car wheels even though I am crawling along. They really are silly birds - sorry - God's beautiful creatures! As I am again cruising at very low speed, through the narrow country lanes towards Veryan they are at it again. This time, a pheasant comes crashing into my driving side window and flies off - fortunately unharmed. I now decide that they are not just silly birds - they really are stupid birds! Having expressed that opinion, I must say they are rather elegant creatures - quite striking in appearance. The male of the species is particularly handsome, with coppery plumage, a white neck ring and iridescent dark green crown and neck, with scarlet wattles around the eye.

TO VERYAN FOR THE CHURCH OF ST SYMPHORIAN AND HOLY WELL.

Driving through the hamlet of Veryan Green, I see that on the well kept green is a delightful small round-house, painted white, thatched and with Gothic style windows. This is one of several in the area, the rest to be found in Veryan. They are early nineteenth century properties, designed and built by a certain Parson Trist, who was a local landowner as well as a vicar. Soon I reach the charming village of Veryan, which is just a mile to the north of Veryan Castle. It is great to discover a traditional village with all the amenities; school, inn, shop, church and public conveniences - all positioned within the most beautiful setting of many pretty thatched cottages. I shall explore the village later - the public conveniences I investigate immediately!

I alight from the car and step onto a bed of scrunchy leaves, a reminder that autumn is upon us and the equinox has just passed. On my drive through the Cornish lanes I have been witness to trees alight with vibrant autumnal colours; burnished golds, russets and reds. It is the Season of Remembrance and Thanksgiving - a time to remember all the blessings we receive from the great Brotherhood of life and be thankful. It is a time to remember that we too can be a bringer of the harvest of good things to others, through our kindness, generosity and in offering unconditional love.

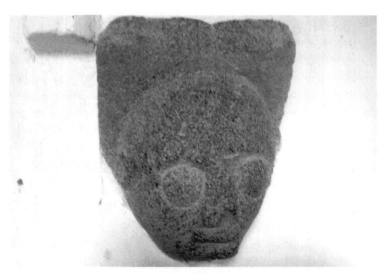

An ancient face at the Church of St Symphorian, Veryan

The thirteenth century CHURCH OF ST SYMPHORIAN which nestles within a surround of mature trees, is in the centre of Veryan around the old Churchtown. Walking the narrow pathway to the church which is lined with pink and mauve large-blossomed hydrangeas, I think how unusual for a church entrance. St Symphorian appears to be a French martyr rather than one of the many Celtic missionaries associated with Cornwall. The church itself looks rather grand for such a small village, but then I often find this to be the case. No doubt a statement was needed to be made about the power of the Christian Church and its position within the community.

I enter into the sanctuary of this Holy place through heavy oak doors. During the Victorian era the church was extensively restored, yet obviously with considerable forethought, because the result is extremely pleasing. Many of its old architectural features have been maintained. There is a row of white granite Gothic arches running the length of the aisle. The barrelled roof of the nave is formed of beautifully carved wooden struts. Its white stone medieval font, which is believed to be a copy of an early Norman design, has ancient carved faces around its rim, which could have their roots in Celtic design. The stained glass east window depicts St Mary the Blessed Virgin, the Master Jesus represented as the Lamb of God and St John the Divine. Sitting in a pew to absorb the peace within this sacred building, I can feel the stillness enveloping me. From somewhere - these words.

A Celtic Cross in St Symphorian's Churchyard, Veryan

THE SOUND OF SILENCE

Dwell in the silence
Dwell in the all encompassing sound of silence
In that silent place wait - you will receive deep peace
In that silent place, the Cosmic rays will flow into your whole being
You are aglow with the warmth of everlasting love
Open up your heart to that perfect love
Open up your mind to the wonders of the Universe
For all that tender love and wonderment can be yours
If you are still and tune in to - The Sound of Silence.
Be at one with the vibrations of all life
Be at one with the sound of the great 'Aum'
Let that sound within you pour out as a great mantra to your Creator
All shall be revealed within - The Sound of Silence.

A moving tribute to the peace and stillness of the ages held within the fabric of these ancient churches and reflected in their holiness: *"Thank you Angels."*

Leaving the church, I walk up some old stone steps through the churchyard where there are several Celtic cross granite headstones. I discover what is purported to be the longest grave in Britain, wherein lies buried the crew of the German Barque 'Hera' which ran aground on local rocks in 1914. Leaving this sanctified area, I wander downhill via a narrow mossy path through some magnificent beech trees. I am saying: *"So many beautiful trees. I bless you all."*

The path takes me to a stream running at the edge of a field, with a children's play area at the far end. I cross the little stone clapper bridge to reach a most stunning aquamarine lake, which is the Water Garden of Remembrance. This was given to the village as a memorial by a local lady in 1929. The dedication on the old high-backed wooden seat reads *'Presented to the people of Veryan for all time'*. Rising high over the lake at either end, are two delightful Japanese style wooden bridges. All around are tropical plants, rhododendrons, weeping willow and other lush greenery. I notice a series of lights set up around the waters edge, which at night-time must transform this lake into a place of enchantment.

Now I have a special task to undertake. I go back to my car, collect my bottle of water from Holy Brook and return to the little stream just below the churchyard. I stand for a moment musing and watching the clear water as it trickles over the pebbles at the bed of the stream and on under the stone-slab bridge. For the stream: *"Dear little stream flowing into such everlasting beauty of the lake, I offer you this water from Holy Brook, near Hembury Castle. Beloved Mary herself has drunk of this pure water (see Chapter 11). It is my offering to you."*

DEVA OF THE STREAM

"What a privilege. What a joy. Bless you human pilgrim. We do indeed thank you for the offering of water from Holy Brook. It will bring new life to our waters. It will enhance our beauty. Thank you." I ask permission to collect some water in another bottle - the reply from the **DEVA** is: *"Yes. We will bless it for you."*

I am in a state of great reverence going back to the village alongside the lake. I walk slowly, feeling the earth beneath my feet - my heart immersed in this ancient land. I now take a look at the village well which I discover close to the school. It has a stone surround with a small Gothic arched entrance protected by Victorian iron railings. I peer into its dark interior to discover it to be in a rather sad state, as within its sludgy waters, sweet wrappers have been thrown in. Due to the railings, access is denied and I am unable to retrieve the offending objects. I offer the 'waters' a blessing and throw in a lovely fir cone which I have brought with me from a Devonshire woodland. It is recorded, that this was probably the original water supply for the village rather than a Holy Well. My impression however, is that an ancient stone Celtic figure representing the Holy Trinity, placed rather incongruously on a pinnacle at the top, would indicate that this was indeed an ancient Holy Well which true history has been lost in time. Could the water from an original spring here have been sipped by the Lady Mary and Naomi on their journey through Veryan?

VERYAN CASTLE ATLANTEAN TEMPLE CEREMONY

I am in my own home and it is 12.00 noon on my dedicated Ceremonial Day for Place Sacred Hill, Veryan Castle and Golden Fort. My Ceremony for Place Sacred Hill is complete and I have taken a coffee break, yet still remain in the quiet of my sacred space. Veryan Castle was the first settlement where Mary and Naomi stayed in The Hinterland. I have been reliably informed by my spirit messengers, that the position of the ancient settlement is exactly where the castle is marked on the map today. I am now ready to perform my Light Ceremony. As before, I prepare myself with dedication, asking for protection and guidance for the work I am being asked to do here, which is to earth the ancient Atlantean Temple.

As I settle down before my altar and re-light my candle, I become very still. I am ready. In my imagination I return to the pretty village of Veryan with its little thatched cottages and peaceful lake. I didn't have physical contact with Veryan Castle on my visit, but now into my inner vision comes the ancient castle site. I begin my Ceremony with *'The Great Invocation'* then call in all the beloved Masters and Angelic protectors, each crystal being laid in turn on my altar cloth. The energies are powerful indeed as I invoke the Cosmic Light and voice the sacred words for the Atlantean Temple Ceremony. As before, I have a vision of the Temple from Atlantis resting on Mother Earth, this time at Veryan Castle. On completion, I bless and thank the Wise Ones for their protection and accomplishments this day. I now picture myself burying the two pieces of quartz crystal - one white and one pink, within the hallowed ground where the Temple now stands.

I am humbled at being used as an instrument to earth this ancient Light Temple of the Stars. I am visualizing the Cosmic Rays penetrating right through the Earth, deep deep to reach the Great Crystal at its very core. I find myself thinking of the significance of the Atlantean Crystal Energy and the Grid Lines of our Planet. My understanding is that stage by stage the Crystalline Grid is being re-awakened and its vibrational frequencies strengthened, in preparation for the higher dimensions of our Earth Plane, which will begin to manifest during the Aquarian Age. The Solstice, December 2012, is a time given when it is purported that the Grid will be fully functional throughout our Planet. While I am pondering these things, a flash of the Continent of Australia comes into my vision and a Master is with me. I am just able to grab by pad and pen which is at my side, before he speaks:

MASTER OF LIGHT

"My name is of no importance dear Sister of Light. I come in the name of Love of whom He is all powerful, all gracious, all perfect understanding.

This day is good. We all thank you and respect your work for the Light beloved Earth person. We are all co-creators with God - He who has always been - He who always WILL BE - for ever and ever. There is no end. For life is eternal - alpha and omega - no beginning and no end. It is this, that we in the Land of Light consider life is - the eternal round - one incarnation leads us neatly and seamlessly into the next incarnation.

Beloved child, we will speak with you later about the Great Crystal and its work. For now we wish to share with you all the profundity of Creation. For in the beginning it was all a mistyness - there was no solid matter. As the mists began to clear so the Great Being - that almighty power whom you speak of as God - brought into existence - into physical manifestation, your Solar System and your Planet. They all came from the Sun - from the Light. The energy of such power and brilliance is so vast. We do know how difficult ALL this is for you Earth people to comprehend and so it will be for some time to come, BUT the knowledge and Ancient Wisdom goes forth and enters your ever expanding consciousness. This, beloved Earthlings - is only the beginning. At one time many eons ago this Planet of Earth was inhabited by Golden Beings - the ones who lived in the Light of the 5th Dimension. Those days as you know beloved Brethren are long past, BUT they will return - we KNOW they will return. There are many many souls incarnated on Planet Earth at this time who were part of that ancient civilization of Atlantis and many more will be born, so that very gradually your Planet will be filled with Light Workers - beings of past times. This is a precious time to be incarnated on the Planet.

We wish you to be aware of the ancient Aboriginal Brethren in that great continent of what is now called Australia. These people were of the past, the original humans to inhabit Planet Earth. Their knowledge is vast - their wisdom immense. Look to their wisdom Earthlings, for these people are of Pleiadian descent and are wise beyond comprehension. Their inner wisdom has been long regarded as Infinite Wisdom and as coming from the Stars and - IT IS SO. The people of Planet Earth will, as is beginning to happen, recognize and acknowledge that ancient Aboriginal wisdom.

As we speak, into your Earthly mind dear sister, comes the being whom you knew as TAIBU. He made connection with you a long time ago in your Earthly life, but a split second in Cosmic time This being - this soul from the Island of Birds - Tasmania as you know it today, will have more to share with you sister as your journey with Beloved Mary progresses. For now, he wishes to make his presence known to you again, in order that you and he can work together in the future. In your days as Naomi, you knew him then beloved sister. More will be revealed of this as time passes on this pilgrimage. Welcome Taibu into your life. Your beloved husband Gordon, Brother Justus, has brought this link for you at this time. For he too is working on the inner planes with Taibu, and this connection Sister Peace Rose, is yours for all time. Brother Justus is one of the beings held in high esteem by the Beings of Light. He is a pure living entity of Light. He is working with your beloved White Eagle to bring your precious Planet into the Light of new beginnings. Think on these things Sister of Light. Know that part of your work will be with Brother Justus and Taibu. More will be revealed in time.

For now dear sister, we wish you to take rest, for you have done much and there is much more to be done before this day is out. May God's perfection and blessed wisdom and gracious love rest in your heart as always. Amen."

I thank the dear Master who has proffered these words. What a revelation. Well - this really IS getting personal now. My Mission with Mary is certainly taking me into some fascinating territory. Originally, in order not to destroy the essence of the work, I made a decision to keep all personal words received, in the text. I realize this last is particularly personal, but still feel justified in doing this as it is pertinent to my pilgrimage. My husband was an integral part of my spiritual journey through this life and past lives and I feel has been instrumental in bringing Taibu to my attention: *"Thank you Brother Justus."* Emotions are a little close to the surface at the moment. At my husband's funeral a few years back, I 'saw' him standing in the church with his back to the altar facing his coffin and the congregation. He was wearing a white robe, his arms were outstretched as if encompassing all before him and he was offering a blessing. He was full of compassion and I knew then that he was a wise soul - an Elder of past times. There is no death. I have known this all my life since a child and now here was my husband proving once again that profound truth to me. Enough of that!

I now close my psychic centres, ground my physical body and surround myself in Golden Light. In the silence which follows I reflect on the past. These words have brought back distant memories which take me back thirty-five years. I recollect the regular weekly spiritual meetings my husband and I shared with a small group in our own home. A trance medium friend of ours joined us and on one occasion the spirit entity Taibu, whom we recognized then as an ancient soul, made his presence known. He offered us intriguing insight into past times, in what he called *'My World'* which we were to discover was during the Age of Atlantis. At the time his words were taped and tomorrow I shall find them and include them in the text at this point.

The following day I listen once again after a gap of many years, to the old recording on cassette, wherein Taibu offers facets of the Ancient Wisdom, which I now share with you. Please respect the fact that the information given us from the Land of Light, was received in the 1970s. I am fully aware that esoteric knowledge has expanded over the years on many levels and that our inner awareness and understanding is perhaps a little more advanced in this present day. However, perhaps we all have some way to go before we can fully comprehend the concepts expressed by Taibu, which during his time on Earth would have been everyday occurrences. These are the original words from Taibu given thirty-five years ago:

TAIBU - ANCIENT BEING from the ISLAND OF BIRDS - TASMANIA

"I wish to speak with you today of what you call MENTAL TELEPATHY and also THOUGHT TRAVEL.

May I deal with in the first instance MENTAL TELEPATHY. This gift was widely used in what I shall term as 'My World'. It was born to us all and as we grew older it was improved upon until finally it was perfect. Let me take you now to your day of what YOU know. Have you never wondered why a shoal of fishes will all veer in one direction or another instantaneously? Have you not watched a flock of birds pitch and turn instantaneously? Have you not noticed when there has been a passing, at times a relative or close friend will say afterwards - 'at the moment of death I KNEW that my friend had passed?' Have you not noticed cases of identical twins being able to think together although a world apart? This gift my friend lies dormant in you even now. With the new born infant, just from the Spirit World, it KNOWS how to transmit. The mother knows not how, but she can receive, as can we all. In the case of the dying, when they are on the threshold of death the gift returns and they can transmit. To explain I must return to my World. Telepathy could only be done between you and the person you have known or have met. You see, the human mind or soul, transmits vibrations and as no two fingers prints are the same, nor are these vibrations. But to practice this Telepathy, one must meet and know the person to whom you transmit or receive. In other words you find out their cycle, their frequency and from then on you can identify and use it. Again with the case of identical twins, they are so close together that they can transmit at will. In my day - in my World - Mental Telepathy was widely used when necessary, but alas in your World today I dread to think what it would be used for!

I now wish to continue unto my second and last subject for this evening - THOUGHT TRAVEL. This again was used with regularity in my World, but unlike Mental Telepathy which could be used at will, this had to be done through the Elders. Thought Transport was not of the flesh body but of the Etheric. If a person wished to make use of this Thought Travel, then they would go to the Shrine of the Elders in a forest glade and there make known their reason. With the help of the Elders, in a short while their Etheric body would leave them and travel to the destination required. The use of the

Shrine is obvious - that the flesh and blood body must be protected in its absence. There it could lie dormant until the return of the Etheric body. Again returning to your World, this is what you call ASTRAL PROJECTION. This is indeed happening here today - everyday - you have all heard of it, but it is usually uncontrolled. In my World it was a controlled gift, put to good use and properly conducted. God Bless you."

At this juncture there was a pause, then the following from **TAIBU**: *"If you wish you may ask me upon the subject."*

QUESTION: *"I would like to ask. If a person is asleep and his Etheric body travels, does it travel into the Spirit World only or can it travel to another part of the Earth? Would you have a mission for it in another part of the World?"*

TAIBU: *"It can indeed travel to another part of the Earth. Sometimes these are mistakenly called dreams. It was sometimes used to visit a wise Master or to attend a great gathering. In my world, Thought Travel was freely used as you would use an aeroplane, for we had not the transportation in the material term which you have today."*

QUESTION: *"When the Etheric body is back in the physical body, does the person know that their mission has been completed?"*

TAIBU: *"The Etheric knows - the flesh and blood body gets to know eventually. Very few people are privileged to know straight away."*

QUESTION: *"Was Thought Travel restricted to this Planet or could you go elsewhere - to Venus for example?"*

Following this question there was a long pause. Obviously much thought was given as to how much could be revealed at this time! Then...

TAIBU: *"I will simply state now, although this leads us to another vast subject, that indeed there is life elsewhere."*

Taibu's words coming from the past have opened up a raft of questions for me today, so I tune in to the Spiritual Realms and asked the following questions:

MY QUESTION: *"When the Etheric body left the physical and went to its new destination, did it produce a temporary physical body at that place?"* I did not get a clear answer at the time, but later as my pilgrimage progressed, I received confirmation that this was so.

MY QUESTION: *"Could you confirm that the gathering and subsequent meeting might be in the Etheric Realm?"* Here I received a *"yes"*

MY QUESTION: *"In ancient Atlantis, were these gifts of Mental Telepathy and Thought Travel for ALL or just for the Elders?"* I seem to be answering this one with a *"yes for all who were trained."*

MY QUESTION: *"Is this what we are to expect as we move into the 5th Dimension and beyond, as we make the shift towards a future Golden Age?"* Again I receive a positive response.

All very interesting. I had certainly forgotten the content of Taibu's words, but they are so relevant to my journey with the Lady Mary today and my discoveries of the Temples of Atlantis in Cornwall. The concept of Mental Telepathy is not new to me, as I suspect would be the same for many. I am sure most of us have had experiences to this effect. For example - the telephone rings - you know EXACTLY who is at the other end - and you were just about to phone them anyway! When Taibu talks about a shoal of fishes or a flock of birds moving together as one, could this be what we today might call swarm intelligence? The idea of Thought Travel, this too I have always 'known' to be truth. Could this explain some of The Mysteries, as for example myths pertaining to the Master Jesus, who was purported to have been seen all over the Globe after his 'death' (see Chapter 7).

Following the unveiling of this past communication from Taibu and as I am tuning in to his energies once again, he is with me. I prepare my altar and wait in the silence:

TAIBU

"Dear child - we meet again after a long gap of Earth years. It is with great joy that I make contact with you my child. I was an Elder in Druidic Society at the time when you were in Wales as Naomi. I was your mentor and you would come to me at times of need.

Child you ask of Thought Travel. I can confirm that this method of travel was used in the days when I was Taibu on the Island of Birds. I can also confirm that this was many eons ago as you would understand time. In those days of the 5th Dimension - the so called Golden Age, we were able to travel across the Cosmos - out into the starry night skies, in order to reach any Planet we wished. The subject is vast. Even with your new knowledge my child and the new knowledge being shared on Planet Earth as the Aquarian age approaches - the subject is vast.

The Golden Age you talk about is a time when the Continent of Atlantis still existed. I was in the Island of Birds at that time. I was able to Thought Travel across the globe of Earth in order to attend a World Council meeting in Atlantis. There were huge cities there, beautiful gardens, high mountains - some snowcapped. It was a place of beauty and magnificence and splendour. There were great lakes and extensive waterways and systems of irrigation, in order that crops could be grown to feed its people. A World Council would be held in that vast continent from time to time and I as Taibu, was able to attend. Decisions were taken as to the process of the Planet of which we were all a part. Even in those days we were very aware of the vulnerability of life on Earth and knew it had to be protected at all costs. Atlantis itself was under one overall Council, whose Elders and Priests protected the rights of ALL its people and who ruled with gentleness and kindness and much wisdom. Everywhere was a state of perfection - a Garden of Eden you might say.

But then changes came - dark clouds in the metaphoric sense - were gathering. Things were not boding well. The Priests were over-riding their power and became greedy and ultimately ruthless. There was danger in the magnetic forces supporting the Earth. Change of thought patterns within the minds of some of the Priests brought about material change to the land. The vibrational energy and the Earth's axis which had been static for many eons of time, was changed with the experimentation of nuclear fusion. This was the beginning of the end of the magnificent continent known as Atlantis.

BUT - the energies of that once great Continent are still here. Those purer energies still inhabit the land - the soil of your Planet Earth. This place - these beloved sacred Isles of your Britain, is all that remains of the once great Continent of Atlantis. BUT - Atlantis WILL rise again - not in a physical sense, but in an esoteric sense - ATLANTIS WILL RISE AGAIN. The great beings of golden magnificence and illumined beauty who were there then, all those ages ago, WILL return - ARE returning. It is beginning - Atlantis IS rising. The New Jerusalem is happening and it is happening NOW. You and many Light Workers in incarnation at this time, are instruments for the new beginnings.

My child, I will speak with you again. I am working with your White Eagle and Brother Justus and many others in the Land of Light for Universal Peace. Goodnight."

I thank Taibu for making his presence known once again at this precious time in my life. With these words he has brought further enlightenment to life on that ancient continent of Atlantis. The connection is being made from the ancient past to Mary's Mission 2,000 years ago, through to my Mission in this present day in the earthing of the ancient Atlantean Temples. However, Taibu's initial remarks concerning Naomi in Wales means I have yet more questions! At present I know little of Naomi's journeying through Wales after the crucifixion. Where did she meet with her Druid mentor Taibu? Was he with her at all times? Where did she go? Did she settle anywhere or travel around? Did Naomi travel with Mary her mother? (see The Epilogue).

After performing this sacred Atlantean Ceremony, I take a light lunch and dwell in my own thoughts. Following their own Ceremony of Light at Veryan Castle, Mary and Naomi left this area. They retraced their steps to the coast and travelled by boat around Nare Head, across Veryan Bay to the promontory of Dodman Point, where they stayed at a settlement called Dodman Fort. Once again Mary performed a Light Ceremony with the Druid Elders. After a brief stay here, they took a boat to Porthluney Cove for Caerhays, which is where I pick up their journey in the physical sense.

THE CHURCH OF ST MICHAEL AND ALL ANGELS AT ST MICHAEL CAERHAYS

On reaching Caerhays, I drive into the beach car park making my way to the seafront, driving carefully in order to avoid the many deep potholes filled with muddy water. Obviously very little attention has been afforded this car park for some while, BUT it is free so I can't have it all ways! I am looking over a vast expanse of sandy Cornish beach, which because of the lateness of the season, is quite deserted. Getting out of the car I take a few deep breaths of the VERY bracing sea air and - jump back in again! Eventually I decide to brave the elements and a short walk takes me to the impressive garden entrance of Caerhays Castle, which has two stone towers with arrow slits and castellated outer walls. Through the gates I can see well kept grounds which I understand are open to the public in April and May, when they are at their best with camellias and rhododendrons. The castle itself, which is set within a huge grassy area against a backdrop of pine and beech woodland, is however not open to public viewing. Caerhays Castle is apparently the only surviving Gothic castle designed by the architect John Nash, who built it in 1808 for the Trevanion family.

Driving on up the hill I pass the main castle entrance. It is here that I first met with the local pheasant population blustering their way across the road. Eventually I reach the Parish Church of St Michael and All Angels, which is situated in the hamlet of St Michael Caerhays, high above the castle. How 'coincidental' that I am here within a couple of days of the 29th September, St Michael's sacred day! I enter the churchyard through the lych gate and follow a gravelled path leading to the church. I am stopped in my tracks as I see the most beautiful yew tree. My thoughts - oh I have not got an offering: *"I will be back"* I say to the deva. Once, when walking through some ancient woodland in Wales, I was 'told off' by the little people who said to me *'where is your offering - where is your gift?'* So I am thinking that I don't want to get into trouble on this occasion! Back at the car I choose a lovely white feather and a small red stone from the stream flowing down from the Llyn-y-Fan-Fach lake in the Black Mountain area of Wales. I feel these will be acceptable. As I place the offerings under the yew tree, I acknowledge the deva saying: *"Here you are beautiful Tree Deva my special gifts for you."*

DEVA OF THE YEW

"Thank you dear human person for your loving gifts. I welcome you to this sacred place. I am very happy here gracing and nurturing this ancient churchyard. In years I am not as old as some yew trees, but I am proud of my position here as guardian of the St Michael Church. St Michael is OUR protector and looks after all Angels, Humans AND Nature Spirits. So I feel I am very blessed to be in this position. Dear human - St Michael awaits you."

My response: *"Thank you so much for your welcoming words."* On my journeying, time and time again, I am made aware of the pride which the devas have in their guardian status and in their beautifying of the landscape around them. They so welcome our acknowledgement and respond to our love.

I enter the ancient St Michael Church with veneration, feeling that my contact with the deva has somehow shifted my awareness. My first thought is - what a gem. I sit in a pew for a short while taking in the ethereal beauty of this little church. Out of the corner of my eye, I see what I think is someone sitting off to the left in one of the side chapels. I do a double-take when I realize that it is a life-size stuffed figure, dressed in smart clothing, which includes a rather natty matching waistcoat and tie - tartan no less. This figure is to haunt me all the while I am exploring the church, as every time I look round - there he is!

The church is a sturdy little stone building which has much to recommend it. It dates back to Norman times, of which there are still remains to be seen in the north wall and in the porch doorway, which has a tympanum above it, depicting the Lamb of God. The Norman font on a single stem, is of white stonework with large carved leaves in flat relief. There is a fifteenth century corbel showing a shield-bearing angel with scallop shells, a possible link with St James and the pilgrim route to Compostella in Spain. I am now moving to the east end and stand in reverence before the altar. I do have an offering for St Michael of a large piece of white quartz, but this does not feel the appropriate place to leave it. The stained glass window above the altar depicts the baptism of our Lord and is exquisite. The left section of the window says *'This is the Son of God'* and the right section reads *'Behold the Lamb of God'* with our beloved Master at the centre. There are other delightful windows, but the two which stand out for me, are those with different illustrations of St Michael slaying the dragon. On the north side, St Michael is shown in his Angelic form slaying a green dragon. On the south wall, he is clothed in his armour slaying a red dragon.

I return to one of the pews and make an inner connection: *"Blessed St Michael I come into your presence with thanksgiving. Beloved Archangel I offer you this beautiful quartz crystal as my gift. Once again I ask for your protection on my pilgrimage."* I receive the following words from this wondrous Being of Light:

ST MICHAEL

"Welcome dear Pilgrim of Light. I welcome you to this little church dedicated to my name. I thank you for your very special offering. I bless your journey. As always I am your protector. The love in your heart is the joy which we receive as we watch over your pilgrimage. Bless you dear Sister of Light.

Now - we would wish to say unto you, tread this sacred landscape graciously. Tread lightly over the Earth - this sacred Earth - where Mary herself has trod with the blessed Jesus. Those many years ago I know that as Naomi, you were part of that little group of pilgrims to this ancient land. You and the blessed Jesus were enthralled with what you discovered and excited by such an adventure. For Jesus this first voyage to these Holy Isles was to set the scene and prepare the way for his many future visits. On this occasion as a young boy moving into manhood, he was especially 'impressed' with all the experiences. I use the word 'impressed' also in its esoteric meaning. He was FILLED with the Holy Spirit as he stepped ashore. His pilgrimage with Mary his beloved mother, was paramount to future journeying to this land. He brought his Divine essence to this sacred land and as such, wherever he walked the land itself was alight with that pure essence of Spirit.

You have already been impressed yourself with visions and awareness regarding Beloved Mary's reasons for this pilgrimage. I have just to say dear pilgrim, your insights are accurate. Mary's role was to reactivate the ancient Light Centres of Atlantis. There will be more for you at a later time. It was also necessary for you dear Naomi as Mary's daughter, to visit these ancient Isles on this occasion, to prepare you for the future after the crucifixion.

I confirm, that Britain is indeed the last remnents of that ancient civilization of Atlantis and as such holds the key to the future for your Planet. So much will be revealed as the Aquarian Age moves along. This, my dear Pilgrim of Light IS the New Jerusalem. It is the sacred Isle of ALL TIME. You are indeed blessed to be a part of this great awakening. I and my Archangels and the Masters of Light bless your efforts and we bless the efforts of ALL our precious Light Workers who have offered themselves in service for this work.

(My thoughts intruding are resting on a question. Why a green and why a red dragon - do they depict different things)? *I see you have a question for me. Hmm.....interesting. What can I say. It is my understanding that the different interpretations reflect different opinion and influences of the time in which they were made. I have been portrayed on numerous occasions in my full armour slaying the red dragon. This is particularly so in Wales. The red dragon here would be representative of the human quelling of the fire within and bringing it into the heart through love. The other interpretation represents the sacrificing of ones envy - you know green for envy. This is part of Universal Law. We must ALL overcome these aspects of our nature. This is a simple explanation. It will suffice for now dear one. I will speak with you again on this subject. For now we would wish you to continue your pilgrimage this day. I offer you my blessings and protection."*

I have a vision of this beautiful Archangel in all his glory, his hand raised in a benediction. What an honour. I am privileged indeed that he has shared so much with me: *"I thank you blessed Michael. I offer my deepest gratitude."* I now go to each of the stained glass windows which have a representation of Michael and the dragon in turn and offer a blessing of love with my hand on my heart: *"Great Being of Light. I honour you. I bless you. I thank you."*

Every time I turn around HE is there - that strange little 'man' sitting in the pew in the side chapel. I purchase a small folder of A5 laminated leaflets called *'Church Trails in Cornwall'* which gives information on local churches, this one covering the Truro area where I am at the moment. Out I go into the welcome sunshine. As has happened before, the cold of the church and the dropping of energies have got to me. Just outside the porch entrance I see a large granite rock and gently lay my white quartz crystal on top for St Michael. It looks to be in its rightful place. It is in full view of any visitor and I wonder how long it will stay there, but can't help feeling that it will be well protected!

Behind St Michael's Church are extensive views out to distant hills. The valley portrays a patchwork of hedged fields with a predominance of long fields. Could this perhaps be the remains in the landscape of a medieval field system? There is a bench seat - just right for a quiet moment. The air round here must be exceedingly pure, as this wooden seat although relatively new, has already got lichen beginning to form on it. I sit down, sun warming my face. A vast arena of blue sky and white clouds is spread out in front of me. The clouds seem to be hanging there as if in suspended animation Any movement is almost imperceptible and what there is, is on mass, as if some giant Divine hand is slowly moving them across a colossal stage. This is a moment of utter serenity.

It is coming up to midday and perfect timing for an attunement. White Eagle has given us some special prayers for World Healing which we can all use either individually or in a group. One of the recommended times for sending out the Light is 12.00 noon. At this time of the day, it would appear that people from many different spiritual traditions make their link with the Universal Christ Light and pray for World Peace. Such cumulative prayer can be extremely potent. The following words, which are taken from a White Eagle Leaflet *'There is Something You can do Now'* may be spoken out loud or said in the silence of your own heart. I am visualizing the Sun-Star high above my head shining down rays of Golden Light to our Earth Plane.

STAR HEALING PRAYER

'We hold all humanity in the golden light of the Christ Star and see the power of the Son of God working in the hearts of all people.
We see the light of the shining six-pointed star reaching to all who suffer and inspiring all who seek to relieve suffering.
We hold all who have asked for help or healing within the healing light of the Star.
We hold all animals, the world of nature and Mother Earth herself within this healing light.
May God's blessing be upon this work. Amen'

I now ask for the blessing of the Christ Light, that ancient Cosmic Light, to shine down over our blessed Isles of Britain. This would seem to have particular merit at this time on my pilgrimage with Mary.

JOURNEY TO TREGONY

Following the account of my visit to Caerhays and its St Michael Church, I continue with Mary and Naomi's pilgrimage through The Hinterland. From Porthluny Cove at Caerhays, they travelled by river, which in their day was navigable, to Tubbs Mill, thence by horseback to Rosevallon Druidic settlement for an overnight stop. The following day they continued overland to Tregony on the River Fal, then took a boat up-river to Golden Mill for the Druidic Tree Temple site of Golden Fort.

I initially connect with them at Tregony on Day 3 of my physical pilgrimage, having left St Just-in-Roseland and before making my way to Golden Fort. I drive into the small town of Tregony where I wish to visit two churches. First, the Parish Church of St Cuby in the town's centre, then an earlier church dedicated to St Cornelius, which is in the valley just below the town. My reason for these choices is that apparently both churches have representations of St Anne, Mary's mother and I feel drawn to take a look. It is said that in St Cuby's church, one of the painted panels on the organ illustrates her and at St Cornelius' there is an altar dedicated to her. At this stage of my pilgrimage I wondered why St Anne in particular, is depicted in these two churches. I could only think the memorials would be in honour of an ancient memory of Mary's visit. It is much later I learn that Cornwall is St Anne's ancestral home and that it is not far away from this area (see Chapter 4). I shall gloss over the next hour as I am to be thwarted in my attempts to visit both churches. Very briefly, I discover that the Parish Church is locked so off I go in search of a key. I walk up and down the high street knocking on doors and calling into shops, following instructions from various people - but to no avail. Likewise, the St Cornelius church is locked and again - no key. Obviously I am NOT meant to make these visits - a shame, but I have to accept it.

A well documented fact about Tregony is that in the Middle Ages it was a large port on the River Fal, which is now silted up. This was caused because much of the water in olden times was diverted for washing tin. Ah - so this was another tin mining area. If Joseph owned tin mines around here and paid a visit, it would have been on a separate occasion - he certainly didn't come with Mary and Naomi.

GOLDEN FORT

I am now on route to Golden Fort settlement. I cannot obviously go up-river as Mary would have done, so I drive there along an exceedingly narrow road. Eventually, with careful scrutiny of the map, I reach a point where I am able to identify a possible base of the fort. I park the car and scramble up through very dense woodland sometimes bent double, apologizing to any branches I have to break off in order to get through. In the course of time, I reach a field of maize at the top. By now I have clambered up and over several earth embankments, so know that I am in the correct place for the hill fort. As the ground levels out I see a circular area which insight tells me is the ancient site. Sadly, there is no evidence left in the landscape of its past except for the embankments. The Light surrounding this hill-top however is still here - it is not lost - it can be reawakened and will be.

Golden Fort lives up to its name with the sweep of gold-topped maize spread out before me. I stand quite still at the field edge sensing the atmosphere. Closing my eyes, I listen to the swishing of the maize in the warm gentle breeze and allow the sound to fill my senses. Mary WAS here - she is telling me. I 'know' as Naomi I was here. I am now getting the impression of Golden Rays of Light being poured down from the Heavens to the Earth in what would be the centre of the field. I can see figures perambulating the flat hill-top area. Once again I have returned in vision to ancient times. I know that by my making this brief contact, I am able to revitalize that Cosmic Light. Later at home in an attunement, it is confirmed that Golden Fort IS an ancient Druidic Temple site and Mary wishes me to perform a home ceremony. I leave an offering of a piece of white quartz crystal for the ancient ones, to reconnect our present day to past times.

GOLDEN FORT DRUDIC TEMPLE CEREMONY

At home now, I continue with my sacred 'Day of Ceremonies'. After my Ceremony for Veryan Castle I am having a light lunch. Looking out into the garden, I see it still displays plenty of beautiful greenery, even in October. However, some of the nearby trees have lost their leaves completely with the recent high winds, yet somehow there is a stark beauty in the shapes of the bare branches. The sky is - oh so blue. Indeed a perfect day for so late in the season. I open the window to breathe in some lovely fresh air as I have been rather closeted today. A short walk would be welcome, but there is no way I can leave this Sanctuary of Light right now.

It is 3.00 pm and my Ceremony for Golden Fort is to begin. I return to sit in front of my altar, once again lighting my candle and making the link with the Christ Light. In my inner vision, I follow Mary's journey from Veryan Castle to Golden Fort. I create a mental picture of the hill fort with its field of waving maize. I remember so well my feelings when at this ancient site - the sense of almost loss at the realization that the embankments were all that was left in the landscape of past times. As I call on the Masters and on Archangel Michael, I feel as if I am now being totally enshrouded in Golden Light. The Ceremonial words flow from deep within. Somehow the words of *'The Great Innovation'* seems to be particularly germane here and when I come to *'Let Light and Love and Power restore the Plan on Earth'* I am moved to feel the powerful vibrational energies go right to the sacred heart of this hallowed place and below the Earth to the Great Crystal. The Druidic Temple is truly restored and reactivated at Golden Fort and my Ceremony complete. As before in my imagination, I take the white and pink quartz crystals and secrete them in the earth, as close as I feel would be the central point of the ancient Temple site. I am now conscious of the presence of one of the Druid forefathers:

DRUID ELDER

"Thank you dear sister for your dedicated work this day. You have asked of the Crystal Energy (a past question). We can share with you just a little of its magnificence and its power. It was as you know, the Crystal in the seas off Carmarthen Bay, which guided Joseph of Arimathea to the shores of Wales after the crucifixion. The same Crystal Energy guided him and others to the shores of the South West. As a Crystal Master he was well aware of the powerful vibrations and energies of the Crystal. This Cosmic wisdom was not for him alone. Many many Beings of Light - the Masters who trod the Earth - knew of its power and magnificence, and that powerful energy was used for good.

It was in the ancient times - in Atlantean days - that the Crystal Energies were used prolifically for healing of the body and of the mind, and indeed of all the subtle bodies of Earth people. It was in those ancient times, that the vibrational energies of the Crystal were used to secure healing energy within the very land itself. It was in those days that we, as Beings of Light in incarnation, were able to maintain the Crystal Energies to the very highest degree. We were able to travel all over your Earth Plane, being guided by the

Crystal Energy. In those days we were able to travel etherically as your Brother Taibu has explained.

Things did change - the darker energies entered in. There were those who would wish to destroy the Crystal Magic and use the power for their own ends This powerful energy was in the hands of some of the Priests of that ancient continent, who used their powers for dubious purposes, which took precedence over the healing power for good. It was time for the Atlantean civilisation to move on - to pastures new - you might say. It was decreed from the highest level of Cosmic life - from the Godhead - that this once precious civilization should be sacrificed for the good and safety of Planet Earth. So it was done.

Many of those who worked from the heart level of purity and truth, travelled to other areas of the Planet before the catastrophe, taking with them the Ancient Wisdom and knowledge of spiritual truths. These people set up the foundation of new civilizations all over the Globe; Egypt, the Andes and Tibet, to name but a few, and the Ancient Mysteries were saved for future posterity. Much as I believe you know, is still 'lost' to the eyes of humanity. Much is to be revealed as time passes.

The Crystal Energy is part of the structure of your Planet. It is the Crystal Energy which helps keep Planet Earth on its axis. It is the Crystal Energy that brings a balance to all aspects of Earth life and links it inextricably to Cosmic life. It is Crystal Energy deep within the crust of the Earth, which will expand in its power and beauty and help Planet Earth to rise once again to greatness - to the Golden Age. This Crystal Energy is to be found in the Grid Lines and within the Ley Line system of your Planet. We can say that Planet Earth is a Crystalline Sphere. We wish ALL Light Workers to tune in to this Crystal Energy as they offer themselves in service to that great Cosmic Light. The Crystal of Light contains all the colours of the rainbow and many more subtle harmonious shades of which you could hardly imagine Earth People. The Crystal Energies are pure and destined to assist in the recovery of your precious Planet. I say again, tune in to the Crystal Energy dear ones and you will be instrumental in bringing forth the Golden Age.

Always we will ask, that you have about your person a pure white quartz crystal, for that is what will link you, not only to your Druidic past, but to ALL your ancient heritage. Goodbye my friends, my fellow Pilgrims of Light. Goodbye."

I thank this Druid Elder for his exposition of the Crystal Energy. My 'friend' leaves and I am alone. I sit absorbed in the pervading silence. Thus ends my sacred 'Ceremonial Day' wherein I performed three Ceremonies, for Place Sacred Hill, Veryan Castle and Golden Fort. Before closing, I visualize the rays of the great Sun-Star shining over the Roseland Peninsula and The Hinterland, with special focus on these three reactivated Star Temples. I thank the Archangel Michael for his presence and offer my utmost gratitude to those beautiful Light Beings, especially the Lady Mary, who have graced me with their presence. I am enveloped in the soft energies of the pink rose of Divine love. My beautiful Mary - my Rose of the Heart is here with me:

MARY

"Dearest daughter. We enfold you in our loving arms. God Bless you."

I close my centres, earth myself and go for a hot drink. It is now that I decide on a brief walk to the estuary through Hackney Marshes - no I am not in London - I am in Devon - this is my local nature reserve. The last of the day's sun warms me as I scuffle my way through the many fallen oak leaves - how appropriate after my day with the Druids. As I return up the little lane to my home, I can smell wood-smoke from the nearby cottages. The sun is setting in a rather wild looking atmospheric sky - dark clouds scurrying by against a backdrop of crimson - what a marvellous end to my sacred day.

Meanwhile back in Cornwall. I return from the Golden Hill Fort site, this time by a rather easier route - a track - which I stumbled across on my upward scramble. The track leads me to a locked gate over which I climb. There is a *'Private'* notice on the other side ....Whoops! I walk down the road to my car. Time has run out on me this day. I am now to travel on to Penzance and Cape Cornwall for Men-an-Tol Atlantean site (see Chapter 5).

For Beloved Mary and Naomi, their pilgrimage continued. They left Golden Fort, taking a boat down the River Fal for the next Druidic settlement near Borlase Wood. This was a time of rest and preparation for their journeying further west into Cornwall.

CHAPTER 4
ACROSS THE RIVER FAL
Deeper into Mystical Cornwall

We pick up the Lady Mary's trail at Borlase Wood, which is situated to the north of the Roseland Peninsula. I am told that Mary and Naomi spent several days at Borlase, while arrangements were being made for them to cross the River Fal for their next settlement at Cowlands. As they travelled further west and south through Mid Cornwall, they were to stay at Carn Brea Atlantean settlement and Tolcarne Wartha Druidic settlement. But more of this later when I undertake my second pilgrimage to Cornwall.

For now I am studying the map and have hit on the place name Cowlands on the west bank of the River Fal. Could this be another Temple dedicated to Hathor the Cow Goddess? The answer from Mary is: "*yes*". She also confirms an Atlantean Temple in the Etheric Realm at this site. I cannot help but wonder, why there were two Atlantean Temples in close vicinity in this area of Cornwall. I put it down to the shift in landmasses after the destruction of Atlantis, thus designating their position in the Etheric. Apparently, the dedication to the Goddess was at a later date and came out of Druidic and Egyptian wisdom of the time.

Whilst staying at Cowlands settlement, both Mary and Naomi attended a special Ceremony of Light. Mary had two tasks to undertake. First, she was to reactivate the ancient Atlantean Temple. Second, as High Priestess in the Egyptian Temple of Isis, Mary was to rededicate this Druidic Temple of the Goddess. My role at this ancient site, is to earth the Atlantean Temple, plus reactivate the energies of the Sacred Feminine and bring them into balance with the masculine. I am to do this within the sanctity of my own home before my next pilgrimage to Cornwall.

CEREMONY FOR THE ATLANTEAN TEMPLE OF THE GODDESS AT COWLANDS

I have earmarked the 17th January 2009 for my sacred Ceremony. From a numerological perspective this date offers up a number two which is representative of Divine Mother and the feminine principle - particularly efficacious for my Ceremony for the Goddess at Cowlands. A higher vibrational frequency of the number two is an eleven, one of the master numbers and which I feel will come into play this day. Astrologically the number eleven relates to Pluto, the Planet of Transformation, which brings Light to that which is hidden. This is significant, bearing in mind what I am being asked to undertake - to bring into manifestation on Earth the Atlantean Temple. Pluto has further significance here, as this planet is in its second year of an approximate seventeen year transit through the earth sign of Capricorn. Again - what is being asked of me - to earth an ancient Temple. One final point, Pluto is recognized as God of the Underworld and it is my theory that as such, its tremendous power will stimulate the Great Crystal at our Planet's core.

My altar beautifully presented, has a new fresh pink rose for Beloved Mary and the Goddess. One blessing of modern life is that one can buy roses at any time of the year. Having smudged my sacred space, I light my candle and am breathing in the essence of the rose. I am visualizing a Temple site at Cowlands. Although not having visited this ancient place, I see from my map that it is situated just at the top of a creek leading off the River Fal.

I begin my Ceremony: *"Blessed ones, I ask that I am a pure channel for the Light this hallowed day."* Merlin now comes to my inner vision. Standing before me, his bearing is upright and his staff firmly planted at his side. He seems to have arrived straight from the starry heavens. I become aware of the Goddess in the form of Hathor, as a tall white-robed figure, bearing a cow-horn head dress. Her energies I feel are gentle and loving yet commanding. I am now being shown a gathering of Brethren in the Temple of the ancient Brotherhood, each Master wearing a white robe. They are chanting and there is great rejoicing. I am being filled with the utmost power. I know it is IMPERATIVE that I stay very strong in this Place of Power and Light and not waver, as I conduct my Ceremony to earth the ancient Atlantean Temple, and re-enforce the beautiful energies of the Goddess. I invoke all the appropriate Beings of Light and lay down my crystals. My whole space is filled with Cosmic Rays as I voice the sacred words. Now I see a gleaming white-pillared domed Temple, which appears to be very gently floating to Earth from the Etheric Realm, its gossamer-like substance solidifying on reaching the ground. As it comes to rest, the magnificent Merlin strikes the ground with his staff in a sacred rite, thus consecrating the deed.

The Brethren in the Temple are still chanting and I am reminded how the ancients used the vibration of sound to move solid objects. The vortex of sound rising and falling in spirals can change their subtle energy field. This manifestation of the Ancient Wisdom was happening before my very eyes - well before my inner eyes - as I watch this ancient Temple come to Earth in solid form. This is how the large capstones on ancient burial cairns were shifted into position. This is how the enormous lintel stones at Stonehenge and other sacred monuments were lifted into their positions. This is how the great blocks of the ancient pyramids of Egypt were slotted into place - by the power of sound.

I am becoming conscious of the awesome force of the great Pluto. I know this Temple at Cowlands is dedicated to the Goddess, but the entity who now comes forward, is masculine, strong and imposing. It is as I thought, Pluto is to be an important component of this Ceremony:

PLUTO

"I am PLUTO the Planet of Destruction and Change. I MAKE change happen when Earth people ignore the warnings. I am at the CORE of this Earth. I make manifest great mountains and vast seas. I am thunder. I am power. I am strength. I am vibrational energy of the most powerful kind. I am the Being which brings the Planet of Pluto into your awareness if needs be, through violent happenings. BUT, I am also your protector Earth people. For without my protection - without my outbursts of sometimes seemingly uncontrolled fury, your Planet would not exist. I am the fuse and yet I am the plug, which prevents vapourisation and bursting forth of such powerful energies, that would have dissolved this Planet many eons ago through mans' foolishness and greed for power. However, IT WAS NOT TO BE. I am your conscience Earth people. Remember me well. Remember my power. Remember my actions. BUT, also remember my protection. It is up to you Earth people. YOU and only you, hold the destiny of your Planet in YOUR hands.

The Angels who enfold this Planet in their 'wings' of perfect bliss, are there for one mission and one mission only, that is to embrace yourselves and your Planet Earth and other Planets of the Solar System, in LOVE. As you aspire to their essence Earth people, so you will touch the very highest vibration of love. LOVE is the KEY that will turn fear and destruction into peace. The power of love will save your Planet. Remember this Children of Earth. I go now. Remember my energies. Remember my power. BUT above all remember my protection and my compassionate understanding. I am Pluto the slayer of dreams or the maker of visions. Choose Earth people. Choose your pathway carefully. FEAR or LOVE - which is it to be?"

Pluto has left me. Phew - that is a powerful message. I got it - so you get it! A warning perhaps, but maybe necessary as we can not help but be aware of conditions in our World today. I believe though, that the true message through all this drama is one of HOPE. Let us all put aside FEAR and embrace LOVE. Love - that pure sacred energy of the Rose in the Heart. Something which is coming to mind, is that Merlin the great alchemist took an active role today in my Ceremony and one of Pluto's expressions is said to be magic - how fitting.

I close my Light Ceremony at Cowlands. In my imagination, I carefully place both pink and white quartz crystals within the Temple and withdraw. I offer my blessed thanks to Pluto and all the Ancient Brethren who have participated in this Ceremony today. I especially thank and bless Beloved Mary for her gentle presence. I seal my physic centres and earth myself VERY firmly.

Eventually I wander off for a cup of tea. My plan now is to type up my notes and write down my thoughts while they are fresh in my memory. A little later today I am to visit two special White Eagle friends for a bit of paper collating and envelope stuffing! I am to assist them in putting together '*Smoke Signals*' the magazine of the White Eagle Star Centre South West. I shall be treated to dinner for my efforts! It is now 10.30 pm and I have returned exceedingly replete and very well grounded!

MAKING PLANS

We are nearing the end of January. Winter this year has brought to Devon as with much of Britain, bitterly cold weather. Despite conditions however, today I am off for a very short local walk. The fields, hedgerows and skeletal trees are covered with a thick hoar frost. I am completely bewitched by the transcendental beauty of this frosted landscape, which is lit up by the sun's rays. A day or so later, I realize that the weather is beginning to release its wintery grip, so its time for travelling once more. This turns out to be a window of opportunity for my second pilgrimage to Cornwall, as when I get back, the wintry weather returns and we are frozen up for a further two weeks!

I will enter into this pilgrimage with two differences from the last. One is that I have now had the opportunity of charting Mary's journeying through Cornwall, so I know where she went in advance. Secondly, at this juncture in my association with Mary, I am more aware of what she requires of me. On this occasion, she has requested that I visit the Druidic settlement of Carn Brea near Redruth, in order to earth an ancient Atlantean Temple. After this assignment I have no specific plans, but am sure to be guided. For my accommodation I have booked three nights in a B & B near Carn Brea, as youth hostels are closed during the winter for single travellers, and the weather is a bit inclement for a camping barn! Radio Devon this morning has issued flood warnings, so the icy weather has given way to rain - lovely. But it will be better in Cornwall - ever the optimist!

For Mary and Naomi, after their time at Cowlands, the next leg of their journey took them on to Roseworthy settlement via the river from Truro. After a short stay they went on through Salem (Jeru/salem) to Carn Brea. It is here that I myself encounter Mary once again.

The day before I leave for Cornwall, I have an attunement and am blessed with the presence of the Master Jesus, this radiant, gentle Master of the Christ Light. The message is exceedingly long, so I will give you the crux of the message. He first offers a blessing on my pilgrimage to ancient Kernow - Cornwall. Then:

THE MASTER JESUS

"There is in the central area of Cornwall a crystal deep deep within the Earth. This crystal is directly linked to the Great Crystal of ancient times within the centre of your Earth's crust and as such can receive its power and distribute that energy throughout the sacred land of ancient Cornwall. Of course, ALL crystals at node points of what you call the Ley Line System, are connected. You will know of Merrivale on your Dartmoor and of Carmarthen Bay in Wales and Strata Florida, the heart centre of Wales. And - there are more - many more. You and many dedicated workers for the Light - for the upliftment of the vital energies of your Planet through your dedication and sacred work - will enliven the crystals of old. The crystals will bring balance to Planet Earth - they will bring healing to Planet Earth - they will bring protection to Planet Earth. They MUST be at the core of your future work. They ARE your future. In ancient times - in the days of Atlantis and beyond, crystals were used for all these things. The ancient people, of which you were one my child, knew of the protection and healing power of the crystals and worked with them. For many, memories of such are returning. There are those who today are working with the Crystal Energy, but this sacred work MUST be undertaken from the heart not through any ideas of curiosity or of gaining power. By power we mean, the personal ego as well as a dominating power. The power of the crystal is real and is to be respected. The Crystal Masters of old will return and guide the younger souls on the Earth - they will share their knowledge with you. Use the power of the ancient Crystal Energy VERY carefully and only from that deepest point of the purist Love. Let love - the Rose in YOUR Heart, rule supreme my children of Earth. Remember this.

Blessed are the meek, for they shall see our God. Blessed are those who seek to serve the one Universal Christ Light, for they shall truly inherit the Earth and other Planets of Light - those Planets of pure Golden Energy and Perfected Beings. Judge not my beloved Brethren, lest you be judged Give unto others as you have received. Let not fear enter your being or be a part of your life. Live only in the place of perfect understanding, divine wisdom and tranquil peace. Love your neighbour as yourself. Let no man take that divine essence from you. YOU are the Master of your emotions. YOU are Master of your physical body. YOU are Master of your mental body. Indeed - you are Master of ALL your subtle bodies. Let love over-ride fear. Let the divine essence of our Father-Mother God be within your sacred hearts."

This beautiful Master then offers a blessing and I can feel the love emanating from his Divine Being. The blessed Mary is standing alongside him - two Perfected Beings. Both are wearing white robes of ethereal material and yet looking so solid. Each has a jewel at their heart centre. For Mary, it is a rose crystal. For Jesus - an amethyst crystal. As I return to physical consciousness, a feeling of profound joy envelops me. I am imbued with the deepest love.

I always have a glass of water close to my altar and as I sip this now magnetized water, I picture its healing properties rejuvenating the physical cells of my body. I blow out my precious candle, sending the Light into the

World and especially into Cornwall, where I shall be travelling. I turn my telephone back on, which I had switched off in order not to be disturbed during my attunement, to hear on the messaging service *'hello granny'* from my three year old grandson. What a delight. I smile to myself. The children are truly amazing - they offer unconditional love, are non-judgmental, accepting you for what you are, in complete trust. We could all learn so much from the little ones. There are many enlightened souls coming into incarnation at the cusp of the New Age; Indigo, Crystal, Star children to name a few, who are bringing in anew the energies of the Ancient Wisdom.

MY PILGRIMAGE OVER THE FAL

Before I leave I have a short link with spirit, as preparation for the journey ahead. I step over the threshold into my sacred space and seat myself before my little home altar. Some pink roses for Beloved Mary are close by. Some of these will come with me to Cornwall as offerings. My prayer: *"Beloved Mary - walk with me on this pilgrimage through the sacred heart of Cornwall. Be my guide and comforter. May the Light of all Eternity shine on our Mission. I trust in your wisdom and I offer to you my deepest love. Amen."* I receive a beautiful acknowledgement from Mary.

My first goal on this my second pilgrimage over the border, is to be the Druidic settlement of Carn Brea south-west of Redruth. My B & B is at Rosgroggan Chapel in South Tehidy nearby. It is through Rosgroggan, that Mary travelled on her journey along the north coast of Cornwall (see Chapter 6). I had booked another property from the Accommodation Guide, but on arrival was told that I would be staying at their second property called, Rosgroggan Chapel (Ros/Rose). I also learnt that the owner was appropriately named Rose! In this region, I will be heading right into the heart of tin mining country. Indications on the map, give the impression that this area of Cornwall, is one vast underground cavern, which brings a vision of many huge crystals within the Earth itself.

My car is loaded. It is 9.00 am and I am ready. I leave my little home in the care of the Angels. It is raining - very heavily! Driving along the A38, I pass Dartmoor which today is looking dark and foreboding, yet strangely mysterious as the tops are shrouded in mist. I can just make out some familiar shapes. I cross the bridge over the River Tamar which divides Devon and Cornwall. Tamar - could this be named after the daughter of Jesus and Mary Magdalene? There are some sources which say that Jesus and Mary were married, had a daughter Tamar and that they travelled in the South West of the British Isles. If so, this naming of the river, would be quite fitting. Well into Cornwall now, I pass St Austell sky-lined with its easily identifiable clay pits. Further on and I am witness to a couple of wind farms, the tall generators looking for all like big white birds. Today they are in full action, whirling round in the high wind. There is much controversy over the placement of these new features in our countryside. To some, they are monstrosities, not in keeping with the natural landscape and emitting disturbing noise levels. To others, they are our environmentally green future.

CARN BREA SETTLEMENT

Approaching Redruth, I see before me the heights of Carn Brea. While the sky all around is grey and overcast, Carn Brea appears to be miraculously topped with light. I see a huge tower and another large structure, which I am to learn, are a monument and a castle. At this first sighting of the sacred hill, my heart misses a beat and I feel that I am being inwardly prepared. I shall go direct to Carn Brea to perform my Ceremony.

Now in Redruth - map to hand - the ancient hill-top rises up right in front of me, but can I reach it - no. I keep stopping and checking all the little roads, which according to the map will take me to the summit, but it's impossible. The reason - there is a wacking great modern industrial estate built just below the northern flank of Carn Brea, which has blocked every available entrance from this side of the hill. At one point I see a narrow road signposted '*Druids Hill*' - this will take me up I think - well it doesn't. Instead, it peters out into a public footpath next to a factory. I ask Mary and the 'powers that be' in the next World - with no joy. By now frustrated, I am probably not tuning in correctly or perhaps this is a test! Eventually, a kind lady, a walking angel of this world, puts me right and sends me off on a roundabout drive of three sides of a square until I spot a sign '*To the Castle*' - success. I take a very winding narrow lane, which soon runs out of tarmac and becomes a stony potholed dirt track. I keep going slowly until I reach the car park - here at last. The castle on Carn Brea's heights is an amazing stone edifice built into a natural rocky outcrop. It is a restaurant, supposedly open seven days a week - today it is closed - no doubt due to the time of year.

"*Well Mary, my beloved one, I am here.*" It is at Carn Brea settlement that Mary and Naomi met up with Joseph and Jesus after their independent journeying. They were apart for some months and were now to spend three weeks together before once again going their separate ways. At Carn Brea they celebrated the winter solstice and the Lady Mary performed a special Ceremony to reactivate the ancient Atlantean Temple.

I step out of my car into a howling gale and slanting rain. All change then since my earlier viewing. Where has the light gone? Perhaps it was an Etheric Light I saw from the distance? I get all togged up - boots, fleece, anorak, over-trousers, woolly hat and gloves - that's it. I am ready - what a pretty sight! I have a small tin from Brittany which used to contain sweet Breton biscuits. Now it is my special container for all my Ceremonial items. Of course, Brittany is another landscape filled with ancient Celtic sites and monuments, so the use of this tin is quite appropriate. In it I have my little pouch of crystals, a small white cloth, candle and matches, my silver six pointed star and a picture of Beloved Mary, along with the words for my sacred Ceremony.

Where am I to go? Carn Brea is an extensive area, but insight tells me to head off in an easterly direction. Walking through muddy puddles and over slippery rocks, I reach an enormous triangular granite stone, which is indicative of an ancient settlement - this is feeling to be the right area. The ancient stone is high on the outer edge of Carn Brea and must have been an excellent landmark in days past. Today it looks out over Redruth and that wretched modern industrial estate. Fortunately, I can see beyond this to the north Cornish coast. In full view on the eastern hills, are the chimney tops of old derelict buildings standing as testimony to a once proud mining heritage. How come these are not a blot on the landscape as are the modern industrial buildings? Instead, they seem to merge with today's landscape quite aesthetically. I come to a long ridge of enormous boulders leading out to the edge of the hill. Walking carefully across the top, being nearly blown off in the process, I reach a huge granite boulder at the far end. In the valley below me is a little village and a church. The space behind the boulder is in the lee of the wind - I do believe I have the most sheltered spot on Carn Brea. There is no-one around - not much of a surprise on such a wet and windy day - which as it happens adds a certain atmospheric element to my Ceremony.

CARN BREA ATLANTEAN TEMPLE CEREMONY

I settle down behind the boulder and prepare my travelling altar. On my small cloth I lay a white quartz crystal, my silver star and a pink rose. I attempt to light the candle, but even though it is in a small protective tin, the air element is the winner and out it goes. So I will have to visualize a living flame. I make ready my crystals - the pink quartz for Beloved Mary, the turquoise for Is-Ra and for Merlin the merlinite. I am saying: *"Beloved Mary - gracious Beings of the Higher Realms, I offer myself to you in service this day. Grant that the sacred work I am to undertake is secured for all times."*

As I begin my Ceremony, a raven flying high above my head croaks in recognition. The raven is a sacred bird to the ancient Celts and very much associated with Merlin. This is a good omen: *"Thank you Merlin for making your presence known."* I visualize a great Sun-Star high up in the Heavens. I become aware of the Golden Light energy pouring down encompassing Carn Brea. I proceed clearly and methodically, voicing the words of my Atlantean Ceremony, submitting each crystal as an offering and laying it on my altar. In my imagination, I see the ancient Temple returning to Earth and I am saying *'As above so below. As on Earth so beneath'*. For there is a Cosmic Thread of Light reaching from the highest point of Universal Light to the Earth and going deep into the Earth's crust, which will be strengthened with the newly earthed Temple. The original well-known saying comes from the Emerald Tablets circa 3,000 BC and reads *'As above so below. As within so without'*. This is my version which seems appropriate at this moment in time. Merlin wishes to speak:

Carn Brea showing the Castle Headland where the Atlantean Temple is earthed

MERLIN

"I endorse this Ceremony at Carn Brea this day. I endorse the ancient Atlantean Temple and its physical presence on sacred Mother Earth. IT IS DONE. The Light from this place as pure energy, WILL travel across the British Isles and beyond. The Light from here will link with the Global Light. The Light from this place will bring healing and peace and harmony to your Planet. I and the Druid Elders of the old times, thank you sister for your work this sacred day"

The message I receive is shorter than others during Ceremonial days, but 'THEY' are aware of physical conditions and that I am freezing! Towards the back of the boulder is a deep crevice in the rock. It is here I place the white quartz crystal for the Druids, with the pink quartz crystal and single stem pink rose for the Lady Mary. They will be visible only to the curious and hopefully will stay there, but whatever happens, their essence will remain. I thank all the beautiful Beings of the One Light and close my Ceremony, ensuring that I am sealed and well grounded.

Gathering up my Ceremonial items, I put everything back in my pack. I retrace my steps but this time avoid the windy top of the big bouldered ridge and take a lower route along a narrow peaty brackened footpath, which eventually leads me up to the castle. Now a brisk walk across the top of Carn Brea takes me to the monument. This is dedicated to Lord Dunstable of the Basset family, who once owned Tehidy Manor, now a country park just to the north of Redruth. All around this area are giant slabs of rock, recumbent standing stones and evidence of hut circles. This ancient settlement is not marked on the map as such, only as a fort. However, I am told this is where Mary, Jesus, Naomi and Joseph stayed. Later at home, I am wondering where the Temple came to rest as I did not have a vision of a precise spot on this occasion. One obvious place is at Carn Brea's highest point where the castle now stands, which I believe to be the site of the ancient Druid Temple. So with my dowsing crystal I ask the question: *"Is the earthed Atlantean Temple positioned on the castle hill-top"* I received an affirmative. Back to the reality of the now - it really is too cold and blowy to linger. I have completed my Mission for Beloved Mary and the Masters. I return to my car, divest myself of my outer gear and have a hot coffee. It is 3.30 pm and I would like to reach my accommodation before 4.00 pm if possible.

ROSGROGGAN CHAPEL

I am staying in this fascinating old ivy-clad chapel with Gothic windows, which was cleverly converted about forty years ago, while keeping many of the original fixtures. For example, on the ceiling of my first floor room, is a long strip of dark wood with two wheels attached, one either end, which I am told was used to raise and lower the lights from the original chapel floor. The present owners obviously chose to retain the old theme, as most of the furniture and fittings are antique, with many curios around the place, including a very talkative parrot! Not quite me this décor, but a very welcome place of rest at the end of the day. During my stay I discover a few other 'interesting' features. One is that the huge brass bedstead, which is free-standing, bangs against the wall with the slightest movement in bed. I really did 'put a sock in it' or in this case 'socks over them' - the bed knobs that is. Also, the door has no lock or key and would without warning unlatch and fly open. Therefore, at night I set up a formidable 'Les Mis' style barricade! Further, there are three extension leads each having four socket outlets to house the various bits of electrical equipment in the room. When it was converted some years back, obviously one wall socket outlet per room was considered adequate.

After a hot drink I decide on a walk as there is about an hour before dark. The lady of the house suggests I might like to visit their local beach. When I ask if I can walk to it, the reply is *'Goodness me no'* which I am to learn is good advice. So it's into the car avec trusty map. Well, I thought local meant local, but I am to undertake a three mile drive which takes me first to Hells Mouth. I park up and walk across a grassy cliff-top to discover a great gaping indent in the sheer cliff-face with pounding seas at its base. I retreat from the edge rather rapidly. A further two miles on is Towans beach, obviously their local. Once again I park, take a quick breath of air, a look at the wild seas and get back in the car. This reminds me of conditions at Caerhays beach in the autumn. An amazing sunset catches my eye. As the sun is beginning its drop into the horizon of the sea, behind a layer of dark navy and lavender cloud formation, so it throws up the most glorious molten-gold fringe. Returning now in dimpsy light, my final delight of the day is to come across a field of golden daffodils, which bring vibrant colour to the otherwise grey dusk. Whether the daffodils are trumpeting me I do not know, but I herald their bravery at this cold time of the year. The snows returned after my journeying and I cannot help but wonder how those plucky little flowers blooming so early, are faring

Driving to my B & B earlier, I passed the turning to Tehidy Country Park identified by a large triangular green. A huge articulated lorry was trying to negotiate the corner bringing down branches from overhead trees in its wake. On my return from the beach, I managed to get one of these branches latched up underneath my car! So there I was - night drawing in - on my hands and knees - crawling under the car to retrieve the intrusive object. Behind me a car had pulled up, its driver politely waiting for me to finish my task No help was offered, but at least I didn't get run over. This is only the first day of my pilgrimage and what excitements I've had! Later, as I settle to sleep my thoughts return to my Light Ceremony on Carn Brea and the wonders which unfolded.

TOLCARNE WARTHA DRUIDIC SETTLEMENT

This is Day 3 of my pilgrimage and it is set aside for exploration of Tolcarne Wartha settlement, which was on Mary's journey south from Carn Brea. This had been planned for my second day, but yesterday came in wet and misty and it would have been fruitless to go up into the hills in search of the ancient site Instead, I took a drive round Illogan and the surrounding area which focuses in Mary's pilgrim route along the north coast (see Chapter 6). Today I have awakened to clear blue skies - all mist and rain miraculously vanished. Tolcarne Wartha - here I come. Beloved Mary has asked that I undertake a home Ceremony to reactivate the Cosmic Light at this ancient site, so this is not part of my directive today. But I am eager to visit the ancient site and link-in to the energies of past times.

Before I leave my accommodation, I sit before my makeshift altar and light a candle for a link with Mary. Making my way to South Tehidy I now drive through Pool until I am in the area of Nine Maidens. I make a brief stop to search for any evidence of a stone circle or standing stones - I find nothing. I call in at the Nine Maidens Adventure School for assistance. It is like Fort Knox getting in, but when I eventually do, the two girls at reception have no idea where Nine Maidens is: *"I just come to work by car"* one says rather lamely. Not a lot of good then! With much unlocking of doors, I am eventually released. For the next thirty minutes, I explore the surrounding countryside, in the car, on foot and with binoculars - with no luck. However I must be careful not to digress too much because my priority today is Tolcarne Wartha, so I press on.

According to my map, just a couple of miles to the south should be Tolcarne Wartha. But as with Carn Brea, seeing and finding are two different things. There it is before me, but as I turn a meandering Cornish lane - it has shifted! Along the roadside are some grassy parking places, but it could be tricky to get off after all the rain yesterday. As I am deliberating my best move, I find myself at Stithians Resevoir. On this bright sunny day with a good stiff breeze, it is as if sparkling diamonds are dancing on the rippled surface of the lake. Windsurfers are scudding along at the rate of knots, riding across the water with ease - an exhilarating sight. A lady in the Recreational Centre informs me that for Tolcarne Wartha I need to return to the village of Penmarth, from where she believes there is easy access.

Following her instructions, I park up by the chapel in the village. Pack on my back and booted up, off I go. I take the road back through the village and pick up a stony track, which according to my map should lead to the settlement. I come to a very narrow path heading off through scrubland of gorse, heather and brambles, - this seems to be going in the right direction. Carefully picking my way over straggling brambles which cut across the path and finding no evidence in the landscape of an ancient settlement, I return to the main track. Now, I am not adverse to a challenge, but so far this one has got me beat. A bit of help is needed. I get out my dowsing roads. Standing very still I speak with Mary and the Druid Elders. I ask for directions to the ancient settlement. The rods indicate to the right. I turn around and ask the same question - the rods indicate to the left. Thank you - the confirmation I need. The information points to a plateau of scrub in the far distance. Armed with improved knowledge, I take the same path through the brambles. I come to a recumbent standing stone approximately three metres in height. This is of significance. I see a very faint outline of what could be a huge raised circular bank, the whole completely covered in undergrowth. THIS IS IT! I eagerly head across to it, wading up to the tops of my thighs in the tangled web of dense scrub. Feeling like some intrepid explorer, I eventually reach the high stone bank, which is almost completely covered in the scrub.. By now my trousers are snagged and my legs jabbed by brambles - I am in a pretty sorry state. Climbing on top of the bank, I see a complete circle of about twenty metres in diameter In what looks to be the middle of this circle is a large yellow gorse bush. I trudge once more through the undergrowth, thinking I may find something of evidence there, get halfway across and suddenly stop. This is the settlement alright but this is NOT the Druid Temple. I retrace my steps back to the path - I need a rethink.

THE DRUIDIC TEMPLE

I retrieve my dowsing rods from my pack, this time asking for the ancient Temple. Once I am happy with the result, I go off in the direction the rods tell me. Hey presto - a little way off from the settlement and about seven metres from my path, I see a very large flat granite stone covered in moss and heather with some surrounding stones. I am unexpectedly overcome with emotion at reaching this sacred place: *"Bless you and thank you ancient ones for your guidance this day."* I scramble my way across to the stone and step up on it. From this high point there are distant views to both the south and north Cornish coasts. I pull out a small mat from my pack and sit down on the stone in contemplation. The sun is out and there is a warm wind. It seems a perfect moment, but this is not the time to perform my Ceremony of Light. I am becoming aware of those from the old times around me and a magnificent Being steps forward:

HIGH PRIEST

"You are most welcome sister. We admire your dogged determination to rediscover our settlement and the ancient Temple of Light (I 'feel' a certain gentle humour emitting from this ancient one!). *It was at this place we brought down from the Cosmos, the ancient powerful Christ Light, to heal the land and help our crops to grow. You dear Naomi with the blessed Mary, joined us on one occasion, a long long time ago by your Earth standards, yet just a fleeting time by our standards. You travelled from Carn Brea that ancient Atlantean settlement of Light and yes dear child you are right, on this journey you did travel on the backs of donkeys* (on my way to Tolcarne Wartha I had come through a village called Burras and somehow I made a connection with the word Burro the Spanish for donkey, with Mary and Naomi's mode of transport). *We knew of your pending visit through the Ancient Wisdom in the long distant past. We also knew closer to the time by Joseph of Arimathea and your Celtic family. Your grandmother, Anna joined you here at what is now called Tolcarne Wartha settlement, for she was not living very far from here* (where I am eagerly asking)? *We are permitted to tell you sister it is close-by. This is why it was destined for you Naomi and Mary to travel to this area of ancient Celtic Cornwall and stay at Tolcarne Wartha. And this is why you have returned now dear sister, to tune in to past memories. It is not right that you know precisely where - you will have to be satisfied with my answer dear sister.*

We know you have a Ceremony to perform on your return. We will ALL be with you on that occasion. We will gather here in the ancient Temple, physical presence of which has all but disappeared. BUT you have found the Altar Stone. Bless you sister. We will be here. You will know this. Thank you for your pilgrimage this day. May the peace of all Eternity rest with you and may you alight from your pilgrimage wiser, happier and at peace within yourself. (I hear the raven croaking above my head just as I did at Carn Brea and receive) *you will know that Merlin's raven is indicative of his presence."*

Coming into full consciousness, I realize that where I am sitting IS the Altar Stone of the ancient Temple. I thank the Druid Elder for his contact. I hear a buzzard mewing its cat-like cry. I look around and there it is, soaring across the sky using the strong air currents for up-lift. Now a stonechat, a very handsome bird, black and white with a russet breast, is chatting away at the top of a nearby gorse bush. This is all going on, yet there is a stillness in the air. I am so happy here. It is 1.30 pm and I take a drink of water and enjoy a crunchy bar - very healthy I don't think - but just right for the moment.

Still curious, once again I take out my dowsing rods and ask the question: *"ancient ones are you allowed to tell me - was Anna born within a five miles radius of this place?"* The answer comes back: *"Yes"*. I narrow it down to within a two mile radius. I offer my thanks and leave it at that. However, at home curiosity once again got the better of me and I went over the area on the map very methodically and - nothing. It was obvious that as the Druid Elder intimated - it was not for me to know!

Sadly I am to leave. I return to the path noting the many large granite stones almost lost to the scrub, obviously all part of the ancient Temple complex. At the recumbent standing stone, I check out a theory that has come to me, that there must have been a second standing stone which would have formed a gateway. I am told there was and that it is still on site, but hidden. Now of course it registers, that THIS must be a beginning of a precessional route, a double stone row leading to the Temple. Using my compass I discover that it is rather unusually, on a south-north alignment.

I start back down the wide track, when I realize that I have forgotten to leave a white quartz crystal for the Druids. It is a bit of a hike, but return I must. At the Altar Stone I carefully place my crystal in the centre on the soft green moss saying: *"I honour you ancient ones. I honour you all."* The Druid Elder is really trying to rest my 'dogged determination!' With much satisfaction I take my leave. I can now visualize the ancient Temple site when I do my Ceremony at home.

ST EUNY CHURCH

I walk the couple of miles back to my car. While having a snack and hot drink I take a look at the map and decide on a visit to St Euny Church in Church Town, the village set in the valley below Carn Brea, which I viewed from the top. The church is closed - how disappointing. This has an air of familiarity about it - at Tregony I had fared no better. I take a wander round the churchyard and find myself drawn to a large ancient yew tree, which I recognize as the guardian of this holy site. I have with me a most beautiful white stone from Yarner Woods on Dartmoor, and as an offering I place this under the tree. I am rewarded by a few words:

DEVA OF THE YEW

"I thank you for your kind offering. You are correct. I AM the guardian of this ancient churchyard. I and my helpers keep this sacred place peaceful and free from disturbance. The little people tend the grasses and the flowers hereabouts. I bring them protection. Thank you for your offering and your presence. You may go now."

Okay. This is typical of what I receive from tree devas - they are so matter of fact! I find it quite amusing. I thank the deva and offer my blessing. It is very peaceful here in this late afternoon sunshine, only broken by the melodic tones of a song thrush. Among the gravestones are snowdrops, celandine and even a few early primroses. The dear little daisies have closed their petals for the night.

I return to my accommodation full of joy. Having journeyed with Mary to Tolcarne Wartha, tomorrow I shall leave for Devon. My journey home takes me via Perranporth and St Piran's Church and Oratory. Mary arrived at

Perranporth after a short sea trip from Portreath, and followed this stretch of coastline to Cubert settlement (see Chapter 6).

CANDLEMAS/IMBOLC

Today is the 2nd February, the beginning of the ancient Celtic Fire Festival of Imbolc, embodying the Fire Goddess, Brighid - 'the Bright One'. It is the awakening of Mother Earth from its winter slumbers to the rebirth of the Light of a new spring. For us all, it can be a time of renewal and transformation, a letting go and releasing old energies and concepts and embracing a new understanding of ourselves and the Ancient Wisdom. Maybe Candlemas can be seen as an opportunity to re-enforce our New Year resolutions. As we step forth with utmost trust into fresh pastures - into new ways of being - so we embrace the secret of Imbolc.

In the Christian Calendar, the Virgin Mary symbolizes Candlemas, which is seen as a time of cleansing and purification before Lent. Its purity is epitomized in the snowdrop, that delicate stalwart little flower, which pushes forth its shoots, often through the snow, at this the coldest time of the year, producing pure white Candlemas bells. For me at this time, to celebrate Candlemas with the Lady Mary, is to be especially cherished.

Back in Devon after my pilgrimage to Cornwall, the cold weather has returned and I awake to find a white world of glistening, pristine snow, just in time for Candlemas. What could be better. Mind you, my planned trip with a local Gatekeeper group (the Gatekeeper Trust who pilgrimage to sacred places in order to enhance the spiritual energies within the landscape), to Snowdrop Valley on the heights of Exmoor later this week, has had to be cancelled due to heavy snow and icy conditions. However, I do manage to get out and about in my own area and have seen the mass of snowdrops gracing the gardens at Dartington Hall, near the town of Totnes. What a lift to the heart this brings.

It is 12.00 noon on this hallowed day dedicated to Our Lady, to the Goddess and to rebirth. I sit in attunement. On my altar, as a special tribute is a beautiful pure white candle shaped like a cylindrical tower with a silver six pointed star marked on it. Before me is a single stemmed white rose. As I light my candle I say: *"Blessed Mary I light this candle in your honour. In my sacred space I acknowledge our Celtic past as we celebrated Imbolc together at Tolcarnr Wartha."* For I have learnt that Mary and Naomi were present at the Imbolc Ceremony at this site, following their winter solstice celebration at Carn Brea. This is the Ceremony in which Anna joined them from her home in the vicinity. Both Mary and Anna are with me now, but it is Anna who chooses to speak this day:

ANNA

"My Sister of Light. Thank you for your remembrance. This time of the year in ancient times we would await the coming of the spring. Our celebrations and our Ceremonies would be to awaken Mother Earth to all her potentialities. All the unseen below the Earth is stirring into life in anticipation of the new life in the sun. When the

time is right for each tiny flower and each tree, then they put forth their blossom and their bud, which will colour your world. Dear sister this is the hidden time when preparation is made for future growth and future beauty.

So it is with us dear sister. There is a time of inner preparation before each human soul expresses itself in its true magnificence - in its true beauty. We are so blessed sister to have this knowledge and to be aware of the deeper esoteric meaning of growth and life. It is a privilege and yet it is our right. Once this is recognized, the human heart begins to expand with an ever increasing glow of a soft warm light, which in turn expands to fill the whole being. We must all eventually reach the stage of complete at-one-ment with that Universal Light, that pure Love of the Sacred Heart. We can all absorb these pure energies. Let us now bring forth into our own lives this secret of eternal joy, recognizing that the pattern of growth in the tiniest flower from the tiniest seed, is a blessed manifestation of the ancient mystery of life. From the smallest seed can grow the fullest manifestation of God's magnificence. Bless the little flowers - bless the grand trees - the recurring wonder of everlasting and ever-returning life. Bless the fairy folk and all those in the Elemental Kingdom, for they tend these delicate flowers and trees with so much love and dedication.

We are aware that there is talk on your Earth Plane of the disappearance of the precious bees. Rest assured this will never happen, BUT as with all things within the Nature Kingdom, there is a fine balance between greed and bringing forth blessed abundance. The little people know this and are working extra hard at this moment in time, to attempt to shift the emphasis of greed and misunderstanding, which is occurring on your Planet. As I say, there is a delicate balance to be maintained.

Whenever - wherever - you walk on your Earth, be it on your hills or moorlands - around your towns and gardens, we ask that you bless each footstep as you allow it to tread lightly on the Earth We ask you to bless all you see and hear around you in order to bring in that Universal Light. We ask you to walk in the purist love, blessing the Elemental Kingdom and always being aware of their truly magical, but essential work for humankind. These little people are the saviours of your precious Earth and the abundance thereof. So my Brothers and Sisters, celebrate this unseen manifestation of new life. Welcome its manifestation as the little green shoots first appear. Look always to the Light as they do, and you too, will rise in inner consciousness to that everlasting and eternal life. Let your pilgrim feet walk gently Let your pilgrim feet heal the very soil Let your pilgrim feet bring blessing to the landscape. Amen"

I thank this dear soul for her special communication. I sit quietly connecting to Anna's words and reflecting on them. Once again, this is a reminder of how fragile is the balance in the natural world. It is a reminder of the role of the Devic Kingdom, and of how our part in it is paramount. As I close my attunement, I offer the flame from my candle for healing of the great Earth Mother and for the Elemental Kingdom.

TOLCARNE WARTHA DRUIDIC TEMPLE CEREMONY

Following Candlemas, I prepare for my Ceremony at this sacred Druidic site which I visited recently. It is 3.00 pm on February 4th 2009, which just happens to be my birth-day, so I am to have an extra special celebration. The Gods are shining on me and the Angels are holding me in their protective wings of luminescent light.

Looking at my Ephemeris, I see that transiting Venus is conjunct my natal Venus in the earth sign of Capricorn. This is very appropriate for the work I shall be doing this day, which is to bring love and harmony to the Earth at Tolcarne Wartha, by reactivating the ancient Light there. I also notice that two of the travelling Planets, Mars with its firey energies and expansive Jupiter are trined the Moon today, which will generate strong positive influences to bear on my Ceremony.

Everything is ready. A six pointed star and a white quartz crystal are placed on my altar. Today it is also adorned with my Candlemas candle. I breathe gently and rhythmically - now I am perfectly still. I link with the Druid Elder who spoke with me at Tolcarne Wartha. He said that all the Brethren would be present as I perform my Ceremony, and indeed I am feeling a multitude with me now in this room. I picture myself at the Altar Stone within the Tolcarne Wartha Temple. I ask a blessing as I bring this sacred Ceremony under the Christ Star.

I proceed with my Druidic Ceremony. As I lay down my merlinite crystal, this time I have a very strong vision of the great alchemist Merlin. Offering my turquoise crystal, my inner vision moves to Is-Ra, High Priest of ancient Egypt. With my pink quartz crystal I become conscious of Beloved Mary and the Sacred Feminine. The energies are very powerful. My inner vision takes me back to past times, as I watch the Druid Elders precessing the sacred circle, activating the Cosmic Light. Merlin is standing within the group of ancient ones. When the time is right, he very forcefully strikes the ground with his staff, thus sealing the vibrational energies. In my imagination I hear his raven croak. His words:

MERLIN

"Let not the World of yours weep. Let joy be its prime manifestation. Help to turn the tide of misery which we see Earth children and bring in the new wave of Light. Let not its people turn their back on the old ways, rather let them recreate the Ancient Wisdom as perpetuated by those ancient ones. Let that Light so shine in your hearts Earth children, that all kingdoms respond to that Light. Let the love of your precious hearts, so flow out to your fellowmen and to your creatures that ALL may dwell together in harmony. Let not hearts be hardened in ignorance of the Elemental Kingdoms lest the little people and their precious work is forgotten. Pay heed my Earth children to these words. (once Merlin has got that message over, his tone changes).

There is great rejoicing in the Heaven World as more and more Earth men and women take up the Banner of Light in order to spread Cosmic and Mystical Wisdom abroad. This is fine work my Earth children and we, all the Masters of Light, applaud your efforts. We watch over you and protect your journeying on Planet Earth. We watch over you and guide your footsteps as they move forward into the Light. We watch over you and offer you our deepest love and blessings Earth children. Be aware of our presence as you go about your Earthly duties. Tune into our magnificence which is YOUR magnificence also. For, we are ALL made in the image of God. We are ALL, co-creators with this great Cosmic energy. Understanding this means that we understand our responsibilities. My Earth children - ALL IS WELL. We wish you good fortune and joy as you progress ever upwards, towards that Universal Cosmic Christ Light, that Christ Star which is the epitome of perfection. Its Rays of Light bring Power, Wisdom and Love to your Earth Plane. THIS dear children of Earth, is the Triangle of Light which is expressed in each human heart as the perfect Rose or Lily. Gather ye in the lilies of the field for none is lost to the Great White Spirit.

Today the Light has once more reached the heart of this ancient Druid Temple of Tolcarne Wartha in sacred Cornwall. It will combine with all such reawakened magical and mystical energies, to enhance and invigorate the land. It IS done. I bless you my Earth children."

I thank the great and magical Merlin for his presence and for the powerful yet loving message proffered. I thank all the Druid Elders who were present. I sense much rejoicing. In my imagination, I place the two crystals on the Temple Altar Stone. A thought - I am struck by the similarity of *'Tolarne Wartha'* and *'Arthur.'* Also, I remember seeing on the map a *'Carn Arthen'* north of Tolcarne Wartha and south-west of Carn Brea. Plus, Merlin has put in an appearance at both sites. The question arises - is there a link in this area with Arthur? I am being told that this is so, but at this point no further information is forthcoming - perhaps later. I offer my beautiful Candlemas candle, this time to reactivating the Light in Britain. I close my attunement and sip from my glass of water in order to re-energize myself.

DILIGENCE

Dear reader, during my Mission with the Lady Mary, I have shared with you many delightful personal experiences and some filled with emotion. However, now I am prepared to share a moment of carelessness, which even though it is not a good reflection on me, could be of value for any who are working with the Light, especially in tricky circumstances. The aberrations happened during my Ceremony for Tolcarne Wartha. In the first instance, I did not prepare my sacred space by smudging. Secondly, I failed to seal my physic centres and earth myself at the end of my Ceremony. How could I be so negligent? These failures allowed a dark element to enter my aura and attempt to take over. In my defence I have to say that this was linked to something else going on in my life at the time, which I subsequently learnt was karmic and had an ancient Egyptian connection. But, lessons have to be learnt. So here we go.

MY NIGHTMARE

What brought things to my notice was something which happened in my sleep state. It began with a nightmare where I was being 'CONTROLLED' is the only way I can describe it. The actual experience of a dream or nightmare is very difficult to explain, yet it is always so real to the participant, but I will give it my best shot. There were three sections to the nightmare. In the first, I was driving my car along a stretch of main road known to me. My eyes were shut and it was if someone else was controlling the car. I was going faster and faster and faster and couldn't stop - it was so real that I even felt cold spray from an open window on my face. I sort of woke up, but then went back to sleep almost immediately, whereupon the second part of my nightmare occurred. On this occasion I was standing in my bedroom. I couldn't open my bedroom door or draw the curtains back or in fact perform any physical action. Once again, I was in somebody else's control. By now I was in a state of semi-consciousness and feeling scared. I tried to open my eyes which was exceedingly difficult to do, but eventually managed it, noting the time as 1.06 am. Almost immediately I returned to my sleep state. This time in my nightmare, I was lying flat on my back unable to move my legs or hands, unclench my fist or open my eyes. I can feel now as I am writing this, the effort I made, but to no avail. I did eventually wake up but couldn't my eyes. There seemed to be a heavy weight on them as if I was not to wake up. By now I was in a state of sheer terror. Somehow I forced my eyes open, propped myself up on my pillows and put the light on, absolutely determined to get myself fully awake. I knew I just HAD to wake up. That's my story. The key to this whole episode is that I was in the control of someone or something else.

Eventually I get out of bed - it was approximately 2.00 am. I take a few drops of Healing Herbs Five Flower Remedy for shock and make myself a hot cup of tea with honey. I immediately write down any reasons I could think of to cause this happening, one of which was that it could be past life stuff. Next, I decide to do an attunement making a decision that I would not go back to sleep this night. I smudge ALL the rooms of my flat in order to cleanse and clear any unwanted attachments. At my altar with everything prepared, I seal my physic centres and put myself at the centre of a Cross of Light. I visualize the Christ Star above my head shining down Golden Light and ask for the protection of Archangel Michael. In my imagination I take myself off to the Healing Temple in the Heavenly Spheres. Now comes in the most powerful Being. I do not know who he is - I say he - because the energies are very strong and it feels like a male presence. My whole demeanor changes as I sit in my chair. I receive:

BEING OF LIGHT

"Child we are with you. All is well. We would wish that you continue your work for the Light. We have released the soul attachment - you are free. (as this was being said I was aware of something being drawn from me. I felt and saw a sort of black sticky substance being removed and knew that it was going - kicking and screaming - it did not want to leave). *We would wish you now to cleanse your body through diet. We would wish you to ensure you are protected and sealed always. And always work from the heart - that place of love. This work you are being asked to do - which you have chosen to do - is sanctified. It is blessed from the very highest - IT IS SACRED WORK. Always respect this. Be diligent my child - ALWAYS be diligent. You KNOW. You have found the answer. There are those who oppose the work you are doing for the Light. There are those who would wish you harm BECAUSE of your work* (a vision of ancient Egypt comes in and I know for definite this all has a karmic connection), *BUT we will always protect you."*

I thank this Being of the Christ Light for his contact. Mulling things over, I remember White Eagle telling me that I have no need for protection as I work from the heart, though here I am being told to ensure that I am protected and that my centres are sealed. White Eagle is with me now:

WHITE EAGLE

"Dear Peace Rose. We have said to you before, that if you are working from the place of purist love of the heart, then no harm will come to you and you have no need for protection, BUT you are working with powerful energies, and because you are up against dark forces who do not wish the Light to rise, then to overcome that dark element it is prudent to protect yourself. These are not normal circumstances. Never forget this my child - care is to be taken - please be diligent."

My thanks now go to White Eagle. It is as these two Masters are speaking with me I realize my errors. This occasion at the Tolcarne Wartha Temple Ceremony was a blip, for which I suffered and could have paid most dear. I had to be made aware of the potential danger if I failed to be vigilant. How clever/devious are the dark forces to prove their influence over me.

To close this rather unique attunement, I very firmly seal all my chakras and affirm: *"I trust in the Power of the Light. I am protected. I am safe. I am strong. I am in control of all my subtle bodies. I am immersed in the purest love."* When I had woken up earlier I made a decision to stay awake for the rest of the night. After this contact, I decide to put aside my fear and 'walk' in the Light. I return to my bed under the protection of Archangel Michael and sleep well for what is left of the night.

The next morning I put together a practical plan - an Affirmation Mantra, which I shall say each night before I sleep. It is rather extensive, but vital at this stage of my work. I will use it for as long as I consider necessary and adjust as I see fit. These are the words I shall use with visualizations:

- *Protect me Archangel Michael from control and harm from beings unknown.*
- *I am enfolded within a Sphere of Golden Light from the Christ Star.*
- *I am at the centre of a Cross of Light within that Golden Sphere.*
- *I close each of my physic centres individually and ground myself.*
- *I am immersed in the love of the Rose in the Heart.*
- *I have complete trust in the Creator - our Father-Mother God.*
- *I am safe.*
- *I have no fear.*

I hope this admission and these ideas may be of use to other Light Workers.

This has been new territory for me, in spite of many years of spiritual discipline, wherein I have been used as an instrument in the serve of the Angels and Masters to bring about personal healing, earth healing and on one occasion being instrumental in releasing a dear soul from the Astral Plane. I am usually very thorough with my preparation - this time not so. Whilst being unable to give her details of my Mission, I felt it a wise move to share this occurrence with a special supportive friend, whom I can trust implicitly. On arrival at her home, I received a beautiful contact healing in her sanctuary, which she had prepared so lovingly. I was also given an angel flower remedy for protection, courage, strength and divine peace. Before I arrived, she had intuitively picked out two cards from her angel pack. One was '*Share with a friend*' - the other '*Mother Mary*' . How appropriate! "*Bless you and thank you Angels.*"

I feel I should make record of something which I learned yesterday regarding Tolcarne Wartha. I attended a meeting of our White Eagle Astrology group in Totnes. The speaker was a well-known local astrologer. Lo and behold as our morning session draws to a close, he comes out with information about a large Arthur figure of approximately eight mile radius, mapped out in the landscape in the area of Tolcarne Wartha settlement. So I have my link with Arthur which I suspected, yet still feel that I am only just scratching the surface. Then to cap it all, he mentions Mary the mother of Jesus as being connected to that area. Insights like this are coming at me from all directions at the moment, but at this stage I must take them on board, treat them as validation of my discoveries, but carry on working quietly in my own way. .

MARY'S CELTIC CONNECTIONS

So far in this work, reference to Mary's Celtic-Cornish heritage, has arisen on several occasions. I will try to pull the threads together and clarify what I have gleaned through personal insight and spiritual messages.

1. Mary tells us that she with Jesus, Naomi and Joseph of Arimathea were welcomed at Place in the Roseland Peninsula by their Druid family.
2. There are two churches in Tregony with memorials to Anna, Mary's mother and I learn that this is not far from Anna's ancestrial home.
3. At the Tolcarne Wartha Temple site, the Druid Elder tells us, that they knew of Mary's forthcoming visit from Joseph of Arimathea and her Celtic family.
4. He goes on to inform us, that Anna lived close-by and joined Mary and Naomi for a sacred Ceremony.

All this has led me to do some research. I was eventually lead to a book by Stuart Wilson and Joanna Prentis *'The Essenes - Children of the Light'* which resonated with me and confirmed much. Joanna is a Past Life Therapist whom I have met in Devon - a most inspiring lady. In this book she makes contact with five subjects who lived in the Holy Land at the time of Jesus, two of whom are friends, Daniel Berezza and Joseph of Arimathea. Speaking about Mary's mother, on Page 229 of their book, Daniel informs us that: *'she was a very special person, a princess from a Celtic family in Britain.'* He confirms her name was Anna and that her husband was called Joseph. On Page 230 Daniel says: *'Joseph's (of Arimathea) father began the trading in tin, and he went to the western part of Britain. When he went there he was already a rich merchant and he impressed those in that country with his wealth. The Celts there were looking to make alliances with other lands and so the match* (with Anna) *seemed good to them.'* So what we have is an alliance of two Royal Houses, Joseph from the Holy Land of the House of David, and Anna from Cornwall, a Celtic Princess. Further, these few words would explain Joseph of Arimathea's interest in the tin trade, as he would have inherited a thriving business from his father.

I have been told that Anna travelled with Joseph her future husband to the Holy Land, where they were married and settled. Also, that many years and several children later, after her husband's passing and Mary's marriage, Anna returned to Cornwall. I have learnt that Mary brought Naomi, her first born, as a baby to visit her mother in Britain. Once other children came along, Mary could well have found going overseas difficult, which would make sense of St Michael's words given at the Caerhays Church, when he talks of this present pilgrimage being the first trip of Jesus to Britain. So for Mary, this trip with Jesus and Naomi as young people was possibly the first opportunity to visit her mother since Naomi was a baby. I realize that this present theory would alter my original hypothesis put forward in the 'INTRODUCTION TO THE SOUTH WEST' that: *'It is quite feasible that excursions from the Holy Land might have been made over the years to meet with family.'* For Anna, having returned to her homeland after Mary's marriage, it would mean that effectively she was there at the time of Mary and Naomi's visit to Tolcarne Wartha, as the Druid Elder tells us. A theory - could there be some link with the knowledge that the settlement at Tolcarne Wartha had close family connections to Jesus the Christ

- the Light Bringer - and the actions of the darker elements, who wish to prevent the Light from being reactivated there at this time, hence my salutatory experience after my Ceremony?

THE ESSENE LINK

Joseph, Anna's husband was a member of the Essene Brotherhood. On arrival in her adopted country, Anna would have embraced her new life as wife of an Essene Jew. Of course all their children, including Mary, would have been brought up within that culture. It would be quite natural however, that Anna would have also shared with them much of her own Celtic background and the Druidic form of worship. So what do we know of the Essenes who were to play such a vital role in the family's lives? Much has been written about them and their way of life, so from me just a brief overview.

Historically, the Essenes were a Jewish sect living in the Holy Land, which held equal prominence to the Saducees and Pharisees. They began to make their presence known around 150 BC and by Anna's time they had communities right across the Holy Land, one of their key centres being at Qumran on the Dead Sea.

So, where did they come from? It is said that the Essene Brethren were an ancient people - legend has it that they originated from Ur in Babylon. In *'The Essenes - Children of the Light'* (Wilson and Prentis), we are told that their mystical knowledge came from a people called The Kaloo, an ancient race of Atlantean descent, who had brought their knowledge of the Ancient Wisdom held within crystals and scrolls, to Egypt. If they were from this lost continent, then as Britain became the last remnants of that civilisation, the same wisdom would have been held within the Cosmic memory of the ancient Druids.

What was their belief system? According to Baigent, Leigh and Lincoln in *'The Holy Blood and the Holy Grail'* Page 332: *'they used the Old Testament, but interpreted it more as allegory than as literal historical truth. They repudiated conventional Judaism in favour of a form of Gnostic dualism - which seems to have incorporated elements of sun worship and Pythagorean thought.'* In this respect they studied the Cabbala alongside the Torah, the Jewish Holy Law, but also drew from a font of recorded wisdom passed down through the ages. Their name means 'Holy One' and the inner core were the custodians of the Ancient Mysteries. The Initiates worked on the inner planes projecting the Cosmic Light and used the vibrational energies of crystals for healing. As well as the Initiates, were those who lived everyday lives within the towns and villages of Judea.

Their centres which held vast libraries, were places of learning where Priests and Teachers instructed in many aspects of knowledge such as; Pythagorean principles, philosophy, astrology, astronomy, medicine and arts and crafts. Study was also made of ancient Egyptian texts, with emphasis laid on preserving them for prosperity and producing up-to-date texts. Essene Brethren from all over the Holy Land would visit these centres for study and research. Scholars would also travel from far flung places, as did the Druids from Britain, who came for instruction and to exchange ideas, hence the transference of knowledge between the Druids and the Essenes. As has been well documented, it was at Qumran, that many of their ancient scrolls were discovered in 1947. My spiritual sources tell me that these contained only that information which was destined for the World in that era. Other scrolls with secrets of The Mysteries are still being kept hidden, until the Wise Ones consider the time is right for them to be made available for humanity.

The Essenes knew of a forthcoming great Teacher. They waited and prepared for his coming. They recognized Jesus as the Messiah and provided a support network for him and all those accompanying Essene Brethren - his family and disciples. They took care of arrangements after the birth, assisting with the escape of Mary, Joseph and the baby Jesus into Egypt. During and after the crucifixion, the part they played was crucial to sustaining the life of the Master and in providing a flight route for him and his followers from the Holy Land (see Chapter 7).

UNICORNS

Before I return to my pilgrimage and Mary's travels in Cornwall, I am going to introduce a short interlude. I can not believe that I am writing this. I have been directed to tune into the unicorns. This comes following all the dramas of the Tolcarne Wartha Ceremony and is a beautiful note with which to end this chapter. I became more conscious of their majesty and purity on being guided to Diana Cooper's book '*The Wonder of Unicorns*'. I have just read the first few pages and find I am sobbing - shedding tears of joy. What is going on I ask myself? As my sobbing ceases, I settle down to look at the reason for the strength of my feelings. I know the unicorns are making themselves known to me. They have found me and I have rediscovered them. I am now experiencing physic shivers through my whole being. This is only just the beginning I am thinking.

Diana Cooper intimates that Divine Mary has a special affinity with unicorns and immediately I understand the connection - my beloved Mary has been instrumental in bringing them into my consciousness. In her book Cooper tells us that unicorns are brilliant white horses with a Golden Horn of Light at their centre of enlightenment - the brow chakra. We are also informed that the Unicorn Kingdom is Lakuma, which is found on the higher planes of the constellation of Sirius. On Page 2 of her book, Cooper writes of what she received from a unicorn: '*He told me that they were etheric beings, seventh dimensional ascended horses, fully of the angelic realm. He said they had been present in Atlantis during the Golden Times, when everyone was able to connect to them, just as they did to their Guardian Angel. Unfortunately as Atlantis devolved into a low frequency, the beautiful unicorns could not bring their energy down to such a low level, so they withdrew.*' Reading these words I have entered the realm of soul memory.

In this life too, the unicorns have occasionally made themselves known to me in subtle ways. I can remember a few pointers of more recent times. The first was at Hembury Fort in Devon in 2008. A lady walking her dogs told me of one snowy winter's day when she saw a white horse on the top of the fort. My visual mind immediately shot to a unicorn. I thought better of mentioning it to her in case she thought me quite mad. Then a special friend who does exceptional stained glass work, produced a unicorn - the most perfect representation of this mystical being. My heart leapt out to it - I just had to have it, but was obliged to wait quite a while before the time was right for it to come into my possession - now is that time. My friend only made one - and it waited for me. Next, the charming Megan Wingfield, author of *'The Grail Journey through Wales'* told me about a dimensional gateway for unicorns near Holy Mountain in Anglesey and I am to meet with her there when it can be arranged. Further, my mind leaps to the white horses formed in the chalk landscape of Wiltshire by the ancient Celts who venerated horses. For the Celts, I suspect that their collective consciousness was awakened to the Cosmic memory of when unicorns visited our Planet in Atlantean days. For me, the white horse has always been an expression of the unicorn. In the Daily Telegraph, February 11th 2009, there is talk of a huge white horse - one hundred and sixty-four feet in height - to be constructed in the Kent countryside. This will be visible in the landscape for all to see, including those who come into Britain and alight from Eurostar. The Kent horse (unicorn?), is to be started in a year's time, so perhaps will be in place by 2012. What a wonderful symbol of hope, reconnecting us to our ancient past at the beginning of the Aquarian Age.

Since Diana Cooper's book has made its way into my possession, my association with the unicorns this incarnation is cemented. My life is being totally immersed in the joy of LOVE, which they express so genuinely. There is nothing outside Love. Everything is an illusion outside Divine Love. Everything is transient except Divine Love. As we seek to express that perfect love in our own lives, so we can ALL re-establish our connection to the Universal Light - that Christ Consciousness. Let each action - each word and each deed be one of kindness offered with loving intent. White Eagle expresses it so beautifully when he says: *'You can give love in very simple ways; by the gentle word or smile, the kindly touch, the comfort which can be offered to everyone you meet on life's journey - because every human being needs love. Is it not a wonderful law and provision of God, that God provides every one of His-Her children with the opportunity and the means to give the divine quality of love to their companions on life's way?'* - Page 111 of *'On Living in Harmony with the Spirit'*.

I have said it before, that by writing this book, I have embarked on a personal journey and this is so true. The more I am with Beloved Mary, the more I realize how she is directing me to even deeper awareness of the Divine, opening up for me, even more truths of the profound mysteries of life. Now it is the turn of the mystical unicorns of the 7th Dimension to enter my consciousness. How can I stop - the die is cast. It was cast before I came into incarnation. It was cast long ago in the Holy Land - it was cast back in Atlantis. It has always been.

MESSAGE FROM A UNICORN

Ever since my reconnection to the unicorns, the Unicorn Energy has been tugging at my heart strings and at last I am able to have an attunement with them. I wished to have time without distractions and for a couple of days life's commitments were against me. Then I could wait no longer. On waking one morning, after a glass of warm water and cup of herb tea, I decide to forgo breakfast and attune at 9.00 am this very day. So it is that I set up my sacred space once more, this time with my new magical stained glass unicorn on the altar keeping watch over me.

I speak with Mary: *"My beloved one, thank you for directing me to these magical Beings. Help me now to tune into the Unicorn Energy. I just want to BE within this sacred energy.'* To the unicorns: *'Let me express deep love from my heart to reach out to all in the Unicorn Kingdom. If there is one unicorn who would wish to make himself known to me - then let it be so."* I am now astounded, as not only do I have an inner vision of one of these magnificent creatures, but some words. The vision is of a shining white horse with a Golden Horn at the front of its head - very ethereal and yet full of substance. There seems to be a plume of feathers rising from its back as a sort of second mane. A plume of feathers in the Ancient Wisdom indicates a wise and enlightened soul. I am receiving:

LUDAKA

"I am Ludaka your unicorn. Thank you for calling me. I roam the Higher Worlds of Infinite Light. I come from the Stars. The Planet which you know as Sirius is my abode. I bring you blessings and joy from ALL the Unicorn Kingdom. I will guide you through your life and I will protect you on your journey with Mother Mary. She of infinite wisdom and bliss who manifests now in the simple white robe before you. (I see my blessed Mary dressed in white with a gold buckle at her waist. She has a blue cloak resting on her shoulders tied at the neck with a clasp. At her heart centre is a rose-pink jewel. Her hair is light brown, shining and hanging quite simply over her shoulders. On her head she has a garland of flowers which is indicative of the Sacred Feminine. The last time I saw with my inner vision, the flower garland, was for Brighid, the Goddess, at St Brides Church at Llansantiffraed Cwmdeuddwr near Rhayader in Mid Wales, on my pilgrimage in 2008. It is represented in fabric hangings within the church. In meditation there, I had a vision of several young females wearing light floaty long clothes, each wearing on their heads a pretty garland of wild flowers, dancing in a circle on a grassy area. Seeing Beloved Mary here in this similar vogue, brought to mind my previous experience and is a reminder of the potency of the Goddess Energy). *My child of the Earth Plane, this beautiful Master of the 'Rose in the Heart' is part of the rose in YOUR heart. She comes to share much with you at this time. Welcome her gentle presence Earth child. You have before you a visual representation of me. Let this*

shining translucent effigy be always with you. It will bring the Unicorn Energies to surround you. I am indeed privileged to have this opportunity to speak with you Earth child. You will be always close to the centre of my being - close to the heart centre of Light and Love.

Forever is forever. Your beautiful ancient Aboriginal folk walked the Pathway of Forever. Our Kingdom is especially close to these ancient peoples. You yourself have walked that land a long long time ago. It is your spiritual home which has ever been. You went there from Atlantis on one of your incarnations. I know you also have an affinity with your precious British Isles, which is also a place of special significance to you, for you have lived many lives in that place (I believe Ludaka means when it was Atlantis and subsequently). *The people from Atlantis left their domain at different successive times. Think on this my Child of Light* (migration then did not all happen in one big mass at one upheaval). *I have to tell you that you also have an Atlantean link with Egypt. This link is particularly strong and deep in your soul. How great thou art oh beloved Child of the Universe. For are we not ALL Beings of Universal Cosmic Light.*

In my World of the Unicorns, we live in a place of joy and musical light, the Sounds of the Spheres fill our world. I bring you that joy. I bring to you ALL beloved Earth children who will listen, music from the 7ᵗʰ Dimension, so that Heaven can return to Earth in all its magnificent glory. My children of the Earth plane I plead with you to LISTEN. Listen to the music - to the sounds of all life - in all spheres - in all dimensions. Tune in I say, to the Unicorn Kingdom and this will bring the joy into your precious lives. Take the time Earth children to recognize other dimensions - other beings a little different perhaps to yourselves in appearance, but whose heart beats in synchronicity to yours. We are ALL ONE. All kingdoms are one. There is no separation, only that which you yourselves devise. I bow before you in recognition of YOUR light and YOUR wisdom Earth Children (I have a vision of this magnificent creature bending his head). *Goodbye my friend of the Light - my friend of the Universe."*

As he closes with these words, I see him turn and move off across the skies, into the limitlessness of space. I watch until he disappears into the beyond - into infinity - to return to his domain. My beautiful unicorn Ludaka. What a privilege - what a blessing: *"Thank you Ludaka. I bless you. I bless you. I bless you."* I am completely bowled over by this most magical Light Being, who has seen fit to grace me with his presence.

I complete my morning with brunch as breakfast-time has long gone!

MIRACLES

Soon after this encounter, two magical unicorn happenings came into my life at the time when my daughter had her first baby. What a joy, this newly incarnated soul, this precious little babe, making his presence known to us all. My daughter had, let's just say, a long and difficult labour and I kept a healing vigil with the Angels and the unicorns, with my candle lit. Just before 11.00 pm on the 21ˢᵗ February I said to the Angels, that when the candle goes out I will know everything is alright. I looked up and a wisp of smoke was just rising from the spent candle. I was told that the baby was born at 10.57 pm! My second miracle was on my drive up the motorway the following day to visit my daughter and new baby. In front of me across a huge expanse of sky was a unicorn. I could hardly believe it and wished I could have got a photograph. It was amazingly clear - this huge white cloud horse galloping across the sky at pull pelt. It appeared to have wings streaming out, above and behind it. Seeing the wings I immediately thought of Pegasus, but no, I could see the horn of the unicorn VERY clearly. In her book *'The Wonder of Unicorns'* mentioned, on Page 29, Diana Cooper says: *'The roles of the unicorn and Pegasus are slightly different. The unicorn's is to inspire, give hope, empower and enlighten, while that of the heart centered Pegasus is to comfort, succour and enfold.'* In my vision the two were blended as one. My impression was that Ludaka had brought in the gentle Pegasus energy for mother and child. As I watched, within a short space of time it disintegrated.

I return to my present pilgrimage and Mary's travels through Cornwall. After a stay at Tolcarne Wartha settlement, Mary and Naomi journeyed south to the coast via Hendra, Trewennick and Holy Well to Helston. They then took a boat down-river leading to The Loe, but stepped off at the little inlet of Penrose. From there they went north to St Elvan settlement where they joined with Joseph and Jesus.

CHAPTER 5
WEST TO THE CAPE
Revelations of the Sacred Stones

From St Elvan the next stage of the Lady Mary's pilgrimage in Cornwall sees her heading west. Her main destinations were to be the Druidic Temple on St Michael's Mount and the Atlantean Temple at Men-an-Tol in Cape Cornwall. It was to Men-an-Tol that I went on the final day of my first pilgrimage to Cornwall, where my sacred task was to earth the ancient Temple. This I will come to in due course. It is while looking at my map, the thought is dropped into my mind: '*Did Mary visit the Isles of Scilly on her pilgrimage in this area?*' An affirmation is given and again this I will take a look at further into the chapter.

We first make the link with Mary at St Elvan settlement, which according to the present day map, is approximately two miles inland from Porthleven on the south Cornish coast. What a joy it must have been to meet with her son and brother once more after their parting at Carn Brea. There was great rejoicing at the reunion and much to talk about. They stayed at St Elvan for a week or so. There was no Druidic Temple at this settlement and they did not take part in a specific Ceremony - it was just a convenient meeting point. Mary, Naomi, Joseph and Jesus left together, returned to Penrose, then took a boat down-river via The Loe. My understanding is that the river was much wider in those days and flowed through the present day Loe Bar. They left the river and travelled on horseback across land (now sea - see below) to Praa Sands, thence on inland about three miles to the settlement of Memi. I puzzled why they did not go from St Elvan to Memi settlement via the direct shorter route as it appears on the map, and was told that the terrain was too difficult. Once again, there was no Temple at Memi and no Ceremony to attend, but I learn it was there that they met with other family members. They stayed at Memi for a few days before moving on to Marazion settlement for St Michael's Mount. I was impressed that it was essential the four travellers visited the Druidic Temple on The Mount together, where Mary was to initiate an ancient Ceremony to reactivate the Light on the full moon.

ST MICHAEL'S MOUNT

St Michael's Mount is a towering rocky castle fortress jutting out into Mount's Bay on the south coast of Cornwall. Historically, its position has meant that it was strategically placed to control shipping in the bay and through the centuries it has been the focus of many battles and sieges. The castle has been lived in for over three hundred years by the St Aubyn family, but is now owned by the National Trust. It is an island at high tide, giving way to a wide stony causeway for access as the tide ebbs. Legends abound regarding The Mount. Just one illustration - it is recorded that in AD 495, witnessed by local fisherman, that a vision of St Michael in all his glory was seen standing on the rock. St Michael's Mount once a monastery, has attracted pilgrims throughout the ages, as it does to this day.

The access point to St Michael's Mount is the village of Marazion, which is built over the settlement where Mary and her family were accommodated. Mary is letting me know that in her day, 2,000 years ago, St Michael's Mount was not an island, but that the land stretched out as far as the eye could see. Subsequent research tells me that in fact today, there is evidence of an ancient sunken forest, in the form of very large tree stumps, visible at some low tides in the waters around The Mount. Apparently, the old Cornish name for St Michael's Mount is *'The Hoar Rock in the Wood'*.

St Michael's Mount

THE LEY LINE SYSTEM

St Michael's Mount houses a junction or node point for many Ley Lines, of which the four main identified ones are, the St Michael Line merging with the St Mary Line, and the Apollo Line with the Athena line.

For those who do not have knowledge of the Ley Line System, I pose the question - what is a Ley Line? In brief, a Ley Line is an invisible energy line - a line of power criss-crossing the landscape, travelling through sacred prehistoric sites such as ancient settlements, stone circles and earthen mounds. Later as Christianity took hold, churches were often built on top of these ancient sites. I see Ley Lines as a great Cosmic web - a matrix of alignments - interwoven within the landscape of the Earth, but also connecting the Cosmos to below the Earth's crust. They portend to deep mysteries hidden within the landscape, of which we are just learning. Could this system of invisible energy lines have been used by the ancients of Atlantean times, in their process of Thought Travelling, as expressed earlier by Taibu? A node point is a junction of more than one Ley Line, which would be situated at places of great antiquity and power. It is my conjecture, that they are portals to other dimensions and an integral part of our planetary vibrational energy system. We know from information given earlier by the Druid Elder and the Master Jesus, that the Ley Line System supports the Crystal Energy of which the node points are extremely powerful vortices of energy and as such their intensity would be immense.

Alfred Watkins whom I think of as the father of the Ley Line System, produced a very early book in 1925 entitled *'The Old Straight Track'*. I came across his work over forty years ago and at the time was very exited by the contents. During my pilgrimage with Beloved Mary, this is another book which has been dusted off, once again to see the light of day! Watkins lived in Herefordshire and it is understood, that while riding on horseback over the hills above the village of Bredwardine, as he looked out over the landscape laid out before him, he had a flash of insight. His vision was of a network of interconnecting lines stretching out across the countryside, which he identified as ancient trackways. In later life he began to suspect they held much deeper significance and suggested links with many ancient civilizations including the; Egyptians, Babylonians and Grecians. The astronomer Priests within ancient Druidic society would certainly have been aware of such ancient energy lines.

Hamish Miller and Paul Broadhurst in their book *'The Sun and the Serpent'* expand the Ley Line picture initiated by Watkins very much further, and have given us a comprehensive study on the St Michael and St Mary Leys. Using the science of dowsing, they charted the St Michael Ley Line from its point of origin on the mainland at Carn les Boel near Land's End in the far South West. From here, it connects to St Michael's Mount and Marazion before travelling through Cornwall, Devon, Somerset and on across the south of Britain, taking in the great henge at Avebury, to eventually exit in East Anglia. It is within the Avebury complex that Miller and Broadhurst were made aware of a female energy - the St Mary Line - joining the St Michael current, creating a node point. Regarding these two Ley Lines, on Page 114 of their book they say: *'the energies themselves were apparently of different polarities. One type was Solar in influence, traditionally associated in the Christian ethos with St Michael, the other was Lunar, indisputably feminine and connected with the Earth Goddess whose Christian counterpart was St Mary.'* Further more, this led them to the realization that the two energies weaved in and out of each other in the landscape like great serpents. No longer was a Ley Line only thought of as a straight track as Watkins had interpreted. Page 117 of their work tells us: *'we had glimpsed an important aspect of the ancient and universal symbol of the Caduceus'* - the Magical Hermetic Rod of the Ancient Mysteries which was encircled by two serpents.

Power Rock on St Michael's Mount

This discovery took them back to the beginning of their quest at Carn Les Boel in Cornwall, to fully chart the St Mary Line, as it interwove with the St Michael Ley across the south of England. It is then they learnt that the St Mary Ley joins with the St Michael Ley at a node crossing on St Michael's Mount. Further, they ascertained that this node point was not at the castle-church on the summit, but met at a massive rock - *'We had been led to the most prominent natural feature of the island - a great rock, balanced on a horizontal platform on the western side, looking out across Mount's Bay to Penzance'* (Page 126). I have been to St Michael's Mount on a number of occasions and stood on a path looking up at this Power Rock. Even from this lower elevation, I could feel the powerful energies emitting from it.

MY LEY LINE INVESTIGATIONS

Now for some things I have unearthed as I browse the map. Following the St Mary Ley through Cornwall, I realize that it goes directly through Tolcarne Wartha settlement - interesting bearing in mind the Mary connection. Taking my line of vision further west, I am wondering, does the St Michael Line or the St Mary Line go out to the Isles of Scilly from Carn Les Boel? If so this opens up the possibility of the line then flowing across what I hypothesize, is the now flooded Land of Lyonesse. This leads to even wider implications. Could their energies flow right into the heart of the ancient continent of Atlantis itself? I collect my dowsing crystal and my map of The Scilly Isles. On the island of St Agnes I spy a well - St Warna's Well. Knowing that the feminine Mary line will often travel through Holy Wells, this is my start point. I get a positive response from my crystal. I carefully study the island of St Mary's followed by the other islands, but there is nothing else of significance. So time for some simple questions. I began with the St Michael Ley Line. I asked if this line went to; 1. the Isles of Scilly 2. Lyonesse and 3. Atlantis. I get a NO for all three. Now for the St Mary Ley Line. I asked the same three questions and received a YES for all places. A little strange I thought. Why did the St Michael Line stop at the Cornish mainland and the St Mary Line continue? I couldn't come up with a clear answer. I have to leave it there for now.

ST MICHAEL'S MOUNT DRUIDIC TEMPLE CEREMONY

While staying at Marazion, Mary and Naomi with Jesus and Joseph, were to attend a special Full Moon Druidic Ceremony on The Mount. In my home sanctuary I am to perform a Ceremony to reactivate the Light at this ancient site as requested by Beloved Mary. My chosen date is 25th February 2009 - a new moon - a new beginning. This, combined with Pluto's ongoing stirrings within the Earth's core, will today assist in a transformation of the fiery energies at St Michael's Mount. Over time there have been many who have visited The Mount and revitalized the ancient Light in this sacred place. During the middle part of the last century, the seer Wellesley Tudor Pole (W.T.P), author of several books relating to the sacred South West of the British Isles and its many legends, envisioned that very thing - that pilgrims would visit and re-energize the St Michael Light Centres of Britain, which includes St Michael's Mount. W.T.P. had strong associations with Glastonbury and Chalice Well and we shall meet with him when Mary reaches Glastonbury

Making plans for my Ceremony I decide not to link at 1.36 am, the time of the beginning of the waxing moon. Instead I will act on whatever time of the day or night presents itself. As it happens, the Angels see fit to wake me at 5.00

am, therefore 6.00 am, one of the powerful energy times, it is then. I am woken with a vision of the Power Rock on St Michael's Mount, opening to a vortex of great magnitude. Into my mind comes the remembrance of a previous vision. This was of a huge circular Light System hovering above our Planet. This Ring of Golden Light appeared to have tubes slotted in around the circle, the whole, vibrating with Light. They were receiving the Crystal Energy from the Cosmos, collecting and storing it within the tubes, then distributing it as powerful Rays of Light to the Earth and below, through the vortices.

I rise, have a cup of tea, cleanse my physical body and get dressed. Now I am particularly diligent in my preparation of my sacred space including smudging, bearing in mind my last episode at Tolcarne Wartha. For some reason, today I find I am putting something representative of the four elements on my altar. For Fire I have my candle; for Earth a large white quartz crystal; I choose a beautiful stripy buzzard's feather for Air; then put a little Water in a pretty container. With my Ohm CD quietly playing, I leave the room for a short while to allow the energies to build. Now, seated before my altar I prepare myself. First I ensure I am well protected. Then I bring into balance my chakra system. My quite simple method is to visualize the Libran scales aglow with Light at each energy point. I allow the scales to settle naturally into perfect balance until each bowl is quite still and in alignment.

I tune into the Higher Beings offering myself in service this sacred day. I picture in my mind, the Power Rock on St Michael's Mount. With reverence, I carry out my Druidic Ceremony to reactivate the Light there. Following this I balance the Michael Solar, and the Mary Lunar, energies. I am saying: '*Let the Light Shine*' as a mantra over and over again. I am now seeing the great Archangel Michael standing on top of The Mount - his arms outstretched. As my Ceremony draws to a close I hear the sound as he strikes the Power Rock with his sword, thus formally implanting the Cosmic energies. It is done. I now say: "*Let me be master of myself and servant of Thee. Great Archangel Michael speak with me. I am your servant of Light.*"

ARCHANGEL MICHAEL

"*Child of the Universe. I am YOUR servant. We are ALL servants of the one Light - it is so. Welcome and thank you for your work this day. It is good. At St Michael's Mount, at the point of the Power Rock, is a vortex of vibrational energy going deep into the Earth's core. This is connected to the Great Crystal at the Earth's centre. It can be seen by those with the inner eye as a great spiral of fiery Light with the power of magna, drilling its way deep within the Earth's crust. It gives out tremendous power and energy and helps to recharge the energies of your Planet. This power vortex at St Michael's Mount, is connected to the Grid System of your Planet and as such, is a vital component for repairing the Grid. The Grid System over a long long time - millions of years - has gradually become damaged. Now is the time to begin the repair work.*"

The Grid System is a web - a huge web of interconnecting lines of tremendous energy, which hold the structure of the Planet in place. If they become out of kilter, then imbalances happen within this structure. This has happened on numerous occasions in the life of your Planet, one you are all aware of, is that once great Continent of Atlantis. The Grid was damaged by the hand of man and the result was catastrophic for your Planet. However, repairs to the Grid System are on-going and this is VITAL work Light Worker. (How can we do this?). *Regularly focus the Cosmic Light to the Grid System and see it being made whole - SEE it complete. The Grid is like a series of lines interconnecting east to west and north to south, totally encompassing your world like a gigantic web. The power of Arachne* (the Spider), *has a part to play. She, with the great Pluto, have taken it upon themselves to restore the Earth's Grid System and thus transform and renew the essential vibrational energies to restore your Planet to a working whole. This work MUST be done. It is vital for Earth's survival. It WILL be done. There are many today working to this effect with Arachne and Pluto from the great Cosmic Life and from your world. IT WILL BE DONE."*

He has gone. I thank Archangel Michael for this confirmation and further disclosures of the Grid System which is synonymous with the Ley Line System. I am feeling a drop in the energies as usual after such a powerful connection. To complete my Ceremony, in my imagination I transfer my white and pink quartz crystals to the Power Rock at St Michael's Mount. I am in a shivery state and put a wrap around me. I take a few sips of water and stay completely still for a long time. Finally, I close each physic centres, earth myself and enfold myself in Michael's blue protective cloak I offer my candle - the Flame of Eternal Truth to St Michael and to the great Power Rock on The Mount. Now for a little sustenance.

TO MERRY MAIDENS

The Ceremonial day at St Michael's Mount completed, Mary, Naomi, Jesus and Joseph were free to continue their pilgrimage. Together they travelled west to the river inlet marked on the map as Lamorna Cove. In my judgment, this section of coastline linking to Mounts Bay, was not under water in Mary's day so the journey would have been over land. They then took a boat up the Lamorna river valley to alight at the settlement of Merry Maidens.

Merry Maidens today is a well preserved stone circle of approximately eighty feet in diameter. In close vicinity are many standing stones - the largest two are called The Pipers, one of which is some fifteen feet in height. Legend has it, that the Merry Maidens were merry revelers turned to stone!. Mary and her family do not attend a Druidic Ceremony here. They only stayed for three days while plans were being put into place for Mary, Naomi and Jesus to undergo the next stage of their journey over to The Scilly Isle. This time it is Joseph alone who leaves the group to deal with his business interests in the area. He rejoins the family at Men-an-Tol at a later date.

THE SCILLY ISLE

Mary, accompanied by her children and their Druid companions, returned to Lamorna Cove, then travelled on horseback a short distance across land, which is now sea, before taking a boat to The Scilly Isle.

The Isles of Scilly as we know them, comprise of five inhabited islands; St Mary's, Bryher, Tresco, St Martin's and St Agnes, with hundreds of islets and rocks. In Mary's day, the late Iron Age, it would have been one large island called The Scilly Isle. Rising sea levels produced the fragmentation of the original island, leaving the outline we have today. In AD 240, the Roman Solinus was writing of *'The Scilly Isle'* indicating one island rather than many. Paul Ashbee on Page 66 of his book *'Ancient Scilly'* tells us that: *'Marine transgression may, by Romano-British times, (AD 43 - 410), have made considerable inroads into the large island'* and *'In Romano-British times and for a period following, Tresco, St Martin's, the Eastern Isles and St Mary's were joined.'* As attestation of this inundation, at low tides there is today visible evidence of man-made walls and roads running out into the sea. Alongside this, excavations on some of the islands carried out in the 1950s, have found ancient Bronze Age and Iron Age burial cists, stone huts and wells below the now high water level.

It is reckoned that in Roman times, the harbour for The Scilly Isle, was on its eastern flank - what is now called the Eastern Isles. This would have been where Mary and her children alighted from mainland Cornwall. From there they travelled across what is now St Mary's, to stay at the Druidic settlement of St Mary's Pool. This is marked on the map as being situated within the present-day bay of Hugh Town, which of course was dry land before the sea encroached. St. Mary's Pool was one of numerous settlements dotted all over the island. The abundance of chambered tombs still in evidence, would indicate a large community with a vast burial ground. I happened on a booklet by John Michell called *'Prehistoric Sites in Cornwall'* wherein he says on Page 4, that the Greeks described The Scilly Isle as: *'sacred territory, the seat of Chronus and the western paradise reached by the souls of the blessed.'* How very apt!

There was no Druidic Temple at St Mary's Pool settlement and no Atlantean Temple in the Etheric either. I could not help but wonder why a decision was taken to visit The Scilly Isle. I went through many possibilities without success, when I suddenly hit on the question: *'Did they do a pilgrimage to honour the ancestors?'* -*'Yes'* came the answer - eureka! Is there evidence to support Mary's visit? While we have no concrete proof as with mainland Cornwall, we do have place names. First of course, the island of St Mary's itself and on it St Mary's Pool, Holy Vale and a St Mary Church. It is referenced by Charles Thomas in his *'Explorations of a Drowned Landscape'* *(Archeology and History of the Isles of Scilly)*, that the Vikings on a raid to Old Town on St Mary's, where their intention was to gain possession of the church plate and altar fittings belonging the Church of St Mary, after their victory, called it Mariuhofn. *'Mariuhofn is Old Norse for 'Mary's Haven'* Thomas (Page 212). All possible signs of long lost memories of Our Lady.

IN SEARCH OF LYONESSE - MY RESEARCH

Many legends have truths locked away in them which have become lost in the mists of time. To differentiate between myth and historical fact, is in itself a minefield. Much has been written about a fabled lost land of Lyonesse. But what can I glean about a possible submerged landmass of this name and is there a connection to The Scilly Isles? Where do I begin my research?

My first port of call is to browse my own bookshelves. Here I did find some very old books on ancient lands, but not specifically Lyonesse. Next it was to the famous 'Google'. As you would expect, there was masses of information, much to sift through and anomalies galore! However, I needed a map and 'Google' didn't give me that. The next plan - my local library at Newton Abbot. They had no maps, but offered me a book on Lyonesse - a work of fiction, which included a conjectural map - no good for my purpose. While there I did look at their computer list of possible books and chose one by Nigel Pennick *'Lost Lands and Sunken Cities'* which they kindly ordered for me through their inter-library service. They also suggested I might find more information at the West Countries Studies Library in Exeter. So a trip to Exeter was called for. I drove the twelve miles or so from my home along the main road in record time, then endured a couple of miles of queuing traffic to reach the city centre, followed by negotiating all the new one-way street systems, parking up and walking the distance. Hurrah - made it - but they tell me they have no maps of Cornwall and that I needed the Cornish Studies Library at Redruth or the Cornwall Records Office at Truro - wonderful! The next morning, Saturday, I make contact with the Cornish Studies Library. They do have old maps, but none going back 2,000 years to Mary's time. A very helpful lady is to do some research and get back to me. On the Monday morning I give their office a bell. The person to speak with is on leave until the following week. However, it is confirmed that no maps go back to that era. Any map would be speculative - what the experts call 'predictive modeling', whereby they view the contours, plus or minus the degrees, then come up with a conclusion! It's all beyond me. I have to say, that eventually I was able to talk with a Mr. Bryn Perry Tapper, who true to his word, sent me a whole screed of information which he had been working on called *'Rapid Coastal Zone Assessment for The Isles of Scilly'*. It was a manuscript of some hundred and sixty-four pages and full of technical jargon and graphs. It gave an overview of The Scilly Isles, but no reference to Lyonesse and therefore no map. Eventually, I collected from my local Library Nigel Pennick's book which gave me my illusive map - see information below.

THE LOST LAND OF LYONESSE

So down to the nitty-gritty - what have I gleaned from my research? First, what are the indicators which could suggest that a land called Lyonesse ever existed off the southern tip of Cornwall? Initially, we have evidence of sunken land in this area supported by the submerged tree stumps in Mounts Bay which are visible at low tide. Also at low tides, walls and dwellings can be seen in the shallow waters around The Isles of Scilly, further evidenced by excavation. Then there have been reports over the years of fisherman dragging up pieces of ancient buildings in their trawling nets within the assigned area. Alongside this, Lyonesse features in the Arthurian Legends. It is chronicled, that some of King Arthur's knights came from there and also that it forms a part of the Tristram and Iseult story.

That established now to my second question. Where is ancient Lyonesse reputed to be? It is said to be situated between Land's End on the furthermost tip of Cape Cornwall and The Scilly Isles. This is too vague. I need more detail. Page 64 of Nigel Pennick's book *'Lost Lands and Sunken Cities'* gives us a map (at last) put forward by Agnes Strickland, which was recorded in Beckles Wilson's *'The Story of Lost England' (1902)*. This map is a simple representation scribed in pen and ink. It indicates a large landmass stretching from Land's End, west to the Longship's Lighthouse, going thirty miles south-west to include The Scilly Isles. From there it rides round the southern perimeter of the islands, taking a fifty mile sweep, curving around to reach the Lizard Point. For now I shall take that map as a credible basis to work from.

What was Lyonesse like? It is thought to have been prosperous and fertile land with many villages, a few towns and over one hundred churches. The terrain must have been identifiable with that of present day Cape Cornwall, which is cloaked in evidence of its ancient past. It does sound as if it really was an intrinsic part of *'England's green and pleasant land'*.

I am curious about the name 'Lyonesse.' In my research, I have found that there was purported to be a City of Lions on Lyonesse. The ancient Egyptians venerated the Lion which was personified in the Sphinx. I have just come across a book *'Secret Places of the Lion'* written in the late 1950s by George Hunt Williamson. On Page 6 he points out that: *'The Lion symbolizes secret wisdom (King Solomon was often symbolized as a Lion)'* and Page 5: *'The Lion denotes the fearlessness of one who is imbued with Divine Truth.'* Astrologically, Leo the Lion is the King and for the Egyptians was representative of the Divine essence of Kingship. Perhaps the Lion of Divine Truth will roar once more and bring into the Light those elements of the Ancient Mysteries which have remained hidden. During the Aquarian Age could the sunken land of Lyonesse offer up its secrets? Could the sea unleash its long held mysteries of other lost lands? There is still so much to be discovered. Perhaps a new age of exploration below the waves, will reveal more of our mystical past - how thrilling to consider.

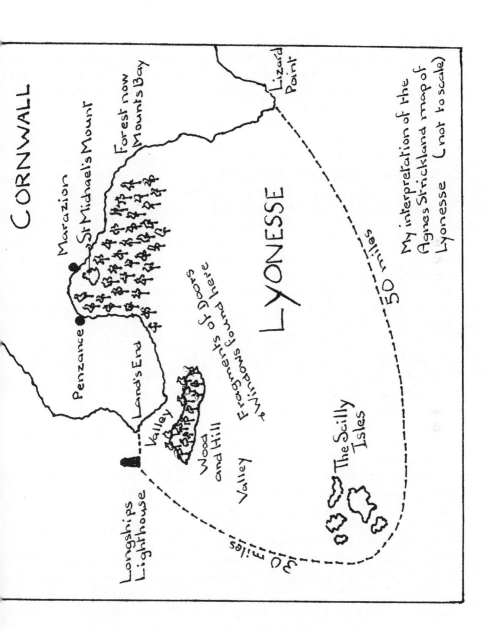

What happened to account for the rise in sea levels that obliterated Lyonesse? Could there perhaps have been a single catastrophe? Many theories have been put forward, some in the *Kithra's Krystal Kave site on Google*. One possibility set out in an article by Andrew Rothovius, is that a shorn-off piece of Halley's Comet smashed into the Earth in AD 530. There is also apparently evidence of an old volcano beneath the waters between Land's End and The Scillies, which could have caused the rift from mainland Britain. Finally, a perspective which supports a possible earthquake. Pennick on Page 63 of his book, talks of the corpus legends known as *'The Matter of Britain'* in which a theory is put forward that: *'The final apocalypse which eliminated this vast territory was, according to the story, a sudden and final cataclysm. Possibly as the result of an underwater earthquake which lowered the level of the land suddenly and drastically, a huge wave-front swept across Lyonesse, destroying all in its wake.'* So three viewpoints of which to me Pennick's holds most water - if you'll excuse the pun!

Okay - so when could such a catastrophe have happened? If it was Halley's Comet we are looking at AD 530 which ties in with Pennick who says on Page 70: *'The date of the inundation of Lyonesse is usually reckoned at sometime in the sixth century of our era, perhaps concurrently with the similar destruction along the Coast of Wales, where the lost Lowland Hundred known as Cantref y Gwaelod was overwhelmed by the sea. It is possible that the Breton coast also suffered a similar fate, with the destruction of Caer Ys.'*

Did any of the inhabitants survive the inundation of Lyonesse? It is recorded that one man called Trevilian escaped on his white horse, to reach the higher ground of Perranuthoe east of St Michael's Mount on Cornwall's southern coast. He went on to found the Cornish Trevelyan family, whose coat of arms shows a horse coming out of water as tribute to his survival.

So far so good. But after many weeks of research and studying data, I have a dilemma. One thing does not sit easy with me and that is an inconsistency with the timescale. How could Lyonesse have disappeared as late as the sixth century as Pennick purports, when the Roman Solinus talks of 'The Scilly Isle' three centuries earlier, indicating that the landmass in the form of one island, was already detached from mainland Cornwall and not called Lyonesse? Further, how can the Arthurian tales relating to Lyonesse be accurate, because in Arthur's day during the fifth century - same thing - it was known as The Scilly Isle not Lyonesse? It is my supposition, that an earlier upheaval, perhaps an earthquake, separated Lyonesse from mainland Britain, leaving its hill-tops to form the one island - The Scilly Isle. A further earthquake in the sixth century would then have fragmented this single island, bringing into being The Scilly Isles as we know them today. It would have been this sixth century earthquake which also caused the flooding around St Michael's Mount and other sections of the Cornish coastline. This massive water surge would also have spread along the whole of the western seaboard of Wales and Brittany and accounted for the loss of land in those areas.

Taking all these things into consideration, I would guess that The Scilly Isle of Roman times and ancient Lyonesse of the Arthurian tales, have become interwoven in a mix of legend, historical record and storytelling.

For some while I have been mulling all this over. Then - middle of one night - surprise - I was woken up at 1.00 am - again! I hear: *'You have many questions beloved one - we would like to help you.'* It was dear White Eagle. So gathering up some warm clothes and collecting a pen and notepad, I light my candle and waited:

WHITE EAGLE

"You have so many questions beloved one. We will attempt to give you some answers. We start off with Lyonesse. This ancient land was once part of that great continent of Atlantis. At some time it was part of your British Isles as you know them today. There was a time of major catastrophe when the land sank around the shores of Britain in certain n places and the seas rushed in. It was mostly on the western seaboard. Whole areas of land disappeared under the waters, great cities were lost, many people lost their lives. Some were fortunate and were able to move quickly to higher ground. Those people gradually dispersed throughout the Isles of Britain. (This is different to one man Trevelyn escaping).

The people of Lyonesse had their own language, which we can tell you was very similar to the Cornish of today and which was widely spoken throughout the land. There were other tongues spoken in different areas of Lyonesse Lyonesse traded with places of far flung shores as for example, the Phoencians, very much as they traded with Cornwall and other areas of Britain at a later date. In Lyonesse there was mining of precious metals. Gold and silver were to be found there. All manner of materials were mined including tin. Trade was two ways, as the Phoenicians brought in spices and beautiful artifacts which were exchanged for things of value in Lyonesse. The people of Lyonesse were great voyagers and travelled the Globe in small, but very stable well built wooden sailing craft.

Within reason there was relative peace on the Earth Plane in those days. Petty squabbles perhaps and light skirmishes locally, but not the global wars we see today on the Earth. The great Beings of Light watched over the Land of Lyonesse, which was a part of the Sacred Isles (of Britain), *and a part of that ancient continent of Atlantis, for a very long time.*

Those living in Lyonesse worshiped the one God. They lived very close to the natural world sharing their bounty with all. There was no poverty. People lived a simple life but everyone had enough for their needs. There were no rich or poor. All there was, was shared equally between all. There was no crime as you know it today. Once again occasional disruption in ones life but easily and quickly remedied. It sounds an idealistic existence doesn't it dear one. Well in many respects it was. The dear souls who lived their life on Lyonesse were gentle, wise and generous of nature. There were Temples for healing but not as would be in the dynastic time of Egypt. There was no King or Queen. 'Top' people, the hierarchy as one might say, would be the Healers and the Priests and Priestesses. But again in name only, not of hierarchal grandeur but rather of equalitarian wisdom. (So why did this perfect Land have to go - my unspoken question?*).*

Because dear one it had outworn its purpose. The quality of life was so pure and perfect that life became too easy. The dear ones living there were becoming TOO comfortable with their lives of beauty and harmony with all life. In a way their perfection was their downfall. It led to a kind of complacency where it was thought life would always be the same - perfect and joyous. What were they learning? Where were the challenges? Were they progressing? As I said, a kind of spiritual complacency set in and it was decided from the Cosmos, that this land should be forfeited for the sake of spiritual advancement. (This is a new slant on spiritual enlightenment!). *So earthquakes happened and seas rushed in. It was more a gradual happening over a period of about a hundred years, until eventually the land held still and settled to what we have in place today.*

I can tell you dear one, that in the not to distant future, there will be discoveries made as to the precise detail of life in the lost land of Lyonesse. Already it is known that there are roads and buildings beneath the waters of The Scilly Isles, and more will be discovered. More will soon be explored in the seas around these British Isles, and many discoveries will be made.

I can tell you also that there is a link with Egypt as you intuitively know. Part of that ancient civilization manifested itself in Lyonesse, but the culture was of a more gentle nature, not so powerful and hierarchical - and it was blessed."

White Eagle suddenly leaves me as another strong, yet loving entity comes in. It is a Priest/Elder of ancient Lyonesse and these are his words:

ELDER OF LYONESSE

"Dear companion of Light. We welcome your interest in our ancient land. Indeed, it was a pleasant place in which to live out our lives, but its time as a great nation had to go. We knew this. We were pre-warned by the Higher Beings and many of the people escaped the disasters. We will share in your journey with Beloved Mary for she, even in our day, was a Being of Light who visited our lands in another incarnation. She and the Master Jesus were with us in a different guise, but still working for the Light and bringing healing to the sick. Dear sister, you also had your part to play in our ancient land. Of this you will learn more in time. All the connections are being made. All the pieces of the jigsaw are gradually being put in place as you progress on your special Mission with our Beloved Mary. We are watching over you dear Sister of Light. We are ever your protectors and loving friends. Thank you for making this pilgrimage with Mary. It will lead you to a greater understanding of Cosmic truths."

I have the impression of a kind benevolent Being. He appears to be wearing some sort of white robe of light material, loosely tied at the waist with a rope belt. What a delight to have this connection with the soul and people of Lyonesse. I offer deep gratitude and thanks for the communications from both White Eagle and the ancient Elder. Still pondering this whole question of Lyonesse/The Scilly Isle saga, a few days later in another attunement I receive:

HIGHER BEING

"Child - you were with Mary many many years ago. You were her hand maiden and served her faithfully in ancient Lyonesse. We would wish that you cast your mind

back to those ancient of days. Child it was many thousand of years ago, back in what you would term antiquity in your world today. Read again very carefully the words you have been given. You will discern the hidden truths contained therein. Be your own judge. You will find the answers. The ancient Land of Lyonesse is more than 10,000 years old. Its demise was caused by a catastrophe, a Cosmic happening, which penetrated deep down into the depths of your Planet. Many of its people did survive and went off to colonize elsewhere."

The '10,000 years old' threw me a bit, until I realized that this landmass, being the remains of Atlantis, WOULD have been that old. Trading with the Phoenicians would have transpired much later, probably around 4,000 years ago. Once more I thank the dear soul who has communicated with me. I accept all the words offered from all these beloved Masters and put my trust in them implicitly. If there is something I am not understanding, then no doubt answers will come in time. For now the subject is closed, because I have gone as far as I can with it. But, it has been a fascinating area of study, which I will pick up on at a later date. I must return to Mary and her children on The Isle of Scilly 2,000 years ago.

Before I do though a little aside. I remember two memorable family holidays in The Scilly Isles. The first, when my children were very small. We shared a bungalow with friends and spent two magical weeks in hot sunshine, each day clambouring aboard a rickety old bus, down to the harbour and off to different islands. Our second trip was in 1979 and began in a howling gale, at the time when many boats in the Fastnet Race were sunk and lives lost. When we arrived at Penzance quay to alight on The Scillonion ferry, we were told:*"Welcome aboard. God (forgive me) knows where you'll get off!'* Obviously we survived!

CAPE CORNWALL

On leaving The Scilly Isle, Mary, Jesus and Naomi returned to Merry Maidens. From there they did much travelling around The Cape, this mystical land which has layer upon layer of tangible evidence of its ancient past. While exploring this mysterious area one has the feeling that the fairy folk are watching your every move and ensuring that you respect their precious domain as you walk your pilgrim ways. Over the years I have explored much of Cape Cornwall. This time my main focus is to be Men-an-Tol with Nine Maidens.

CARN BREA

After a few days Mary's pilgrimage continued north-west through St Buryan to the Druidic settlement of Carn Brea (a second one in Cornwall). One sunny August day in 2005, I found myself at this sacred place with two dear White Eagle friends. We had walked the dirt track through a mass of purple heather and yellow gorse, to eventually reach the crest of the ancient settlement. At the topmost point is a cairn on which is nailed a plaque bearing the words *'Chapel Carn Brea, site of The Hermitage Chapel of St Michael. The pilgrimages of Margaret Keturah Fulleylove Thornley, Bard Maghteth Myghai (servant of Michael) led to the acquisition of this hill presented to the National Trust 15 May 1971"* The words speak for themselves. From this high point, one can scan 360 degrees, out over Cape Cornwall's ancient landscape and seascape. We each chose our own secluded place for an attunement. I was seated on the soft green turf with my back to an ancient stone, absorbing the deep place of this breathtaking hill-top. The hot summer air was filled with the evocative scent of the wild gorse and heather and the buzzing of honey bees. This was a blissful moment. I was aware of the presence of the Master Jesus and received from him the most beautiful words of welcome. I knew then that he had walked in this ancient place. For Mary and Naomi with the boy Jesus 2,000 years ago, being on this high plateau of Carn Brea, they would have had panoramic views around The Cape, south to St Michael's Mount from whence they had come and north to their prime destination Men-an-Tol.

CARN EUNY

Leaving Carn Brea, Mary travelled east through the settlement village of Carn Euny. In the same year, 2005, I visited this fine example of a well preserved village of the late Iron Age period. Extensive excavations carried out between 1964 and 1972 shed much light on this site and unearthed stone built houses, each of which would have supported a thatched roof. The village itself is built around a fogou. In Cornish a fogou means a cave and these subterranean structures of which there are many around Land's End, are unique to Cornwall. They usually consist of a long passage leading to an inner chamber. For this one at Carn Euny, one can enter the inner chamber via one of two entrance passages, coming in from opposite directions. I remember bending down and walking almost double underneath a large granite lintel through one of these passages to arrive at its centre. I was in a small circular chamber and could now stand up. Ahead of me was a niche in the bouldered wall. I sat in silence on a large stone slab. Theories abound as to the purpose of a fogou. The impression I was receiving was that this was a secret hidden place - a womb - where new life could be blessed and offerings left in thankfulness in the niche provided. On a deeper level my insight was telling me that this was a sacred place - an inner sanctum - wherein one could tune in to the Sacred Feminine energies and pay homage to the Goddess. I left a small pink quartz crystal as my offering, asking a blessing for the ancestors.

St Euny was a sixth century Irishman and near this ancient village is a Holy Well dedicated to him. I also came across St Euny on my second pilgrimage, at a little church dedicated to him in the village of Church Town in the valley below the other Carn Brea near Redruth. On Mary's pilgrimage, going east through Cape Cornwall is another Holy Well at Sancreed. This is a truly magical place. On an earlier visit I descended the old stone steps into a luminescent cavern of mosses and ferns to reach its crystal clear waters - its enchantment rising to meet me.

REVELATIONS AT PENZANCE

Beloved Mary and her children arrived at their next settlement of Rosehill, which is on the northern outskirts of present day Penzance This is where I connect with my first pilgrimage to Cornwall for my ongoing Mission. What I didn't know at the time, was that the Penzance Youth Hostel where I stayed, was in the area of Rosehill. I wondered how close I was to the ancient settlement.

After exploring the Roseland Peninsula and its Hinterland, I had travelled west to Cape Cornwall as yet unaware of Mary's wishes, but knowing it was where I was to be. I remember it well. I had had a nightmare journey from Golden Hill Fort, in rush hour traffic, against a dazzling setting sun. Eventually, I arrived at Penzance for the hostel, but finding it was tricky. After a long search, I found myself passing the local Police Station - ah they'll know I confidently thought. Following their directions, I turned into the road mentioned, to find at its end my way was barred by concrete posts - this was the pedestrian access! Turning around was interesting! However, I finally arrived at 7.00 pm, very happy to be there.

My words of the time take up the story. The hostel is a large country house and tonight there is a school party of about fifty young people in residence, so it is busy and noisy. I book in and discover that my bedroom which is shared with three other ladies, is fortunately tucked away at the back of the building. I head for the self-catering kitchen for a spot of refreshment and it is not too long before I am abed.

Guess what - middle of the night - two snorers are competing in my room. So, gathering my duvet, putting in a bag my notebook, pen, map and dowsing crystal, I am off downstairs to the lounge to sleep on the sofa. But everything as I am to discover, is for a reason. It is about 1.00 am - 'Mary's time' - and she wishes to speak with me! Before I am aware of this, I spend about half an hour browsing over the map trying to plan my tomorrow using my crystal. This time, I am asking Mary where SHE wishes me to go rather than making my own decision. As I receive a positive response over Men-an-Tol, I believe I have it right. I also believe I have found the settlement where Mary stayed which is in the valley below Nine Maidens. But, what does Mary have to say:

MARY

"Dearly beloved. There is only one area I would wish you to visit tomorrow, that is Men-an-Tol with Nine Maidens. You may find the settlement I identified if you wish. I want you to go to this special sacred Druid Ceremonial Complex of Men-an-Tol. There is a link with Merrivale in Devon. They are both Light Centres of a marked degree. Each has in place very powerful vibrational energy held within the landscape surrounding them.

Nine Maidens as is Men-an-Tol, is a power house of Light and as such has a part to play in bringing into manifestation the New Jerusalem in these sacred Isles. As with Merrivale and Hembury Castle, (see Chapters 10 and 11), your task is to reactivate the Light held within the very soil. There is an Etheric Temple of ancient past. We went you to be instrumental in bringing this Light Temple of ancient Atlantis to physical manifestation, to take its rightful place on the Earth once again. When this has happened, it will gradually be prepared for great happenings over the next years. With the physical eye it will not be seen but to anyone with the inner vision it will be there. This beloved one is ALL we require of you.

There will be changes to your Planet which are already beginning. There has already been a slight shift of the axis of the Earth Plane in order to bring it into alignment with future needs. This is nothing to be alarmed about beloved one. No disaster will occur, but the energies of your Earth Plane will be fine-tuned shall we say. You and the many many Light Workers will be our special helpers who will give service to bring this about. It is happening NOW. It has begun beloved one. Play your part. Your reward will be in the knowledge that you as a physical instrument now in incarnation, will have played your part. Do not shrink from this task. Michael will be with you and protect you. All we ask of you is that you open your heart in the purist most profound love. Let the Rose in your Heart truly be your saviour. Rest in that pure essence of perfect love beloved one and all will be well. I know that your beloved White Eagle is waiting for you as are many Masters and Angelic Beings.

Once again I say unto you, play your part in this magical event under the guidance of the Alchemist Merlin. Merlin is indeed the transformer of energy and is your helpmate on this occasion. Beloved one I will be with you. You will sense my presence and you will KNOW that I will be there. Your pure heart of love will be your passport to the work which you have undertaken to do before coming into incarnation. There is nothing to fear. All is well. You will be filled with that pure Cosmic energy from the Universal source. Rest now beloved child as we have need of you. May all the Angels and Archangels surround you with the love essence beloved one. Goodnight. We would wish that you time your Ceremony for 12.00 noon. We will ensure that the area is clear for you. May God's purist blessings fill your heart.

My response: *"Thank you Mary for this confirmation and for all your communication contains."* I pose the question: *"Beloved one you talk of a link between Men-an-Tol in Cape Cornwall and Merrivale on Dartmoor. Is there also a link to the heart of Wales at Strata Florida?"* From Mary:

MARY

"This we will tell you more of on another occasion. Good night beloved one."

Wow - what can I say. This is why two snorers have been placed in my bedroom and I had to beat a hasty retreat. So it is to Men-an-Tol I am to go and I have my instructions. Furthermore, Men-an-Tol is one of the ancient Atlantean Temples. Don't forget, these were early days in my Mission with the Lady Mary and this was the first Atlantean Temple I had been asked to earth. I thought I was to go to sleep, but my frontal mind is working overtime It is now 4.00 am and I find myself asking: *"What was the purpose of the Men-an-Tol?"* I think Mary gives up encouraging me to rest and returns with the following:

MARY

"Beloved you ask of Men-an-Tol. This ancient stone did have a specific purpose. Once a year at the summer solstice when the sun was at its highest point in the Heavens, a great and important Ceremony was held. This was to invoke that Great Light, the Light of the Cosmos, the Light which has always been since the World began. The Light was shot out of the Cosmos as a great shaft of energy. It would go right through the centre of the stone and strike the Earth beneath, thus sealing the Light in and below the ground. This Light would have kept the Earth on its correct axis. The Men-an-Tol stone in ancient times, was at a slightly different angle to what it is today. Also as you have already discovered the stone has been moved. It would have been in the centre of the circle

I thank the Lady Mary for her presence and 'patience' with my questioning! How fascinating - when I was at the Men-an-Tol some years previously, I had intuitively picked up that the stone had been moved from its central position. Now for a few hours sleep before the 'big day'. A momentous decision has been made. My original plan for Cape Cornwall, was to visit as many ancient sites and churches as I could, but now I shall head for home after my Ceremony at Men-an-Tol today. My Mission which Mary and the great Beings of Light have entrusted to me must be my main focus and I am not to be sidetracked.

MADRON - THE CHURCH, BAPTISTRY AND HOLY WELL.

On her pilgrimage around Cape Cornwall, Mary travelled from the settlement at Rosehill, through Madron to Men-an-Tol. My pilgrimage to Men-an-Tol takes me from Penzance, along a route close by Madron. Honouring my decision to be one-pointed, I reluctantly refrain from visiting this sacred place, but an earlier pilgrimage took me there.

The Parish Church of Madron is the Mother Church of Penzance. It is dedicated to St Maddern who hailed from Brittany in the sixth century. Within are so many treasures and fine features. I will just name two. First, it houses the bell from the Ding-Dong Tin Mine which was closed down in the late nineteenth century. Then there is an inscribed stone which is said to be of Pagan origin but later adopted as a Christian memorial. Two interpretations are put forward of the inscription which it is reckoned could commemorate a Cornish princess:

1. QONRA FILIA TAENNAE and
2. AIA HELNOTH.

A little to the north of the village is St Maddern's Baptistry and Holy Well. A narrow pathway, delightfully lined with wild flowers and grasses leads the way. A sign *'Celtic Chapel and Wishing Well'* is engraved on a grey slate plaque fixed to a large piece of granite. I first reached the Holy Well which was overhung by a bush sporting offerings of masses of brightly coloured ribbons. I walked on to the Baptistry/Chapel which is surrounded by ancient woodland. I remember entering its quiet sanctuary, and feeling the holiness of past times embedded within its old stone walls. In the far right hand corner is an old baptismal font where water collected as it ran from the Holy Well. At one end, is what is purported to be the original stone altar. I had picked a few wild flowers along my route and carefully placed these on the altar as my offering, with a blessing.

ARRIVAL

I am parked up on a little grassy area which serves as a car park for the Men-an-Tol and Nine Maidens, having taken the northern route in from Morvah. On my journey, I have passed derelict chimneys of the old tin mines, standing out starkly on the skyline, a reminder of Cornwall's historical mining past. It is 10.00 am and as I step out of the car, I am already feeling the warmth of the sun on this early October day. I prepare my pack. In my Ceremonial tin I have all I need for my Atlantean Temple Ceremony, including words which I have drafted out, for this is before I formalized my three Ceremonies. Job done, I sit back in the car for a drink and biscuit.

The sky is a vibrant blue, with white clouds looking for all like gossamer, just hanging there. I can see a flying saucer! Cloud shapes can be quite breathtakingly beautiful. I remember while on a retreat holiday in Pembrokeshire with a group of dear friends, we were standing overlooking Fishguard, when the most perfect Cloud Angel was spotted in the evening sky - we all thought what a very special blessing. Do you know that there is a group who call themselves The Cloud Appreciation Society? They photograph cloud formations and make postings of them on their web site, thus producing an exemplary cloud photo gallery.

Pondering and coffee finished, I now have time for an attunement before I set out for my walk to the Men-an-Tol. I place over my shoulders my beautiful scarf and go into the stillness: *"Great Beings of Light, Masters of the Universe, I offer myself in humility and dedication for my sacred task this day. May I do justice to what is being asked of me. I honour all the Masters of the Light and Higher Beings."* I sense that the Ceremonial site is being prepared, and that the Masters and Angels are waiting. I place myself in the Merkaba, that spiraling body of crystalline energy, which protects and links us to other dimensions of reality. I am conscious of Beloved Mary and reminded that she and her family would have found their way to this sacred site, as I am about to do. Her brother Joseph rejoined his family for their Ceremony at the Men-an-Tol.

TO THE MEN-AN-TOL TEMPLE SITE

All is ready. I have my pack on my back. Cars have arrived, and I calculate nine people have headed off in the direction of the ancient site, so it could be getting quite busy there. But I have complete trust in Divine organization and am sure the area will be cleared for me at the appropriate time. I pass through the kissing gate at the start of the track to Men-an-Tol asking the Druid guardian permission to enter their sacred area. I am treading steadfastly as if on a precessional route. My hands held in front of me appear to be enfolded in some sort of garment. It is a white robe - I have gone back in time. The ancient ones are walking with me. I am Naomi and have an impression of the presence of my family of past times, Mary with the boy Jesus, and Joseph are at my side. On I go, walking between hedgerows sprinkled with tall grasses and red campion, until I reach a stone stile with a small directional sign *'To Men-an-Tol'*. Another notice carved on a large granite stone reads *'This site is cared for by Cornish Ancient Sites Protection Network'* and the thought provoking words *'Don't change the site, but let the site change you'* I like that.

Climbing over the stile, I am on open moorland amongst ancient landscape so familiar to me. The golden bracken of autumn is in evidence, alongside the last of the mauve heather. The chimney of the old Ding Dong Mine is sky-lined on the distant hill. The Men-an-Tol comes into view and my heart misses a beat. Men-an-Tol is Cornish for 'Stone with a Hole'. It is said to be between 3,000 and 4,000 years old, and there is much speculation as to its purpose. Some say it was used for astronomical purposes. Others suggest the stone is part of the remains of a Neolithic tomb. Mary has told me of the summer solstice Ceremony, and how the Men-an-Tol was used to direct the Cosmic Light to the Earth and below, in order to keep the Earth's axis stable. I also learnt from a Druid Elder when at Nine Maidens later, that the Men-an-Tol: *'was centred at the ancient Temple of Atlantis'* and that it was a point where the Light went through the Earth to the Great Crystal.

The Men-an-Tol

As I draw close to the ancient site, I feel as if the powerful energies emanating from the stones are drawing me in. I reach my first standing stone which I deem to be the guardian. I ask permission to move forward. The main feature is a very large circular stone standing on its end with in its centre, a huge hole of approximately eighteen inches in diameter. THIS is the Men-an-Tol. At either side are two small standing stones, which I dowse, to discover are male and female. The male stone would have represented the Father aspect of the Godhead - the Will, while the female stone would be symbolic of the Mother - the Wisdom. However, I am being shown three standing stones not just the two visible today. A third missing stone would have completed the ancient geometric symbol of the Triangle, bringing into being the Son - the Love aspect. This powerful Cosmic Truth links to the ancient Egyptian pyramidal structures, which were four equilateral triangles built on a four-square base. Here at Men-an-Tol, surrounding the whole, would have been a stone circle, but now most of the stones have disappeared. This was a hallowed place for the ancient Druids.

There is a group of people at the site. They gradually begin to leave and wander off back down the path. I counted nine persons in so I shall count nine out. There is one gentleman left sitting slightly away from the stones. I take a few photographs and do my dowsing. I decide to go over to the guy and engage him in conversation. We have a chat about the ancient site, during which time he tells me his trip to Cape Cornwall is an annual pilgrimage. I deliberately bid him farewell, saying I shall sit on the grass for a while. I think he is now ready to leave - he does leave! I have Men-an-Tol to myself and it is 12.00 noon. The Angelic Ones - they are quite wonderful.

MEN-AN-TOL ATLANTEAN TEMPLE CEREMONY

My Ceremony here is dedicated to earthing the ancient Temple of Atlantis. Near to the outer circle of stones is a small flat square granite stone - perfect I think for laying out my 'equipment'. But first I take from my pack a small bottle which contains water from the St Just Holy Well and slowly pour it over the top of the Men-an-Tol with a blessing. I now sit on the grass in the warm sunshine, my makeshift altar before me. All is still and the atmosphere is filled with expectation.

It is time to begin my Ceremony. I first visualize the great Cosmic Christ Star in the Heavens, high above my head shining its pure Light down, to encompass me and the ancient Men-an-Tol. As I do this, I am remembering that Mary 2,000 years ago reactivated this Atlantean Temple of Light. Now I am playing my part. My prayer: *"Beloved Masters and Angelic Beings, I call on your presence this sacred day asking for your protection and guidance. I humbly offer myself in service. Let me be worthy of the task in hand."* I voice 'The Great Invocation'. I feel as if I have moved into an altered state of consciousness as I submit each of the crystals to the Masters, speaking the sacred words. With great reverence I proceed with my Ceremony, being very aware of the potent vibrational energies around and within me. I am finalizing with: *"Let the Light Shine…Let it be Done"*. Merlin is indeed present and I hear a mighty clash as his staff impacts with the earth, securing the Light at this sacred place. The ancient Atlantean Temple is earthed at the Men-an-Tol, which can now be used for its true purpose, as a conductor for the Cosmic Light as the Age of Aquarius comes upon us. My Ceremony is complete. I now go into a deep meditation. Finally, I close my Ceremony and ensure I am protected and grounded. I speak the words: *"Oh Great Beings of Light, I honour you all and I thank you for your presence this day."*

Into my consciousness comes the buzzing of a single honey bee. It is my understanding that bees are messengers from spirit, so I am going to accept this as telling me that all is well. Also Merlin's raven is croaking loudly over my head - I open my eyes and watch as he flies off into the distance. Yes - all IS well. I am hearing voices from far off. Quickly before anyone comes into view I go to the great Men-an-Tol. I first put a large piece of triangular shaped white quartz collected from the estuary beach of St Just Pool, on the stone itself within its holed centre. This gift from the Angels is returned with love. I now bury two small pieces of white and rose quartz within the earth and grass at the edge of the Men-an-Tol. Perfect timing - two people appear a little way off coming across the moorland. I put away my prayer items and sit quietly. They arrive, wander round the stones taking their photographs and leave. Mary is to speak with me:

MARY

"Bless you my child. IT IS DONE. We all in the Land of Light, thank you for your dedication and your offering of service to humanity. It is recognized that you have left the quartz crystal which will link Men-an-Tol to the Heavens above with the Earth beneath. It is also recognized and accepted with special blessing your offering of a pink quartz crystal for me as a token for the Sacred Feminine."

From me: *"Blessed Mary, I am honoured and humbled by this experience. Amen."*

NINE MAIDENS STONE CIRCLE

I now confirm with Mary that she is happy if I visit the ancient circle of Nine Maidens, and possibly view the settlement where she and her little party stayed. I check the direction with my map and compass, then head off in search of the Druidic site. I retrace my steps a short way and at an old stone wall start off along a track, which soon becomes a sea of mud, so I revert to moorland. I am very happy, feeling light of foot as I pick my way through the rough turf. I come to a derelict stone cottage with some very handsome black cows in the 'garden'. Here I take a short rest to have a sandwich before moving on. Now the path sweeps off to the right, and I begin the gentle climb towards my goal, passing a small hut circle identified by its familiar triangular granite stone. The Nine Maidens stone circle is now before me. As I first glimpse the ancient circle, Cosmic memories are stirred once more. The site is situated towards the top of the hill in the midst of a large black peaty area. I pick my way carefully across to the stone circle, jumping onto tufts of grass trying not to end up to my knees in the bog.

I stand at the entrance to Nine Maidens which Mary has told me is associated with the Men-an-Tol site. I first bless the two male and female guardian entrance stones. These very tall stones are in a direct south-east/north-west alignment balanced by two smaller male and female stones at the far side of the circle. Now I look more closely at the site. It is obviously called Nine Maidens because of the nine vertical granite stones in evidence. But I know there are more. I go round with my dowsing rods and discover a total of twenty-four stones plus the two entrance stones, each stone being approximately one metre apart. I return to stand between the two guardian stones. My inner vision is showing me great Flames of Light rising up from the tops of each of these two huge granite pillars, as if the very stone itself has been imbued with that ancient Cosmic Fire. I am now feeling a very positive link and strong influence of ancient Egypt and names from Dynastic times are coming in, which include Akhnaton and Nefretiti.

Somewhere within this peaty bog I find a grassy patch not too far from the stone circle entrance, to sit down for an attunement. It is a bit damp, but I can put up with that. A Druid Elder is standing before me robed in a long white garment:

DRUID ELDER

"Pilgrim of Light we welcome you to this ancient site. As you have discovered, I can confirm the twenty-four stones with the two guardian stones at the entrance. Men-an-Tol was centred at the ancient Temple of Light of Atlantis. Nine Maidens as this circle is called, is where we performed our Druidic Ceremonies. From the settlements below the hill, we would precess as a group of Elders and lay people at special times of the year - at the summer and winter solstices and at the spring and autumn equinoxes, in order to bring the Light down from the Cosmos to heal our ancient Land. There was a legend of these ancient Isles being all that remained of the lost Atlantis. It was known. We as a Druid group considered we were upholding that ancient Light in our Ceremonies and did all in our power to preserve its sanctity and power.

Beloved Mary with Joseph of Arimathea and the blessed Jesus and you Naomi, DID visit us here and were cared for in one of our settlements below the hill This visit by the beloved Mary and the great Master was known. We were prepared. The boy Jesus was, all I can say, an exceptionally beautiful and gifted child. His bearing was calm for a boy of his age. He appeared completely at-one with all the elements of the natural world. He was a blessed child and a blest child. The Light of all Creation shone out of his face. On one occasion he did offer us a few words of wisdom, which I can only say was when the Christ Light entered his body and he was illumined. He had just completed the first part of his Temple training as a young person of the Essene Brotherhood community. In coming to Britain this time with his mother Mary, he would have been beginning his many years of travelling the Earth, including many visits to these sacred Isles, before he began his Ministry in the Holy Land.

Beloved Mary had a very special Mission. That was to reinstate that ancient Light and Power of Atlantis in the land at Men-an-Tol and elsewhere. The Light went deep, deep within the Earth's crust where you will know is an ancient Crystal, embedded there at the beginning of time. This Crystal is being reawakened for the Aquarian Age and the Ceremony you performed Sister of Light, was a part of that great awakening. We thank you for your service this day. God Bless you Sister of Light."

I am so happy to receive confirmation from this Druid Elder at this my first sacred Ceremony: "*Thank you and bless you for your wisdom and beautiful words. A part of my heart will remain here.*"

I walk to the edge of the site and look into the deep valley below Nine Maidens, searching for the settlement where Mary stayed. However, I realize that for today it is too far for me to go as it is getting late, and I have my journey back to Devon. Another time perhaps? I offer a final tribute to Nine Maidens and rather reluctantly leave this sacred hill-top. It is only on arriving back home, that I realize I am missing my dowsing rods. Wondering where I left them, I could 'see' them stuck in the peat at Nine Maidens! Too far to return to retrieve them. Never mind, my loss is another's gain - a gift for a pilgrim traveller.

I retrace my footsteps across the moorland and pick up the track to my car. I pass the stone stile entrance to Men-an-Tol and acknowledge the Atlantean Temple, once more firmly placed on Mother Earth, with a blessing of my hand on my heart. I KNOW that the power of the ancient Temple Light will be instrumental in healing our precious Planet.

Back at the car, it is 4.00 pm. Amazingly the sun is still hot. I believe this day has been hotter than any we've had during the summer. I see that the car park is filled with visitors - who can blame anyone for wanting to make the most of the October sunshine. I put my pack in the boot of my car and take my leave.

At home I reflect on my travelling and make the link once more with Beloved Mary. I thank my gracious Lady and all the blessed Beings of Light for their guidance and protection on my first sacred pilgrimage in Cornwall.

The sunny days I experienced in Cornwall this October have brought to mind a little personal story. My Dad was and still is very dear to me. He used to take a week's holiday each year in this early part of October as the weather was always fine. He called it '*St. Luke's Little Summer*'. Goodness knows where he got this from. His office colleagues called it '*Graham's week*' and knew they were in for a sunny spell. He passed over to the Land of Light on October 4th at the juncture of '*St. Luke's Little Summer*'.

ON RETURNING TO DEVON

It is now after my first pilgrimage, while trying to chart Mary's journey through Cornwall, that I become aware of the huge task ahead of me. I tried not to panic and received comforting words from Mary (see the 'INTRODUCTION TO THE SOUTH WEST'). The following day I was sitting in meditation, for I was feeling the need to seek communion with the inner world and rediscover my focus after my slight glitch the day before. I lit my candle and had some soft music playing. I was focusing on the pure light of the sacred flame. I entered the eternal silence. The Golden Flame seemed to fill my heart centre and in my imagination I was gradually rising, as on Wings of Light, right into the Temple of the Golden One. The beloved Master Jesus spoke with me and his message reflected my need for solace and wisdom, but is addressed to us all:

THE MASTER JESUS

"I come in on the Ray of Divine Love. Dear Peace Rose we bless you. Your recognition of the situation is important. Your way is clear now for further revelations. We welcome the joy and love within your heart.

Now we wish to say, hold steadfast to that still centre. Always work from the Heart Centre of the Rose Light. These words which we say unto you, you know are not for you alone. They are for all humankind. We applaud your efforts dear sister as we applaud the efforts of each and every one of you, to master the intricacies of the physical body. The physical is indeed the Temple of all your other subtle bodies. It is your centre of perfection whilst on the Earth Plane. So dear Brothers and Sisters, respect the vehicle which you have chosen to do your work in this lifetime. The Divine essence of purity and truth abides within all your subtle bodies and can be reflected through the physical, which is so precious. This is why to respect and nurture the physical is of vital importance. It is your vehicle during your incarnation for the manifestation of love and perfect joy. Thank you dear sister for all your efforts in this respect.

We move on to other things now. We, that is I and the Brothers and Sisters of the Living Light, would wish that you take one step at a time in the Mission which has been presented to you. You will be guided every step of the way. The only thing for you to do is to listen to your heart and abide in the wisdom there. Let the Mind of the Heart ever be your travelling companion. This dear ones is the way for you ALL to live your Earthly lives - through the Mind in the Heart, as your beloved White Eagle tells you. With this you cannot go wrong. We know that challenges will beset you, but challenges are along the pathway of ALL our lives and no-one can escape them, least of all the great Masters, those Beings of Light who have passed this way before you. So we say to you ALL - all who are reading these words - to reflect on their meaning and endeavour to live your own lives within their context. Your World is full of many many souls in need of sustenance on all levels. Let this be your guide dear ones. You are your own Masters of Light Let that truth reflect in your actions while on Earth. You are all so blessed with the opportunity to serve the one true Light from the place of this precious Planet. So, live your life in purity and truth to the best of your ability. Love your neighbour as yourself and the peace which passeth all understanding will truly be yours.

I respect the difficulty of your Earthly journeys, but you will grow ever closer to that Divine presence as you pass through your Earthly initiations. My dear fellow Light

Beings, always - yes ALWAYS - be that still centre of perfect love. Always - go into the centre of your being. Enter that Sacred Heart in times of trouble. You will surely receive the sustenance and peace of mind you need. Dwell dear ones in the Heart of that Perfect Rose - ALWAYS.

I give you my blessings and perfect love. I offer you my heart. I am that pure love. Know that YOU are also. Live in the love. Love your life. Know that there is always a hand offered to hold you up when things are difficult. I offer you MY hand. I am YOUR Friend. Walk in MY footsteps dear Brothers and Sisters and all will be well for you. You will BE that place of stillness and perfect peace. You will be comforted, for I am The Comforter and I will never leave you. You are ALL so precious to me and will dwell in my heart for ever. Amen."

From me: *"I am humbled. Bless you dear Master and thank you for your profound words."* I am in a place of wonderment. The Master Jesus has always been a living part of my life. I acknowledge and welcome his words of wisdom. Now Mary is drawing close, smiling and bringing an air of gentle serenity and perfect understanding. She just says:

MARY:

"My child - my blessed child."

After Men-an-Tol Joseph sallied forth once again on one of his own adventures. Meanwhile Mary, Jesus and Naomi completed their travelling around Cape Cornwall. From the settlement below Nine Maidens they journeyed east to Chysauster, now a well preserved stone-walled ancient village of the Roman period, but where evidence of an earlier Iron Age site has been discovered. From here they went north, over Lady Down, to Rosewall Hill settlement, then south over the heights of Trink Hill and Trencrom Fort to reach the Druidic settlement indicated on the map as being just south of St Erth.

CHAPTER 6
TRAVELLING THE NORTH COAST
Arrival of the Saints

After a few days at St Erth the Lady Mary with Jesus and Naomi began their pilgrimage along the north Cornish coast. Passing through Geal, they met with Joseph at a settlement called Merry Meeting (appropriate name), which is to the west of Cambourne. After a two day stay here, they all travelled further east through Roscroggan and Illogan, to reach the Druidic Temple settlement on the hill above Portreath. I notice that from St Erth to Portreath is a good 'rose' trail starting with Rosewarne, Roseworthy Barton, Roseworthy, Roskear Croft, Rosgroggan and Merrose Farm. From here they took a sea trip around St Agnes Head to Pertanporth and on to a settlement at Cubert.

It is at Illogan that I pick up Mary's footsteps in the physical sense. As a reminder, I stayed at Roscroggan on my second Cornish pilgrimage at the end of January. At that time I was able to get to Carn Brea Atlantean Temple site and Andrew Wartha Druidic settlement. Day 2 however, came in wet and misty, so I decided to explore locally, knowing this would connect with Mary's journey in North Cornwall. So this is where we are now.

It is fortunate I am in B & B accommodation that I may have an attunement in my own little bedroom haven. Yet if I judge by the noise in the house today, it appears to be over-run with children, which I discover on going down to breakfast, is one two year old! I light my little candle which travels with me and settle down saying: *"Mary help me to put aside all the disturbances and tune in to your essence."* I am quite calm and as I rest my lovely pink scarf over my head, I feel as if I am in ancient garb of a women of the Holy Land 2,000 years ago - Mary/Naomi? Mary is here:

MARY

"My blest child, pay no heed to outer conditions. Today I would wish that you listen to and be guided by your intuition. I shall be with you every step of the way. Travel to one place and from there you will be shown the way. Bless you my dearest child Naomi."

ST ILLOGAN PARISH CHURCH

Initially I feel drawn to the little village of Illogan. I travel the few miles along peaceful country lanes enjoying the greenery in spite of the murky conditions. I arrive at the Parish Church and park in the small space designated for church visitors. As I alight from the car, the stillness hits me. The air is filled with bird song; robin, chaffinch, blackbird and song thrush. I open the gate leading into the churchyard, asking permission of the deva guardian to enter this hallowed ground, to be greeted by an ancient Celtic wheel cross. I then notice something most unusual - the church tower is separate from the main church - I have never come across this set-up before. Why should this be? A little later, in conversation with a very kind local gentlemen of eighty-two years, so he informs me, I learn that this tower was part of the old church, which was pulled down in the mid nineteenth century, because it had become too small for its congregation. When the present church was built forty metres away, the tower remained in situ, because it had been scheduled as a landmark on Navigational Charts by Trinity House. The old church was built on top of a small ancient Celtic church long since disappeared. Using my dowsing rods, I discover that the original church, probably of daub and wattle structure, was built by St Illogan a seventh century Celtic saint, somewhere between AD 630 and AD 640.

A Celtic Wheel Cross at St Illogan's Church

I arrive at the church entrance to find the door locked. It is now that I make contact with my elderly gentleman 'friend' Peter. Noting my disappointment, he unlocks the back door for me and we enter together. It is always a special moment coming into such a Holy place, where vibrations of ages past come alive. Unfortunately I could find no leaflet in the church to tell of its history. Peter did a thorough search and concluded they were all gone. A little later in the day on his advice, I met with a lovely lady from the village called Gill, who informed me that the brochure was being rewritten by the rector, following his research in the Truro archives. She said when it became available she would post me a copy, so I left her my address and some cash.

Peter gives me a tour of the church, coming up with a great deal of fascinating information. He shows me the Basset Arms. It would seem that a noble - Lord Dunstable of the Basset family, lived at the local Tehidy Manor. The house no longer exists, but the estate remains as Tehidy Country Park, with nine miles of beautiful woodland and lakes, a sanctuary for wildlife. Lord Dunstable was at the time, the fifth wealthiest man in England and his cortage used to travel down from London quite regularly. The monument on top of Carn Brea which I saw yesterday, was built by local people after his death in his memory. I wonder if the money for it came from the people or from the Basset coffers!.

I now take a look around by myself. The stained glass windows are exquisite. They depict many of the saints including St Mary and St Michael, but oddly, not St Illogan. The granite font which is most impressive, comes from the old church and is set on four rounded granite pillars, each sporting a most beautiful carved angel. And - the best bit - at the back of the church I find an ancient panel, so old that the wood is blackened. It is about three metres in height and depicts a full length standing dragon.

I offer my thanks and say my farewells to my helpful guide. As a parting note he tells me that although he has lived fifty years in Illogan, he was born under the lee of Carn Brea. The vulgar industrial units, which I came to whilst trying to negotiate a way to the top of the hill, were not there then and all around was the natural beauty of the countryside. As I wander through the churchyard, I come across the Basset Vault, made of concrete and looking very dilapidated. On top is a large rather sombre solid box-like structure of black ironwork, with a familial inscription. As a complete contrast to this dour memorial, I now discover on a grave, some pure white snowdrops enhanced with their slender green leaves. In the yearly calendar, we are coming up to Candlemas, the 2nd February, so this is a blessed reminder of Our Lady - Mary.

I return to the car for a hot drink from my flask. The misty rain is still doing its stuff and gets you wet as soon as it looks at you! I choose a beautiful feather and two fir cones from Lustleigh Cleave in Devon and return to the church tower. I offer each of my gifts in turn to honour the Celtic missionaries and especially St Illogan. The rooks high up in the bellfry, are noisily telling me of their presence. Standing with my back to the tower, I chant the well known Celtic Prayer, of which there are different versions. This one is from 'The Celtic Morning Worship' booklet I purchased from St Illogan Parish Church, copyright the Archbishop's Council 2000.

CELTIC PRAYER

The peace of the running wave to you;
the peace of the flowing air to you;
the peace of the quiet earth to you;
the peace of the shining stars to you;
and the peace of the Son of Peace to you.

As I leave the churchyard for a short circular walk to the village by a designated footpath, I am conscious of being overshadowed by a presence of past times. I am walking slowly as in meditation, blessing the land with each footstep, my hands before me within the sleeves of a brown habit. Could this be St Illogan? The saint leaves me and I am myself once again. I continue alongside an old stone wall, which is covered with shiny green ivy, delicate ferns and foxgloves in waiting. I reach an area of parkland which has been very carefully managed, leaving the appearance of natural woodland. A high canopy of mature oaks is interspersed with young beech and holly. A rotting tree trunk lying in the soft brown earth left as it has fallen, is displaying some beautiful fungi. There is a traditional design oak bench-seat, a resting place for villagers and visitors alike. My feeling as I amble through this magical place is of deep peace. I am aware of the presence of the nature spirits and am filled with delight. I exit through some elaborate black wrought iron gates at the far end on which is a plaque *'Welcome to Maningham Wood opened by Lady Mary Holberow 23rd October 2004'*. The woodland is part of a Parish Regeneration Scheme with the Illogan Parish Council, but used to be the grounds of the old vicarage until it was given to the townsfolk. The gates were the start of a wide driveway to the house which can be seen in the distance through the trees.

In Illogan square I pop into a local shop for some goodies. This is followed by a brief visit to Gill to introduce myself. Apparently Peter has already 'phoned to warn her of my pending visit! Gracious it's nearly 2.00 pm and I have been all morning exploring this church and village just three miles from my B & B. Back at the car I am very wet and looking rather dishevelled. Thoughts come to mind: *"Oh Mary you must have been so weary at times - you must have been cold and wet and tired."* A traveller/pilgrim's life would not always have been a bed of roses, even for the *'Rose in the Heart'*. I lunch in the car, just fruit and dark chocolate digestive biscuits - my favourite - with some coffee from my flask.

TO PORTREATH

I am now on my way to Portreath in the hope of discovering the settlement where Mary stayed. As I approach the village, I find myself being funnelled down through a narrow road leading to the harbour. The weather has really closed in and there is only the faintest outline of the hills rising up either side of the road. The Druid site is on the hill to my left, but to go in search of it in these conditions would be foolish. Instead I park at the waterfront and sit quietly, bringing to mind Mary and her family's time here. It is from this area of coastline they took a boat to Perranporth. To conclude this day, I have a wander around Portreath. I come to the St Mary Church which Peter told me about. Shock - horror - it is a modern building and it is closed - end of story. Enough's enough. Time to return to my cosy accommodation to dry off.

PORTREATH DRUIDIC TEMPLE CEREMONY

We shall continue with Mary's journeying along the Cornish coastline shortly. First I shall perform my sacred Ceremony for the Portreath settlement at my home sanctuary. The day and time I have chosen is 9.00 am on the 16th March 2009. Does my Astrological Ephemeris indicate anything auspicious about this date? I notice that three Planets are transiting the air sign of Aquarius - my sun sign; Mercury, Jupiter and Neptune. Each will be beneficial in its own way. The Planet Mercury, the Winged Messenger of the Gods, will be instrumental in reactivating the powerful energy of the Cosmic Light and for myself, will effect good communication with the Masters and Angelic messengers. The ever expansive Jupiter, Bestower of Good, will give my Ceremony joy and added impetus. Finally, Neptune the God of the Sea, will take that Cosmic Healing Light into the very depths of our Oceans.

I am woken at 6.00 am. The Angels know that my physical body is in need of healing and balancing. I will admit that my energy levels have been rather low of late and it goes without saying, that I need to be in 'tip-top' condition for my Ceremony. To begin my day I have a relaxing bath with a few drops of lavender oil. Then a glass of water and two cups of herb tea. Good start I think. Lighting my candle I sit before my altar with my spine straight and bring all my sacred centres into alignment. I now play my beautiful healing CD *'Cellular Alchemy'* by Lyn Edwards and Gay Robinson of our White Eagle Lodge in Maleny, Australia. With the CD finished my healing is complete and I am in a place of inner calm. I take a light breakfast then prepare my sacred space.

Today my altar is cloaked with a white cloth embroidered with purple iris. On it among my usual sacred articles I have two fresh iris in a small vase. White Eagle is identified with the iris and I have often wondered why he chose this particular flower as his 'emblem'. For the first time I find I am drawn to study it in detail and maybe my deliberations can provide an explanation. The iris is quite lovely - its petals forming a six pointed star, the symbol of the White Eagle Lodge. The three large open petals give an exact as near as flowers can, triangle, with the upper petal pointing Heavenwards and the other two forming the base. Each has a distinct gold-yellow centre open to receive the

Light of the Great Sun. The edges of this central section seem to be slightly feathered. This could be representative of White Eagle's feathered headdress as he presents himself today in the guise of his American Indian incarnation and also of the plumed serpent of the Initiate. The other three smaller purple petals balance the three main ones in a further triangle. The two triangles merge to complete the six points of the star. Finally, the purple is the colour of kings. In this respect, let us never forget that White Eagle the wise sage and teacher, is much more than this one incarnation. He is a great Being of Divine essence who has had many blessed incarnations. Two more popularly known of, are as the High Priest, Is-Ra of Egyptian Dynastic times and Hah-Wah-Tah, a Priest King of an early Mayan Indian tribe in the Andes of South America. As I am writing this and making these simple but profound observations, this beloved Master is with me.

I smudge my room and leave it to still. When it is time I sit before my altar. I visualize the Christ Star, its rays of Golden Light pouring down to encompass me. I ask for the protection of Archangel Michael and put myself in the Merkabah. I feel as if I have Wings of Light and am flying in some sort of chariot of flames through the Cosmos. Then the significance of my vision hits me. Of course THIS is Elijah's fiery chariot, wherein he ascends in his Body of Light. Later I find the book *'The Essenes. Children of the Light'* wherein Stuart Wilson adds to our knowledge of the Merkabah by telling us, that the name has been handed down through the Order of Melchizedek and that - Mer-Ka-Bah: *'translates as 'Light-Spirit-Soul' (ie: the Light Body which, when empowered by the Spirit becomes the vehicle of the Soul)'* - Page 276.

In my imagination I now picture the ancient Druidic settlement at Portreath on its misty hill-top. As I watch, I see a great Light descend and shine through the mists to reach this ancient Temple. I begin with a prayer to the Masters of the Universe. I utter my Ceremonial words, setting on my altar each of my crystals in order - the merlinite, the turquoise and the pink quartz. I continue my sacred rite. When I mention *'The New Jerusalem'* I am hearing bells ringing out and can 'feel' the joy of Jupiter. Today my inner sight is showing me the Cosmic Light focusing as a central point of a compass at ancient Glaston - Glastonbury. This Light is now spreading out across the whole of the British Isles. As my Ceremony is drawing to a close, I become aware of a powerful presence It is Mercury:

MERCURY

"We thank you oh pilgrim of ours for your service given freely, in love and unconditionally, this sacred day. IT IS DONE. The Light has been restored at Portreath Sacred Druidic Temple site.

Yes - you too can fly in chariots of fire throughout the Cosmos. All it needs my Brethren is a loving heart, trust in the Divine alchemy and the desire to take that first step. There are no limits to where you can go, except for the limits you yourselves may put on your travelling - on your Cosmic experiences. The Heavens are there for you to explore in your meditations and in your sleep state. There are NO LIMITS I say again. There are Planets and Stars and Universes of all natures for you to travel to and gain knowledge and experience. Knowledge is the key to understanding the Cosmic wonders, but knowledge must be tempered with a loving heart. Knowledge alone is not enough. Knowledge without love feeds the ego and can lead the unwary into sometimes difficult circumstances. Come with me my Brethren - for you are all my Brethren - I know each one of you. Come with me my pilgrims - for so you ALL are, as you journey through your incarnation at this time on Planet Earth. The Cosmos is yours - your birthright. Seek and ye shall find. Explore and you will discover. Open your heart to the pure love of the Masters of Light. You can ALL fly. You can ALL learn of deeper things. And so you will as you open your heart to Divine Love and let your Light shine forth. Whatever you do in your life Earth Brethren, do it in purity, in trust and with love. I come before you now as the great Mercury, to bring you this wisdom that you may understand that to work with the intellect alone is not enough. ALWAYS seek Divine purpose in each action and ALWAYS seek that action through the heart.

Our Lady Mary - Isis - was the epitome of that Divine Love and sacrifice, which was made as she offered herself in the totality of loving service to your human race, under the protection of the Divine Masters. She - whom the Christ Light shone in abundance. Her heart was full, not only of love, but sheer joy as represented by my Brother Jupiter. She would be called upon to hit the very depths of despair and yet her heart shone in pure everlasting love.

Earth Brethren, there are many changes happening at this moment in time and for some time to come as your planet shifts into the new consciousness. The Grid System is being repaired and prepared. The vibrational energies of your Planet are being lifted. Each precious human is being offered the opportunity to raise their own vibrations through understanding, knowledge and love. Go forth my valiant pilgrims into the Light.

I, the mighty Mercury, hold your Planet in the Cosmic Cup of life, which now is overflowing. Sip of its nectar my Brethren and you will be refreshed."

As this Golden Being takes his leave, my insight shows him flashing away into the Universe, so fast that sparks are flying off wings of fire - all this set against a backdrop of a jet-black night sky. I see Stars and Planets going on and on and on for ever. Alpha and Omega - there is no beginning and no end. It always has been and it always will be. I express a devout thank you and blessing to Mercury. White Eagle has so often talked of 'The Mind in the Heart' and here Mercury is expressing this very succinctly and embracing Mary as being the embodiment of this perfect state of being. As I re-enter the world, I am once again reminded of the privilege and joy of this work which I am being asked to undertake. I offer an acknowledgement and blessing to all Angels and Archangels and to the Masters of the Great White Light. I close my Ceremony in the appropriate manner, as befitting the nature of my powerful Cosmic connection. With my crystals placed at the Portreath Druidic Temple site, I now seal my physic centres and ensure that my whole being is protected with Golden Light. I blow out my candle offering the Light for World healing. I leave the room in its stillness for some while as a token of reverence and in order not to disturb the beautiful energies.

TO THE CUBERT SETTLEMENT FOR MARY

After partaking in a Druidic Light Ceremony at Portreath, Mary, Jesus, Naomi and Joseph took a short sea journey around St Agnes Head to Perranporth beach. Just before St Agnes Head marked on the map, is a place name 'Tubby's Head'. Ever the curious one, I wondered what this meant, as I had come across a similar place name before - 'Tubbs Mill' at the head of an estuary leading from Caerhays Castle on Mary's journey *'Into the Hinterland'*. I looked up Tubb in my Chambers dictionary and this is what it say: *'A pit-shaft casing; a bucket, box or vehicle for bringing up coal from the mine.'* Of course a tub is a bucket everyone knows that! I just did not connect the name to the tin mining in Cornwall.

Around Perranporth the 'rose' place names flourish, in the form of Rosehill, Rose and Lower Rose, but try as I may, I could not get Mary staying anywhere in this area, so I had to look further afield. I found her at a settlement to the south-east of the village of Cubert and inland from Penhale Sands. On the coast nearby is a place named Holywell with a Well marked on my map. This would all seem to tie in with my insights.

MY JOURNEY TO ST PIRAN'S CHURCH AND ORATORY

It is the final day of my 2nd pilgrimage and I intend visiting St Piran's Church and Oratory in Penhale Sands In order to reach these Holy places, I drive from Perranporth along the narrow coast road and park up not far from the hamlet of Rose. According to my map, the church and oratory look to be in the middle of Penhale Dunes reached by a dedicated footpath. Guess what - it is raining once again, this time combined with a howling gale. Well wrapped up, I stride forth, valiantly battling against the elements. At first I follow some low white posts which have been placed at intervals along the start of the track. However, these soon die out and going becomes difficult, because being unfamiliar with the terrain, out here one sand-dune looks the same as another. The few walkers out on this blustery day are in the far distance, so I send out my spiritual antennae to guide me. As I trudge purposefully along a grassy sandy path towards Penhale Sands I am beginning to feel as if I am walking the way of the saint in sandalled feet and simple garb. Then I see it - a massive granite Celtic wheel cross identifying the position of St Piran's Church.

ST PIRAN

Who was St Piran? St Piran was a sixth century Irish saint. Legend has it that he floated across the waters on a millstone landing at Perranporth. He is acknowledged as the Patron Saint of Tinners and the National Saint of Cornwall. The Cornish flag bears St Piran's Cross, a white cross on a black background and his feast day is the 5th March. St Piran founded his oratory at

Perranzabuloe, after which he built his first church and then a monastery. The monks who lived a simple, devout life of obedience, chastity and poverty would have been housed in cells within the monastery. During the sixteenth century the whole community was gradually invaded by sea-sand driven by north-west winds. A second church was built further inland, but that too became a victim of the elements. Eventually in the nineteenth century a new church dedicated to St Piran was built on the hill above Perranporth, but still within the parish of Perranzabuloe.

ST PIRAN'S CHURCH

At the ruined St Piran's Church is an excellent descriptive plaque. After a quick read, I walk down the few stone steps into the relative shelter of this hallowed place. It is roughly oblong in shape narrowing at the altar end. The stone foundations laid deep within protective turf walls, have been very well preserved. There is little left of the original building except the remains of one rounded pillar. It would seem that the main fabric of the church such as the roof, pillars, window frames, altar, and font, were removed and utilized in the new church. By the early twentieth century this derelict church had been enveloped by sand, but excavations carried out made big improvements. The real preservation came from further work done in 2005 by Cornwall County Council in partnership with the Piran Trust. I sit on a low stone wall. The energies of St Piran are compelling:

ST PIRAN

"Welcome pilgrim. I was a pilgrim once travelling the ancient land here in Cornwall and in Ireland. It is a blessed thing that you do. By walking the land in reverence, one brings a blessing to the Earth and to the landscape. The concept of the simple way is recognized. It is in living the simple life that one can uphold the true values which our Lord Jesus Christ imparted to us. It is not in the trappings of the Roman Church. It is in the pure love and simple worship of the ancient Christianity as taught to us by Jesus, which ever was and ever shall be. This is the joy. This is the peace. This is the way to live your life pilgrim. I travelled far in my search for truth and I found it within. This is a blest place. Thank you for undertaking the pilgrimage sister. Go in peace."

An inner vision shows me St Piran offering a benediction with the sign of the Jesus cross drawn in the air. I offer my profound thanks to this saint of old who has spoken with me. I leave the ruined church and amble round amongst the dunes until I find a beautiful triangular rusty-red coloured stone as my offering. I return and place it gently at the altar end with a blessing in honour of St Piran.

ST PIRAN'S ORATORY

I now head off to seek out St Piran's Oratory. A notice directs me to a very large mound. I climb the steps to discover a small granite stone with a tablet at its base which reads *'This Stone is dedicated to the Glory of God and in memory of St*

Piran, Irish Missionary and Patron Saint of Tinners, who came to Cornwall in the 6th Century. Beneath this stone is buried the oratory which bears his name erected on the site hallowed by his prayers.' One cannot see the oratory itself yet I am visibly moved as I stand before the inscription, picturing the saint spending hours at his devotions in this very spot. As a sacred gesture I place six little stones close to the tablet in the shape of the six pointed star.

I withdraw from the oratory and go in search of any remains of the monastery which might be visible in the sand dunes. It is quite exhilarating walking in the dunes with the high wind buffeting me. The tall pale sand-dusted maram grass is leaning almost to the ground. I spy some beautiful shiny sea-snail shells with their perfect spiral formation. They are pink and bluey-grey and look as if they have been bleached by years of exposure to the sun. I collect a few to take away with me. After a bit of a search I find nothing and return to my car. Before leaving for Devon, I decide to take a look at the St Michael Church in Perranporth and the new church dedicated to St Piran on the hill. However I am to be disappointed on both accounts, as they are closed and there is no key available - familiar tale! This is the end of my day - lack of time prevents me from visiting Cubert and Holywell - they will have to wait until my next pilgrimage.

RETURN TO THE NORTH COAST

It was to be some weeks before I was able to revisit this area to complete my explorations. Eventually an opportunity to return to Cornwall for my 3rd pilgrimage arose about the middle of March, after my home Ceremony for Portreath. I was asked by the Lady Mary to conduct a Light Ceremony at Castle-an-Dinas which I did on Day 1 (see Chapter 7). But for now - my second day, we rejoin Mary at Cubert, in order to keep her pilgrimage in logical order. My plan is to look for the Cubert settlement where Mary and her family stayed, visit Cubert Church, go to Holywell Beach and find the Holy Well.

This time I am based at Treyarnon Bay Youth Hostel and a glance at my map tells me the distance to Cubert as the crow flies, is about thirteen miles. I plan a good easy route in order to avoid the large and busy town of Newquay. But then hey presto, what do I do, change my mind - well it's the car actually - it turns right at the first junction from the hostel rather than left! I am therefore now taking the quiet winding coastal road which goes through Newquay, which turns out to be a very pleasant route. The sun has its work cut out today in order to penetrate the thick sea mist, but it does eventually break through. I drive on via Porthcothan, Trenance and Mawgan Porth to eventually reach Newquay town where I discover that the directional signs for *'Through Routes'* are clear and simple to follow - even for me!

ST CUBERT PARISH CHURCH

The Church of St Cubert stands in the centre of Cubert village. On a hill, it is three hundred feet above Penhale Sands and is visible for many miles. In actuality I see the church spire well before the church itself. It is not the norm for a Cornish church to have a spire, as most display Norman towers. I pull up nearby, step from the car and walk the few yards to the church. On entering a feeling of utter peace descends on me.

St Cubert was a Welsh missionary of the seventh century, who crossed the Bristol Channel to establish a church in Cornwall. He eventually returned to Wales to become abbot of his monastery. It is thought that the first church here would have been a small building of simple wooden structure with a thatched roof, later replaced by a stone built church with a slate roof. The present church was built around the fourteenth century, with later additions in the fifteenth century - its spire being added sometime later. I look around this beautiful little church with its oak barrelled roof and two rows of white stone arches running down its length. The stained glass windows which are exceptionally fine are memorials to members of the local Hosken family. By the altar is an embroidered banner depicting a haloed St Cubert dressed in a brown habit, with his staff. There is legend that his relics were placed in a tomb, in what is now a vacant recess in the south transept of the church.

I find myself at the Lady Chapel, wherein the sun is making waves of light as it shines through a clear glass window. There is a statue of Our Lady holding the infant Jesus on her lap. I pay my 10p for a votive candle and place it in a wrought iron holder. I light it and as the flame leaps into life, I am saying: *"Beloved Mary this is for you. I honour you."* I look at my watch - 12.00 noon - perfect for a short attunement. The interior of the little church is cold, but a warm pink glow fills my heart centre as Mary draws close:

MARY

"Welcome to this little church of St Cubert. Thank you for your offering. We are pleased that you have made this pilgrimage. I will guide you to my Holy Well and to the settlement where we rested you and I many years ago. You will find much inspiration and joy in being here. There is much in this area of Cornwall which will bring back past-life memories for you. This land holds sacred memories for us all dear daughter. Our physical journeying was quite arduous at times, but we all felt filled with the Holy Light, yes even you dear Naomi, as a child was aware of the Cosmic Life (in answer to my unvoiced question). *We were a small band of travellers, but we had much protection on the physical level and from the Angelic Beings and Masters of Light. There were times when we were ALL overshadowed by the ancient Cosmic Light. This knowledge bound us together in everlasting love and humility. May the Angels of Light walk with you on your pilgrimage as shall I dear sister. Amen."*

I acknowledge Beloved Mary's precious words and offer a heart blessing. I leave this little sanctuary in silence. Outside sparrows are happily chirruping away in the March sunshine, welcoming a new spring. Before moving on I do a little explore of Cubert village. It appears to have all a village should have for a thriving active community; a church, church hall, shop, café, pub, school, playing fields and so forth.

TO HOLYWELL BEACH

I carry on to the coast at Holywell, an evocative name given that Beloved Mary and the boy Jesus would have graced this area with their Holy presence. As I am driving down the hill to the bay, what a vista befalls my eyes; a white sandy beach, high dunes, sea rolling in across shimmering sands, blue sky - picture postcard perfect. With my car parked, I walk a track of fine silvery sand towards the beach over a tiny wooden bridge which crosses a gently flowing stream. The small pebbles in the stream's bed are sparkling in the sunlight. On the banks of these clear waters are some little daisies, white petals fully opened to absorb the sun's rays, yellow centres like golden jewels. I am now following the stream down to the beach. The wild cry of seagulls is coming across on the still air. This ancient land is enveloping me. I am soon 'lost' in an inner sense with the wonder of this place and am already running out of superlatives.

Lovely seashells are everywhere on this beach. It could have taken its name from Shell Island near Harlech in North Wales. I pick a few choice ones to keep by me for offerings and in order to transfer their energies elsewhere on my pilgrimage. Walking down to the sea, some magnificent pyramidal shaped rocks come into view, rising like great grey whales out of the greeny-blue waters surrounding them. These bring to mind another memory of Wales - this time South Wales. There is a beach which has similar huge grey triangular rocks in exactly the same position, and that is Three Cliffs Bay on the Gower Coast, which is for me truly one of the most splendid places on Earth. Deciding to take a closer look at the rocks, I head off across the shallow stream which has by now spread out across the beach. But after attempting a rather precarious crossing sinking ever deeper into the shifting watery sands, I beat a hasty retreat. It is as if the whole beach is one vast quagmire at this point. Instead, I turn and trace the waters edge its full length, before walking back through the sand dunes. The sound of the sea gives way to the silence of the dunes. A pure white feather is presented to me on route by the Angels.

ST MARY'S HOLY WELL

I am ready now to look for Mary's Holy Well. It is written that St Cubert could have baptized his converts at this well, but I believe the dedication goes back much further - to the Lady Mary. According to the map, the well is on a hill overlooking Holywell Beach, so I began my ascent of the little road out of the village. Rather than go on a wild well chase amongst a huge estate of houses I see before me, I ask a gentlemen tending his garden for assistance - he gives me clear directions. He also tells me of two magical caves on the beach itself. Perhaps if there is time and the tide is right, I shall return to the beach later.

Entrance to St Mary's Holy Well, Holywell Bay

St Mary's Holy Well, Holywell Bay

It is a bit of an uphill pull but my slow pace allows time for me to observe the hedgerows, which are filled with hazelnut catkins, today lit up by the sun and dancing in the breeze. I turn left into the Golf Course as instructed and ask the 'nice lady' on the reception desk if she can inform me where the ancient well is. She is very helpful and directs me across the golf course, but warns that I could be up to my knees in deep water at the well. I carefully cross the green keeping an eye out for flying golf balls. I think I can see it - down in a little valley. Excitedly I walk down the hill until I reach the gateway to the Holy Well.

The entrance is a large granite-stone edifice with a Gothic arch on top of which is a white granite Jesus cross. There is a recess at the bottom right which could possibly have held a statue. I look through the arch into the old stone well a few feet away. Ahead of me is the deep water I was warned about. However, it turns out to be only ankle deep which I manage to negotiate by jumping on stones and large chunks of turf. As I peer into the inner world of this Holy Well I am quite mesmerized. Directly ahead of me crystal clear water is trickling down through incandescent mossy greenery, which over centuries has become melded together. No sun reaches this little sanctuary, but somehow it is glistening in the light. There is a stone arch on top of which are two small recesses, obviously meant for offerings. Once more I attempt a water crossing, until I am seated on one of two narrow stone seats within the confines of this inner world. I am feeling now as if time is standing still in my little secret dell. Others have been here before me and left offerings and messages on the walls.

I ask of the water deva if I may collect a little of the pure well water, which I do. Then as an offering, I pour some of the water collected from St Just's Holy Well in the Roseland Peninsula. For my beloved Mary, I leave the white feather which I received from the Angels earlier. For the saints of old and especially for St Cubert, I lay down a small white quartz crystal. I sit quietly for a long time tuning into the past times and feeling the vibrational energies of this sacred place. Obviously, when Mary was here, there would have not been all this stonework surrounding what was probably a small natural spring coming from within the Earth. I have a vision of Mary drinking of the waters. I am sure Naomi, Jesus and Joseph would have done likewise? I dip in my fingers and gently flick a little of the healing waters over my head then touch my brow centre. I have already offered a blessing for this sacred place and now receive these few words from its protector:

GUARDIAN OF THE WELL

"Pilgrim you are most welcome. You have reached this ancient place by dint of perseverance and trust. Enjoy the sanctity and peace of Mary's Holy Well."

TO THE MAGICAL CAVES

I acknowledge the guardian then reluctantly take my leave. The water from the well gathers in a pool, which in turn feeds into a small stream running through a narrow valley to the beach. This is my return pathway which as I set off I realize is seldom used, as overhead branches form low arches, under which I have to stoop to pass through. A robin is serenading me and a chiff-chaff is calling from the hedgerows. The sound of the burbling stream reaches my ears. This bewitching realm belongs to the little people who obviously nurture it with much dedication and love. As I follow this little secret way by the stream I can imagine travellers of old - pilgrims and saints - coming from Holywell beach and finding their way up a path such as this, to drink of the waters of the well. What welcome refreshment after perhaps a difficult sea voyage or tiring overland journey?

Eventually my path opens to an expanse of rabbit-warrened field. I am at the bottom end of the golf course though outside its confines. I walk through a little gate onto the coastal footpath. From here I have choice. I can either take the track to the left, which would lead me back to Holywell village or go to the right and seek out the caves. The right wins. Two ravens croak an acknowledgement. Merlin's energies would be very powerful here, as there is much ado about Arthur throughout Cornwall, and in this area particularly so, as we are not far away from Tintagel Castle, King Arthur's alleged birthplace. I cross a field to the cliff top which takes me to the sand dunes. I run down the last high dune with such exuberance that I arrive at the beach at a rather faster pace than I would have wished!

I have been told that the caves are at the far side of the beach and can only be reached at low tide. Bearing this in mind, the water looks too high for me to reach where I think the caves could be. I stare at the distant rocks with the waves crashing over them, thinking that it is not meant to be, but then something makes me spin round and look to cliffs at the back of the beach. I do believe I can see some caves and as I get closer - yes I am right. I enter a magical world. The roof and the walls are covered with indescribable beauty. Water percolating through the minerals within the rocks, has generated scintillating colours; yellows, golds, vivid pinks, blue-greys and shades of green - all blending in. Combined with this, the calcium carbonate deposits have produced formations of the most fascinating shapes. I am entranced.

I walk back over the beach and dunes to my car. I have found much joy in being here as Mary predicted. Returning to Cubert I now attempt to find the settlement where Mary and her family stayed. According to my map, the road leaving Cubert runs right through it. I stop and do a search, but there is just nothing - nothing visible in the landscape that could denote an ancient site was here. This happens of course in many places - fields ploughed up - stones cleared for the farmer's convenience - that's the way it is. I am sure that Mary has guided me to the correct place, but I have tried and can do more. It is the end of my day and time to return to Treyarnon. Mary's pilgrimage along the coast of North Cornwall has come to an end.

CHAPTER 7
CAMEL CORNER
Celtic Churches in the Landscape

From Cubert the Lady Mary accompanied by Jesus, Naomi and Joseph, continued her pilgrimage east to a settlement at Porth, then on to Castle-an-Dinas Hill Fort. After participating in a Ceremony where Mary reactivated the ancient Atlantean Temple in the Etheric, Joseph and Jesus left the group once more. Meanwhile, Mary and Naomi journeyed over St Breock Downs, across the River Camel to Brea Hill Druidic settlement. They met with Joseph and Jesus at Port Issac before they all headed south to Castle Killibury.

It is the 17th March, St Patricks day, as I begin my 3rd pilgrimage to Cornwall. I worked tirelessly last evening into the wee small hours in order to bring all my notes up to date. My accommodation is booked at Treyarnon Bay Youth Hostel on Cornwall's north coast. My priority on this pilgrimage as 'instructed' by Mary, is to earth the Atlantean Temple at Castle-an-Dinas, so this will be my first stop. Conscious of my forthcoming Ceremony, before I leave this morning, I speak with Beloved Mary and the Master Jesus, this blessed soul who seems to be drawing ever closer as my Mission with Mary progresses: *"Beloved ones, let me walk in your footsteps. Let me share in your vision for our ancient British Isles. Let me be a pure channel for this sacred work. Let me be mindful of the task ahead and worthy of the honour bestowed upon me. I offer this sacred day to the Great White Spirit and all Angels. As above so below."* I receive:

BELOVED MARY

"My beloved child. Walk with your hand in the hand of the Master - our blessed Jesus, and all will be well. May the blessings of the Great Spirit be upon you as you walk this sacred land."

JOURNEY TO CAMEL CORNER.

My pilgrimage to Cornwall begins in sunshine which is to be the pattern for the next four days. Spring has really sprung into action at last. Outside my window golden daffodils bring a lift to the soul and pale yellow-petalled primroses are gracing our country lanes once again. Trees in bud are making preparation for their fresh green mantle. Mother Earth is indeed awakening from her slumbers as evidence of new life is all around.

I set off about 10.00 am, my aim to reach Castle-an-Dinas in time for 12.00 noon. I drive west along the southern fringe of Dartmoor, which today is lit up in the morning sun. I pass the sign to Buckfast Abbey and I am remembering one of my early encounters with Our Lady in the Chapel of the Blessed Sacrament within the abbey (see Chapter 11). This chapel houses the wonderful stained glass mosaic east window of the Master Jesus. Once again his presence enters my consciousness. I cross the River Tamar over the road bridge, glancing to my left and right to see the sunlight dancing on the vast expanse of water far below. Happy am I to be back on Cornish soil.

I think all is going splendidly until I try to turn right from the A30 for Castle-an-Dinas, just two miles from the village of Victoria. There is no way off! I am puzzled, because looking at my map, there appears to be turnings off this road in that direction. I do have an old map, so perhaps the road design has changed or maybe I have just misread the map. Whatever - I sail past my planned exit. Glancing over to my right, I see a hill which instinct tells me is Castle-an-Dinas. I continue on to Indian Queens, turning right to Rosewastis, after which another right takes me to the turn off for Castle-an-Dinas. Driving down a dirt track I eventually reach the car park for the castle.

CASTLE-AN-DINAS HILL FORT

I have misjudged my timing today as it is now close on midday, the hour I had scheduled for my Ceremony. By the time I walk to Castle-an-Dinas, explore and find a suitable place to hold my Ceremony, it will to be very much later. I have to accept this - I am sure the Angels will understand. This acknowledged, the pressure is off and I can relax. I tune in to the Land of Light to send out healing for our World, then to Beloved Mary asking for her blessing on the sacred Ceremony ahead of me. Now for some refreshment.

At the start of the track which leads to Castle-an-Dinas is an information plaque by Cornwall Heritage. It tells me that this hill fort dates from between 400 BC and AD 150. As evidence of this dating, excavations in the 1960s have revealed post holes for a circular timber house near the main castle entrance and some pieces of pottery. However, two Bronze Age barrows within the main circle of the fort, would take this date back even further, to at least 2,000 BC. The castle standing at seven hundred feet commands extensive views over the surrounding countryside, which in times past would have secured this site as a valuable strategic position. Elsewhere I have read that in Arthurian legend Castle-an-Dinas was one of the hunting lodges of King Arthur.

I begin the short walk up the track entering the ancient site through a five-barred gate. At this point I speak with the guardian and feel a welcome from the ancestors. As I reach the hill fort itself, I see that the ramparts and ditches look to be in good order. I take the little path leading through the ramparts to its grassy top. Up here the air element is certainly working overtime, as I am being nearly bowled over with the high wind. I walk over to investigate the two burial mounds, standing for a few minutes at each one sensing the past. On the earth at my feet I see a lovely flat circular stone imbued with sparkly bits, which I pocket, saying a thank you to the ancients. There is a pond indicating an obvious source of water - possibly a well. I cross the diameter of the fort and through to one of the ditches on its far side. I am now feeling impressed to walk its whole circle, so begin a slow perambulation in a clockwise direction. As I go I am visualizing the ancient Atlantean Temple in the Etheric Realm. The air is filled with the sweet song of a skylark and the sound of the rushing wind. I reach the original castle entrance and find myself thinking of weary travellers of times long ago, as Mary and her little group would have been, wending their way on horseback into the sanctuary of this then Druidic settlement.

CASTLE-AN-DINAS ATLANTEAN TEMPLE CEREMONY

Back on the summit, I am wondering where to perform my Ceremony. Up here it is too exposed to the wind and people watchers, although I must say that at this moment in time I have the place to myself. I drop down to the far side once again and into the outer ditch, settling down underneath a rather wind-worn hawthorn tree. I ensure that my space is cleared of bracken and rough grasses apologizing to the little people for any disturbance. This is perfect - I am in the lee of the ramparts on either side. As I look up all I can see is my little section of a vast azure-blue sky. A large curious bumble bee comes to pay me a visit and flies off. Sitting on my mat facing east, I carefully lay out on my small white cloth all the accoutrements needed. A miracle and a blessing - the living flame from my candle within its protective tin stays alive during the whole of my attunement.

Let my Ceremony begin. I visualize the Cosmic Light in the form of a huge Star at its highest point in the Universe, pouring the Christ Light down to encircle this sacred site. Each of my crystals have been blessed and offered to the highest good; for the Lady Mary and the Goddess energies - the pink quartz crystal, for Is-Ra and ancient Egypt - the turquoise crystal, for Merlin - my merlinite crystal, and for our Druidic ancestors, a large white quartz crystal. My link with the Angels and the Masters of Light is pure and powerful. I become aware of our connection with the expansive Cosmic life and of the Great Crystal at the centre of the Earth. This is sacred land - land before time as we know it. The ancient civilizations of Lemuria, Hyperborea and Atlantis are forming in my consciousness. As the sacred words are spoken, my inner vision shows me the ancient Atlantean Temple, its columns glistening white, riding the airwaves as it comes to rest on the top of Castle-an-Dinas. An Ancient One is standing before me, in long white flowing robes, as if he has stepped right out of the past:

PRIEST OF THE OLD TIMES

"We welcome you Sister of Light. Thank you for the service you have extended to all humanity this day. We bless your endeavours. All the Masters of the Light thank you. My child you are right, our beloved Jesus the Master of true compassion and everlasting love, did indeed come to our sacred centre here at Castle-an-Dinas as it is now called, with his beloved mother Mary and you dear Naomi. It is here at Castle-an-Dinas he received inner knowledge of his pending journey and ministry. He was just a boy, but one through which the Light shone out to all he touched. The boy Jesus was as in tune with the Elemental Kingdoms as he was with the Angelic Realms. There was nothing beyond his reach - nothing beyond his care and compassion He was a friend to all and master of himself - even as a boy.

He came but once to this place but his essence stays - it is embedded in the soil - in the rocks - in the very earth on which you are now resting. The boy Jesus was a great joy to his mother. It was she also who made a profound sacrifice in order to 'lose' her precious son to the cross. Mary was very human and the loss for her was almost unbearable. She was from the higher realms of Cosmic Life, but had offered to undertake this profound and sacred task of bringing this blessed Master of ancient times, into the world - to temporarily lose his physical presence. Mary the mother, the Goddess, was of ancient lineage. We knew of her pending visit with the boy Jesus. It was written in the Stars and held in the Cosmic memory. May the Cosmic Light and Divine Love always be a part of your pathway dear Sister."

For a while all was silent immersed as I was in my inner world. But as this Elder leaves me I am picking up external sounds. There is a tractor chugging round a nearby field, which as it moves closer, seems to be almost on top of me. Thankfully the driver can not see me as I am in one of the ditches! A light plane is overhead. Once more I am aware of the wind and the lark's song. I offer my gratitude for this blessed communication. I thank the Cosmic Beings for their presence and protection this sacred day. I now ground myself and ensure all my psychic centres are sealed. I continue to sit in contemplative thought for at least half an hour so reluctant am I to leave, but eventually leave I must. It is later on reading my notes that I am drawn to the words: *'to 'lose' her precious son to the cross'* and *'to temporarily lose his physical presence.'* This 'loss' has been mentioned before by White Eagle during my Christmas Reflections. It does not sit comfortably with me, as it is my belief that Jesus did not die on the cross (see end of this Chapter). I can only think that maybe the interpretation of 'loss/lose' is different to our understanding of it. Perhaps the very human Mary, being witness to her precious son on the cross, caused a temporary loss of faith, for that intimate moment? Or perhaps she knew they would be physically parted for the rest of that lifetime?

I return to the central plateau. At the pool I pour into the still clear waters with a blessing, a little of the sacred water recently collected from Becca Brook below Hay Tor on Dartmoor. There is an enormous granite stone and it is here that I bury my pink quartz crystal for Beloved Mary. For the ancient

Druids, I place on top of the stone a large piece of granite containing feltzpar and particles of crystal quartz, from an ancient settlement in the Becca Valley of Dartmoor. Mission accomplished, I take my leave with a final benediction.

After Mary's sacred Ceremony for the Atlantean Temple, Joseph and Jesus went their own way, while Mary and Naomi took a journey east to a settlement at Rosehill, which on the map is north of Lanivet. I knew they had visited this settlement, but wondered how they had reached it, because by then I had charted most of Mary's pilgrimage around Cornwall and there was no way I could see her staying at Rosehill as she went south from Port Isaac. I pondered this for some while until I hit on the idea that she and Naomi could have travelled on an unrelated journey from Castle-an-Dinas. Once I 'sussed' this out and was given a positive answer, I wondered why they should make such a journey and chanced upon the notion - to meet with family. Thank you Mary.

Continuing their journey north from Castle-an-Dinas, Mary and Naomi rode over St Breock Downs to a settlement at Brea Hill on the far side of the Camel Estuary. Me - I now leave Castle-an-Dinas for the hostel at Treyarnon Bay stopping off to visit St Columb Major Church.

ST COLUMB MAJOR CHURCH

The Parish Church of St Columb Major is a well restored fourteenth century church dedicated to St Columba, a Celtic Holy woman from Ireland. Inside is a beautiful statue of St Colomba with her dove emblem, the symbol of purity. The Lady Chapel also has a statue - a striking bronze of the Lady Mary. On the north wall, is a flagpole with an emblem of a chough, the bird making a comeback in the Lizard Peninsula. It is the standard of the 11th Battalion of the Home Guard. Onward....

TO TREYARNON BAY

The way takes me via a series of quiet country lanes lined with row upon row of sunlit daffodils on grass verges or as borders to cottages. On reaching the village of Treyarnon, I take the narrow no-through road to Treyarnon Beach, then up a little track to the hostel which is situated on a low cliff-top overlooking the bay. Memories come flooding back. I have stayed here on numerous occasions, but had forgotten what a wonderful position this hostel is in. I see that the rather shabby building of old has been 'poshed up' and includes a new extension incorporating a café, which may also be used by the general public. Before I enter I walk out onto the cliff. A splendid sight opens before me of a magnificent expanse of sandy beach with white-crested waves rolling in. No wonder this hostel is the haunt of families and surfers alike. It is also a regular stopping off point for walkers doing the South West Way long distance coastal footpath from Minehead in Somerset around Lands End to Dorset. A startlingly bright sun hovering in a blue blue sky offers a line of silvery light over the sea. I think I have just arrived in paradise!

At the hostel I settle in and before it gets dark wander down to the beach. The sands offer up a treasure - a gift from the Angels of a beautiful large chunk of sparkling white quartz. I do a thorough search of the sands but it appears to be the only piece around as if it has just materialized from the ethers. I saunter across the beach and watch the waves pounding over the rocks on its far side - the wild spray rushing in, forms deep watery pools. Scrambling up over the rocks I reach the top of the cliff and return to the hostel. The sun is now a huge red ball of light framed within a tangerine sky, which is pouring into the horizon of the sea, sending a pathway of golden light across the waters in front of me. What a climax to an incredible first day.

ON ROUTE TO ST BREOCK DOWNS

The next day I paid my visit to Cubert and Holywell which I have already documented. It is now Day 3 of my pilgrimage and my plan is to seek out the settlement on St Breock Downs through which Mary travelled as she proceeded to the Camel Estuary and take in a few churches on the way. What an understatement - as this turns out to be a 'day of churches'.

ST MERRYN CHURCH

A couple of miles inland from Treyarnon is St Merryn which lies in the direction of Breock Downs settlement, so my first stop is its Parish Church. To my delight I discover it is open, which turns out to be the same for most of the churches hereabouts, unlike those in the Redruth area. St Merryn was a sixth century Celtic missionary priest born of a noble family in West Wales. He studied at Bangor before undertaking his missionary work in Wales, Cornwall and Brittany.

There is quite a contrast as I move from the bright sunshine into the cool dark interior of this little church. A fine arcade of seven pillars and Gothic arches separate the nave from the south aisle. Looking up I see an impressive fifteenth century wagon roof with some rather strange bosses, which appear to represent the Green Man. I stand before a beautiful Mothers Union hanging tapestry in rich blue, illustrating the Virgin Mary. I offer a special prayer and blessing for our beloved Mary and leave a small pink quartz crystal.

CHURCH OF ST PETROC MINOR, LITTLE PETHERICK.

I have just pulled into the car park on the old wharf and quay at the centre of the village of Little Petherick, which lies at the top of a now silted up river valley running down to the Camel Estuary. One would assume that in days past, the river would have been free flowing, thus allowing much trade to pass this way. I look up at the church of St Petroc Minor, which seems to be woven into the fabric of a beautiful wooded hillside. Rather than entering the church immediately, I find myself following a little pathway through the trees into the graveyard. I am greeted by a carpet of primroses, the petals open to receive the sun's warmth. I sit down on a bench seat, face to the sun and have a few moments of bliss. As an offering and thank you for this peaceful little place, so obviously well tended by the nature spirits, I lay down a white feather and a seashell from Holywell Beach.

I enter into the sanctuary of the little church. The outside has given me no indication of the splendours I am to behold within. Its interior is quite awe-inspiring and dominated by an exquisite gilded and coloured rood screen. This was carved by one man J. Ninian Comper, to become Sir Ninian Comper. In the late nineteenth century he was employed by the then patron of the church with a remit to restore the dilapidated church to its former glory. What a masterpiece he produced, bringing back some idea of the wonders of this medieval building. It was dedicated in 1908. The chancel section of the rood screen heralds a central figure of our Lord, to his left the Blessed Virgin Mary, on the right St John, each flanked by six winged Seraphim. The section over the Lady Chapel portrays an image of: *'The Thrones, a wheel in the middle of a wheel full of eyes, round and about four winged and flaming'*. This description from *'Church Trails in Cornwall - The Padstow area'* is a Biblical phrase from Ezekiel 1 & 10. Here is my interpretation of what I see before me: *'This wonderful gilded image portrays two interlocking wheels each surrounding a central feature of a Human/Angelic sun-face, which in turn is placed at the centre of an eight pointed cross. Within the circumference of each wheel are sixteen eyes and on its outer edge two pairs of wings.'* To me the whole is representative of the vast Cosmic Plan in ancient symbology - the Great Sun, the Circle of Life and the All Seeing Eye. Within the Lady Chapel, is a fine carved and gilded reredos, with our Lord magnificent at its centre and figures of the Virgin Mary, St John the Divine, St Frances, St Petroc and St Anthony of Padua. I sit in the pervading stillness looking at the wonders before me, thinking of the dedication and patience with which Comper must have carried out his work. For everyday folk of the past, to enter such a magnificent building, must have seemed that they had truly encountered Heaven itself. Before I exit I stand in front of a most beautifully carved white stone statue of St Petroc with his tame wolf and offer a benediction.

ST ISSEY CHURCH

A short way down the road I come across the splendid Church of St Issey. I pull into the parking area and take an early lunch break. The car park is surrounded by tall trees topped with rookeries. Rooks are very vocal birds at the best of times, but in the springtime it would seem that their volume increases ten-fold. Funny birds rooks - birds of duel personality! I consider them to be quite stalwart creatures as they build their nests of bits of twig at the top of tall trees, very precariously placed for high winds. However sitting in my car, when I throw out a few little bits of bread for them, they become scaredicats! They are big birds so can't very easily sneak up on me, but I have the camera at the ready just in case. I enter the churchyard through the lych gate offering a blessing. Standing beneath one of the magnificent trees I thank the nature spirits for their dedicated work in keeping this sacred space so beautiful. I hear:

DEVA

"Thank you pilgrim for acknowledging our presence and the work we do to care for this little churchyard. You may leave us now to continue your journeying with Mary."

I salute the deva, metaphorically speaking, thinking that his words are short and to the point as so often happens.

Opening the old oak door I step over the threshold of St Issey Church. I was expecting it to be immersed in silence, but instead the atmosphere is married slightly by the murmer of voices. However, a lovely lady comes out of the vestry and asks if I would like to join them for a coffee. How kind - but I politely refuse.

The Church is dedicated to St Issey, Virgin and Abbess, who hailed from Ireland. There is no actual record of St Issey having visited Cornwall, but her nephew was a disciple of St Petroc. Issey or Itha means 'thirst' and St Issey was endowed with this name because of her thirst for the living waters of Holy Truth. It is written that there has been a church on this site since the seventh century. I note a couple of things of particular interest. Around the arches of the chancel is charming decorative Victorian stencil work portraying the rose in a delicate pink and the lily in very pale green, both representative of the Lady Mary. In the Lady Chapel is a fourteenth century pieta of the Blessed Virgin with the body of Christ in her lap, one of only nine in the country. It is carved from Catacleuse stone and its beauty is marked by its devout simplicity. I take time for a short attunement before leaving this delightful little church. As I sit in the silence I am aware of Mary and am able to hold this precious link for a short while. Near the porch I lay two small beautifully formed white stones from Dartmoor, which I have brought with me as offerings.

TO ST BREOCK CHURCH AND DOWNS

Back in the car I open up my map for I need to choose my route to St Breock Downs carefully in order to avoid Wadebridge and decide the best way is via Burlawn. However, I come unstuck because the little road from Polmorean to Burlawn has a '*Road Closed*' sign and diversion signs take me through - yes Wadebridge! I find myself close to St Breock Church so decide to take a quick peek before heading up to the downs. I turn into the narrowest of Cornish lanes but one of the prettiest, lined with spring flowers; celandine, primroses, daffodils and violets. The little church nestles amongst the trees in a peaceful secluded valley. This delightful scene comes alive as the spring flower theme runs through the churchyard. There is a stream - its waters sparkling in the sunlight, over which is a small stone bridge. The church is closed. I see a tiny cottage set within a rose garden at the end of the churchyard path. I am sure I shall be able to get a key here. At a rather rickety entrance gate some dogs rush up barking and snarling. I talk nicely to them - they calm down and wander off. I am about to enter when I see a scrappy little notice *'Beware of Dogs - please ring bell'*. I ring the bell twice but no answer. I decide to err on the side of caution as I am not very valiant when it comes to dogs, especially the snarly ones. Sorry, but I shall have to give this one a miss.

The Menhir at St Breock Downs

Eventually I come to the windmills on the hill, which I am told is one of the identifying features of St Breock Downs. According to my map there is a standing stone, a longstone, a burial chamber and several tumuli, all indicative of an ancient settlement. I pull up where I believe I may gain access to the burial chamber, to realize that I am at the gated entrance to the E-On St Breock Wind Farm. This is private land so no joy here. Looking in the other direction, there are just no visible landmarks of a settlement and the whole area is one of thigh-high impenetrable gorse and brambles. Then I see a little track which I think could take me to the standing stone. A car is parked up at the beginning of the track, which looks to be a fire inspector's vehicle. I ask the off-duty fireman sitting at the wheel having his lunch, if he knows of a standing stone or ancient settlement close-by. He looks at me blankly and says: *"sorry"*. It is obvious he has no idea what I am talking about, so I give up on him. I am about to walk away, when I turn and in the distance behind his car is what I am looking for - my standing stone - success. I walk up the track saying: *'thank you - thank you'* to Mary and the Universe. The menhir is magnificent - about ten foot in height at a guess. I lean with my back against this massive stone feeling its powerful vibrations and beautiful energies. From a certain angle, the stone has a face which appears to replicate those on Easter Island in the Pacific. In the long grass at one side of the stone I tuck in a black and white feather and small piece of white quartz to honour the Druids. I return to my car. Even though I have been unable to discover any more of the ancient site, it has been good to be on these high downs over which Mary journeyed.

I see two other interesting names marked on my map - Nine Maidens and The Fiddler, a few miles to the west of St Breock Downs and just off the main road to Wadebridge. I think I'll take a look on my return to Treyarnon. I leave the downs taking the little road to Roseannon and eventually to Winnards Perch where I pick up the A39. However, once on this road which is fancifully called *'The Atlantic Highway'* - a rather grand name for a Cornish two lane road - can I get off it to where I wish to go? No way. There are no turnings or lay-bys in the right vicinity - never mind. Back at Treyarnon I have memories of a happy day.

TAKING LEAVE OF TREYARNON

I come to the final day of my pilgrimage and I am to say a sad farewell to this magnificent part of Cornwall with its vast beaches and wild seas, for my home county of Devon. Once again, I am blessed with a sunshiny day as I prepare to take my leave of the youth hostel. To keep the cost down I self-cater and have packed just enough food for four days. This morning I am using the last; dribble of milk, teabag and two pieces of bread with a little cheese for my sandwich - sad isn't it! I don't do full-scale meals when hostelling, but live economically and have very simple fare which seems to suit me. Perhaps this frugal way of being is indicative of my travelling past.

Today promises to be a full one. My aim is to visit the ancient Druidic site of Brea Hill where Mary and Naomi stayed. From St Breock Downs they had journeyed through Bodellick to the Camel estuary, where they took a boat across to Cant Hill and on to the settlement. Before I reach Brea Hill I shall no doubt do a round-about trip via a few churches! My first stopping off place is to be Padstow where I especially wish to visit the Parish Church of St Petroc. I drive the short distance through St Merryn which brings me directly into Padstow and park up at the top of town.

CHURCH OF ST PETROC, PADSTOW.

Leaving the car park a sign directs me to St Petroc's Church. I follow an easy track above the town at the edge of well established woodland. The church, of which I am getting tantalizing glimpses, nestles within a tranquil wooded haven in the valley. St Petroc was a Welshman of noble birth educated in an Irish monastery. It is documented that on arriving in the Padstow

Estuary, he established his church and monastery here in the sixth century. In AD 981 it was destroyed by Vikings and the monastery removed to Bodmin. A second church was built in the twelfth century, which due to the material used - beachrock and sandstone - did not last. The present church with its Norman tower dates back to the fifteenth century.

As I enter the church through its heavy oak door, my first impression is one of space and light. It has the traditional white Gothic arched columns. There are many fine fittings and memorials. Not least among them is the Jacobean wineglass style pulpit which dates from the sixteenth century. Well placed for viewing, is the memorial to Sir Nicholas Prideaux who built the local Prideaux Place in that same century. Then there is a medieval font which has sculptured figures of the twelve apostles in niches around it and at the four corners, angels each holding the book of life. To my eye a marble carving of Jesus and his disciples is quite stunningly beautiful. The stained glass east window shows Christ in Glory, St Petroc and King Arthur. The Lady Chapel has a striking modern oil painting of Our Lady by a local artist, which illustrates Mary dressed in a blue robe standing against a background of vibrant colours; golds, oranges and reds. Sitting in one of the pews I am aware of the silence percolating through this Holy place. I sense a presence close to me. It is St Petroc and he offers me the following few words:

ST PETROC

"Welcome pilgrim to the sanctity of my church. In my day as men of the cloth, we travelled far - long distances over land and across the water to bring the Word of the Lord to the people. I myself brought the Message of Christ to this part of Cornwall and set up initially my little church at Petherick. Now this beautiful church in Padstow is dedicated to my name. However, it was not in the trappings of grandeur or in the comforts of such places that we found our destiny. Ours was the simple life, the open road, the generosity of those around us who gave alms to support us and bread as sustenance. There was always somewhere to rest our weary bodies. As I said, we travelled far and wide. I myself came from what is now called Wales to Cornwall, then on south, by river and overland to the south coast of Cornwall and on into the Breton country. My life was filled with the Holy Spirit and I was greatly blessed. Walk on dear pilgrim. May the blessing of our Lord walk with you."

I am saying: *"thank you blessed St Petroc for your communication this day."*

St Petroc tells us that: *'I......set up initially my little church at Petherick.'* This is controversial, because history has it that his first church was at Padstow. In *'The Church of St Petroc - Visitors Guide '* Page 1, it says of St Petroc, that after his arrival at Padstow Estuary: *'he began to build at the top of the creek, the sea level coming further in than at present, first a church, and gradually other buildings, enlarging the establishment into a Celtic monastery.'* At that time even taking account of higher sea levels, Padstow would hardly have been positioned at the top of a creek, whereas Little Petherick has a well defined creek leading to it and better fits the bill. I suggest that St Petroc's original landing place and first church was where he states, at Petherick and that at a later date a second church was established in Padstow, the first one having gone unrecorded.

As I step out into the sunshine, the sound of birdsong fills the warm March air. In the churchyard is a sign *'This is God's Acre'*. This aptly describes this little oasis filled with beautiful trees, underneath which bloom daffodils, narcissi and primroses. I walk along one of the paths and sit on some curved stone steps overlooking all this beauty. St Petroc is with me still. I am also becoming aware of the presence of the elementals who care for this special place. There is a lovely yew tree one of many fine specimens. I have three fine shells which I have brought with me from Shaldon Beach in South Devon. I gently place them in the centre of its hollowed-out trunk for the deva and all his little helpers, with a blessing.

PADSTOW TOWN AND HARBOUR

On leaving the church, I take a lovely pathway through the trees heading down to Padstow seafront. The rhododendrons are being cleared and at the moment the woodland looks to be in a state of disarray. A woodsman tells me that this is being done in order to allow space for native plants to flourish, which will present a more natural look.

Padstow is a bustling little fishing port with narrow streets and little alleyways leading off from the harbour. It is a popular place with visitors and even today early in the season, there are plenty of people meandering around. I remember going through Padstow when walking the South West Way. I reach the harbour with its fishing boats, and small sailing and motor craft moored up. It is here that Rick Stein the well known chef has his famous fish restaurant. Not for me though - I opt for a raspberry and cream icecream with chocolate flake! I enjoy this treat sitting in the sun keeping a sharp lookout for marauding herring gulls. Strolling round the harbour, I come to what looks to be an Elizabethan house built of stone and slate, with granite block doorways and lintels. There is a legend attached to this property, which tells of a secret passage leading up to Prideaux Place, the manor house on the hill above Padstow. It is said that centuries ago an elderly female eccentric had a young lover, who went up through this tunnel in order that they may secretly keep their tryst. Who knows? Walking up a little rise overlooking the harbour I can see across the Camel Estuary to the village of Rock and Brea Hill, my destination later today.

One of Padstow's claims to fame is the famous 'Obby Oss' ceremony which takes place on May Day each year. Its origin goes back to Pagan ritual wherein it is reckoned to be a fertility symbol. So what is an 'Obby Oss?' *'Your Guide to Padstow'* gives a good description: *'The fearsome mask of today's 'Obby Oss' regalia is set into a body covering costume built around a six feet wide circular wooden hoop. This is carried on the wearer's shoulders and covered in sailcloth that is draped down to the ground'* (Page 11). The wearer dances and swirls around the streets of Padstow accompanied by a teazer who leads the dance with theatrical movements. There are followers, their white costumes decorated with ribbons and sprays of cowslips and bluebells, alongside accompanying musicians and drummers. In their wake come any who may wish to join in the parade - old and young alike - dancing and singing the traditional May Day song

ANCIENT TRADE ROUTE

Padstow at the entrance of the Camel Estuary, was the beginning of an ancient trade route to Fowey on the south Cornish coast, which was used by merchants, pilgrims and missionaries. Aerial photography taken between 1965 and 1990, indicate that there were ancient settlements on both sides of the River Camel. Of course one of these could have been Brea Hill where Mary and Naomi stayed. Further, within this northern area of 'Camel Corner' close to the trade route, there is a profusion of old churches, the foundations of which would have been established by the early saints as small daub and wattle structures.

The trade route followed the River Camel to Wadebridge, through the heart of Cornwall via Polbrock to Bodmin. Here the river turns north for Camelford. Travellers wishing to go south from Bodmin, would pick up their lightweight coracles and carry them on their heads the short distance overland, to re-float them in the River Fowey at Newtown, close to Llanhydrock House. From Newton the route was downstream to Lostwithiel and on to the coast at Fowey. From here they could navigate across the English Channel to Brittany and on through France to the Mediterranean. Since prehistoric times, the safe estuary of Fowey would have also been one of the recognized trading routes into Cornwall from foreign parts.

This trade route of the past is today's well signposted long distance walk called *'The Saints Way'*. It was opened in 1986 and goes for approximately twenty-eight miles, following in the footsteps of the early Christian saints and pilgrims, taking in ancient churches, settlements and crosses on route. As yet this trail has eluded me, but it is on my list of 'to-dos' and could perhaps resurrect past life memories.

JOURNEY TO BREA HILL

Tearing myself away from Padstow, I now venture forth to the far side of the Camel Estuary aiming for Brea Hill settlement. On my way I visit three churches in this sacred little corner of Cornwall at; St Kew, St Endellion and St Minver, all of which are within Mary's travelling area. Initially I considered leaving some of these churches out of this work, but to be quite honest, each has merit - treasures - which I would like to share with you. Leaving Padstow I once again drive through Little Petherick and St Issey to Wadebridge. Out the other side, I take a narrow country road to the left just before St Kew Highway for my first church.

CHURCH OF ST JAMES THE GREAT, ST KEW

The St Kew Church can be found in the pretty hamlet of St Kew Churchtown. It is situated next to the village green with its lone weeping willow and myriad wild flowers I park by a little brook.

This fifteenth century church was originally dedicated to St Kew, a Celtic Saint. However in the late nineteenth century, St James became its Patron Saint. I enter by the most amazing oak door whitened with age, which is supported by a substantial modern oak door of the same size attached to the back, the whole held together with an iron strip wrapping around both doors. The front of the door has what looks to be the original iron nails. I carefully creak my way in, to be surrounded by the silence of ages. Historical interest and fascinating artifacts alight before my eyes. Looking up I see the original wagon-beamed roof with carved angels at each main beam. The pulpit has a small square frame with a carved wooden figure of a man up a tree, which it is said could possibly be King Charles II hiding from the Roundheads in the oak tree. In the chancel a fine Edwardian stained glass window depicts St Kew, St Peter and St James with his scallop shell. In honour of St James, I place a small scallop shell within the church porch as I leave - I knew there was a purpose for me bringing this. The window in the South Chapel portrays the 'Tree of Jesse' indicating the genealogy of Christ. Jesse's hand is holding the vine, Mary is cradling the infant Jesus and depicted below are Solomon and David. There is a medieval stone lantern cross which has rather worn carvings of the Resurrection, the Virgin Mary and Child and two saints.

The Ogham Stone at the Church of St James the Great, St Kew

In the south-west corner of the church is an Ogham Stone. Ogham is an ancient Irish script and can often be found marking out a name on a grave or cross. In this case, alongside the ancient script is the same inscription in Latin. No interpretation is offered however of the name imprinted here. As I am set to leave, two people enter the church, take a brief look round and are about to walk out the door without seeing one of its precious artifacts - this Ogham Stone. I am sorry, but I couldn't help but point out this jewel to them, whereby they went over to investigate. I often find that people spend very little time in these wonderful ancient churches, whizzing in, whizzing around and whizzing out again. They do miss so much.

In the churchyard is a single yew tree and for a few minutes I stand beneath its branches offering a blessing for the deva guardian.

THE COLLEGIATE CHURCH OF ST ENDELIENTA

My next visit is to the Collegiate Church of St Endellion established in the thirteenth century. A Collegiate Church is one which has a College or Chapter attached to it, with a dean or provost presiding. St Endelienta was one of the twenty-four offspring - twelve male and twelve female - of a sixth century Welsh King named Brychan, all of whom became saints. Legend has it that her Godfather was King Arthur.

Close to the altar is what remains of the shrine of St Endelienta. The surviving elaborately carved and painted base would have once been topped with a magnificent pillared wooden structure with a reliquary containing the saint's bones and other relics. What particularly draws my attention are two very beautiful icons. One is of St Endelienta and the other of Christ Pantocrator, both 'written' by the Iconographer, John Coleman in 2005. St Endelienta is presented as a young women, dressed in a green mantle over a scarlet inner gown, with expressions of her life in the background. The Greek name Pantocrator means '*All Powerful*' and the Christ figure, wearing mauve and red, over which rests a blue robe, is holding a sacred book.

ST MINVER PARISH CHURCH

A few miles on and I reach the village of St Minver and its Parish Church. St Minver or St Menefreda, is said to have been a sister to St Endelienta. She was one of those saints who with many others of her time, established the ethos of the Christian Church in Cornwall. A church of simple construction has certainly been on this site since Saxon times. The greater part of the present church was built in the fifteenth century.

I am struck by a feeling of absolute calm in this lovely church. There are many examples of beautiful carvings on the old dark oak pew ends. One which is rather amusing, is a sculpture of a 'very devout bird' his head bowed before the altar. I have my quiet time and offer a little prayer before leaving.

THE AGE OF THE SAINTS

During my pilgrimage through Cornwall, I have been drawn to visit some of the extraordinarily large number of churches in the county, especially here in the north close to the River Camel. Churches equal saints and there is an old saying: *'There are more saints in Cornwall than in Heaven'* writes James Mildren in his book *'Saints of the South West'* (Page 11). He suggests that this has been contributed to by King Brychan of Wales with his huge family. I decide to research into this period of British history, a timescale of almost two hundred years, from AD 425 - AD 600, which became known as the 'Age of Saints'.

The Romans had withdrawn from Britain in AD 410, leaving the country with no protection, thus open to raids from across the waters. The Germanic Angles and Saxon invaders, to become known as the Anglo-Saxons, were able to surge through Britain, crushing all in their path. They failed however, to subjugate Cornwall, Devon and Wales, due to difficult terrain and pockets of resistance. For Britain, as for the rest of Europe, this historical period is registered as being the 'Dark Ages' yet in point of fact, it was an age of enlightenment for the ancient Celtic World of the West. By the middle of the fifth century, conversion of the Celts from their ancient religion to Christianity was in progress. It is St German of Auxerre in France, who was the spiritual father of Celtic Christianity. The Celts embraced Jesus the Christ and the Latin liturgy, while maintaining their ancient Druidic belief system and the two were interwoven for over a century.

Wales was the birthplace of many saints such as St Dubricious, St Padarn, St Illtud and St Teilo. A key upholder of the Christian faith in Wales was St David who became its Patron Saint. In AD 430 St Patrick went to Ireland from his native Wales, to begin the conversion of the Irish to Christianity, and subsequently became their Patron Saint. Other Holy men and women from Wales travelled far and wide as missionaries, in order to spread the Gospel of Jesus Christ. Some travelled by boat to Cornwall, where one of the main entry points was the Camel Estuary, from which area they spread throughout the county, evangelizing. There were those who journeyed the route through Cornwall to its south coast at Fowey, and across to Brittany which was once called Amorique. The ties between Cornwall and Amorique were very strong, so much so, that the name given to the south-east of Amorique in those days was Cornouaille (Cornwall).

These Celtic Christian saints rejected the trappings of the Roman Church, but instead chose to live a life of austerity and righteous existence devoted to worship, meditation and prayer. Their base was often a hermitage, from where they would travel the local countryside, preaching. From such an unpretentious beginning, monastic communities were sometimes established, as for example those set up by St Petroc at Padstow and St Piran at Perranzabuloe.

The Christian ministry of these Celtic saints during this 'Age of the Saints' prevailed until AD 597, when St Augustine arrived in Britain with his great mission to convert the whole of Anglo-Saxon England to Christianity. He failed however, to resolve the disparity within the Roman and Celtic Churches, which had to wait until the Synod of Whitby in AD 664, when the resolution came down on the side of Roman Christianity.

JESUS WELL

I now drive on to the village of Rock via the delightfully named hamlet of Pityme. Making my way along the coastal road to the car park at its far end, I feel as if I have arrived in the French Riviera as I pass the fashionable waterfront apartments. Jesus Well close to Rock is on a line with Brea Hill. This is not my route today however, as I shall take the beach and dune pathway. But some years ago I crossed the golf course to reach Jesus Well. I recollect the joy of making my way over the sandy green to this sacred place. The Holy Well is situated in the centre of a square grassy area surrounded by a neatly built, dry stone wall - three feet high and topped with turf. The crystal clear waters are encompassed within what looks like a little stone house. Green fronds of ferns are hanging from its roof. The stonework is covered in yellow and white lichen proving the purity of the air here. I will never lose the memory of this visit. I knew then of the Master's journeying to Cornwall and to this place in particular. The energies of pure love which I felt, linger deep within my psyche. Mary and Naomi would I am sure, have stopped here to drink of the cool refreshing waters of a natural spring.

ST ENODOC CHURCH

From Jesus Well, the track over the golf course continues to St Enodoc Church. Again sadly, it's not for me today. During the nineteenth century, this little church was in such a state of disrepair and often almost buried in the sand that the locals took to calling it *'sinkininny church'* such was their conviction that it really was sinking! However, as time went by it was cleared of sand and renovated. Remains of a village have been found between the church and the sea at Daymer Bay, apparently with furniture still in the houses, giving rise to the conjecture that they had to be abandoned in a hurry, possibly at the same time as the church.

Passing through the old lych gate one immediately comes to the grave of Sir John Betjeman. It is marked with a quite plain but most beautifully engraved dark slate gravestone which reads *'John Betjeman 1906-1984'*. At the time of my visit there were a few wild flowers placed in a little pottery container. Sir John Betjeman often worshipped at the Church of St Endelienta where there is a memorial to him, but chose to be buried here at St Enodoc's Church.

St Enodocs' Church is a long low building with a spire. I remember crossing its threshold for the first time and being immediately immersed in its extremely dark interior. I still have a few photographs of the church which I took at the time. One shows a small rood screen with predominant colours of dusky pink and the softest blue with gold embossment, giving the appearance of being very old. Others show some tiny but exquisite stained glass windows and a very ancient Celtic wheel cross. Little is known of St Enodoc, but it is recognized that he was someone of great prominence within the Bodmin Priory. There was a gentleman by the name of the Reverend William Henry, who felt sure that this present church was built over St Enodoc's cave. Some years later it was noticed that dampness was seeping into the church at the eastern end. Some flagstones were dug up and a spring was found underneath. The conclusion was that St Enodoc could have had his hermitage in a cave here by this spring, thus confirming the hypothesis of the Reverend. Further, it has been said that the saint may possibly have baptized his converts at the nearby Jesus Well.

BREA HILL DRUIDIC SETTLEMENT

I take the little pathway at the edge of the dunes towards Brea Hill. There are some National Trust yellow acorn markers on posts, indicating the route as a public footpath, which are helpful. It is late in the day, but the sun is still quite warm and there is a gentle breeze wafting around me. To my left I have the clear blue waters of the Camel Estuary with the huge sweep of Daymer Bay in the foreground. On the opposite side of the estuary I see Padstow lit up in the sunshine. I am thinking of Mary and Naomi, having crossed the waters to Cant Hill, now travelling on horseback along this stretch of coastline, eager to be in the safe haven of the settlement.

Ahead of me is a large white and yellow house tucked into the trees at the base of Brea Hill. I skirt the house and begin my ascent. At the summit the gentle breeze has become a fierce gale. From here the views are magnificent in all directions, inland and across the estuary. At this ancient site there is little left to tell of its past, the only things being three circular enclosures indicated by partly hidden granite boulders, two of which are domed and one with a dip in its centre, possibly due to land submergence. Within the relative shelter of this indent, I settle down for a short attunement and become aware of the vibrational energies of this sacred Druidic hill-top. Although I have not been requested to enact a special Ceremony here, my inner vision instantly brings into action the great Universal Light, which I see pouring down to Earth. I am conscious of Beloved Mary with me and I tune into her essence. Moving on across the ridge, I am now looking down at the Church of St Enodoc in the valley below and feel a great pull to go there, but the evening is drawing in and I need to return to my car before the light fades.

I leave the Camel Estuary and make my way back to Devon as darkness falls. In my own home sanctuary I once more make the link with the Lady Mary and the Masters of Light. I offer my blessed thanks for their guidance, inspiration and protection which I have received during my four day pilgrimage to Cornwall. I hear: *"Bless you my child - bless you."*

From Brea Hill Mary and Naomi travelled to Port Isaac to meet up with Joseph and Jesus who have come in by boat. Together they all journeyed south, via St Endlellion to their next stopping place at Castle Killibury, which is their final settlement in Camel Corner.

EASTER REFLECTIONS 2009

Before going on my next pilgrimage, this time to Bodmin Moor, the calendar is unfolding into Easter. Having regard to my Mission with Our Lady, this time of the year is to hold a deeper meaning for me and will perhaps open my inner awareness to new understandings. I feel the need to have a quiet few days in my own sacred space this Easter, in meditation, contemplation, reading, listening to music and walking in the natural world.

Today is <u>GOOD FRIDAY</u>. After a light breakfast I dress in clothes which reflect my mood. I decide to wear something completely out of character, one of those long flowing things - you know - it's called a skirt! My friends would not recognize me as I am a 'trouser girl' at heart. Maybe they would think a new woman has emerged - maybe a new woman is emerging. How could this not happen with my encounters with Beloved Mary. I choose my apparel with infinite care. The colour theme is mauve and is completed with a mauve chiffon wrap with small pink roses embossed on it. I am ready for my day.

At my altar for my morning attunement, I light a new large white church candle. I am to keep the flame burning all day. After my attunement, I collect my Bible and read the four Gospel accounts of all the events surrounding the crucifixion. The story is well known or can be easily accessed, so I will not detail it. In all my years I have never read the relating sections of Matthew, Mark, Luke and John, in one continuum. The thing that strikes me very clearly is the difference in the text of each Gospel. Of course, the words were not written down at the time, memories fade and interpretation of events differ. There would also have been mistranslations and lost words. For example in AD 325 at the Council of Nicaea Constantine, the first Roman Emperor to be converted to Christianity, decided which Gospels should be the basis of his adopted religion. This day I am feeling such a strong connection with the past and am riding the waves of events with the characters as incidents unfold. The Lady Mary and the Master Jesus are at my right hand gently walking the journey with me.

DID JESUS DIE ON THE CROSS?

In brief the main tenet of Orthodox Christianity hangs on the belief that Jesus the Christ died on the Cross at Calvary, ascended in his glorified body, to his Father in Heaven, thus sacrificing himself to save the World and ensuring that we all have Eternal Life. The belief is upheld by most churches of Christian denominations. In more recent times, much has been written on this subject giving alternative viewpoints. I list just a few of the books which come to mind - some I have read - others I have not.

1.   *The Secret Teachings of Mary Magdalene'* by Claire Nahmad and Margaret Bailey
2.   '*The Essenes, Children of the Light'* by Stuart Wilson and Joanna Prentis
3.   '*The Essene Heritage'* by Martin Larson
4.   '*The Fifth Gospel'* by Rudolf Steiner
5.   *'Jesus and the Essenes'* by Dolares Cannon

The authors offer their own interpretation of the crucifixion, the empty tomb and what finally happened to the Master Jesus. What I have read, offers credible but different explanations of events, but all reflect a deeper hidden meaning. I offer you a few words from White Eagle on this miraculous event, which speak to my heart. He talks in mystical terms and says the true meaning can only be understood with intuitive wisdom. The quotation is taken from an article in '*Stella Polaris'* the White Eagle Lodge magazine - April/May 2007. The words were first spoken by White Eagle, channelled through Grace Cooke on Easter Sunday 1933. Page 100/101: *'And he was taken from the cross, and his bones were not broken. His side was pierced with a sword, that is all. And those who loved him, took him down from the cross......They laid him with care, and with great love, in the sepulchre, and it was sealed, and they went away. The next morning they hurried to the garden, for they had much to do; and the first arrival at the garden was Mary, who loved him. And she was sore afraid, for she found the stone rolled away.....the body of her Master had gone! But there were two shining forms - angel forms - guarding the place. Jesus, in his Mastership had acquired the power of triumphing over death. He performed miracles.....he raised a body from death. The Master, the Christ, could command the Universal Creative Forces. No-one understands this until he or she is in touch with the Cosmic Consciousness, and these things become simple. When the body was placed in the sepulchre, it rested, asleep; it was not dead, and those powers by which Jesus had been able to resuscitate others were set working by his own consciousness. He drew to his body the universal power of healing and life, and he became whole........And Jesus Christ walked forth. His physical body had certainly undergone a change - it had become etherealized, of finer texture. He had heightened the vibrations of his body. It was the physical body of Christ which had risen from the dead and which went forth to demonstrate to his disciples that those who know God's power can triumph over death. Truly, truly I say, there is no death'* Finally from the same article on Page 102: *'Jesus withdrew into heaven. He withdrew from the multitude, but he was not dead; and he lived for many years after that, on your earth plane, in seclusion in what you call a monastery - still in touch, but not of the people, for he was able to direct his rays of power and love to humanity. He directed the formation of the first early Christian Church.'*

Following my reading and my deliberations, I am feeling the need to sit quietly in attunement with my dowsing crystal. Perhaps I may be allowed to receive a clearer picture of events in the Holy Land at that time. In my chair before the living flame, my pink scarf resting over my head I link to the Wise

Ones. I have many questions which I have written down. I offer you some of the answers which I can give testament to through the rose crystal of my heart.

Jesus did not die on the Cross. As White Eagle expresses, Jesus changed his physical atoms by his own consciousness in order to resuscitate his body. He was secreted away through a hidden entrance at the back of the tomb where Essene healers also ministered to him. Joseph of Arimathea, an Essene Master, had the tomb built in his own garden especially for this purpose. He asked for the body of Jesus and as a trusted member of the Sanhedrin, permission was granted. So the whole dangerous plan was put into action. As quickly as could be acted upon due to Jesus physical condition, the Essene Brethren activated the escape route to Egypt. Jesus went on to live in a monastery high up in the desert hills, where he spent the rest of his life, teaching and continuing his ministry. He did travel across the Globe and met with Mary, his mother, Naomi and Mary Magdalene and many others. However, this travelling was undertaken on an Etheric level. The method used we have learnt from the ancient one Taibu and is called '*Thought Travel*' whereby the body would be protected by the Elders/Priests, as the subject travelled to distant places on Earth or elsewhere. I have been able to establish that these advanced souls were able to manifest another temporary physical body at their destination - this was one of my earlier queries. Thus, the Master Jesus was able to meet with others and be seen in many different places throughout the world.

But what of the Lady Mary, the Mother of Jesus? This great Being of Divine proportions, with full knowledge of the Ancient Wisdom and its relation to the present happenings, was living in a human body with all the emotions of a human heart. Her anguish at seeing her son on the Cross must have been almost too much to bear. She was sorely tested. All her Temple training and her trust in Divine deliverance, must have had to come to her aid. She with Naomi and other family members, alongside those closely associated with Jesus, were also spirited away in the safe keeping of the Essene Brotherhood to Egypt. From there, in time each went their separate ways to travel the Globe to preach and to teach the words of the Master. Mary and Naomi, with some of their family voyaged to the South of France then on to the south coast of Wales, under the protection of Joseph of Arimathea As these insights are coming in I am aware of Mary's presence. Can she help me now with a clearer understanding of events at that time? Her words:

BELOVED MARY

"My child, my dear, dear child. We have given you ALL that we are permitted to do. We would wish you to contemplate our answers and seek for truth within your own heart. The Masters of Light are showering you with blessings at this sacred time of the year. It is pleasing to them that you have chosen this sacred pathway over the Easter time. You have learned much. You have remembered much. Your being is being enlightened to receive even greater and more profound manifestations. I bless you, all the Masters of the Light

bless you my child. Go in peace. May the blessings of our Father-Mother God rest in your heart for all times and open the doorway to further enlightenment."

I accept Mary's words and thank her and the Masters for guiding me to the insights received at my attunement.

Good Friday is passing very peacefully and appropriately. It is later in the day that I listen to a CD by Daniel O'Donnel *'Faith and Inspiration'*. It fits my disposition today. One tune *'The Rose'* (A.McBrown Warner Chappell Music Ltd. Arranged by John Tate), goes right to my heart and for some reason I find myself weeping as I listened to the words. This is the third time I have had a 'weep-in' since my Mission with Beloved Mary. The first was when Mary initially came into my life at the St Michael Church, Trefenty in South Wales, then recently when the unicorns made themselves known to me and now today. Each happening must have touched a chord. I give you the words of *'The Rose'* . You may recognize it.

THE ROSE

Some say love - it is a river that drowns the tender reed
Some say love - it is a razor that makes your soul to bleed
Some say love - it is a hunger an endless ache in need
I say love it is a flower and you it's only seed.
It's the heart afraid of breaking that never learns to dance
It's the dream afraid of waking that never takes the chance
It's the one who wont be taken who can not seem to give
And the soul afraid of dying that never learns to live.
When the night has been too lonely and the road has been too long
And you think that love is only for the lucky and the strong
Just remember in the winter far beneath the bitter snow
Lies the seed that with the sun's love in the spring becomes 'The Rose'.

I am sure many of you as myself, will relate to the sentiment of these words. As they are expressed, they appear to indicate the emotional challenges in our Earthly lives, as through often painful personal experience, we find our way to the 'Rose in the Heart'. The Rose - the seed of eternal truth, planted deep within our being, which as we overcome life's challenges and seek mystical answers buried within our subconscious, opens the way to pure love and becomes the Heart-Rose. It is then, that we can recognize the Divine element of Universal Love within our own tender sacred hearts. It is then, we can genuinely offer unconditional love to those along our pathway. It is then, we will arrive at a state of emotional balance. It is NOW we can accept and trust in God's perfect plan without condition and can truly say: *'Thy Will not Mine Oh Lord'*. We become more aware that the Angels and our beloved Masters walk with us along our pathway, gently guiding and helping us on our Earthly journey, full of compassion and benevolence. With this knowledge our pilgrim journey continues without fear and in perfect trust of the Divine.

As this day draws to a close, I offer a prayer to the gracious and beloved Masters for their presence and wisdom. I bless Beloved Mary, the Master Jesus, Mary Magdalene and the many Masters of Light who when in incarnation, taught us 'The Way' - the way of Eternal Truth - and often with such sacrifice. I bless those who came after - the saints - who continued their journey towards the Light. ALL still working from the inner planes to secure the enlightenment of our precious Planet Earth. I bless the Angels and Archangels, who enfold us within their 'wings' of protection, as we travel our Earthly journey. My whole day has been spent in a bubble of sacredness and joy and afforded me the privilege of new knowledge, thus bringing me ever closer in understanding of Universal Truth.

On <u>EASTER SATURDAY</u> in the outer world I visit St Mary's Church at Wolborough, high up on a hill overlooking Newton Abbot and with a distant view of Dartmoor. How lucky am I that two ladies are doing the flowers in preparation for the Easter Sunday service, so it is open. The church is rather a fine building with some magnificent stained glass windows, depicting as central to the Easter story - Jesus the Christ, the Virgin Mary and Joseph of Arimathea, alongside a plethora of saints. I sit in one of the pews and hear:

MARY

"Welcome dear child. We are pleased you have found sanctuary in this sacred place. It is rather grand don't you think! It doesn't hold the simplicity of our ancient Essene way of life or my Celtic background. But it serves a purpose dear child and that is to bring people a little closer in understanding and witness to the Divine. May the peace of God's understanding be with you at Eastertime."

My response: *"Bless you my beloved Mary."*

The sun is very hot and high in the sky as I take a stroll around the beautiful churchyard. It is full of marvellous old trees and today of course spring flowers take precedence; celandine, primrose, wild garlic and one or two of the first English bluebells just peeping through. I offer a blessing for the elementals and leave a small gift at the base one of the trees. Sitting on a seat in the sunshine I have a view over open farmland and am hearing the laughing call of a green woodpecker, the 'yapping gale' of country folk, in the distance.

WALK TO OGWELL

I go downhill on a narrow non-vehicular road to Bradley Manor Woods and stroll along the woodland path until I reach the River Lemon. Everywhere shouts of new life. Birds are heralding in a new spring as their song fills the air. There are hedges of blackthorn in their new season's dressing of little white flowers, preparing for the autumn fruiting of sloes - good for sloe gin! I follow the gently flowing river shining in the sunlight. In due course, I reach the pretty village of Ogwell, which supports an old thatched pub and many thatched cottages. The Parish Church of St Bartholomew is open, so I enter into its still darkness for a quiet moment. There is a striking modern stained glass window illustrating St Bartholomew adorned in vivid colours. He wears a turquoise robe, over which is a rich blue mantle with reds and golds. I climb the little hill to Ogwell Green and sit on a seat overlooking the village. From here I can just make out the outline of Buckland Beacon on the distance hills of Dartmoor, where I know are placed the Ten Commandment Stones, two huge granite blocks on which is inscribed the Biblical message. I am hearing a buzzard cry and see him circling overhead in the clear blue sky, gliding on the warm thermals. I return to my car with joy in my heart.

It is <u>EASTER SUNDAY</u> and I take a walk to Buckland Beacon. It is much later when I am charting Mary's journey through Devon that I discover she and her family went to Buckland Beacon as they travelled through East Dartmoor (see Chapter 12).

This Easter weekend has been one of profound delight and deep peace. My choice for seclusion has been reflected in all my activities. In the quiet of my own home, alongside listening to religious music and contemplation, I engaged in things associated with Easter on the television. First I looked at the film about Jesus *'The Greatest Story Ever Told'*. I watched the Pope's Easter message from the Vatican, and engaged in 'Songs of Praise' and 'Handel's Messiah'. The Lady Mary and the Master Jesus have graced me with their presence throughout. I offer a silent thank you for this sacred time.

To close my 'Easter Reflections' I can tell you of a rather amusing incident. I suppose it had to happen at some time. I have in my refrigerator a selection of bottles with water collected from Holy Wells and special streams. However, today I took a bottle out of the fridge which I thought was white grape juice, poured some into a wine glass and took a sip. I then realized, but not before I had swallowed some, that it was water not juice. Strange I thought - then I looked at the label *'St Mary's Holy Well.'*. I could not stop laughing. Oh well - I will either live or die - anyway it is supposed to be pure and holy and have healing properties!

CHAPTER 8
TO BODMIN MOOR
The Ancient Moorland Beckons

The Lady Mary's pilgrimage through Cornwall is drawing to a close, but she still has two vital sacred acts to carry out, both on Bodmin Moor. First she was to undertake the role of a Druid Priestess for the celebration of the summer solstice at the Druidic Temple of The Hurlers. From there she was to travel to Dozmary Pool in order to reactivate the Atlantean Temple in the Etheric.

With Castle Killibury behind them, Mary, Naomi, Jesus and Joseph stayed at three Druidic settlements on route to Bodmin Moor; Temple, Goonzion Downs and Liskeard. After The Hurlers and Dozmary Pool, Mary and her family crossed Bodmin Moor to arrive at the Cornish coast at Millhook Haven, for a sea trip to Maer and on to Hartland for the county of Devon.

Taking a look at the map for this section of Mary's journey, I see that it is just littered with place names associated with Mary and the Holy Land. I list just a few; Merrymeeting, Tumrose, Goonzion, Lady Park, Bethany, Herod Wood, Dozmary Pool, Jacobstowe, Week St Mary, Rosecare and Maer.

THE KNIGHTS TEMPLAR CHURCH AT TEMPLE

I am making preparations for my final pilgrimage to Cornwall. I shall be unable to reach the Temple site which I have identified as being just to the south of Merrifield, but can offer you a little of a pilgrimage I made a couple of years back to the St Catherine Knights Templar Church at Temple. I was with some friends from my White Eagle Lodge Centre South West and the local Gatekeeper group, when we paid a visit to this special little church, which nestles in a most peaceful and secluded valley surrounded by trees on the western fringe of Bodmin Moor. On arrival our group had an attunement and offered a special blessing to the Spirit of Place. On entering the church, I was struck by the simplicity which somehow emphasized its sacredness. One of our party laid on the altar, a fully opened dark rich-red rose, its petals like soft velvet.

The Knights Templar were a religious-military order founded in 1118, associated with the Temple of Solomon in Jerusalem. They were established to protect pilgrims on their journey to the Holy Land at the time of the Crusades, and were active in the South West of England. Temple would have been a place of hospitality for such travellers. This church built in the twelfth century, has indications of its Templar heritage a-plenty. A section of one of the stained glass windows over the altar, displays a Templar shield, white with a red cross. In the tower, a window shows a knight on horseback. On the walls of a small stone building in the churchyard are crosses engraved with recognizable Templar symbols.

A Templar Symbol at the St Catherine Church, Temple

In contemplation before the rose, remembrances of times past were reaching deep within. I was not to know then the significance of my visit or of the insights received. Subsequently of course I was to learn that as Naomi, I was in Temple with Mary in the incarnation I am presently exploring. During my attunement, I was conscious of the presence of Our Lady and received some very moving words from her. So as at other places, the link was being made for this present Mission.

TO GOONZION DOWNS SETTLEMENT

After Temple, Mary's next settlement was Goonzion Downs. I paid a brief visit here before returning to Devon on this final pilgrimage to Cornwall. I recollect driving uphill out of the village of St Neot to the ancient site. From the hill-top, magnificent views of Bodmin Moor were laid out before me. I searched for any identifying features of a settlement. The whole area was one of mounds and dips, spread out across a gorse filled landscape, but no significant standing stones or hut circles. Further investigation was out of the question, because it was too late in the day. However, I climbed to the top of one of the mounds and was able to have a few quiet moments, allowing my inner vision to bring it to life. I left a white crystal next to a large heart-shaped stone which I found lying on the ground saying: *"Beloved Mary - in memory of our time here."*

As I turned to leave, I spied a rather large rectangular grassy area, surrounded on all sides by a low earth embankment. This must be the 'crow pound', of which a lady tending the graves in St Neots' churchyard had told me. The legend goes, that St Neot became somewhat aggrieved as the local farmers were not coming to church because they had to stay on their land to protect their crops from crows. So he had built a 'crow pound' to imprison the crows, so that the farmers had no excuse to miss the church services - great stuff!

Mary's next settlement was Liskeard, all remains of which have disappeared, but I understand it was to the east of the town. I notice just below Liskeard on the map is a place called *'Roseland'* on the river. Another Roseland and another puzzle. How could Mary have landed here when she came across country? I considered she may have taken a short river journey, but this was not the answer. Then an inspiration - could this name have arisen because it was designated as *'Rose's Land'* in memory of the presence of 'Mary the Rose' all those years ago? A tenuous link I am sure you will agree, but I was told that this was so.

From Liskeard, the journey to Bodmin Moor took Mary via Merrymeet to a settlement at The Cheesewring, set above The Hurlers Druidic Temple site. For the duration of their journeying around Cornwall and on into Devon, the four travellers, Mary, her children and Joseph stayed together, except for one occasion when Joseph made a brief visit to a place called Pensilva just south of the moor. Its name had led me to wonder if Joseph had interests in silver mines in the area, which was confirmed.

MY PILGRIMAGE TO BODMIN MOOR

It is the end of April and I am off on my last adventure in Cornwall with the Lady Mary, this time to Bodmin Moor. My six year old granddaughter will walk distances, climb up hills, scramble over Tors on Dartmoor with great enthusiasm as long as it is 'an adventure'. Me, I love an adventure and each pilgrimage I undertake turns out to be one - of varying degree! My plan for

Day 1 is to go to The Hurlers where I shall enact a Druidic Ceremony for the Light. On Day 2 my intention is to perform an Atlantean Ceremony at Dozmary Pool. The last day sees me searching out the actual settlement where Mary stayed in the area of Dozmary Pool, before moving on to St Neot's Church and Goonzion Downs. My whole pilgrimage turns out to be quite an endeavour with a few twists and turns along the way!

The day begins with an early morning attunement, wherein I dedicate myself to my first sacred Mission at The Hurlers. I leave in plenty of time to be on site by 12.00 noon my allotted Ceremonial hour. The distance is shorter than on previous trips to Cornwall. I drive the main road west, which today is lined with mile after mile of yellow gorse and primroses. Shafts of sunlight are breaking through a rather grey sky. On this occasion, I have booked two nights at Boscastle Youth Hostel on Cornwall's north coast. Unfortunately, there is no hostel on Bodmin Moor, so I had the choice of Golant on the south coast or Boscastle. I intended tossing a coin, but knew that on whichever side it fell, Boscastle would win, as it is one of my heart places - so decision made.

Driving through the busy streets of Liskeard, I can't help but wonder if I am close to the ancient settlement of my past life. I take the B3254 north to Bodmin Moor, go left at Upton Cross and pick up a quiet country road to the pretty hamlet of Minions with its white and colour-washed cottages. I park in the car park for The Hurlers, which is in the centre of Minions. I have done the journey without incident this time! There is one hour before my Ceremony. I take a swig out of my rather damaged plastic water bottle. Damaged because, one winter's day, I decided to do something really clever and top up the cold water with a little boiling water from the kettle. My aim failed and it hit the sides hence its unusual shape.

THE HURLERS

I walk across the soft peaty moorland turf to The Hurlers. In the far distance high up on the hill, I can see The Cheesewring settlement where Mary stayed, marked out with its distinct granite tower. The song of the skylark filters across the pure moorland air, bringing joy on its every melodious trilling note.

The Hurlers is a triple stone circle lying in a NNE-SSW direction towards Stowe's Hill, with two outlying standing stones to the south-west which are called The Pipers. Surely not more merry revelers turned to stone as at Merry Maidens. Is it possible that in past times, The Pipers were in some way, channels for the use of sound, activated by the Druid Priests, in order to increase the vibrational energies for their Ceremonies of Light. If so - an apt name.

One of the Stone Circles at the Hurlers

*The Pipers at the Hurlers with Stowe's Pound (the Cheesewring Settlement)
in the background*

Standing before the first stone circle in reverence, I am thinking to myself, so this was where I came with Mary 2,000 years ago. I ask permission of the two tall granite guardian stones to enter their sacred circle. As I do I am almost overwhelmed by the powerful vibrations emanating from within. I walk the complete circle in a clockwise direction, noting that each stone is one metre apart. Some stones are of course are not visible, but I dowse and they are there. Why a total of twenty-nine stones? As I explore the other two circles, I find that each has a similar anomaly of twenty-nine stones. This perplexes me and I do not have an answer. In the centre of the first circle is a flat stone which I perceive to be the Altar Stone. There is a standing stone to one side. There must be another one to balance this? Again dowsing, I confirm a second stone. The feeling I am receiving, is that this first large circle at The Hurlers is the original Temple where Ceremonies for important days in the Druidic annual calendar would have been carried out.

Later at home, I found a little book hidden away on my bookshelves, by Cheryl Straffon called *'The Earth Mysteries Guide to Bodmin Moor and North Cornwall'* in which she discusses The Hurlers. On Page 9 Straffon tells us that: *'The south circle* (my first circle) *is now quite ruined, although its original diameter would have been about 104 ft. and it would have been an important site from which to have observed the Beltane/Lughnased sunset going over the ridge to Craddock Moor circle (or alternatively the Samhain/Imbolc sunrise would have been visible rising over the ridge from the Craddock Moor circle). The centre circle has 14 uprights (out of 29 original.....The north circle also has 14 uprights out of 29 original.'* This information ties in with my discoveries - three circles, twenty-nine stones in each. But still I have no answer as to why that number of stones.

Straffon also mentions, that during excavations, it was discovered that the central circle had a floor of quartz crystals. Again I am a little mystified, because I thought the crystals would have been embedded in the first circle, which I have identified as being the main Temple site. However, I later read in the *'The Sun and the Serpent'* (Miller and Broadhurst), that they ascertained the St Michael-St Mary Ley Lines, cross at a node point at the centre of the central circle of The Hurlers. So, the crystals here would have acted as a powerful conductor to link with the Great Crystal within the Earth's core.

It has been written that there is a fourth circle. I can not get any information on this at present. However, I do believe I have been able to identify the use of the three circles visible. Circle No.1 is for general Druidic Ceremonies, hence The Pipers in close vicinity. Circle No.2 is where Initiations took place, which Ceremonies would have made full use of the powerful Crystal Energy. Circle No.3 is for burial rights and for releasing the soul to the world beyond. In this regard, leading away from the third circle are burial chambers, placed between The Hurlers and The Cheesewring settlement.

THE HURLERS DRUIDIC TEMPLE CEREMONY

When Mary was here, it was pre-ordained that she take the part of a Druid Elder at the time of the summer solstice. Today, I am to perform my own Druidic Ceremony to reactivate that ancient Light. I have chosen my position carefully, away from prying eyes, slightly hidden by a gorse bush and close to the Temple site. I lay out all I need for this sacred undertaking. The wind, even in this sheltered place, is blowing out my candle, so I hold the vision of the Golden Flame rising up, linking the Cosmos with Planet Earth. I offer a prayer to the Higher Beings and proceed diligently through each stage of my Druidic Ceremony.

Suddenly my inner sight is showing me a snake and I realize that I have tuned into the Serpent Power of the Ancient World. The serpent represents the invisible energy current that flows through the Earth, recognized by Miller and Broadhurst, which would be stimulated by the ancient Druids at sacred sites such as this. Sometime later it comes to me, that the 'Obby Oss' as it winds its way through the streets of Padstow on May Day, is a portrayal of the serpent. So an ancient custom being played out today, is keeping the Earth Spirit alive. Is the Serpent Energy about to be stirred in the rocky outcrops of this ancient landscape as I perform my Cosmic Ceremony? I can feel mighty forces swirling all around. My inner vision now shows me the Christ Sun - the Eternal Light - beaming down directly onto the Altar at the centre of the stone circle, from where it is shooting forth, lighting up all the outer stones. It is shining out across the land and spreading throughout our Planet, pouring into the unseen energy channels within the Earth. An ancient Druid is at my side:

DRUID ELDER

"Pilgrim we welcome you. Thank you for your sacred work this day. Dear Naomi you were with us all those years ago and now you return to grace us with your presence. In those days you were still a child but growing fast into womanhood. You shared in our summer solstice Ceremony with your mother, the blessed Mary and the boy Jesus. When the solstice is upon you this year we would ask that you return in thought to this sacred place. We shall be waiting for you."

I now become aware of a very vivid green colour focused on my brow centre. I mentally ask the significance and receive the answer, that this colour is bringing cleansing and healing to the Earth and that I am being used as a channel for that Light. White Eagle confirms this:

WHITE EAGLE

"We wish to speak with you Peace Rose. You, as can many others, be instrumental in bringing cleansing and healing to the Earth. Use this colour from your inner vision. It is very strong and very potent. It is time. The Earth will be cleansed of all unwanted debri. Steps will be taken to cleanse and revitalize your Planet for new beginnings. Play your part dear sister and you will have done what is being asked of you. Keep on keeping on in service to humanity, as you have been directed from the Masters. Your beloved Mary is ever at your side as your Mission progresses. You will feel her presence even more strongly. Open your heart to her pure love energy, and joy and fulfillment will be yours. Your journeying in this Celtic Cornwell is almost at an end, but as you know, there is still much work for you to do. There is much research for you to carry out on the physical and inner levels before you can continue your journey with Mary at the physical level. During your research, you will be guided to be witness to ancient truths, and deeper understanding and significance of your present Mission will be offered to you. For you are not alone on

your Mission, even though you are physically working alone. The Heavens are filled with Brethren offering their deepest love and protection, their support and love unparalleled. God Bless you sister."

As White Eagle leaves me, the vibrant green once more fills my third eye chakra, which seems to be bathing in its Etheric Light. The green mass spins around in strange shapes. I allow it to float out gently but purposefully, to heal the land and the seas and the atmosphere. All at once it is gone - as quickly as it came

I thank my beloved White Eagle and the Druid Elder for the words expressed today. My closing ritual follows and I surround myself with a lovely protective sphere of Golden Light. I gather up all my Ceremonial items and put them away. Stepping into the circle I advance towards the Altar Stone. I discreetly bury a pink quartz crystal for the Goddess and leave on view, a piece of white quartz crystal for the Druids. My work here is complete.

THE CHEESEWRING SETTLEMENT

As I walk the line of the ancient precessional route from The Pipers to The Cheesewring settlement, I see on the skyline, perched high above the old quarry, the enormous tower of flatish granite slabs called The Cheesewring, alongside which is a huge triangular granite stone. As I draw close to The Cheesewring I can feel the energy radiating from it. A raven on the wing croaks a welcome - thank you Merlin for your presence. Between the great slabs of rock, I insert a small piece of white quartz which I have recently obtained from Brent Tor in Devon, in order to link these two powerful energy centres. I leave a single pink rose for Mary and the Sacred Feminine. I also acknowledge the large triangular stone.

Exploring the ancient settlement, now commonly known as Stowe's Pound, I note it is a flat circular grassy plateau covering an extensive area. From here it stretches out over the surrounding moorland. There are many granite boulders which are lichened with the most beautiful colours of green, pink, black, yellow, grey and white. There is one solitary hawthorn bush, near horizontal from the prevailing westerlies. Up here the World is standing still. I have views of 360 degrees across Bodmin Moor, but the one which catches my eye is Dozmary Pool to the west, my destination on the morrow. I am now hearing my first cuckoo of the year calling from the trees in the valley. I sit in solitude in this magical place, looking across the ancient landscape, visualizing the past, when this settlement was for a while, the abode of four travellers from the Holy Land.

As I make to leave this wild and wonderful spot, I can see a family running amongst the ancient stones of The Cheesewring settlement, the children shouting 'cheese' - they are having such fun. I return to The Hurlers across open moorland where once again, the lark's joyous song is thrilling me. I am thinking that up on the hill is the domain of the raven, but on these lower slopes is where skylark abides. Horses are galloping free across the open moor and cattle are gathering in one of the circles. I am remembering the exhilaration of open air worship. At the summer solstice we were filled with Heavenly Light - the natural world adding another dimension. I offer a final blessing at The Hurlers as I pass by and am aware of the presence of my precious Mary. Returning to my car, I note that it is 3.30 pm.

The Cheesewring

ST CLEERS -THE CHURCH AND HOLY WELL OF ST CLARUS

I drive on to the village of St Cleers which is just a short distance away, and park up behind the church. As I go through the lych gate into the churchyard, I see a grassy bank under the trees, drenched with a thousand pale-lemon primroses. The fragrance arising from them is quite overwhelming as it hangs in the warm late afternoon air. It brings to mind, that in days past in certain parts of the country, it was custom to dress the graves in parish churchyards with primroses and other wild flowers at Eastertime. The Reverend Kilvert of Clyro in Radnorshine, writing in one of his famous diaries in 1870, expresses delight at the continuance of this old custom. He himself, very early one Easter Sunday morning, went off around the country lanes 'primrosing' and made primrose crosses to adorn some of the graves in his churchyard.

The fifteenth century Parish Church is set within all this natural beauty. Close to the south porch stands an early rendering of a Celtic cross. Little is known of St Clarus other than that he was an Englishman of the eighth or ninth century, who became a monk in Normandy, and while there was murdered by a local noblewoman. Within the church is a beautiful depiction in stained glass of the Lady Mary, robed in blue and magenta. Alongside this, are other Victorian stained glass windows, where no less than twenty-four female saints are personified. Some of these are; St Lucy, St Cecilia, St Catherine, St Hilda, St Agatha, St Barbara, St Margaret and St Agnes. Interesting features are the eighteen wooden boards on which are scribed Biblical texts, plus the old parish stocks from 1744, which can 'house' three miscreants at a time!

I buy the church booklet and read that behind the vicarage is the Biblical Garden, a project created as a quiet garden for the New Millennium by local craftsmen and gardeners. The whole is designed to form a Biblical narrative from Creation to Calvary. In the Garden of Eden, is a Serpent Stone, a reminder of the Old Testament story and of the Serpent Power of the ancients which I touched on at The Hurlers during my Ceremony. The garden is unfortunately closed today.

After a short attunement, I leave the quiet realm of this ancient church for the Holy Well, which is not surprisingly situated in Well Street. You can not miss it as it stands alone within a small courtyard next to a large granite cross. The framework is a miniature stone building, its open walls pillared and with curved lintels. A plaque tells me that it was restored in 1864. In a niche in the apex is a small statue of St Clarus. The well itself is covered by old iron grating so one cannot reach the water, but close-by I leave two large fir cones and a triangular stone as an offering to the deity of the well and in remembrance of its saint.

Back at the car I am preparing to leave St Cleers for Boscastle, when I hear a distinctive sound I have not heard since I was a girl - the soft whirring of a push/pull lawnmower! I peep through the hedge and yes I am right.

ON TO BOSCASTLE

Leaving Bodmin Moor and travelling north, I am soon in familiar territory, driving down the steep hill through a verdant valley to the gem that is Boscastle. I park up opposite the Cobweb Inn, gather up my bag and walk the short distance along the River Valency to the youth hostel, which is positioned right on the harbour. The smell of the sea - the cry of the gulls - the sound of the gently flowing river - what more could I wish for. Once you have been hooked with the enchantment of Boscastle, you will always return - and I do.

This peaceful scene of today was not always so. In August 2004, Boscastle had 'The Big Flood' when the gentle river became a raging torrent. The River Valency coming from the high ground above the village, burst its banks and poured down Valency Valley to unleash a ten foot wave of destruction, wrecking havoc on all in its path; shops, houses, the harbour bridges and cars, leaving total devastation in its wake. Cars were found part submerged in the harbour and I remember seeing a picture of the youth hostel with a huge tree stuck in one of its upper windows. The once tranquil village of Boscastle resembled a war zone. What caused the disaster was apparently a unique combination of factors, which included seven inches of rain falling in a two hour period and the hills above Boscastle becoming waterlogged. Thankfully there was no loss of life, this put down to amazing rescues by the Emergency Services and by locals, who were all recognized as heroes. People were dragged out of cars which were floating down-stream in the torrent, while others were rescued by helicopters from roof tops. I did pay a visit about two months after the ravages of the water and was saddened at what I saw. It took nigh on two years before all was cleared and the rebuilding completed.

The village has now returned to its former tranquil haven and I am so glad to be back and staying in the refurbished hostel. I sign in and as it is such a lovely evening, after a drink, I take myself off for a walk. First I cross one of the new river bridges to the inner harbour, which is graced with a dozen or more small fishing craft moored up. Hundreds of little-gulls are thrashing about amongst the green seaweedy rocks in the clear shallow waters. They are making such a noise and seem to be delighting in sprucing up their feathers. On reaching the outer harbour I am reminded of the famous 'blow-hole'. This is a phenomenon known to Boscastle, where at certain states of the tide, a noisy burst of water shoots forth from a hole in the harbour cliff-face, its spray sending a waterspout halfway across the harbour entrance. It is caused by water exiting from a long tunnel, which runs through the rock deep below the cliff-top from the wildness of the open sea to the relative calm of the harbour.

I am now walking the cliff path. Amongst the masses of bright yellow gorse bushes, a carpet of spring flowers covers the grassy cliff; primroses, bluebells, sea pinks, deep purple violets and the tiny pretty blue squill. I begin the ascent to the little whitewashed lookout tower at the top of Willapark promontory. At just over three hundred feet high it has fine views in all directions, including along the coast to Tintagel. I look down at the waves crashing on the rocks far below me. I hear the wild cries of seabirds as they wheel about. Some are sitting on nests precariously perched on the steep cliff-face. The horizon is spread with the beginnings of a glorious crimson sunset. This is truly a place of the Gods.

On returning to the hostel, I take a little supper and that night go to sleep with the haunting sound of the river running past the hostel.

WAS KING ARTHUR BORN IN TINTAGEL?

I cannot be in Boscastle without making mention of the well documented Arthurian legends which abound in the Tintagel area, and which seem to be held within its ancient landscape. On her journeying through Cornwall the Lady Mary did not visit Tintagel. However, it is recorded that the Master Jesus with Joseph of Arimathea did visit the Island Castle of Tintagel on a subsequent occasion. For me, this time a visit is not on the agenda because of my other 'duties' but it has been a place of pilgrimage in the past.

Cornish folklore speaks of King Arthur having been born in Tintagel Castle and given into the care of Merlin. Excavations on the island indicate a Celtic monastery, but no tangible evidence has been found to make the Arthur connection. On a recent visit I was standing on the cliff-top looking out to Tintagel Island and heard the words: *'Prince among Princes - King among Kings'.* I knew this related to King Arthur. On the island itself, I felt a strong connection with Arthur and my insight told me he was indeed born at Tintagel Castle. I also knew that this sacred island was a powerhouse for the Cosmic Energy. I wrote at the time: *'From the centre of the island, I am aware of a huge shaft of Light spiralling round anticlockwise and shooting up from below the Earth into the Heavens. It seemed to be grounding the Cosmic Light being directed in its downward spiral.'* There is a tunnel at the island's centre and my intuition told me that below ground used to be a hallowed space - an inner sanctum - perhaps a kind of Temple, where Light Ceremonies were held. As I looked for some evidence of an entrance in the rocky wall, a messenger bee alighted on a section of the wall in front of me. There was no obvious indication of a way in, yet my dowsing rods confirmed that this was the ancient entrance.

The Labyrinth in Rocky Valley, Tintagel

Below Tintagel Island is a cave known as 'Merlin's Cave' through which one can walk at low tide and where the waves come pounding in at high tide. Exploring the cave on one occasion, I was looking through the lens of my camera and became aware of a remarkable purple light. A friend who was with me experienced the same marvel, yet nothing came out on any prints. Was the light caused by the sun shining through the cave exit onto the water and rocks below, causing some sort of trick of the light? I don't know. Whatever it was, it had an ethereal quality and was quite magical. Perhaps it was Merlin's 'trick of the light'.

It is not the remit of this work, and lack of space denies a full description of all the wonders around this area of Tintagel, but for the dedicated pilgrim, I bullet-point some of the sacred places. Please visit with respect for Mother Earth and with respect for our ancestors. Enter in love, light a candle, make an offering and leave with a peaceful heart.

- Tintagel Parish Church of St Materina overlooking Tintagel Island.
- The Chapel of Our Lady of Fontehrault - a hidden gem of peace in the little valley on the way to the church.
- St Nectan's Glen - a walk through ancient woodland following the stream, to reach a sacred waterfall, where legend has it that King Arthur and his Knights came to pray and receive the healing waters.
- St Nectan's Hermitage and Shrine close-by.
- St Piran's Chapel at the entrance to St Nectan's Glen.
- Rocky Valley - a picturesque wooded valley leading to the coast, where you will find an ancient labyrinth inscribed on granite stone.

MY WANDERINGS AROUND DOZMARY POOL

I have left Beloved Mary and her family at The Cheesewring settlement. After the summer solstice at The Hurlers Druidic Temple site, her pilgrimage took her west across Bodmin Moor, over the River Fowey to reach the settlement of Dozmary Pool. On the map you will see it as being slightly to the north and west of Higher Langdon Farm and in the lee of Brown Gelly Downs. When there, Mary performed a Ceremony to reactivate the Light within the Atlantean Temple in the Etheric. It is Mary's wish that I go to this site and undertake the sacred act of earthing this ancient Temple.

I begin this second day of my pilgrimage, with an attunement asking my dearest Mary for her guidance and protection. It is the 23rd April, St George's Day. I wonder if this will hold any significance? I set off in lovely sunshine, travelling back south to Bodmin Moor from Boscastle. Driving along the two lane A395, now passing through the Windmill Farm, I have managed to collect a trail of vehicles behind me - yet again. I pull in to let them all pass, then head off along the road until the next lot arrive! I am in no rush - my time is my own - relatively speaking. Banks of vivid yellow gorse once more line my route. I reach the A30 and soon take a road off, two miles past Jamaica Inn at

Bolventor, made famous by Daphne de Maurier in her tales of Cornwall. It is a peaceful little road circumnavigating Colliford Lake, and after a short while I see Dozmary Pool in the distance across the main body of the lake. From here Brown Gelly Hill rises up before me, to a height of approximately three hundred and fifty metres. I am now parked up just off the roadside close to Dozmary Pool. I have planned my timing once again for 12.00 noon. My day's Mission has begun - and what a peculiar day it turns out to be.

I gather the equipment for my Ceremony. I put my large scale map into its plastic cover, for I have a premonition that I may be doing some exploring this day. My instincts turn out to be correct. From the woodland directly behind me another cuckoo bursts forth its familiar springtime call. I set off the short distance to Dozmary Pool along a wide stony track. The grassy bank is covered with bright yellow dandelions. I think the 'humble' dandelion is so often overlooked. To me it shows the golden face of the sun. It is also a fine herb, rich in minerals and nutrients which have distinct medicinal properties, including acting as a detoxifier. Therefore this so-called weed is valuable indeed.

My track opens to Dozmary Pool. At the waters edge, a notice tells me that *'This is a Bird Sanctuary Area'*. I can see wildfowl at the far reaches of the lake and hear the evocative cry of a curlew as it rises out of the marsh. I have stepped into a little sanctuary of peace. I look around and see Brown Gelly now to my right. Ahead of me, I can just make out King Arthur's Bed on Bodmin Moor, with Smallacombe Downs plantation in the foreground. This was Mary's route back to the high elevation of the moor. I hear the cawing of a rook as it flies across my vision over the lake. I would like it to have been Merlin's raven but it's not! As I am thinking this, a raven DOES put in an appearance, swirling around the lake and hinterland, croaking loudly.

THE 'LADY OF THE LAKE'

I stand in reverence at the lakeside. Whatever the legend - whatever the truth - I am now tuning in to the 'Lady of the Lake', whom I see as representing the Sacred Feminine aspect of the Godhead - the Goddess. She is Isis - she is Hathor - she is Mary.

Anyone who has read of Arthurian legend will be familiar with the 'Lady of the Lake' stories. Dozmary Pool is one of the claimed locations for this Cornish lore. Some traditions see The Lady as benevolent. In this guise, she is purported to be the foster mother of Sir Lancelot, raising him below the waters of the lake. She is also said to have extended her arm up through the waters of the lake, presenting the magical sword Excalibur to King Arthur. It is here that Sir Bedivere was commanded by the dying Arthur, to throw Excaliber back into the waters, thus returning it to the Lady of the Lake. In another tradition, The Lady is of deceptive character who enchants and entraps Merlin after he has taught her his magic, and thus is responsible for his demise. She is an enigma. She is most certainly linked to pre-Christian Celtic mythology. In this estate, her name Viviane, would derive from the Celtic 'Co-Viana' another name for the Celtic Water Goddess, Coventina. She would be seen as a water fae in this realm. The modified version of Viviane is Morgan le Fay, who with two other Queens, escorted King Arthur to the Isle of Avalon, to have his wounds healed following his battle with Mordred.

Is there a deeper meaning to all of this? Perhaps - we have the Goddess offering the Sword of Righteousness to King Arthur, in order for him to go forth and cut through the dark vibrational energies which penetrate our world. Perhaps - the 'Lady of the Lake', residing within the still waters below the surface, reflects the mysterious water element, which tests young humanity, bringing to our awareness that if we too can go within, through attunement, our emotional bodies can be stilled. Perhaps - The Lady's contact with Merlin, indicates abuse of power from a feminine perspective. Things to ponder.

LEGENDS OF LLYN-Y-FAN-FACH

At this point I feel compelled to make mention of another Lake of Legend in an area which has strong associations with King Arthur and Merlin AND where Mary and Naomi visited after the crucifixion. It was in the summer of 2008 and I was on pilgrimage following Megan Wingfield's *'Pathway of the Beloved'* through Wales, when I chanced upon the stories. From my copious notes I give you a brief summary of the legends and my journeying. I was staying at Llandeusant Youth Hostel, which is situated on the northern slopes of the Black Mountain in South Wales.

The lake in question is called Llyn-y-Fan-Fach. In fact there are three legends relating to this lake all connected through healing.

1. A Lady of the Lake
2. The Physicians of Myddfai
3. The Healing Waters of the Lake.

Although much of this folklore dates from the twelfth century, my belief is that it stems from the arrival of Mary and Naomi with their healing gifts and knowledge of the Ancient Wisdom, combined with Druidic wisdom of the time.

The first legend tells of a local herdsman called Rhiwallon, who lived at an upland farm Blaen Swadde, in the parish of Llandeusant. Rhiwallon fell in love with a beautiful maiden who emerged from the waters of Llyn-y-Fan-Fach. The story goes that they eventually married, had three sons and lived at a farm Esgair Llaethy. A warming was given, that The Lady would return to the lake if her husband struck her three blows without cause. As time passed, three light playful blows (taps) were struck. She returned to her watery world Rhiwallon never saw her again. On my pilgrimage, I walked the little mountain track to the lake which is tucked in below the dark imposing heights of Bannau Sir Gaer. I was impressed to perform a special Ceremony for The Lady of this magical lake and for the Guardian of the Mountain who watches over this sacred land.

A second legend relates to the three sons. They grew to adulthood and The Lady appeared to them. She was renowned for her knowledge of the medicinal properties of plants, herbs and flowers, which wisdom she taught to her sons. She gave them a bag of instructions and prescriptions for healing telling them that their work on Earth was to cure the sick. They became skilful doctors, whose descendants were known as the Physicians of Myddfai. Myddfai is a small village just below Llyn-y-Fan-Fach, which I was able to visit on my pilgrimage. I was immediately drawn to the St Michael Church, to discover that in the porch there is a large stone memorial plaque dedicated to the last Physician of Myddfai, who died in the early eighteenth century. On display inside the church, is the most beautiful large piece of stained glass work in sections, which shows aspects of the local area and its legends.

Now to the third legend, the purported healing properties of Llyn-y-Fan-Fach which I had cause to test and can verify! I had taken the track through the Afon Sawdde valley to the lake, passing through the ancient settlement at the edge of the stream where Mary and Naomi stayed. After my lakeside Ceremony, I took a rather precarious scramble where I had to keep my wits about me, up to the high ridge of Bannau Sir Gaer. From here I could look down at Llyn-y-Fan-Fach far below me. By the time I returned to the stream I had completed an approximate five mile hike. It was a scorching day and I was extremely hot. I flushed lots of lovely cold water over my face, arms and legs then took my walking shoes and socks off and paddled in the stream. I sat down on a large rock in the middle of the water. When I got off the worst happened - the rock wobbled and fell onto my right ankle. I could feel it moving, but it was as if everything was in slow motion and I was powerless to prevent the inevitable. A few explicit words were expressed! I looked down at my ankle which had a huge graze and by now had become black and swollen. I remember thinking to myself '*this is not good*'. I decided to treat it like a burn and kept my ankle immersed in the cold water for at least ten minutes asking for healing. The pain diminished a little, but the swelling and bruising remained. I suddenly remembered the 'alleged' healing properties of Llyn-y-Fan-Fach. Sitting on the bank, I gently dabbed my ankle dry, then got out my bottle which contained water I had retrieved from the lake and poured a little onto my ankle asking that I receive help. WELL - all I can say is that as I watched, the swelling was visibly reducing! The pain was completely gone: "*Blessed ones I thank you.*" It was amazing - if I had wanted proof of the healing properties of the lake, then here it was, BUT they (Spirit) did not have to go to such lengths to prove it to me! I put a plaster pad on the graze, then very gingerly put my sock on and eased my damaged foot back into my shoe with the laces loosely tied. I managed to hobble the mile and a half back to the youth hostel along the little mountain road. I took a shower and put on flip flops so that there was no pressure on the ankle. It was looking very black and had a nasty graze, but the pain had gone and the swelling was right down. Again: *"Thank you Blessed Ones for your healing grace. Thank you Lady of the Lake for the healing properties of your sacred waters."*

Finally - my insights, plus words from the Lady Mary at the time, confirmed my discoveries in this area. To Llyn-y-Fan-Fach came Mary, Naomi, Joseph of Arimathea and others from the Holy Land. Also, the presence of Arthur and Merlin echo throughout this ancient land. And guess what - not far away is a place named 'Bethlehem' with 'Carn Arthur' and 'Merlin's Hill'.

BACK TO DOZMARY

Where shall I hold my Ceremony? I begin my preamble around Dozmary Pool, passing the neatly presented Dozmary Pool Farm on my left. There is a small duck-egg blue rowboat hauled up at the lake edge close-by. The wind blowing across the surface of the lake is causing frothy ripples as it laps against the sandy shoreline. The notice board told me that the surrounding grassland is called a mire. I would second this, as I jump from tuft to tuft to avoid the bog. Some dear little mauve violets are pluckily rising out of all the mud and muck around me. This is cattle country - they are everywhere. Two fields further on still walking around the lakeside, I now find my way blocked by a barbed wire fence. The peace I was at first experiencing on arrival at the lake, belies the feelings I am now having. I am not happy in this area at all. I make a momentous decision - not to hold my Ceremony at Dozmary Pool, as it not conducive for the work I am to do.

Before leaving, I scatter some rose petals on the surface of the lake for The Lady and for Beloved Mary who is at my side, with a benediction. From my pack I take a small glass phial containing the healing water I obtained from Llyn-y-fan-Fach. I pour a little into the lake. I ask the water fae of Dozmary Pool for permission to collect some water from its sacred waters.

I begin my return walk and bravely go where men and of course women, HAVE gone before. There is a herd of heifers heading down to the lake edge for a drink. Can I make it in time or will I get caught up in the stampede? I am learning to be brave around cattle. I visualize them slowing down and myself walking fearlessly at the lake's edge! I just manage to get in front of them before they arrive at the water. I have a friend with whom I holiday on occasions, who would have considered me to be particularly courageous. Once in Wales we came to a field of 'big' heifers which had to be negotiated. At first I refused point blank to enter. In the end I had to as there was just no other way round. We sallied forth resolutely, brandishing sticks and making strange scary noises. The cattle were right at our heels - not a good experience, but we did reach the farm gate in one piece.

WALK TO BROWN GELLY HILL

A decision has to be made as to where I shall hold my Atlantean Ceremony. I take a look at the map and consider that the top of Brown Gelly will be perfect because I shall have a clear view of Dozmary Pool. I set off on my three mile trek to walk the distance as every good pilgrim should! Twelve noon has well past by now so I elect for a 3.00 pm time. To reach Brown Gelly, I follow the little by-road around the side of Colliford Lake, which will take me to a point where I can pick up a farm lane, then moorland track to reach my destination. The day is sunny and the walk pleasant alongside the lake. A tiny rabbit runs across the road just feet from me. A little further on I see an adder in the road. It has the identifiable dark zig-zag stripe down its back. I am careful not to go in too close. I remember one occasion on a cliff path, when I was young I hasten to add, that I was so excited at seeing an adder that I put my hand down, the adder bit me and I spent the night in the local cottage hospital! So this time I am a little more cautious. But as I am looking intently at it there is no sign of life. It has sadly passed away into snake heaven. Feeling suitably foolish, I gently hook it with a stick and lay it to rest in a field.

I find myself singing *'To be a Pilgrim'* as I march along the road. By the end of today I shall surely be a most exhausted pilgrim. I hear the words: *"Well done brave and valiant warrior."* This is a bit premature I am thinking. What do 'They' know that I don't! I am already feeling this journey could be a test of dedication and endurance. Undaunted I soldier on, but the hard surface of the road is beginning to take its toll. I realize I have a problem with my right hip which is affecting the way I am walking. It is very painful but I decide to walk through the pain. It is not improving, so - Plan B. With my inner vision, I focus my attention on the great Healing Star and see Rays of Light pouring down encompassing me. I then direct the colour blue for pain directly to my hip area, followed by a warm golden colour, asking the Angels and the Master Jesus for healing. Knowing that I can do no more and determined to continue with my day's plan, I walk on, maintaining the healing concentration. After a further mile, I reach the farm lane and realize I have no pain in my hip and am walking normally: *"Thank you Beloved Ones."*

The farm I pass on my way to Brown Gelly is called *'Lord Park'* - not especially significant unless one is aware that our Lord would have passed this way 2,000 years before. For when the following day I reach the Druidic settlement where Mary with Jesus, Naomi and Joseph stayed on the far side of Brown Gelly, I am to learn that the boy Jesus would wander off into the surrounding hills to commune with the Angels.

Walking uphill through ancient settlements, I come across some beautiful rusty-brown large-horned Highland cattle with soft brown eyes - they are quite lovely and more afraid of me than I am of them. I climb up and over a high stone wall and begin the steep ascent to the summit of Brown Gelly. Eventually after negotiating several false hill tops, I reach the trig point at the top. Up here there appears to be evidence of ancient burial mounds, hut circles and cairns all around me. From the top as I predicted, I can see Dozmary Pool in the valley directly below me. THIS is definitely the place for my Ceremony.

DOZMARY POOL ATLANTEAN TEMPLE CEREMONY

After a short relaxation and spot of lunch, I make ready for my Ceremony. I find a sheltered position out of the wind. It is close on 3.00 pm. The sun is now illuminating the sacred land around Dozmary Pool. Peace and stillness descend. I lay down all the Ceremonial articles needed. I begin my Ceremony to earth the Atlantean Temple with a special prayer. As I ask Archangel Michael for his protection, I become conscious of a great company from the Land of Light with me this precious day. I speak *'The Great Invocation'* then offer each crystal in turn, calling on Merlin, Is-Ra and Beloved Mary.

Dozmary Pool and Farm indicating position of the earthed Atlantean Temple – to the left of the farmhouse

As I voice the words: *'Let the ancient Temple of Atlantis be brought down from the Etheric Realm where it now resides and be securely grounded on Mother Earth'* my inner vision fixes on a Temple of Light with shining white pillars, resting on the western side of Dozmary Pool. In Atlantean days, I understand that where the pool is now, was but one part of a vast Temple complex, so this positioning of the newly earthed Temple is perfect. At home I checked with my dowsing crystal its exact location, which is just before Dozmary Pool Farm near the lake edge, Grid Ref 193748. For any pilgrim wishing to visit this sacred site, park on the little road close to the property Pinnockshil and take the track opposite to the lake, turn left and walk along the shoreline to the farmhouse. Please bear in mind that the Temple although earthed, is still Etheric in nature and can only be seen by those with clairvoyant sight. As I voice *'Let the Light shine'* the valley is filled with Holy Light. Archangel Michael is in attendance. It is his trusty sword which, as it hits the ground, sets the seal on this sacred act - *'Let it be done'* and it is done. The Temple of ancient times has returned to play its part in the New Age and in the New Jerusalem, now being established within the mystic British Isles. A voice loud and clear resonates within:

ARCHANGEL MICHAEL

"Blessed pilgrim. You have travelled far this day to do your duty by the Cosmic forces. Well done my valiant soldier (so it was he who spoke with me earlier on my walk, I should have known). *The Temple is nestling alongside Dozmary Pool. The Light is returning to Britain. The New Jerusalem will emerge out of the old chaos and destruction. We do not mean destruction in the physical sense beloved sister. We mean destruction of those salient things which humanity holds most dear and which feed the ego. It is the breaking down of barriers of the inner being, whereby each individual identifies with the concept of love and not fear, generosity and not hatred, rebuilding and not destruction.*

For your Earth's resources are finite and over many many years, greed has destroyed much of your precious metals and resources. Greed has taken over the desire mind of many. This greed then leads to abuse of power and cruelty. THIS MUST STOP - it WILL stop. Man is at last beginning to recognize the result of his greed. The New World will rise like a phoenix out of the ashes of human greed and power and will bring into being the New Jerusalem on Earth. This is moving your precious Planet through time as one age passes into the next, each one a step further to the Golden Age. Yes, a long long time you may think (reading my mind) *but this is a part of the great Cosmic Cycle of Life and we are ALL part of that Cosmic Cycle and we each play our part precious pilgrim. Live each day with valour. Have no fear.*

Life eternal is for all not just for the chosen ones. BUT you dear pilgrims, should choose your pathway through your life very carefully. Now is the time to put aside foolish things, put aside personal greed and take up the banner, take up the Sword of Righteousness, plough your way with valour and gentleness through your life dear pilgrims. My sword is with you always. I am the Archangel of pure Light. I protect your every move pilgrims. The Light is yours. The Right is yours. The way forward is yours - for the choosing. So - TAKE UP YOUR BANNER - HOLD IT HIGH and GO FORWARD INTO THE LIGHT."

As this Great Being leaves me, I have a vision of Michael on his steed dressed in full armour, with his sword held up high in his right hand, riding off into the distance across a deep-blue starlit sky. I am saying: *"Thank you great Archangel for your words of wisdom and for your protection this sacred day."*

I hear Merlin's raven croak and watch as it flies off in the direction of Dozmary Pool. I sit for a very long time in the silence until I eventually begin to feel the chill of the wind. As I look down into the valley to my right, I believe I can see the settlement where Mary and her family stayed. Tomorrow I shall go in search of it. I rise, take my rose and white quartz crystals and bury them beneath a large granite boulder offering a blessing. As I have been made aware of the positioning of the earthed Atlantean Temple, I repeat the same gesture in that locality before I leave the area.

I retreat off Brown Gelly hill to the farm track and walk along the road beside Colliford Lake. As I make my way back to the car I reinstate the blue and gold healing colours for my hip, which now feels strong and without pain. There are some deep purple violets almost hidden within the tall grass at the edge of the road. I can remember the time when small sprigs of Devonshire violets were sold in shops all over the country. The nursery which produced them was on the road between Dawlish and Starcross in South Devon. But like many things it has closed down - sadly no more little bunches of violets for sale. My journey back to Boscastle is an easy drive and uneventful.

JOURNEY TO DOZMARY SETTLEMENT

The last day of my pilgrimage to Bodmin Moor sees me returning to the same area as yesterday, the intention being to attempt to find the Druidic settlement where Mary and her family were accommodated. Sadly I am to leave Boscastle but I will return. I drive south and this time leave the A30 just before Jamaica Inn, onto a narrow country road which signpost directs me to '*Sibley Lake*'. This runs parallel to the road I walked along yesterday and is to the east of Brown Gelly. My map indicates that there are several settlements on the lower slopes of Brown Gelly and in the vicinity of Dozmary Pool. I hope to be guided. I am driving through the most picturesque valley beside the gently flowing River Fowey - a quiet and delightful backwater. The stream-side of the road is lined with small standing stones. I suspect that this little valley has been much the same for hundreds of years.

I come to the start of the track leading to Higher Landon Farm where I believe the settlement to be and park in a small off-road area. After a coffee and biscuit I emerge from the car into the morning sunshine. Before I set off, I stand on a little bridge over the River Fowey, looking into its clear waters. A sheep and her lambs are taking a drink. The cuckoo's clear note is once more filling the valley.

I begin the walk up the long dusty dirt-track towards the farm, the heights of Brown Gelly rising before me. The area to my right and left is marshy land and I remember seeing a sign '*Road liable to Flooding*'. We humans think we have tamed the landscape, but we still have to contend with the forces of nature. Among the long grasses there is delicate little pink plant indicative of a boggy area, known as lady's smock, so called because it was apparently a favourite colour for lady's smocks in the Middle Ages. Its other name is cuckoo flower as it begins to flower when the cuckoo arrives in April.

To my right, I see on the brow of a slope, an area of gorse and boulders. My heart leaps, because cognizance tells me this is what I am looking for. I walk on up the hill past the farmhouse with a sense of returning to a place once known to me. Soon I am nearly overcome with excitement as on my right is clear evidence of an ancient settlement with stone circles and large granite triangular stones, almost hidden amongst the gorse bushes. How on earth can I get in as the area is enclosed with barbed wire. Saved from any rash action, a little further on I am able to walk through a broken-down open gate. Access - the Gods are kind to me. I ask permission of the ancient Druid guardian to enter their sacred domain. It is hard to express the joy I am feeling - I have returned to an age long gone. I WAS HERE. I just know it. As I begin my explorations, I realize that this settlement is huge - a vast area of hut circles, dolmens, recumbent standing stones, one of which is over four metres in length. I stand in amazement at all the visible evidence of a past era. There are times, when I can't quite get over the wonder of being guided to discover places of my past life and this is one of them. I sense a presence:

DRUID ELDER

"You are so welcome once again dear Naomi, Sister of Light. This Dozmary settlement was your home for a short while 2,000 or so years ago. However, you have returned here in previous lives since, so this landscape is well known to you. (at this revelation my eyes are whelming up - I feel so at home here. I now ask the question with my inner voice: *"Why did I have to make such a difficult journey to Brown Gelly yesterday?"* because I can see that if I had taken a drive to this side of the hill the route would have been shorter). *My dear child we wished you to understand from a very physical aspect, the journeying of the ancient ones and the saints of old, of which you were one.* (I am asking which one?). *I am not permitted to say but you will discover in your own time.*

To continue - the journeying for those of the past was quite arduous and many a time great sacrifices had to be made. You my dear Naomi know of this very well. You journeyed through Cornwall with your mother, our blessed Angel Mary and you shared in the hardships of the times. As a young girl you were strong and forthright. Mary was at times a little overcome with the strenuous nature of the travelling. You were her loving and dedicated support at all times. Our blessed Jesus as a boy, was also strong but the character was more gentle. When he was at this settlement, he would go wandering up to the hills by himself - yes even as a boy he felt drawn to commune with his Father in Heaven, with the Angels and Cosmic Forces - for he was of their ilk. We understand dear Naomi, this today has been a profound experience for you. You will learn more as this day manifests itself. We bless you my child. Beloved Mary is at my side."

In contemplation now, I am reliving the words of the Druid Elder. As I rest within the confines of this sacred circle, I become aware of protective wings around me. I look up to Brown Gelly remembering my long pilgrim journey yesterday. I am not alone - this place is thronged with the ancient ones and I feel their joy at my presence. My heart is full - my grail cup over-floweth. I am now hearing a skylark singing its song of exaltation as it is poised between Heaven and Earth. The wild cry of the curlew comes across the moorland from the sanctuary of Dozmary Pool. Never have I wanted to stay in a place so much. I lay down an offering of a small white feather and quartz crystal with a silent prayer. I have a thought - could I be sitting in the very circle where I resided in my past life as Naomi?

As I make my way through the ancient stones, a snipe rises abruptly from the ground in front of me. I watch as it zig-zags across the blue sky. Moving on over the terrain, I reach what I believe to be one section of an enormous stone circle. Is this the ancient Druidic Temple site? I walk the whole circumference jumping from stone to stone. Then, trying to get some idea of the diameter, I step it out in a hundred and four large strides. Accepting that one stride would be approximately one metre, we have a diameter of one hundred and four metres. In the centre on a rise I see an extremely large granite stone with several stones piled around it. I am elated - this must be the Altar. I hear: *"You are so diligent young Light Worker we applaud you."* For confirmation - oh ye of little faith - I dowse and it is correct. I am now receiving a vision of a Druid dressed in white robes. In the distance I can see Dozmary Pool and a picture of the newly earthed Atlantean Temple forms in my mind. From my pack I take out a beautiful shiny shell from Llansteffan Beach in Carmarthenshire. I carefully but firmly wedge it between two of the boulders, alongside which I place a white quartz crystal for the ancestors. I now pour some of the water which I retrieved from Dozmary Pool over them. I offer a blessing for this sacred site and for the newly earthed Atlantean Temple with the words: *"I honour you all blessed ones of my past. Thank you for guiding me to this sacred place."* How I would love to share my amazing and profound discoveries with special friends, but at this stage in my Mission with Mary it is not to be - I will be patient.

Regrettably I am to leave. I walk back through the stones towards the track. On route I spy a large triangular white-granite stone with miniscule crystals embedded within its surface, which sparkles in the sunlight. Would I be allowed to keep this one for myself? I stand quite still for a moment with my eyes closed, ensuring it is acceptable to take this special stone with me. As this is granted, lo and behold another one appears. I graciously 'accept' this one also, because I believe there is a place for it, although I know not where at this moment in time. As I load up my two gifts into my pack it has become decidedly heavier.

Returning down the farm track to the road, I find myself having to walk through cattle once more which have wandered off the surrounding marshland. Okay I am getting used to them now, but then to test my resolve, I am suddenly confronted with a real ring-in-the-nose bull on my track - lovely. I erect a stone-wall Etheric barrier between him and me with the hope that he won't be able to see me! I then put myself in the Light and 'calmly' carry on. Phew - that was a close one I think, as he lumbers past me.

TO THE CHURCH OF ST NEOT

Back at the car, I munch my way through a delicious crisp green apple before driving on to the nearby village of St Neot, my aim to visit its Parish

Church and Holy Well. I pass an enticing looking track to Golitha Falls - but resist the temptation. I see a herd of deer grazing in a field and pull in to take a photograph. I stop again, this time at an old bridge over the River Fowey, which is not in use today. A plaque informs me this is '*Treverbyn Bridge. River Fowey. Circa 1412*'. This ancient packhorse bridge with its vee-shaped sections for pedestrians, is amazingly well restored. Dropping down the hill to St Neot I drive through a dark sunken lane with tree roots clinging to the high rock wall above me and a mass of bright yellow celandines growing along the banks. I park up in the local car park and take a saunter around. I pass a shop and pub then come to a fascinating 'hole in the wall' close to the church which features two standing stones supporting a dressed lintel. Within the space is a pyramidal shaped granite stone and built into the rocky wall is a small receptacle, perhaps for an offering.

I walk up some old stone steps to the Church of St Neot. The first thing that catches my eye is a well shaped yew tree, which feels to be the guardian of this sacred place. Alongside, are four ancient stone crosses of different Celtic design. I sit on a stone bench offering a blessing to the Deva of the Yew. Something awakens within me and I know that here is to be the home of the second of the beautiful white sparkly granite stones from the Dozmary Pool settlement. I lay the stone in the semi-darkness under the tree in recognition of the deva and St Neot. I hear:

YEW TREE DEVA

"Thank you pilgrim for your sacred gift from the settlement near Dozmary Pool. I am the strong guardian of this ancient churchyard and protect all wayfarers. My felicitations to you dear pilgrim as you journey to discovery. Your namesake, St Neot is awaiting your presence. Goodbye."

Well - what am I to make of that? Suddenly the light dawns - a flash of inspiration is telling me that St Neot was one of my past incarnations. I do not know about the word 'namesake' but maybe this is 'deva-speake'. At Dozmary settlement I was told by the Druid Elder, that I would discover more as I journeyed on this day and he was right. This for me is a major revelation, for which I thank the Masters.

The Church of St Neot is superb, with many features of interest, such as a battlemented porch and south aisle which date from the fifteenth century, plus its original wagon roof. However, the main focus as I enter its sanctuary is the medieval stained glass windows of dazzling colours, most of which contain original glass. Remembering that yesterday my Ceremonial day at Dozmary Pool was St George's Day, I am particularly drawn to a window at the west end of the north aisle which depicts '*The Legend of St George*'. St George as the Patron Saint of England is well known, but this association goes much deeper. How many are aware that he is the Guardian of the ancient Light in Britain and as such he would have a supreme objective in the manifestation of that Light. From the Higher Realms his influence would have been brought to bear in the reactivation of the Light at Dozmary Pool as at other ancient sites. Another excellent stained glass window illustrates St Neot with his staff. St Neot is also depicted in a fabric hanging with an antlered deer at his feet and what have I passed on my way here - a field of deer - coincidence?

WHO WAS ST NEOT?

What do we know of this saint, whom insight has just told me is a past life of mine? Later at home I did some investigation and learnt that St Neot was a ninth century monk who was ordained in Glastonbury Abbey. In the abbey his role was as a sacristan and as such he had the care of the sacred vessels. It is claimed he was an Englishman, a relative of King Alfred the Great, and that he had visited Rome. In his search for solitude, he retired to this part of Cornwall where he is said to have became a hermit. Numerous stories have grown up around this saint, including his ability to live on one fish a day taken from the Holy Well, hence his title as the Patron Saint of Fish. In art St Neot is often portrayed as an old monk with a pilgrim's staff and hat. He died in AD 870 and his relics are said to have found their way to St Neot's in Huntingdonshire.

Sitting in one of the old pews in the church with eyes closed, my inner vision shows me St Neot dressed in a long grey-blue robe, holding in his right hand his staff which has a Celtic cross at its apex. He speaks with me:

ST NEOT

"My child, my soul mate - for we, you and I, are as one. My staff was your staff. My Light was your Light. My pilgrimage was your pilgrimage. I travelled this ancient land bringing to those who would hear me, the words of our Lord - the Master Jesus, who taught us 'The Way' - the true way. Love your neighbour as yourself. Do good to those who despise and abuse you. This is the way of the heart dear pilgrim. We have to return incarnation after incarnation to learn and proffer this sacred truth. And so it is now for you my child. The way of the pilgrim - the seeker of truth, is everlasting. So be it. The road is long. The joys many. The hardships great. BUT we each overcome the vagaries of Earthly life and move ever forward into the Light. I know this. You know this. You are still in your present Earthly incarnation, being presented with challenges. How you deal with those challenges is of vital importance. Always bring them into the Light of Cosmic truth and understanding and the way will be made straight for you. Always bring them into the Rose in the Heart and you will receive redeeming love. THIS IS TRUTH fellow pilgrim. This is 'The Way' my soul mate. One day when you have completed your Earthly journey, you will return to the whole, and perfect understanding will be yours. I await this time. You will go to my Holy Well now pilgrim. I offer you a blessing. (A question: "did you have an oratory nearby?"). I didn't have an Oratory as such, but I settled very close to my Holy Well."

St Neot has left me. I find this all quite fascinating. I have made brief reference to reincarnation before. One can presume from this, that St Neot is another aspect of my whole soul which resides in the Heavenly Spheres. I am feeling the sacredness of the moment. I offer my profound thanks and blessings to St Neot for his remarkable words. To have been granted this awareness of a past incarnation, is extremely precious and I leave the church inspired and gratified.

I take a wander round the churchyard, which is sparkled with primroses around the many magnificent trees. It is now that I meet with the lady who tells me of St Neot's 'crow pound' on Goonzion Downs.

ST NEOT'S HOLY WELL

As I walk to the Holy Well, I find I am taking a steady pace, with my hands clasped in front of me as if in the sleeves of a cowl. I am on a narrow road by a stream, the banks of which are covered with bluebells and wild garlic. At a gated entrance to a field marked with small standing stones, I see St. Neot's Well, set against the back-drop of a huge rocky cliff-face. I take the well trodden path across the grass to its entrance, which has a surround of granite stonework. Engraved on the lintel are the words *'Restored in 1852'* and the top supports a small Celtic cross. A stone slab at its base, indicates a further restoration has taken place as recently as 1996. Now I am looking at a small very old faded-oak door with a large iron latch. My heart sinks momentarily thinking it to be locked, but - no. I draw the latch to one side and as it squeaks open I see a slate altar supported on an old iron frame. There are niches in the stone walls. From the back, crystal clear water is trickling forth into the little stony pool beneath. Rather irreverently I am thinking, that St Neot must have been exceedingly clever to have received a fish a day out of this, but it is a great story and there is a stream close-by! I walk down the three old stone steps and gently place my offering of a small quartz crystal and posy of wild flowers on the altar, offering a blessing for this sacred place. I re-fix the iron latch on the old well door and bid farewell to St Neot.

Back in the village I pop into the shop for an ice-cream. The choice is rather limited so I 'make do' with a Magnum! Before I take my final leave I am to go to the hill-top settlement of Goonzion Downs where Mary stayed, as recorded earlier. My day has come to a close. My pilgrimage has come to a close. It is nearly 6.00 pm as I begin my drive back to Devon, bringing with me the new knowledge gleaned this sacred day.

ON MY RETURN FROM BODMIN MOOR

The day after my pilgrimage, I make the spiritual link and thank the Lady Mary and all the Masters of the Light who have guided and guarded me on my travelling. On this occasion I receive a beautiful message from White Eagle and then it is St Neot who comes to me:

ST NEOT

"You may speak with me at any time. You may ask of me anything. For I am your twin soul Peace Rose. I work on the vibration of love. I have learnt much since my return

to the Heavenly life. I know, because you know, how difficult Earthly existence can be. I WILL always be here to help you."

THE HIGHER SELF

So my higher self manifesting through St Neot offers help. The Higher Self then, is not just a higher expression of the individual, but is of the whole soul, which holds the total of learned wisdom of each of its many separate incarnations, whether on Planet Earth or elsewhere in the Universe. This is most valuable and puts a different perspective on spiritual guidance. In times of trouble, not only can we ask our Father-Mother God - not only can we make that link with the Angels and Masters - not only can we speak with our Guides and Helpers, but in the silence of our own hearts, we can tune into our TOTAL soul wisdom and allow our Higher Self to be our helpmate. This might be quite obvious to everyone else and I am now wondering if I am the only one who hasn't caught on. In my own meditations, I tune into my Higher Self, but until now the full extent of its subtleties - its knowledge and wisdom - has not registered.

BELTANE/MAY DAY

Today is May 1st - May Day, which day in the annual calendar, welcomes in the ancient Celtic Fire Festival of Beltane. In past times fires would have been lit on beacons throughout the land, as the Sun/Fire Goddess awakens from her slumbers to promote the full flowering of new life and hope. It is springtime welcoming in summer with its show of sweet smelling flowers such as rose and honeysuckle, which scent is very potent in the warmer air. It is celebrated by the merriment of traditional activities such as dancing around the maypole and May queens on floats riding through villages. The Padstow 'Obby Oss' will be whirling its way through the streets of the old town today. At this time of the year at Malvern, in Welsh-English Border Country, ancient custom was and still is today, to dress the wells with wild flowers to honour the water deities.

MARY'S FINAL JOURNEYING IN CORNWALL

To complete her travelling in Cornwall, Mary with Naomi, Jesus and Joseph, leave Dozmary Pool settlement and climbed back to Bodmin's heights. First the journey took them to King Arthur's Bed and on to stay at Nine Stones settlement. They then went over Fox Tor and Trewint to a settlement at Braydown, thus keeping to the high ground. From there they journeyed north, coming off the moor for Warbstowe Bury settlement and on through Rosecare for Trengayor and the coast at Millook Haven. Two short sea trips took them first to Bude Haven for Maer settlement, then on to the mouth of the Abbey River for Hartland and their first step onto Devonshire soil.

Before I continue with Mary's pilgrimage, this time through my home county of Devon, I am to take a trip to Wales with a special friend. We shall be based near Abergavenny relatively close to Border Country. I was very reluctant to take this break, as I thought it would intrude on my Mission with Beloved Mary, but suddenly found myself saying 'yes' to my friend and getting excited at the prospect. As it happened, this was not a deviation from my Mission as a higher purpose emerged. Unbeknown to me, Mary had obviously masterminded this journey, in order that I pay a visit to the ancient settlement of Aconbury, which is situated just to the south of Hereford - now in England but once in Wales. It was here, she and Naomi met with their Welsh family at the end of their South West pilgrimage. My original thought in this regard, fell on Priddy in Somerset, but during this holiday, new insights emerged. This story is documented in The Epilogue.

CONCLUSION TO CORNWALL

So draws to a close the Lady Mary's pilgrimage through Celtic Cornwall. It seems a long time back since I was made privy to Mary's Mission of 2,000 years ago at the beginning of the Piscean Age, and her Mission for me in this new Age of Aquarius, which began my own pilgrimages in Cornwall. Mary's role in the South West of Britain was to reactivate the ancient Atlantean Temples in the Etheric Realm and perform Light Ceremonies at Druidic sites and those dedicated to the Goddess. I have picked up the Holy Baton and followed in her wake, bringing in the Cosmic Light and earthing the ancient Atlantean Temples. You will see from the list in 'INTRODUCTION TO THE SOUTH WEST' that by far the majority of the sacred sites in ancient Dummonia were in Cornwall - thirteen in all.

To conclude I give you a brief summary of the pilgrimage undertaken by Beloved Mary and her two children Naomi and Jesus with Joseph of Arimathea. Their journeying began with the landing at Place in the Roseland Peninsula following a sea voyage from the Holy Land. The family travelled extensively around Cornwall but were not together the whole time. There were occasions as we have learnt when Joseph took the boy Jesus with him on his mining inspections.

Mary's first Cosmic Ceremony was at Place Sacred Hill Atlantean site. While staying at Place settlement, Mary and Naomi went across to the Lizard Peninsula for Cow-y-Jack Druidic settlement, which was dedicated to the Goddess Hathor, and which had an Atlantean Temple in the Etheric. Here once again she enacted a sacred Ceremony. Onward through Roseland's hinterland, she performed two more Ceremonies of Light at Veryan Castle Atlantean site and Golden Fort Druidic settlement. Crossing the River Fal, her pilgrimage took her to Cowlands, another Druidic Temple site with a dedication to Hathor and an Atlantean Temple. Then Mary journeyed to Carn Brea Atlantean site and thence to Tolcarne Wartha Druidic settlement - at each of these a special Ceremony was undertaken by Mary. Their time at Carn Brea and Andrew Wartha coincided with the winter solstice and Candlemas respectively. It is at Tolcarne Wartha Mary met with Anna her mother, who had returned to her Cornish homeland after the death of her husband and the birth of Mary's first child - Naomi.

Heading further west Mary and her family, stayed at Marazion settlement in order that Mary could perform a Ceremony at St Michael's Mount, before moving on to Cape Cornwall. Following a trip to The Scilly Isle with Jesus and Naomi, Mary's pilgrimage proceeded around The Cape to eventually arrive at Men-an-Tol, where she was instrumental in reactivating an Atlantean Temple. Joseph joined them for this Cosmic Ceremony. The journey along the North Cornish coast took Mary to Portreath Druidic settlement for a further Light Ceremony. From here Mary and her companions continued east, and on reaching Castle-an-Dinas in Camel Corner, she performed a sacred rite for the Atlantean Temple in the Etheric. Journeying over St Breock Downs and crossing the Camel Estuary, Mary with Naomi arrived at Brea Hill settlement. A little to the north of this site is Port Isaac where they reconnected with Jesus and Joseph. Now the four travellers went south and east to Bodmin Moor for two final Ceremonies, one at The Hurlers Druidic Temple site and the other at Dozmary Pool Atlantean settlement. Mary was at The Hurlers for the summer solstice. The final stage of her Cornish pilgrimage saw Mary and her family going north across Bodmin Moor for the coast and on by sea to Hartland in Devon.

The Lady Mary's Mission in Cornwall was at an end. What an incredible journey. I would suggest that as she was nearing the completion of this the Cornish section of her sacred pilgrimage, she would have been physically and emotionally exhausted and yet very much at peace with herself. The last part of her journey which was uneventful, would no doubt have allowed her time for recuperation and reflection. Perhaps she was already contemplating and preparing for her pilgrimage through present-day Devon? Whilst writing these words I am receiving confirmation of my insights. I am also hearing: *"a job well done my trusty and faithful servant."* This accolade from on high, not for me, but for Our Lady.

My Mission throughout Cornwall as you have witnessed, has so far brought me the most profound and rewarding experiences, with new insights and ever increasing knowledge. With dedication I have undertaken my sacred role. I honour Beloved Mary - my *'Rose in the Heart'*. I thank all those Masters and Angels who have walked at my side and who have offered protection and words of wisdom. I tender my humble gratitude for this opportunity to serve the One Light. For me also - what an incredible journey!

Part II – Devon

Introduction to Devon

A t the beginning of my Devonshire chronicle with the Lady Mary and her family, I initially prepare with an attunement. I light my candle: *"This is for you Beloved One. I ask for insight as I plot your journeying through Devon. I ask a blessing on my beautiful dowsing crystal. I ask for guidance as to where you wish me to go and which ancient sites you wish me to reactivate or earth an Atlantean Temple."*

I settle down, maps laid out before me and keep my candle vigil as I plot Mary's pilgrimage through Devon. It took me three days, as at times there was the need to break up the concentration, have refreshment and get some sleep! I take a section of the map at a time as I methodically chart her travelling. It soon becomes clear that Mary's Devonshire journeying was very different from her Cornish one. As in Cornwall, she had to make contact with specific Druidic settlements in order to fulfil requirements from the Masters. However, they were less in number and the distance between each site was greater. Some of the settlements were used as sanctuaries of rest on her wide-ranging journey. My own experiences in Devon also turned out to be quite dissimilar from my adventures around Cornwall. This was due to several factors. One - except for my initial pilgrimage, I could undertake my trips on a daily basis because they were relatively more localized. Secondly - each Light Ceremony was to be performed on site. Further - I was in more familiar territory

An outline of Mary's pilgrimage shows her travelling through Devon from Hartland on the north-west coast, south to the Druidic settlement of Brent Tor. From here she climbed to Dartmoor for two Druidic settlements which had an Atlantean Temple in the Etheric, the first at Merrivale Ceremonial Complex and the second at Hembury Fort. From Hembury she turned north along the eastern fringe of the moor to a Druidic settlement at Hound Tor. Finally Mary went through Mid Devon and on into Somerset. A fuller picture of her journeying is given in *'MARY'S JOURNEY DEVON'*.

I had been asked to perform Ceremonies of Light at four ancient sites in Devon, all of which are on or close to Dartmoor. The first was a Druidic Ceremony at Brent Tor. The second Ceremony was to earth an ancient Atlantean Temple at Merrivale Ceremonial Complex. Towards the end of August 2008 on my return from Wales and before I was fully alert to my

Mission, I was impressed to visit Merrivale settlement and undertook a short Ceremony to link Merrivale with Strata Florida, the heart centre of the Welsh Grail. I returned in June of the following year to perform my Atlantean Ceremony. In August 2008 I also went to Hembury Castle and enacted my very first Atlantean Ceremony. It was in the previous year, I had made pilgrimage to Hembury Castle and received a message from White Eagle, informing me of a Temple in the Etheric that I was to reactivate, and I would know when the time was right. I assumed that it was a Druidic Temple, but in due course learnt it was Atlantean and I was to earth it. The Ceremony I used on that occasion was a simplified version of the one I subsequently devised. My final Light Ceremony in Devon was at Hound Tor Druidic Temple site.

Devon as with Cornwall has a multitude of place names which could have association with Mary - derivations of either; 'Mary' 'Holy' 'Rose' or 'Heart'. Using the pattern these names were forming, combined with insight and dowsing had helped me identify her route. I list just a few for you, following in order of Mary's pilgrimage. Starting in the north of Devon, we have Hartland, Rosedown, Rosehill and Holwell. Further south, there is Mary Tavy, Merrivale, Hart Tor and Holybrook. To the east I see Holwell Tor, Holcombe, Down St Mary, Maire (Mary), Rosemoor and Rose Ash. Near Rose Ash is Marionsleigh, which is another accepted name for Our Lady. Now read into these names what you will, but possible evidence of Mary's once presence in this ancient land cannot be ignored, especially when one comes to 'Virginstow' - Grid Ref. 380926.

My pilgrimage through Devonshire beckons. My intention is to follow Mary's route as near as I can. I feel that this time my pilgrimages will be easier in some respects. In the first instance, my knowledge has increased and secondly I am primed to Mary's wishes. However, throughout my travelling I have to remember to listen to Mary's guidance and be constantly alert to my intuition. I can make my plans but must allow for flexibility. So - off I go on my Devon experience - a new phase has begun and anticipation is great.

Mary's Journey - Devon

CHAPTER 9 FROM HARTLAND TO BRENT TOR
BRENT TOR - DRUIDIC Ceremony on site

The four travellers, Mary, Jesus and Naomi with Joseph of Arimathea have sailed from Cornwall along a stretch of coastline which shoreline was further out 2,000 years ago. On arrival at the mouth of the then much wider Abbey River at Hartland, they went up-river to a Druidic settlement at **ROSEDOWN**. Here they all took time to recuperate. Following this Joseph took Jesus with him on one of his business trips, while Mary and Naomi travelled on south through West Devon. With their Druid companions, they journeyed across land to Hollaford where they picked up Seckington Waters. I notice on the map an area of marsh marked out, which could be an indicator of land under water in past times. For the two pilgrims, this was the beginning of a good navigable river system which connected to the River Torridge. Mother and daughter then journeyed by boat south-east to Newton St Petrock, where a Holy Well is indicated on my map. At this point they left the river and headed overland to the **ROSEHILL** settlement. From here it was to be south through Holroyd, across the River Torridge, on over hilly country for some miles, to stay at **BROADBURY CASTLE**. Mary and Naomi continued south to take a break at Burley Wood settlement. Travelling on they dropped down into the valley of the River Lyd, to finally climb to St Michael of the Rock, the **BRENT TOR** Druidic settlement. It was here, that Joseph and Jesus rejoined Mary and Naomi. It was here also, that Mary took the role of a Druid Elder, and performed a sacred Cosmic Ceremony of Light.

CHAPTER 10 CLIMBING TO ANCIENT DARTMOOR.

MERRIVALE - ATLANTEAN Ceremony on site

Leaving the Brent Tor settlement, Mary and her family began the steady climb to Dartmoor, going east through Mary Tavy, then crossing the River Tavy to Peter Tavy. After Peter Tavy, they made their way over Cox Tor keeping to the high ground, using ancient tracks through the then afforested landscape. Now it was a short ride to **MERRIVALE CEREMONIAL COMPLEX,** an ancient Druidic settlement, which has an Atlantean Temple in the Etheric. Mary undertook a special Ceremony to reactivate this ancient Temple.

CHAPTER 11 MOORLAND TRAVERSE FOR HEMBURY CASTLE

HEMBURY CASTLE - ATLANTEAN Ceremony on site

Their next destination was the settlement of **HEMBURY CASTLE**. another Atlantean Temple site. For Mary and her family, this was to be a long arduous journey across Dartmoor on horseback. From Merrivale they travelled south over Walkhampton Common and Cramber Tor to Hartor Tors. Now their way took them east, dropping off Hartor Tors, crossing the River Plym and continuing downhill to Broad Rock at Erme Head. From this point, the going would have been quite treacherous, as they had to negotiate boggy marshland, using specially laid out trackways to traverse the dangerous terrain. Continuing in this direction they journeyed on to the ancient settlement of Huntington Warren which is north-west of the now Avon Dam, where they rested. Eventually, the little party dropped down off the moor at Water Oak Corner, over Lambs Down to cross the River Mardle and Holy Brook before they climbed to Hembury Castle settlement. Mary was very weary by now. However, after a period of rest she was to reactivate the Atlantean Temple as designated from above. The last part of Mary's journey in this area, saw her and her family return to Holy Brook and travel east to reach the River Dart close to Buckfast Abbey.

CHAPTER 12. DARTMOOR'S EASTERN FRINGE

HOUND TOR - DRUIDIC Ceremony on site

For Mary and her companions, from Buckfast now began a long journey north through East Dartmoor. First they made use of the waters of the River Dart which connected to the River Webburn, travelling by boat upstream to Buckland in the Moor. They climbed out of the river valley to Buckland Beacon and over Buckland Common. On now, they went through Foals Arrishes settlement, across Seven Lord's Lands, over Holwell Lawn to reach the Druidic settlement of **HOUND TOR**. Once again Mary and her family took part in a Druidic Ceremony of Light. Their journey continued north over Hayne Down and Easdon Tor. They crossed the River Bovey at North Bovey, went on to Mortonhampstead, through Holcombe, to reach **CRANBROOK CASTLE** on the south bank of the River Teign. Following a short stay at this ancient hill fort, they negotiated the deep gorge of the Teign Valley. Their pilgrimage led them on a direct route north, through Drewsteignton. They left Dartmoor just north of Windscombe.

CHAPTER 13. THROUGH MID DEVON FOR EXMOOR

I have not been asked to perform a Ceremony at either of the settlements in this section of Mary's pilgrimage.

For Mary and her family, their journeying took them in an approximate northern direction through Mid Devon for Exmoor. During this part of her pilgrimage, Mary was not required to undertake a Ceremony at either of the settlements where she stayed - it was just a convenient travelling route through Devon for Cow Castle and Culbone Hill in Somerset. Beginning at Hole Farm, Mary, Naomi, Jesus and Joseph first went through Thorne Cross then passed by Hittisleigh Mill. From here they crossed the River Troney at Coltsfoot Farm, on through Landsend Barton, Lammacott Farm to Down St Mary. Now their journey took them in a NNE direction through Morchard Bishop to **BERRY CASTLE DRUIDIC SETTLEMENT**. After a short stay they went on through Washford Pyne and Nomansland, over Rose Moor, across the Little Dart River to a second Berry Castle. A break was taken here before Mary and her family continued on through Maire and Rose Ash, to cross the Crooked Oak River at Ash Mill. After a few miles they went over the River Yeo and climbed to their last settlement in Devonshire - **WHITECHAPEL FORT**. The final leg of Mary's journey in Devon, saw her continuing north, through Higher Ley to reach the present day Exmoor National Park at Millbrook. Climbing all the time, Mary and her family went via the now Holy Well Reservoir where there is a Holy Well, then over Darlick Moors close to the source of the River Mole. A mile or so further on they crossed the border into Somerset.

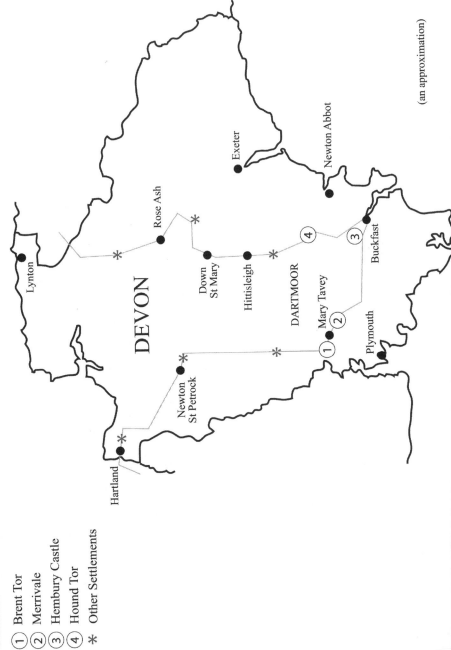

CEREMONIAL TEMPLE SITES IN DEVON

① Brent Tor
② Merrivale
③ Hembury Castle
④ Hound Tor
∗ Other Settlements

(an approximation)

CHAPTER 9
FROM HARTLAND TO BRENT TOR
Land of the Sacred Heart

It is the beginning of June 2009 and I am in North West Devon walking in the wide valley of the Abbey River near Hartland. In the early evening the stillness is beginning to descend. Having wandered through ancient woodland, I come to the crystal clear waters of the Abbey River. Now standing on the shingly river beach, I am listening to the river as it happily burbles its way through a deep narrow rocky gorge. This is the mystical realm of the little people, and I can almost feel them watching me from every nook and cranny of the dripping mossy banks. This is truly a magical and joyful place. I am thanking Beloved Mary for her guidance in bringing me to this little haven of peace. Memories are being re-awakened once again. This was a place of my past - in another existence - 2,000 years ago. I am Naomi, Mary's young daughter of those past times. My pilgrim adventures through my home county of Devon have begun.

JOURNEY TO HARTLAND

The Lady Mary and her family have left Cornwall for Devon. Travelling by sea, their sail craft has entered the mouth of the Abbey River, to begin the journey up-river to a settlement at Rosedown, just inland from Hartland. This is the beginning of their pilgrimage through Devonshire. In Mary's day this would have been a wide navigable river going deep into the hinterland. In this chapter I wish to connect with Mary at Hartland and follow her journey south to Brent Tor Druidic settlement. In order to do this I have first to reach Hartland. Therefore my plan is to travel north this first day, visiting one or two places on route, and linking it all up on the morrow as I journey south with Mary. I have booked in one night at Elmscott Youth Hostel which is on the coast near Hartland, in order to explore the area and gain some appreciation of the surrounding landscape.

Before I set off, as always I prepare myself for the journey ahead. I have my quiet moment with Beloved Mary, asking for her guidance. As I become aware of her presence, a feeling of love and compassion enfolds me. I walk out of my door into drizzly rain, never mind - ever the optimist - it will improve. In spite of the weather I decide to go over Dartmoor for West Devon. As I begin my drive to the moor, I pass fields of bright yellow oil seed rape spread out across the landscape, like liquid sunshine. Not my delightful observation, but a term phrased by my dear Welsh friend's father. I leave the main highway at Ashburton and after negotiating the ancient narrow stone Holne Bridge across the River Dart, I go over a cattle grid and into The National Park. After New Bridge, I sweep up to the high moors, carefully avoiding the wandering black moorland cattle looming up out of the atmospheric mists which are swirling around. I feel a bit like 'Pilgrim in the Mist' as I journey onwards. Knowing the road however I am quite comfortable in these conditions. The pervading mist brings to mind that crossing these moors would have been an extremely risky business for Mary and her companions in past times, trying to pick their way on horseback over rough moorland turf and bog. Their Druidic guides would no doubt have been familiar with the terrain and brought them to the safety of each settlement.

As I pass Princetown to my left, with its infamous prison tucked in just below North Hessary Tor, I am reminded of a story which tells of escaping prisoners in centuries past, who after becoming lost in the moorland fog and trying to surmount the boggy terrain, were glad to be rescued and returned to their cells! As I travel on I can't help but wonder, if there are any intrepid walkers out on the moors in this foggy weather. I have heard it said, that if you do get lost on the moors in the mist, an infallible solution is to follow a little stream down-hill until you reach a road. I can't vouch for that one, but would suggest it might be a case of - first find your stream, which could be a bit difficult if you are stuck on the top of a tor when the mist rolls in! The most sensible solution is to learn to read a map and have a compass. One rather frisky lamb leaps out into the path of my car and an emergency stop is called for - lucky lamb. I love this moorland in all states, including the wild mysterious face it is showing this day. I feel so at home in this ancient landscape.

MYSTERIOUS TALES OF DARTMOOR

Driving across Dartmoor today has brought to mind some of the many legends which have come down from days of yore, and which are still regaled today. I am sure that most have heard of the Arthur Canon Doyle story set on Dartmoor '*The Hound of the Baskervilles*'. In conditions such as today, one could well imagine a slavering beast coming out of the fog and leaping at the car. Further, there are many tales of the Hairy Hands of Dartmoor. In the 1950s, a motorcyclist was crossing the moor at night, on a road I have just been on I would add, when a pair of hairy hands closed over his, forcing his bike off the road. Of course stories of spectres and apparitions abound. One tells of a driver who was crossing Dartmoor near Dartmeet, when out of the mist, he saw a lady dressed in old fashioned clothes standing holding the reigns of her horse, looking quite bewildered. He stopped and asked if he could help and she said: *"I'm looking for my horse - have you seen him?"* and promptly disappeared. Of latter years there have been many sightings of big cats, which some say are pumas, bought as pets and let loose on the moors when they became too big and dangerous, which are now breeding. Fact or fiction - you decide but these tales do enliven the imagination

Off the moor now, I drop down to Tavistock and begin the drive north. The weather is lifting and the skies are lightening, offering a fine view to my right of the majestic heights of Dartmoor. I make a stop at Newton St Petrock for its Parish Church and Holy Well, which experiences I will share with you on my return journey tomorrow.

HARTLAND - LAND OF THE SACRED HEART.

I arrive at Elmscott Youth Hostel by 5.00 pm and sign in. After a cup of tea and snack, I am off to explore the Hartland area. I drive through narrow country lanes with vegetation running down the middle of the road. The high hedgerows are filled with tall grasses and wild flowers left to grow naturally. Tonight and tomorrow morning I wish to visit the following:

- The estuary entrance to the Abbey River where Mary's boat sailed in.
- Rosedown settlement where Mary stayed.
- Hartland Quay
- Hartland Abbey.
- Stoke Parish Church.

As finding ones way round these lanes is quite intricate, I shall go to whichever place presents itself first! It happens to be Stoke Parish Church, which I am not surprised to find closed this time of an evening. From the outside I see that it has a magnificent tall Norman tower which I subsequently discover is quite a landmark in the surrounding countryside, and I should imagine from the sea as well. So only a brief visit and on now to Hartland Quay. I have been here before on two occasions, one whilst walking the South West Way and another, staying in the hotel on a few days away with my local ramblers group. The quay which houses the hotel is built high up like a fortress, overlooking jagged rocks and often wild seas, being on the west coast of Britain. I look around and take stock. I suspect that 2,000 years ago the rocky shoreline even though it was further out, would be very much the same, making landing of a boat precarious at this point, which confirms my hypothesis that Mary's ship would have entered Devon via the Abbey River estuary. Leaving the quay I pass the driveway to Hartland Abbey. A notice tells me that it is not open today - Friday, or tomorrow - Saturday, so I will have to give that one a miss.

GATEWAY TO THE ABBEY RIVER

The now overcast skies will bring an early close to the day in spite of it being June. Keeping this in mind I set off in search of the river estuary. Studying the map, I decide that a place called 'Berry' will give me my best entrance point for the river valley. However, as usual I am to be taken on a challenging walk rather than a direct route. This I realize in retrospect is the way it is to be, in order that I may comprehend the lie of the land. I park at Berry, wisely taking note of a *'No Access to Motor Vehicles'* sign. At Berry House I can see Stoke Church, standing out on the skyline on the opposite side of the valley, above dense woodland.

The Abbey River Valley at Hartland showing probable width of river 2,000 years ago

My walk takes me downhill on a very narrow road its banks graced with huge green ferns. In the valley I alight at the far side of Hartland Abbey. The beautiful abbey grounds are grazed by a herd of black sheep, while drinking from the river are several donkeys. Pheasant are calling from the undergrowth. As I turn, I see there is a path through a field with a sign indicating one mile to the sea. From this point, it is very easy to identify the extended width of the original Abbey River, now a landscape of green fields bounded on both sides by steep woods. For some reason rather than walking the valley floor set out before me, I choose to continue on the uphill road. This takes me along the most amazing old green lane, with trees growing out of the top of moss-covered dry stone walls, their arched branches making it very dark and dank. As I enter the woodland and take the pathway leading to the sea, I find that I am now walking the ancient river valley at a slightly higher level. This is bringing back profound memories for me. I am saying to Mary who has come into my inner world: *"Beloved one - thank you."* I receive:

MARY

"My dear Naomi, we all are so very happy at your journeying today. Thank you for returning to this valley of the past. You will see the wide valley where our journey took us by boat up-river to our settlement. My dear child, this is a day of great sacredness. Re-live it whenever you can. You will never lose the memory. Let the Rose of Divine Love ever dwell in your Sacred Heart beloved one. For it is so."

From me: *"Thank you dearest Mary. I am truly blessed."*

My path which now runs alongside the Abbey River, is overhung with sweet scented wild honeysuckle. I scramble down to the river's edge and here I am immersed in the sound of the running water as it is channelled through a rocky gap. I stand for some while staring into the sparkling water, then out of the corner of my eye, I become aware of water sprites dancing with joy as they frolic in and out of the water. I take the mossy butterfly shape, which I found in Newton St Petrock woods earlier in my day, and with a blessing, gently lay it on the surface of the water, watching as it is taken downstream. I am now as close as I can get to the mouth of the Abbey River. Standing in reverence, I 'see' a small sail-craft enter the estuary and ply its way up-river on its way to the Rosedown settlement and I know the pilgrims from the Holy Land are on board.

It is time to leave as it is getting late and becoming quite dimpsey, the darkness of the woodland is closing in on me, so I beat a hasty retreat, feeling quite relieved when I reach the lane which will take me back to my car. My walk to the sea was enhanced with the sweet song of a thrush and on my return in the twilight, he is still serenading me. I see Stoke Church on the hill above me with a good pathway leading to it - a much quicker route to the valley, which I was not allowed to take! I am more than happy with my little evening pilgrimage and my discoveries in this area, which begins Mary's journeying through Devon. I arrive back at the hostel at 10.00 pm to find the door locked - an oversight I am told as I am allowed entry!

IN SEARCH OF THE ROSEDOWN SETTLEMENT

Leaving Elmscott the next morning, my intention is to look for the Rosedown settlement close to Hartland, where Mary and her family stayed. I take the road out of Hartland in an easterly direction, and at the hamlet of Rosedown searching painstakingly for any signs of the ancient site, stopping at intervals to look over hedgerows and to scour fields - but to no avail. There is simply no physical evidence left in the landscape. Rather disappointed, I must now leave North Devon to follow Mary's journey south.

WOOLSERY CHURCH OF ALL HALLOWS

After Rosedown, Mary and Naomi journey south from Hollaford using the river system of Seckington Waters and the River Torridge to Newton St Petrock. In Mary's day the rivers would have been a good mode of transport through this part of Devon. Meanwhile, Jesus with Joseph leave for their own travelling. On my way south I pay a call at Woolfardiswothy, or Woolsery as the locals call it, because I see a church marked on the map. What a delightful village this turns out to be as are so many round here. Hurrah, the Parish Church of All Hallows, originally Holy Trinity, is open. As I approach, I see that the church tower is very grand. Tiered in four layers, it apparently reaches to a height of seventy-four feet four inches to the top of its pinnacles. I walk into the porch, and what stands out for me is the Norman door arch, surrounded with stone effigies of universal ancient faces, strange birds and beasts, probably of Celtic origin, very similar to the corbals around the outside of the ancient church of Kilpeck in Momouthshire. The church has been modernized and carpeted throughout, but fortunately the old dark oak pew ends, depicting saints and old implements of farming and carpentry, have been kept and incorporated into the new pew benches.

THE RIVER TORRIDGE AT WEST PUTFORD

I am now at West Putford, approximately five miles south of Woolsery, right in the depths of the Devonshire countryside and close to the River Torridge. I have been trying for some while to access the river, in order to honour Mary's river journeying with a gift and to collect some water. I have crossed over this river back and forth on several occasions during my two days in North Devon, but somehow getting close has been denied me. I walk down to the bridge. Once again there is no way I can reach the water, so will have to forgo my collection, but I stand on the little stone parapet gazing into the effervescent waters below. I have made a posy of wild flowers securing it with a soft grass tie. This I drop into the water, offering a prayer and blessing for my Mary. So many times on this journey of mine I am saying: *"My dear Mary we travelled this way before you and I."*

NEWTON ST PETROCK - CHURCH AND HOLY WELL

From West Putford, the River Torridge flows south to Newton St Petrock. It is here that Mary and Naomi left the river and went overland to the Rosehill Druidic settlement, which we'll connect to in a moment. Meanwhile, I am heading for Newton St Petrock on this the second day of my pilgrimage. I am driving under cobalt blue skies filled with a flurry of white clouds of tantalizing shapes. I take up the story of my adventures there on my journey north yesterday, completing the tale with today's escapades.

I arrived in this sleepy little backwater, in order to visit the Parish Church and look for the Holy Well. On the village green is an ancient pollarded oak with a huge girth. I park up opposite the church. On entering the churchyard, I stop to offer a blessing and gift of a small triangular shiny white stone for the magnificent beech at its entrance. For my 'pains' I hear:

TREE DEVA

"Thank you dear pilgrim for your gift and for recognizing my presence. I wish for you to enjoy your visit to this ancient church. Search and you will find the Holy Well. Goodbye pilgrim."

The church is locked - no surprise there then. I have a wander round the churchyard, then head off in search of a key. Initial stop - a dear little cottage covered with pink roses by the church - there is no-one at home. A gentleman in the next door bungalow, directs me to 'Linny Park' where - there is no-one at home. The vicarage next to it - again no-one at home. Obviously another Mary Celeste.

Okay, I shall leave it for now and go in search of the Holy Well. I think I have pinpointed its position on my map, as being on a tiny tributary of the River Torridge. I wander off down a lane bordered with majestic pink foxgloves, then across a field spread with white clover. The public footpath sign which turns out to be at the wrong angle, directs me to the edge of some mixed woodland. I step over a rough bank into its dark interior, to be faced with a very steep slippery path leading down to a stream at the bottom. Is the Holy Well down there? Eventually I reach the stream to find no evidence of a well - holy or otherwise. I clamber back up through the woodland, now seeing the entrance to a badger earth, which I had missed on the way down as I was concentrating on trying to keep upright. I stop in my tracks, as I spy a most beautiful piece of pale green dried out moss in the shape of a butterfly. I carefully collect this and put it in my pack, thinking that it will have a future use and as you know, it was for the Abbey River later that day.

Back in the clover field, I see a footpath sign. This time, although the path through the woodland is steep, it is more established and a little easier to negotiate. The birds are suddenly very noisy and then I see the reason.. They are mobbing a bird of prey high up in the tree tops. It is a sparrow- hawk, which even without binoculars, is easily identifiable by its shape, size and its loud 'kek kek kek' cry. As I watch, it lurches from one tree to another trying to avoid the angry mob, until it eventually flies off defeated. All is quiet once more. Down I go as silently as I can through this ancient woodland, but still manage to disturb a deer drinking from the stream at the bottom. How splendid to briefly see this wild animal. The footpath takes me across a little stream on a narrow wooden bridge into a field, whereupon I step forth into grass up to my waist. This is obviously NOT a well used path! Struggling through the grass, then under an electric fence, I reach the river tributary at last, but of the Holy Well there is no sign. At this juncture I dowse, asking Mary if the well is nearer the church and receive an affirmative reply. I walk back uphill on the little path through the woods. Once more I am rewarded, this time with a beautiful white quartz/granite mix stone, which I accept with a special *'thank you'* to the Universe.

THE PARISH CHURCH OF ST PETROC

I return to St Petroc's Church, in order to look in that vicinity for the Holy Well and discover that it is now open, as a lady called Lesley is doing the cleaning I have entered through the old faded oak door, which features most unusually, a Gothic arch. It is written that St Petroc was a greatly revered man. We have met with him at Padstow in Cornwall, but he also had strong association with this part of Devon. This is a lovely old church, though the once gleaming white Gothic pillars and arches are now pale grey and crumbling. I am feeling its sadness, almost as if it was crying out for some loving attention. But of course as is often the case, there is no money available. It must be very disheartening for those who tenderly care for the little church, and for all the parishioners who worship here. The church has two redeeming features. One is a striking stained glass window in the chancel, depicting our Master Jesus with St Petroc and St Dorothea. Then there is a Norman font, which at its base has a large stone slab divided into small squares, each square marked out with ancient symbols including the rose, the fleur-de-lys, circles and strange mythical creatures. I have a moment's silence sitting in one of the pews, but with another person present, it does not feel conducive for a lengthy attunement. On leaving, I place a wild pink rose collected from the lane and a beautiful buzzard's feather, in the porch as an offering for Our Lady and St Petroc.

THE HOLY WELL - FINALLY

I learn from Lesley that the Holy Well is on private land belonging to a lady named Gwen Leonard, who lives at a house called 'Lenhaven' close-by. On reaching the house I knock on the door, but there is no reply. I 'cooy' around but can raise no-one - again! Leaning on a gate looking across a field in the direction I believe the well to be in, I am rather reluctant to trespass. Instead I decide to leave a note for Gwen, indicating that I shall return the next day, in the hope that I may be permitted to view the well. On my return this charming lady is waiting for me. She tells me that her husband knows of the well's existence and that it never dries up, plus he has apparently considered restoring it. We talk for some while as Gwen shares with me a little of village life. I then explain to her that a 'Holy Well' marked on a map would often indicate the one-time presence of a saint - here probably St Petroc - and is often purported to have healing properties, as opposed to a 'well' which could just be a village pump. I choose not to mention that the Virgin Mary may have sipped from the waters of this Holy Well at Newton St Petrock!

I set off through a little gate, over the newly cut hay field in the general direction of the well, telling Gwen that I shall call in on my return to report on my findings. Her parting words are that a Holy Well on her land could be a tourist attraction! I reach an area of dense undergrowth. Battling my way through and after much climbing over and under tree branches, I eventually reach a little pool of water in a secretive spot underneath the trees, where water seems to be bubbling up from below ground. I am now hearing my name being called from the distance, as Rita another local lady, who has heard of my exploits, excitedly rushes across the field to see if I have found anything. I don't know quite what she was expecting, but I could tell that she was a little disappointed when I pointed out what was little more than a puddle. She returned and I was left to my own devices. I am now standing on dodgy sinking tufts of grass and scrappling around in the water. I check with Mary who confirms that this is the Holy Well from whence she and Naomi drank. I find myself feverishly beginning to clear some of the grass and muck from the water with my bare hands. I discover some good size black stones which I use to form a very simple horseshoe shape outline to the well, leaving an open end to allow any excess water to trickle out. I am getting wetter and wetter. Before I leave, I ask permission of the deva to collect a little of the sacred water, then pour in some water retrieved from St Neot's Holy Well in Cornwall.

My 'Horseshoe' outline for the Holy Well, at Newton St Petrock

After my 'good deed' I return rather wet and dishevelled to my car. I dare not enter Gwen's delightful home in such a state, so I have a quick change of trousers, shoes and socks before knocking on her door. I tell her of my findings and my initial restoration work! She seemed amazed. You never know, my enthusiasm might rub off on the locals and produce the impetus needed for restoration of the Holy Well.

THE ROSEHILL DRUIDIC SETTLEMENT

One final port of call before I head for home and that is to see if I can find the Rosehill settlement, which is nearby. I travel on and in order to look at my map, I stop my car at a wide road junction with indicators flashing. A 4x4 pulls up alongside me and the lady, looking down on me says in her best voice: *"Can I help you."* Me: *"No thank you. I've just stopped to look at my map. I think I've got it sorted."'* Whereupon country lady says: *"You should get 'Sat Nat' - it's brilliant - just put in your postcode and away you go."* Me: *"Thank you so much."* And away I go. However it's stretches the imagination, to consider that an ancient site might have a postcode!

Examining my map, I identify the settlement as being a small piece of woodland between a Tumulus and a place called Alscott Farm as near as I can judge, on a Grid Ref. 458115. I decide to approach from the east through the farm. Having parked up, I walk up a track and into the farmyard, where three great dogs barking ferociously, come rushing towards me. I am standing quite still, talking quietly to them, when a lady comes out of the farmhouse to see what all the commotion is about. I apologize for the trespass, though it is actually a public right of way, and ask her the best direction for the section of woodland I am seeking. I start off across a field coming to the remains of what was once a small copse of ancient oaks. They are very old, very faded, all uprooted and entwined higgledy-piggledy with each other. What is left is just the barebones of a once proud piece of ancient oak woodland. At a guess I would say, they would be well over 1,500 years old, but could they possibly go back to Mary's time? My insight tells me that these oaks would have lined one of the old trackways into the settlement. I walk on and after about ten minutes, something tells me to approach from the other direction. I retrace my steps back through 'doggy' farm to my car.

I drive to a position the other side of the woodland, which I realize will give me easier access than from Alscot. I park and make my way along a track, through a five-barred gate, across a field of cows towards the woodland. As I approach, my intuition lets me know that this is the Rosehill settlement. I step into the silence of the trees and tune in to times past, feeling the presence of Beloved Mary very strongly. As is so often the case, I see nothing left in the landscape to indicate there ever was a settlement here. But the energies are still vibrant. I lay down a white quartz crystal for the ancient Druids and a rose-pink crystal for Mary, with a blessing. I thank Mary for her guidance to this sacred place.

This is the end of my two day pilgrimage in North Devon and I begin my journey home. From Rosehill, Mary and Naomi travelled south through Holroyd, over Chilla Moor and Hollow Moor to reach Broadbury Castle. From here they continued south through Burley Wood, crossing the River Lyd in its deep valley. The Lydford Gorge is truly magical - cascading water pouring into deep green luminous pools - the river cutting through tall rocky walls covered with mosses, lichen, ferns and wood sorrel, all drizzled with misty spray. In the miniscule bit of sunlight which reaches this place, the waters give off a silvery light. This is a mystical, sacred place - nurtured and protected by the nature spirits. Climbing out of the gorge, Mary and Naomi reached Brent Tor Druidic settlement on the western perimeter of Dartmoor where Joseph and Jesus joined them. I choose not to pay homage at Brent Tor this day, because my plan is to perform a Ceremony of Light on a day set apart, which will combine with the same at Merrivale.

I arrive home, memories in tact, eager to type up my notes. First though in order to honour my pilgrimage, I light a candle for Mary. My heart is full of the deepest love. I am conscious of her presence and of many dear ones from the Land of Light, among them, my guide and mentor White Eagle. I offer special thanks for the insights received on this my first pilgrimage through Devon and receive a short acknowledgement:

MARY

"Beloved one - we are with you at all times. We guide and comfort you on your journeying. Go forward with our blessings and purist love"

PREPARATION FOR CEREMONIES AT TWO SITES

1.   ST MICHAEL OF THE ROCK, BRENT TOR. Druidic Ceremony
2.   MERRIVALE CERMONIAL COMPLEX. Atlantean Ceremony

On my return from Hartland, I am to make preparation for a Ceremony in situ at these two ancient Druidic settlements. The first requirement is to purchase some new pink quartz crystals, purify and bless them. For the time being I have sufficient pieces of white quartz. On a short walk through my local nature reserve, I spy some delicate pale pink wild roses. Asking of the deva, I take two perfect specimens for Mary, one to be left at each site.

My aim is to perform both Ceremonies within one day and my chosen date is 19th June. Why this date? Well first of all the weather looks set fair - no rain, gales or fog! Also, I wish my sacred work to be undertaken as close to the summer solstice as possible. Sunday, 21st June is out of the question due to a White Eagle Centre South West commitment. I now look at the date from a Numerological perspective and see that it relates to the number nine, which on a personal level, indicates selfless humanitarian service - that's good enough for me. I aim to be at Merrivale for 12.00 noon, then move on to Brent Tor for 3.00 pm.

Early in the morning of my departure day, I make time for an extended attunement. I quietly prepare my altar space, light a candle and set some gentle music playing. I leave the room for ten minutes in order for the power to build, while I assemble my Ceremonial tin of 'goodies', checking its contents and ensuring I have all I require. My two precious wild roses are encased separately in wet cotton wool and placed in a protective cover for the journey. I step back into the room, sit before my altar and lay my delicate pink scarf over my head: *"I pledge myself to thee Great White Spirit in service for humanity. I enter your presence with the most pure love - the love of the rose within my heart. I pray that any insights received come from a place of Divine Truth. My beloved Masters and Angels, I ask that you be fully present this sacred day. Beloved Mary, I ask that you are at my side throughout this sacred Mission. Great Archangel Michael, I ask for your protection at all times."* As my consciousness shifts to a deeper level, I am feeling my heart centre expanding to receive the pure love energies. I am in a place of deep peace and hearing dear White Eagle:

WHITE EAGLE

"Beloved Peace Rose. We are ALL with you right now. We will follow your progress this sacred day. Go forth without fear. We will guide and protect you. Walk forth with your hand in the hand of God, the Great White Spirit. Walk forth with your heart open to receive the beauties of OUR World. God be with you my Pilgrim of Light. This day is sacred - so mote it be."

White Eagle is standing before me as Is-Ra of his Egyptian incarnation, dressed in a white robe with a beautiful golden star at his heart centre. His right hand rises in a blessing, as he draws in the air the ancient symbol of the Equal Sided Cross of Light encircled by Light. From me: *"Dear White Eagle and all my dearly beloved Brethren in the World of Light, I thank you for your presence and protection this blessed day. Amen."* Spirit will play their part - I will play mine.

MY JOURNEY

As I set off across Dartmoor, there is good visibility today with the sun attempting to work its magic and break through the cloud level. I am full of joy and yet quite calm as I cruise along. Leaving the main highway at Ashburton as before, I take the narrow road to the moors, where there is a notice which tells me that this road will be closed on the 21st June, so a very practical reason why I was not to go on that day. It is not long before I catch up with a gigantic log bearing lorry, which is causing utter chaos, as it is totally filling the road. Any on-coming vehicles have to pull into lay-bys or driveways to allow it to pass. Me - I am just patiently following, staying well back, wondering with interest how it will negotiate the narrow Holne Bridge over the River Dart. As it reaches the bridge it swerves out, to what I think is to take a good angle, when instead it stops at a gate opening to some woodland. Thank goodness for that, because I really do believe the lorry would have been too wide for the bridge! After this debacle a little further on - another hold up. A huge digger and two lorries are working on a very narrow stretch of road. A man with a *'Stop/Go'* sign indicates that I can move forward. By pulling in both wing mirrors I just scrape through with a hairs breath of the vehicles and the stone wall! Good job I am in a state of utter peace and serenity - obviously another test!

As I cross the River Dart at New Bridge and take the rise out of the valley to the high moor, I am remembering a wonderful walk not far from here called 'Dr. Blackall's Drive' which now forms part of 'The Two Moors Way' long distance walk. Dr. Blackall had the track cut out of the rock face, high up above the River Dart, in order that his invalid wife could take a carriage drive, which gave her outstanding views of the valley and woodland below. I am now traversing open moorland, where remains of ancient settlements abound. I pass Two Bridges, the ancient clapper bridge, although not in use today, is still in excellent condition. I am on time for my 12.00 noon Ceremony at Merrivale Ceremonial Complex (see Chapter 10).

ST MICHAEL OF THE ROCK (ST MICHAEL DE RUPE) BRENT TOR DRUIDIC SETTLEMENT.

Meanwhile, on to Brent Tor. I continue across Dartmoor eventually dropping down into Tavistock, to leave this busy market town via the country road for Brent Tor. One of the derivations of Brent Tor is *'a high rocky place'* - Brent being a common name for a hill-top. There is variance in the spelling of the name. The civil authorities spell it 'Brentor' whereas the ecclesiastical name for the parish is 'Brent Tor.' I shall use the latter as this is the name given on my map.

As I approach, I see to my right, St Michael's Church in its imposing position perched atop the high rocky outcrop. Today it is lit up with the sun's rays as a Golden Beacon of Light, symbolically seeming to be holding the power within this ancient landscape. For the ancient Celts it WAS a Beacon, whereupon fires would have been lit to celebrate certain dates in their annual calendar. Then for centuries after, it was used as a Beacon to give warning of invasion.

St Michael of the Rock, Brent Tor from the western elevation

What else can we learn of Brent Tor and its St Michael Church? On Page 23 of her book *'Prehistoric Hill Forts in Devon'* Aileen Fox tells us that: *'Brent Tor is an isolated hill of volcanic origin, 300m high and visible for many miles around; it is crowned by St Michael's church founded in the twelfth century by Tavistock Abbey, restored in the late nineteenth century. The Iron Age fortifications are visible on the slopes facing, north-east and south, consisting of two close-set ramparts and ditches with an in-turned entrance worn and spread. A third line with stone facing lower down the slope appears to be a later property boundary. Most of the site has been dug over for manganese.'* Further information to hand, narrows the timescale for this hill fort down to the late Iron Age, between 150 BC and AD 50.

So the St Michael Church has stood on this isolated volcanic hill-top for over eight hundred years, dominating the landscape. It is said that the dedication to St Michael the Archangel was common for churches built on a height spot, notably because of the association with the Angelic Realm. It reminds me of another St Michael Church on the isolated hill-top of Ysgyryd Fawr (Holy Mountain) just outside Abergavenny in South Wales. There is little remaining of that ancient church, but as with St Michael of the Rock, it is a place of immense power and calls many a pilgrim to visit. For St Michael on the Rock, Hamish Miller and Paul Broadhurst tell us in their book *'The Sun and the Serpent'*, that Brent Tor is a node point where the St Michael and St Mary Ley Lines cross, so perhaps this could explain its compelling energetic presence within the landscape.

Earlier this year three dear friends and I undertook a pilgrimage to this enigmatic St Michael Church. At the time, our pivotal focus was to make contact with the Michael energies at this ancient place. Today, my criteria is the Druidic Ceremony for the Lady Mary and the Masters. Having parked in the dedicated car park, I gather all I need for my Ceremony and set off. I pass through a rather dilapidated kissing gate, to meet with a very large rock on the path, the guardian of this sacred domain. I put my hand on the rock and feel it vibrating. I ask permission to enter as before. The St Michael Church rises up to my right. A little green pathway winds round to eventually reach some steps leading to the church building where I shall go later. For now, I begin my perambulation in a clockwise direction around one of the ramparts. I am identifying two key ramparts and ditches, with evidence of a further boundary in the distance - this before reading Aileen Fox's words. The near embankment appears to be stone built and well camouflaged with turf, which at this time of year is crested with bright pink foxgloves. As I walk along, I see two tiny moorland flowers peeping out from the long grass and bracken - the pretty blue heath speedwell and white eyebright Along my way there are a few large granite stones and one incumbent triangular shaped stone.

BRENT TOR DRUIDIC TEMPLE CEREMONY.

This Druidic Temple settlement was a place of some significance for Mary. It was the first destination in Devon, where she and her family participated in a sacred Druidic Ceremony to reactivate the Light and offer a Holy blessing. Now this sacred rite will be played out once more.

Part way round my perambulation, I come to the perfect position in which to undertake my Ceremony. I have stepped through a gap in the rampart, to discover a lovely grassy area close to a row of huge old beech trees. I have views out across to Dartmoor. I lay out all my special things. Soft fluffy cotton-wool clouds are hanging in the blue sky. For a fleeting moment, I see a cloud formation of the most perfect Celtic cross - an equal sided cross of blue sky surrounded by a white cloud - a beautiful omen. I am quite alone. I sit in the warm sun, absorbing its energizing rays, remembering that we are close to the ancient Sun Festival of the summer solstice. It is almost 3.00 pm my designated Ceremonial time, so I begin.

I ask for the protection of Archangel Michael, which seems very appropriate at this St Michael's Church on the Rock. I reverently speak the words of my Druidic Temple Ceremony, invoking the beloved Masters and Angels. I intone *'The Great Invocation'* then place each of my chosen crystals on my small white cloth. As I utter the final words from my Ceremony *'Let it be done'* I hear the Sword of Michael impact with the top of The Rock, the sound resounding all around me. All my sacred words having been expressed, I close with: *"Oh Great Beings of Light I honour you all and I thank you for your presence this sacred day."* My inner vision shows me a great assembly of ancient ones dressed in white robes. One steps forward from the group:

DRUID PRIEST

"Most blessed Light Worker. We welcome your presence this day and thank you for your service. St Michael on the Rock is indeed a great powerhouse for the Cosmic Light to be received into the Earth. As you know, it is at the centre of the junction of the Michael-Mary Leys and as such, the power is great and can be more readily accessible and activated. The Cosmic energy here at this point links into the Grid System and is instrumental in its repair. The Grid System of your precious Planet IS gradually being strengthened and repaired to withstand and to manifest the vibrational energies of the New Age. It has been a slow process beloved one, but with the dedication of many workers for the Light, it is speeding up. By 2012 the work will be complete and Earth people can begin the long process of moving ever closer to that Great Cosmic Light.

We of the Higher Realms, are watching with great interest, the unfolding of the ancient ways once again. We are guiding you dear Earth people. We love you all. We honour and respect each small effort made by each individual to progress a little further along the pathway to the Cosmic Sun. You are ALL blessed from on high. Amen."

I thank this Higher Being for his treasured words. My Ceremony finished, I quite deliberately close my chakra centres with the ancient protective symbol, then using a great spiral of Golden Light, ensure that I am well and truly earthed. This has been for me another unforgettable Cosmic episode.

After carefully putting away all my Ceremonial articles, I continue my preamble around the ramparts, then take a little pathway leading diagonally up the steep slope towards the church on the hill. Climbing ever higher, panoramic views now open up before me. I am drawn to the side of the hill well below the church summit. Standing on a rocky ridge, I am facing west to Cornwall with the heights of mysterious Bodmin Moor in the foreground. On my last pilgrimage I stood alone at this very spot. I remember feeling that I was being overshadowed by a Great Being, as my arms were rising up involuntarily, at either side of me. At some deep level, I was connecting Cornwall to Devon - vibrational energies being transmitted between Bodmin Moor and Dartmoor. The power was reverberating through my physical body as I offered an Invocation to the Light. Returning today and having enacted my sacred Ceremony, has I believe, strengthened the Ley Line energy link between The Hurlers on Bodmin Moor and Brent Tor on Dartmoor. Today I know this is where I am to place my white and pink quartz crystals. I gently place them in the long grass at the back of a great granite rock. This final act completes my Ceremony for the Light here on Brent Tor.

SANCTUARY OF THE ST MICHAEL CHURCH

I continue my climb to the church. At the summit a narrow stone pathway leads me round to the entrance. As I enter this simple, humble, yet quite beautiful little church, whispers of the past seem to be calling to me, as if they are embedded within its ancient walls. My focus is immediately drawn to the magnificent stained glass window at the east end, depicting a winged St Michael holding the Sword of Righteousness and the Scales of Justice. His sword is pointing downwards rather than rising to invoke the Light. For me, this is indicative of him striking the Earth, in order to seal in the energies at times of profound Cosmic occurrences, much as has happened this day. On my knees before the Altar, I gaze at this beloved Archangel for a long long time. I offer a dedication of love with my hand placed on my heart. I leave my wild pink rose for Mary on the altar base. I rise and sit in one of the pews wishing to be still. On my earlier visit with my companions, I remember reaching into my bag for a notebook and pen as St Michael came in very close. His words then, line up with what I received today from the Druid Priest. St Michael:

ST MICHAEL

"Welcome my little pilgrims to this church on the hill-top dedicated to my memory. The Angels of Light are shining down pure Light energies to this sacred ground and deep into the Earth's crust to reconnect with the Great Crystal at the Earth's centre. As above so below. This site is what you would call a node point for the vibrational energies from the Cosmos. This point in the landscape is very powerful indeed. There is a blending of the male and female energies here at this Ley node. The Michael and Mary Leys joining at this point produce enormous energy, which as received through the human vehicle, can be utilised for healing your precious Planet. It is good that you are here at this special sacred

time, as new DNA codes are bring connected to the Earth's Grid System. We, the Beings of Light, thank you for your dedication in this regard my Pilgrims of Light."

Stained Glass Window of St Michael in the St Michael Church, Brent Tor

At that time, I also heard Michael's sword strike The Rock, imprinting the Grid with dynamic Cosmic energies. At this juncture, I knew I was to return to this sacred place very soon, yet knew not for why. My insight then showed me a vision of the Earth's Grid System, similar to one I received in a meditation some while back. I saw a huge Circle of Light, of such brilliance that it was nigh impossible to look at. It was hovering above the Earth and was implanted with tall tube-like crystals, which were receiving Light from the Cosmos - the Crystal Energy then being poured deep into the Earth. There is a message from the stars which needs decoding. I don't know what it is at present. I do know that here at Brent Tor is a sacred site of great importance. I had a vision of an upward winding spiral of energy like a vortex. The thought which came at the time, was that this indicated the Earth Plane aspiring to the higher vibrations of Cosmic Life, slowly and assuredly moving in that direction. I then saw a great water spout - the Fountain of Life - shooting upwards, spraying out its pure water to cleanse Planet Earth. My words: *"I honour you my Masters, Angels and Archangels. Let me be used as an instrument for your healing light. Let the Light forever shine."*

Returning to the now, I leave this hallowed place, stepping out into the sunlight. Walking thoughtfully down the stone steps, I offer a final acknowledgement to the guardian and am soon back in my car. After a moment's contemplation, a drink from my flask and a glance at my map, I make a decision to revisit the local Castle Inn at Lydford.

THE SACRED HARES OF DARTMOOR

The Castle Inn is at Lydford, a few miles from Brent Tor. Today I feel drawn to take another look at a small stained glass window set within its entrance door, which depicts the Three Hares. It was on our recent pilgrimage to Brent Tor, that my friends and I came across it. On that occasion, asking permission of the landlord, I took a photograph of the window, which vision has haunted me ever since. So what does this ancient symbol look like? It shows three hares in a circular configuration, prancing around each other, their ears interlocking at the centre forming a trefoil, giving the very clever illusion that they have six ears between them, when in point of fact only three are depicted. This symbol is to be found in profusion across Dartmoor especially in church roof bosses. I name just a few places where it can be seen.

Stained Glass Window of the Three Sacred Hares at the Castle Inn, Lydford

- St Andrew Church, Sampford Courtney north east of Okehampton.
- St Pancras Church, Widecombe-in-the-Moor
- St Mary Church, Mary Tavey
- St John the Baptist, North Bovey

On Dartmoor the hare was associated with the Dartmoor tinners, who claimed the ancient symbol as their own. For them, hares were synonymous with rabbits, possibly as a connection to warrening on the moors, which activity the tinners employed.

However, the emblem of the sacred hare is ancient and is to be found within different cultures and countries worldwide. For example, hares can be seen all over Europe, in Nepal, China and Southern Russia and they also appear in hieroglyphics on the walls of Egyptian Temples. In ancient Celtic mythology, the hare is the Goddess - the messenger of the Moon Goddess, shifting across the skies by moonlight between the Heavenly Realms and our world. In this regard, the hare is the archetypal symbol of femininity and womanhood, which is associated with the lunar cycle, fertility and birth, epitomized by the laying of the Cosmic Egg. The first Roman Christians in Britain were smart enough to align their festival days with established Pagan belief, thus their Goddess of Spring - Eostre, became Easter, with the Cosmic Egg becoming the Easter Egg. Beloved Mary is in essence the Mother Goddess, and her pilgrimage through Devon would surely have enshrined the Divine Sacred Feminine for all time. My insight tells me that the Three Hare symbol denotes the Holy Trinity and as such, embodies the concept of the male and female as Divine Beings, embracing and nurturing the Christ Child.

TO NORTH BRENTOR AND MARY TAVY

After my visit to the Castle Inn, I decide to drive on to North Brentor and Mary Tavy, to view their Parish Churches, both of which are within a few miles radius of Brent Tor and on my route home. Whilst looking at the map, it is only now that I notice a place called 'Holyeat' just a stones throw south of the Brent Tor settlement where Mary stayed - hmm - interesting.

Driving into the pretty hamlet of North Brentor, I park in the centre and make for its Christ Church. I pass a small conservation area, which is obviously well tended by the local community. Nearby I see what looks to be a well established yurt homestead on a small piece of private land. The church is a Chapel-of-Ease to the Parish Church of St Michael, Brent Tor. It was built in the nineteenth century as a more convenient place to worship. Although its energies are very peaceful, they are not comparable to the ancient church on the hill.

The Lady Mary passed through Mary Tavy on her journey from Brent Tor to the Merrivale settlement. I am standing outside the little church and can see no dedication to any specific saint, so can only presume it to be to St Mary. The church dates back to the fifteenth century and as I enter, the holiness of the ages surround me. The stained glass windows are exceptional images of colour and light. They include representations of a multitude of saints, among which are; St Andrew, St George, St Patrick, St Alban, St Stephen, St Benedict, St Agatha, St Bonafice, Paul the Apostle and Joseph of Arimathea. In the churchyard is the grave of William Crossing, who lived in Mary Tavy, and who in 1909, wrote the definitive book for walkers and explorers on Dartmoor called '*Crossings Guide to Dartmoor*'.

This is the end of my full and wondrous day, which saw me undertaking two sacred Light Ceremonies, at Merrivale and at Brent Tor. I leave for home with the knowledge that my work for the Masters of Light has been satisfactorily accomplished. Driving back across Dartmoor, I have the final delight of witnessing about fifteen moorland ponies and their foals by the roadside. I stop for a moment and wind down the window. This encourages one foal to put its head right into my car and I can stroke his soft brown muzzle. Of course, the plea for food is why he is being so charming, but the advice is not to feed the moorland ponies, so he is to be disappointed. However, I have a nice little chat and tell him how beautiful he is.

At home now, I am able to close my Ceremonial day with a precious link with Beloved Mary and the Masters of Light.

CHAPTER 10
CLIMBING TO ANCIENT DARTMOOR
Awakening its Druidic Past

From Mary Tavy, the Lady Mary and her family crossed the River Tavy to Peter Tavy and began the steady climb to Merrivale Ceremonial Complex on Dartmoor. Their journey on horseback would have taken them along ancient tracks through almost impenetrable forest. Looking at the map of the Merrivale area, I can't help but notice the place names, Lower Godworthy and Higher Godworthy and being conscious that our blessed Lord as the boy Jesus, passed this way. Also - could 'Roos' Tor to the east of Peter Tavy, be a derivation of 'Rose'? Before we embark on my explorations and insights at Merrivale, a little about Dartmoor.

DARTMOOR NATIONAL PARK

In 1951 Dartmoor was designated a National Park, thus protecting the land and securing its future heritage. Dartmoor is a place where people live, work and play, with its traditional farming community, tourism and a variety of outdoor leisure pursuits. Also controversially, the Army have access to three designated sections of upper moorland. To The Dartmoor National Park Authority falls the unenviable task of keeping all participants satisfied - they have to perform a difficult balancing act. The Authority runs Visitor Centres, placed at strategic localities on the moor, which provide a wealth of historical and geological data regarding Dartmoor through the ages to the present day.

The topography of Dartmoor today offers a diverse landscape. From the wild peat-bogged high moorland, to vast areas of easily accessible good walking terrain, to the fringes where excellent market towns are situated. For refreshment there is a good choice of 'oldy-worldy' pubs with open fires set in huge inglenooks. There are granite tors, quiet lanes, tranquil reservoirs and ancient woodland. Delightful wooded river valleys are spread with daffodils and bluebells in springtime. August brings in swathes of purple heather and yellow gorse on the open moor. One can become immersed in this magical landscape, which is a solace to the weary soul. Attestation to Dartmoor's past can be discovered in its present landscape. Evidence of the Bronze and Iron Age periods abound, as for example - pound settlements, Ceremonial sites, chambered tombs, hut circles, menhirs, triangular standing stones, dolmens, stone rows and hill forts. Then there is evidence of medieval villages, some thoughtfully restored. As witness to its industrial past, are the remains of smelting houses, mines, pillow mounds, granite quarries, blowing houses, ice-works, and the old stone tramways which were built to bring goods off the moor. All this would indicate Dartmoor as a hive of activity and a dynamic, ever changing landscape. Echoes of that past call out to you as you explore this ancient land.

THE MERRIVALE AREA

What could the landscape around Merrivale have looked like 2,000 years ago in Mary's day? The general terrain would have been that of dense woodland, extending to the high central moor, with oak and alder the predominant species. Deer and wild boar would have roamed the forests. Merrivale settlement was a vast clearing, set within this ancient woodland. Tors such as Roos, Great Mis, Great Staple, Cox and Kings which surround Merrivale, were either well hidden or peeping up through the trees.

What can we see of the actual settlement today? The main features consist of two double stone rows running either side of the Prison Leat, so called because it was constructed by prisoners from Dartmoor jail in the early nineteenth century. There is a large stone circle with an adjoining great menhir. This whole area is awash with hut circles, burial mounds and impressive standing stones. Unfortunately the B3357 runs rather disrespectfully through the site, completely dissecting it in two, but was no doubt constructed over an original dirt track. However, it does appear that the main Ceremonial Complex is in tact to its south. According to my map, just below Rundlestone, is Hollow(Holy)Tor which indeed is not a hollow. It is within, yet slightly off-set from the main complex. Could this naming be a memory left in the landscape, as recognition of and in honour of, the visit by the Lady Mary and the Master Jesus? Could the hut where they stayed have been on this actual spot?

MERRIVALE CEREMONIAL COMPLEX

Merrivale Druidic settlement was a key focal point for Mary. It is here, as a High Priestess, she performed a sacred ceremony to reactivate the ancient Atlantean Temple in the Etheric. My knowledge of the importance of the Merrivale site built up gradually over a few months in 2008. I walk regularly on Dartmoor and have explored the ancient site on numerous occasions, but I have never been fully cognizant with its full significance. I shall keep the narrative of my discoveries and insights in a logical order for clarification. You will notice that I bring in Strata Florida Abbey, the reason soon becomes clear. This was the sequence of events for me in **2008** - my **Pilgrimages**:

May To Merrivale with a White Eagle group.

August To Strata Florida Abbey in Mid Wales.

End August To Merrivale after Wales to honour Beloved Mary and enact a Ceremony at the Illumination Chamber.

I have discovered many similar features at Merrivale Ceremonial Complex in Devon and Strata Florida Abbey in Mid Wales. My list for both centres:

- In the first instance, both Merrivale and Strata Florida, encompass the embodiment of the sacred heart.
- Secondly, Mary made a pilgrimage to each site, in order to bring the Divine teachings of 'The Way' of purity and truth to this ancient land.
- A connection was made with ancient Egypt, particularly with the Temple of Kom Ombo and the Egyptian Mystery Schools.
- There is a link with the Pleiadeans, who according to Divine plan, implanted on Planet Earth, the 'Star Seed' at holy centres such as these, in order to enhance the advancement of the human race.
- Both sites are connected on an Etheric Triangle of Light with the Temple on the Hill at the White Eagle Centre at New Lands in Hampshire.
- Finally and most important, there is an unusual indentation in the earth - a stepped pit at both places, which had a specific purpose. It was an Initiation/Illumination chamber.

May 2008 TO MERRIVALE WITH A WHITE EAGLE GROUP

My words of that visit:

On a warm sunny day our small group visited this ancient site. We began with a link to the Light and I asked the Druid ancestors for permission to enter their sacred land. As pilgrims dedicated to the Light and the purest energies, we walk the earth with clear purpose and this was our experience on this memorable occasion. During the day, we all received information through intuitive insight and dowsing, which was confirmed within the group.

The huge stone, which was situated at the beginning of the long double stone row set on an east-west alignment, we understood to be the Anchor Stone - the guardian of the site. In silence, we began walking in single file the precessional route between the stones. It would seem that from each of the stones on either side along the length of the rows, was emanating either male or female energies alternatively.

On reaching the central point we came upon a small square hole in the earth, with two stone steps on either side, surrounded by a circle of stones. This had to have special significance. Each of us in turn sat within its centre and tuned in to the energies. Between us we received intuitively the following; a vortex/spiral of energy, pure feminine energies, feelings of emotion and the awareness that our ancestors were here with us. Then I realized that for the anciet ones, after the preliminary walk, this point was a place of Transition, where the individual would be imbued with powerful energies and illumined to a changed state of being. This was also a place of Initiation. This was the womb wherein one became reborn into the higher consciousness before continuing the precessional route. This was the HEART OF THE MOTHER. I shall call this an 'Illumination Chamber'. My insights in this regard were confirmed by one of our Druid ancestors who spoke with me:

Beginning of the Double Stone Row with Guardian Stone at Merrivale Ceremonial Complex

The Illumination Chamber at Merrivale Ceremonial Complex

DRUID

"*Dear ones. Welcome. Welcome. Welcome. We welcome you to our sacred place. Please enjoy your time here in the beautiful energies of the Heart of the Mother. We would wish that you have your periods of stillness as of now. Walk forward along our precessional route, with added purpose and stillness and you will receive.*"

Continuing our precession, we all felt more attuned to the higher energies and 'knew' that it was imperative we stay within the stone row perimeters. It was as if there was an invisible barrier to the left and right of us. I was aware of vibrations coming off the stones - my hands feeling electric. I felt that what was in evidence in this sacred landscape today, was but a very small part of the original site. At the end of the second section of the stone row, I walked between two huge stones, one male and one female, which I knew were to ground and balance the powerful energies. What a treasured experience.

To complete our day we explored the rest of the ancient site. As a final blessing, one of our party drew our attention to a remarkable aura of rainbow light completely encircling the sun.

<u>August 2008</u> REVELATIONS AT STRATA FLORIDA

I was on pilgrimage following '*The Pathway of the Beloved*' as depicted in Megan Wingfield's book '*The Grail Journey through Wales*' and staying at the Black Lion Inn at Pontrhydfendigaid, a short distance from the Cistercian Abbey of Strata Florida. It is here that I had the extraordinary encounter with my two White Eagle friends, where the connection was made with the Lady Mary at Merrivale, which began my pilgrimage in South West of Britain (see Preface). In her book, Megan shares experiences and insights received at Strata Florida Abbey, many of which link in with my own findings.

From my notes of the time. My pilgrimage to Strata Florida Abbey from the inn begins along a quiet country road on a beautiful sunny morning. The only intrusion to the peace which is most welcome, is the sound of a red kite making its strange whistling call from a little copse in the valley. On this sacred day, I feel I am walking right into the heart - my heart is filled with the essence of beloved Minesta (Grace Cooke), White Eagle's medium, who is beside me and speaking blessed words.

Within the now ruined abbey, I walk across to the large stone Altar at the east end, and with a prayer gently lay two precious offerings for Mary and the Goddess. First a pink rose 'acquired' from a derelict garden in Tregaron on my way to Strata Florida, and second, a heart-shaped stone which had been 'presented' to me by the devas who care for '*Garden Cottage*' at New Lands - both accepted with gracious thanks. I receive a communication from Beloved Mary, who made pilgrimage to the ancient Druidic Temple site over which the abbey was built. Mary, the '*Rose in the Heart*', blessed this sacred land on her journeying through Wales. She speaks with me. In this instance however I have picked out a few relevant sections of what was a very long message:

The Initiation Pit at Strata Florida Abbey

MARY

"We would wish that all people become aware of the LOST GODDESS and allow her to return. When I came from the Holy Land through Egypt, I brought with me from the Temples of Egypt, in particular from Kom Ombo, that essence of Purity and Truth and Dedication to 'THE WAY'. Here in Wales, the link was once more made with our Druid ancestors and protectors and we followed the Pathway of Peace and Love. A simple philosophy but true. As with all things of truth it was subjugated, but it is beginning to rise again in the hearts of humankind. It will succeed. Ultimately Love and Light always triumphs over Fear and Darkness. Then.....

The GRAIL CUP ever full of perfect Light and Love will rise again. This Grail Cup will heal hearts - calm minds - purify all the subtle bodies of the individual This Grail Cup will bring the Light once more into Britain - into the World. This is the goal - this is the ultimate goal of the most High and all the Archangels and Angels of Light. They and the Masters are holding the whole World - indeed the whole Universe - in the Light of Purity and Truth. For your Earth Plane, enlightenment will come - yes dearest one - it WILL come - there is no doubt of that. Your World will be as that other World of Light - Venus - which in its own time followed the same pathway of progression as Planet Earth. Finally......

And the CHILDREN - the special children - they are as you know, being incarnated at this present time - and the present time spans hundreds of years - this new generation of enlightened souls are bringing to humanity a new vision - a vision of hope - a vision of joy - a vision of love. And it is good. It is decreed. It is happening - NOW. They, the Blessed

Ones, are returning from their place of the very highest, to instruct humanity during this forthcoming age, which will see good, purity, love and light ultimately succeed. Enlightenment is here for you all dear one - it is your birthright."

I now move to the Initiation Chamber described by Megan in her book. On Page 68 she tells us: *'There is a strange 'pit' inside the abbey which is unknown anywhere else. It has steps down. You walk through the water at the bottom, and up the other side. No one knows what it is for.'* This is followed on Page 69 by: *'It is part of an initiation ceremony in which the monks passed into a new life or were 'reborn' - you must do this yourself and you will understand. The energies are still there and they can be re-energised by people born of the light. Some of the monks understood this connection, but because of the fear of Rome, they said it was a baptismal font. It was one of the ways in which an underground covert religion was practiced. Welsh religion was practiced as the Druids would have done. Try it. Test the energies and you will know.'*

I realize that White Eagle is at my side. He shares with me many words of great profundity - again due to lack of space, I can offer you but a taster:

WHITE EAGLE

"All is one in the eyes of the Great One. The Masters know this and this understanding brings perfect peace and clarity of vision. All is one - there is NO SEPARATION - we each of us are a part of the whole. What each of us thinks, speaks or does has an effect on the whole. It is THE LAW. The Law of Perfect Understanding - the Law of Love - the Law of Consequences - the Law of Cause and Effect. So much is

incorporated in this understanding. The underlying principle is LOVE. We mean Love in its purest sense dearest one. We are not saying it is easy, but the challenges and experiences of your earthly life are so valuable for the future transformation of your soul. This is a wonderful opportunity to progress along your Pathway of Love and Perfection."

White Eagle, now as Is-Ra of my Egyptian incarnation, takes my arm and guides me through the Initiation Chamber. Standing within the sacred space, I have a profound sense of that Oneness he has just talked about. I feel empowered, as Divine Light and Energy pours into me from the Cosmos. I visualize this Light flowing out to the Illumination Chamber at Merrivale and in another direction to the Temple of the Heart on New Lands Sacred Hill, forming a vast Triangle of Light Now follows a feeling of deep peace, and as I experienced on my first pilgrimage to Merrivale, a sense of being reborn, as if I have undergone a hallowed experience.

I return to sit quietly near the Altar when another entity comes in - it is Merlin:

MERLIN

"I am the Druid Guardian of this sacred place. I am the forefather of Druid worship. I am still the Bearer of that Light. I keep the Light burning here constantly. I am the protector of this land. This Heart - this Grail of Wales. You are welcome pilgrim for you bring the Light. Be at Peace. Blessings."

The croak of Merlin's raven accompanies my departure. I thank all the blessed ones who have drawn close this sacred day.'

End August 2008 TO MERRIVALE ON MY RETURN FROM WALES

Back in Devon, I have been rather busy sorting photographs and writing up my notes of my Welsh pilgrimage. I awake to a new dawn and all of a sudden I have a strong pull towards Merrivale. I wish to honour the Lady Mary and enact a little Ceremony on site, so I gather together a few Ceremonial items and some offerings from Wales. I leave at 7.00 am in order to be there before it gets busy.

As I drive over Dartmoor, I am aware of a keenness to be at Merrivale, yet find myself making an unscheduled stop at Dartmeet. I park up wondering why I am here. I walk over to the East Dart River and sit on a large boulder on the river-bank, staring into the frothy water, bubbling over its rusty-tint peat base. I am here to tune into the energies of the river and balance my own energies with its purity. My attention is focused on a little flow of water, as it swirls eagerly between two of the boulders, like a mini waterfall. As I watch, it seems to go faster and faster, then appears to flow in slow motion. I am mesmerized with this rather strange illusion. I have some water collected from Gregennan Lake in the Cader Idris area of Mid Wales and pour in a little as an offering with: *"I bless you dear river."* The river is calling to me - speaking with me:

WATER DEVA

"You are most welcome to be here, please stay a while and listen to our voice. Thank you dear human for your gift of the sacred water from Wales. Thank you also for your blessing and your love. We offer you OUR blessing. Our water flows through the land carving out its pathway as we go, over thousands, nay millions of years. We are part of the changing pattern of the landscape. As such, we can be strong and powerful and destructive. But we can flow gently and can be VERY STILL"

The words - perhaps a reference to my illusion. I acknowledge the deva and ask if I may collect a little of the pure energized water.

Close-by is an ancient granite clapper bridge which has a central block missing, riding high above the water level. In times past this narrow bridge would have provided a precarious yet substantial crossing, for those on foot or horseback. I wonder how such a crossing would go down if it had to be used in today's world? I suspect that modern safety regulations would require there to be a rail on either side to prevent the unwary falling into the water, combined with a notice warning of the dangers and indicating that you cross at your own risk!

ON REACHING MERRIVALE

Driving on to Merrivale, I am now picking up the gentle energies of Beloved Mary - she is travelling with me. I reach Four Winds car park, which is set back from the B3357 within two dry stone walled areas, where the old school house once stood. On go my walking shoes, fleece and anorak and with my pack on my back I venture forth.

I step through the narrow stone exit of the car park into a further walled area. The ground here is a quagmire and I have not reached the open moorland yet. Mind you, we have had a summer of persistent rain. Perhaps my boots would have been more appropriate today. I know someone who will remember a situation like this very well. A small group of friends were visiting the Merrivale site with conditions under foot much the same as today, added to which the rain was lashing down. This lovely lady, wearing a pair of lightweight shoes, managed a delightfully delicate and very ballerina-like slip on the wet muddy grass. What a game girl - she got up and carried on, finally paddling in the water with not a care in the world! She will know who she is.

A gap in a second stone wall takes me onto the moor itself. The settlement of Merrivale is laid out before me. I acknowledge the Druid Spirit Guardian of the ancient site. I stand quietly for a moment, taking in the atmosphere of this enchanting place set below the mighty Kings Tor. The morning air is cool and fresh and the sun is struggling for recognition in a rather grey sky. The eagerness and excitement is almost overwhelming, yet I must stay very calm inside: *"I'm here Mary. I'm here ancient ones."* My day's quest has begun.

Crossing the Prison Leat by way of a small granite clapper bridge, I am walking over what should be a lovely grassy section of moorland, but instead is a river. A male wheatear flashes past me. This little bird is one of the most striking summer visitors to these moors. I think that I get my fair share of adventures, for I now come across a sheep lying on its back with feet waving in the air. I am led to believe, that when a sheep gets in this position, it can't get up. Well I am not sure whether this is true or not, but as I watch from a distance, it does seem to be floundering. After a little while I go across, being careful not to frighten her and gently but firmly, push her back on to her feet. As I touch her woolly back, I am thinking how loose the wool is and wonder how long she has been in that position unable to feed. She walks off a bit shakily, but doesn't seem frightened. A baa of acknowledgement is issued forth. She is probably very grateful to be upright once more. I am sure St Francis was watching over her until my arrival!

Paddling along, I follow the leat until I reach the Guardian Anchor Stone at the head of the main double stone row. I am being pulled in very strongly now and aware that my whole inner world has shifted - I am in a different space. I can still hear the leat rushing by, but its sound is muffled. I hold out my hands to feel the vibrations coming off the stone. It is warm to the touch even though the air temperature is cool and the sun has not put in an appearance yet - a sign that the stone's energies are dynamic and full of Light. I am saying: *"Blessed Stone."* I am also asking permission to enter this double stone row. I hear:

GUARDIAN

"Welcome I will guard and protect you."
My words as I stand away from the stone: *"Blessed Mary be my guide."*

MARY

"Beloved child, now precess between the rows."

CEREMONY AT THE ILLUMINATION CHAMBER.

I walk steadfastly between the two rows of ancient stones, aware of the powerful energies drawing me forward. I am now standing before the Illumination Chamber. This time, on closer inspection, I realize that it is slightly off the east-west alignment. This is most interesting. My compass tells me it is a good ten degrees off-centre. What can this mean? I look at the pit again and also notice that one of the flat step-stones looks to be set in a slightly different direction to the others, which again does not fit the pattern. Perhaps it has moved over time with the Earth's upheavals or a shift in the Earth's axis? I take a few photographs then settle down for my Ceremony.

I sit on a flat granite stone at the edge of the Illumination Chamber. On a pretty white cloth, I place a candle which will not stay alight due to the breeze, so I use my imagination to visualize a pure white flame. On the second step of the pit, I put a white quartz crystal acquired from the stream running from Llyn-y-Fan-Fach in the Black Mountain and a grey miniature standing stone from Strata Florida Abbey. I have a beautiful shell from Llansteffan beach in Carmarthenshire, which I place in the centre directly on the Earth. Thus I have my links with Wales. Finally I lay a pink rose for Mary. My words: *"I offer these gifts from Wales with the deepest love. Mary my precious one, I honour you and our pilgrimage in that ancient land."* I then chant *'The Great Invocatino'* followed with: *"May the link between Merrivale and Strata Florida be strengthened and may the Triangle of Light between Merrivale, Strata Florida and New Lands Temple be secured for all times."* I see the great Light from the Cosmos, pouring down on each centre, re-enforcing this blessing. There is a great multitude of Ancient Beings with me. My short Ceremony is complete. - all is well - the links have been reactivated. I am speaking with the Lady Mary: *"Beloved one. Is there any more you can tell me of the connection between Merrivale Ceremonial Complex and Strata Florida Abbey?"*

MARY

"Dearest child I can tell you a little. First of all, welcome to this most sacred place. Now as you have so rightly realized, there is a powerful energy link between Strata Florida and Merrivale. You know and understand about Grid Lines or Energy Lines. Strata Florida is the Centre of the Heart of the Welsh Grid System and as you have 'seen' the energy lines flow out to other smaller centres as Rays of Light. I say smaller ones, that is not to say they are any less important, but there has to be a central point. This heart at Strata Florida is the heart of the Grid of Light which beams out all over the British Isles and beyond. It is like a Lighthouse. In time more will be shared with you, more is to be discovered dearest one. We are just at the beginning. Merrivale is a very powerful Centre of Light here on Dartmoor. It has been so since time began. Merrivale is part of the old path and the ancients here were part of that Golden Age of which you have heard. This land, these settlements go back far far beyond 4,000 years. There were people here many AGES ago, right back to the beginning of time. This land, this ancient land which you now call Dartmoor, was once part of Atlantis. (Is this possible I was thinking at the time? Please bear in mind, that these were early days with Mary and my knowledge was limited, alongside which, somehow my memory of any past understanding of all this, had been conveniently erased). *Hard to believe dear one I know, but what I say is truth from the very heart of the Cosmos. Ceremonies were undertaken on this actual land in the dim distance past. It is sacred and it is full of Light and shall always be so. Yes, there are places where Light Energy has withdrawn but it will return. With your help dearest pilgrim and with the help of other Light Workers, it will be done. The Light will return and in abundance. This Light will shine once more on your ancient land.* (I ask Mary about the unusual angle of the pit, but receive an evasive reply - I am obviously not meant to know at present).

(Another question: *"Was I here at Merrivale?"* again - early days). *Yes my beloved daughter you were here with me. It was long before I finally made my home in Wales. I came to these ancient Isles with Joseph of Arimathea and my beloved son Jesus. It was necessary for me to make physical contact in preparation for my future journeying. My Druid ancestors and family welcomed us and guided our journey. I will tell you more of this dear one on another occasion. On THIS occasion I am to say, that you dear daughter were with us. We were a very small band of travellers. We were guided by the Light which was here in the British Isles and by the alchemic power of the Druids. And yes,* (this thought had just come to me) *there is another Crystal you know - this one within the earth here-about on Dartmoor. Yes dearest one, ON Dartmoor, actually HERE at Merrivale. In fact I am sure you are beginning to realize that the Crystal Energy is WITHIN the Earth's crust and is at all the key sacred sites. The system is vast. The sacred sites are built at energy points where the Grid Lines cross, where the vortex of energy is very powerful and the Cosmic forces are able to bring that Light down from the Cosmos, through the ethers to the Earth Plane, deep deep into the crust of the Earth. This Light Energy illumines and brings vital fire energy to the Earth. There is much more to say dear one and I will contact you again very soon. For now I bless you. I offer you my most blessed and pure love. Let this love meet with your heart love and dwell within your being for all time blessed daughter."*

Mary finishes and I start to return to normal consciousness. I hear the raven croak - Merlin's raven is with me here on Dartmoor today. Looking up - there he goes flying high over Great Staple Tor. I am now hearing the sound of the water in the leat once again and feeling the sun's warmth on my back. I rise and stand at the edge of the Illumination Chamber. Beloved Is-Ra is by my side as he was at Strata Florida. He is taking my hand saying:

IS-RA

"I will always guide you and protect you dear Peace Rose."

I step down onto the near step, aware of intoxicating energies coming in. A beautiful feeling of love rises from deep within my heart - I am in the Heart of the Mother. The Divine Feminine essence is very strong. I am immersed in pure Light energy as I stand within the Illumination Chamber. I BECOME illumined - this is an initiation. I receive a sacred blessing from the great Earth Mother. Upon the moorland turf once more, I continue my precessional walk, down between the last section of the double stone row, feeling as if I am floating. As before I must stay within its perimeter. I walk through the taller male and female stones at the end of the rows and stand quite still for a moment adjusting to the change in energies. Then very deliberately, I seal each of my psychic centres and I surround myself totally with a beautiful Golden Light with a cross at its centre. Finally I ensure that I am well grounded.

Back to reality. I decide against any more exploring - for today, my time here is at an end. The wind has sprung up and suddenly I am very cold. My feet are wet and I need to return to my car. I jump across the leat and walk back up the other side, listening to the song of the water. I reach the second double stone row which runs parallel to the larger main one. I have often puzzled as to the reason for two stone rows in this position. The answer I came up with, is that perhaps the second row was for the ancestors? Maybe more will be divulged on another occasion.

It is coming up to 11.00 am and the car park is filling up. Certainly it was the right decision to be on site early. I change my shoes and have a warming cup of coffee from my flask. My journey home takes me back through

Dartmeet and off the moor at Ashburton. On reaching Newton Abbot, I am amazed that folk are wandering round in shorts with skimpy tops or short sleeve shirts. The difference in temperature up on the moors compared to the town, is astonishing.

At home it is 11.45 am. A quick change and I prepare my sanctuary space for a 12.00 noon attunement. I go into the silence, breathing in the love energy of the Sacred Rose right into my heart centre. I am very still now and voice: *"Blessed ones I thank you for your love and guidance on my pilgrimage to Merrivale this sacred day. I thank you Is-Ra for walking beside me. My beloved Mary, I especially thank you for your presence and for your words of wisdom, accepted with great joy and humility. I honour you all."*

I am reliving some of the words received today and at this early association with Beloved Mary, I know there is so much more to learn regarding her pilgrimage to Britain. It is like weaving a cloth - as each new thread is inserted, the pattern becomes clearer, brighter and ever more beautiful and I am that little bit closer to realizing truth. I find myself thinking of past times, when as Naomi I travelled in the South West of England and Wales with Mary - and marvel at it all. Now, she is very close, my dearest Mary:

MARY

"Dearest child, it is good that you contemplate the past, because you as you know, were part of that great time. After the tumultuous happenings in our land and subsequent travelling, it was a blessed relief to have landed safely on the shores of what is now South Wales. We, all of us, were physically exhausted and our emotions still very near to the surface. Yet we knew that this was a deep deep Cosmic happening, for which we had been prepared during many physical lifetimes on the Earth Plane. For it was necessary for the spirit on such occasions, to reach down to be filled with the Earth's vibrational energy as preparation. The bonding of our subtle bodies with the Earth's vibrations was part of the design. Beloved child, rest now we will talk again."

I feel my hands rising in prayer and I am saying: *"I honour you beloved one. Let the Rose of Love ever bloom in my heart. I bless your Divine presence."* I close this attunement with my hand resting gently on my heart.

MERRIVALE CEREMONIAL ATLANTEAN TEMPLE CEREMONY

It is **June 2009**. A lot of water has gone under the bridge since my last visit to Merrivale, when I performed a Ceremony at the Illumination Chamber. My Cornish pilgrimages are finalized and I have entered Devon with the Lady Mary at Hartland, thence undertaking a journey through West Devon. The day has arrived when I can turn my attention to Merrivale once more, this time to earth the ancient Atlantean Temple.

I arrive at the Four Winds car park at 11.00 am - perfect time for a quiet drink and to be in position for my Ceremony for 12.00 noon. Booted up with pack on my back, I step out of the car into a high wind. Walking through the narrow stone wall onto the moorland, I connect to the ancient Druid

Guardian. I cross the little clapper bridge over the leat, its waters today shimmering in the sunshine which has suddenly burst forth. Along its banks, I spy some fluffy-topped cotton grass and pretty pale-blue water forget-me-nots, both indicative of boggy land. As I set off, the moorland turf is soft and springy underfoot. However, this time the going is relatively dry, except for a small seepage from the leat, causing a wet mossy area, which is glistening in the bright sunlight. A skylark is singing its joyous welcome. No sheep in distress today!

The Lady Mary is at my side. This landscape is so familiar to me in this life and from the past. I am feeling the pull of the energies emanating from the Ceremonial area of the ancient site as I near the beginning of the double stone row. I acknowledge the Anchor Stone, then precess slowly between the two rows until I reach the central Illumination Chamber. I stand at its edge looking down and notice that my white quartz crystal and miniature standing stone have disappeared, but my shell from Llansteffan beach is still here. I replace the crystal and lay down a delicate wild pink rose, offering a blessing for Mary with the words: *"I honour and bless you my beloved Mary of the Sacred Heart."* This truly is the Heart of the Mother. As I step within the Illumination Chamber I feel as if I am connected to that great Universal Heart. I attune to the Higher Beings in order to prepare for my Mission this day. As I continue my precession along the last part of the double stone row, I feel as if I am in a heightened state of awareness.

Leaving between the large male and female standing stones at the end, I turn left and find myself making my way in a direct line to a tall standing stone linked to an ancient circle next to it. This menhir is over ten foot in height. As I come within its presence I feel utter reverence: *"Bless you beautiful stone."* Resting on the grass close to the stone is a pale grey and white moorland pony with its pure white foal. As I arrive, both stand and the foal suckles from its mother - what a delightful scene. A little white foal is a blessing in deed and brings to mind my unicorn.

Where shall I perform my Ceremony? My often asked question. At first I am thinking at the menhir would be just perfect, but then I could be disturbed, even though I am alone at present. So I move towards the dry stone wall just a short distance away and settle myself down in its lee. All is so very still - it is as if the Masters and Angels are waiting. I am now more strongly aware of Our Lady. As Naomi I would have been here with her and the boy Jesus 2,000 years ago. Into my inner vision comes a scene of joy - there are small hut circles - children are running round laughing and screaming with delight. At what I can not see - perhaps it is just with the sheer exuberance of life.

I prepare for my Ceremony laying out all my precious items. In the silence spread across this open mystical moorland, I make my Divine connection. With my pink scarf around me, my head bows in prayer, then lifts to behold the great menhir. This is a sacred moment. I am conscious of waves of energy being transmitted from the tall stone before me. As always I begin with 'The Great Invocation.' I now call on the Higher Beings to be present as I submit my precious crystals for this hallowed work.

The Great Menhir at Merrivale Ceremonial Complex

At the point in the proceedings when I say: '*Let the ancient Temple of Atlantis be brought down from the Etheric Realm where it now resides and be securely grounded on Mother Earth*'. I am seeing a beautiful white-pillared Temple gently coming to Earth and settling within the nearby stone circle. After: '*Let this Temple act as a powerful energy link between the Cosmos, our Earth Plane and the great Crystal at the Centre of the Earth,*' I feel a great wave of emotion coming over me. I complete my Ceremony then hear:

MASTER OF LIGHT

"*My child - we, all the Masters in the Land of Light, wish to honour and thank you for your dedicated service this day. This sacred site has the most powerful connection to the Great Crystal at the Earth's centre as we have told you before. Your work today will strengthen this connection Light Worker. Your presence here today has brought into being a new Temple in the landscape. Yes - we are aware, that it is only those with the clairvoyant eye, who will see clearly this vision, but many will come and be aware at an inner level of the presence of this ancient Atlantean Temple. It rests on the Earth, as testament to a once proud nation of beautiful Light Beings. Honour its presence all you Light Workers. May the Angels and Master of Light be with you, each and everyone of you, as you pilgrimage to this ancient sacred site. Amen.*"

I was just slightly puzzled by the use of the word 'nation'. I could only assume that the Master was using modern terminology. However, on looking it up in my Chambers Dictionary it gives - paraphrasing: '*a body of people marked off by common descent, language, culture or historical tradition…the people of a state…a federation of tribes...a set of people etc.'* - so quite a legitimate use of a word for the Atlanteans! Sorry for querying a Master, but I do like to have a clear understanding of things.

I thank all the Masters and Angels of the One Light for their presence and protection, and offer a blessing on all which has taken place this hallowed day. I sit quietly in contemplation before I close my Cosmic link. I ensure that each of my energy centres are sealed and that I am very well grounded. Quietly I gather all my articles and return them to their special tin.

MERRIVALE STONE CIRCLE - ATLANTEAN TEMPLE SITE.

I rise and go to the nearby stone circle, which now houses an ancient Atlantean Temple. As I step into its inner sanctum, it is like going back in time - perhaps to a Golden Age - ancient voices fill the silence of the present day and it becomes alive once again. With my dowsing rods, I walk the circle in a clockwise direction, checking how many stones are in situ and picking up on the missing ones. I wonder why there is an unusual twenty-eight - I know of no reason for this particular number. On Bodmin Moor, I came across twenty-nine stones making up each of the three circles of The Hurlers. Is the menhir the final stone here? Even so, the reason for twenty-nine is still lost to me. I now go into the centre of the Temple, at a point which instinct tells me the Altar is situated. It is here I am to bury my white and pink quartz crystals. However, the ground is a very firm and unweilding. I suddenly remember I have a small pair of scissors in the deep recesses of my pack - they'll do - always something to hand - regular little girl guide that's me! I retrieve them and with apologies to Mother Earth, hack away at the ground in order to produce two holes large enough to secrete each crystal separately. My work here today is finished.

My return across the moorland takes me back to the entrance of the double stone row, through the male and female stones and along its entire length to the Anchor Stone. At the old stone wall, I stand looking out once again across the Merrivale settlement, visualizing it now graced with an Atlantean Temple. These ancient Temples, being thus returned to their rightful place, combined with the many many dedicated souls playing their part to bring Light and Healing to this ancient land, are all part of the Divine Plan. ALL is preparation for the New Jerusalem in these sacred British Isles. No raven today, but I know Merlin has worked his alchemy. Back at my car, after a sandwich and drink I now continue on my journey to Brent Tor and my second Ceremony of the day, which I have documented (see Chapter 9).

WISTMAN'S WOOD

Wistman's Wood is just a few miles from Merrivale, and to draw this chapter to a close I wish to share with you two visits I made in 2004 and 2008. The reason - the Lady Mary with Jesus and Naomi visited this ancient woodland and its connecting Druidic settlement. They with other Druids, precessed from the settlement to deep within the woodland to worship at the High Altar.

Wistman's Wood situated on the West Dart River, is one of just two areas of indigenous oak woodland left on Dartmoor. As one crosses the threshold into this sacred wood, one enters a mystical realm. The gnarled stunted oak trees are twisted into strange mysterious shapes; tree trunks and stones entwine as one entity; over-hanging ferns spray forth from crevices in the rocks and trees; ancient moss and lichen-covered stones, are a dominant feature. The whole, gives an air of deep spiritual intensity. On warm rainy days in summer, the impression once gets, is of being within a Celtic rainforest.

I have visited Wistman's Wood many times. As briefly as possible, I shall relate just two of those pilgrimages with my insights, in order to build a picture of what it must have been like in Druidic times, when Mary was here.

A PILGRIMAGE IN 2004.

I am feeling a great sacredness on entering the ancient woodland which is Wistman's Wood, after asking permission of the Druid Guardian. As I wend my way through the gnarled oaks and mossed stones, I am drawn to an enormous triangular stone with a huge base-stone. The feeling of reverence increases now, as in the stillness I stand before these awesome stones. In order to honour the ancestors, I step up onto the base stone, facing the triangular stone and rest my hands on it. I can feel its pulsating energy. As I turn around, the power lifts my arms, so that they are outstretched to each side of me. I am wearing a white robe and impressed that I am a Druid Priest. People are gathering and I seem to be offering a blessing. This is the High Altar. This is the 'Holy of Holies' entered by just a few Priests and Elders, except on special occasions. My intuition tells me, that here was a vortex of energy for invoking the Light. I am aware that the vibrations within this woodland in this present day, are what can only be described as - 'dark energies' so I ask what had happened here and am told that the Light had been withdrawn a long long time ago. I did not receive a reason for this. At this point in time, I feel that this woodland is bereft of the little people, even though to me it is such a magical place. I ask whether it is ready to be opened up again and get a resounding: "*NO*". After this, I continue my walk through the woodland, to discover many huge granite stones; triangular, pyramidal and dolmen type cap-stones, which seemed to be set in patterns.

Wistman's Wood showing the Triangular Atar Stone and Base Stone

A PILGRIMAGE IN 2008

Early in 2008, some special friends and myself are undertaking a pilgrimage to Wistman's Wood. Our journey takes us first through the ancient settlement to its boundary. I become aware that at this juncture are two Cardinal Stones either side of the path, which I learn are male and female. I find myself saying: *"This is an ancient gateway in direct alignment with Wistman's Wood."* With respect, we go through the gateway. My inner vision shows, that I am dressed in white and walking with great reverence, the ancient precessional route. Each measured step is a sacred one - with each I am blessing the Earth. I am feeling a pull and an almost yearning, to be at the High Altar, deep in the heart of the woodland. At the entrance we have a short attunement. We honour the guardian and silently enter this ancient oak-wood and into fairyland. I make my way to the triangular Altar Stone. I have some wild flowers and gently place my little posy as an offering on the large base stone. With a small piece of white quartz, I do likewise. My friends and I each choose a boulder to sit on and attune to the Higher Beings. These are the words I receive:

ANCIENT DRUID

"Beloved child, you are so very welcome to our sacred place. Be still now - be very still and listen to the sounds of nature all round you. Tune your inner senses to the inner sounds of this sacred woodland. This is YOUR sacred place dearly beloved one - dearly beloved pilgrim. You were here many eons ago and now you return - welcome - welcome

- *welcome. Remember if you will."* (I realize now that this could be a reference to my time here as Naomi with Mary and maybe confirming an incarnation as a Druid Priest).

I enter into a deep state of meditation. I am registering that there would have been special times in the Celtic calendar when the Cosmic Light was invoked here in Wistman's Wood. I become aware of many people dressed in white robes, wearing sandals, standing encircled by these ancient trees. There is a feeling of great joy among them. The Druid who spoke with me, took his staff and drew on some sandy soil the ancient symbol of the Celtic cross, as a benediction. How privileged and how blessed I feel at being a part of this wonder. As I emerge from my meditation, I ask if the Light is now ready to be reawakened and this time receive a: *"YES"*. So in the silence of my own heart, I make a sacred request that it be done, offering myself as an instrument for this Divine act. I am fully aware, that over time many have been the Light Workers who have made pilgrimage to this ancient wood, each adding their own blessing of grace - sanctifying and re-energizing the Light. Today I am picking up these words: *"the darkness is subsiding."* So we have each played our designated role. Also, the little people have returned and I feel their immense delight. I offer a blessing for the ancient Druids and for the fairy folk.

I have a theory - that when the Light energies were withdrawn from Wistman's Wood, the trees stopped growing, hence the stunted woodland we have today. Am I right? Who knows? However, I feel that this ancient woodland sanctuary, is now full of Light and the energies are pure.

There was much more to this day and subsequent days, but as usual space is limited. However, just to note, that my friends and I were aware of a link with the Pole Star, the Pleiades, Pluto and other wondrous Planets and entities.

So ends the narrative of two pilgrimages I made to the mystical Wistman's Wood. For any who may wish to make pilgrimage to this sacred site, here are the instructions. Park opposite the Two Bridges Hotel on the B3357. Walk through the gate and along the track going north. At a farmstead named 'Crockern' the track becomes a path, leading you up a rise passing to the right of the house and below Crockern Tor. Crockern Tor was the site of the first Tinners Parliament formed to deal with their affairs. The path continues gently uphill, through the ancient Druidic settlement and on to Wistman's Wood which is situated below Littaford Tors. All the way, you are travelling above the West Dart River, within the most beautiful ancient landscape. I suspect that in Mary's day the whole river valley would have been one vast oak woodland

CHAPTER 11
MOORLAND TRAVERSE FOR
HEMBURY CASTLE
Landscape of Light

From Merrivale the Lady Mary and her family travelled across Central Dartmoor to Hembury Castle. With their guides they set out on horseback to climb Cramber Tor and Hartor (Heart) Tors to reach Broad Rock. From here the little party would have been met with an extensive area of marshy terrain. This region today is the head of several rivers, a swampy area with deep peat bogs and quite hazardous for the unwary. However, one does have the advantage of an ancient route, which the monks took to travel between Buckfast Abbey and Tavistock Abbey. This is a twenty-two mile long-distance walk called 'The Abbots Way' which I have completed on two occasions. In Mary's day 2,000 years ago, this territory was even more waterlogged and I suspect would have had wooden walkways across it, rather like those discovered on the Somerset Levels. On reaching Huntington Warren settlement, Mary took a much needed rest before continuing. The final part of their moorland trek led them over Lambs Down, to cross the River Mardle and Holy Brook for the climb to Hembury Castle settlement. I am amazed that they undertook the journey in one day, a distance of approximately sixteen miles, bearing in mind the terrain, but can't discover anywhere they stayed overnight on the central moor.

Focusing on the map in this vicinity, I discover many place names with Druidic association; Ashburton, Highgrove, Aish Tor, Druid, Water Oak Corner and Two Oaks plus a Merryfield and Holy Brook for Mary!

HOLY BROOK

We now pick up Mary's trail at Holy Brook. It was in the autumn of 2008, when I was looking at the map in order to plan a pilgrimage to Hembury Castle, that I suddenly came across the name 'Holy Brook'. A flash of intuition told me that this had a connection with Mary. I was already privy to information about her having stayed at a settlement at Hembury Castle, but knew little else at the time, so seeing this name was a bonus.

I went in search of Holy Brook following my visit to Hembury. Driving the mile or so downhill I park close to the little stone bridge over the stream, which I had crossed earlier on my journey to the castle site. Standing on the bridge I notice that the dreaded mechanical hedge-strimmer has had its wicked way and sadly decimated the hedgerows. What trauma this must cause the plants and how sad for the elementals. Where are the old hedge-laying skills? I am now looking over the low stone wall into the clear water of Holy Brook. I have in a bottle about my person, some water collected from the East Dart River at Dartmeet. I pour a little into the stream with a blessing saying: *"Dear little brook, may this offering help to keep your water pure as it flows through the land."* I stand very still - past memories are returning. My inner voice tells me: *'we drank from here.'* I know this refers to Mary and Naomi on our journey to Hembury. Now the voice of the water is talking with me:

WATER SPRITE

"Bless you Pilgrim of Light. Thank you for your offering. We are indeed blessed as the Holy Mother did sip of our nectar. We were running freely and very happily in those days. There was no bridge, no road, just a track to the top of the hill. We didn't see many travellers, but those we did see were on their way to the Temple at the top. There were some who went on to what is now called Buckfast Abbey, to the ancient centre which has long gone. However, the energies can still be picked up. The abbey itself is built very close to the ancient Druid site. Maybe you will find it one day. You will have guidance Pilgrim of Light. For now - this day is good. You have fulfilled your destiny at the Temple (that is at Hembury Castle, details of which are coming up) *and all is well. Let our voice sing to you as you remember past times."*

I offer a blessing to the water deva and my grateful thanks for confirmation of my insights.

A thought - I might collect a little water from Holy Brook. The water level is far below the bridge and it may be impossible, but where there's a will there's a way. I spy a little gap to one side of the bridge. Gingerly I climb down the bank clinging on to holly branches. As I reach the water level, I feel that I am in a secret world down here, well hidden from the country road. With one foot placed on a rather wobbly stone in the middle of the stream causing me to almost fall in the drink, I just manage to collect some water. As I scramble back up the bank and return to my car, I am laughing at my efforts, thinking - I must be mad. I suspect the little people of the woodland and the water undines are having a quiet chuckle also!

ARRIVAL AT HEMBURY CASTLE DRUIDIC SETTLEMENT

Mary and her family finally reached Hembury Castle settlement. It was after my recent pilgrimage to Hembury, that I went into a deep meditation at home. I had felt inspired to sit for an attunement, when my inner awareness took me back to the ancient site. I found I was asking Beloved Mary if she could throw any more light on the Hembury settlement in her time. This is what I received:

Hembury Castle

MEDITATION ON HEMBURY CASTLE

'I have a vision of Mary, Joseph of Arimathea and the children, Jesus and Naomi on horseback at the bottom of the hill leading to the Hembury Druidic Temple site. The little band of travellers are now crossing Holy Brook and beginning the long pull uphill to the Temple. When they reach the settlement, they are greeted by their Druid Brethren. I am conscious of Mary being very weary. Both children concerned for her welfare, go over to help her off her horse. I feel the weariness, but she smiles in gratitude. She is saying: "how blessed am I to have such kind thoughtful children." The little group are taken care of and given sustenance and a place to rest. I am aware that the journey was not without dangers and they were pleased to be in this place of safety at the end of their day. I could see that it was still daylight, so their long trek over Dartmoor had obviously been completed before darkness fell.

Mary rested for a few days until she was fully recovered. Then at the next full moon, a special Light Ceremony was enacted by her at the Temple. I see a group of Druid worshipers in their white robes. It comes to me, that there is no difference between the Elders and what shall I say - the lay people. They are all dressed alike and I felt were considered of equal worth. Just before sunrise on the day of the full moon, the great trail of white robed Brethren circumnavigated the Hill Temple in a spiral, winding their way up to the top.

The time has come for the Lady Mary to perform her sacred Ceremony. First, she is re-energising the Atlantean Temple in the Etheric, bringing the Light of Atlantis back to this ancient land. Now I see her invoking the Cosmic Light for the Druidic Tree Temple on the hill. I see Mary standing in her white robe at the highest point, ethereal like, her arms raised high offering a great blessing. I am aware that the hill-top is completely enveloped in Light. The Light energy is causing the land to vibrate and Mary herself seems to almost have disappeared within its powerful core. She is illumined. The Christ Spirit has entered her physical body, as we understand happened on numerous times with the Master Jesus, as he went about his ministry.'

My vision leaves me and I am back in my sanctuary - I close my meditation. For me, it is again early in my association with Mary, and yet I knew that THIS WAS HER ROLE - this was her Mission during her pilgrimage in the South West. of Britain. What a blessing to have received this image of Mary enacting the role of Light Bringer: *"Thank you Beloved Mary for your insights this day."*

PILGRIMAGE TO HEMBURY CASTLE 2007

Hembury Castle is an Iron Age hill fort dating from between 500 BC/AD 50. The name itself would certainly indicate this, as 'bury' corresponds to the Anglo-Saxon 'burh' meaning fortification. It is situated high above the River Dart just to the north of Buckfast. It has a predominance of fine oak trees set within a large area of mixed woodland. Careful searching will discover the stumps of much older oaks, from which their size would suggest, are well over 1,000 years old.

It was in 2007 on an early pilgrimage to Hembury that I received a prophetic message from White Eagle. I was sat at the mossy base of one of the oak trees, when I became aware of him being close at hand:

WHITE EAGLE

"Welcome to this sacred place. Dear one, we would wish that you be still now and at every available opportunity. This will give US the opportunity to prepare your physical body, alongside your other more subtle bodies for the task ahead. Listen to the wind in the trees, be aware of the birdsong all around you and be conscious on an inner level of the devas and other elementals, who reside in this sacred grove. For this was a place of Druidic worship a long time ago, but the energies still abound and the Temple has been lifted above the physical into the Etheric. The energy and the power which was once here, only lies dormant. It will be reactivated when the time is right. You will know dear one - you will know. Meanwhile, we would once again ask that you be very still and absorb the atmosphere of this sacred place. Dwell in the silence always dear sister and deep peace will be yours. In the silence you will open to the inner worlds and receive. God Bless you dear Peace Rose. God Bless you."

I thank White Eagle for his contact. As he finishes I couldn't help but wonder what he meant by 'the task ahead'. No doubt time will offer an explanation I thought. And it did, as a year later the Lady Mary had made her presence known and so began the next chapter of my life. The impression I am receiving, is that Hembury Castle was a Temple of Light where the Light was so bright and pure, that it formed the Rainbow Bridge linking to all dimensions. Sitting quietly among the trees, I become aware of the Lady Mary and the Master Jesus. Before leaving I feel the urge to perambulate around the lower slopes of the hill fort. As I follow a clockwise spiral, I realize I am dressed in a white robe and know that I have done this before at this sacred site. Again I am sure that more will be revealed in time. For now I am happy that I have made this pilgrimage, and am sure that I will return when the Masters wish me to.

PILGRIMAGE TO HEMBURY CASTLE 2008

Re-reading White Eagle's words of 2007, I realize there is a job to be done here. When White Eagle talks of a Temple being lifted into the Etheric he implies that it is a Druidic Temple. It is possible that the energies of the Druidic Tree Temple have been lifted. However, it is my contention with fresh insight, that he is referring to an ancient Atlantean Temple which Mary re-energised. Today I am to earth this ancient Temple. This is the beginning of my Mission and before I have prepared my three Light Ceremonies, thus for my Ceremony at Hembury, I draft out some words, which although briefer than my subsequent one, are no less sacred. The evening before I make preparation, gathering together a few precious items, including my little pouch of crystals.

After an early attunement, I leave my house at 6.00 am, the idea to be at Hembury with plenty of time for my Ceremony before I could be disturbed. From Buckfast I take the country road signposted for Hembury Woods and before long, am turning into the gravelled area which is the car park for Hembury Castle. Alighting from the car, I am struck by the stillness and silence, only broken by early morning birdsong. There is an air of expectancy.

My pilgrimage begins. As I walk the well defined track through the trees towards Hembury Castle, I feel that I have gone back to Druidic times. I have my hands before me, as if encased in the sleeves of a robe. I am in a walking meditation, feeling the energy of the earth beneath my feet. On through the woodland, I arrive at a little gate and ask the Druid guardian permission to enter. Now at the base of the Temple site, I have stepped into a sacred space. I reach my first oak tree. I put my pack down and stand with my back to the tree, offering a blessing and hearing:

DEVA OF THE OAK

"You are so welcome Light Worker. We have been waiting for you. Feel the energy. Feel the life through my trunk. It will sustain you. We are so happy you are here today. This is a special blessing on this ancient land. And yes, Mary WAS here. You will learn more."

From me: *"Bless you dear Tree Deva."*

HEMBURY CASTLE ATLANTEAN TEMPLE CEREMONY

I climb to the top of the inner bank of the ancient fort looking for a suitable place to conduct my Ceremony. I choose a lovely old oak tree on the far side. I set out a small cloth and light my candle. Already I am kneeling in reverence. With a blessing, I lay down four items, one for each element. For Fire, it is a cut-out star/sun, then a white quartz crystal for Earth, followed by a pure white feather for Air. For Water, I pour a little of the water I collected from Becka Brook below Hound Tor on Dartmoor, into a small glass bowl. I also have a rose-pink quartz for the Lady Mary and the Sacred Feminine.

I make the Cosmic link with Beloved Mary, the Divine Masters and with those from the Angelic Realms. I now voice *'The Great Invocation.'* Then in rhythmical steady tone I speak the following words:

"Beloved ones. Great Beings of Light, let me be a channel to bring the Light back to this sacred place.

Let the Atlantean Temple in the Etheric, return to its rightful place and grace Mother Earth with its presence once again.

Let this Temple be used to send out Light and Healing to this sacred land and beyond.

Let this sacred site be blessed and healed. LET THE LIGHT SHINE."

St Michael the protector of our ancient land seals this Cosmic act with his flaming sword. I have completed my Ceremony.

Being a little conscious of the open nature of the hill fort I close my Ceremony and decide to clear away all obvious signs of anything 'odd' going on! I remember thinking. that I would have wished to have been able to give a little more time for the Ceremony. However, I sit quietly and continue to attune and maintain my Cosmic link. Now I am feeling that there are so many dear ones from the World Beyond clambouring to talk with me. First Mary comes in, but takes a step back for White Eagle:

WHITE EAGLE

"Welcome dear Peace Rose. We have been waiting for you. Bless you. We understand that circumstances are not perfect, but you have done what we have asked of you (Bless you White Eagle for allaying my doubts). *The Temple is gradually returning to this sacred hill-top. It will stand as a Beacon of Light. It will be invisible to the human eye, but visible to all those with the inner sight. We in the Land of Light - all the Masters and Beings of Light - appreciate your pilgrimage today. You are one of our precious Light Workers in incarnation at this time. You know the value of pilgrimage and the joy of healing the land. Dear Sister of Light we bless you. I will leave you now because our blessed Mary wishes to speak with you."*

I thank White Eagle for his presence this hallowed day Now from Mary, a rather long message, but essential to my understanding during these early encounters and even now, can serve as a reminder of some of what we have learnt so far:

MARY

"*My dear dear child. This is such a special occasion. Once again we meet in this sacred place where we have travelled to before. You were then, as you know, my beloved child Naomi and with us was my beloved Jesus. Joseph of Arimathea was our protector and our guide on our journey to this land. It was important that we ALL visit for this one occasion together, in order to lay the foundation for future journeying. I knew I would be returning after I had 'lost' my beloved Son in the future time* (see Chapter 7). *My insights and visions told me this would be so. Of course on that occasion I went to Wales and not to the Westcountry. I was fortunate in some ways to have the reassurance that after the crucifixion, I would be taken and guided eventually to a safe haven.*

Indeed, although the Roman Empire at that time stretched far and wide, the area of sacred Wales was very remote from its tentacles. However, as we were to learn later to our cost, the great might of Rome, did eventually destroy nearly all traces of our ancient wisdom - what you today call Celtic Christianity. This was 'THE WAY'. This was the true and pure way to live as had been brought to us by our beloved Jesus. This was the way of love which we all knew and understood. It was a way of peace and gentleness and caring for our brothers and sisters. It was a way of worshiping the Great Ones and nurturing the land, our precious Mother Earth and all therein. It was THE WAY OF PEACE.

Our journey to this land was fraught with dangers. We first of all, through much subterfuge and protection, had to leave the Holy Land. Then on to our Egyptian guardians, finally across the sea in a perilous voyage till we landed on the shores of Wales, now Carmarthen Bay. You know some of this, but I will share more in a future time.

For now dear Naomi, we would return to the voyage undertaken by you, Jesus, Joseph of Arimathea and myself in those early years. In a vision, I was shown a pilgrimage that we must all make to the South West of these sacred Isles. You and Jesus were very excited at the opportunity for freedom from your studies and confines of Temple life. However the journey had a special purpose, which was to bring these two young people and of course myself, to the Heart of the Grail and to walk on the soil of our ancestors, in preparation for future visits By touching the Earth in this way, the Light was able to be brought down to invigorate the Earth and heal the land. It was a precious journey and one which we undertook with joy. We were fulfilling our destiny to bring Light to this ancient land. The power and energy from the great Angelic Beings, is to revitalize the Earth Planet and bring in the Light. We, our little group, were just instruments for that purpose.

We knew we would return. Beloved Jesus returned as a young man with Joseph of Arimathea. Later, he and the beloved Mary Magdalene journeyed to Britain as part of their pilgrimage to the sacred places of our Earth. That is another story dear one. You and I returned after the happenings in Jerusalem - after our great loss.

Jerusalem - THIS is the New Jerusalem. Here in these ancient British Isles is the New Jerusalem. It is from here, that the Light of all Eternity will ignite hearts everywhere and once again bring that Golden Age into manifestation. This sacred land houses the blue print for the future of the Earth Plane. There is so much hidden at the present time, but gradually minds and hearts will be awakened to this Light and much will be discovered. In the Etheric above this precious land, is a store of magical ancient texts which will at some time come to light. In the Etheric, is so much waiting to be called down to the physical, where once again, as in olden times, it will be used for regeneration and uplifting the land and its people. Truly I say unto you, the New Jerusalem will return. This ancient land will once more be a Light Beacon for the World. It will once more be filled with the power and essence of the ancient ones. It is happening. It is beginning. Atlantis will return. The vision is real. It is beginning to happen - now.

Yes, these precious Isles were once part of that great continent of Atlantis. And dear daughter we were there, you and I and many others who walk this pathway of Light. Many of those in present incarnation were there. Memories will return as the heart opens to love. As the heart opens so will the inner mind, the mind behind the earthly mind, transpose that pure love of the Heart Rose, to bring forth manifestations in a physical sense. Much will be revealed through the Mind in the Heart. We know this. You know this. You DO KNOW. We are ALL part of that one true Light of all times. The mysteries of our Universe are so profound by earthly understanding and yet so simple to grasp when in the Land of Light.

Enough for now beloved daughter. We bless you for your pilgrimage to this place of ancient times - to the place where we once journeyed. Yes we did come here from the Light Centre at Merrivale of which you will learn more (this in answer to my intuitive thought and way before I had charted Mary's journey across Devon). *God bless you Sister and Daughter of Light."*

I acknowledge Mary's beautiful words and her visitation, realizing once again how blessed I am. I believe Mary had even more to say, but I think it was registered on the inner planes how cold I was becoming. I was aware that the energies were dropping, possibly due to my discomfort. I gently but firmly close my physical centres and ensure I am grounded.

Time to leave this Ceremonial spot on Hembury Hill. At the base of the oak tree, I place the star and the feather, then bury the white quartz crystal for the Druids. I pour the now blessed water over them. I collect my things and put them away. I am about to leave when I notice my pink quartz crystal lying on the earth. Well - I KNOW I put it back in its little pouch, placed it in my tin of special items and put the tin in my pack, BUT there it was on the ground! My thought - maybe I am to leave it for Mary. I take the pink crystal and carefully bury it with the other crystal. I thank Mary for bringing it to my notice. This is the reason why I always leave a rose-pink quartz crystal for Mary and the Goddess at all the sites I visit. I have also learned that together with the white quartz crystal, it ensures that the male-female energies stay balanced.

As before, I perambulate around the base of Hembury Castle being conscious of the newly earthed Atlantean Temple on the hill. I am aware once again that my hands are within the folds of a white garment. I reach the point where I started my perambulation and stand quite still in contemplation. The landscape around is flat and green with purple heather set amongst rusty-brown bracken. I am suddenly filled with emotion. This place was once home to me and I feel as if I have become an integral part of the landscape. Now I am to leave, but a part of my heart will remain here.

I walk up the slope and reach the centre of the Castle/Temple which is hollowed. I wonder why. In Druidic times, I suspect the top would have been rounded. Has the land here sunk over time? Could there have been a secret chamber underneath for sacred inner Ceremonies, which has caved in due to land-slip? Who knows? There has never been an archeological dig here at Hembury. I stand facing east in prayer. Things are being brought to my notice. Firstly, that Jesus as a boy on that journey with Mary, would have preached here to the people. Also, that they, the Druid Elders, knew of his coming. For me, this mystical hill holds deep Cosmic memories. I return from my reveries slowly. But by now even with the little bit of warmth expended by my perambulation, I am shivering. I have been at Hembury for over three hours.

Suddenly I am rather rudely awakened from my musing, by a bark and the appearance of a little dog - a Yorkshire terrier - at the top of the bank. The dog has a shock at seeing me and I jump - I don't know who was the most surprised! I walk off the hill fort and greet its owner. I have completed my time here so it was pleasant to share conversation with this lady. We talked about the peace of the land hereabouts, the old oak trees and I brought up a possible Druidic link. This lady said that she was from Buckfast, just a mile or so away and walks her dog here regularly in all seasons. As mentioned in Chapter 4, one winter she was up here when everything was covered with snow and she saw a white horse on top of the fort. My mind pictured a unicorn and I nearly verbalized it, but thought better of it. Talking of Druids is sort of okay but a unicorn - well I would surely have been given a strange look! She then said, that on another occasion she saw a fox coming out of the nearby bushes with a rabbit in its mouth. It was startled when the dog barked at it, dropped its prey and rushed off into the undergrowth. The rabbit scampered away unhurt - free to live another day.

As I leave the ancient site, I again say a thank you to all the Beloved Ones. I am visualizing the whole of the hill-top enshrouded in Golden Light. Feeling elated and full of joy, I skip along, a bit different from the slow reverent pace with which I entered this sacred place. A hot drink back in the car revives me and eventually I warm up. Now for some breakfast of a little fruit. My thoughts keep returning to the Temple on the Hill and its revelations. I leave the car park to spend that precious time at Holy Brook.

At home typing up these pages, I am aware of the presence of Beloved Mary and White Eagle. They in the Land of Light are very satisfied with today's outcome at the Temple. Here endeth my report on this, the first of many sacred Ceremonies enacted in the South West of Britain for the Lady Mary and the Masters.

THE NEW JERUSALEM

During the writing of this book, the concept of the New Jerusalem has been interwoven on numerous occasions, either through personal insight or received messages. But what is this New Jerusalem? At the beginning of the Piscean Age, the Master Jesus, the Light of the World, through his Divine knowledge of the Ancient Wisdom, laid down a set of guidelines by which we should live our lives. He brought The Way of Divine Truth through the purity of love within the Sacred Heart. The New Jerusalem, as I see it, is the transference of those Cosmic Energies and ancient truths to Britain from the Holy Land, at the beginning of the Aquarian Age. This was set in motion 2,000 years ago, by the Master himself with Mary Magdalene during their pilgrimage to Britain. The Lady Mary also had her part to play with her Mission to re-energize the ancient Druidic Light centres and reactivate the Atlantean Temples in the Etheric. So, preparation was being made at the beginning of the Piscean Age, to bring into manifestation the Ancient Wisdom and reinstate the Light in these sacred British Isles for the Aquarian age. As that New Age is upon us, many are the Light Workers playing their part in this renaissance - in this Great Awakening. The New Jerusalem is beginning - NOW.

St Michael when he was speaking with me at Caerhays Church in Cornwall, talked of the British Isles as being the New Jerusalem. At Hembury the Lady Mary herself confirms that: *'Here in these ancient British Isles is the New Jerusalam'* But why Britain? For me, the answer lies in the understanding, that these ancient Isles form the last remnants of the lost continent of Atlantis. This is mentioned on numerous occasions by Mary and St Michael. As such, Britain would hold within its energetic nature, the ancient power and vibrations of that lost civilization, so often talked about as being the Golden Age.

I reconnect to *'The Light in Britain'* by Grace and Ivan Cooke. This is a book I deliberately refrained from re-reading, until right at the end of my Mission with Mary, when the ancient civilization of Hyperborea was brought to my notice at Glastonbury, as I had no wish to be influenced in my thoughts. I have returned to it now on the completion of my travelling and on my investigation of this subject. In this book, White Eagle talks of the Brotherhood of the Light and tells us on Page 104 that: *'the origin of this Brotherhood of the Great White Light is here, here in the mystic isle of Britain.'* He tells of the God-men who once inhabited the ancient land of Britain and who responded to the Source of all Wisdom - the Universal Cosmic Christ. So the Light in Britain has always been. Therefore the re-birth of that Light in these sacred Isles, through the New Jerusalem, will be built on strong Cosmic foundations and its influence will reverberate throughout our Planet.

I notice White Eagle says *'Isle of Britain'* giving indication that he is referring to an era when Britain was a single landmass. We've heard that Britain could be the high ground of ancient Atlantis. A premise - what do we think of the possibility of Britain, as that single landmass, actually being an island off the main Atlantean continent? The problem of all this, is the vast timescale of prehistory. The opinion of chroniclers differ as to the age of Atlantis, and give us dates of anything between 10,000 and 21,000 BC. But whichever is accurate the age of the continent makes it is almost impossible to come up with any definitive conclusion.

Mary's message to me at Hembury says that Britain: *'houses the blue print for the future of the Earth Plane'* and that ancient texts are held in the Etheric above Britain. This infers to me, that they are held in trust, until such time as we - the human race - are ready to receive them and will not misuse them. We need to reach a stage in our development and understanding of the Ancient Wisdom and the Universal Laws, that the texts can be accessed and acted upon through the Mind in the Heart. Then, and only then, will the secrets and mysteries be unveiled.

To conclude - a few words from Mary. First she talks of Atlantis, then:

MARY

"But there is more dear one. The British Isles as they now are, have secrets of other past civilizations Lemuria - Hyperboria. To this day, much can be discovered beneath the seas surrounding these Isles, evidence of roads - evidence of buildings. The ancient civilization of Lemuria is so close to being rediscovered. At present very little investigation has been done on this account, but believe me dear one, it will happen. The seas around your British Isles are waiting to be investigated. I feel your excitement and I do understand dear daughter, because what I am telling you or should I say confirming, is awakening soul memories for you in this present incarnation, as if you are living in these ancient times. Gradually memories will begin to return as you release yourself to spirit wisdom. Listen to your heart Be awake to intuitive insight and you will discover more.

I bless you dear sister. We all love you for your enthusiasm and the love expressed in your life. God Bless you my Sister of Light. God Bless you.'

I thank dearest Mary for enlightening me a little further.

THE HOLY GRAIL

This issue of the Holy Grail has also popped up in this work and perhaps now is the time to take a more in-depth look at it (see also Chapter 17). Much has been written about the Holy Grail. Some view it as the physical cup of the Last Supper, brought to Britain by Joseph of Arimathea. Both the Lady Mary and Mary Magdalene, have been identified with the Holy Grail. At Hembury, Mary talks of a pilgrimage to the South West of the British Isles, which she, Jesus and Naomi undertook *'to the heart of the Grail'* (this present journey). With these words Mary appears to be saying that BRITAIN is the Holy Grail.

Suddenly it comes to my understanding that the Holy Grail is the pure essence of Divine Love within each human heart, represented by the Sacred Rose. Whether it manifests as a physical vessel, or as a Divine incarnated being, or within the sacred landscape - it is LOVE. It is the Chalice of the Heart, and

Love is the key which will unlock the door and allow The Rose to unfurl, to receive the Golden Light from the Godhead - thus we become filled with Divine Fire. Love doesn't choose where it will abide. It just IS. It is there in the heart centre of every man, women and child, awaiting recognition, ready to be activated through our expression of unconditional love. Our happiness, our joy and our peace of mind, can become a reality through this unconditional love. We have lost ourselves in the materialism and greed of worldly desires. Until we can ALL realize the true value of the Sacred Heart, we will continue down the pathway of self-destruction and World destruction. Our personal salvation is the Rose in the Heart and is in our own hands. The salvation of our Planet, is in our hands. Know this my Brethren. This is TRUTH. Now a beautiful Being is offering a benediction for us all:

BEING OF LIGHT

"We in the Land of Light offer to you now the Grail Cup of your own heart - sip its nectar, bathe in its perfect essence - it is yours for all times. It is within you. It is the Rose in the Heart of each and every one of you. God Bless you dear Pilgrims of Light. God Bless all your endeavours to maintain your equilibrium and for every effort you make to manifest that Grail Cup of Love in your own lives."

From Mary a beautiful confirmation of my insights:

MARY

"Dearest sister. We respect your own inner wisdom, for that has truly brought you to an esoteric understanding of the Holy Grail. I CAN say to you that THE GRAIL is LOVE It is the Love within each human heart - the heart as it opens to love, overflows with this Divine essence. Thus we have the concept of a Grail Cup overflowing with Golden Light. The Light of Love exudes from each human heart centre, bringing into being ultimate perfection within the human vehicle. So, wherever that Grail Cup is filled with pure Love and Light, it is there we find perfection. It can be attached to an object also, if that object is imbued with Love. We do not wish to take this any further at this time dear sister, because there is also a much deeper Cosmic answer. It may be deemed that this can be imparted to you in the future. For now dear Sister of Light, we entrust this information to you and are happy if it is shared."

From me: *"Bless you Beloved One."*

JOURNEY TO THE RIVER DART

To conclude Mary's travelling in this area, she and her family leave Hembury Castle settlement on horseback, riding back down the hill to Holy Brook, then follow the line of the brook to the River Dart by Buckfast Abbey. You may remember we have been told that there was once a Druidic centre here, evidence of which is long gone. Mary did not stay at the settlement, but took a boat up the River Dart for her journey north through East Dartmoor. For us however, we shall tarry a short while at Buckfast Abbey as I have things I wish to share with you.

BUCKFAST ABBEY

The autumn of 2008 following my pilgrimage to Merrivale Ceremonial Complex, sees me on the road to Buckfast Abbey. I don't know why, but I am to go there. All I know, is that I have been impressed most strongly in this regard. So - ever the obedient one - well to Spirit's wishes - here I am turning into the abbey car park.

Statue of the Lady Mary and baby Jesus in the Lavender Garden, Buckfast Abbey

Buckfast Abbey, which is dedicated to St Mary, today houses a community of Benedictine monks. The abbey has had a chequered history as with many in the British Isles, not least at the hands of Henry VIII through his Dissolution of the Monasteries, which is well documented historically. The present Benedictine community returned towards the end of the nineteenth century and rebuilt the abbey on its medieval foundations. However in times past it was home to the Cistercian Order. The Cistercians hailed from Burgundy and were quietly reshaped by Bernard of Clairvaux, in order to assimilate aspects of Romano-Celtic Christianity. They arrived in Britain in the twelfth century, their first Holy centre being Fountain Abbey in Yorkshire. In Wales the Cistercian Order was supported by Lord Rhys a Welsh Prince, who held the

Anglo-Norman houses of the Benedictines and Augustinians of the time, in poor regard. Cistercian monasteries were established throughout Wales, the most sacred centre being at Strata Florida. In time, the Cistercians travelled south and became prominent throughout Dummonia, with Buckfast Abbey of prime importance.

A few days previous to this present pilgrimage to Buckfast Abbey, I had met with a dear friend there, at the start of a Dartmoor walk. While waiting for her to arrive, I wandered into the Physic Garden within the abbey grounds, enjoying the pervading scent of the different herbs and lavenders. I noticed a beautiful white stone statue of Mother Mary and the baby Jesus - I was entranced. I have been to Buckfast Abbey on numerous occasions, yet this statue had never registered with me before. I had no camera this day but knew I had to return to take a photograph. I also knew that there was an urgent need to once more sit in the peaceful confines of the Chapel of the Blessed Sacrament within the abbey itself. It is here there is a huge and quite remarkable stained glass window dominating the east end, portraying the blessed Jesus, arms outstretched as if to encompass the whole world. Also portrayed in the window, are the Grail Cup and the ancient symbol of the Celtic cross, both illustrated in Golden Light.

The morning of my special pilgrimage begins with an attunement. The room is filled with the gentle presence of White Brethren and a great stillness befalls me. I ask a blessing on my sacred day. I hear from Mary:

MARY

"My dearest sister, my daughter. I bless you for your dedication. We all bless you. Beloved one, already we have brought to your attention the thought of Buckfast Abbey. We know you wish to return to take a picture of my statue. But, we would like you to go into the abbey, through to the quiet room with the beautiful mosaic of our beloved Jesus and be still there. We shall be with you and you will be aware of our presence. You will receive guidance and a special blessing. Bless you my child. Bless you."

This mosaic of the Master Jesus, has always had a profound effect on me so I am eager to oblige. I now go into a deep Meditation.

MY MEDITATION

'In the stillness I am looking at the magnificent window of the Master and I have the impression of Ascension. The figure of the Master is rising. He is floating up high above the Earth Plane, arms open wide to form a beautiful arc of Rainbow Light. He has the appearance of a solid human form, but angelic and celestial in nature. He really IS holding the whole World in the Light. He really IS encompassing us all in his healing grace and offering a blessing for each one of us. As I watch, the Lady Mary joins him. They link hands and together in unison, they float above the Earth, beaming down Light and Healing Rays in colours of immeasurable beauty. Beloved Mary has now left Jesus and he gently returns to his position as the Master of the illumined window in the abbey.

I offer a blessing and prayer of thanks as I return to physical consciousness.

My thoughts now turn to how I can get hold of a rose for Mary. I live in a block of flats with a communal garden, so can't go out and just 'nick' a rose! I know I can go to the local supermarket, but than I have to buy a bunch which I am happy to do, but they will not be opened fully as I wish. So with these thoughts in mind, I go down to the garden to water my own pots of flowers and herbs. I meet with a person who is just the right one to ask permission to take a rose. I explain that the rose is for a very special lady, who has a need for a loving gesture right now! That is the simplest explanation and it is half true, because she is my very special lady. The answer is yes and I have my rose. I choose a delicate pale pink one. I am ready for my visit to Buckfast Abbey.

INSPIRATIONS AT BUCKFAST ABBEY

It is 12.00 noon as I park up. The bell is tolling for the hour. This ancient sound brings to me a feeling of stillness and deep peace. I send out the Light for World healing. I now make my way to the Physic Garden. There are a few people within the garden confines. I sit on one of the seats at the entrance in the sunshine, with Mary's statue in full view, waiting patiently. A few minutes later the garden becomes quiet and I walk purposefully along the path through the lavender beds to the statue. As I look at it intently, I see it is rather in need of some loving attention and that the baby Jesus has lost the lower part of his arms. But this does not detract from the almost ethereal beauty of this solid white stone statue. I see the faces of both Mary and Jesus as being most beautifully portrayed. I stand in silence, offering a prayer and a blessing for the Holy Ones. I offer Mary my purist heart as I lay the pink rose at her feet. I take my photograph, which is before me constantly during my writing.

THE ST MARY CHAPEL

As I enter the main body of Buckfast Abbey, in spite of there being many visitors, I am enfolded in its peace. I walk directly down the left hand side to the St Mary Chapel. Many candles have been lit for the blessed Mary and the candle holders on the candelabra are full. So while I wait for a space, I sit looking at her effigy within the exquisitely decorated chapel. After about five minutes, one of the candles goes out and it is my turn. I pay my coin and collect a pure white votive candle, light it from another and place it in position: *"Mary my beloved, I offer you this candle - this Flame of Eternity with my deepest love."*

CHAPEL OF THE BLESSED SACRAMENT

I now move to the Chapel of the Blessed Sacrament. There is a notice informing me that this chapel is for quiet prayer and contemplation. I enter through the large heavy glass door and take my place on one of the long wooden pews. There are two or three people sitting in the silence. One gentleman is reading from what looks to be the Bible. Ahead of me is the stunning stained glass mosaic window depicting the Master Jesus. He is robed in the deepest pink and purple, with a surround of iridescent blues and greens.

Everything about it is perfect and his inner beauty seems to shine out. I am mesmerized by his eyes. I am filled with peace and joy. A lady comes and speaks with each of us, quietly informing us that the monks will be chanting for ten minutes at 1.00 pm in the main hall of the abbey and that the barriers will go across and we shall be unable to leave. She gives me the option of coming to listen to the chanting or staying where I am for the duration. I choose to stay. As the others leave I am alone. This is perfect. Is this all co-ordinated by Mary? I am saying: *"Beloved One alone at last"*

MARY

"Dear child I welcome you to this beautiful chapel, for here is where you can be very still and tune in to the Infinite. I wished you to be here today so that I could share more insights with you of a deeper nature. I wish you to travel physically to the places you went to in the past in the South West. As I have indicated, you dearest Naomi, were part of our small band of travellers to these sacred Isles a very long time ago. Joseph of Arimathea as a Druid master was our protector as we voyaged over seas and travelled across the land. You dearest one were a young girl of fourteen and this was part of your inner journey working towards the Light. You were given leave from the Temple in Egypt in order to take this journey. Our beloved Jesus was twelve years old and had completed the first part of his Temple training. This journey was to prepare him for his future journeying with Joseph of Arimathea and for his future ministry. You dearest one were blossoming into a beautiful young women. This was the time for you both to travel and touch the soil and the heart of these blessed Isles. We all welcome you again now dear Naomi and will guide you where we wish you to go. Be at peace now dearest one. Be at peace.

This gives me great joy to be able to make this contact with you. It has been possible because you have reached a point of time in this incarnation, when the heart is fully open to receive. Let it always be so dear daughter. You are completely in tune with your beloved White Eagle, our Is-Ra of Egyptian days. You knew him then dear one, as a loving strong father figure of great stature and kindness. He is here with us now and will always be part of your journey. For he, like us, is a part of that great Brotherhood of life, which enfolds us all in the simple pure love of devotion. My beloved son Jesus is with us now. He too is close to your heart and will always be so.

Now dearest one, the moment has come for your stillness and peaceful time. I thank and bless you for the beautiful pink rose you have placed as an offering for me. How blessed we are you and I to have been able to make this connection in this your earthly lifetime. Thank you for making it possible through your loving heart. I am your true Heart Rose for ever, as you are mine. Bless you. Bless you. Bless you."

I thank the Lady Mary for her contact, and my inner vision opens to her offering a loving blessing with her hand over her heart.

As Mary leaves me, the chanting which I had initially been hearing in the background, has come to an end and people begin to re-enter the chapel. Once again - excellent timing. I sit quietly pondering her words. It is time to go. I rise and discreetly acknowledge the beautiful Master of the east window with my hand on heart. I return to the St Mary Chapel for a final benediction for my blessed Mary.

I am in the car taking a little refreshment. I need to be in my own space for a time and must immerse myself in a cocoon of stillness. Later I visit the gift shop, buying a book about the Lady Mary's feast days, a few post cards and a book mark illustrating Mary. I then walk up to the monastic shop at the top of the abbey grounds. I purchase a small bottle of perfume from the monks on Caldy Island and a miniature bottle of green chartreuse from the French abbey of that name. Of course I just HAVE to have that! A momento which didn't last long once I decided on my 'treat' evening!

At home the following morning, I am reflecting on Mary's words. She tells me that she wishes me to visit certain places in the South West - this was my first indication of her plans for me. Secondly, it was news to me that White Eagle - Is-Ra - was my mentor during my incarnation as Naomi, for I thought our association went further back in time. More of that later. For now I have a quandary - that is, the ages of Naomi fourteen and Jesus twelve, which has obvious implications for the 'Virgin Birth'. I need to speak with Mary. I prepare myself for an attunement and receive the following:

MARY

"Bless you dearest one. For now we would wish you to go about your research and your daily life placidly. In due time I will share more insights with you. For now you have much to do, much to write up - much to transpose to paper (I agree). *So I would wish that you, as your beloved White Eagle would say, 'keep on keeping on' calmly, working always from the heart, never allowing the mind of everyday to intrude. For you ARE pure spirit living in a human vehicle. We are ALL that when in incarnation. This being the case, your physical and mental well-being is paramount. There is only so much information one can absorb at any given time dear sister. Enjoy your day. All is well. All is very well, dear Sister of Light. We bless you. Be still now and receive the peace which passeth all understanding."*

Well - that told me. Wise words as always. I have to learn patience and do this in Mary's time not mine!

THE IMMACULATE CONCEPTION

Finally some weeks later, after yet another reference to the ages of Naomi and Jesus, I need some answers. Mine and perhaps your understanding of this is important, so I will devote quite a chunk of text to it. This is the sequence of events.

I decide to have an attunement with the Lady Mary. As usual I put on some soft background music, light my candle and relax in my chair. Immediately Mary comes within my aura and my hands rise in prayer: *"Beloved one. Can you help me understand the ages of Naomi at fourteen years and Jesus at twelve years in the context of the 'Virgin Birth?"*

MARY

"Dearest one you WERE my child with Joseph. Listen to your heart. Read between the lines. Your beloved White Eagle has explained the process very well in one of his books. Do look at it once again. It is difficult for the human mind with its questioning and reasoning to fully comprehend. It is as White Eagle has said. The blessed Jesus was conceived without the desire element in place. Joseph and I, each Priest and Priestess within the Temple, knew our destiny with this great soul and abided by the request of the Higher Beings. I think you are beginning to understand. However, we know it IS difficult to understand the Virgin Birth as your Bible depicts it. Of course you also realize, the word in itself has been mis-translated.'

At Mary's request I decide to look up White Eagle's words on the Immaculate Conception. I shall also investigate what Graham Phillips has to say about any mis-translation.

The two following quotations are taken from *'White Eagle on Divine Mother. The Feminine and the Mysteries'*. White Eagle gives an explanation phrasing it in different ways. Personally I have read and re-read all his words. One minute I think I've got it and then it is gone! It seems so simple and yet very complex to the earthly mind. As the following quotations are only a part of a chapter entitled *'Mary, Mother of Jesus'* you may wish to read the whole chapter, in which case the book is available from the White Eagle Lodge.

Quotation No.1. Page 68 This section begins by White Eagle telling us that both Mary and Joseph are members of the White Brotherhood. Then: *'Of this White Brotherhood, Joseph was an 'elder', a pure and highly-evolved soul, an Initiate. Mary the mother was one of those pure sisters who have certain work allotted to them by the Brotherhood. Both were pure in body and in desire and it was their mission to be guardians - we use that word on purpose - guardians of Jesus the Master. We trust that there will be no misunderstanding of our words. The Holy Ghost, the Inner Wisdom, is the wisdom of the spirit which raises the desire body and the physical body to a plane of power and beauty. This inner wisdom raised the vibrations of the two chosen for their holy office, and in the conception of the Master Jesus, no vibrations of desire nor thought of self marred this holy consummation of God's will. So much for the outer story of the birth of the Master Jesus.'*

Quotation No. 2. Page 69 White Eagle begins by talking of God, the Holy Ghost, the Holy Breath, the Life Force and then: *'The truth of the Immaculate Conception is beyond anything physical, in that it has to do with the Divine principle of life, the union between the First and Second Principle. It has to do with the union between the Divine Will and the embracing Love and Wisdom of the Holy Mother. The two Principles bring forth the perfect child, the Christ. This is really the meaning of the Immaculate Conception. It is outside all physical vibration, but it has been brought down into a human concept because men and women want to have things explained for them in a physical way. You must try to comprehend from a spiritual level. Yes, any conception can be immaculate insofar as it can be removed entirely from the desire body and the will*

- 300 -

of a man and women. Such a birth is the result of purity of body and soul and freed from all desire of self.'

Now to Graham Phillips and his book *'The Marian Conspiracy'*. Phillips has obviously done a vast amount of research into the Virgin Mary. He credits the theologian Rudolf Bultmann who questioned the authenticity of the Gospels in the 1920s, with bringing much to light. Phillips, on Page 61 of his book, says and I quote: *'In the Bible story, as it now survives, God is portrayed as Jesus' true father by direct intervention of the Holy Ghost; Joseph merely acts as Jesus' guardian. Mary, we are told, was a virgin when she conceived and bore Christ.'* He continues…*'Incredibly, the idea of the virgin birth appeared to have arisen from a simple mistranslation of the Isaiah prophecy.'* Then Phillips tells us, Bultmann has discovered that mistakes had been made when the early Christians translated the text from Isaiah. Phillips again Page 62: *'The original text did not employ the Hebrew word for 'virgin'- betulah; it used the word almah - 'a young woman' The original Hebrew passage had predicated that a 'young woman'- not a 'virgin'- would conceive and give birth to the Messiah.'*

I bring you up to date. There has been a week's gap so plenty of time to assimilate all that I received and read. This subject is still on my mind and I feel ready to delve a little deeper. I choose 12.00 noon for an attunement and settle down in front of my little altar. The golden flame of my candle becomes very still as I relax into meditation. I begin with White Eagle's Star Healing Prayer for Humanity. I am being shown the most beautiful Chalice with Divine Light rising up and pouring rays of its golden essence out to the world. The Lady Mary and White Eagle are both with me: *"Beloved Mary - Dear White Eagle - I honour and thank you for your presence and for all the guidance which you have brought to me in connection with the Immaculate Conception. In the silence I await your words of wisdom:"*

WHITE EAGLE

"Dearest Peace Rose, there is no simple way that the earthly mind can comprehend the mind of the Cosmos. We understand your dilemma. We know that you want it clarified. I will do my best. Mind you I may make it worse for your understanding (I sensed a sort of benign amusement as he said this)! *The Immaculate Conception is part of the Holy Breath. It is the breathing in of the Breath of God. This Holy Breath is from deep within the Mind of God. It is part of the Secret of the Cosmos. As we breathe in the Holy Breath, so it fills all our subtle bodies with Divine Fire and vibrational energy. Both Mary and Joseph were imbued with that Holy Breath. It was a part of their being which has always been. They were able to draw on its magical power to bring into being this Immaculate Conception. Both Joseph and Mary were Priest and Priestess of the very highest degree in the Temples of Egypt. Their inner knowledge of Universal Law was paramount to their being able to put into practise Divine Law, which is represented in the Immaculate Conception. The normal way for conception to take place was not on the agenda when it came to the soul of the great Master Yesu coming into incarnation. The desire element was lifted into the very highest place of perfect reception of that Holy Ghost,*

the Holy Spirit. For indeed THIS is what it was - the coming into incarnation of the Holy Spirit. This dear one is very profound. I do hope you have a glimmer of the magic of this event. Regarding your own personal incarnation as Naomi, Joseph and Mary were your parents through the normal way of conception.

We are happy dear Peace Rose, to share these insights with you, as we believe you have reached a point of understanding of spiritual matters, which will indeed help you to be able to receive a clearer picture of Universal Law. Yes we are happy if you wish to share these things and write of them in your book (my inner question). We offer these words of inner wisdom from deep within the Cosmos to guide and help humankind comprehend truth. We are happy that you are seeking for inner wisdom, but please do not get 'bogged down' with detail. The journey you are undertaking with Beloved Mary will obviously bring certain questions into the frontal mind, but PLEASE enjoy your journey and relate TRUTH as you are given it. Dear Peace Rose, I offer you my deepest blessing of the loving heart. Beloved Mary is close-by and she wishes to speak with you. I bless you now."

White Eagle leaves with the benediction of the equal sided Cross of Light within the Circle of Light drawn on high. Mary:

MARY

"My dearly beloved daughter. We ALL in the Land of Light, welcome your questioning mind, but as White Eagle has said and as I have said on a previous occasion, do not let the earthly mind take over my spiritual journey with you dearest one. There are certain Divine truths and wonders which are beyond the comprehension of the earthly mind. We offer these thoughts to you with the deepest love and may I once more use White Eagle's words, to 'keep on keeping on' dear Sister of Light. ENJOY THE JOURNEY. God Bless you."

Mary offers a heart blessing as always. From me: "Thank you dearest ones for your sacred words."

PERSONAL THOUGHTS ON THE IMMACULATE CONCEPTION.

If Naomi was conceived in the normal way, Mary was not a virgin when she conceived Jesus. However, the concept of the Holy Breath - the Holy Spirit - is part of the magic of Universal Law held within the Cosmos. The Immaculate Conception is thus a profound Divine truth. I accept this Divine element in relation to the conception of the Master Jesus, but keep asking myself, how CAN we when incarnation, fully comprehend such a deep Cosmic truth? Perhaps by making the link with our Higher Self, we can access the Mind in the Heart, wherein we may intuitively receive a clearer understanding of this wondrous happening.

CHAPTER 12
DARTMOOR'S EASTERN FRINGE
Legends Abound

The Lady Mary's pilgrimage continued north through East Dartmoor. The first stop was Hound Tor Druidic Temple site, where Mary performed a Light Ceremony. From here, Mary, Naomi, Jesus and Joseph proceeded in a northerly direction to Mortonhampstead and Cranbrook Castle, then onwards to leave Dartmoor for their journey through Mid Devon In a recent attunement Mary has confirmed that she wishes me to enact a Druidic Ceremony at Hound Tor, which I shall undertake on a day trip, as it is only about ten miles from my home. After this sacred act, I will attempt to follow Mary's journey north. .

BUCKLAND IN THE MOOR AND BUCKLAND BEACON

Mary and her family left South Devon by taking a boat from Buckfast up the Rivers Dart and Webburn, which in Mary's day would have been wider and navigable, to Buckland in the Moor. Today this is a most picturesque hamlet situated in the sheltered wooded valley of the River Dart. Here we are just a few miles from the busy A38, yet a world away - the peace is tangible. A crystal clear moorland stream running off Buckland Common, tumbles its way down through a cluster of thatched cottages, nestling within a green oasis and on underneath an old stone road bridge, to feed into the main river in the valley below. This little hamlet tucked away on the edge of Dartmoor, is one of God's sweet havens - a lush tranquil gem where time has stood still. Talking of time, the twelfth century St Peter's Parish Church in the village, offers an interesting artifact in its clock, which was a gift from William Whitely in the 1930s. It is dedicated to the memory of his mother and bears the letters 'MY DEAR MOTHER' in place of the numerals on its face.

Climbing out of the steep valley from Buckland in the Moor, Mary and her party would have alighted at Buckland Beacon. The views from here are far reaching - down into the valley and the little church far below, then on to the south coast of Devon. In the other direction, one can take in the expanse of southern Dartmoor with its distinct granite tors. A feature of The Beacon today, are its two commemorative rocks, with inscriptions from the Ten Commandments and other verses of Scripture, cut into the large granite slabs, which are known as the Ten Commandment Stones. Only yesterday I heard that the Dartmoor National Park Authority has employed a stone mason to preserve the engraved words.

A WALK TO BUCKLAND BEACON

It is Easter Sunday just past, when during my quiet spell, I chose to take a walk in this area. The day before, I had spied Buckland Beacon in the far distance from Ogwell Green, near Newton Abbot and felt called to pay a visit once again, unaware at the time of Mary having passed this way on her journey through East Dartmoor. I drive to Dartmoor parking up at Cold East Cross above the town of Ashburton. The car park is almost full but there is no-one around. It always amazes me how people just disperse into the surrounding moorland and except at popular 'hot spots' one has the moor to oneself. The sun's warmth is on my face as I walk the ancient land to Buckland Beacon. I am feeling the energies of Mother Earth beneath my feet as I tread the soft moorland turf. On reaching Buckland Beacon, I first take a look at the Ten Commandments Stones, then climb to the upmost point of the tor to sit in the sunshine, surveying the landscape and taking time for contemplation.

I move on to explore below the hill. Partly hidden in the undergrowth, I can see dolmens with collapsed cap stones and some huge recumbent standing stones, one of approximately twelve foot in length, then there are some roughly formed stone hut circles - all indicators of a substantial settlement. On reaching the bottom of the hill, I see a stone circle in tact but well disguised, covered with bracken and blueberry bushes. I hurry across and ask the Druid guardian for permission to step inside. A large bumble bee comes buzzing in to investigate this stranger in its midst and spends at least two minutes checking me out. I stand very still and let him get on with it. As I close my eyes, I can feel the energies emanating from the surrounding stones and am conscious of the ancient ones. Moving on now across the brackened moorland, I sit on a large rock where I am slightly hidden behind a scrap of holly bush, to take a drink from my water bottle. I hear nothing, but out of the corner of my eye, I catch a glimpse of a large dog fox silently jumping over the gorse bushes past me, completely oblivious of my presence. He turns to take the little path to where I am sitting, sees me and decides to head off in another direction. Wow - thank you - a moment to treasure.

Mary's journey from Buckland Beacon to Hound Tor settlement, took her across open moorland, via the Iron Age settlement of Foale's Arrishes, through Seven Lords Lands and over Holwell Lawn.

SEVEN LORDS LANDS

On Seven Lords Lands is the old farmstead of Emsworthy. In Maytime the landscape around here, offers field upon field of bluebells, their deep blue/purple flowers, which on mass exhibit a mystical mauve carpet, are spread as far as the eye can see. I was there this year with my family and we were all immersed in the magic. The colour presents an almost ethereal beauty and with the scent drifting across the still warm air, one has the feeling of having stepped into a heavenly idyll. Emsworthy Farm is today deserted, but in a good state of repair as it is used as a shelter by a local farmer for his sheep. One time I was walking past the farm when a ram confronted me standing stock still, stamping his foot. I beat a hasty but careful retreat! I didn't wish to antagonize him and be butted by a very cross ram. On another occasion, I was walking in this area and heard a plaintive baa-ing, to discover a sheep had got its horns lodged in some square wire fencing. After a bit of sheep-whispering to keep it calm, plus much shoving and pushing, I eventually managed to manipulate the horns back through its wire prison. And then two minutes later there was another one, same thing - stuck - same procedure!

HOUND TOR DRUIDIC SETTLEMENT

Arrival at the Hound Tor settlement, gave Mary and her children an opportunity for rest and refreshment - another long day travelling completed. And rest they must, for a special Light Ceremony was to be conducted soon after their arrival.

Hound Tor

Hound Tor itself is a splendid granite rock formation - an impressive cluster of horizontal chunks of granite, piled on top of each other. In its lee lies the remains of the medieval village of Hundatora, mentioned in the Domesday Book. Excavated during the 1960s and 1970s, four Dartmoor longhouses and many smaller houses, plus three grain storage barns were discovered, which have been well preserved. There is an easily accessible car park for both Hound Tor and the medieval village, therefore they are well visited.

The name Hound Tor relates to its shape, as it is said to resemble a pack of hounds in full cry. It is alleged to have been the inspiration for Conan Doyle's *'The Hound of the Baskervilles.'* Legends of apparitions are rife, including a cavalier horseman and a large black dog. A modern legend is the 'Hound of the Basket Meals', a mobile vehicle which provides snacks and is parked up daily in the nearby car park. It is a popular venue at any time of the year, but in winter in the 'old days' if you happen to be a solitary walker, you might be offered a free tot of whisky or brandy in your coffee! On Boxing Day a few years back, my daughter and I headed out there, not for the chance of a tipple I hasten to add, but to have a hot coffee before a walk on the moor. The narrow moorland roads were icy and traffic was heavy - all seemed to be heading in the direction of the 'Hound of the Basket Meals'. On arrival we saw that the queue stretched out of the car park, so we decided to give the coffee a miss, and as the weather was closing in scotched the idea of a walk also. Instead we did a U-turn and struggled our way back uphill slipping and sliding on the treacherous road against all the incoming traffic.

Hound of the Basket Meals' at 'Hound Tor

Evidence in the landscape surrounding Hound Tor, shows a vast area of what was once a Druidic settlement, however the ancient stones are all over the place. I am feeling that since Mary's time, the land has shifted quite dramatically, perhaps as a result of a ground tremor. I came here some years back with a dowsing group and they intimated, that to the south of the tor was a large burial complex, incorporating two or three outer stone circles leading to several small family inner tombs. This might be so, but my insight also tells me that this was a Temple site of some distinction. While exploring the area, I saw a huge upright boulder which appeared to link to what I believe to be an Altar Stone near the main bulk of the tor, at a distance of about sixty metres. For our Druid ancestors, this was a place of worship, a place to invoke the Cosmic Light to enrich the land and THIS was Mary's role as she joined with her Druid Priest counterparts.

MY JOURNEY TO HOUND TOR.

Today is for my Ceremony of Light at Hound Tor which begins as always with an attunement in my home sanctuary. I light a new pure white candle. As the golden flame licks into shape it stills and yet as I focus on it, it appears to grow taller and taller. When I close my eyes, the flame shoots right up into the Angelic Realm to connect with the Everlasting Flame. The Angels gather up the Light from my little candle and multiply it a million-fold, sending it out to heal the Universe. Now that Light is filling my own heart centre and encompassing my whole being. I offer myself in devout and loving service this sacred day. My Beloved Mary, my Angel of Light will walk with me. This is to be a day of Angels. My Mission with Mary continues.

I leave my home very early in the morning, my aim to be at Hound Tor before any visitors arrive. I have chosen the time of 6.00 am for my Ceremony this day. The date is 7th July 2009. From an astrological perspective, on this date, Mars is in the fixed earth sign of Taurus, perfect for the fiery Martian energy to bring that Cosmic Light into full play within the Earth and secure it for all time.

I am driving to Dartmoor on quiet roads as one would expect at this time in the morning. I take the back road from my home to Bovey Tracy, a delightful edge-of-moor town. From here it is an uphill drive along a tree-lined country road. Once over the cattle grid, I am on the open moor. I pass the usually busy Hay Tor with not a soul in sight today. All around, the black moorland cattle and calves and Dartmoor ponies with their foals are still resting. Before long I see the towering heights of Hound Tor to my right. I am now feeling an eagerness to be on site. Never before have I pulled in to this particular car park to find it empty - even the 'Hound of the Basket Meals' has not arrived!

HOUND TOR DRUIDIC TEMPLE CEREMONY

I have all my precious Ceremonial articles in my pack which I put on my back. I am suitably kitted out in warm gear this early morning as I set off on the short walk to the ancient site, over a moorland spread with white clover.

On through an array of hut circles and dolmens, I keep Hound Tor on my left, then skirt around its base to where I wish to be. As I settle down in a secluded position close to the Altar Stone, I am already feeling the presence of the Blessed Ones. The awakening overcast sky seems to be filled with Mary's Angels of Light, welcoming this new day. Completely alone, I make preparation. Before I begin, I take the time to contemplate the vista spread out before me. My eyes are led to the rise at the far side of the Becca Brook valley, noting the majestic Hay Tor with Smallacombe Rocks and Black Hill. In the middle distance is Greator Rocks and just below me is the medieval village. The whole panorama is feeling atmospheric and mystical. As I look to my right across Holwell Lawn, my thoughts turn to the little group of travellers perhaps weary, riding ever onwards to reach this settlement.

My Ceremony follows its normal pattern beginning with 'The Great Invocation' which somehow today has special significance, as I am able to voice it quite clearly, measuring each phrase. Each of my crystals are set out before me. I call on the Masters of the Christ Light. I have a strong vision of those from the Angelic Realms encircling this ancient land within their all embracing 'Wings of Light'. There is a great Ray of Light pouring forth to the Hound Tor Temple site and the words: "*Let the Light Shine*'" hold a deep esoteric meaning this sacred day. As at Hembury Castle, I am aware of the Rainbow Bridge linking the Heaven World to our World. It is coming to mind that on one stormy day, it was over Hound Tor, as I stood across the valley on Hay Tor, that I saw the remarkable complete arc of a physical rainbow of astonishing clarity of colour, echoed by a paler version. I had the impression that it was reaching deep within the Earth to enliven the Great Crystal. Is the fabled pot of gold the Earth Star Crystal? I remember being moved to almost tears by its magical beauty. From the back recesses of my psyche I am hearing Merlin's raven croaking loud and clear many times. I close my Ceremony, honouring all the beloved ones, giving thanks for their presence and protection this sanctified day. Our beloved Master Jesus wishes to speak with me:

THE MASTER JESUS

"*My dear sister - Sister of Light. A great rejoicing has gone forth in Heaven on this sacred day. Thank you dear Sister of Light. We speak with you today of past times and future times.*

The travelling we as a family group did to these sacred Isles, was planned a long long time before its actuality As children you and I, were beloved brother and sister not knowing of future events, but gradually becoming aware of the enormity of what was to be. My insight as a boy told me much. At times I was able to commune with my Father in Heaven. Our Temple training led us both into deeper levels of consciousness, so that we were able at a young age to commune with the Angels and Masters of all times. It was a sacred road which we travelled. It was a dangerous road which we travelled. It was a road to salvation. My life and 'death' were necessary for the upliftment of this Earth, in order for the Earth to shift into a higher dimension at that time. On my 'death' the atoms of my physical body changed, so that I was able to resuscitate myself to physical wholeness once again. A miracle you would say and yet this gift we all possess to a lesser or higher degree. My sister, it was then I was to be secreted away and spent my remaining years in seclusion, working from the inner planes to further the upliftment and enlightenment of Planet Earth. (what a wonderful confirmation of events by our blessed Master - see Chapter 7).

Now dearest sister it is 2,000 years later and I have returned, to once again bring enlightenment and hope and love and compassion at this age of changing times. I have never left you dear people of Earth. I have always been close to your every move, your every dilemma, your every sadness, your every pain and suffering. For I am the Light of the World. How could I have left you dearest ones. It is our wish that as the Age of Pisces gradually merges into the Age of Aquarius, that you dearly beloved Brethren, look to yourselves and see how YOU can be instrumental in furthering the work of the Great Spirit. See how YOU can further the Light within your precious Planet. Dearest Brethren, my Brothers and Sisters YOU are the Saviours of your World. It is in your hands - the upliftment and enlightenment of your Planet is in YOUR hands. We the Masters, are always on hand to assist you and you may call on us wherever there is a sacred need, BUT the upliftment of your Planet is YOUR responsibility. Dear Brethren, take hold of the Sword of Michael, cut through the darkness and the Light will explode into being. God Bless you my Brethren of Light. May the Light and the Joy of the new salvation be your way forward. Let the Light so shine forth from your precious hearts, that the healing of your Earth Plane is complete. Amen."

My beloved Master has gone - gone for this moment but always there for each of us when we call on him. I thank the Master Jesus for his compelling message. I have felt him drawing closer of late, but never before has he made direct reference to our past life relationship in the Holy Land.

My eyes now open, focus once again on the moorland landscape as displayed before me. I see the cattle grazing on Holwell Lawn. I am conscious of a gentle wind, of birdsong, of a dog barking from a nearby farmstead. I seal all my psychic centres and ground myself. I am enfolded in protective Golden Light. It is now time to release into Mother Earth my white quartz crystal and my rose-pink quartz crystal for the Druid ancestors. I carefully tuck them in behind the long grass at the base of the Altar Stone. My work here today is finished.

Before I take my leave, I climb to the heights of Hound Tor, from where I have an excellent view of Hayne Down and Easdon Tor towards North Bovey, which is Mary's continuing journey across Dartmoor. I come off Hound Tor by the 'interesting' route, making my way down one of the steeper sides, just to add to the excitement of my day! The sky has lightened considerably with glimpses of blue amidst a mix of white and grey clouds - the Heavenly Angels are doing their utmost. Back at the car, it is time for a hot drink and a little sustenance. It is 9.30 am and there are half a dozen cars parked up. A police car pulls in, which turns out to be a little early for the 'Hound of the Basket

Meals' vehicle - it arrives five minutes after they've gone - so no morning snack for them here today.

TO JAY'S GRAVE

My Light Ceremony accomplished, my plan for the rest of the day is to follow Mary's journey north as near as I can, by a combination of car and on foot, culminating at Cranbrook Castle, Mary's next settlement. This is the first time for a while, since I have released myself from my computer, so a full day exploring is most welcome.

My first calling is to walk the mile along the road from Hound Tor to Jay's Grave. Mary and her family would have passed within yards of this spot. The air is now warm and it is good to be stretching my legs. The roadside abounds with summer flowers; tall pink thistles, foxgloves, sweet smelling honeysuckle and purple vetch. Blackberry and elderflower bloom in profusion, with many honey bees doing their precious work, to prepare the plants for their autumn berries. A cow and her calf standing on the grass verge are joined by more of their kind, with much moo-ing in greeting.

I reach Jay's Grave. The story which is well known goes.....in the nineteenth century Kitty Jay a young servant girl, fell pregnant by the son of her farmer employer and was thrown out of the household. Her reputation in tatters and with nowhere to go, she hanged herself. She was just fourteen years old. Suicides could not be buried on consecrated ground but had to be interred at a crossroads. For Kitty, this was to be on an intersection of road and moorland track. The grave today is a raised stone mound topped with grass and a small granite headstone. A local phenomenon associated with Kitty's resting place, is the daily appearance of fresh flowers on her grave - from whence they come - no-one knows. However, today it is my turn to add to the legend and place an offering. I have chosen a pure white rose for Kitty. I know Mary would have wished this - in fact I am sure it was her influence, which brought this flower to mind. So for Kitty - a symbol of purity and female compassion. I gently place the rose against the headstone amongst the foxgloves and other offerings there.

BOWERMAN'S NOSE

Bowerman's Nose is part of the Hayne Down settlement which Mary would have passed through on her way to Easdon Tor. This is a huge stack of weathered granite, its top section showing an easily identifiable face and head with a cap. There is a legend from 1,000 years back, that a mighty huntsman by the name of Bowerman who lived at Huntor, the ancient Saxon village below Hound Tor rocks, ran foul of a coven of witches because he insisted on hunting on a Sunday. One young witch followed him and turned him into stone - hence this formation became known as Bowerman's Nose. She also turned his hounds into stone thus creating the nearby Hound Tor.

Bowerman's Nose

NORTH BOVEY AND THE CHURCH OF ST JOHN THE BAPTIST.

The journey now for our Holy family was to cross Easdon Tor and drop down to the River Bovey at North Bovey. Attempting to follow their route, I drive along the narrowest of moorland lanes, made even more so with the summer vegetation. How on earth did the coach, which I fortunately meet at a road junction, get through? Over the cattle grid I leave Dartmoor, passing an out of use red telephone box on my left, almost lost within tall grasses. Finally I reach North Bovey, park on the hill and walk into the centre of the village. I discover it is a delightful place still immersed in a bygone age. There are rows of pretty colour-washed thatched cottages, many dating back to the seventeenth century. The village green with its lovely specimen trees, houses an old water-pump with a stone trough, and an ancient granite Celtic cross

As I enter the lovely old Church of St John the Baptist, I feel its overwhelming aura of peace. The building dates from the thirteenth century with of course some additions. The rood screen installed in the fifteenth century is a point in question. Although today it is quite handsome, in its original state, painted, gilded with its panels illustrating figures of the saints, it must have been very striking. The original flagstone flooring is most unusual, embedded as it is with several large engraved slabs of commemoration, of which each has a heart design. In the barrelled roof above the chancel are some interesting medieval bosses. One is a head which represents King Edward 1 and two more are of his Queens - Margaret of France and Eleanor of Castile. It is here I come across another roof boss of the Three Hares. There is also a most striking painting of the Lady Mary, robed in blue with a haloed baby Jesus. On leaving I put an offering in the porch of a beautiful shell from Shaldon beach in South Devon.

I take a wander through the churchyard, then leave by a gate framed by two standing stones. I find myself on a deep mysterious path, riding between a high stone wall to my left and a bank of tall beech trees, with overhanging branches, on my right. The path drops steeply to the road and to the River Bovey at the bottom of the village. It is here into its clear water that I am to pour the last of the sacred waters retrieved from St Just's Holy Well in the Roseland Peninsula with a blessing, thus furthering the link between Cornwall and Devon. Mary crossed this river I would say near enough at this point, on her way to North Bovey. I climb the hill back to my car above the old village.

THE CHURCH OF ST ANDREW, MORTONHAMPSTEAD.

On to Mortonhampstead. I thought a visit to the Parish Church would be of value in order to absorb its atmosphere. The St Andrew Church is situated in the centre of the old part of Moretonhampstead. I can see the church tower above the houses from the car park, but can I find it? As I round each corner, it seems to disappear! On eventually reaching the church, I am to be rather disappointed - for me it is too modern and there IS no atmosphere. Its saving grace is, that today the church is festooned with brightly coloured banners made by local school children, to mark the celebration of 1100 years of Christianity in Devon.

On closer inspection the church does have some redeeming features. Two rows of beautiful shiny white Gothic arches run its length. The traditional stained glass windows are excellent, but the one which speaks to my sense of aesthetics, is strangely enough, a modern one dedicated to *'St Luke - beloved physician'*. St Luke is standing, robed in purple and blue holding a serpent staff and a Holy Book with a Celtic cross on it. At his feet is a Winged Bull - his sacred animal. The whole is set amongst a country scene and encompassed within a green circle entwined with vines. Finally, at the rear of the church on its south side, I discover three ancient stone slabs engraved with interesting symbols, which are very difficult to identify, because the carvings are very worn. However, I can just make out what might be the 'Tree of Life' on one, while others seem to be engraved with a Celtic face, spirals and circles.

Walking back to the car park I pass a house with the name *'Unicorn'*. I have never come across this as a house name before. So these magical 7th Dimensional Beings have arrived on Planet Earth, if in name only.

CRANBROOK CASTLE DRUIDIC SETTLEMENT.

On leaving Mortonhampstead, Mary and her family, took a steady climb through Holcombe in order to reach Cranbrook Castle. This proved to be an ideal place to stay before they left Dartmoor and travelled on into Mid Devon.

I leave Mortonhampstead on the A382. After four miles I turn right onto a narrow road with grass running down the middle and very few passing places. I drive on winding ever upwards - a drive which is accompanied by much tooting of the horn. I park opposite Uppacott House close to a farm entrance. Due to the state of the road and not knowing if there is to be parking further on, I decide to go on foot the next 1½ miles to Cranbrook Castle. I set off up the hill on my little pilgrimage, feeling very happy and quite relaxed in the warm afternoon sunshine. After about ¾ mile I am leaning on a five-barred gate, looking out across a hay field, when I see directly in front of me what I am sure is one of the ramparts of the castle. Walking on excitedly, I turn left onto a stony track directing me to *'Cranbook Castle'* and *'Fingles Bridge'*. An interesting granite standing stone, well hidden in the long grass, is marking the entrance to this right of way. It is obviously an old directional way-mark. Looking at the map I try to link the letters with their destination. Its south side presents an 'M' for Mortonhampstead. On the north side is a 'D' for Drewsteignton. The west has a 'C' obviously for Chagford. While the east side is rather difficult to distinguish, but the letters could be a 'C' and 'B' for Clifford Bridge. Having got that sussed - I think - I walk on, passing a Trig Point, then follow the track through woodland.

Cranbrook Castle which sits high above the Teign gorge, is one of the best examples of a stone built Iron Age hill fort in Devon. There is a large circular enclosure with a stone-faced rampart approximately four foot in height, and a deep ditch, with outer ramparts to the south-west Excavations in the early twentieth century revealed some Iron Age pottery. Cranbrook is but one of two hill forts set above the Teign river valley - its counterpart being Prestonbury on the opposite bank. Walks in this valley are quite wonderful. A most rewarding one begins at Fingle Bridge and follows the north bank of the River Teign west for some two miles, from where a path leads upwards to the National Trust's Castle Drogo. The return walk takes you high above the wooded valley, which offers up the most magnificent views. Pick a clear day and you will not be disappointed.

It is not long before I am turning into a field through a little wooden gate for *'Cranbrook Castle Iron Age Ramparts'*. I speak with the guardian of this ancient site asking permission to enter, and offer a blessing. Walking along a narrow grassy pathway through five foot high bracken, I note that there are many recumbent standing stones spread around. On reaching the first rampart I find a place to sit in relative comfort in spite of the high wind - the air element is having full play up here and it is exhilarating! I am hearing a voice which is saying: *"Well done my industrious pilgrim."* Words acknowledging achievement are always acceptable! The views from here are outstanding in all directions. I can well imagine Mary looking north from this point and considering the next stage of her journey through Mid Devon. I am thinking of the Lady Mary and her daughter Naomi. I am thinking of the Master Jesus and Joseph of Arimathea. So long ago - in another lifetime - we were here. When finally I rise, I lay a small bunch of honeysuckle which I had picked from the hedgerow, as an offering to the four pilgrims with a prayer and almost a sigh of remembrance. In turn I am presented with two beautiful buzzard feathers.

The landscape of Cranbrook Castle stretches out ahead of me as I start out on a perambulation of the circumference of the ancient fort. Patches of early purple bell-heather are sprinkled amongst the yellow gorse and tall dried grasses. There are butterflies aplenty, but most are little 'brown jobs' which do not stop long enough for me to identify them. After circumnavigating about half of the circle, the very tall bracken and dense gorse bushes, prevent me from going any further. I retrace my steps. I try taking the narrow path to the centre of the site, where I think could be an Altar Stone, but again I am stopped by the vegetation. My plan is to return during the winter months when the bracken has died back that I may investigate further. However I become too busy and it just doesn't happen.

Coming off the castle fort I suddenly realize I have lost my watch. It must have slipped off my arm - it was rather loose. Oh well never mind - it only cost me a fiver. I make my way back through the bracken and on reaching the entrance gate, what should I spy, but my watch on the grass. Thank you Angels.

I return to my car at Uppacott and negotiate the narrow lane back to the Mortonhampstead road and on home. What a special day, beginning with my Druidic Light Ceremony at Hound Tor, then taking me to some of the places Mary and her family would have gone through on their journey north, to finally reach the ancient settlement of Cranbrook Castle their base for the night.

TO DREWSTEIGNTON AND SPINSTERS ROCK

On leaving Cranbrook, Mary dropped down into the valley close to Fingle Bridge, where there is now a delightful inn - a very popular watering hole - nestling on the banks of the River Teign. Climbing up through Drewston Wood she travelled via Drewsteignton to leave Dartmoor round about Hole (Holy) Farm.

I connect with Mary at the ancient village of Drewsteignton, which antiquarians identify as 'Druid's Town on the Teign'. I undertake a visit as part of a day's pilgrimage following Mary's travelling through Mid Devon (see Chapter 13). On that day, from Mortonhampstead I take the A382 and at Shilstone, turn off onto a country road for Drewsteignton.

I do however make a slight detour to visit the well preserved Neolithic burial chamber of Spinsters Rock, which is believed to be part of a large complex of ancient circles and stone rows. The tomb, which stands sentinel in the middle of a field, has a huge cap stone of fifteen foot by ten foot and rests on top of three supporting stones. In *'The Sun and the Serpent'* Miller and Broadhurst shed a little light on this tomb by telling us that the St Mary Ley Line goes through the stones, then in relation to the three supporting stones, that: *'in the old Celtic religion the 'three maidens' or 'three sisters' were a symbol of the Goddess in her three distinct phases of Virgin (new moon), Mother (full moon) and Crone (waning moon)'* - Page 146. Of course the same allegory of the three phases of the Goddess here would also apply to the Three Hares. The St Mary Line running through Spinsters Rock, which is situated so close to the Lady Mary's route through Devon, would indicate to me that her essence is strongly embedded in the landscape.

Spinsters Rock, near Drewsteignton

On I go and am soon pulling into the charming old village of Drewsteignton with its stone and thatched properties, plus cafe which does an excellent Devon cream tea. I park up in the village centre, close to the church and opposite the legendary Drewe Arms Public House. Legendary because, until relatively recently the pub was owned by a lady, quite a character, whose name if my memory serves me right, was Auntie Mabel, who was still pulling pints at one hundred years old! On entering the pub one had a feeling of stepping back in time - it was as if nothing had changed for almost a century. Folk used to make their own little pilgrimage there to drink with Auntie Mabel! After her passing obviously things did change. However the new décor and excellent food still makes for a well visited pub today.

HOLY TRINITY CHURCH, DREWSTEIGNTON

I make my way to the Parish Church of Holy Trinity. In the churchyard my eyes alight on a most handsome fir tree, which girth tells me that it is several hundred years old. I pick a few wild flowers and gently lay the little posy in one of its crevices with a blessing and hear:

FIR TREE DEVA

"Thank you dear pilgrim. It is not often I get noticed. You are so welcome to walk this ancient land. Our Lady Mary welcomes your presence in the church. This day will be blessed."

I thank the tree elemental for the blessing.

My first impression as I open the church door is one of utter shock. Internally it appears very damp and obviously restoration work is going on. A lady comes in to prepare for morning worship and tells me that water has been pouring in like a river. How very sad. For me personally, notwithstanding the damage, it has little to recommend it, as so much has been modernized. The church has records going back to the early thirteenth century, but I suspect that it was built on the foundations of a much earlier Celtic church. The roof of the nave and the aisles are of the traditional Devon wagon type. Of particular interest are the carved wildlife pew ends, which include a hare, ducks, a fox and two fish. I notice that one of the long kneelers in front of the Lady Chapel is dedicated to the Rev'd Keble Martin who wrote a most comprehensive book '*British Flora*'. In his latter years he settled in the village of Woodbury in East Devon, where my husband and I who were living in the same village, became acquainted with him.

As I step before the altar, a sense of reverence comes over me. A divided stained glass window offers on one side, a most beautiful depiction of an Angel with the Three Marys' - the Virgin Mary, Mary Magdalene and Mary Cleophas. On its other side, is Mary Magdalene in the Garden of the Tomb. Written below are the moving words: '*He is risen. He is not here. Jesus said unto her 'Mary I am the Resurrection and the Life.'*

Sitting silently in one of the pews, I receive the impression that Mary is here. In my heart I am saying: *"Dearest Mary you are with me this sacred day. Thank you."* She speaks with me:

MARY

"Beloved child. I never leave you. Welcome to this Church of Holy Trinity in this ancient village of Drewsteignton. It was very close that you and I journeyed 2,000 years ago on our pilgrimage to these ancient Isles. Thank you dear one for making this pilgrimage here today. As you travel, soul memories will be revived for you dear Naomi. They are never lost but hidden within the deep recesses of ones psyche. The soul holds all our memories and in the right circumstances can issue forth those memories of a long distant past.

On this part of our journeying we travelled north through this sacred land, our destination to be the ancient settlement of Cow Castle dedicated to the Goddess, that feminine aspect of The Trinity which has for so long been lost in the landscape. Now it is to be reborn as we enter the Age of Enlightment - the new Aquarian Age. She - the Goddess - will find her rightful place alongside her male counterpart and together they shall rule the World for all eternity. The time is here dearest Naomi. It is degreed from within that highest Divine place of Eternal Life. The Light of the countenance of the Goddess will shine forth and be recognized. It will dwell in the hearts of each soul on your Earth Plane. The Rose in the Heart has returned and her loving energies and vibration will permeate all darkness and grief. Sister of Light - my child - all is in place. The Goddess is here. She is being recognized and hearts are being opened to her Divine wisdom and blessed love. I say unto you all - welcome this beautiful energy into your own heart and let it fill your whole being with perfection and joy. God bless you my Pilgrims of Light."

I am thanking this dear soul for her message of love and hope. Our beloved Masters so care for our World. Let us acknowledge the blessings they bring with loving gratitude? I leave a gift of a large white triangular stone as a representation of the Holy Trinity; the power which is God the Father, the wisdom of Divine Mother and the Christ Child - pure love. I step out into the sunshine. This completes my sojourn of Mary's journeying through East Dartmoor.

A DAY FOR THE SOUL

Before I continue with Mary's pilgrimage through Mid Devon, I am putting aside some time for a 'Soul Day' - a day to replenish the physical and mental bodies and revitalize all my subtle bodies. We all need to take time out on occasions - a day just for ourselves - and this is one of mine.

I have set up my quiet room with soft music and candles. After a relaxing soak in the bath, with lavender and geranium oils, I am awaiting the arrival of a very special spiritual lady for a deep healing massage. My day will continue with meditation, music and if it ever stops raining, a leisurely stroll in my home vicinity. No car - no computer - no brain-work. This is to be a day of peace and stillness - I recommend it. For even if I am connected to the inner planes, much of my work is focused at the physical and mental levels, as eagerness to move along with my pilgrimage is great at this stage of my Mission with Beloved Mary. Today I may even go so far as having a inner cleansing day with lots of pure water and herb teas - we shall see.

It is 3.00 pm and the fly in the ointment of this well planned and so far perfectly executed day has arrived, in the form of an Engineer, who is telling me he is testing all the fire alarms in the building including my flat! So - end of quiet relaxing time. I can deal with most background noises when meditating, but not the sudden intermittent piercing sound of the fire alarm going off. I cannot even escape into the great outdoors because I am needed to be here.

However, my day until this point has maintained a stillness and clear focus and I am feeing very much at peace. No doubt this is one of the many little tests - no challenges - in life, in this case, of acceptance and thankfulness for the time I have had!

CHAPTER 13
THROUGH MID DEVON FOR EXMOOR
Over the Rolling Hills

Having left Dartmoor this part of the Lady Mary's pilgrimage was relatively straightforward - a continuous ride north, her main objective to reach the Druidic settlement dedicated to the Egyptian Cow Goddess Hathor, at Cow Castle in Somerset. On this stretch of her journey Mary and her family stayed at two settlements - first Berry Castle and then Whitechapel Fort, before reaching Holywell Cross on Exmoor, and on into Somerset. Mary performed no Light Ceremonies in Mid Devon.

In order to cover this section of Mary's travelling I undertook three separate day pilgrimages during a period of a few weeks in August 2009. Each of these days were extended ones with early starts and late finishes. I also have not been requested to enact any Ceremonies here.

I have charted Mary's route through Mid Devon very carefully and perceive many place-name indicators of her presence in past times. To list just a few in some semblance of order; Harepath, Down St Mary, Berry Castle, Merrifield Hayes, Hole Farm, Bethem, Rose Moor, Maire, Rose Ash, Hares Down Cross, Mariansleigh and Holy Well Cross. It goes without saying that Druidic names like ash, oak and aish abound.

ON MY JOURNEY NORTH

Mid Devon is an area of quiet natural beauty nestling between Dartmoor and Exmoor. This my first pilgrimage, which goes roughly to plan, takes me to Hittesleigh Mill, Down St Mary and Morchard Bishop, all on Mary's direct route, with a brief stop at Colebrook and Nymet Stacey. I have selected a few offerings which I think might be appropriate and collected some containers of holy water which I keep in my fridge. My sandwiches and flask of coffee are ready, plus a bottle of filtered water - my wibbly-wobbly water bottle is still my trusty companion. Before I embark, a prayer at my sacred altar: *"My dearest Mary - my fellow traveller. Let me listen to and be guided by your Divine wisdom this precious day. Let this day bring to me a sense of achievement and inner satisfaction combined with a feeling of deep peace. Let the Rose of Divine Love rest within my heart beloved one."*

Leaving my little flat in the care of the Angels, I set off at 7.00 am. This being a Sunday and early in the morning, the roads are quiet. From Bovey Tracey I take the A382 road to Mortonhampstead. I am driving through the most beautiful countryside, following the line of the old railway, which runs close to the thatched village of Lustleigh. The River Bovey winds its way through the dense woodland of Lustleigh Cleave, which is just littered with gigantic granite boulders and evidence of ancient settlements. When one walks through this enchanting landscape, one feels the interconnectedness of all life - as if time has stood still

There has been much controversy over the years about this stretch of the A382. A certain Lady Sayer now deceased, owned much of the land between Bovey Tracy and Mortonhampstead and refused point blank to allow any road widening, a decision with which I was in full accord at the time. However, over the years traffic has become heavier and the size of vehicles larger, all using a very narrow windy road with long single line stretches, which can cause driving havoc. The council in their wisdom, have now marked out the road with mile after mile of white lines, directing traffic into a central point each time it narrows, which is of some help, but still snarl ups occur. The best bet is to get behind a row of traffic and just keep following through. It is relatively quiet this morning and I catch up with a nice little green car which leads me onwards - most convenient. I drive on by way of the old market town of Mortonhampstead, past the White Hart Inn, to rejoin the lush green countryside on its far side. My first stop is Drewsteignton (see Chapter 12).

HITTESLEIGH MILL

I leave Drewsteignton along the quiet back roads through farm land, to eventually drop down to Hittesleigh Mill, pulling in opposite Hittesleigh Mill house. This is the most picturesque property - thatched and painted a very pale lemon, with roses round the porch and the most charming well tended garden. The stream which would have originally fed the mill and still runs alongside, is a tributary of the River Yeo. Standing on the little bridge I am in paradise once again - the stillness, the peace, the holiness - as it registers that as Naomi I was here with Mary. A great feeling of reverence comes over me. My heart is full of past memories as I stand looking into the little babbling brook. I return to my car and collect a bottle of sacred water acquired from Mary's Well at Holy Well Bay in Cornwall. Pouring a little into the stream, I offer a short benediction and collect some water in exchange. Climbing out of Hittesleigh Mill, I stop to look down into the valley and can see a line of trees identifying the position of the stream, along the route Mary and her family would have taken.

TO HITTESLEIGH AND THE CHURCH OF ST ANDREW.

My next port of call is the St Andrew Church at Hittesleigh. I park opposite Hittesleigh Barton, a very old property which has ancient barns sited around a courtyard paved with large stone slabs. On the opposite side of the road is a most attractive garden belonging to Hittesleigh Barton. There is a long trellis with arches supporting vegetables and brightly coloured flowers. On a buddleia is a single peacock butterfly, its rusty-reddish wings open wide to absorb the warmth of the sun, have striking black eye spots tinged with white, blue and yellow. How the natural world has changed. When I was a girl, a buddleia in any garden would be heavy with butterflies of all descriptions - peacocks, red admirals, tortoiseshell etc.

The church is situated behind Hittesleigh Barton. As I walk up the path through a section of the churchyard dedicated to a wild flower garden, the morning service has just finished. A gentleman standing outside kindly offers me a cup of coffee which I respectfully decline. The congregation of eight or nine, appear to be a very dedicated happy bunch of people. The church is quite small and simply adorned. The whitewash on its walls I am led to believe, cover medieval wall paintings. There are old fashioned brass gas lamps - now electric - hanging below a wagon design roof. No information leaflet is available, but I am told that the church dates from the thirteenth century. I am proudly shown a most beautiful painting by a local lady, whom I was introduced to, of St Andrew as a fisherman on the Sea of Galilee. I asked her whether she thought St Andrew may have visited this area because of the many churches dedicated to him, which I have discovered. The lady doubted whether he did, but told me that Joseph of Arimathea and Jesus Christ did come to the south-west - hurrah for ancient knowledge being kept alive. All is now quiet as the good folk have left and I am able to have a moment of stillness.

On leaving the church, I place a beautiful large fir cone as my offering in the corner of the old stone seat in the porch. Running down one side of the churchyard are the remains of ancient trees with huge girths. Hens are pecking in the grass amongst the gravestones. This is a place of peace - a little rural idyll. I take a stroll around the outside limits of the small graveyard. I seem to be wearing a cowl, my hands held within its sleeves in front of me. Now sitting on a bench near the church porch in the sunshine, I realize that for a short space of time I WAS St Andrew - he was overshadowing me. I am to take out my notepad and pen as words flow forth:

ST ANDREW

"You are most welcome pilgrim. We have met before at Lilstock and we will surely meet again before too long. As you know, I travelled to these sacred shores of Britain in the South West. My hermitage was at Lilstock, but I travelled far and wide preaching the Gospel of Love as our beloved Master Jesus taught us. Love of the simple things. Love of

the natural world - the nature kingdom - which is all around and part of us. I loved the little people and communed daily with them, as I did with my Father in Heaven.

The Universe is vast. How CAN we comprehend it - even now (indicating to me that even in the Land of Light he finds it amazing). *When I was on Earth I looked up into the Heavens - at the skies - filled with a million shining Stars and Planets, all of inestimable beauty and mystical proportions. The vast night sky shimmering across my head in all directions, filling my consciousness. As I watched I saw more and more. The whole sky appeared to be hanging in space, then dropping down to encompass me. My being was filled with a sense of holiness and wonder* (I couldn't help but think what a joy to have lived in a time with no street lights - but of course I did!). *The little animals of the woodland used to commune with me. The birds of the air joined in my worship. The great trees shaded me in times of hot sunshine and provided shelter in times of rain. All part of the great Universal Life. I was one with all life in those moments of pure beauty. Bless you my child."*

How wonderful to once again make contact with this beloved saint, who made his way to these shores such a long time ago. My heart goes out in love and thankfulness. A little earlier in my travelling, I had come across St Andrew at Lilstock in North Somerset and my insights identified him as another St Andrew rather than the Biblical one (see Chapter 16). Reluctantly it is time for me to leave. I enjoy a sandwich and drink in the car before moving on.

FOR COLEBROOK AND NYMET TRACEY

From Hittesleigh Mary crossed the River Troney at Coltsfoot Farm and on through Lammacott to Down St Mary. To reach Down St Mary, I shall go via Colebrook and Nymet Tracey, each of which is a mile or so off Mary's route, in order to visit their Parish Churches

I drive into the sleepy little village of Colebrook to discover its church is another with a dedication to St Andrew - yet so very different. I enter a very tall building with pinkwashed walls, which to my way of thinking, appears to be a strange choice of colour and a little incongruous. A reference booklet tells me that its history goes back to the twelfth century and interestingly, that in earlier times St Mary was one of its Patron Saints.

Moving on, I am in the small hamlet of Nymet Tracey at St Bartholomew's, which is actually the Parish Church of Bow, a mile away. One possible reason for its positioning, is that the word 'Nymet' means sanctuary and in this context could refer to an ancient Druidic grove, suggesting it was built on an original place of worship. Another rationale is that until the nineteenth century, Nymet Tracy supported a larger population than Bow in over eighty houses, which were all destroyed by fire. It is an engaging little church with a fine carved rood screen topped with tracery, which has maintained its original colours of blue and green. A lovely stained glass window shows an image of a haloed Virgin Mary, adorned in a deep ruby-red robe, over which rests a blue cloak.

Looking at the map I notice that the ancient hamlets of Sampford Courtney and Honeychurch are approximately ten miles to the west of Mary's journey north. Although not on her route I feel I must make mention of them because they have dedications to St Andrew and St Mary respectively. It would appear that these two saints are inextricably linked in Mid Devon and North Somerset. The church at Sampford Courtney features on its roof bosses, amongst many ancient symbols, the Three Hares and the Green Man The tiny church of Honeychurch, has hardly been altered since the fifteenth century. Both are fascinating and quite special places of worship.

THE CHURCH OF ST MARY THE VIRGIN, DOWN ST MARY

Time to continue my pilgrimage with Mary as she reaches Down St Mary and to pay a visit to the church dedicated in her Holy name. This church is an absolute delight and has stood the test of time. A pointer to its antiquity is that the churchyard is higher than the surrounding lanes, due to layer upon layer of burials over the centuries. Its history is well documented in tangible evidence. For example, the village cross would support an age back to St Petroc's mission in the sixth century. An indicator to its Saxon heritage is the carved tympanum above the south door, depicting the triumph of good over evil - the interpretation shown is St George slaying the dragon. The subsequent Norman church is recognized by its tower and the presence of a small window aperture in the north wall of the sanctuary. An extensive restoration programme during the Victorian era, upheld its ancient character.

In a stone recess above the entrance porch is a statuette of Mother Mary holding the baby Jesus. A sense of deep peace fills my soul as I step into its quiet interior and take a look around. There is a beautiful carved chancel screen of the North Devon School style. A series of the most striking stained glass windows from the nineteenth century grace the church. In the church booklet '*A description of The Parish Church of St Mary the Virgin, Down St Mary*' scribed by Gerald Miller, a very full description is given of the stained glass windows, which is most unusual.. I shall pick out two windows which speak to me. In the west wall is the impressive 'Jesse Window' portraying the ancestry of Jesus through David and Jessie to Adam. Then the three-light window in the Lady Chapel features: '*the Blessed Virgin and Child over a base panel of the visitation of Mary to Elizabeth . . . the three Kings of the Adoration over a panel depicting the Annuniciation . . . the three Shepherds above a panel of the Nunc Dimittis. The complete window can be viewed as being appropriate to the Epiphany*' (Page 11 Miller). I would like to complement the author on the most comprehensive church information booklet I have come across.

In the churchyard I am conscious of how well cared for it is and am reminded that a friend of mine cuts the grass here. He and his wife, dear friends of long standing, live in the village and play their part in the nurturing of this sacred place. There are some splendid yew trees which I acknowledge with a blessing. Why are yew trees so often found in churchyards? On Page 2 of the church booklet Miller says that the yew is: *'a survival of ancient pagan beliefs and before conversion to Christianity considered sacred. The yew's evergreen foliage is still regarded as symbolic of everlasting life.'*

DISCOVERIES AT MORCHARD BISHOP AND THE CHURCH OF ST MARY THE VIRGIN.

On leaving Down St Mary, the little party of travellers journeyed in a NNE direction, through Morchard Bishop and on to the Druidic settlement of Berry Castle. What I am to learn at Morchard Bishop is most enlightening. I park up at the St Mary Church and wander into the churchyard where the evocative smell of freshly cut grass assails my nostrils - the groundsman is at work. For some reason I don't go into the church immediately as would be my norm, but am being drawn to the eastern end of the churchyard. I walk through a little gate onto an open grassy area with fine old trees. The impression I am receiving is that I have stepped into another time and space

The St Mary Church, Morchard Bishop, linking to the ancient Celtic settlement

Coming towards me is a lady with two dogs, which I discover are rescue dogs and rather timid. This is a fortuitous meeting - obviously designed from above. Her name is Pamela and she is a font of knowledge. First we get into deep conversation about Ley lines and ancient history, completely on each others wave length. Then she says that this green area was a Celtic settlement, indicating to me the position of the dew pond close to a small copse of trees. Further, she informs me that underneath the grassy path on which we are standing, is an ancient stone trackway which goes to Berry Castle. So on reaching Morchard Bishop, Mary would have connected to this trackway and ridden the distance to Berry Castle settlement. Pamela and I walk out through the gate at the far end of the site and she points out to me in the valley below, a large field which is called 'Lady Plain' - a reference to 'Our Lady' she tells me. Finally, my new acquaintance mentions that between Morchard Bishop and Down St Mary, there is a place name 'Slade' which is another derivation of 'Lady' indicative of the Lady Mary - would you believe!

Beloved Mary's presence appears to be well upheld within this sacred landscape. It is all quite amazing: *"Thank you Mary for guiding me to this ancient site and trackway."*

I feel I have secured the information I need here and any desire to enter the church has left me - how strange. However, I do go in because it is here and I am on its doorstep. I have little to report about its internal structure which is fairly traditional. There is though the most lovely pale-blue Mothers Union fabric hanging, which illustrates the Virgin Mary and Christ Child. A leaflet gives details regarding the church and local history. Apparently, there has been a building on this site since Saxon times. It is written, that the old Celtic name for Morchard is 'Morchet' meaning 'Great Wood.' In AD 739 King Aethelred gave the Bishop of Sherborne land which included Morchet to build a minster, which was subsequently built at Crediton. Hence - Morchard Bishop. It is recorded that archaeological excavations have revealed an Iron Age settlement to the north-west of the church, but no mention of a site to the east, of which I've just heard.

I did consider trying for Berry Castle settlement at the end of my first pilgrimage in this area. I start on the road to Black Dog for the castle, when I make an abrupt and very sensible decision to head for home. It is late in the evening and raining very hard now. I wouldn't do Berry Castle justice. It is best left until the start of my next pilgrimage.

TO BERRY CASTLE DRUDIC SETTLEMENT

In order to cover the next stage of Mary's journey through Mid Devon, during this second pilgrimage I shall follow in her wake as closely as possible. I will begin at Berry Castle, then move on to Washford Pyne, completing my day at Rose Ash, with a few interesting 'twiddley' bits in the middle.

After my early morning attunement with Beloved Mary and the Masters of Light, I am ready. The prospect of a warm sunny day is ahead as I set off beneath a lightly mottled fair-weather sky. Initially I shall aim for the village of Black Dog in order to seek out the Berry Castle site. Driving the main A380 from Torquay I see in a field alongside the road, a very large and rather bizarre orange elephant statue which is an advertisement for a local ice-cream company. It normally supports an ice-cream cone in its trunk which today seems to have disappeared - it has no doubt melted away! I drop down Telegraph Hill and from Exeter take the main road to Crediton, soon to be following a country road for Black Dog. The countryside is dressed in its green summer mantle and in the fields, tall yellow corn is swaying in the light breeze. I pull in for a coffee break near some woodland. As I alight from the car the silence is palpable broken only by the gentle 'coo-coo-coo' of a collard dove.

My car is safely parked at Black Dog and I start off in search of the ancient settlement. With my pack on my back I am strolling along under now brilliant blue skies. I soon reach the little farm lane which according to my map should lead me to the site. I keep looking into fields through the hedges for any sign of the ancient castle. I come to a huge oak tree at the edge of a small copse of mixed trees, which include a handsome mountain ash with its bright orange berries. Something tells me I am here and I dowse to confirm. I speak with the deva of this lovely oak and hear:

OAK TREE DEVA

"Welcome pilgrim to the ancient site of Berry where you and Mary made camp for the night. You were most welcome then and you are most welcome now. Thank you for your journey here. Go in peace."

I leave an offering of a smooth round stone for the deva at the base of the oak tree. From this point there is nothing of the site visible in the landscape. I walk a few yards down the road and reach a gated entrance to a field. On a diagonal line, I see in the distance what looks to be a mound. Climbing over the gate I cross the field until I reach my goal. Yes I am right - a very definite embankment with many large oak trees, ancestors of the original ones no doubt. Clambering up to the top, I note that on the far side the ground drops away steeply and I am looking into a huge circular field surrounded by tall hedgerows. I suspect this could be the circumference of the ancient site. I try to walk in both directions along the earthwork until brambles bar my way. It is impossible to do the round but I am satisfied. I am here. I have found Mary's settlement.

Powerful energies of the ancient past are now hanging on the warm summer air. I have an inner vision of the ancient travellers, Mary and Naomi with Jesus and Joseph, being met and welcomed to this safe haven. They slide off their horses seeming to be quite exhausted. Is this my imagination or is this reality - the two merge as one. To think I am standing on the embankment of the ancient Druidic settlement where I stayed with Mary 2,000 years back. Memories are released from soul level once more and I am filled with wonderment. From somewhere deep within - a voice:

MARY

"My dearest daughter Naomi. Welcome to our settlement of Light - this ancient site which has always been. The energies here are still strong and your presence here today imbues the ancient landscape with renewed energy and vibrations, which will reverberate throughout the land Thank you dearest one."

I thank Mary for her warm welcome, and now visualize this Druidic settlement of Berry Castle in the Light - seeing a pure ray from the great Universal Light pouring down to bring healing to the land. Within the earth below one of the oak trees, I place a small white quartz crystal as an offering for the ancient ones. After a period of stillness tuning in and sensing past influences, I return to my car.

ST PETER'S CHURCH, WASHFORD PYNE

I am heading now for Washford Pyne. An exceedingly narrow road with virtually no passing places takes me there. This is haymaking time so goodness knows what large farm vehicles I shall meet on the way: *"Angels keep the road clear for me please."* I pull up at the village green with its old fashioned chain-link fence, in front of the tiny church of St Peter. A public footpath sign informs me that I am on the Two Moors Way. This is a one hundred and two mile long-distance footpath which runs from the town of Ivybridge in South Devon, across Dartmoor, through Mid Devon, over Exmoor to Lynmouth on the north coast. I must have passed this way some years back when I walked this route with a friend, but really can't remember this particular spot. I suspect my head was down, because what I do remember in Mid Devon, was trudging through very mucky red Devon soil in the pouring rain for two days!

My first impressions on seeing this little church is - what a treasure. It is a low building with an unusually squat bell tower supporting a square conical roof, the whole positioned within a churchyard which backs on to fields. As I approach the entrance, I see that in a niche above the porch is a statuette of St Peter. Pushing open the old faded oak door and stepping inside, I am touched by its serene atmosphere. Just as I am about to browse around a lady comes in to empty the humidifier, which as she shows me is completely full of water, so it proves its worth. Expressing my thoughts on what a delightful church, I ask her how many were normally in the congregation. She said around ten to twelve persons except on special occasions - so a very small parish indeed.

The layout of the chancel is most unexpected. The altar is cloaked with brilliant white material which has a red Celtic cross prominently displayed on its front panel. On either side are two matching curtains, each embroidered with St Peter's keys - again in red. I am feeling that this little community is very proud of their association with this rather special saint. A noteworthy feature is the lectern which is fairly modern and well crafted. It stands on four feet which show the emblems of the evangelists. On its front length is the 'Angus Dei' and on its back panel the 'Sword of Michael'.

In order to try and date the church I take a look a wall plaque, where it tells me that the first recorded Rector was Adam de Morcetre on 2nd May 1280. Sitting in one of the pews I have the feeling that I am not alone - the building is filled with previous parishioners - souls who have worshiped here. There is much rejoicing - maybe because their presence has been recognized. Into my mind comes the list of Rectors I have just read, so perhaps it is one of these who speaks with me:

RECTOR FROM THE PAST?

"Welcome - welcome pilgrim for taking the time to visit our ancient church. We wish you to leave in peace and joy dear traveller. Go in peace."
He leaves me with the sign of the cross. I offer a blessing to him and to all those who have drawn close. On my way out I see the church leaflet with a note *'please take one'* - a free leaflet - surprising. Alongside are a few small bottles of drinking water with another sign *'please help yourself'*. What a kind thought for any parishioner, or perhaps walker on the Two Moors Way, who may be thirsty. I pop a donation in the wall safe for the upkeep of the church.

Before I leave the little hamlet of Washford Pyne, I walk a wide green path alongside a thatched cottage, its gardens laid out with country-garden type flowers - blue delphiniums, roses, lupins, foxgloves and big white daisies. Now, leaning on a fence looking across a field, the peaceful landscape reflects my mood. My pondering once again brings to mind Mary with her family, travelling through this area, and I am wondering where the ancient trackway could be - very close I think, because I am certainly on relatively elevated ground here. I notice on the map to the east of this point, an interesting place name - 'Merryfieldhays' - is the past coming alive once more?

TO ROSE ASH PARISH CHURCH OF ST PETER

Mary's journey took her on through Nomansland, across Rose Moor to the second Berry Castle, then on via Maire to Rose Ash. Over the next few hours I follow this route the best way I can. From Washford Pyne I find that I am negotiating miles of windy country lanes, stopping every now and then to get a 'feel' for the area and try to identify significant places. I manage to encounter a recently laid road surface, running the risk of stones becoming lodged in the tyre treads. The nightmare of this happening in the worst possible way was in East Devon a few years back and it still haunts me. In brief, I took a newly surfaced road, and the stones covered with sticky black tar stuck to my wheels. I called in at a local garage for assistance. The mechanic drove my car, wiggling the wheel vigorously back and forth so that the car went all over the road, in order to dislodge the stones. He had got rid of the worst, but I then had to travel the fifty miles back home with noisy, still stone-filled tyres, park outside my house because I had a gravel drive, and spend hours picking off each disgusting stone! Whatever - this was not in the same category, so on I go with just a little trepidation.

I drive into the village of Rose Ash and come to a halt underneath a massive oak tree by a green, where the church, the old school house and several cob and thatch properties are in the immediate neighbourhood. All is very still here and the heady fragrance of summer flowers hangs in the warm air. This is a place of refined energy which holds the memories of centuries.

At this next St Peter Church I see that a bench seat has had to be chained to the wall, a sad reflection of these modern times. Putting this aside, I go through the Victorian wrought-iron kissing gate into the churchyard. There are many lovely trees and I notice that a small area has been designated a wild flower sanctuary. I offer a blessing for all the nature spirits who work tirelessly and lovingly to nurture the plants and thus bring about this haven of peace.

On entering into the domain of the church, I am immediately conscious of the gentle ticking of an old Victorian clock. This doesn't intrude as the quiet sacred energies engulf me. The church is very ancient, but received a major restoration in the late nineteenth century. There is much to admire here, not least the craftsmanship in the two magnificently carved screens. The old screen dating back to the fifteenth century which separates the nave and chancel, was meticulously restored in 1935. Then there is a fine Jacobean screen dating from the early seventeenth century at the head of the north aisle. As is often the case, I am bowled over by the stunning beauty of the stained glass windows. They are the crowning glory of this church and focus on the life of our Lord - space precludes a full eulogy! However, I come to one which moves me almost to tears. It is on the south side of the church, and depicts Jesus with Mary Magdalene in the Garden of the Tomb. Within its framework are plants of all descriptions, including a magnificent lily. In the distance are the hills of the Holy Land. Mary Magdalene is robed in scarlet and purple, cloaked in white - the Master in scarlet, cloaked in white. The words: *'Jesus saith unto her - Mary. She saith unto him - Rabboni.'* So touched am I by this holy scene that I sit down in a pew to continue my adoration. The Master Jesus is with me - I bow my head in reverence offering a blessing with my hand on my heart. He offers this sacred message:

THE MASTER JESUS

"My child - my pilgrim sister. You are nearing the end of your pilgrimage with our blessed Mary (these words because this is my penultimate pilgrimage before I take the road to Glastonbury, as by this stage I have covered much of Somerset). *The road you have travelled has been long - at times you have been weary and yet you carry on, knowing the precious journey you are making. My dear child, I will talk with you again at Glastonbury - very soon. This day is for your memories to be reawakened as always and this is sacred.*

My sister Naomi - go in peace. Tend to your flock - for each of us are gatherers of men - each of us have a part to play in the great scheme of things This is YOUR role for now sister dear. I will protect and guide you and build your strength (I have been ill) *that you may continue your sacred pilgrimage. My heart is your heart - for we dear sister are one - we are ALL one. Each a part of that great Cosmic Being you call God. Each a part of the Universal Light. Each a part of ALL humanity. For where I go - you go also, what I think - you think also, and what I experience - so such experience will be yours. We each are to be crucified on the Cross of Matter, that we may rise in full consciousness of the Divine Heart and its manifestation within our human Brethren - as with the Angelic Realm and the Deva Kingdom. ALL IS ONE my child - all is one. The blessings of my*

Father in Heaven be upon you this sacred day. Let your Father-Mother God be your guide and helper always. My child - go in peace."

The Master is standing robed in white, his right arm raised, drawing in the air with two fingers, the blessing of the cross. I am totally immersed in his vibration. I am so humbled. The emotion of the most profound transcendental love I am feeling, is whelming up from deep within. Blest am I: *"Beloved Master - I thank you for your grace this sacred day."*

As he fades away it is time for me to go also. Wandering outside: *'where am I to leave my offerings?'* I am being impressed to leave two gifts to enhance the already well balanced male-female energies in this hallowed place. I chose a small white quartz crystal discovered at Brent Tor and a pink quartz crystal. Behind the church I spy a lovely yew tree. I tune in to the Spirit of the Tree and with some special words, bury both offerings at its earthy base.

Although it is late in the afternoon the sun is still warm, so back at the car I take out a rug and lay it down on the grass beneath a large beech tree. On my back, looking up through the greenery, with the warm breeze gently moving the leaves and the sun's rays shining through them, it seems I am seeing a million little sparkling stars. I am absorbed in its magic. My thoughts - yes I HAVE come a long way and I HAVE been weary at times - but mine is the joy also. I could stay in this hallowed place with its peaceful energies for ever. On completion of my Mission with Mary, I shall return to walk the highways and byways of Mid Devon. To think that about forty years ago my husband and I nearly bought a property in Rose Ash!

My day has drawn to a close and I wind my way back through the country lanes to Crediton then head for Exeter and home.

ST MARY'S CHURCH, MARIONSLEIGH.

On leaving Rose Ash the Lady Mary's journey took her north to Whitechapel Fort settlement. My third pilgrimage sees me returning to the Rose Ash area in order to visit two places which I see marked on the map close to Mary's route - Marionsleigh and Morchard Bishop, then on to Whitechapel Fort and finally to Holy Well Cross for St Mary's Holy Well.

After my morning link with Beloved Mary I am ready. Today I am driving along the A380 in quite misty conditions, which by the time I emerge from Haldon Forest at the top of Telegraph Hill, has lifted its misty mantle to reveal the River Exe lit up by the morning sun in the valley below me. On now through Crediton for Black Dog that I may link to the E3137 for Marionsleigh. The road approaching the village is extremely narrow with the proverbial grass down its centre. It is quite dark and mysterious under the overhanging trees. As I round a bend all of a sudden a buzzard flies up from the road in front of me with a little creature in its talons and gives me a bit of a start.

In the village now I park up at the church entrance opposite an old farmstead with hens and cockerels running free. Two of the cockerels wander over to take a curious peep at me then set-to for a brief fight.

I felt drawn to visit Marionsleigh because of its evocative name-link to Mary, and on arrival discover the church is dedicated to St Mary. The name Marionsleigh is said to refer to 'Marion's Meadow' connecting to St Marion, whom it is understood built a small oratory here in AD 600.

I go through a little wooden gate into the churchyard, unusually devoid of trees, and enter the sanctuary of this ancient church. Inside is a fact-filled booklet regaling its history. It is said that the present day Norman church established in AD 1250, was built on top of the original oratory. Over the centuries the church has been enlarged and undergone various restorations. Apparently much of the original building work was undertaken by local people, evidenced by the poor materials used and indicating a parish without the money to employ a well-known mason of the period. Perhaps another hint of lack of local funding, is that many of the interior fitments have been gleaned from other churches, such as the rather plain oak pews, the pulpit and the lectern. These were acquired following a fire in 1932 which gutted the church. What catches my eye is the chancel ceiling. Flanked by two beautiful angelic figures painted in white, pink and blue are bosses, which depict many interesting artifacts, among which are; the sacred triangle, the crown of thorns, a harp, an old fashioned oil lamp and a Kings crown. Before the altar I offer a heart-felt blessing and take rest in a pew. Mary is before me robed in the softest blue and delicate rose-pink attire which covers her head. Her words:

MARY

"Welcome to this church dedicated in my name. We know of the historical background of St Marion within this landscape, but the dedication goes back so much further dear Naomi. How close we were you and I, to this sacred place on our journey through Devon to Whitehchapel Fort Druidic settlement. Immerse yourself dear one in the silence. Feel as if you are in the inner sanctum of the most Holy of Holies - for it is so. This is your sacred space this precious day. The pilgrimage you are undertaking this day is most important, for I know you are to seek out my Holy Well near Whitechapel Fort. Search diligently dearest Naomi and the reward will be yours for you will know the way. Bless you my child."

I thank my beloved Mary for her contact. Outside the church I walk to its east end and gently tuck into the earth, a rose-pink quartz crystal in her memory.

THE PARISH CHURCH OF ST MARY THE VIRGIN, BISHOP'S NYMPTON

I now continue my journey and drive across the Crooked Oak River to Bishop's Nympton. On reaching the Parish Church with its very tall Norman tower sectioned in four layers, once again I discover that its dedication is to St

Mary. I walk the path to the church entrance through a series of five yew trees, which by their spacing should be eight in number. Pushing open the heavy oak door, I expect to find myself in the church but instead walk into complete blackness - I quickly realize that there is a second inner door to the church! It is a splendid church with a strong Eastern-Roman influence in its many effigies of the Lady Mary and the Master Jesus. Two stunning pictures illustrate one, Jesus the Christ holding the Russian cross - the other, the Virgin Mary dressed quite simply in a blue robe, with the Christ Child on her lap. In the Lady Chapel facing east, the stained glass window depicts from left to right; Sanctus Paul, Sanctus Maria, and Sanctus Peter. On its south side, another window shows Sanctus Celia sat at her spinet. She is robed in blue and scarlet, her haloed head adorned with long brown hair, garlanded with flowers.

Through the silence in this holy place, my ears pick up the sweetest sound of singing - a female voice. This strikes a chord with me, as I had a similar experience at the ruined St Michael's Church, Trefenty in South Wales on my first encounter with Beloved Mary. Today she is once again making her presence known to me in this very special way. My heart opens in love.

Walking back to my car across the village green, a beautiful white feather 'leaps' from my bag. I had forgotten to leave an offering - so here it was: *"Thank you Angels for the reminder."* I return to the church and place it close to one of the yew trees.

TO THE WHITECHAPEL FORT DRUIDIC SETTLEMENT

About three miles north of Bishop's Nympton is Whitechapel Fort and I am soon pulling into a small lay-by at the entrance to Garliford House, just to the south of the settlement. I am studying the map in order to get my bearings and identify the best way into the fort, which does not appear to have a public footpath going to it, when a car pulls up. The young lady driver wonders if she can be of assistance so I ask if she can tell me the best route up to Whitechapel Fort. *"Where?"* she enquires. I show her on the map and she is visibly surprised at there being a fort on the hill, but can't help me - even though it would seem that she lives here. So I make my own plan.

Gathering up my pack and bits and bobs, I start off up a steep hill, struggling a bit in the mid-afternoon heat. The sun has stayed out all day - a miracle after my misty start this morning. At the top of the hill is a good parking area which would have saved me a ½ mile uphill trudge! On down the other side I go until I reach a lane, at the end of which the woodland track should take me to the site. Only snag - there is a *'Private'* notice at the lane entrance. But I am prepared to assume this means for cars. A huge oak tree at the entrance invites me in - so that's all right then! I sally forth - with confidence.

The lane crosses a boggy field, as testament to the low level of the land at this point. Looking at the map, the contour lines suggest that Whitechapel Fort could once have been surrounded by water, as it is situated close to the River Yeo, and river levels in Devon were higher 2,000 years ago. At the end of the lane is a small cottage almost hidden amongst the trees. I turn to the right hoping not to be seen and follow the wide forest track through the woodland. A quad bike is coming towards me along the track with two very barky dogs running alongside. A countryman of indiscrimate age with a weather-beaten face tells me: *"This is private land - I live at the end of this track."* Whoops! Me: *"I'm really sorry but I'm trying to reach Whitechapel Fort. Can you help me?"* He very kindly gives me directions. I ask him for permission to go to the fort bearing in mind he has just informed me that this is all private. He just nods and chugs off.

I follow a very muddy path to an old dilapidated five-barred gate. On the far side of a field of several acres, I can see what I believe to be the fort on a distant rise. Up and over the gate I go, coming underneath those disturbing electric pylons which still run cross-country in some parts. On through a small copse of young beech and silver birch trees, I now walk directly across the field climbing steadily, hoping against hope that there is no 'mad' farm animals lurking in the hidden surrounds!

I reach an embankment topped with great oak trees - success at last. I am hearing an inner voice saying *'Well done'* but this could just be me giving myself the proverbial pat on the back! From the extent of the boundary of Whitechapel Fort as portrayed on my map, I suspect that what I am seeing is only a fraction of the original site. I make the sacred link with the Lady Mary and the Masters of Light. I honour the ancient trees and embed in the earth a white quartz crystal for the Druid ancestors. It is wonderful to be here - the last settlement for Mary and her family in Devon. I don't hang about, as not too far away I can see farm hands working on some machinery and I would rather not be confronted. I leave this ancient place a very happy pilgrim and begin the long return trek to my car, which by now seems a million miles away, but is only about three. Nearly back to base I stop to look over a gate and across a field of golden wheat. High up on a hill in the distance I can place Whitechapel Fort, which with hindsight is easily identifiable.

TO ST MARY'S HOLY WELL

My last call of the day is St Mary's Holy Well. I believe that as Mary and her family travelled north from Whitechapel Fort, they connected to a tributary of the River Mole which they followed along an ancient trackway to Exmoor then over the border into Somerset. This stream today runs into Holy Well Reservoir and it is in this valley I shall go in search of St Mary's Holy Well.

I plan a route from Whitechapel Fort through South Molton and North Molton. At Holy Well Cross I take a right onto a narrow lane high above the stream and park my car in an old quarry by the roadside. I have previously checked the map for a footpath to the Holy Well and there is none. I considered that I may be able to drop down to the valley from the quarry, but before me a steep densely afforested area ringed with a stone wall which is topped with barbed wire, bars any entrance.

I start walking along the lane soon reaching a bridge, which doesn't give me a sight of the valley in its entirety. Around the sharp bend I go, constantly peering through the thick hedgerow hoping for a better view. Eventually I stop and bash my way through tall brambles and bracken at the side of the road, step over a small ditch and climb an old stone wall. Great - now I have a picture of where I think the Holy Well could be. Excitement starts to mount - I can almost 'see' it. Mary did tell me at Marionsleigh: "*you will know the way.*" I look to see if I can possibly scramble down the wall on the field side but it is too steep. So I decide to continue up the lane to seek another entrance to the field before me.

View of the valley which houses St Mary's Holy Well, on the trackway to Exmoor

Then IT happens - disaster strikes. I am coming down off the wall, when my foot catches in a bramble and I take a tumble. This is an understatement, because one moment I am vertical - the next horizontal. I have landed on the grass at the side of the road, the left side of my jaw taking the full impact of the fall - it is a split second happening. The pain from my jaw's contact with the ground shoots right up into my head - it is excruciating. I am completely stunned and lay still for some while hoping against hope that I've not broken anything. Somehow, still reeling from the shock, I manage to stand up and it is then I realize how much worse it could have been, as my face was an inch from the road. I gingerly feel my jaw - it is in tact. I check my eyes - yes still in their sockets. I ask the Angels for healing, enfolding myself in very gentle gold and pink, focusing the blue healing ray to my jaw and head for the pain. I have no Rescue Remedy which is a pity. When a little recovered I make the decision to go on, because I am so close now to discovering the Holy Well. I cannot help thinking though, as one does, why did this have to happen. I appreciate that I was eager and excited, but not to the extent of acting foolishly and not taking care. It was a pure accident - or was it - is there some deeper reason for this drama? Who knows - I never did work it out! At home later the thought comes to me: *'did I feel the slightest uplift as my face hit the ground?'* I couldn't be sure, but I know the Angels protected me because I came away virtually unscathed.

A short distance down the road I reach a field-gate, on which there is no 'Private' sign nor 'Public Footpath' signpost. I take a chance and go through the gate into a field of sheep and lambs. In order not to disturb them, I keep close to the perimeter as I walk down into the valley. I am now picking up the sound of the stream trickling through the coombe. At the bottom of the field is an old ford. I paddle my way across. A row of magnificent beech trees follow the line of the stream, their trunks encrusted with pale green lichen running into rich green moss at the base. Strangely shaped gnarled tree roots left to rot where they have fallen, offer homes for the small creatures of the woodland. Here is a place where the little folk work their magic. I extricate my dowsing rods from my pack and ask Mary to direct me to her Holy Well - both rods move together in the direction downstream. I check from another angle and yes - this is correct.

Following the line of beech to the right of the stream, I arrive at the field boundary where I find my way blocked and discover nothing, so I return to the ford. I now climb over a wooden fence and try the left side of the stream, walking through a field with many tall purple thistles, until I come to a marshy area with reeds. This feels better. In front of me is a massive uprooted rotted tree, its three main trunks fallen across the water. I dowse and the Holy Well is three feet away. I believe the tree has fallen over the old well. My impression is that at one time it was the guardian and that the deva is still watching over this sacred place. I look in earnest at the base of the tree waterside, but there is no evidence left of any well. Sitting down on a mossed root of a beech tree I feel a tranquility of spirit. Now I am aware of Mary:

MARY

"Diligent searching once again has brought you to the place you seek my child - my Holy Well. We rested in this little dell and drank of the crystal clear stream as we made our way north to Cow Castle. We were tired and weary and the water gave us refreshment. Once refreshed, we kept on climbing to our destination. Bless you Naomi."

I thank Mary for her guidance. I offer with a special blessing, a little water from St Neot's Holy Well in Cornwall, asking permission to collect some of its precious liquid in return. I now focus on the water before me. Cascades of sequined sunlight are dancing on its surface producing myriads of tiny sparkling lights. A large yellow dragonfly with blue-green iridescent wings, is hawking its way through the reeds. In this little dell I am in fairyland and very conscious of the nature spirits. It comes to mind that here in Mary's day, close to the stream was a rest house, for pilgrims on the trackway to Cow Castle. All of a sudden the wind has a wild moment. I can hear it whooshing through the trees on an otherwise completely still day. Perhaps my intuition is being acknowledged by the air element. It is gone as quickly as it came and all is still again. My time here has come to an end, so I retrace my steps through the field at a slightly different angle. I come across a grassy stone round with an indentation, which I recognize as the shape of a hut circle - of course - this whole area was an ancient settlement, hence my insights at the stream.

Back at the car I have a drink from my flask and bit of relaxation before I leave. It is the end of a long day. I did consider that if time permitted I would take a look at the churches in North and South Molton. However due to my earlier accident, my instants tell me that it would be a wise move to return home without further delay. I drive the narrow switch-back of a road to Holy Well Cross and begin my long journey south. I reach my little abode at sundown, after being witness to a magnificent evening sky streaked with burnish gold, reds and oranges.

My pilgrimages through Mid Devon are complete. Before we leave this area please note the number of St Mary churches which I have been guided to visit at; Down St Mary, Morchard Bishop, Marionsleigh and Bishops Nympton - and I know there are others. Mary and her family have covered quite a distance and stayed at just two Druidic settlements - Berry Castle and Whitechapel Fort. Now a new venture is to unfold as they go over the border into Somerset for Cow Castle.

CONCLUSION TO DEVONSHIRE.

This brings to a finale my pilgrimage with the Lady Mary through Devon. I thought I knew my home county relatively well, but Mary's Mission for me has opened up new vistas and more wonders. It has enabled me to explore much of the countryside, taking me to many of the ancient sites, traditional villages and sacred churches.

By way of a brief synopsis let us take a general look at Beloved Mary's pilgrimage through Devon. With her precious family - her children Jesus and Naomi and Joseph, her brother - Mary entered Devon by way of the Abbey River near Hartland. From there the Holy Family began their long journey south through West Devon for Brent Tor Druidic settlement. By now I have solved a question which has been puzzling me. Why did Mary travel to Hartland in the north of the county in order to reach Brent Tor in the south, as no special Light Ceremonies were carried out during this section of her pilgrimage? Would not a quicker route have been from Millook Haven on the north Cornish coast, east in a direct line through Cornwall and Devon to Brent Tor. I wrote a lot of possibilities down and after tuning into Mary, I methodically dowsed the list. The answer I gleaned, was that although no

Ceremonies were undertaken, her role was to bring her Divine presence and that of the boy Jesus to the sacred landscape of West Devon, thus imbuing it with Cosmic Light and vibrational energy.

On arrival at Brent Tor settlement Mary was to re-energize the ancient Druidic Temple, then move on to Merrivale Ceremonial Complex to revitalize the Atlantean Temple in the Etheric. After crossing the wilds of Darmoor, she reached another Atlantean Temple site at Hembury Castle, where once again she performed a Ceremony to open up the energetic vortex of Cosmic Light. The last sacred act for Mary in Devon, was a Ceremony at Hound Tor Druidic Temple settlement in Eastern Dartmoor. With the key part of her Mission in Devonshire complete, Mary was free to travel north, over East Dartmoor, through Mid Devon for Exmoor and on into Somerset.

An observation - during their pilgrimage through Devon, the family stayed together for the duration, whereas in Cornwall Joseph left the little group on a number of occasions, sometimes taking the boy Jesus with him, to attend to his tin mining operations.

I have followed in the Lady Mary's footsteps as closely as possible, faithfully playing my part in the scheme of things by performing sacred Ceremonies of Light, to reactivate the ancient Druidic Temples and earth the Atlantean Temples, as directed by her. It is as I undertook the last part of Mary's pilgrimage through Mid Devon that I became aware of her progressive fatigue, which I appear to be matching. By now Mary had been journeying for over a year and still had some months to go. Although she had her Divine connection, the constant travelling must have taken its toll physically. I do know that at Culbone Hill settlement in Somerset just a short way ahead, she becomes ill.

Thank you my blessed Lady for being my constant guide during my travelling through Devonshire. I honour you. I honour ALL the Beloved Ones who have been my companions and protectors during my journey. My pilgrimage has been one of immense satisfaction and deep profound joy. As I enter Somerset what more wondrous revelations are to unfold?

Part III – Somerset

Introduction To Somerset

The Lady Mary has left Devon far behind. She is focused on her next two very important spiritual charges. The first - to perform a special Ceremony of Light at the Druidic Temple for the Goddess at Cow Castle in the heart of Exmoor. Secondly, her pilgrimage was to take her to Culbone Hill Atlantean settlement, named K'SH'B'H by the first Sumarian teacher to arrive there approximately 4,000 years before Christ. The ancient Atlantean Temple had been lifted into the Etheric, as had others, of which we are now aware, and Mary's role designated by the Higher Beings, was to prepare and reactivate this sacred Temple for future ages. This was to be Our Lady's last sacred Ceremony before Glastonbury, where I learnt there was an ancient Hyperborean Temple in the Etheric. It is at Glastonbury that Beloved Mary accomplished her final Cosmic Act in the South West, which was to conduct a Light Ceremony of profound proportions, to fulfil the Divine Will of the Illumined Brethren of the Christ Light

I have now tracked the whole of Mary's pilgrimage through Somerset, which is documented in *'MARY'S JOURNEY SOMERSET'* - so just a précis. Together with Naomi, Jesus and Joseph, Mary travelled over Exmoor to Cow Castle, then on to Culbone Hill settlement. This is where her illness meant that the little party had an enforced extended stay. On her recovery, Mary and her family headed for the North Somerset coast west of Porlock Bay, where they took a ship to Blue Anchor Bay for the Hungerford Druidic settlement, which was a few miles inland. Leaving Hungerford, they went by sea once more, this time from Watchet, to reach a place called Kilve a little further along the coast. Their journey then took them overland via Holford to The Quantock Hills for the high peak of Trendle Ring settlement. After a brief stay, they travelled the ancient trackway almost the entire length of the Quantock ridge, dropping off at Lydeard Hill for a Celtic settlement near Broomfield. Finally, they crossed the Somerset Levels to Glastonbury.

On the map are many place names which could well have association with Mary. Here are a few. Beginning at Cow Castle, there follows; Lillycombe House, Faircross, Holford, Lady's Edge, Paradise Farm, Merridge Hill, Treble Holford, Merridge, Great Holwell and Rose Hill. Also, a little to the south of The Quantocks at Kingston St Mary and Stoke St Mary, their Parish Churches are both dedicated to Mary. Across the Somerset Levels there appears to be little evidence of Mary's presence in the landscape. I suspect this is due to the fact that 2,000 years ago during the Iron Age period, much of this area of Somerset was under water.

By this stage in my Mission with Mary, I have already completed many of my pilgrimages in Somerset on separate day trips, as opportunity presented itself whilst staying at my daughter's home in Wellington. I shall gather all my travelling experiences together and systematically document them in the order of Mary's pilgrimage around the county. When this is complete, I shall set off on my final pilgrimage to Glastonbury.

To date I have conducted two sacred Light Ceremonies, both on site. The first was for the Goddess at the Druidic settlement of Cow Castle. This was followed by a pilgrimage to K'SH'B'H - Culbone Hill, in order to earth the Atlantean Temple Finally at Glastonbury, I shall earth an ancient Hyperborean Temple. This will bring to a close my Mission with the Lady Mary in the south-west of these mystic Isles During my travelling in Somerset, I have visited and shall continue to visit, places and churches of particular interest, on or close, to Mary's route, combined with the other settlements where she and her family stayed.

Mary's journey through Somerset took a different turn from that in Devon. For example, the overall distance covered is much shorter. And - although she had travelled by river through parts of Devon, now she was to spend a fair portion of her time on the water, either sailing along the North Somerset coast or taking a small craft across the Somerset Levels. For me however for obvious reasons, my pilgrimages are land based. Throughout my own journeying I know that Beloved Mary and the Masters of Light have been, and will continue to be, my constant companions, and attentive loving guides.

Mary's Journey - Somerset

CHAPTER 14 SURMOUNTING EXMOOR'S HEIGHTS

COW CASTLE THE GODDESS Ceremony on site
CULBONE HILL/K'SH'B'H ATLANTEAN Ceremony on site

Together with Naomi, Jesus and Joseph, Mary left Devon crossing the border into Somerset just after Darlick Moors. They then rode NNW over Horsen Hill to the Druidic settlement for rhe Goddess at **COW CASTLE.** They stayed there between two and three weeks, during which time a special Ceremony was enacted by Mary and the Druid Elders to revitalize this ancient Temple. On accomplishing this Mission, Mary and her little party took a boat up the River Barle, which was a wide river in her day, to Simonsbath. They went across the River Exe, followed by a steady climb to Tom's Hill Barrows and Mill Hill, and on to Weirwood Common for the **CULBONE HILL SETTLEMENT** in the Vale of K'SH'B'H. Here in this sacred place Mary performed another Cosmic Ceremony this time for the Atlantean Temple in the Etheric.

CHAPTER 15 THE NORTH SOMERSET COAST

No Ceremonies are to be performed on this stretch of Mary's journey.

Due to Mary's state of health, it was expedient to make a prolonged stay at Culbone Hill, but finally the little party were ready to continue their pilgrimage. They dropped down through the Culbone Valley to the coast near Porlock Bay. The water was further out 2,000 years ago, evidenced by a submerged forest in the bay, much the same as in Mounts Bay on the south coast of Cornwall. Mary and her family embarked on a sail craft which took them along the North Somerset coast, passing Minehead, to pull in at the eastern end of Blue Anchor Bay. From this point a journey was made on horseback inland through Old Cleeve, for the Druidic settlement of **HUNGERFORD** where Mary joined with the Druid Elders for a Ceremony of Light. After their time here, they all returned to the coast by boat along the Washford River to reach Watchet, for a short sea journey to Kilve.

CHAPTER 16 OVER THE QUANTOCK HILLS

Once again no Ceremonies are to be performed in this area.

On leaving Kilve, Mary and her family travelled inland to Holford, from where they accessed the valley of Hodder's Combe set below Lady's Edge, to go over Black Ball Hill and Thorncombe Barrow for the Druidic site of **TRENDLE RING** on top of The Quantock Hills. Here was an ancient Tree Temple and Mary performed a Cosmic Ceremony to revitalize the site. From Trendle Ring, Mary with her companions travelled the length of The Quantocks along the high ridge, following a route through Thorncombe Hill, above the aptly named Paradise Farm, over Hurley Beacon, through Crowcombe Gate passing the ancient Triscombe Stone. The journey continued over Wills Neck to Lydeard Hill where they left the ridge. They then went east to Merridge and Great Holwell. Finally, it was over Broomfield Hill to a settlement on the south-eastern flank of The Quantock Hills which I shall call **BROOMFIELD.**

CHAPTER 17 ACROSS THE SOMERSET LEVELS TO GLASTONBURY

GLASTONBURY TOR HYPERBOREAN Ceremony on site

The last leg of Mary's pilgrimage in the South West took her through the Somerset Levels for Glastonbury. Leaving Broomfield settlement, Mary and her family went directly east to North Newton. At this juncture they took to the water and continued in an easterly direction to Glastonbury, which is well documented to have been an island 2,000 years ago. This section of the journey is rather difficult to chart because the little boat, probably a dug-out canoe, would have weaved its way through water channels around hill-tops. With Mary's help I have dowsed and picked up a sort of route which goes via Burrow Mump, Othery and High Ham to **DUNDON HILL,** their last settlement before Glastonbury. From here they journeyed through Butleigh Wootten to the Druidic settlement of **GLASTONBURY TOR,** which was actually situated below The Tor. This concludes Beloved Mary's pilgrimage through the South West of Britain. Her Ceremony to revitalize the Hyperborean Temple in the Etheric Realm at Glastonbury Tor was to be her last Mission. She stayed at no further settlements in Somerset.

TO WALES

From Glastonbury, Mary and Naomi with their guides, took a boat through the Somerset Levels to the coast at Burnham-on-Sea. From here mother and daughter sailed on to the mouth of the River Severn and entered the south coast of Wales at the River Wye, which they followed all the way to a settlement at **ACONBURY FORT.** The plan was to meet with Druidic family and especially with the Druidic Priestess Mair, in order to establish a physical link for future travelling around Wales after the crucifixion. In the

Epilogue I record my experiences at Aconbury and chart the journey undertaken by Mary and Naomi along the River Wye. The boy Jesus and Joseph stayed at Glastonbury to make ready for their future visits there. They all reconvened at Burnham-on-Sea and journeyed on through ancient Dummonia to the south coast at Lyme Bay, in order to pick up a sailing boat for their return to the Holy Land.

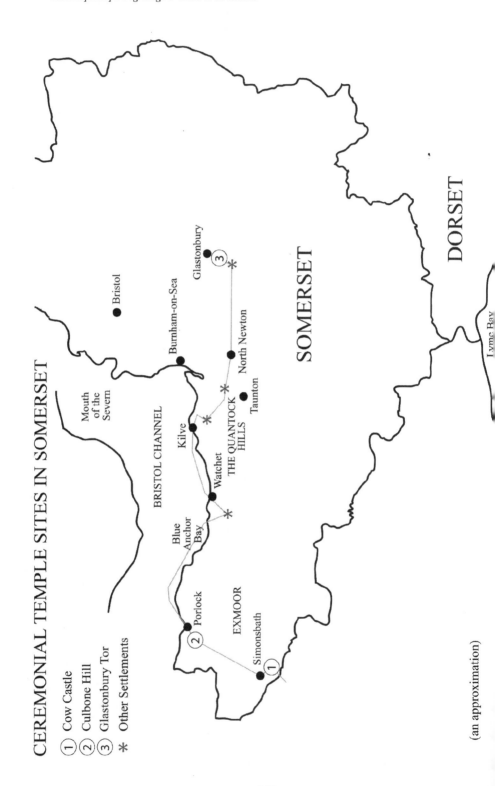

CEREMONIAL TEMPLE SITES IN SOMERSET

① Cow Castle
② Culbone Hill
③ Glastonbury Tor
✳ Other Settlements

Mouth
of the
Severn

BRISTOL CHANNEL

Bristol

Burnham-on-Sea

Glastonbury

Kilve

Watchet

North Newton

THE QUANTOCK
HILLS

Taunton

SOMERSET

Blue
Anchor
Bay

Porlock

EXMOOR

Simonsbath

DORSET

Lyme Bay

(an approximation)

CHAPTER 14
SURMOUNTING EXMOOR'S HEIGHTS
Its Cosmic Past Unveiled

I am walking in the most peaceful sacred valley of Cow Castle on Exmoor, alongside the clear sparkling waters of the River Barle. I hear within: *'oh ancient land - my land'* as once again memories of the past come flooding back. I am Naomi travelling with the Lady Mary through this ancient landscape. Together with Jesus and Joseph of Arimathea, they have left Devon and arrived at the sanctuary of Cow Castle Druidic settlement which is dedicated to rhe Goddess and the Sacred Feminine. The specific dedication is to Hathor the Cow Goddess of ancient Egypt whom we've met before at Cow-y-Jack and Cowlands in Cornwall. My beautiful Mary, the *'Rose in the Heart'* is a part of that long history of Divine Feminine essence of compassion, pure love and gentle strength - she is the personification of Isis. A few days before my pilgrimage to Cow Castle, during a meditation I received the most profound words from Beloved Mary, which sacred concepts I shall carry with me today. She talks of the Law of Oneness and the Sacred Feminine:

MARY

"My dear child we would wish you to understand that your heart is a part of that Great Heart. It is the Mother - the SACRED FEMININE aspect of the Christos. This Sacred Feminine is not the prerogative of the female sex - it is the pure love aspect within each human heart. There has been much said and much written about the Sacred Feminine by people. What they fail to understand is that this is for ALL. It is so easy to pigeon-hole God's plan. Since passing and through many incarnations, I have grown to understand the true meaning of certain aspects of the Godhead. The Godhead, this Almighty Being - this Power - this Light - this Love - IS ALL ONE. There is no division in male and female and there is no division in the grand scheme of things. We can ALL aspire to the highest.

We in the Land of Light are not separate from you on the Earth Plane. The Masters and Angelic Beings are not separate from their human counterparts. The Nature Spirits are not separate from the rest of Creation. ALL IS ONE. This is a tricky concept to comprehend, but I give you only truth dear one. This concept of non-separation, then fundamentally means that the action of one affects us all. This is why we are learning to live in the purist energies of the Sacred Heart.

I say unto you dearest one, I say unto you ALL - never forget this. Love your neighbour as yourself. Bless those who condemn you. Honour your Brother and Sister. Nurture Mother Earth and all therein. This is the way dear ones. This is 'THE WAY'. This is the way to eternal life and everlasting love.

We in the Land of Light - ALL the Beings of Light - honour and love the endeavours of you ALL. We acknowledge the difficulties of Earthly incarnation, but we bless and honour each effort made by ALL our Brothers and Sisters to live with the purist intent. We are your true Brethren. Once again I do emphasize there is NO SEPARATION. All is one in the eyes of the Great One. We, that is you and I and every living soul, are pure Light and Energy. We vibrate together in the Sacred Heart of all life. There is so much we would wish to share with our Earthly Brethren. In time more will be revealed to you dearest one for ALL humankind to understand. We have so much love to offer. We give you ALL our pure Sacred Heart of Divine Love. Take this blessing and let it merge with your understanding as it is at this time.

Remember always, ALWAYS dear children of Earth, live the Way of Peace - live the Way of Love - Live in the Heart of the Rose. This is THE WAY dear children for you ALL. Bless you my children."

Mary held up her hand then touched her heart in a blessing as she closed. Once again I am overwhelmed with the beauty and sacredness of Mary's words and offer her my deepest heart: *"Let me be worthy of your love beloved one."*

MY JOURNEY TO COW CASTLE

It is July 2009 and I am on a week's house and cat sitting 'duty' for my daughter in Wellington, an ideal opportunity to explore Somerset with Mary. Cow Castle on Exmoor, is one of the places she has requested that I visit in order to perform a Ceremony of Light. I have been there on numerous occasions, but today's sacred pilgrimage is of special significance. My day-pack ready, I now light a candle for some inner time with Mary: *"Beloved One, may I walk in your Light this precious day as I continue my Mission with you in the South West."* I am conscious of a 'full house' as here in my room with Mary are many other Light Beings.

I alight from the house into wild blustery rainy weather. THEY - the famous weathermen/women - told us we were to have a hot dry summer this year. To date, this prophecy has gone out of the window. However, I am full of Light even if 'the sun don't shine'. Leaving Wellington I am soon driving along a country road to Milverton by dint of a deep dark lane cut through red-sandstone rock, which today with the heavy skies, is particularly atmospheric. On through open countryside which is showing the lush green face of summertime. No doubt the onslaught of continual rain has much to do with the magic I see around me. The Quantock range of hills rising out of the mist to my right, I recognize as being part of Mary's journey through Somerset.

Turning left just before Elworthy, a notice tells me that I am in the Exmoor National Park and I begin the steady climb to Simonsbath. The distinctive Dunkery Beacon at a little over five hundred metres, looms up before me through the inclement weather. Without warning the rain becomes torrential - it is going to be an 'interesting' Ceremony at Cow Castle! For mile after mile the country lane hedgerows are graced with tall bright pink rosebay willow herb, which brighten up the otherwise rather drab conditions. I drive on by way of the popular tourist centre of Exford and it's not long before I am pulling into the car park at Simonsbath.

The skies have cleared just a little and the sun is beginning to peep through the dark clouds. All kitted up, I set off on the three mile hike to Cow Castle, on a pathway indicated by the *'Two Moors Way'* directional sign. The first part of my pilgrimage takes me through mixed woodland with a predominance of beech and oak. Here fallen trees have been left to rot, providing a natural habitat for little woodland creatures. Leaving the wood I am high up now above the River Barle, and walking on a narrow track lined with the ethereal-blue sheep's scabious and bright pink bell heather. The going under foot can be politely called a quagmire, where much jumping from stone to stone and scrambling up the high bank is called for. Below me the River Barle is slowly meandering its way through this beautiful valley. Looking down at the wide expanse of low land stretching away from it, it becomes clear that the river would have been much wider in Mary's day and therefore easily navigable. She and her family took a vessel up-river from Cow Castle to Simonsbath on their way north. To my right I see a magnificent single beech tree just off my path. I go to it and lay my hand on its trunk. Through the smooth texture of the bark I become aware of its energetic life-force I hear:

BEECH TREE DEVA

"Welcome my pilgrim to this ancient land. The Beloved Ones are waiting for you. Proceed with care and dutiful intent and open loving heart. Mary, the Mother of ALL, is waiting for you." From me: *"Thank you blessed deva."* I leave a small offering.

As I reach the first of many little wooden gates through the valley, the energies begin to change - the feeling of being encompassed in tender loving arms is very strong, as if I am walking into the womb - right into the heart - the Sacred Heart of the Mother. I am filled with compassion and inner happiness - a pilgrim walking through ancient and familiar landscape. The path drops down and I now find myself at the river's edge - a little eddy of clear water before me. Common-blue damselflies, their bodies of iridescent blue with finely veined translucent wings, flit among the grasses which are rising from below the surface of the water. Here the river is gurgling its way over its stony copper-coloured bottom. From my pack I take a small bottle of water collected from the Devon Leat on Dartmoor, which I gently pour into the precious waters with a benediction. Asking permission from the water sprites I collect a little water in another container.

At the gateway to the Cow Castle site a huge Guardian Stone salutes me as I pass through yet another wee gate. I return the salutation asking a blessing on my forthcoming ritual. I now enter the magical kingdom where one feels the presence of fairy folk. A row of very tall beech trees, their branches spreading out and hanging low, border the river. Last time I was here on a Gatekeeper pilgrimage, a ewe had just given birth and we watched with great delight from a safe distance so as not to disturb mum and lambkin. As I walk this final section by the river, with the enchanting sound of the water in my ears, my heart is expanding. My pace slows to a methodical amble and I can feel the anticipation of soon reaching my destination - Cow Castle.

I have left the river and am now climbing up a gentle slope alongside an old dry-stone wall. I am standing on the path facing the low hump of Great Woolcombe hill, with the Cow Castle peak to my left and Flexbarrow peak to my right. Suddenly the landscape is telling me that in front of me, Great Woolcombe is the womb - its rounded shape personifying the belly of the mother with unborn child - the Christ Child. Flexbarrow is the father - the male aspect of the Godhead. The female aspect of the Godhead is represented by the Cow Castle peak itself. Because of the strangeness of the landscape's features denoting these aspects and the fact that I needed to ensure accuracy, at home later I dowse and receive verification.

CEREMONY FOR THE TEMPLE OF THE GODDESS AT COW CASTLE

A look at my Astrological Ephemeris earlier had indicated that this day July 14th, there are two Planets - Jupiter and Neptune - conjunct in the fixed earth sign of Aquarius, the sign where personal motivation is subjugated for the good of the whole, hence perhaps my act of service to come. Jupiter offers an expansion of Universal Consciousness, while the energies of Neptune will clear away any negativity and bring in new spiritual wisdom and understanding. Thus for my sacred Ceremony at Cow Castle, this is an excellent combination of energies, which will help revitalize the ancient Druidic Temple site and which can be instrumental in awakening humanity to the new vibrations.

I reach the base of Cow Castle hill and climb up through the tall bracken along the line of its rocky outcrop, today covered with bilberry bushes, to its apex. Up here it is blowing a 'hoolie' and in this position I am very exposed to the elements. I settle myself down in a little hollow, tucking myself in amongst the gorse and bracken as best I can. All of a sudden the skies darken and big spots of rain begin to fall. This does not look so good for my Ceremony. What shall I do? Then a thought - I speak the words: *"I call on the alchemist Merlin to please clear the skies in order that I may perform my Ceremony."* The wondrous magician does his trick - the rain ceases, the dark clouds are magically blown away and I see little specks of blue appearing. How wonderful art thou!

Cow Castle Hill

I take out of my special Breton tin which holds my Ceremonial articles and place them in position. There is no way as often happens, that my candle will light with the high wind, but I visualize myself lighting the wick and 'seeing' a magnificent flame rising to meet with that Cosmic Flame. My inner vision shows me the great Sun-Star high above my head, shining its Golden Light down to envelop me and this sacred hill. I make the link with the Druid ancestors. My crystals I reverently place in turn on my white cloth, calling on each of the Higher Beings represented by them. On laying down my rose quartz crystal, I invoke Hathor the Cow Goddess of ancient Egypt, for she is the archetype of the Sacred Feminine.and here at Cow Castle is her domain . Today I am especially conscious of the gentle strength of the Goddess energy. Beloved Mary, the embodiment of the purist love - the *'Rose in the Heart'* - is by my side.

I voice the sacred words of my Ceremony for the Goddess at this ancient Druidic Temple. As my Ceremony is drawing to a close I have a vision of ancient Egypt - of the Great Pyramid and of the Sphinx. I am there as Naomi experiencing my own Temple training. Is-Ra is offering his hand to me. I walk forward. We sit on a seat in the garden courtyard of the Temple of the Golden Rose and the essence from the profusion of roses, symbol of the Sacred Feminine, fills my senses. My beloved Is-Ra speaks with me:

IS-RA

"Beloved sister, we welcome you to this sacred heart of the Temple. Open your eyes - your inner eyes that you may see all things. (My inner vision now shows me a heart-shaped pool with water lilies of white, rose and gold. I stare deep into the clear waters of the pool). *We wish you to know dear sister that the ancient energies have*

been relocated to this sacred place - Cow Castle. *When you were in the Temples of ancient Egypt and Atlantis, this work of bringing in the ancient Light was your role as Priestess of the old times. It continues - nothing is lost - nothing changes. Circumstance of each Earthly existence are different, but for you dearest one in this lifetime, the way has been made clear for you to continue your sacred work. This you will continue to do and to a very much deeper degree. There is much still to be undertaken with your chosen companions of Light You will work with the higher dimensional energies to be a part of the great mass of Earth people doing this sacred work today. Your role is sacred. Let it always be so. I and Beloved Mary and the Master Jesus are at your side at all times and are your trusty Companions of Light."*

Is-Ra, standing in the white robe of a High Priest offers me a symbolic blessing. I am filled with utter joy. From me: *"I thank you for your blessing - for your words and for enabling my visions dear Is-Ra. I honour you and all the dear ones in the Land of Light."*

As he takes his leave, clouds are forming once more - rain is coming in. I complete my Ceremony and close down my physic centres, ensuring that I am well grounded. Before I depart this pinnacle of Cow Castle, I place deep in the long grass, my white quartz crystal for the ancient Druids and my rose-pink quartz crystal for the Goddess, thus bringing into harmony the energies of the Sacred Feminine with their male counterpart in this hallowed place. I wedge into the low branches of a gorse bush, a yellow rose which I had brought with me for the Goddess. How was I to know that I was to go in my inner vision, to the Temple of the Golden Rose this day when I chose this colour?

Here it comes - the rain is falling steadily now so I scramble off Cow Castle hill as quickly as circumstances allow. Safely on terra firma I make my way back to the river. Something catches my eye and I see the white flash of a dipper as it bobs up and down on a rock in the middle of the current. As I pass the giant stone at the entrance of the Cow Castle landscape, I acknowledge and thank the guardian. Conditions are getting wetter and wetter, and I hit a brisk pace, making the journey back to the car in record time! Drying off and sipping hot coffee I reflect on my day.

First, I am thinking that perhaps there was some benefit to the inclement weather, as I did have Cow Castle to myself. Then, that this has been another miraculous pilgrimage with my dearest Mary. It is now I realize that when at Cow Castle in ancient times, she took the role of High Priestess in a Druidic Ceremony. As I was leaving the site I had rested my hand on my heart as a blessing for the Temple of the Golden Rose. I am remembering two visions received at that time. The first was of a Druid Priest standing on the highest point where I had been, his arms outstretched invoking the Cosmic Light - a most impressive sight. Secondly, I saw the Hill Temple surrounded by a circle of huge oak trees. My journey home was undertaken in a state of bliss.

In the early hours of the morning on the day I was to leave for Cow Castle, I received the following inspirational words and perhaps this is a fitting place to include them. I had been thinking that the pattern of receiving messages from the Beloved Ones in the middle of the night was drawing to a close - how wrong could I be! I was feeling the energies of a most beautiful Being around me. I don't know whom this dear soul was, but share with you the words I was given, which I shall call the 'Great Awakening'.

BEING OF LIGHT

"The Goddess is awakening and bringing with her a new consciousness - the Christ consciousness is returning to humanity. The arisen Christ as depicted 2,000 years ago by events in the Holy Land, is now bringing forth a new understanding of the ancient wisdom. Arise all you seekers of wisdom - all you seekers of truth - and welcome the Goddess, as once more she takes her rightful place at the side of her consort - equal is the key word. For there is work to be done - there is to be no slacking - the gateway is open now - the New Jerusalem is to rise and makes its presence felt. So what is this New Jerusalem?

The New Jerusalem is the natural extension of what was laid down 2,000 years ago in the Holy Land. At that time alongside the Master Jesus our beloved one, Masters of a very high degree, were in incarnation. So it is today. They are being reborn into the World at this time, for the sole purpose of bringing your Planet into the 5th, 6th and even 7th Dimensions. For it will be so. Unicorns will return to your Planet dear ones. Be ye wise as serpents and gentle as doves. Oh people of the new consciousness, it is your role to bring this Christ Consciousness into manifestation - into its full glory. Begin in the now - begin with yourselves - perfect yourselves so that the very atoms of your physical body are purified. Go into the Sacred Heart. Witness the joy of union with the Goddess, for SHE is your salvation - SHE is your way to eternal life. Through her wisdom and love all things will be. Let the conjoining of the masculine and feminine essences, bring forth the new born Christ Consciousness - the Son - the offspring from a perfect union.

The word has gone forth. The cry of the spiritual warrior is abroad. The union of the sacred essence will bring into physical manifestation a world of song - a world of dance and joy and happiness. But dear ones - it has to be recognized - it has to be earned. The New World Order is waiting in the Wings of Heaven for humanity to rise and take up the Sword of Light, riding forth with its banner of beauty and gentle alliance held high. Trust in your Divinity my valiant soldiers of God and of the Goddess. The World - your World - is on the threshold of the formation of the 'Great Awakening'. Be a part of that New Order my children - for it is your right. Let the Goddess in you awaken to embrace the New Order. We come to you all with such joy in our hearts at this time Earth people for you are on the threshold of great change. AND IT IS GOOD. God bless you my friends - my Pilgrims of Light. Be witness to the new consciousness." A blessing is given.

CULBONE HILL ATLANTEAN SETTLEMENT - K'SH'B'H

Following my sacred Ceremony at Cow Castle yesterday, my visit to K'SH'B'H is to be my second pilgrimage from Wellington. From Cow Castle Mary and her family first took a short river trip through the Barle Valley to Simonsbath. From here they travelled over Exmoor via Tom's Hill Barrows, across Weirwood Common to Oare Post for the Culbone Hill Druidic settlement. A thought comes that there must have been an excellent co-ordinated network of Celtic guides to provide a combination of boat and horses for the different sections of their journeying, as in this short stretch alone they travel by river, land and then leave from Culbone by sea.

I am told that Mary was taken ill at this settlement and subsequently their stay was to be longer than originally planned. I suspect that Jesus and Naomi as resilient young people, were coping well enough with the long and sometimes arduous travelling. But for Mary perhaps not so. Her brother Joseph was their guide and support and I am picking up how concerned he was for Mary's welfare. When recovered, the Lady Mary was able to enact a special Ceremony to reactivate the ancient Atlantean Temple in the Etheric.

Again - and by now you're probably sick of hearing me saying this - Culbone is a place I have visited many times. The first was as a fourteen year old on a cycling holiday with my older cousin, when we took a train to Bristol from Cardiff my home town and cycled the coast of North Somerset. I can still see us now pushing our very modern, for those days, five derailler gear, drop handlebar bicycles up the 1 in 3 gradient (old money) Porlock Hill on the way to Lynmouth. We had heard how notorious this hill was and we were not to be disappointed! Many a car got stuck on Porlock Hill in days past. There was and still is another route - a toll road which is much longer, winding for ever, up and around through woodland from Porlock to Pitcombe Head, called with much imagination 'New Road'. But of course way back then, we were young, fit and full of enthusiasm and nothing would have induced us to take the easy route. This holiday offered me my first opportunity to visit Culbone Church. I have walked the path through the woods to the old church often over the years since, either alone or with special friends. Each journey has been in the form of a pilgrimage. During a short break staying in Porlock with a dear friend a while back, I also reached the ancient settlement on Culbone Hill and saw the incised Culbone Stone.

THE HISTORY OF CULBONE/K'SH'B'H

Yes - the energies of this sacred place kept calling to me and I had to return time and time again. Of course when I was younger I was unaware of the true significance of the area. Eventually, it must have in the nineteen seventies I came across a book by Joan D'arcy Cooper *'Culbone - a Spiritual History'* which unfortunately I do not have in my possession any more and it is now out of print. However, for those pilgrims who know nothing about Culbone and yet feel drawn to learn more, it can be accessed through 'Google'. I deliberately chose not to research this before my pilgrimage. When I did finally reread D'arcy Cooper's words, I was truly astounded at the miraculous happenings in this sacred valley - I had completely forgotten. Some of which I subsequently read, had become apparent during my time there. I can give you but a glimpse of the magic of this Valley of Peace - the Valley of K'SH'B'H. If you chose to make your own pilgrimage to this sacred place, your spiritual insight will surely be awakened to the perfect sacred energies in the vale.

So, to a little of its history. It was approximately 4,000 BC when a wise sage and teacher from Sumeria, landed on the North Somerset shores to set up a School of Learning in the place he called K'SH'B'H. One of the meanings of this Sumerian name is 'The Trinity of Holy Action' referring to its spiritual function. The teaching expressed from its Divine source, was to offer comprehension of humanity's spiritual evolution and the nature of the Universe. Emphasis was laid on the personal disciplines of healing, yoga and meditation, in order to realize Divine truths. After the Sumerian's passing there was a long gap when itinerants visited the valley. Around 2,250 BC people who wished to learn and live the life of the wise Masters came from Wiltshire, Dorset and Somerset to settle in K'SH'B'H. Once more it became a centre of civilization - in fact it is said to have been THE principle teaching centre in Britain at the time, which lasted for seventy-five years. During the next 2,000 years or so there were long periods when K'SH'B'H was left undisturbed.

We can move forward to 65 BC when a wise man from Somerset arrived in K'SH'B'H with a special mission to prepare the people and cleanse the valley for the coming of Christ. As an aside, I notice how similar are the names of 'Sumeria', 'Somerset' and 'The Summerland', (one spiritual tradition's concept of where we go on physical death). The man from Somerset lived there as a recluse for fifty years. His successor was a spiritual teacher with pupils from far and wide, who continued the preparation for a visit by the Master Jesus.. D'arcy Cooper tells us he inhabited K'SH'B'H from 15 BC until his death forty-five years later in AD 30. If this was so, then he would have been there when Jesus first visited as a boy of now thirteen years with Mary, Naomi and Joseph, AND when he returned in AD 25, D'arcy Cooper's date for the visit of our Master in adulthood. Intriguingly she refutes the possibility of Jesus having visited Britain before AD 25. So once again it is a case of discovering ones own truth. On his return in adulthood the Master Jesus was at K'SH'B'H for eight days. His role alongside teaching and healing, was to implant his own Divine spiritual essence in the form of the 'Flame of Caring'. He performed a sacred Ceremony to implant the 'Seed of Caring' in the then teacher, which would be passed on to his successor. It was our beloved Master Jesus who spoke of a Temple of Light in the Etheric.

The following extract is taken from Joan D'arcy Cooper's *'Culbone - a Spiritual History'* which is part of *'Joan D'arcy Cooper's Collected Works* offered on the Internet by The Neith Network Library. Page 19 - her words: *'Christ spoke also about the Temple of Light which was to be built in the Etheric sphere above K'SH'B'H and whose foundations he was to lay spiritually. The plan for this Temple of Light was first formed and laid out about nine thousand years before the coming of Christ. It was originally designed for the purpose of making man whole as an Etheric being, that is, the healing of people in Etheric bodies for the continuation of their spiritual evolution.*

But with the coming of Christ, this purpose was altered to include the possibility of healing physical mankind as well, in the future. This would require the fulfillment of a number of conditions to make possible the descent of the Temple of Light at a later time, so that it rested on the Earth - although still in the Etheric sphere and invisible to physical sight. (It was not until about a thousand years after the physical time of Christ that the construction of the spiritual Temple was complete, and it could begin to function in terms of its original purpose. And it was not until nearly another thousand years had passed, that the conditions were right for the Temple to commence its descent onto what was by then called Culbone).

I have read this and the rest of D'arcy Cooper's work very carefully and note a couple of things. When she talks of the plan for the Temple having been formed 9,000 BC, this would to my mind be one of the ancient Atlantean Temples which was lifted into the Etheric and held within the Etheric membrane, until such time as Jesus the Christ visited K'SH'B'H in AD 25, in order to prepare it for physical manifestation 2,000 years later. Further, I can see nowhere in her writing where she says that any action has been taken regarding its descent into matter. The timescale mentioned of 1,000 + 1,000 years fits with the present age. I trust in the Divine Beings that now is the time for the earthing of this ancient Temple to be accomplished, and acknowledge that I have been entrusted with this sacred Mission. This is my role this treasured day. How wondrous is that. How humble the joy. How blest am I.

MY JOURNEY TO CULBONE HILL SETTLEMENT

My pilgrimage day is July 15th - St Swithins. The weather as I set off is raining which doesn't bode well for the next forty days! Leaving Wellington about 9.00 am, my aim is to reach the settlement in plenty of time to prepare for a noon Ceremony. I check all the contents of my Ceremonial box to ensure I have all I need. Settling for an attunement, my pink scarf resting over my head and my candle lit, I offer these words in prayer: *"Oh Gracious Spirit. I ask that this day I'm of good service to humanity and worthy of the task before me. I ask that the beloved ones in the Land of Light walk my journey to K'SH'B'H with me. Guide me and uphold me on my precious pilgrimage Beloved Mary and Master Jesus. I go to a hallowed place on this sacred day."* My inner vision shows me the valley and hill already alight with Cosmic Light.

I take the same roads as yesterday, but on reaching Exford turn north over Exmoor's open moorland heading for Culbone Hill. I know each pilgrimage - each Ceremony is sacred, but something tells me that this day it is even more so. Touch of the yesterdays regarding the weather - a mix of storm clouds and rain with an occasional flash of the sun. The roads are awash with surface water from the last storm. I take a short coffee break sitting in my car parked amidst a mass of pink heather. The Exmoor ponies which are used to this wild upland landscape are looking rather bedraggled today. Their value as 'hairy lawnmowers' as I have heard them described by a ranger, speaks for itself, as I survey the neatly cropped moorland grass. At the junction to the A39 Porlock-

Lynmouth road, I stop for a short while at the viewing point of Whitestone Post. Looking down into the wide expanse of Porlock Bay, I am reminded, that 2,000 years before, the sea was much further out and that below me would have been a forest.

Now travelling west along the main road, I turn right at the Porlock Stables Pub and pull in at the lay-by at the beginning of the path to the ancient settlement, with its stone row and incised Culbone Stone. Shock. Horror. What was once a public right of way has been barbed-wired and is now private land. I stand staring at the notice before me almost paralyzed, in a complete state of astonishment. The way is blocked to my proposed Ceremonial site. What looks like a relatively new wooden board has been nailed to the post stating *"The Culbone Stone. Access by arrangement only. Details on the National Park Website'.* In the field and a long way from home, I don't have access to a computer so that's not a lot of good! Below this is the original notice much faded indicating that *'The Culbone Stone was discovered in 1940 and is approximately 1metre high. It features an incised wheel cross which suggests it dates from the 7th Century. The stone is a scheduled ancient monument'.* I take photographs of the two notices. On my return to Devon I shall contact the Exmoor National Park Authority and make it my job to get this ban lifted and the ancient site opened up. At home I put my plan into action with a phone call, following it up with a letter. The reply I received told me in a nutshell, that the Culbone Stone is on private land and the landowner has withdrawn permission for access. Plus, there are no legally defined public rights of way through the site. They, the National Park Authority, are apparently working with the landowners to come up with a workable solution to reinstate access. So far so good. However there is an amazing sequel to this which you will read of later.

For now this has absolutely thrown me. What am I to do? I could trespass but something tells me it would be unwise - it all looks to be rather official. I can almost hear Mary saying: *"we wouldn't want you to get arrested would we!"* Perhaps there is another way in where my presence wouldn't be so obvious! A short distance down the road I arrive at a gated entrance. Here another notice tells me that this is *'The Lillycombe Estate. Private Road. Authorised vehicles only.* 'Lily' - a symbol of Our Lady - evidence of her past presence again lies in the place name. Once more I am unable to gain access. A feeling of great sadness comes over me. I am still undecided as to what to do. I return to the first no access point and am able to talk with a local guy who informs me, that the owner only recently had the notice put up because he uses the land for shooting! Just as well I couldn't find a way in then!

A plan is formulating. I shall drive to Porlock Weir, park up and walk the beautiful way through the woods to Culbone Church and perform my ceremony there. I check with Beloved Mary that she is happy with this idea before I proceed. Decision made, I am back in emotional balance. What I do know is that the Atlantean Temple in the Etheric will be earthed at the ancient settlement on Culbone Hill, therefore it is imperative that I try for access for there will be those pilgrims who may wish to pay homage.

A thought has just struck me. Have the powers of darkness who would know of my forthcoming visit and intent, attempted to put a block on the work for the Light. This sudden realisation has made me even more determined to one - set the Atlantean Temple on the Earth in its rightful place and two - get the site opened up. With this insight and remembering past experiences, I immediately put myself under the Christ Star and within the Merkaba, asking Archangel Michael for protection. I know I have to be vigilant today.

I turn my ignition on and notice the warning light stays on indicating a fault in the ignition system. This has NEVER happened before and was perfectly alright before I arrived here. Is my car being esoterically sabotaged? A little concerned, I drive on gingerly to Porlock parking up at the Information Centre to report the closure of the land. The lady is very surprised at the news and says she knows nothing about it and that it must be very new. Back in the car with the ignition still playing up, I drive on to Porlock Weir, deciding that I shall sort the ignition problem out AFTER my Ceremony. I shall allow NOTHING to get in the way of that. I have a two-three mile walk to the church and it is now 11.30 am therefore my 12.00 noon planned Ceremony has gone out of the window.

PILGRIMAGE TO CULBONE CHURCH

Having parked in the harbour car park I am ready to go. Before I leave for my Mission, my eye takes in a view of the area of coastline where Mary and her family would have left K'SH'B'H for Blue Anchor Bay. I begin my pilgrimage by way of a little path behind an hotel, on through a field to a country road which takes me to the Worthy Toll, a point of road access to enable one to reach the higher track for Culbone Church. At its entrance is the toll house, a most delightful neatly thatched cottage. I go under a low stone arch, through a gate and past the cottage to begin my walk to the church. I am in Yearner Wood and am already feeling a change in the energies and a welcome from the little folk. I ask permission of the guardian to enter this sacred domain. The path takes me through a man made tunnel and under a small bridge alongside an old lime kiln. A little further on is a long deep gulley leading to what could have been an old mine, the entrance blocked now with a padlocked gate. I climb the neatly crafted old stone steps, where huge graceful ferns are cushioned by the warm brown earth of the woodland floor on either side. I am conscious only of the sounds of the natural world - the wind in the trees - birdsong - the sea pounding on the rocks far below me, of which I get the occasional glimpse through the dense trees. The darkness of the trees interspersed with little shafts of bright sunlight is drawing me in.

It is here that I took a photograph, which when it was printed, showed an OR within the treescape. If anyone wishes to find out more about Orbs, Diana

Cooper and Kathy Crosswell have written an excellent book with fantastic pictures, called '*Ascension Through Orbs*' wherein they inform us that Orbs present themselves for view as Globes of Light suspended in space, and can be detected in photographs. In the introduction to their book Cooper and Crosswell tell us that: '*Orbs offer keys to higher consciousness to accelerate our ascension.*' They also say that Angels and Guides can come in to help us in the guise of Orbs. They recommend spiritual practices such as meditation, prayer and chanting in order to ingress their Cosmic potential. We can all do this through attunement - just allow the petals of your heart-rose to unfold with love and the connection will be made.

The path gets steeper. Although quite wide and safe I am walking carefully, focusing on each footstep, and surrounding myself with Light in order not to have an accident, remembering my past awareness and taking seriously any potential presence of the darker elements. Would you believe that after so much rain, the day has turned out to be very warm and sunny. Walking through the wood I am hot and sticky and being bothered by masses of flies. They insist on buzzing round my ears and it is most unpleasant, so I stick a bit of tissue in each ear - that'll fool them!"

ST BEUNO'S CHURCH AT CULBONE

At last there it is - the Church of St Beauno - peeping through the trees, set in the secluded valley beneath me, wrapped round and cocooned by a surround of tall trees and vegetation. I have with me a leaflet I obtained from the church many moons ago on my first visit as a youngster, which gives a little of the history of this ancient church. Entitled '*Culbone Church*' it is published by Williton Printers. Much of its content is based on the late Dr. F.C.Eeles booklet, now out of print.

We know of the original Sumerian Master who called this sacred valley K'SH'B'H, and during many subsequent occupations it remained so. But according to the leaflet, by the fifth century and the arrival of the first Celtic monks from Wales, its original name had been lost in time. The monks named it KITNOR - 'Place of the Cave'. The Church of St Beuno was so called after Kil Beaun or St Beuno a Welsh saint of some importance. I had never come across St Beauno before, but by strange 'coincidence' some months later, I was in South Wales and discovered a church dedicated to St Beauno and St Peter at Llanvenoe in the Black Mountains. The church here at Culbone, began its life in the seventh century as a small simple rectangular stone building with a thatched roof. Following hundreds of years of mixed fortunes, including a fire, abandonment, various re-buildings and restructuring, by the nineteenth century it was established much as we see it today. Eeles informs us that Culbone is the smallest complete Parish Church in the country. It has a tiny spire added in 1810 and on Page 3 of the leaflet is an amusing anecdote: '*This quaint spirelet, which waggish people suggest has been snipped off from the top of Porlock church is made of deal and covered with slate.*'

St Beuno's Church, Culbone

I step into the sanctuary of the little church and welcome its cool interior after my hot exertions. It is as I remember it, rather dark, made so by tiny windows set in wide stone walls. There is one balustraded box-pew, other than that the fifteenth century seats are quite plain. I sit in one of the old pews giving myself time for stillness before my Ceremony. I love this little church - there has always been something quite special about it for me.

CULBONE HILL ATLANTEAN TEMPLE CEREMONY

Leaving the church I walk to a seat on a rise in the churchyard which has an element of seclusion, in order that I may conduct my Ceremony. I have the place to myself at the moment and am sure it will be kept that way for the duration by the miracle workers above. I can hear the little burbling stream as it runs past the churchyard on its journey through the Culbone valley to the sea. The astrological data for my Ceremony at Cow Castle still stands.

As I begin my Ceremony, it is only now I am remembering my original reading of the Sumerian Master and the Master Jesus, who in times past visited this hidden valley and laid down the spiritual foundations for the Aquarian Age. Comes to mind now are those Beings of Light who have safeguarded this sacred place over eons of time. I reinstate the protection of the Archangel Michael. My special items are laid out and all is quiet. I voice 'The Great Invocation'. I place myself under the Christ Star and can feel the powerful Rays of Light pouring down. Each crystal is laid on my cloth as I call on the Angelic Ones and Masters of Light. My Ceremony proceeds as ever - the energies here are extremely powerful. This ancient valley is the Grail Cup. The Cosmic Rays being poured down to fill this sacred vessel, will act as a

Fountain of Light, which will burst forth to spread Light and healing far and wide.

My inner vision sees me at Culbone Hill ancient settlement. I am standing with outstretched arms invoking the Light and saying: *"Let this ancient valley be filled with Cosmic Light. Let any negative or dark forces be released from this valley. Let the Light - the Flame of Eternal Truth and Wonderment - be the torch that bears Light to these mystic Isles. Let the 'Flame of Caring' be awakened. Let the Temple of Light - the ancient Atlantean Temple - be earthed in this sacred place."* As these words are being uttered I am in a state of semi-trance. The Temple is earthed - the Light is being reborn on Culbone Hill.

As I come round a little I am aware that there is a black and white cat coming in close to investigate this stranger who is sitting so quietly. He is very pretty with a white blaze, white chin and white paws. He jumps up and climbs over all my 'equipment' then on to my lap, obviously very determined to make his presence felt and not to be left out, probably happy with the vibrations around me. After he receives a gentle stroke - he jumps down and wanders off. Now a very powerful Being is at my side. It is the Master of past times:

SUMERIAN MASTER

"My child you have entered the sanctuary of this sacred valley with a loving open heart. Your work this day is one more step in the long journey back home for your Planet. In our time we each played our part. I visited K'SH'B'H many thousands of years ago and prepared the Light energies in the valley. Your beloved Master Jesus was here and laid the foundation of the Golden Flame for all eternity. You were here child with Mary and you each had your part to play 2,000 years ago.

This is an ancient Atlantean Temple site and as such the vibrational energies of that 'almost' lost continent are still embedded in the landscape. I say almost, because as you have already learned this part of the sacred mystic Isles of Britain is the last remaining land of that once great continent. This is why it is called the mystical Isle, for it holds the mystical magical powerful energies of Atlantis. The great crystals are still at work even though they are laid dormant for a while. They are being brought back to life once more. As we enter the new sphere of Aquarian life much will be revealed to the wise eye and the open heart.

We know of your predicament today sister. It will change - believe in that - trust in Divine providence. It will happen - the ancient Atlantean site WILL be reopened for pilgrims to visit. The dark forces WILL be disbanded. There was much fear in certain quarters of our Universe when it was registered that it was time for the ancient Temple to be earthed. There were those who didn't wish this to happen - who are afraid of the Light and the goodness therein. Light ALWAYS prevails over darkness, but where there is Light, darkness will always be. It is The Law. The Flame of Eternal Light will ever shine forth and draw humanity into Divine Truth.

In the sacred triangle of Love, Wisdom and Power is a Divine message of hope, trust and perfection. The Christ Light at its apex shines down to each corresponding male and female energy. Its base is being strengthened and the energies of the Sacred Feminine aspect of the Godhead, join in unison on an equal status with its male counterpart. Again - it is The Law. What is lost is found. What is subjugated once more comes into being. Let the Divine Light shine in you ALL - my dedicated Light Workers. We praise you. We thank you. We honour you ALL. Amen."

My heart is full as I receive these words. The feeling which comes over me at this moment is of great reverence and humbleness. I offer a blessed thank you to this ancient Master of K'SH'B'H. Nothing gets past them does it! Seriously - the wise Cosmic Masters always know the situation. My experience was all part of the great Cosmic plan - there are no mistakes. Perhaps I was not privy initially to circumstances at Culbone Hill, because they wished to prove my resolve and what action I would take. I hope I've passed the test! Time to positively close the energies down and ground myself.

I have been alone here for almost an hour in this the normally busy time of day - the early afternoon - but now I am hearing voices from across the valley. I quietly but rather hurriedly put things away, keeping out two crystals and other offerings. I am just in time because the voices have bodies to them and they suddenly materialize at the church gate. Some go into the church, others spread out around the churchyard with their dogs. I am thinking, this will be a little difficult for me to lay my offerings without arousing attention. First I leave my seat and wander the churchyard to view the grave of Joan Cooper. On her gravestone is written *'Joan D'arcy Cooper 1927-1982. Let not your heart be troubled'*. I pick a few wild flowers and leave them on her grave with a blessing. I am able to secrete myself behind a large yew tree and lay at its base three shells from; Holy Well beach in Cornwall, Shaldon beach in South Devon and Kilve beach on the North Somerset coast, by way of linking the three present day counties of Mary's pilgrimage in the South West of Great Britain. Now for my crystals. I walk to the east end of the church. This seems to be the right place and I am out of view of any wandering pilgrims here. With a prayer, I gently insert into the soft grassy earth at the base of the stone wall of the church, my pure white quartz crystal and my rose quartz crystal.

My job here is accomplished. I make the return journey through the woodland. As I near Porlock Weir my mind turns to my car. I had left it in a state of doubt as to whether there was something radically wrong. I am saying to the Angels: *"I have trust that you will do your special work and when I turn my ignition key everything is working perfectly."* I have no doubt - well - just a little creeps in but I brush it aside - I must be positive and trust. In the car I sit holding it in the Light for a few minutes then turn on the ignition - a miracle happens - the light goes out this time - all is well once more. Believe me - it is true! Once more a blessed thank you to the Angels passes my lips.

TO THE CHURCH OF ST MARY, OARE

Anything else which occurs today will seem to be routine in comparison to my Cosmic experience, but perhaps a return to normality by visiting the church at Oare will be a good idea before I drive back to Wellington, and of course it is a church dedicated to Mary. From Porlock I take the A39 west and am soon driving up Porlock Hill in second, then first gear! After a few miles I turn off on a narrow road, dropping steeply down into the valley for the village of Oare, parking adjacent to the church. Oare Church was made famous by R. D. Blackmore in his well known novel '*Lorna Doone*'. This is the tragic story of how Lorna Doone of the Doone clan of local outlaws, falls in love with a yeoman farmer by the name of John Ridd. On their wedding day in Oare Church she is shot and killed by Carver Doone one of the clan. Many Lorna Doone fans visit Oare Church and the surrounding area each year, in order to identify places in the book.

St Mary's Church is small with several interesting features. One on the south side is a piscine in the shape of a head held by two hands, an apparent representation of St Decuman, whom we shall meet on the third day of my pilgrimaging in this area. A further point of interest is the most unusual buzzard lectern which was installed in 1999 after their original eagle lectern was stolen. The basin of the font is very old, dating from the twelfth century, but is resting on a rather plain nineteenth century base and stem. Certainly a fascinating little church but I must not linger.

EXFORD CHURCH OF ST SALVYN

Although it is getting late, as I drive back through Exford and come to the Parish Church, I just have to pop in. This delightful little church was originally dedicated to Mary Magdalene, but now to St Salvyn. To my eye the stained glass windows are a wonderful feature. Some of the saints illustrated are; St Salvyn, St Mary Magdalene, St George, St Francis and St Joseph of Arimathea. The information board reminds us that the Christianity which came across from Wales and Ireland, was not of the Roman church which converted Saxon England, but had its roots in Celtic tradition. This church is said to stand on a prehistoric trackway between Barnstaple and Bridgwater, which travels across the hill-tops of Exmoor, perhaps to link with The Quantocks.

I am home at the end of another amazing day with the added bonus that I am not soaking wet! I can hardly believe that earlier this morning I was looking at the notice at Culbone Hill in a right flummox, wondering what to do about my sacred Ceremony. I am filled with a feeling of deep peace and inner elation as I mull over events. The Temple designed by the Higher Powers and planned 11,000 years ago, is holding the energies of an ancient Atlantean civilization - a race of Golden Ones. By coming into descent - by being earthed though still in its Etheric state - it has fulfilled its destiny to date.

It has taken its rightful place within the confines of the ancient Druidic Tree Temple on Culbone Hill. It was here that the Divine plan was put into action by the Sumerian Master 4,000 BC. It was here 2,000 years ago, that the Lady Mary performed a Cosmic Ceremony to open up a vortex of Light for the future. It was here in AD 25, that the Master Jesus put his blessed signature to the Divine plan through the 'Flame of Caring'. Me - I am just an instrument playing my part guided by the Masters of Light - hoping I get it right! And it will be passed on - the Sacred Light - the Golden Flame - will be passed down from pilgrim to pilgrim, to prepare this ancient land for the New Jerusalem. The Light of all Creation will be spread far and wide - and it is good. I am truly blessed - we are ALL truly blessed.

THE SEQUEL. RETURN TO CULBONE/K'SH'B'H

I promised you a follow up to my pilgrimage to Culbone. Here it is - and what a sequel!

LILLYCOMBE HOUSE.

It is early in March 2010 and I have recently returned from a White Eagle retreat based at - you will never guess - Lillycombe House! This retreat was undertaken many months after my trip to K'SH'B'H/Culbone, and when I was told of the venue just two weeks beforehand, bells began to ring. Of course staying in Lillycombe House would give official access to the whole estate THIS was my opportunity to visit the Culbone Stone and Culbone Hill settlement. I shall never cease to be amazed at Divine planning. Lillycombe House is set in the most idyllic situation, nestling on a hillside against a backdrop of coniferous trees, with views down to the Oare valley. On arrival and full of joy I kept saying thank you, thank you and received: *"My dear little Light Worker. You knew we wouldn't let you down. You are so welcome to this sacred area. You have returned to us. We will endeavour to inspire you that you may find the ancient settlement and the newly earthed Atlantean Temple."*

TO THE CULBONE STONE AND TEMPLE SITE.

During our retreat, an opportunity arose that a small group of dedicated White Eagle pilgrims were able to set off for the Culbone Stone and the Temple settlement. I had told them little except for a brief history of Culbone, of which one or two were aware, and that I was unable to access the Culbone Stone the previous year. I kept it that way, not just because my information was not ready to be shared, but also that I was curious as to what their own insights would pick up. On entering the woodland site I asked the ancient ones permission and for a blessing on our sacred day. We walked in silence. Then we saw it - the ancient stone - in a little clearing ahead of us. For me - elation. It was smaller than I remembered from my past visit which was some while back. On reaching the incised stone I rested my hand on it offering a benediction. It was exuding extremely powerful vibrations. I turned to see a grassy well-defined circular clearing surrounded by trees close-by. I told the group that this was the ancient Druidic Tree Temple which it was, but knew it was specifically the position of the earthed Atlantean Temple. It was at this point in time I realized that the Culbone Hill settlement spread over many acres and would have encompassed the land where Lillycombe House stands today. This was a vast Druidic Ceremonial site of great importance.

The Culbone Stone at the Culbone Hill Settlement

We stood in a circle linking hands for an attunement. In the centre I had laid on the earth a large quartz crystal, a small white quartz crystal, a pink quartz crystal and a phial of water from Chalice Well. My prayer recognized and blessed the Sumerian Master, the Master Jesus, the Lady Mary and Mary Magdalene, each of whom had visited this ancient place and undertaken a Divine sacred act. Then followed a heartfelt acknowledgement of the 'Flame of Caring' which had been established here by Jesus the Christ. At that moment I felt we had reignited this sacred flame. Thank you my precious pilgrims. I silently offered recognition of, and salutation to, the Atlantean Temple now earthed at Culbone Hill.

After an exploration of the ancient site where we discovered the rather sorry remains of the stone row, we all gathered around the Culbone Stone for a final Divine link. I can reveal some of our insights received. Directly below the sacred stone secreted deep in the Earth's core, is an immense diamond shaped Star Crystal - the Earth Star. The Culbone Stone is a conductor for the Cosmic Light which links to this Earth Star Crystal. A portal has been opened up and the Light from the Christ Star has pierced and reactivated the ancient Culbone Stone. The Archangel Michael was present with a multitude of Heavenly Beings - profound gratitude was their expression. At the close of our Ceremony I embedded the small white quartz and pink quartz crystals within the grass at the mossy base of the stone. On top of the stone I placed the large piece of white quartz pouring over it a little of the water from Chalice Well. Through our dedication we have undertaken the work of the Holy Grail.

Inscribed on the Culbone Stone is the ancient symbol of a wheeled cross with an extended arm leading below the circle, set at an angle of NNW/SSE. This intrigued and puzzled us. Many possibilities were considered. One thought - could it be a directional sign indicating the route to Culbone valley and the coast just below the site? This idea would seem to coincide with another of our group who knew of a navigational aid for sailing of similar design today, called the Breton Plotter. This could in turn link to my own knowledge, that the Celtic Cross was a mathematical instrument which the ancients used for navigation via the Celestial World, and in particularly the Pole Star. However my immediate response, which came out of insight at the time, was that the ancient symbol here was representative of the Christ Star directing the Cosmic Light through the stone to the Earth Star Crystal, and identifies with the 'Flame of Caring.' My inner voice told me *'the ancient symbol denotes the Flame of Eternal Life.'*

As we left the Culbone Stone a devoted member of our little band of pilgrims felt inspired to close the gateway. She gently rang her two small cymbals three times, and on the third occasion the sound came back to her. She was positive that it was not an echo. She was aware of a Being dressed in white who felt like a spiritual warrior. Could this have been St Michael?

In the quiet of my room at Lillycombe House later, I received some words from White Eagle, after which I had another 'weep-in'. The message is rather long so I give you the beginning and the end - the relevant sections for our day:

WHITE EAGLE

"My dear child we would never let you down you know this. We thank you. We thank you ALL for the sacred work you have undertaken today. The Light is sealed at Culbone. The Stone is once more activated and will be used for future work to enhance and reinvigorate your precious planet. We thank you - we thank you - we bless you all. You have carried out the instructions to the letter. The Light is returning. All is as you left it. All is well. Then White Eagle closes with….Keep on keeping on dearest ones. We thank you ALL. Amen."

TO CULBONE CHURCH

At the end of our retreat five of us who stayed over for a few days undertook a walk to Culbone Church. Being based at Lillycombe House we were able to reach the valley of K'SH'B'H from the top of the estate through a series of fields and woodland. For myself it was particularly interesting, to see how the landscape between the valley and the settlement on the hill linked up. It was the beginning of March and in the churchyard pure white snowdrops were displaying in their thousands under the trees and long slender hazelnut catkins were dancing in the light wind and shining in the sunshine. In the peaceful confines of the ancient church I received the following:

FROM A DIVINE SOURCE

"You are so welcome dear pilgrims. This place - this valley - you know very well. We are conscious of your two sisters who have remained in Lillycombe House. They are with you in spirit. You know you are all blessed. We add a sacred blessing for all your endeavours and your service to humanity. We so welcome you dear travellers of old. This is YOUR valley - you know it - you will recognize it. It is part of your soul wisdom and memory. The Master Jesus was here - our beloved Master - with his Mary. The Magdalene energy fills this sacred valley. Walk on my precious pilgrims into the Light - take the 'Flame of Caring' - MY 'Flame of Caring' - forward into the new Age of Enlightenment. The Rose will ever bloom in the sacred heart and the Lily will open to reveal its true nature - the Flame of Eternal Life. You dear child, of course know of your sacred journey here with our beloved Mary and Jesus in a long gone age. Your essence still remains imbued in this sacred valley. Amen."

When 'MY Flame of Caring' was mentioned in conjunction with 'the Master Jesus was here' it indicates to me that this communication is from the very highest source - from the God energy.

Our 'Heart of the Rose' retreat under the guidance of beloved White Eagle, drew to a close with a final attunement and sincere gratitude to the Masters of Light and the Angels. Many impressions were received, too much to write of here. Incredibly through shared insight, we learnt that the Sumerian Master was White Eagle in a previous incarnation. The presence of the Master Jesus with Mary Magdalene, the Lady Mary and other Beings of Light were keenly felt. At home a final word from Beloved Mary says it all:

MARY

"My Child, my dearest child. Your Light is my Light and my Light is your Light. We are all as one. We know of your profound joy at this time spent in retreat with your companions of the heart. Again we are all of one heart dearest Naomi. Your Heart is my Heart and my Heart is your Heart.

The new revelations at K'SH'B'H have I believe, exceeded your expectations. The work here for the time being is complete dearest one. The Temple is earthed. The Light has been sealed for ever through the Culbone Stone. It is as it is. The great Cosmic Light from the Sun-Star has been directed by the Masters and Angelic Beings through the stone to the great Star Crystal at the Earth's centre. This ancient site at K'SH'B'H is as you have recognized, a vast Ceremonial complex, incorporating the sacred Atlantean Temple of which the Culbone Stone is the guardian. It is a stone of immense power which conducts the energetic Cosmic flow. You dearest child have played your part well. It is now time to be still and absorb the revelations which have been allowed you.

(I ask of the symbol upon the Culbone Stone and receive) *It is a mystic symbol of great antiquity. It is an indication that the stone is directing the Great Cosmic energy to Earth. From the Great Sun the Light shines forth to re-energize your planet. The axis of your Earth has changed over millennia and what is represented in this symbol is the ancient directional line of the Earth's axis at the time of the Sumerian Master 6,000 years ago. It is an indicator of the flow of Cosmic energy. Dearest ones, through your Mission at this time, the energetic love element has been restored to this ancient place. The sacrament of love, devotion and healing is forever embedded within the very soil here at Culbone. We thank you my child, all the Masters of the Light thank you for your dedication to duty - to your devotion to the Light.*"

Postcript. It is my belief that the site at Culbone Hill had been closed deliberately by the Brethren of the Light in order that only the genuine pilgrim will heed its call. For access contact Mr. Bristow, the Lillycombe Estate Manager on (01643) 862534 or The Exmoor National Park Authority on (01398) 323665. Don't forget, you will be on private land so treat it with respect and enter the ancient grove with a loving heart.

CHAPTER 15
THE NORTH SOMERSET COAST
Ancient Landing Places

On leaving Culbone Hill settlement, the Lady Mary and her family made their way down through the valley to the coast and took a sailing boat to Blue Anchor Bay, followed by an overland journey to the Hungerford Druidic settlement. Although not fully recovered from her illness at K'SH'B'H Mary wished to perform a Ceremony of Light at that site. No Ceremony is required of me. The key focus for this third pilgrimage from my Wellington base in the summer of 2009 is to reach this settlement and search for the Holy Well. From here I shall follow Mary's route back to the coast at Watchet where she left for Kilve.

ST MARTIN OF TOURS CHURCH, ELWORTHY.

Where HAS our summer gone? As I set off today it is cold, very wet and the rain is incessant. I travel the same route from Wellington as on my two previous days to Cow Castle and Culbone Hill, but this time turn north at Elworthy for Hungerford

My first stop is the Elworthy Church of St Martin of Tours. I park up on the narrow lane close-by. The church is sheltered within a very overgrown churchyard. Opening the rather rickety gate I walk the narrow path to the entrance through tall wet grass. In the porch a notice tells me this church is in the care of the Churches Conservation Trust. My heart sinks - would it be closed? I hesitantly try the door and to my delight it opens. A look around this charming little church no longer used for regular worship, shows how well looked after it is by the trust. Its history dates back to the thirteenth century and it is endowed with well restored medieval and Jacobean woodwork in the chancel screen. The stained glass window over the altar depicts the four Gospels; St Matthew with a bull, St Mark with the lion, St Luke with an angel and St John the Divine with his eagle. I spend a short time in the silence before I make my exit.

Standing in the church porch looking out, my vision beholds the most magnificent yew tree. Eyeing it up then taking a walk around it, my estimation is that its girth must span at least twenty feet. I am guessing it to be well over 1,000 years old. Its position identifies it as a guardian of this ancient churchyard. One of its lower trunks is embedded around a very old stone coffin of which little is left visible. I reach into my pocket and pick out a heart-shaped white stone: *"I have something for you dear yew"* and lay it gently at its base. I hear:

DEVA OF THE YEW TREE

"Thank you pilgrim. How long have I been here? Many many years. As a sapling I first broke forth from Mother Earth to the light of day. As a sapling I saw much activity in this ancient churchyard. I grew and over the years have nurtured and protected this sacred place. Thank you for recognizing me pilgrim."

Aren't these ancient trees wonderful? They go nowhere yet can we imagine what they must have seen in their lifetime. Making my way back through the churchyard, I am aware that my feet in their walking shoes and my legs and trousers are saturated, and this is just the beginning of my day! So be it. Back in the car I turn on the engine and warm blower to try and dry my trousers a little. Shoes I give up on.

Continuing my journey, I drive under arches of dripping trees which seem to be hanging rather forlornly in the constant rain. I expect though they welcome the refreshing manna from Heaven. I remember on one occasion I was walking in the hills of Mid Wales, when I was informed by the little people that rain: *'refreshes us as it falls on our faces and reinvigorates growth.'* Perhaps we too can express the joy the nature spirits feel when the rain comes! Passing the entrance to Combe Sydenham Country Park, it is not long before I reach the pretty village of Monksilver with its many thatched cottages. I park near the Notley Arms Public House for the church. In the pub car park are five tethering posts for horses - an innovation I haven't come across before. This is the life - the country life! Such an excellent way to arrive for ones pint or ones pimms!

ALL SAINTS CHURCH, MONKSILVER

The path to the church is lined with pink rose bushes. There is a rather ornate Victorian memorial cross resting on the foundation of what was once a medieval cross. At its base are four small stone figures - the bull, lion, angel and eagle - the four Gospels portrayed again.

Above the porch in a niche is a little statuette of the Madonna and Child. I leave an offering of a small bunch of wild flowers for Mary in the ancient stoop in the porch. On entering the church and facing the chancel, one is immediately struck with the asymmetry of chancel and chancel arch - a most unusual feature. It would seem that at some time in the past, the original south wall of the nave was demolished and a new structure built, altering the shape of the nave, thus giving the irregular formation high up in the roof. It is reckoned that some parts of the church date back to the twelfth century - the wagon roof being one. I am drawn to a narrow stained glass window set back within the frame of a white stone arch. It is quite beautiful and shows a haloed St Mary robed in scarlet and cloaked in blue. I sit in one of the Victorian pews, my thoughts turning to Beloved Mary. Monksilver Church is just four miles south of Hungerford where she stayed and by now I am feeling her presence.

IN SEARCH OF HUNGERFORD DRUIDIC SETTLEMENT AND THE HOLY WELL.

Moving on, I leave the B3188 at Fair Cross and take the country road to Hungerford. Mary tells me that there is nothing left in the landscape of the ancient settlement. However, I will see if I can identify its position. First to the HOLY WELL which I understand from Mary was once dedicated to her. It is clearly marked on the map, but when I turn in at the appropriate place by the Washford River, I am confronted by a private road to Torre Fishery with a '*no entry*' sign. I shall leave that for now and see if I can access it from other side of the river. Up and down the minor road on its opposite bank I go without seeing any entry point to the river. Local pub - that's the place - they'll know where the Holy Well is. The barmaid looks at me quite blankly when I ask her. I indicate on the map where it is supposed to be - still nothing. It would appear that the three gentlemen sitting at the bar have also never heard of it: "*Was it St. Decumans's Holy Well I was looking for?*" they enquired. I bid them a friendly farewell. At a house nearby, although the lady is not aware of a Holy Well in the vicinity, she does tell me of a way to reach the river from the little road I have just come down. Back I go and discover a small lay-by next to an open field, which entrance was blocked by a lorry on my previous search!

Parked up I set off, following the line of the river at the edge of a wet muddy cornfield, looking for any sign of a well. By now I am paddling in the mire and totally give up trying to keep dry - I failed with that one at Elworthy Church and of course it's still raining! The river itself is fast flowing and looking very muddied obviously due to all the rain washing the muck off the fields. The only thing which brightens the day is the mass of purple marsh thistles along the river-bank. Eventually I reach a small wooden bridge which crosses the river. The energies are feeling stronger now. I stand on the bridge underneath an overhanging hazelnut tree with my dowsing crystal to hand and discover St Mary's Holy Well was very close to this bridge. Taking a good look around I can see no sign of it - our blessed Lady lost in the annals of time once again. I pour a little of the water retrieved from the River Barle at Cow Castle into the Washford River and drop in a beautiful shell from Holywell beach in Cornwall, with a blessing for Beloved Mary and the ancient ones.

As I turn to leave I see on the hill-top above the valley a clump of tall trees which draws my attention. Mary has indicated that the settlement was close to the river. Looking at the present landscape, the Washford River would have been much broader 2,000 years before, evidenced by the width of the river valley today. Thus, the positioning of this clump of trees on the hill would seem to fit the bill for a settlement close to the river back then. I take the field path away from the river to the road below the hill-top. Diligent searching for the ancient HUNGERFORD site sees me blocked at every turn. It seems impossible to reach and I shall have to leave it for today, as in the appalling weather conditions, to carry on looking would be pointless. I make my way back to my car. I vow to return and eventually do in the following year, this time on a bright sunny June day. On this occasion I park in the village of Roadwater and walk back to a narrow road which I consider will take me to the clump of trees. I am walking in a very deep ancient green lane - roots of beech trees embedded in banks of red sandstone, rise twenty feet above my head. After consulting my map I turn right at the top of the lane onto a dirt track, and soon come to an opening in a large field of ripening wheat just past a derelict ivy-clad house. At this point I see several enormous oak trees alongside the track and also on the opposite side of the field. I am positive this is the ancient settlement of Hungerford. I am so pleased and somewhat relieved at my success, and thank Mary for her guidance. The thrilling sound of a skylark and the more muted yet distinctive song of the yellow hammer, come across on the warm summer air. From this site I can see the Quantock range of hills across open countryside - Mary's destination on landing at Kilve. Before moving on, I embed a pure white quartz crystal at the base of one of the old oaks with a blessing.

Hungerford Settlement with The Quantock Hills in the background

ST DECUMAN'S CHURCH

From Hungerford Mary's river journey took her and her family through St Decumans to Watchet. Returning to my 2009 pilgrimage, I drive the B3190 to this little hamlet as I wish to visit the church and Holy Well. St Decuman came to my notice at Oare Church on Exmoor and his Holy Well was mentioned by the folk in the Hungerford Pub. So I am curious. It would seem that Decuman was one of the many Celtic saints who brought the Christian faith to the South West of England in the fifth and sixth centuries. Legend tells that he sailed on a raft with his cow across the waters from Wales.

I am parked on a wide stretch of unused road which originally led to the paper mill, and take a rather hazardous walk under huge trees which are spewing off branches, left, right and centre, in the now gale force wind. A narrow back lane leads me to the church. As I approach I notice that the wall of the churchyard is round, signalling its antiquity. From the outside the little church is charming, with whitewashed walls and a tall castellated stone tower. As at Monksilver Church, the path through the churchyard is lined with rose bushes.

I enter its quiet sanctuary and am in awe. The church dates from the thirteenth century and has a wealth of gems. Among them the wagon roof supporting angel bosses and the fifteenth century font showing carved angels. Just behind the pulpit are two small well preserved statues built into the stone pillars, one of St George in armour slaying the dragon, the other of St Anthony with his staff. The stained glass windows depicting many different saints are magnificent. One rather special one is of St Decuman (*Monk and Hermit*), St Caradoc (*Bishop and Confessor*) and St Petroc (*Abbot*). Some of the interesting female saints portrayed are; St Hilda - Abbess of Whitby, St Margaret of Antioch, St Catherine of Alexandria and St Anne. I find my way to the Lady Chapel. Here the stained glass window over the altar illustrates Mary with the Angel Gabriel and the words '*Hail Mary Full Of Grace*'. Archangel Michael is watching over Mary. I sit in the stillness of this little chapel with the wind howling outside. Mary is very close to me now, but it is St Decuman who comes to speak with me today:

ST DECUMAN

"Thank you pilgrim for visiting this church dedicated to my name. For a very long time I travelled this ancient land of Britain. Evenutally I settled at Watchet near here. I had my cell and taught the Celtic form of Christianty - the words from the old times. I was well versed in Roman Catholicism, but was in a position in this sacred part of Britain, to be able to combine the teachings, erring in the favour of the old teachings of this ancient land. Our dear Mary is with me and wishes me to acknowledge her. She tells me that you and she have a Mission of great importance - of great value to the future of humanity. Blessed Mary. Beloved Mary. Our Beloved. Most blest of all women. I honour you - your wisdom and compassion. Amen. Go now my child to my well. I will walk with you."

I thank St Decuman for his words and the Lady Mary for her presence.

ST DECUMAN'S HOLY WELL

St Decuman's Holy Well

I have truly walked into a little bit of Heaven on Earth. Only a few hundred yards from the church, down a quiet tree-lined lane, I discover the Holy Well. Nothing could have prepared me for the mystical beauty of this sacred place. Its wooden framed entrance porch, set in old stone, has a small wooden cross above a sign '*St Decuman's Holy Well*'. I unlatch the little gate and walk down the steps through a garden of natural loveliness. The well has two small stone-pillared sides topped with a slab of rock and is surrounded with greenery. Inside its dark recess, crystal clear water from a natural spring has filled a deep pool. I immerse my hands in the healing waters, sprinkling a little over my head. With a blessing for St Decuman and the water deva I leave a small piece of white quartz, one of those I found on the beach at St Just in Roseland, in the soft green moss at the entrance to the well. The water trickles on through the ferns in the dell to fill a little lake in the woodland on the hillside below. There is an arbour with wooden trellis covered with honeysuckle and rose of sharon, Mary Magdalene's flower. I sit on a curved stone seat and give time for contemplation. Just in front of me I see a large stone with a plaque reading '*God breathed and man became a living soul. Genesis.*' Tear myself away from this sanctuary I must.

MARY'S JOURNEY TO THE COAST

I drive the mile or so to Watchet. Today the Washford River runs into a harbour filled with small sailing boats - the whole area being a hive of activity. In Mary's time the river flowed out into the Bristol Channel. My thoughts turn to Mary and I picture her with Naomi, Jesus and Joseph, sailing forth for their next destination - Kilve. Today as I look across Blue Anchor Bay, the waters of the Bristol Channel are churned up into white horses by the high wind. I can't help thinking how wild and desolate this part of the coastline would have been in Mary's time. Even though the little party were not heading into open seas, but staying within the relative protection of the coast, the journey could have been quite risky.

ST ANDREW'S CHURCH

I am returning south to Wellington at the end of an eventful day. Driving through the pretty village of Old Cleeve, which was on Mary's route from the coast to Hungerford, I spot the Parish Church which I learn is dedicated to St Andrew, and decide to pay a quick visit. I am so pleased I did - it really is a lovely little church. The present building dates from around the fifteenth century, though it is recorded that there has been a church on the site since the early eleventh century. There is much of interest but it is the altar cloth which draws my attention. It is quite spectacular, being *most* beautifully embroidered in red, green and gold and bearing the fish symbol of St Andrew. The words emblazoned on its front panel read '*Follow me and I will make you Fishers of Men*'. For me the Master Jesus of the Piscean Age, is moving in ever closer as I travel further east through the mystical South West - maybe in preparation for ancient Glastonbury. The Mothers Union tapestry hanging in blue and gold is decorated with lilies for Our Lady.

CLEEVE ABBEY

Cleeve Abbey which is in the care of English Heritage is close-by. The abbey originally occupied by the Cistercian White Monks, although in a ruinous state, is a most impressive complete range of monastic cloistered buildings. It escaped destruction in the Dissolution of the Monasteries because it was easily adaptable for secular use. One can visit the abbey as part of a journey on the West Somerset Railway, which steams its way from Bishop's Lydeard to Minehead. I have no time for a visit today but have done so on a previous occasion. I could tell you a long salutary tale of a visit a dear friend and I made to Cleeve Abbey. How after both checking our watches without our glasses on, and coming up with the same incorrect time, we missed the last train back to Bishop's Lydeard, a distance of approximately ten miles - AND, after the initial panic as there were no buses on a Sunday, how we gratefully accepted a lift from two charitable elderly gentlemen - voluntary workers on the railway - AND, how when we got back to Bishops Lydeard found the car park locked, or so we thought, and our car the wrong side of the gates - AND, how we were laughing like drains driving back to Devon to her house where I was to spend the night - AND, how we said, no way are we going to tell D...her husband - AND, how on stepping over the threshold, the first thing my friend says was: "D...*you'll never guess what happened to us today*"........but I wont!

As I drive into Wellington the stormy weather has abated and the sun puts in an appearance. For me it is the end of a long wet tiring day as I prepare for a lovely soak in the bath. For Mary at the close of her day at Kilve - no such luxury!

FURTHER EXPLORATIONS OF THE NORTH SOMERSET COAST

We connect to the Lady Mary's pilgrimage on the coast near Kilve. As I reach this stage in her journey, it is September 2009. I can't believe the year's wheel has turned full circle since I was here in September 2008, very much at the start of my Mission and just as I was beginning to comprehend the true nature of my commitment. At that time, once again I was staying in Wellington and planning a day's walk. I had no preconceived idea as to where, until on getting my map out I spy a place named Holford (Holyford) to the east of The Quantock Hills, and a few miles inland from the North Somerset coast. I was suddenly alerted to the possibility of Mary having been in that area. Further more, previously a friend had mentioned a lovely old church at Kilve with a nearby derelict chantry. Suddenly I knew this was where I was to go. My unplanned day was now planned. Before I leave I relax in my quiet space for an inner moment with Beloved Mary:

MARY

"Dear child go with your instinct. Go with your intuition today and I will be your guide. I will journey with you. Bless you my child."

The most beautiful blue light surrounds me. Mary is part of me - that Divine part. At this most precious time in my life, her physical presence is very real. For she and I have a Mission which will not be quelled. I offer a blessing.

TO THE VILLAGE OF KILVE

I begin my pilgrimage north from Wellington and hello - it is raining. Now I am no stranger to the wet stuff on my travels, as you will have noticed, so here goes. From Bishops Lydeard the road follows the line of the West Somerset Railway. At Williton I turn right onto the A39 and on reaching Kilve take a left for the church and the old chantry. A narrow lane takes me to a grassy area where I park up. I have passed the little church and see that it is dedicated to St Mary - what a surprise! I have also passed the derelict chantry which is unfortunately covered in scaffolding. A local lady walking her dog, tells me that it is owned by English Heritage and the villagers are up in arms, because it has been like this for five years. Regarding the church, I ask her whether there is any information inside about its history. She tells me there is nothing at present but that a new leaflet is being drafted. On realizing my interest and enthusiasm, she offers to send this to me when it is done - how very kind of her. I leave my name and address. An interesting 'coincidence' - I learn that her name is Mair the Welsh version of Mary. This dear lady tells me of two more 'Mary' churches in the area - at Holford and East Quantoxhead. I look forward to paying them a visit at some time. For now I am here in this unique place. I am already beginning to feel totally at peace with its soft gentle energies. A wood pigeon is cooing from a nearby tree. A lone horse and rider trot by. All is well with the world.

As I step from the car the sound of water from a little stream running through the village catches my ear - I shall go there first. I put in my pack a bottle of water from the River Dart on Dartmoor. I make my way across the grass to the stream. Standing below the tree canopy I watch the water trickle by. A shaft of sunlight is miraculously peeping through the trees, producing countless little sparkling pin-points of starlight on the surface of the water. I am captivated: *"Dear stream I offer you in love a gift from Dartmoor. I ask that the energies of this water blends with your energies bringing healing to the land."* Permission to collect some water is granted. I sit on a bench seat close to the stream and the voice of the water speaks with me:

WATER DEVA

"Dear pilgrim. We thank you We bless you. We accept with gratitude your offering. Gratitude is dear to our hearts and this concept of gratitude is also dear to your heart pilgrim. We are aware how appreciative you yourself are at each opportunity afforded you in life to heal and to bless. Once again we bless you dear pilgrim Go on your way now for you are to visit the little church. Mary is waiting for you."

My words: *"Bless you Deva of the Stream. Let your pure waters run for ever free and clear."*

I walk back along the lane collecting some beautiful white and pink flowers for Mary on my way, feeling that they should be roses. As I pass the old chantry I take a photograph, trying to avoid the scaffolding around it, which proves to be quite impossible. On closer inspection I see that it is the scaffolding which is holding up the walls! Without it the ruins would have collapsed a long time ago. I later learn the chantry dates from 1329 and that it was gutted by a fire in the mid-nineteenth century, hence its sorry state today. Judging by the lovely Gothic arches still standing, it must have been most impressive in its heyday. I am sure it could be restored - maybe the will is not there or money not available.

THE PARISH CHURCH OF ST MARY THE VIRGIN, KILVE

I reach the little whitewashed St Mary Church nestling within the confines of its churchyard. As I go through the lych gate my eyes alight on a flowerbed in the centre of the grass full of - yes you've guessed it - pink roses. You see I needn't have worried about not having a rose for Mary: "*Thank you*" I voice to the Universe. I enter the church porch, where set into the thick stone walls is a small window with a view out to the rose garden. On the window ledge I lay down my flowers and one of the many shells I collected from Llansteffan beach in Carmarthenshire, which I think will be a lovely link with the two coasts - South Wales and North Somerset, offering them with my deepest love for Beloved Mary.

In the sacredness of the church I am in my haven of peace - MY haven of peace - as I am feeling instant recognition. As Naomi, I have travelled this way and perhaps this ancient church has been built over where I've walked? Or perhaps I have been here in a later incarnation when the church was built? The answer comes with Mary's words later.

Stained Glass Window in the Church of St Mary the Virgin, Kilve, depicting Joseph of Arimathea and the Two Cruets (see Chapter 17)

Mair was true to her word and sent me the first draft of a church leaflet, but there is no indication as to the age of the church. The font dates back to the twelfth century so that gives us a clue. Through the centuries there have been alterations and additions. An example is the very tiny bell tower which was erected in the seventeenth century. Before that time apparently the two bells were housed in a separate thatched building. The stained glass window in the east is quite beautiful and depicts from left to right; St Peter, Yeshu and St John. Joseph of Arimithea is represented in another window on the south wall with the words '*Joseph of Arimathea - a counselor a good man and just. He begged the body of Jesus and laid it in the sepulchre.*' I was inspired at seeing this representation of Joseph of Arimathea in a church dedicated to St Mary and so close to Glastonbury. I notice in the bottom right hand corner of the window are the two cruets purported to contain the blood and sweat of Christ, which it is claimed Joseph brought to Glastonbury (see Chapter 17). My thoughts of the time - is it possible that the little group on pilgrimage from the Holy Land were here? The significance is beginning to sink in - can I really have been guided to this place? Oh ye of little faith! I 'know' the answer which is coming from Beloved Mary. I sit down on one of the ancient pews and wait:

MARY

"My dear and beloved child, you have now reached this ancient centre as part of your pilgrimage to my heart. I thank you and bless you for the offerings of the shell and beautiful flowers which you call wild flowers, picked for me in the lane. How does one differentiate between wild and cultivated flowers? For each has its inner and outer beauty, and each is tended lovingly by the nature spirits. Each has its place in the grand scheme of things. I digress - back to the now and reconnecting to the past.

Dearest one, where you are now is where we made land, not further north as you at first surmised. (I had considered the River Parret at Burnham-on-Sea). *Part of our journey from K'SH'B'H had been by land and part by sea. You will discover more as you explore more. For the here and now you are in this sacred church dedicated to me, but most important, you are at the very place where we came ashore from our sea journey. We hugged the coast because the sea was wild and rough, and we were most grateful to be safely landed. We hauled up on the shore which was further inland at that time. The shoreline was very close to where this little church is now. Joseph was our strong provider and protector and soon we were all settled in a little haven of safety close-by. It has gone now, but not far from here was a little building where travellers from the sea were sheltered.* (My mind stepped in and I wondered where). *We were made most welcome. We were given sustenance and some straw to sleep on for the night. We stayed here resting for a little while until I felt strong enough to continue my journey, for I had been ill at K'SH'B'H. You dearest Naomi, and beloved Jesus, were my dear children and helpmates, and did everything in your young power to care for me.*

While we were here it was an opportunity to bless this precious land once more, and we were able to do a little Ceremony to bring the Light of all time to this special place. We have landed safely and we are truly blessed. Now it is our turn to offer that sacred blessing of thanks. In our prayers we turned to the great ones on high, the Angelic Beings and the Masters of Light, those beloved Brethren who hold this precious Earth in their loving arms. They, the ones on high, protect and nurture this Planet and forever it will be.

I am to tell you that your beloved White Eagle is one of those close to the throne of the Most High. Of course his name is only identified as that for one American Indian incarnation and his manifestation through the blessed Minesta - Grace Cooke in this lifetime As you know he has had many incarnations working with the purist Light energies, some of which you and he were very close in love and purity. In more than one lifetime he has been your friend and mentor. You know of an Egyptian incarnation whereas Naomi, my daughter, you were part of the band of followers of that Essene Brethren in the Holy Land. As a young girl you journeyed to Egypt to be a Priestess in the Temple of Kom Ombo. My daughter, Is-Ra (White Eagle), was then your counselor and you have reason right to this day to be grateful for his gentle presence and benevolent heart. For you, as a very young girl away from the nurturing of the home and family life and familiar things, at first found it very difficult to settle to a life of almost monastic purity. You were used to running in the fields and walking in the sunlight and under the stars. But in time, you dear daughter, came to realize the intense privilege of your pathway and the opportunity afforded you in the Temple life. You learnt much about astronomy and the star patterns. You learnt of higher philosophies of life and ultimately much about yourself.

When you were age fourteen years, this journey you are exploring today, was put before you and you felt overjoyed at the opportunity to travel and be free and journey to the ancient land of our ancestors, of which you had learned much. So dear beloved daughter here we are, you and I once again in very close contact, and it is good. I bless you my child and wish you to continue your pilgrimage. I will guide you."

Mary brought this special message to a close with a blessing of her hand on her heart: "Oh Mary my beloved one, thank you for all your insights and for the revelations which you've shared with me. I bless you. My dear and beloved family and Brethren in the Land of Light - I thank you and bless you." A sense of gratitude is filling my heart and I become aware of the gentle hue of the pink rose, Mary's symbol, and my own peace rose, at my heart centre. This was when I learnt that Mary had been ill at K'SH'B'H. Here also Mary confirms what she told me at Buckfast Abbey quite recently, that Is-Ra was my benevolent mentor and support at a Temple in Egypt during my incarnation as Naomi.

My long attunement is finished - a still silence falls over this sanctuary. It is time to go as the energies have dropped and I am feeling a little chilled. I leave, closing the heavy oak door quietly behind me and feel the welcome warmth of the sun on my face. From the churchyard there are lovely views through the trees and out over open countryside. This area is obviously popular with walkers for there are many footpath signs, one leading right past the church.

DISCOVERY AT KILVE BEACH

As I make my way the few hundred yards back to my car, a few spots of rain are falling and by the time I reach it, the Heavens have opened. So perhaps some lunch while I wait for the rain to abate is a good plan. In the churchyard I had found a small pale grey feather and some cyclamen. I picked three pink and three white flowers and with the feather make a small posy for my next offering, putting it a little vase of water in the boot of my car.

The rain has ceased and this is my cue to make the short walk to the beach of Kilve. From the lane, I take a gravel track to the top of the beach. I now have views around the coast to Minehead, across the water to Lundy Island, and in the far distance can see the Welsh coastline of my youth. Walking is over ankle twisting pebbles which is not easy. Some of the pebbles however are rather lovely and I collect a few small white ones and a couple of beautiful shells. The water even from a long way off looks muddy and uninviting. The little village stream has ended its journey running into a large pool at the top of the beach. I follow the foreshore to a low grassy cliff-top where there is a bench-seat. The skies are still overcast and this dreariness is reflected in the land and sea all around. I sit down for a spiritual link. I have a vision of a small sailing craft close to shore, coming into a safe estuary, which is now Kilve Beach. The boat contains the little party of voyagers - Mary, Jesus, Naomi and Joseph. My impression is that Joseph is at the helm and navigating, as he would have known this coastline intimately from years of travelling in South West Britain.

Leaving the beach I am taking a different path. On a rise enclosed within a small copse of trees, I come across a small ruined circular building covered in ivy. On closer inspection I see the walls are very well built, each stone squared off quite precisely. The shape of the building is unusual, in that it appears to have been purposefully designed and built with a slight inward slant. I wonder what is at the top. I claw my way up hanging on to tree branches and tufts of grass until I reach what looks to be an old well in the centre of the building - there is nothing else. At the base again I sit on a tree stump in a quiet little dingle, trying to puzzle out what on earth this building was for. Perhaps an old fort - it would certainly have been a good strategic position to keep watch over the Bristol Channel. Whatever - I never do find out - but this is not important. What IS important is that realization dawns - this was built over the safe house where Mary and her party stayed overnight after their landing: *"Thank you Mary, thank you for your impression."*

MARY

"Well beloved one you have found our resting place. That is all I have to say for now. Bless you. Goodbye - until we meet again."

Here in this secluded place my inner vision is once again opened up. Mary and her family have landed and I see the welcome afforded them. I suspect this would have been one of the prearranged safe places organized by Joseph. I wonder if those who take the little party in are aware of the significance of this special group of seafarers to whom they offer their kind hospitality - somehow I doubt it.

Walking back to the car, I am conscious that the leaves are already turning and the smell of autumn is in the air. The rooks are cawing noisily. There are no ravens here though I know Merlin is keeping watch over this sacred land. The day is running away with me - already it is 4.00 pm. I have just spied some nice ripe blackberries in the hedgerow, so surely I can allow myself five minutes to pick a few. Why though do I end up amongst the brambles and in a ditch! Life is never easy or is it the way I travel through it? My day concludes with a visit to Holford, which we shall come to at the start of Mary's journeying over The Quantock Hills.

Arriving home at 7.30 pm, I make note that this has been a very happy and fulfilling day. That evening I light my candle and reflect on my experiences. My first thought at the end of this sacred day so early in my pilgrimage with Beloved Mary when I am just learning of her plans for me, is how humble I feel. This turn of events in my life is such a privilege and honour. I am truly blessed. It is at this juncture in my Mission, that I come to realize with ever increasing conviction, although it had obviously registered at Trefenty after hearing from Mary and Gildas, just how important it is to offer this work to the public domain, and do justice to the Lady Mary and her Holy pilgrimage, which knowledge has been hidden for so long: *"I honour and thank you my special Lady. I thank dear White Eagle and all the Masters of Light for this opportunity to serve."*

THE CHURCH OF ST MARY, EAST QUANTOXHEAD

It is the following day and I retrace my steps to the North Somerset coast. I find myself driving down a very quiet lane to East Quantoxhead. This little Somerset village is charming, with traditional thatched cottages and a duck pond. I pull onto a small gravelled area of the car park, taking the one remaining parking space on solid ground. The larger part is grassed over and today, which has turned extremely wet - again - sees a vehicle stuck, its driver struggling to extricate it from the saturated grass.

I have a bite to eat before venturing forth into the elements. Having finished my repast still it rains - I can wait no longer. So on with the anorak and cap, over-trousers and boots - not quite the height of fashion - but practical all the same. I take a little path across the grass to St Mary's Church which passes an ancient square-pillared long-barn. As the church comes into view, I see it is attached to a series of old stone turreted buildings forming part of Court House Farm, which is of the Elizabethan period. The church is a compact building with a small bell tower. At the church gate I turn and look out across the fields, and through a gap in the trees can see the incline of the northern tip of The Quantocks, where the ancient trackway would have run. In the far distance I hear the whistle of the steam train on the West Somerset

Railway. In the churchyard is an ancient Celtic cross and the stone upright remains of an old preaching cross. My eye now rests on a most beautiful yew tree in the churchyard. I go over and rest my hands on its trunk in greeting. The tree is probably a few hundred years old as the trunk is not as thick as many I have seen. I receive some lovely words - the deva has been listening in to my thoughts!:

An Ammonite in the porch of St Mary's Church, East Quantoxhead

Ancient Granite Celtic Head in the porch of St Mary's Church, East Quantoxhead

Bench End with many symbols including a Unicorn,
at St Mary's Church, East Quantoxhead

DEVA OF THE YEW

"Welcome dear human pilgrim. I accept that by yew tree standards I am a relative newcomer, but I have pride of place in the churchyard of this Church of St Mary. I am blessed. You are most welcome. (At the grassy base of the tree I lay a gift of a black and white feather). *Thank you human pilgrim. I respect your offering as it comes from the heart. Thank you. I give you my blessing also. Goodbye for now."*

There are some interesting ancient artifacts in the porch. One is a huge ammonite fossil. Next to it is a stone granite head with a face which has relatively well defined features. Then there is a large granite trough which today has flowers in it. This seems to be an apt place to leave an offering of one of the lovely stones I collected from the beach at Kilve yesterday with a few wild flowers picked on my walk here.

In the church I am struck by the peace held within its walls. The interior is of simple but devout design with some quite beautiful stained glass windows. The bench ends are particularly fascinating, showing a great variety of birds, animals and mythical creatures, which include a unicorn and Noah's dove with a twig in its beak, plus many interwoven geometric shapes. In the silence of this little church dedicated to Santa Maria, I am picking up Mary's presence. She is very happy that I am here:

MARY

"Dearest one, another little pilgrimage to a church of my namesake. You are so welcome to this peaceful domain. The village itself goes back to Doomsday and at the time its influence was felt far and wide across the land. Now it is but a shadow of its former self, BUT the essence of that past is held very strongly hereabout. The essence of my journeying to this area is also held strongly, but for the main in the Etheric. (Can I help bring that essence into the landscape on a more physical level that it may heal the land)? *Yes dear one, by your very presence, by your pilgrimaging, by your loving heart, that Etheric counterpart is being brought to rest in the very earth itself. Mother Earth is accepting this blessing once again. This area around Kilve and East Quantoxhead is, through pilgrimage and love, gradually being reawakened to the Light, that Light which is beginning to light up centres all over these sacred Isles. Rest assured dear one that you are doing what is being asked of you and it is good. Your heart-light of love will enter and permeate the heart centre of this ancient land and will enhance its magic. Merlin is now very close, and aware of the alchemy which is happening through the loving heart and pure intent, not just by you dearest one, but by many many Light Workers, bringing healing to this land.*

I bless you dearest sister. I bless all your endeavours. I thank you for your offerings given in love and with such thought. May the Light of His countenance walk with you and may the love of His purest heart abide with you. God bless you my pilgrim daughter."

I offer my blessings and sacred thanks to Beloved Mary.

As I step outside the rain has at last stopped and the sun has come out. These last two days have been more like April than September. On my return to the car I hear a chiff-chaff calling from the nearby woodland - so they've not migrated yet. Having disrobed of my wet outer gear I decide to explore the village. I first come to the duck pond with - nary a duck in sight! The surface of the water is shimmering with sunlight which lights up not only the pond, but all the surrounding trees and vegetation, bringing the whole area to life - a magical moment. I wander off around the lanes of East Quantoxhead looking at the numerous thatched cottages with most attractive gardens.

THE ST NICHOLAS CHURCH, KILTON

Back in the car a glance at the map indicates that close-by are two villages Kilton and Lilstock, both with a church. I am sure you've got the hang of it by now - I can't resist a church - so off I go. The St Nicholas Church is a small ancient building within a churchyard garden of wild flowers and grasses, deliberately left in their natural state. Although the garden itself is not manicured, there is a neat path with a tidy edge laid out with different coloured natural bark chippings, which runs around the perimeter and through a little copse of young trees. The way the whole area has been nurtured, indicates to me that this place is held in great affection. I suspect that the nature spirits are working in co-operation with their human counterparts to produce such a delightful scene. I stand still for a moment offering a blessing.

I enter this hallowed church to once again be immersed in a calm sacred space. Among many distinctive features are the paintings of Victorian Biblical texts. Behind the altar is a beautiful marble reredos, the figures depicting scenes from the Bible. A booklet documents a brief history of the area and a little information about the church. The first recorded history of the estate of Kilton was in AD 873 when it was handed down by King Alfred to his son, William de Mohun. Later in my travelling of course, I discover that I have a link with King Alfred through my incarnation as St Neot. The church was probably founded in 1100 and the dedication to St Nicholas dates from 1533. There was an earlier building - the little that remains is built into the existing church. St Nicholas came from Patara in Lycia a province of Asia Minor in the fourth century. He has however been adopted by Nordic tradition as the acclaimed Santa Claus, which brings him to the West as Patron Saint of Children, probably due to his benevolence. In the East he is Patron Saint of Sailors, which is depicted very strongly within this little church. The church is called The Wayfarers Church and it is linked to the Apostleship of the Sea, whose Patron is Our Lady, Stella Maris - Star of the Sea. This is an ancient title for the Lady Mary, whom sailors put their trust in for protection and guidance during their seafaring. How apt that this should be so, taking account of her own voyaging. The St Nicholas Church is now about two miles inland, but as with Kilve I am sure it was nearer the coast in past times. In the silence I am receiving:

ST NICHOLAS

"This little church is built on the foundation of what you nowadays call a wattle and daub hut. In its original state it was a place of sanctuary for travellers. A wattle and daub hut was quite simply a small building of straw and mud built around tree branches. The floor would have been the earth covered in straw. There was a well hereabouts where travellers were able to get pure water. This concept of sanctuary and caring for wayfarers has always been so and we like to think it will continue. Within the walls and perimeter of this church built of more recent years, there is a strong element of caring and nurturing. You have read how it has been renovated (which I had done), *and the loving energy which has gone into that creation has been recorded. A blessing has been given.*

When the beloved Mary was here over 2,000 years ago, the sea was much closer to this spot, and the little ships would sail in quite close to the land where this church now stands. Wayfarers were guided here as part of their journey, which even in those days was to ancient Glastonbury. They would have come to walk the route up to The Quantock Hills, and onwards across the lowland, much of which was under water at the time. But there were causeways through the water and villages on stilts in the area. Travellers would have been guided across the causeways and through the waters, for it could be treacherous.

As you progress on your own pilgrimage dear Traveller of Light you will discover more understanding of these things. I leave you now with the blessing of Almighty God and the peace of all times. Always travel in the Light dear pilgrim. Always let the Light shine in your heart. The way will become clear for you Each step you will be guided and each step will take you further towards truth. Amen."

St Nicholas draws in the air the full Jesus cross and I offer him my thanks and blessings. On leaving the church I take a perambulation around the bark-strewn path back to my car.

TO LILSTOCK AND THE CHURCH OF ST ANDREW.

Taking another gander at the map, I decide to walk the couple of miles to Lilstock which is near the coast, for its St Andrew Church. I have in my pack for St Andrew a lovely stone which I collected from Hay Bluff in the Black Mountains. This will I believe, provide a connection - an energy link - between the north coast of Somerset and the southern mountains of Wales, where Mary and Naomi concluded their journeying before returning to the Holy Land. The lane runs alongside a stream between two hedgerows where wild flowers grow in abundance, even in early autumn. There is the delicate pink wild rose - each heart-shaped petal open to receive the sun's rays. Scented honeysuckle fills my nostrils. I spy a very pretty little flower called common cow wheat, which is pale lemon with a rich golden centre. I pick just a few of these last, which I shall offer to St Andrew with the Welsh stone, at the little church in Lilstock. The air smells fresh and sweet after the rain. It is a great feeling to be walking. In the walking - in the actual act of putting one foot in front of the other with dedicated effort across this ancient land - I am feeling the energy of Mother Earth and it is giving me a true feeling of pilgrimage My dearest Mary with Naomi would have walked here. I enjoy a few blackberries from the hedgerows as I go, without falling in the ditch this time!

I have reached the hamlet of Lilstock. In a small booklet I obtained from the church later, I read that Lilstock, which now comprises just a few farms and houses, was in the nineteenth century, a thriving community. It had a harbour and pier, which allowed a sea link across the Bristol Channel to South Wales, from where coal was brought in from Cardiff Docks. Also, pleasure steamers would ply their way to and fro Lilstock from South Wales, and other coastal ports along the northern coasts of Somerset and Devon. Learning this is fascinating for me, because as a girl with my family, I went on the old White Funnel Fleet Campbell paddle steamers which used to cross the channel from Cardiff and Penarth to Ilfracombe, Minehead, Clevedon, and even to Lundy Island. I hasten to add this was in the 1950s not the 1850s! You might like a taster of my first ever experience on board. I clearly remember this trip with my dad. First the thrill of being on the boat and hanging over the bow-rail watching the bow ploughing through the rough waters of the Bristol Channel. Then going below decks to the engine room and seeing the enormous pistons in action. Of course this would not be allowed today with health and safety regulations in full swing. Finally and most memorable, on the return journey the boat made a rather unconventional docking procedure, as it ground to an emergency halt up a concrete ramp on Penarth beach rather than alongside the pier. Why? - in order to prevent a man in a small row boat from going under the huge paddles. This being my first trip and at nine years of age, I thought this was normal docking! During the 1950s increased use of the motor car caused the excursion trade to decline, and by the early 1960s there were only two passenger steamships in operation - the Cardiff Queen and the Bristol Queen. Sailings ceased in the 1970s.

Back to Lilstock. I seem to have a little difficulty in tracking down the church. At this stage I don't realize that I have missed its entrance which is set well back from the road. I spend at least an hour of my precious time searching for it, which could have been avoided had I thought to get my map out and identify its exact position! Having passed through the few properties which make up Lilstock, I am now at the coast walking through a rather waterlogged car park. No joy so back I go. In a field close to the track I came across some very handsome thoroughbred horses. One jet black stallion comes over to the fence. He allows me to gently stroke his soft velvet muzzle. We share eye contact and an instant inner connection is made. It really is a bond of understanding and love - a touch of horse whispering. He just tugs at my heart strings.

I have had to ask directions and am soon retracing my steps up the hill out of Lilstock. Eventually the lost is found, as I discover the St Andrew Church. I am struck by its position - a tiny church encompassed within a large green graveyard almost bereft of visible gravestones and surrounded by woodland. The silence and stillness is tangible - the only sound being the gentle rushing of wind in the surrounding trees. It is so peaceful here, but how could it be anything else - a church which has seen hundreds of years of worship within this natural setting. It reminds me of a dear little church I visited some years ago in Pembrokeshire, which is dedicated to St Justinian. This was also well hidden from view, surrounded by a copse of trees and even more difficult to reach, as it was down a long path, then through a field - with no vehicular access. St Justinian I learnt settled there in his self-built daub and wattle hut, living a very simple life of prayer, fasting and attuning to the natural world. I am feeling St Andrew would have embraced much the same way of life here.

The Church of St Andrew is a redundant church which holds one service a year. The notice on the gate reads '*Welcome to St Andrew Church, Lilstock. There has been a church on this site since on or before the 10th Century*'. The gate is very difficult to release from its hinge, but eventually with much pulling and tugging I manage it. I walk the short distance to the entrance. Two doors later I am inside this quite special little church. I lay my offerings of the precious stone and flowers close to the altar. The information in the booklet tells me that this St Andrew Church was built in 1532 over the remains of a previous church. It would seem that part of the original church, namely the chancel arch, was incorporated into the new building, and is still in evidence today. Even though a redundant church, according to the number of names in a book placed on the altar, it does receive quite a few visitors - the dedicated pilgrims prepared to search it out.

I sit quietly in total isolation in one of the old pews. As usual I have many questions. If this little church is named after St Andrew, then could he have possibly lived here? If so, where would his hut be positioned? Is there a well in the churchyard or vicinity? Is he buried here? AND most crucial - is he Andrew, brother of Simon Peter, who was one of the twelve disciples? This last, because to my knowledge, St Andrew of Biblical 'fame' travelled and preached in Asia Minor and was martyred by crucifixion at Patras. As these thoughts are coming in I am aware of the presence of St Andrew:

ST ANDREW

"Welcome dear traveller. Welcome to my little sanctuary. As you see there is now a little church dedicated to me. Amazing to think that I lived here on this very spot in my little hut which I built myself. Yes, as you have already thought, there is a well here. I will guide you to it. Meanwhile I would wish to thank you for visiting my sanctuary pilgrim. It truly is a haven of peace. It was in my day and still is today. The little people are very happy here and work feverishly to maintain its peace. The stillness felt and beauty seen here, is down to them. They do love to enhance the landscape. Thank you dear pilgrim for your kind offerings. They are accepted graciously.

When I arrived on these shores it was quite barren land. The water from the sea lapped very close to my little hut. I was able to fish in the sea, which waters were much clearer in those days and were filled with produce. I collected berries and leaves from the hedgerows. I chose to eat simply and to drink the crystal clear waters of the stream.

As you already know, I did not come with Mary and her little band of travellers. I came much later. I would say thirty years later, well after the crucifixion of our beloved Master. The times were fraught with danger in that part of our World and to escape was paramount at the time. But I did not want to feel I was running away, so I made a vow, in time to travel to these distance shores of which I had heard, to begin my ministry of preaching the true Gospel of our beloved Master - the Gospel of Love - the Way of Perfect Being. In those difficult times this seemed a tremendous task, but all the way I was under the protection of the great Beings of Light, the Masters of all time, and under the protection of the Angelic Beings. I know I was protected, but still the challenges ahead would prove to be almost overwhelming. However I did it. I arrived on these shores. I built my hut and gradually travelled around the land preaching, sharing my experiences and visions along the way. My beloved Master Jesus, the Christ, was with me (in spirit) and always at my right hand.

I lived hereabouts all the rest of my natural life. I died here at age sixty-six and was buried here. Maybe you could discover where. I will help you dear pilgrim. Thank you for this contact. Thank you for your pilgrimage. Go on your way now. My rod and staff WILL comfort you. I bless you dear pilgrim."

St Andrew offers this blessing with the Latin cross which he draws in the air. My words: *"Bless you and thank you St Andrew for your presence this day. Thank you for your words and the information which you have shared with me."*

He failed to answer the big question - identification. Was he Andrew, brother of Simon Peter? A little while later in the quiet of my own sanctuary, I light my candle and use my pink dowsing crystal and insight to try to ascertain the answer. I learn that he was NOT Andrew, brother of Simon Peter. I suspect there were many followers of Jesus of that name in the Holy Land.

I leave the confines of the little church and go out into the fresh air. In the church was a wooden effigy of St Francis with a bird on his shoulders and one cradled in his hands. I believe that St Andrew would have found the same affinity with the little creatures. He would have been completely at-one with the landscape, with the animals and birds and with the nature spirits. I am remembering the contact I had with St Andrew at Hittesleigh Church, when he spoke of his love of the natural world and his wonder at the Universe.

Now - to search for the well. I retrieve my dowsing rods from my pack. I am guided to an old stone wall approximately nine feet in front of, and thirty feet away from, the church on its north side. Of the well there is no outward sign but this is its position. Once that is established I set off in search of the burial place. I trace this to the north-eastern corner of the churchyard behind the church and very close to a young ash tree. It is a very overgrown area with lots of brambles. I could not get right into the wall corner, but once again I receive confirmation. These discoveries complete my investigations here. I do not look for a possible site for a dwelling as it is now 7.00 pm and I must set off for home.

Foremost in my mind as I walk the country lane back to the car and return to Wellington, are my discoveries, insights and the special messages received from the Lady Mary, St Nicholas and St Andrew.

CHAPTER 16
OVER THE QUANTOCK HILLS
The Ridge of Light

From Kilve the Lady Mary with Naomi, Jesus and Joseph, travelled to Holford for their journey over The Quantock Hills. They stayed at Trendle Ring Druidic settlement, which is positioned at the one of the highest points. From here they took the ancient trackway across the ridge to come off at Lydeard Hill for a settlement at Broomfield. My travelling around The Quantocks was undertaken in the main, on a series of day trips from Wellington and my home in Devon, during quite a spaced out period between autumn 2008 and the summer of 2010 as opportunity arose. The only exception to the day trips was my journey to the Broomfield settlement, which I visited on the first day of my pilgrimage to Glastonbury.

The Quantock Hills is a range of low hills running like a spine through central Somerset from West Hill in the north, SSE to Cothelstone Hill at its most southerly point. Evidence of its ancient past is everywhere with beacons, cairns, tumuli and forts. Place names in abundance support a story of ancient Druidic culture, such as; Hedden Oak, Aishholt, Lower Aisholt, Seven Ash, Ash Prior etc. Mary's presence is kept alive in the landscape with Holford, Lady's Edge, Rich's Holford, Merridge, Rose Hill and more. Even King Arthur is represented here with a place called the Great Bear.

THE VILLAGE OF HOLFORD (HOLYFORD)

Holford is the gateway to The Quantock Hills from the north-east. Before linking with Mary at Trendle Ring, we shall tarry a while at Holford which I visited at the end of my Kilve pilgrimage in the autumn of 2008.

When there I bought a small booklet entitled 'A Brief History of Holford' by A. Hayman 1973. Mr. Hayman has lived in the village all his life and offers a fascinating insight into its history. I begin with the name because this is what first gave me the connection with Mary, and directed me to these parts. This is what he says on Page 5 of his booklet: 'The explanations of the origin of the name Holford are both vague and conflicting, but it is generally accepted that the name evolved *from the geographical situation. The village is in a narrow valley, a hole, a cleave or a combe in The Quantock Hills and originally was clustered around the spot where the old coach road (now locally called the Stowey Road) dipped down to the stream and crossed it at the only fordable place, close to where the thatched cottages now stand. Thus we have the* name *'HOLEFORD.'* However, I maintain my original hypothesis that HOLFORD is HOLYFORD relating to the visit of Our Lady, and that its true interpretation has become lost over the centuries.

Now on to other things. Mr. Hayman tells us that there was a Roman encampment at Danesborough close-by and that many Roman artifacts have been discovered, including a coin of Constantine. Moving forward to the sixteenth century, Huguenot families settled in Holford to open a silk factory and establish the weaving trade. I must also make mention of William Wordsworth and his sister Dorothy, who rented Alfoxden House now an hotel, for a year, writing several of his well known works in that time, such as *'The Ancient Mariner'* and *'Kubla Khan'*.

Finally and as confirmation of my insights, Mr. Hayman supports the theory put forward by Rev. E. Scholl a local Rector in the 1950s, of a 'Pilgrim's Way' running the length of the Quantock ridge along which travellers would journey for Glastonbury.

THE CHURCH OF ST MARY THE VIRGIN, HOLFORD

The Corn-Dollie in the Church of St Mary the Virgin, Holford

Parking by the church and standing before the lych gate I look up and see a small wooden statuette of the Blessed Mary in the roof apex. A little pathway leads me through a pretty well kept garden with a rustic seat. As I approach the church itself, I notice that the tower is quite unusual, in that it is squat and has a sloping roof. I am overjoyed to see an imposing yew tree in front of me. There are others further off, but this is the one which catches my attention. From me: *"oh you are so magnificent"* and the response:

DEVA OF THE ANCIENT YEW

"I AM the guardian of this churchyard. There are other yews here but I stand sentinel protecting this ancient land. I have been here for a very very long time. You may enter pilgrim and enjoy the peace of MY churchyard."

My reply: *"Bless you and thank you wonderful tree deva."* Again a sense of pride, which the nature spirits attach to their work of protecting and beautifying the landscape, emerges with these words.

This church is presently named the Church of St Mary the Virgin, yet the 1285 Charters of Athelney Abbey, referred to the Church of St Mary Magdelene. Either dedication would be applicable, as it is my understanding that Mary Magdalene with the Master Jesus, travelled the pilgrim path along The Quantock Hills on route to Glastonbury, many years after the Lady Mary's pilgrimage with Jesus as a boy.

Walking through the main door into the vestibule I see before me a marble font. Here I lay my posy of cyclamen and a feather prepared earlier this day at Kilve, as an offering for the two Marys. I enter the main body of the church and my attention is immediately drawn to a huge corn dollie hanging high up in the central aisle. This straw figure in its original context is put into place to indicate the final cut of the corn at harvest time. How good it is to see the old ways acknowledged and brought into manifestation today. The walls of the church are whitewashed which makes me think that they may well be covering medieval wall paintings. A stained glass window over the altar depicts the Christ figure, flanked on the one side by the Virgin Mary in robes of blue and white, and on the other, Mary Magdalene in red and white. On the north wall is a charming picture in a gold frame, which could well be a representation of Mary, very simply dressed as a maid, hands held lightly together in prayer.

I sit in one of the narrow wooden pews for a short attunement. I ask a blessing on this church and envisage a Ray of Light from the Cosmos pouring down to heal the land. In my meditation Mary is welcoming me. I am aware of my own Grail Cup, my Heart-Rose, opening to receive her pure love - the pink Rose of Divine Love is filling my whole being. I am calm and full of wonderment. White Eagle comes to mind and I feel he is sharing the joy which I am experiencing in this little sanctuary. There is complete and utter stillness. This truly is the sound of silence and within that silence one can hear the voice of all Eternity. I express: *"Most blessed - thrice blessed Mary thank you. Dear White Eagle thank you."*

TO TRENDLE RING DRUIDIC SETTLEMENT

From Holford Mary and her family travelled up Hodder's Combe and over Black Ball Hill for Trendle Ring settlement. After my visit to Holford I had considered I might walk this route to Trendle Ring, but as usual time had marched on and evening was upon me when I left the church. Would you believe, it was not until June 2010 that I finally reached this ancient site. It was following my second trip to Hungerford settlement in North Somerset that I headed cross-country to The Quantocks. It was late in the day, but being high summer I had a long evening ahead of me. On route I stopped at the Spa shop in Williton for extra refreshments. I then took the A358 south for Bicknoller and the back lane to Chilcombe. My plan was to approach Trendle Ring from this, the west side of the hill, rather than take the long trek from Holford.

Having parked up I begin my pilgrimage. I pass by a little cluster of buildings comprising Quantock Moor Farm and cottages, huddled together within the lee of the hillside. From this point I see the Trendle Ring hill rising up steeply directly in front of me. There is a dedicated path through tall green bracken to the top. At a little after 7.00 pm with the sun still hot, I struggle a bit as I make the climb. Now walking through an area of wild whortleberry bushes, I hear but fail to see amongst the heathland, a stonechat. Eventually I reach the high plateau for the Trendle Ring settlement where our ancestors once lived. The views are quite stunning - Exmoor to the west, the Blackdown Hills to the south and to the north, the coast at Kilve and across to Wales. To the east, if I could but see far enough into the distance, would be Glastonbury. Far below me in the immediate vicinity, fields in a kaleidoscope of natural colours, are spread out like a patchwork quilt.

Trendle Ring Settlement on The Quantock Hills

But what can I see up here? Actually, as is so often the case, very little of the ancient site appears to be showing in the landscape. I come to a curved grassed-over earth mound which has a stone foundation. This might well be a section of an original circle, of which I cannot identify a complete round. I have the impression that the site covered a vast area of this open hill-top, which would perhaps be more easily identified from an aerial photograph. There is a further similar mound - a long straight stretch - but I am wondering if this latter is a reave, a more modern boundary line, rather than a part of the ancient settlement.

I have this isolated sacred place to myself. I sit quietly and reflect on Mary and Naomi's time here, again tapping into past remembrances. For Beloved Mary, arriving at this settlement would have allowed her time for recovery after a hard ride from the coast. I now see her with her Druid companions, invoking the Cosmic Light to be directed to this ancient site. Mother Earth receives and welcomes the influx of the pure healing ray. With joy in my heart and linking with the great Cosmic Angels, I offer my own Invocation to the Light. Before leaving, I gently break open the soft earth and insert a pure white quartz crystal to uphold the ancient Druidic energies here.

Finally, I make my way downhill to my car and undertake the long journey back to Devon. As darkness is falling I arrive home. In the quiet of my own sanctuary I offer a special thank you to Mary for her guidance, at the end of what has been another satisfying full day's pilgrimage to the settlements of Hungerford and Trendle Ring.

WALK FROM BICKNOLLER TO WEACOMBE HILL

Bicknoller and Weacombe Hill are in the vicinity of Trendle Ring. On one of my day trips from Wellington in the autumn of 2008, I did a circular walk which incorporated both these places, in order to explore the area and to get a feel for the surrounding landscape over which Mary and her family travelled.

Arriving in the tiny village of Bicknoller, first on the agenda is a visit to ST GEORGE'S CHURCH. As I step into the churchyard I am greeted by a yew tree reckoned to be over 1,000 years old, and stand for a moment under its spreading branches, tuning into the energies of the deva, receiving a beautiful and welcoming response. I now enter the calm interior of the little church. Its history goes back to the thirteenth century, when it was built as a Manorial Chapel for the Bishop of Bath and Wells, the tower being added two centuries later. It underwent modernization during the Victorian era, when unfortunately much of its original glory was stripped out. However, one ancient treasure remains and that is the original stone altar, which was found by chance in the 1950s buried in the churchyard. It was restored to its rightful position at the east end of the church. As it now stands before me, its only adornment is a simple wooden Jesus cross. I have a moment of silence before heading for the hills.

From the by-road I take the track running between Bicknoller Hill and Weacombe Hill alongside a trickling stream. It is a happy day to be out in the countryside - the sky is blue, the bracken turning a rusty-brown, and birds are singing in the nearby hawthorn bushes. It was on a previous occasion while walking through this little valley with my daughter, that we saw a herd of red deer on the skyline of Weacombe Hill high above us. Today there are no deer in the physical, but is Cerunnos the mighty stag, which in Celtic mythology is the Lord of the Animals, guarding these ancient hills? As I take a gentle pace climbing ever upwards, I am conscious that Trendle Ring settlement would be off to my right about half a mile, though well out of view from this low elevation. At the top of the valley I reach the ancient trackway which takes me to the trig point on Beacon Hill. Here at this high point the blustery wind is quite exhilarating and the views take in 360 degrees.

Dropping off the hill slightly, I settle down in the bracken and fading heather for a brief lunch stop. I am relaxing in the warm sunshine, out of reach of the high winds. Now lying prone, I feel as if I am merging with the ground beneath me. I become conscious of the throbbing lifeforce of Mother Earth. Somehow the hills are coming alive - the Spirit of the Hills is welcoming me into an Inner World. I drift ever deeper into the secret place of the Inner Kingdom, wherein a dynamic bustle of activity of great magnitude, hidden from the human physical eye, is ongoing. I am being shown the workings of the Earth Star Crystal. I can see it pulsating with the Cosmic Light, which it has gathered to its bosom. I am aware of energetic vibrations emanating from it - reverberating throughout Planet Earth. It is the lifeblood of our Planet - the hub of a vast network of interconnecting energy lines - the key to our Planet's survival. How can I look at it in all its bright scintillating magnificence?

I awake from my deep profound reverie with a start. Just checking - I AM still here on the solid earth. What a vision - thank you Masters. Some brief lunch stop! My route down takes me through Staples Plantation to Weacombe, from where I return to Bicknoller along a little pathway skirting the lower slopes of Weacombe Hill. On reflection at home, I am remembering the magical, mystical and powerful experience up in The Quantock Hills, amongst the heather and bracken. The deep sacred connection with the Earth Star Crystal is with me forever. On another level, I am feeling closer to being a part of the ancient energies of these hills, over which Mary and Naomi travelled.

TO CROWCOMBE AND THE TRISCOMBE STONE

Mary and her family have left Trendle Ring and began the trek along the Quantock ridge. I connect to her journey a little further along her route by undertaking a second day's walk in the area. I plan a circular walk from the village of Crowcombe below the ridge, to the Triscombe Stone and back, but somehow find myself heading off to Wills Neck and Lydeard Hill, Mary's leaving point for Broomfield settlement, giving me a hike of approximately ten miles!

At Crowcombe I first take a look at the CHURCH of the HOLY GHOST. The church, although of ancient origin, does not have quite the atmosphere of the smaller St George's at Bicknoller. However, I do take a look around and find some fascinating old dark oak carved bench ends with strange carved heads, figures and ancient symbology, which I cannot decipher.

I have chosen a calm sunny day in early spring for this visit to the hills. Walking the quiet country road, I rejoice in the beauty and fragrance of the wild flowers, especially the delicate pale primroses, which are once more gracing our hedgerows. Just past the Crowcombe Estate I take a right and follow a little pathway between some cottages. In a nearby garden are the largest, fluffiest and most beautiful golden coloured hens I have ever seen! My route takes me across a field to reach a track running alongside a row of grand old trees - a perfect place for a coffee stop. Climbing higher I turn right for Crowcombe Gate where I link to the trackway, which soon enters deep into woodland. As I make pilgrimage through this ancient landscape, I am very much in tune with the energies of the past. I am a solitary walker - alone yet not alone - I am walking with Mary and Naomi, Jesus, Joseph and other travellers of the olden times. The trackway widens at the edge of a car park and I see the TRISCOMBE STONE directly in front of me. It is a small, almost triangular shape granite stone, part covered with green moss. I can find no information about it, but intuitively understand it to be a marker stone to identify the way and is very ancient - it was on this pilgrim path 2,000 years ago. I rest my hand on the stone - it is warm to the touch - I feel vibrations emanating from its aliveness and offer a blessing. The Triscombe Stone is at an intersection, from where I had planned my way back off the hill to complete my circular route. However instead, I am urged onwards and continue in the direction of Wills Neck and Lydeard Hill. The Lydeard Hill tumulus at three hundred and sixty-five metres is the highest point on the ridge. I stop and take a long hard look at the map. Suddenly my inner vision is opened up and I realize that this is where Mary comes off the ridgeway to drop down to Merridge for Broomfield settlement. THIS is why I was to continue to this point: *"Thank you Mary for your directions."*

At this point I am just a mile away from Cothelstone Hill the last height spot on the ridge, and can see it in the distance. I am tempted to try for it because again something is telling me I have to go there, but decide that judgment is the better part of valour, bearing in mind the length of my walk back. It will have to keep for another occasion. And - another occasion does arise many months later when I am staying over with my daughter in Wellington. It is suggested as the weather is good that we take a walk to Cothelstone Hill. Hurrah - at last the opportunity I have been waiting for. We set off - daughter and her husband with baby on back - and me. We take the 'scenic route' through the woodland and soon emerge close to the hill-top near the tumuli where a beacon once stood. This is quite marvellous as from here I am looking across to Lydeard Hill Mary's leaving point from The Quantocks so am able to get my bearings. We walk over to Merridge Hill just a few metres away and although it is a hazy sort of day, I can see in the distance the wide expanse of the inlet of Burnham-on-Sea, which was an ancient port and trade route for Glastonbury. From this coastal estuary Mary and Naomi left the South West for Wales after their time in Glastonbury, in order to make the journey to Aconbury settlement (see Epilogue). From Merridge Hill I can also scan the surrounding landscape and envisage a picture of their route to the coast. This chance afforded me to visit Cothelstone Hill and Merridge Hill, has put me a little more in the picture regarding Beloved Mary's journeying.

Back to my earlier walk. I return via Wills Neck to the Triscombe Stone, thence downhill on a very potholed road, marked '*Not suitable for Motor Vehicles*' to the hamlet of Triscombe. Would you believe it, there is a car coming up the narrow road, desperately trying to avoid all the potholes! I have a very pleasant walk through the country lanes to Crowcombe, but am rather pleased to be back at my car and take a rest after my long foot slog.

THE CHURCH OF ST THOMAS OF CANTERBURY.

Just below Cothelstone Hill on its western side is the Elizabethan Manor of Cothelstone Court, the Church of St Thomas of Canterbury and a Holy Well. Shortly after my trip to Cothelstone Hill with my family, I am able to return to investigate this region. When I arrive however, the owners of The Court are hosting an antiques fayre and in this quiet little corner of England, there must be a couple of hundred cars in the car park. I don't get to see The Court, but am able to access the church. The Church of St Thomas of Canterbury is a gem, set in a churchyard of beautiful mature trees, against the backdrop of The Quantock Hills, just behind Cothelstone Court. I would say that its crowning glory are two great table tombs both in fine condition, showing effigies of members of the Stawell family who owned the Manor throughout the Middle Ages. One is of Sir Matthew de Stawell and his wife Eleanor Merton - they died in 1379. The other is of Sir John Stawell and his wife Frances Dyer and is dated 1603. Marked on the map is a Holy Well close-by. I go in search of it, but it is absolutely impossible to find and there appears to be no-one around to ask - they are all at the auction. However, dowsing tells me that it was originally called St Mary's Holy Well.

IN SEARCH OF THE BROOMFIELD DRUIDIC SETTLEMENT.

The Broomfield settlement is where the Lady Mary and her family stayed on leaving the ridge. I visited this ancient site on the first day of my three day pilgrimage to Glastonbury. My inner voice had directed me to this specific area, and my map showed a settlement high above Haswell Farm, plus a place name 'Rose Hill' near Broomfield, so I felt I was on the right track.

I first reach the entrance to Fyne Court which offers nature trails, but there is no time for a walk here today. On the Fyne Court estate at Broomfield, is a church dedicated to ST MARY and ALL SAINTS - here I do decide to pay a brief visit. A notice in the porch says *'Let the Light, Space, Peace of this place enfold you. Pause. Reflect. Listen to the Voice Within'* - a warm welcome indeed with words of gentle wisdom. The little church is simply and most beautifully adorned. I spend just a few moments in this most lovely sanctuary of peace.

Now for the settlement. I drive to where I think I can get a good vantage point and possible access. I am standing at an open gate and looking across a huge field of tall green and gold maize which is waving in the light breeze. My instincts tell me this is the right place. However, to reach the main site area which I believe I can identify in the far distance, I decide to investigate from a different angle.

With my pack on my back, I head off down a very dark old sunken lane. The stony track is lined with ancient beech trees, which have lush green ferns growing out of their moss covered root system. I am mesmerized as I look into the secret spaces between the tree trunks, and my imagination runs riot. It is a magical fairy kingdom - I see dwellings for the little people everywhere. On passing by I offer a blessing. Deeper and deeper I go into the gloom, until eventually I come to a five-barred gate, which opens to a field rising to a tree lined horizon. Up there I am sure is the settlement. Just inside the gate is a magnificent oak tree. Could this king of trees be guarding the southern approach to the ancient site from the lane? I start up the steep slope through long grass, nettles and pink thistles, puffing my way uphill higher and higher until at last I reach the top. From here I can see in the distance the long dark ridge of The Quantock Hills running down to its most southerly point. Somewhere in that direction is Lydeard Hill where Mary left the ridge. I follow the line of the hedge, trying to peer through its thick dense tangle until at last a gap allows me a look into what is beyond. There is a field cropped with golden maize which I realize is the far end of the very large field I saw from the gate. THIS is the Broomfield Druidic site. I hear the deep-throated croak of Merlin's raven and see it way up in the sky - I accept this as confirmation. I learnt recently, that ravens fed Elijah in the wilderness, so their association with us humans goes way back. Unfortunately it is not possible to break through the barbed-wired hedgerow, but from what I am witness to from this side, there is literally no evidence to suggest an ancient settlement was in existence here. I pull out a small mat from my pack and settle down with my back to the hedge for a link with Mary and the Masters. It is with great reverence I make this inner connection. I hear the following from Beloved Mary:

MARY

"Welcome to this our settlement at Broomfield beloved one. (Then the famous words) *Be still my child - be still."*

This is short and sweet, but something is telling me that the Masters are saving their words for Glastonbury on the morrow.

I retrace my steps to the sunken lane. As I am sauntering back up, I have a strong sense of days gone by - Mary and Naomi are travelling with me as I walk this ancient way. Once again I become aware of Mary's physical tiredness, this time at the end of a long day journeying across The Quantocks from Trendle Ring settlement. However, I am also feeling with her, an eagerness - almost a need - to push on to Glastonbury. Broomfield was to be their last settlement before they began their crossing of the Somerset Levels to ancient Glaston. Back at the field entrance I can see far off, the steep slope which I climbed linking to the extensive maize field. I now choose a large piece of white quartz and place it in full view on the wooden gate post for the Holy Family and the Druid ancestors, with a sacred blessing. It is well noticeable and I expect the local farmer will be a little puzzled as to how it got there when he comes to harvest his crop.

As a follow up to this pilgrimage, it is a year later and I am visiting Fyne Court with my son, his wife and two children, where we do one of the nature trails. The youngsters aged seven and four were having great fun, running around, exploring, climbing trees, laughing and generally being very loud! It brought to mind my vision at Merrivale Ceremonial Complex on Dartmoor, which opened to a scene of ancient times, where children were playing and running everywhere with much joy, laughter and noise - nothing changes! Driving away from Fyne Court, we come to the maize field entrance and I notice that the piece of quartz which I put on the post has disappeared. I must have subconsciously known, because in a stream running through Fyne Court grounds, I had come across a beautiful piece of quartz/stone mix - just perfect for a replacement. I asked my son if he would kindly stop the car. I laid the precious piece gently on the post with a silent prayer. My family probably thought I was totally mad, but so be it!

FINDING THE STILLNESS WITHIN

At the Broomfield settlement I am once again reminded to withdraw into the silence, as Mary tells me to *'Be still my child - be still.'* How often has Mary or another Master requested that I - 'be still'. How often have I said through this work, that the silence is tangible? For it is only in the stillness that our inner senses can be enlivened and we can achieve heightened awareness. It is then that the Etheric counterpart of each of our senses awakens and allows our consciousness to move to a deeper level, wherein we can go beyond the physical and be in touch with our true inner nature.

By way of an illustration, I shall paint you a simple picture, which should you wish, you can use in the form of a meditative visualization at home or when you are out in the natural world. It might help to awaken your own sense of sight, hearing, smell, taste or touch. There are many ideas for each of our senses but I list just a few. Here goes - this is the picture I would like you to visualize... *'It is springtime and you are sitting with your back to a tree on the mossy bank of a stream which is running through a bluebell wood. The sun is shining and there is a gentle breeze.'*

What might we be **seeing**? The crystal clear water of the stream running over its stony bed; a dragonfly flitting amongst the grasses rising from beneath the waters; tall trees seeming to reach for the sky; the sun shining through the tree canopy sparkling on the surface of the water; the light green beech leaves of early spring; a mauve carpet of bluebells; a squirrel running up a tree.

What might we be **hearing**? The gurgling sound of the water; the whooshing of leaves in the trees being blown on the breeze; a little creature scurrying across the woodland floor; a woodpecker 'drumming' in a nearby tree; the cat-like cry of a buzzard overhead.

What might we be **smelling**? The collective scent of a thousand bluebells; the pungent wild garlic; the damp rich brown earth; the distinctive smell of a fox.

What might we be **tasting**? The sweet fresh cold water of the stream as we take a sip; perhaps we may chew on one of the stems of garlic; a juicy peach from our lunchbox.

What might we be **touching** and how does it **feel**? The soft velvet green moss alongside us; the smooth or rough bark of the tree; a crisp rusty-brown leaf from autumn past; a wet shiny stone from the stream; the warmth of the sun's rays on our face where they penetrate the tall trees.

This meditative experience opens the door to the Etheric Realm. Our clairvoyant vision may open up to see the little people - perhaps a fleeting glance out of the corner of our eye, or we may hear the voice of a Master, whispering words of wisdom. THIS is the real world - the inner world - the world we know, but have all but forgotten as we live out our lives in the physical. By invoking that stillness - by going into the silence - we are making the connection to the life beyond, and to the world within. We have made our union with the Divine essence. It is now we can discover and develop inner peace, harmony and deep compassion. This is the way to perfect love, as in that state of silent being our Heart-Rose opens to receive. A Master can do this, but are we not all Masters in the making?

St Francis of Assisi, that gentle brother, epitomizes the ability to be still and go into the deep silence. Through mastery of his physical senses, he was able to tune into the Infinite and make that link with the Great White Light, that he may commune with the birds and all the creatures of the natural world. His compassion shone through his actions, brought about by stilling the mind and opening his heart to love. His special prayer which I love, says it all for me. This version is from a devotional card.

The Prayer of St Francis

'Lord make me an instrument of your peace.
Where there is hatred, let me sow love.
Where there is injury, pardon.
Where there is doubt, faith.
Where there is despair, hope.
Where there is darkness, light.
Where there is sadness, joy.
Divine Master, grant that I may not so much seek
to be consoled, as to console.
To be understood, as to understand.
To be loved, as to love.
For it in giving that we receive.
It is in pardoning that we are pardoned.
And it is in dying that we are born to Eternal Life. Amen'

And - we can achieve this state of mind in The Stillness. While contemplating these things Beloved Mary comes in very close:

MARY

"This is pure truth. It was the way of the Master Jesus our beloved son while on the Earth Plane. It is the way of purity and truth. It is the way of The Heart dearest one. Let the Rose of Love ever bloom at your heart centre and it will absolve all pain - physical and emotional. It will allow only beauty and truth to prevail and it will give you, as we have said before, that peace which passeth all understanding. Dearest daughter THIS IS TRUTH. Everything outside this is an illusion. The Law of Perfect Love is truth and within this Law, all Laws abide. The Rose in the Heart is the rose in the heart of every man, woman and child. It is that Divine element of the spirit which is opening to love in its human form. That Divine element links one to the Divine Being, our Father and Mother God and to all Angels and Archangels and to the Masters of Light. KNOW this Heart Rose our beloved Brethren.

So dearest one. Let there be Light. Let the Rose ever bloom in your Heart. Let the Rose in your Heart be your Grail Cup, open to receive, open to give to ALL. Today at the end of our little session dearest daughter, I give you words from dear White Eagle which you know very well - 'keep on keeping on'. Seek truth and truth you will discover, not always in the way you expect, but always from the deepest and purest level of Infinite Wisdom - from the most high. Bless you my child. Bless you."

What more can I add. I offer a heartfelt thank you and blessing for Mary's special words.

CHAPTER 17
ACROSS THE SOMERSET
LEVELS TO GLASTONBURY
To the Isle of Avalon

After leaving Broomfield settlement, the Lady Mary and her companions travelled overland to North Newton from where they took a boat through the Somerset Levels to Glastonbury. Mary had a sacred Mission to undertake at Glastonbury Tor, which was to invoke the Cosmic Light and prepare the Hyperborean Temple in the Etheric for the future. I have put aside three days for my pilgrimage to Glastonbury, to include; travelling, visits on route, exploration of ancient Glaston and the undertaking of my Mission to earth the Hyperborean Temple. Taking a look at my map of the Somerset Levels I can find no place names associated with Mary. The watery nature of the landscape probably prohibits this. However, a street map of Glastonbury gives me Paradise Lane and Maiden Croft Lane. On this section of my pilgrimage through Somerset, I connect with the St Michael Ley Line, as identified by the dowser Hamish Miller, at no less than six points of reference. First is at the Wellington Monument, which I pass close to on my journey east along the M5 motorway. Then I visit the five following places:

- The St Michael Church near the hamlet of North Newton
- Burrow Mump - the ruined St Michael Chapel
- Othery Church of St Michael
- Wearyall Hill - the Sacred Thorn
- Glastonbury Tor - the ruined St Michael Church

I MAKE PREPARATION

Before I begin my pilgrimage, unusually I take a couple of days to scan any reading material I have regarding mystical Glastonbury. Normally I would set off with an open mind, but something is telling me that this time I have to be more aware of the significance of what I am about to undertake.

There has been so much written about Glastonbury that I hesitate to add to the hundreds, nay thousands of works. The market is awash with books covering almost every aspect of historical data and archeological discovery, all merged with myth and legend. It does make for exciting reading, but one has to sift through it all and decide what sits comfortably with oneself. My plan as I visit a sacred location, is to give a brief dossier of its history, combined with my present day insights.

My two day research is followed up with a walk on Dartmoor. I have a need to be somewhere away from people, away from traffic noises, and in the silence, where I can be in-tune with the natural world and commune with the Heavenly Spheres. Following a rather blowy walk over open moorland, I settle down within the shelter of an ancient hut circle. First I hear:

BEING OF LIGHT

"Preparations are being made Pilgrim of Light. All is being set in place by the Higher Beings. There will be a Host of Angels and Masters with you We have everything to hand. Have no fear - just open up your sacred heart to the Rose of Divine Love - the Flame of the Cosmos will enter therein."

Now my inner vision is opened to reveal Glastonbury Tor. A great Light from the Cosmos is pouring down to completely encompass the tor, which has disappeared within its brilliance - the Light is piercing deep into the Earth's core to the Great Crystal beneath. Back in physical consciousness at the hut circle, in the dark green lichen of a granite stone before me, is outlined a dragon which stimulates my mind to these thoughts. Soon the age of the dragon of materialism will be stayed for all time. A font of new understanding will ascend as a Fountain of Light from the Well of Ignorance. The phoenix will indeed rise from the ashes. The Ancient Wisdom through the eagle of John the Beloved will soar on high, ushering in the new Golden Age. The Flame of Truth will not be quenched. The New Jerusalem is emerging.

At home later I book my accommodation at Street Youth Hostel, which on arrival due to some sort of promotion, I receive a £4 reduction on each nightly booking - a lady who booked a week or so back had to pay the full wack! The Angels are looking after my financial welfare as well as everything else!

The morning of my departure I light my precious candle and rest my pink scarf over my head for an attunement: *"My beloved Mary - Lady of Light - ancient Goddess, I come before you now in thanksgiving for this opportunity to serve the Cosmic Christ. Let me be worthy of the task set before me. My gracious Lady, walk this sacred pilgrimage with me. I offer myself to the Great Spirit in obedience to His will. I honour ALL the Masters and those of the Angelic Realms as I set forth on this journey to Glastonbury."*

MY JOURNEY FROM DEVON

My pilgrimage to Glastonbury begins. It is September 2009. Today I shall visit the Broomfield Druidic site, Mary's last settlement on The Quantocks.

Tomorrow is to be my sacred Ceremony at Glastonbury Tor. Setting off from South Devon on the A380, I almost immediately run into thick fog. I drive attentively. An illusion I know, but I feel as if I am driving through the mists of time, so enveloped am I in the misty elements around me. On the motorway now, the Blackdown Hills which would normally offer a fine view of the Wellington Monument, are today shrouded in low cloud. The monument, which is quite a landmark as it dominates the skyline, is an Obelisk of a hundred and seventy-five feet high, and presents the ancient Egyptian symbol of the winged disc above the entrance door. It is the first St Michael Ley Line energy link as it enters Somerset.

THE PARISH CHURCH OF KINGSTON ST MARY.

Leaving the motorway and skirting Taunton, I soon pick up the country road for Kingston St Mary on route to Broomfield settlement. Amazingly the mists have lifted, the sun has come out and the dark rise of The Quantock Hills is coming into view. At the quiet little village of Kingston St Mary in the lee of the hills, I park up next to the thirteenth century church underneath an oak tree, and am immediately bombarded by acorns! As I enter the churchyard I hear the raucous cackle of the yapping gale close-by. I am struck by the sight of a magnificent yew tree around which is a semi-circular stone seat, with the dedication *'In loving memory of the Bryant family'*. At the base of the yew, is a simple wooden cross and some flowers. I offer a lovely white and grey feather for the deva, inserting it carefully amongst its lower branches. As I look into the depths of the tree I see a tiny robin hopping around not a bit afraid of my presence. I sit down on the seat and the tree deva speaks with me:

DEVA OF THE YEW TREE

"My dear pilgrim you are most welcome. I am the guardian of this ancient place. Over hundreds of years I've stood sentinel watching the changes taking place in Kingston St Mary. I am most beautiful. I help the other nature spirits in this churchyard to produce of their best. I give them encouragement and bless their efforts. Sometimes the little pixies are quite mischievous and I have to reprimand them. BUT they are all - we are all - a part of our Creator and as such are blessed in every way. Mary is awaiting your pleasure. Goodbye."

Stepping into the church porch, I look up to see the most striking pale yellow fan-vaulted roof with a rose at its centre. The clock strikes 12.00 noon as I enter into this glorious church. I am drawn to walk down the central aisle with its large handsome chandelier, to view the impressive three-light stained glass window over the altar. The central window shows the crucifixion of Christ with the words *'God so loved the World'* which I always find most poignant. The window to the left depicts the Virgin Mary and St George, and the one to the right - St Elizabeth of Hungary and St Johannes. The well crafted sixteenth century oak bench ends show old country scenes such as an oxen and yoke. Seated in one of the pews, through the pervading silence I can hear the distant steady tick of the church clock in the tower. I drift deep into my inner world soon to be being overshadowed by my blessed Mary:

MARY

"My dear child - welcome to this final part of your pilgrimage with me beloved one, here in the ancient South West of these mystic Isles. I and my beloved Jesus will walk all the way to Glastonbury with you. You will never be alone. In fact there will be many of the Heavenly Hosts with you at Glastonbury. They are waiting your arrival eagerly. All is in hand. All is in place. The Masters are preparing the way for the transformation of the ancient Cosmic energies for the new era on your Planet. The Cosmic Light which has never died, is reawakening to usher in the New Jerusalem in Britain - for the whole World. My child - Naomi - go in peace."

Returning to normal consciousness, I pay homage and thank Mary for her sacred words. I realize the enormity of what is to be the climax of my Mission with the Lady Mary and yet a certain calmness comes over me.

Taking an amble around the well kept churchyard with its mix of lovely trees I notice that it is full of mole hills. The local mole population are obviously having a 'field day' or in this case a 'churchyard day.'

TO ST MICHAEL'S CHURCH, NORTH NEWTON

From Kingston St Mary I make the pilgrimage to Broomfield settlement (see Chapter 16). From there Mary's journey took her in a direct line east to North Newton along an ancient trackway. I follow the narrow country lanes through Thurloxton to North Newton for the Church of St Michael. According to my map the church is situated just south of the little hamlet of North Newton. I am having a little difficulty in finding it as the lanes wind every which way. I stop and ask a lady working in her garden for directions, which is very fortuitous, as she informs me I shall need a key which can be obtained from her neighbour Sarah. With said key in hand, I drive on, park up and am now looking for the church, which I have been told can't be seen from the road. I eventually find it down a track tucked away behind a row of barns. This wee church set within its own small enclosure of greenery, has a miniature tower topped with a square roof running to a point. As I approach I am sensing almost mystical properties emanating from it, as if it has an aura of protection around it.

Unlocking the door with the huge key I am holding my breath as I enter. Although unadorned, this little church is an absolute jewel with some exceptional stained glass windows. Taking central stage over the altar is St Michael slaying a bright green dragon. It brings to mind my lichen dragon seen on the granite stone on Dartmoor recently. This is only the second east window I have come across on my pilgrimage, with an illustration of St Michael - the other being at the St Michael Church on Brent Tor. It is a reminder that the St Michael Ley Line connects to both churches. Through two tiny Gothic arches on its south side is a small chapel with rather special windows. To my right is the armoured and winged figure of St Michael, this time quelling an orange dragon and to my left a most beautiful portrayal of the Virgin Mary robed in white, turquoise and pink. They are opposite and compliment each other, as if bringing into balance the male and female energies. I am completely awestruck and sit for a short attunement within this peaceful sanctuary. As my offerings I lay down two crystals - a rose-pink quartz and a pure white quartz, with a special prayer.

TO BURROW MUMP

For Mary and her family, on leaving North Newton their mode of transport changed. They transferred to dug-out canoes and were guided by local Celtic tribes-people through the marshy waters of the Somerset Levels to Burrow Mump.

I am soon on the road again driving south to pick up the A361 to Street, which takes me to Burrow Mump, another stage on the St Michael Ley Line. Burrow Mump is a rather strange conical hill topped with a ruined St Michael Chapel, which apparently used to belong to Athelney Abbey up until the thirteenth century. As the mump becomes visible in the flat landscape, it appears to be a smaller version of Glastonbury Tor. Parking in the dedicated car park, I put my walking shoes on and make the short trek to the top through a herd of rather large heifers. I reach the ancient chapel and stand in silence absorbing the atmosphere. Up here it is wonderful with the sun warming my face and an invigorating wind. A buzzard with its wild mewing cry is quartering the skies on the uplifting air currents. There are spectacular views. Within the distance landscape, I can see Glastonbury Tor crowned with its ruined St Michael Church. I can also make out the coast at Burnham-on-Sea, one of the entrance points for trade vessels from the Bristol Channel to Glastonbury in the Iron Age. I return to my car to continue my journey.

THE CHURCH OF ST MICHAEL, OTHERY.

The ancient church of St Michael at Othery is close to Burrow Mump. I am told that the meandering path the canoes took through the waters, would have brought Mary very close to Othery. I therefore chose to pay it a visit on my homeward journey. The old village of Othery is set back from the main A361. Its church is hidden away at the top of a narrow leafy no-through road. In the churchyard I pay my respects to a magnificent yew and receive a gracious acknowledgement. The sweet smell of roses comes drifting across on the warm air as I take a look around. The graveyard is on a raised site, suggesting as I learnt at Down St Mary in Devon, a place of some antiquity. I see that the church has the unusual feature of the tower being at the chancel end. On each of its four sides in niches are stone figures of St John, St Mary, St Michael and a crowned King.

As I enter the south porch I become aware of the most powerful vibrations, and look up to see a stone statue of Archangel Michael dispatching an enormous dragon by ramming a spear down its throat. Inside the church are many intriguing features, including numerous carved bench ends of different character - all bloodthirsty stuff! One depicts Archangel Michael slaying the dragon, this one seeming to have a human head. Another is of David holding the head of Golaith. A third shows Abraham about to sacrifice Isaac. A discovery made in 1897 of a fifteenth century cope hidden beneath the pulpit which has the Archangel Michael embroidered on it, is now on display in a glass case at Glastonbury Abbey. I take time for reflection in the quiet haven of this little church on the St Michael pilgrim route to Glastonbury.

Archangel Michael dispatching a Dragon at St Michael's Church, Othery

DUNDON HILL FORT AND ST ANDREW'S CHURCH, COMPTON DUNDON.

By now Mary and her family were rapidly approaching Glastonbury. From Othery they went through High Ham before reaching the safety of Dundon Hill Druidic settlement. It is on the third day of my pilgrimage to this area that I am able to view from a distance, the wooded hilltop which makes up the settlement of Dundon Hill. Time and energy do not permit a full investigation, but it is enough for me to lean on a gate and focus in the direction of the site. I am visualizing the Holy Family at their last place of sanctuary before ancient Glaston. For Mary, her stay at Dundon would have been a time of preparation for her sacred Mission ahead.

Before I leave the area I pay a short visit to the St Andrew Church, situated in the old village of Compton Dundon to the west of the settlement. It is quite a small church with a correspondingly small Norman tower. In the churchyard another awe inspiring yew tree greets me - the huge girth of its trunk indicates this one to be very ancient. I later read in the church leaflet that it is the remarkable age of 1,700 years - it could almost but not quite, have been here at the time of Mary. On a board inside the church is a certificate of authentication. The yew has a small protective stone wall around it used as seating. I take out a lovely stripy buzzard's feather and immerse it in the soil at the base of the tree with a blessing. As always the deva is overjoyed at being recognized. A small offering is such a simple thing to do, but shows to the Devic Kingdom that we humans do appreciate the work of the nature spirits so lovingly and selflessly given.

Ancient Yew Tree at St Andrew's Church, Compton Dundon

As I attempt to open the old oak nail-studded door, it takes my two hands to lift the heavy iron latch. I enter another place of peace. There are many striking stained glass windows. One depicts a kneeling Mary Magdalene at the feet of Christ in the Garden of the Tomb. Another illustrates St Mary the Virgin with St Michael. A third shows St George with his white horse. Deserving of a mention are the brightly coloured carved roof basses of ferocious creatures including a dragon.

TO STREET YOUTH HOSTEL

The final stretch of my first day's travelling sees me continuing east on the A361, a long straight way across open landscape, interwoven with watery ditches and willow trees, passing the Grey Lake Nature Reserve on my left, to reach Street Youth Hostel at around 6.00 pm. The hostel is a large wooden chalet type building, and my room on the second floor opens to a balcony beneath the eaves. Except for obvious internal modernization, it is just as I remember it forty-five years ago, when I was here as a young person. It is a lovely warm September evening and I sit on a bench seat drinking a cup of tea in the peace of the tree-filled garden. Before me is an apple orchard. I am truly in Avalon - the Isle of Apples. There are commanding views, which in winter time with no leaves on the trees, I am told one can see the St Michael Tower on top of Glastonbury Tor. Tomorrow is to be my Ceremonial day, so this evening I shall spend in contemplation in this idyllic place. The Lady Mary told me she and many from the Heavenly Realms will accompany me on my journey to Glastonbury, and this day I have never felt alone.

MY PILGRIMAGE TO GLASTONBURY - THE ISLE OF AVALON

My hallowed day has begun. I leave the youth hostel around 9.00 am after an attunement with Our Lady. My plan is to first visit Chalice Well in order to ensure that I am completely still, and attuned to the Cosmic Beings who will be with me today. Then I shall proceed to Glastonbury Tor in order to earth the ancient Temple of Hyperborea. Followed by an attempt to discover the exact location of the ancient settlement where Mary stayed. After this - we shall see - but I suspect this will be quite sufficient for one day.

As I take the short drive to Glastonbury a very strange feeling comes over me. This is to be my last Ceremony for Beloved Mary. We have travelled far and wide together and it is not over yet, because after Glastonbury, she will be with me in Wales in a few weeks time. But today - this Ceremony - this last sanctified act - will draw to a close my Mission with her in the South West.

The Lady Mary made the journey from Dundon Fort to the Druidic settlement close to Glastonbury Tor, where she was to reactivate the Hyperborean Temple, in preparation for future visits by her blessed son. This for Mary was a most sacred day - this for me IS a most sacred day.

THE ENCHANTMENT OF CHALICE WELL

Having free parked in Bere Lane which leads to Chalice Well and Glastonbury Tor, I set off, my day pack on my back with all my precious Ceremonial items within.

It was the visionary Wellesley Tudor Pole (W.T.P.) who set up the Chalice Well Trust in 1959, in order to preserve this sacred garden for all time. But what is it about Chalice Well that draws people of all callings to seek sanctuary in the serenity of its contemplative gardens and drink from its Holy waters?

Perhaps just that - the peace - but is there more to it? There are two specific legends associated with Chalice Well, each linked to Joseph of Arimathea.

One is connected to the Holy Grail. On Page 122 of his book '*The Silent Road*' W.T.P. tells us that: '*Joseph is believed to have brought with him the Cup used at the Last Supper and to have buried it for safekeeping beneath Chalice Hill within a stone's throw of the well itself. One of the first books published by the Chalice Well Trust is called The Upper Room. This contains what purports to be a description of the Master's Cup, which in medieval times came to be linked in men's hearts and minds with the lovely mysticism of the Holy Grail.*' There is a Cup known as 'The Blue Bowl of Glastonbury' which is said to have been found buried at a Spring near the River Brue and held under the protection of St Michael. Now I have seen this Blue Bowl. I was with a Gatekeeper group a few years back for a special attunement at Chalice Well. As I held for a brief moment the cherished object, the vibrations which emanated from it were very powerful indeed, and the impression I received was of a very sacred vessel. However whether this is THE Cup - THE Holy Grail, I consider questionable. There is opinion that the Holy Cup is in the Etheric Realms, awaiting the right time to come into physical manifestation, a theory which I uphold (see also Chapter 11).

A further legend has it, that after the Ascension of Christ and fifteen years after the Assumption of our Lady, in AD 63, Joseph and his disciples travelled from the Holy Land with two small Cruets containing the blood and sweat of Christ, which he buried at what is now Chalice Well Gardens. These are represented by the Blood Spring and the White Spring, which join to produce the waters of the well.

I have a question. Is the Cup of the Last Supper and the two Cruets, one and the same - the physical aspect of the Holy Grail? My query because different scholars have attributed the Holy Grail to each relic.

MY CHALICE WELL EXPERIENCE

As I approach Chalice Well I first see the Little St Michael House with its Upper Room. It is here W.T.P. sought to create a replica of the Upper Room of the Last Supper. Seeing it again brings back personal memories. It was in the early 1970s my husband and I with a small spiritual group, shared a very special time in meditation in this little sanctuary.

I enter the garden through a little gate formed by the ancient symbol the VESICA PISCIS. This is formed by two interlocking circles - its sacred geometry symbolizing 'Union' - Union of Heaven and Earth - Union of Spirit and Matter. Walking under a shady wisteria arch, a feeling of deep stillness comes over me. The energies here in this timeless place are alive, vibrant and pure. I walk down shallow stone steps and sit on a bench-seat close to where the water from the Holy Well, having come from its subterranean depths and run through the gardens, exits.

From my last visit a while ago, the framework for the water has been redesigned and I must say is now most beautiful. Today it trickles out of what appears to be a stone Tree of Life, with a surround of reeds and greenery, into a Chalice Cup and on through a series of miniature waterfalls to the pool beneath. It is all set in a neat cobbled area. The water continues within a channel making its magical journey on through this Peace Garden.

The Tree of Life Water Feature at Chalice Well

The morning sunshine is warming my face. The sound of the water is filling my senses. My visit to this sacred place is preparation time for me. I visualize the great Cosmic Star in the Heavens as I say: *"Beloved Ones - let me put this most sacred of days under the Ray of the Christ Star and within the protection of Archangel Michael. Let me form the purist link with the Cosmic Christ as represented by our beloved Master Jesus. Beloved Mary - my Heart Rose - the Divine Mother element of that Cosmic Christ - guide me on your most sacred Mission. I call on all Angels and Archangels, and Masters of the Light for your sacred blessing."* As I close I enfold myself in the protective, uplifting Golden Heavenly Light.

I take a stroll up through the gardens which are filled with roses, stopping to rest beneath an arbour of greenery, where a little guardian stone angel keeps watch. Now it is time to drink of the waters. A little further, on the water pours out of a small stone head of a lion, its copper content staining the stones beneath. This brings to mind a link with the Egyptian Sphinx and the remembrance that our Master Jesus who was in this sacred place, was known as the Lion of Judah. Below its head are three glasses. When all is quiet I move forward to take a sip of this sweet nectar. I sprinkle a little over my head and body as a blessing for the day. I also fill a bottle with this pure liquid from its natural source.

At the top of the garden I come to the original Sacred Well secreted under the enfolding branches of a yew tree. It has a surround of stonework with a protective circular wrought-iron grill out of which moss and ferns are growing. Its heavy wooden lid is raised, revealing the Vesica Piscis design and some six pointed stars in black wrought iron. A couple sitting there quietly, tell me that the Vesica Piscis pattern which was once only on the top of the lid, has now been replicated so that when the lid is in its raised position, it offers full view of the symbol, rather than its original plain wooden face. As I take a closer look at both sides, I see the addition of a heart on the raised lid. How magical - the Sacred Feminine is receiving recognition - the Goddess is awakening. The blending of the energies of the Cosmic Christ and Divine Mother is perfected here at Glastonbury. I lay my pink rose for Mary before the heart with a blessing. I return through the mystical gardens via a small rectangular healing pool.

The Chalice Well lid displaying the Vesica Piscis with the Heart

VISIONS OF GLASTONBURY TOR

I make my way now to Glastonbury Tor which entrance is in Wellhouse Street, aptly named as it houses the well-house for the WHITE SPRING which gushes out of a wall outside it. On the opposite side of the road, the RED SPRING similarly spews forth from a wall. The waters come directly from caverns deep within the bowels of the Earth. Both waters are held to have healing properties. It is alleged that the White Spring is cleansing for the body and the Red Spring will clear up stomach upsets. I stop to take a drink from the White Spring

The little pathway of my previous visit, going up through the woods to Glastonbury Tor, has now become a series of wide stone steps. As the tor with its St Michael Tower comes into view, I stand in reverence - a composed kind of excitement mounting. The tower is all that remains of a fourteenth century church built to replace a previous one which was destroyed by an earthquake in the thirteen century.

Glastonbury Tor

So what was the purpose of this mysterious hill? What secrets do the terraces which I can see encircling the tor hold? Is the tor hollow and are there tunnels connecting to some sort of initiation chamber below the ground? All these questions were entering my mind as I sat in contemplation at home following my research and before I set out on my pilgrimage.

During my attunement I first became aware that Glastonbury Tor was an Observatory for watching the Heavens, one of many throughout our ancient British Isles. One other I have come across is at Henab Garn Goch nr Llandeilo on the northern edge of the Black Mountain in South Wales, a place where Naomi visited during her time in Wales after the crucifixion. This is followed by a vision of the ancient Druid Priests and Priestess moving up from their settlement below the tor, winding their way round the hill to the top on a precessional route. They then went BELOW the ground somewhere near the top of the tor, to some sort of Temple - an inner sanctum. I saw a sacred Ceremony invoking the Great White Light being carried out, well hidden from view. The Cosmic Light pouring down from the Heavens, was shooting through the top of the tor into the Earth beneath, to the Earth Star Crystal. Glastonbury Tor was a conductor of the Cosmic Ray. The mystical Merlin was involved with this magical ceremony. Once again the union between the Heavenly Spheres and our precious planet was being cemented. For me, a connection was made with the Egyptian pyramids and the Sphinx, wherein a past life I experienced an initiation Ceremony with Is-Ra below the earth. It is also here at Glastonbury Tor, as a young Naomi with the Priestess Mary, I had taken part in a special Ceremony towards the end of my time in Britain. Once again I know that this revered place will welcome me.

I was reminded of the discoveries of Hamish Miller as he dowsed the Michael and Mary Ley energy currents some years back. The Michael Ley Line winds around the tor looping the St Michael Tower at the top and on down. The Mary current at the tower interweaves with the Michael current, forming what he calls a point of fusion. In their book '*The Sun and the Serpent*' here is what Hamish Miller and Paul Broadbent have to say about this phenomenon - Page 155: '*The Mary energy formed a container which encompassed the Michael current and its bulbous projection around the tower. The symbolism was graphic. The female force enclosed the male energy in the form of a double lipped cup. It was a Chalice or Grail.*' Then: '*Within an hour the secret purpose of the Tor had been revealed. It was a place where the male and female energies of the St Michael Line were ritually mating, the actual point of fusion apparently located at the site of the altar of the old church.*' This concept of fusion would seem to imply several things. First, the union between the Cosmos and the Earth Plane which is being reborn in this new Age. Then, the union between God and the Goddess which has for so long been denied. A third is the union between humankind and its Source. Finally, the union of the Immaculate Conception. As we have learnt, the age-old symbol of the Vesica Piscis in Chalice Well also represents this symbolic Cosmic union.

Back to the present. Looking at the tor my insights come flooding back. Again I have the impression of an Observatory for studying the Stars. Also I am feeling that accessed by underground passages, a secret Temple lying beneath the structure, could well have been a reality. Looking at the terraces I can quite easily imagine a precessional route around the tor, even allowing for the possibility that earthquake damage could have shifted the alignment.

Walking through the kissing gate I begin the climb, resting for a moment on a large stone, one of the few left marking the original pilgrim path to the top. A group of people puff their way past me and I hear: "*they could do with a cable car up here!*" On the ridge I see scores of pilgrims/tourists making their way to the top like a lot of tiny ants. There are too many folk around, so part way up I take a left along one of the grassy perambulation terraces and find myself methodically walking my way around the base, my hands enfolded within an imaginary robe. Looking across the open landscape, white gossamer clouds are hanging in a blue sky, offering up the most magical formations - an angel - a spaceship - oh the imagination - isn't it wonderful! I am suddenly alerted to the raven's croak then am amazed to see no less than five ravens encircling the tree tops close to me. I rarely see more than one - perhaps a pair. My immediate thought is that they each represents one of the Holy Ones linked to Glastonbury; the Master Jesus, the Lady Mary, Mary Magdalene, Joseph of Arimathea and King Arthur. My heart is uplifted. I take this as a sign that THEY, the Beloved Ones are watching over me and that all is well The next day I buy John Michell's recent book 'New Light on the Ancient Mystery of Glastonbury' wherein he says that ravens have left the tor and not been seen for many a year. Well - these sacred birds, symbolic of the alchemist Merlin and Bran, the Grail Keeper in the Christian Grail Romances, have returned.

THE LOST CONTINENT OF HYPERBOREA

As I am walking I contemplate my future Ceremony. How do I know that it is a Hyperborean Temple? Because I was told! At home in an attunement when I had many questions to ask of Beloved Mary, I discovered that there was an ancient Temple at Glastonbury Tor in the Etheric. Okay - my initial thought was it being Atlantean as with previous Temples - but no. I was puzzled for a while until trawling through any previous knowledge, I eventually came up with Hyperborea - - bingo. What can I say but utter astonishment. I checked and re-checked, but yes - the Cosmic Beings wished that I earth an ancient Hyperborean Temple!

What do I know of Hyperborea? Very little. I am aware that as with the ancient civilizations of Lemuria and Atlantis, Hyperborea goes back to another epoch. Suddenly I find myself picking off my bookshelves 'The Light in Britain' by Grace and Ivan Cooke. This is one of the books I chose NOT to pre-read before my Mission with Mary in order not to be influenced. A glance through its contents tells me nothing, but then I see my own note 'Hyperborea' - "Thank you dear White Eagle for your guidance once more." This book tells the story of pilgrimages made by Grace Cooke with her husband Ivan and their grand-daughter, to some of the ancient sites of Britain in the 1960s. Wherever they went Grace Cooke's mediumistic gift brought to life ancient civilizations. On one occasion they were at the earthwork of Uffington Castle in the Berkshire Downs, when she became aware of a great Being of Light wearing a crown, whom she knew to be a Hyperborian King. On Page 23 of their work, White Eagle tells us: 'In the beginning, the earth was peopled by perfect sons of God who came in all their glory as guardians of a young race on a young planet. These God-men, great and wise brothers, brought the knowledge of the power of the spiritual sun or Christ to the earth. They came first to the land of Hyperborea whose very stones became impregnated with the light they brought to earth. In the course of time these great and wise brothers journeyed across the northern hemisphere taking with them the truth of the light of the sun. Knowledge of sun worship, of the power of the light, swept across the world from that original northern continent of Hyperborea, from the great Sun Brotherhood. What you now call Great Britain, was once a part of the ancient continent and later of Atlantis.'

With these few words, the wise sage White Eagle tells us of Hyperborea, its connection to Atlantis and to our mystical Britain.

GLASTONBURY TOR HYPERBOREAN TEMPLE CEREMONY

The date is the 9th September 2009, which I realize has special significance. In the first instance, it is the date of the Nativity of the Virgin Mary - my blessed Lady. Astrological data tells me, that the Moon trines the Sun on this date, indicating that the great Cosmic Light will shine forth in its full glory and bring a positive, harmonious energy to my Ceremony. The great awakening of Planet Earth to the new vibrations will move up a notch. Also the 9th day of the 9th month of 2009 would seem to have a special connotation. I am sure someone more knowledgeable than I could give some deep astrological insight into this. In numerology this date totals a number eleven one of the master numbers, and thus is a visionary vibration which can work through the intuition. All these are good omens for this sacred Mission.

I am now on the north-eastern edge of Glastonbury Tor and looking for a quiet place for my Ceremony. Dropping off the hill slightly I find my way to a field and settle myself down underneath a most beautiful ash tree - perfect. I am to learn later, that I have placed myself in a direct line between the St Michael Tower and the ancient Druidic settlement where Mary stayed, AND at the point where the Michael Ley leaves the tor.

My Ceremonial articles are in place as I prepare with the deepest reverence for my ritual - to earth the ancient Hyperborean Temple. The energies are building as I tune in to the Great Cosmic Star and the infinite wisdom of the Masters of Light. My pink scarf is around my shoulders. I hear the gentle rhythm of drumming coming from the top of the tor, and the smell of incense pervades the warm air. I am voicing: *"Let good work be done this sacred day."*

It is midday. I begin with *'The Great Invocation.'* I tender each of my special crystals to the Masters of Light. For the alchemist Merlin I present my merlinite crystal, for Is-Ra and ancient Egypt - my turquoise crystal, and for the Lady Mary and the Goddess I offer my rose quartz crystal. I proceed with my Cosmic Ceremony as for the Atlantean Temple, but call in the energies of the ancient continent of Hyperborea, and ask that the Temple in the Etheric Realm be earthed for all times in this hallowed place. It is to be grounded at the ancient Druidic settlement on the lower slopes of Glastonbury Tor. As I speak the words: *"Let the Light Shine - Let it be done"* this great Cosmic happening is secured by St Michael at the highest pinnacle of the tor with his sword - the noise is tremendous and the power is immense. My inner vision shows me the down-pouring of Cosmic Light from the great Sun-Star, shooting right through the St Michael Tower - deep deep into the earth - connecting to the Earth Star Crystal at its centre. My impression is of a seed being implanted within the Earth's core at Glastonbury Tor - the Pleiadean Star Seed of Hyperborea is entrusted to our world at the beginning of the Aquarian Age. From here in time, all the Holy places in mystic Britain and throughout the world will be infused with this Star Seed. I say: *"Let the Cosmic Fire spring forth from the belly of the great Earth Mother bringing new life and healing."* The Light now rises like a great fountain to flow out over the whole planet.

The Masters speak First:

THE MASTER OF THE STAR

"Pilgrim of Light. Let thy grace pervade this sacred land. The Cosmic Light from ancient Hyperboria is impregnating this sacred land. The time is right - the time is now - for this ancient sacred energy to be returned to your Earth Plane. Its power is great - its vibrational energy will be felt far and wide. Many will respond to its energy. Many will respond to its call. The Light is getting brighter and purer as I speak with you. It is penetrating deep below your Earth Plane to link with the Great Crystal at its core. The Cosmic energies are sealed for all time. Glastonbury is the central axis for this incoming Light in these sacred Isles. This is why our Divine Mary with her beloved son came here, and this is why Jesus came with Joseph of Arimathea - to set in the ether the great Cosmic Plan for the New Age. This is why Jesus and Mary Magdalene returned - to set in motion the inevitable strengthening of the Grid System of your Planet. ALL in preparation for the New Jerusalem. All is prepared for the great new Aquarian Age to come. So many beloved souls over the centuries have played their part - so many of more recent years. We are aware of the great Initiate - you know him as Walter Tudor Pole - a master of the highest degree - who put into place the foundation for future pilgrims to Glastonbury at Chalice Well - a place of sacred origin. My Pilgrim of Light we must leave you now. Beloved Jesus wishes to speak with you."

I feel the energies shift as this dear Master steps forth:

THE MASTER JESUS

"My child - my beloved Child of the Light. We would wish you to know we have all been with you every step of the way during your Mission with our beloved Mary. It has seen you travel far and wide in your mystical Isles, and the great Beings of Light thank you for your dedication and love. As with OUR journeying in the past when we all came to this ancient land, there have been times of hardship and sorrow. But there were times of great joy and un-relinquished perfect love. The Light we sought to invoke at places of Druidic worship was reactivated by our mother - Mary, in that incarnation. You have followed in her footsteps. We each have a part to play sister - Sister of Light. You have played your part well, with dedication and diligence. Our beloved Mary, the Rose in the Heart, is with me and she too wishes to talk with you."

As this beautiful Master leaves me he offers a blessing in the air, two fingers extended Heavenwards. Our Lady comes in:

THE LADY MARY

"My child - my beloved child. Thank you for your part in this sacred Mission set down 2,000 years ago, when you and I walked the Earth together. This time we've shared has I know, brought back many memories for you on your pilgrimage. We have one more place where we shall meet and that is in Wales at the Aconbury settlement. But

THIS is the end of our time go together in the South West. BUT dearest daughter, I will ALWAYS be at your side - I will ALWAYS be in your heart. In your moments of quiet contemplation - I shall be there. In your times of stress - I shall be there. In your times of joy - I shall be there I WILL NEVER LEAVE YOU. Thank you - all the beloved Angels, Archangels and Masters, thank you for your dedication to this sacred work. The Light of all Eternity is within your being - the love of my deepest heart is with you always my child. Thank you."

I thank the beloved Masters for their treasured words. During my Ceremony I have been conscious of a multitude of Heavenly Hosts - Masters, Angels and Archangels. As Mary is leaving I am feeling such a special blessing emanating from her. My heart is full. She - who has walked my pilgrimage with me for so long. She - whose Mission I have faithfully followed. Overwhelming feelings of humbleness and the deepest love for all the blessed souls who have shared my journey engulf me: *"Beloved Ones I honour you all."* This is almost the end of my personal journey with Mary in South West Britain. My final thoughts I will share with you at the end of my Glastonbury pilgrimage. I close my sacred Ceremony.

TO THE ST MICHAEL TOWER

My Ceremonial things carefully put away, I step out from under my beautiful ash tree into the sunshine, thanking it for its shady protection. I take the walk to the top of Glastonbury Tor in order to implant my white quartz and rose-pink quartz crystals in the good earth. Climbing the steep steps I feel full of Light and joy as if I am walking on air. At the St Michael Tower I join the throng - all the world and his wife are up here today! Also the energies of the ancient tor seem to have attracted a herd of curious cows, who are standing in a mass close to the tower. The drummers dressed in their colourful garb are still going strong - they are giving pleasure to a lot of people. I have a chat with one of them asking if today is a special occasion, wondering if they would be aware of Mary's nativity. I am told: *"well it's the 9th of the 9th 2009 so we thought we'd come up here and celebrate and just have fun."* There's no answer to that. One of their group enters the tower and plays his solitary tune to the Universe on an American-Indian flute - it is quite hauntingly beautiful.

From up here I have a fine view out over the surrounding countryside. Laid out before me, is the way Mary and Naomi travelled through the Somerset Levels to the coast at Burnham-on-Sea, in order to sail for Wales at the end of Mary's Mission in the South West.

THE GLASTONBURY ZODIAC

As I stand on Glastonbury Tor the ancient Zodiac comes to mind. Katherine Maltwood in her book '*Glastonbury's Temple of the Stars*' writes of the Glastonbury Zodiac which she discovered or should I say rediscovered, in the early part of the twentieth century. She indicates that this is a Star Temple, claimed to have been set in the landscape of the Vale of Avalon by the great

Merlin many thousands of years ago. It depicts zodiacal animals and figures incorporating the myths and legends of Arthurian Romances. On Page 5 of her work Maltwood says: *'To realize at all the size of the prehistoric 'Round Table of the Grail' one must think in miles not inches, in millennia instead of centuries; for the Temple is ten miles in diameter, it is about 5,000 years old, and this counterpart of the heavens corresponds with the constellation figures recognized by astronomers today.'* She asserts that in this modern day of aerial photography one can pin-point the separate figures.

However, from this high spot I can see one section of PISCES the Fishes at Wearyall Hill - the other is a little further off in Street and not easily identified from here. Glastonbury Tor is delineated as AQUARIUS the Water Bearer, in the shape of a phoenix or eagle, wings spread out, with its beak in Chalice Well sipping of the waters of life. Interestingly, at the top of the St Michael Tower is a fourteenth century stone carving of an eagle. Jesus the *'fisher of men'* having laid down the foundation of Christianity in Glastonbury at the beginning of the Piscean Age (see my insights at Glastonbury Abbey), heralds now the Aquarian Age with its eagle, symbol of St John the Beloved. Could St John perhaps be the Master of the New Age? Throughout the ages in different civilizations, the eagle has been one personification of the resurrection - man's ascent on Wings of Light into the Higher Realms, free from the restraints of Earthly ties and ignorance. Maltwood tells us, that Glastonbury Tor is the central point within The Zodiac - it is the Mount of Transfiguration for the Christed Man.

When I was in contemplation at Chalice Well, I had a vision of a maid whom I knew to be the Lady Mary, collecting water in a pitcher from the Holy Well, putting the pitcher on her shoulder, and holding it with one hand, she walked up to the top of Glastonbury Tor hill. The saying of the Master Jesus and I am paraphrasing, *'follow the 'man' with the pitcher of water'* came to mind. Mary of the Age of the Fishes was bringing the pure waters of the Holy Spring to flood The Tor of Aquarius with new life. This is OUR journey as pilgrims on our pathway to the Light - to search diligently at the Well of Enlightenment and take that Ancient Wisdom to the highest point of our understanding - to literally *'reach for the stars'*. The Master of the Star spoke with me at my Temple Ceremony. He is guiding each of us, ever upwards to the goal of perfection and comprehension of Divine Truth. Let us then open our minds to Divine Wisdom and our hearts to Divine Love as we enter the new Aquarian Age.

I inspect the ancient tower trying to view the stone effigies. There is no way I can see the eagle high up in its eyrie. But the two within my line of vision are most intriguing. There is a carving of a soul being weighed on a balance by the Archangel Michael. Then St Bridget or St Bride, one of the great Earth Goddesses of pre-Christianity, is seen milking her cow, bringing a link with Hathor the Cow Goddess of Ancient Egypt. In my earlier vision Egypt had played a part. And - isn't it curious that some Glastonbury cows feel drawn to be at the St Michael Tower!

After taking a few photographs, I wonder how I am to bury my crystals without drawing attention to myself. Many folk are sitting around on the grass enjoying the afternoon sunshine. I join them at a discreet distance and sit looking out at the surrounding landscape listening to the drumming. I have a small knife with me and with apologies to Mother Earth, am able to dig two small holes and insert a crystal in each, carefully brushing the grass over the spot. Success - they are hidden and no-one has noticed. I seal the offerings by carefully pouring a little of the water from Chalice Well over the top.

TO GOG AND MAGOG FOR THE DRUIDIC SETTLEMENT

I leave Glastonbury Tor via the same steps to join Stone Down Lane at the bottom. I am now off in search of Gog and Magog, two very old oak trees of which I've heard speak, and which I feel will guide me to the ancient Druidic settlement where Mary and her family stayed. The giant Gogmagog is reputed to have been the last giant in Britain and was slain by Brutus the first King of Britain, who landed with his Trojan army at Totnes in Devon.

One of the two 2,000 year-old Trees – Gog (or Magog)

With the position of Gog and Magog off the limit of the street map, I follow instructions given me by one of the drummers. At the lane I turn right, descend Stone Down Hill, and go left at the bottom along a dirt track. As the track comes to its natural end I see Gog and Magog on my right amidst much shrubbery. These oaks are bleached white with age and are very gnarled, the branches standing out quite starkly against a bright blue sky. From outward appearances there is no sign of life. I climb over the small fence enclosure and rest both hands on the trunk of one of the trees - there is life - maybe Etheric in nature - but I can feel the energetic forces pulsating from deep within. With a sacred blessing, I leave a silver star for the Master of the Star and a white quartz crystal for the ancient Druids in one of the crevices. For Beloved Mary I insert a single pink rose. I subsequently learnt that these ancient oak trees are the only two left of a huge circle of trees, cut down when the farmer wished to clear the land. By counting the rings of the felled trees it was discovered they were 2,000 years old. When I heard all this I went cold, because while standing next to them I knew intuitively that Gog and Magog with the other oak trees, would have formed the circumference of the ancient Druidic settlement of Glastonbury. They were growing when Mary was here.

So what is the exact position of the settlement and where is the Hyperborean Temple resting? Intuition directs me and I retrace my steps a few yards until I come to a stile with a footpath sign to *'Paradise Lane and Glastonbury'*. Over the stile I go. I am in an open field below Stone Down Hill. THIS is the ancient site and before me is the just earthed Temple, though of course still in its Etheric state. To ensure accuracy I dowse, and yes my insight is correct: *"Thank you, oh thank you Angels for your guidance."* I am actually standing within the very settlement, where as Naomi, with Mary, Jesus and Joseph, I was 2000 years ago. I can visualize the Druidic Tree Temple complete. What a blessing indeed to have discovered this. I had thought from the settlement I would have seen Glastonbury Tor, but in this day and age there are too many trees in my view-line. However, my instincts tell me that there was an ancient track to Glastonbury Tor for worship, which went over Stone Down Hill and which would have had wooden walkways laid down over any marshy area. I offer a final benediction before leaving this ancient place.

Suddenly I look up and see a remarkably accurate dove cloud formation in the clear blue sky. For me the dove is a symbol of peace and prophecy - an Angel which brings in the Goddess Energy. At home I have wondered about any further significance. On my book shelf is a work by Mary Caine called *'The Glasonbury Zodiac'* wherein she has built on the findings of Katherine Maltwood. In the Zodiac Landscape of the Vale of Avalon, the dove is represented by the harmonious air sign of Libra, an indicator that the scales of justice can be tempered by mercy. On Page 91 Caine tells us that: *'the Dove of the Holy Spirit.....is undoubtedly a light-bringer, a source of enlightenment and priests in the Mysteries, after bewailing the sun god's death would shout "Hail to the Dove, restorer of Light.'* What a time to have this vision.

I return to Glastonbury by way of Higher Wick Farm, now Paddington Farm, on account of the fact it is presently an activity centre for children. From one of the fields I now have a view of the St Michael Tower on the tor. My route back takes me through Wick Hollow and soon I am in the town. Walking into Glastonbury feels like walking into mystical mayhem after the peace of the ancient settlement and my wander back through quiet country lanes. Everyone is everywhere. Of course being a sunny day people are milling around enjoying the delights of open-air continental style cafe life. A lovely old cart horse is waiting patiently for its owner at one of the cafes. It is around 5.00 pm and my sacred day is at an end. I walk back to my car and return to Street. Reflecting on my Ceremony at Glastonbury Tor and my discoveries, I am filled with profound wonder and great elation. It was my final Mission for the Lady Mary and I shall need a little time to assimilate it all.

EXPLORATIONS OF GLASTONBURY

The following day, once again I take the road to Glastonbury, this time my intention is to do some exploring. My wanderings are to take me to Glastonbury Abbey, the Parish Church of St John the Baptist, The Tribunal, St Margaret's Chapel and Wearyall Hill. I park in Bere Lane as before and walk into town.

GLASTONBURY ABBEY

My first port of call is Glastonbury Abbey, and I arrive this morning as it opens. I have not been here for many a long year and welcome the opportunity to set foot within the beautiful grounds of this ancient ruined Benedictine Abbey. The abbey was established in AD 712 and fell into ruin following the Dissolution of the Monasteries. There are many legends associated with it, some of which I shall look into. In its heyday it was obviously a place of some grandeur evidenced by the extent and design of the abbey ruins. Set out in the new Exhibition Hall is a model of the original structure, pictorial evidence of its internal decoration, and a beautifully embroidered altar cloth and vestments. The Abbot's house must also have been quite grand, with its kitchen having no less than four fireplaces. All testament to the abbey's importance as a monastic establishment.

As I enter its cloistered sanctuary, I am reminded of my own past life connection with the abbey as the monk and sacristan St Neot, which I learned when at St. Neots in Cornwall. I pay homage to the Glastonbury Thorn just at its entrance, which is a cutting from the original tree and is reputed to flower at Christmastime as well as in May.

ST MARY'S CHAPEL (THE LADY CHAPEL)
SITE OF THE VETUSTA ECCLESIA (THE OLD CHURCH)

I walk straight across to the Lady Chapel which was erected in the twelfth century, and enter by a magnificent carved stone archway. A board illustrates its sumptuous colour and beauty before the Dissolution. Legend has it, that here on this site the first Christian church was built I sit on a seat just outside the Lady Chapel and give some thought to the myths surrounding this chapel.

The Lady Chapel in Glastonbury Abbey

I have seen a pen and ink drawing of a small oblong wattle and daub structure, depicting what the original church could have looked like. In medieval tradition it is contended that this church, which was called the Vetusta Ecclesia, is Britain's oldest church. In the sixth century, Gildas the British historian who spoke with me at Trefenty penned, that it is the ancient mystic Isles of Britain at the farthest reaches of the then known civilization, which first received the Christian message. Jesus is said to have dedicated the first church to his Mother - the Virgin Mary. But who built it and who brought Christianity to Britain? Over the centuries many have written on this subject and there are usually two contenders. The first is Joseph of Arimathea, when he returned to Glastonbury with his disciples some years after the crucifixion. Second, that it was our Lord Jesus the Christ, on one of his visits before he began his ministry in the Holy Land. Little is chronicled about Jesus in this regard and yet much about Joseph.

As I am mulling these things over I have a vision. There is a stone - a circular stone - the Master Jesus laid a Foundation Stone for the first church and it is beneath the Old Church. Engraved on the stone is an ancient symbol of an Equal Sided Cross held within the Circle of Eternal Life. It will be discovered further into the Aquarian Age. This sacred act was undertaken by the thirteen year old Jesus at the end of his journeying through South West Britain with his mother Mary, Joseph of Arimathea and Naomi (my story), AFTER his going into the Temple in Jerusalem. This Temple visit was crucial and had special significance apart from his Bar Mitzveh. The boy Jesus was impregnated with the Christ Light, which Cosmic energies he was to transfer with his physical presence to British soil. The Light of the Holy Land was to be implanted in Glastonbury - in preparation for the New Jerusalem. By this act the Master was to earth a Cosmic Current. THIS was the beginning of Jesus' Mission in Britain. It was later with Mary Magdalene that he returned to Glastonbury, where this Christ Consciousness was further upheld and implanted in the Grid System.

The Stone Engraving on the wall of the Lady Chapel – 'Jesus Maria'

On a subsequent visit with Joseph of Arimathea, Jesus built his first church. As I am tuning in to these vibrations, I am having a vision of a small simple round structure of interwoven tree branches with a roughly thatched roof. The Altar is placed directly over The Stone and has on it a lit candle. This place was a sacred Shrine - indeed a Temple of Light. After the crucifixion, Joseph returned to Glastonbury and enlarged the original church by erecting a second circular structure. On the Altar in this enlarged, now firmly established church, my inner world shows me a Chalice with a permanently lit flame - the Eternal Flame. A thought - is this the physical Chalice which could have come with Joseph from the Holy Land, of which so much has been written? Something else has struck me. The church which is now built of two circular 'walls' - could this be another expression of union as is the Vesica Piscis? Could this once again represent the union between the old Jerusalem in the Holy Land and a New Jerusalem in Britain? It was the poet and seer William Blake who prophesied that the New Jerusalem would become manifest in Britain. This could be the perfect place to remind us of Blake's poem of the Master Jesus in Britain - 'Jerusalem' of which many of us are so familiar:

JERUSALEM

And did those feet in ancient time
Walk upon England's mountains green?
And was the holy Lamb of God
On England's pleasant pastures seen?
And did the countenance divine
Shine forth upon our clouded hills?
And was Jerusalem builded here
Among those dark satanic mills?
Bring me my bow of burning gold!
Bring me my arrows of desire!
Bring me my spear!
O clouds, unfold!
Bring me my chariot of fire!
I will not cease from mental fight,
Nor shall my sword sleep in my hand,
Till we have built Jerusalem
In England's green and pleasant land.

Still in contemplation at the St Mary Chapel I hear a voice:

MASTER OF THE STAR

"My beloved child. All we would wish to say is to confirm your intuitive discoveries. There is more - much more dearest one, which in time will become manifest. As always we thank you for your time and your diligence to these questions. The Christ Light was indeed implanted at the sacred Glastonbury by the beloved Master Jesus, Master of the 6th Ray of Peace and Devotion All is as you surmise. Rest assured. This is truth pilgrim. This is an ancient truth. The Cosmos has opened its doors just a little for you to understand some of the hidden secrets at Glastonbury. More will be revealed in time as the Aquarian Age progresses. It is early days. The Master of Light will return, not in physical manifestation BUT in the hearts of all humanity. The Rose in the Heart of the Goddess will enfold the Christ energies, and they will dwell as one - forever - in the hearts of humankind. IT WILL BE SO. IT IS DESTINED. IT IS THE LAW. Heaven will manifest on Earth once more. The Cosmic Star shines its Light for ALL to embrace and live in its pure ray for all time."

My words: *"Thank you Master of the Cosmos. Thank you and bless you."*

As I rise, I see behind me carved on the south wall of the St Mary Chapel, the words 'JESUS MARIA' in archaic letters. This is said to mark one of the thirteenth century medieval stations visited by pilgrims during their tour of the abbey. I am now looking for somewhere suitable to place my pink rose offering for the Lady Mary, which is bit difficult as there is no floor left in the chapel, but eventually I do find a niche.

THE CHAPEL OF ST JOSEPH OF ARIMATHEA.

At the beginning of the sixteenth century the crypt of the Lady Chapel now open to the skies, was excavated to the level of the St Joseph Chapel. I take a wander down and walk its length to an altar at the east end. To my right I see the old well with its small but beautifully sculptured curved stone arch. There are railings protecting it, but I am able to put my hand through and place my offering of a lovely white quartz crystal on a stone slab near the well.

THE TOMB OF KING ARTHUR

I am now standing before the High Altar where there is an oblong stone-framed area. A plaque tells me that this is the *'Site of King Arthur's Tomb. In the year 1191 the bodies of King Arthur and his Queen were said to have been found on the south side of the Lady Chapel on 10ᵗʰ April 1278. Their remains were removed in the presence of King Edward and Queen Eleanor to a Black Marble Tomb on this site. This tomb survived until the Dissolution of the Abbey in 1539'.* Alongside, as documented by the Welsh travelling man of the cloth Giraldus Cambrensis, was found a leaden cross, the Latin inscription of which translated as *'Here lies Arthur, the famous King in the Isle of Avalon'.* There has been a suggestion however, that the discovery of the two bodies, purported to be of King Arthur and Queen Guinevere, came at an opportune time in the Abbey's history, when pilgrim visits were falling! Food for thought.

IS THERE AN ALTERNATIVE ARTHUR?

These discoveries should have been the closing chapter in the life of the historical Arthur. However, it would seem only to have added to the legends which have come down to us through the centuries, and brought into the public domain by a multitude of scribes, offering immeasurable and diverse theories of his life and death.

I give you the following in the tiniest of nutshells, because I am sure most of you are all familiar with the legends relating to King Arthur, and if not, there is much literature to peruse. Arthur was born in the fifth century, son of Uther Pendragon, at Tintagel Castle in Cornwall. With a military background, on the death of his father, he gathered around him a group of young knights whose creed was that of chivalry. He married Guinevere and they set up their court named Camelot at Cadbury Castle in Somerset. It is said that he was brought to Glastonbury for burial. The Arthurian romances also tell of his mighty magical sword Excalibur and the Lady of the Lake (see Chapter 8), and the search for the Holy Grail. But is there a deeper meaning to Arthurian legend?

In Katherine Maltwood's Zodiac of Glastonbury, the Fire sign of Sagittarius is represented by King Arthur. He is depicted stretched across the landscape of the Vale of Avalon in full armour astride his horse, which is taking the place of the Sagittarian centaur. Arthur is Hercules the King of the Constellations, and as such, he is not just delineated within Somerset in Britain, but is represented in many ancient cultures as for example; Babylonian, Egyptian and Assyrian. On Page 42 of her *'Glastonbury's Temple of the Stars'* Maltwood points out that: *'The stars of the constellation Hercules exactly coincide with the effigy and the stars of Lyra, the harp, fall on his back - a reminder of the Hyperborean's god who 'plays upon the harp and dances every night, from the vernal equinox till the rising of the Pleiades', as Diadorus Siculus recounts.'* and *'The ancient Britons called Lyra 'King Arthur's Harp'* - this last perhaps the origin of the Welsh harp. Thus Arthur becomes a Solar Hero - a Great Being of high esteem within the Heavenly Realms.

Further, in *'The Light in Britain'* mentioned earlier, Grace Cook on Page 21 says after witnessing an ancient Ceremony at Uffington Castle: *'I felt that a great being was enveloped within this light and thought it might be the Christ-form. The form gradually became more definite; and then I saw another being appear who seemed like a king, wearing a crown of gold and robed in light, with the points of that crown emitting rays of great brilliance. I thought then about King Ar-Thor, the ancient mythical Hyperborian King, and felt that it must be he who had come to bring blessing to his people'*

So....Ar-Thor - Hercules - King of the Constellations - a Hyperborean Sun God - a 'true' King of Britain! In this context his role on Earth and in other realms, would be to cut through the powers of darkness with Excalibur which now becomes a solar sword, and be a bearer of the Cosmic Christ Light.

RETURN TO MY ABBEY WANDERINGS.

On this beautiful sunny morning I am now taking a relaxing amble around the rest of the abbey ruins. Low stone walls outline the position of the cloisters, the refectory and the Abbot's hall. I go into the grand circular edifice of the Abbot's kitchen which is still in tact. Finally to the Exhibition Hall which documents much of the abbey's history and archeological finds. On display are chunks of ancient stonework from the original building, including a striking rose sculpture. In a huge glass cabinet is the Othery Cope discovered at Othery Church, which dates to the 1470. It illustrates Archangel Michael and is a fine example of the most exquisite medieval embroidery.

Finally, before leaving I sit in the sun underneath a plane tree, which I note has been planted *'In honour of Geoffry Ashe'* who is/was a local historian and writer of many works of Arthurian persuasion. I take time for a little stillness.

THE PARISH CHURCH OF ST JOHN THE BAPTIST

On leaving the abbey I make my way up through the town to the Parish Church of St John the Baptist, taking in a coffee shop on the way. The present church built in the fifteenth century, is an impressive building with a very tall Norman tower and a grandiose castellated porch over its main entrance. Its west doorway is most interesting, as in the spandrels are featured the lamb and flag, a symbol of St John the Baptist, and the eagle, symbol of St John the Evangelist. Little is known of any previous building, though excavations have proved its existence. As with the abbey, this church passed to the Crown with the Dissolution.

On entering, one of the 'lady guardians' ushers me in and hands me a descriptive leaflet, while the other makes a note in the book of my presence! There is much of historical interest within the walls of this church, but I make my way to the north wall for the Shrine of St Joseph of Arimathea. Above the shrine is a huge and most magnificent stained glass window depicting some of the Glastonbury legends. I am spellbound as I stand facing this window. On the left is a haloed St Joseph with his staff, royally robed in purple. Cradled in his hands are the two small cruets, claimed to have contained the blood and sweat of Christ, which it is said, he brought from the Holy Land.

Moving on, I kneel before a small Altar covered by a white cloth with a naturally shaped wooden cross on it. Above is a framed picture of a devout Virgin Mary hands held together in prayer. This is a silent moment wherein I offer a benediction to my beloved Mary at the close of my sacred Mission.

I complete my visit here by going into the St George's Chapel on the south transept, which is quite beautiful and retained as a sanctuary for prayer and meditation. A section of an impressive stained glass window on its eastern wall shows St George and the Dragon, with in the higher reaches, a winged St Michael. In his elevated position, the Archangel appears to be rising into the Light, perhaps illustrating the goal to which we all aspire as we learn to slay the dragon within.

THE TRIBUNAL

Situated close to the St John Church, the Elizabethan Tribunal building doubles as a venue for the local Tourist Office and Museum portraying the Lake Villages of Somerset. I spend a fascinating time wandering round the exhibition, which chronicles archeological discoveries, and shows how life must have been in this area during the Iron Age. On one stand is a diagrammatic map demonstrating Glastonbury as an important port in the Ancient World. In fact it was THE centre for exports and imports in Britain. It was the hub of a huge wheel which saw commodities such as tin, iron, copper, glass and pottery going out in all directions to the rest of the British Isles. Also, these goods went south through Dummonia to coastal ports, thence on to Gaul, the Mediterranean and beyond. Imported items of pottery, glass, spices etc. would have travelled the same ancient routes. In the Museum, of particular interest to me, is the remains of a dug-out canoe protected within a large glass case, which was excavated many years ago. Did it bring back soul memories for me? Yes - as Naomi I travelled in this manner during my pilgrimage through the Somerset Levels to Glastonbury 2,000 years ago.

ST MARGARET'S CHAPEL.

I was hoping to visit St Mary's Roman Catholic Church in Abbey Road but sadly it is closed. Nearby is the rather special little Chapel of St Margaret, which was once a part of Glastonbury Abbey. It is set within the courtyard of the Magdalene Almshouses, and to reach it I take a narrow lane off the main Abbey Road. I first come to the meticulously kept gardens of the old Almshouses, one row of which still stands and is occupied. I enter the little chapel. Its beautiful interior has whitewashed walls with a little of the natural stonework left to view. The Altar is well presented as a simple wooden frame on which is a cross and some flowers. I light a candle for Mary and offer a blessing. This chapel is a sanctuary of peace - a perfect place to spend a few moments in the silence towards the end of my three day pilgrimage to Glastonbury. As I turn to depart I see on a table at the back of the chapel, a most lovely picture of the Virgin Mary and the Christ Child in Eastern Christian style, alongside which are lilies in a glass vase: "*Thank you Mary - my final vision of you in Glastonbury.*"

WEARYALL HILL AND THE SACRED THORN

Before returning to Devon one last pilgrimage completes my time here - Wearyall Hill. Grabbing myself a bag of chips - the best chips ever - and munching away rather irreverently, I stroll up Fishers Hill through the houses until I reach a small kissing gate which leads to Wearyall Hill. Here it is alleged that Joseph of Arimathea and his disciples landed after their long sea voyage from the Holy Land. Joseph set his staff in the ground pronouncing: '*Since we are weary all, here we will rest.*' The staff took root and grew to produce the first thorn tree. The Sacred Thorn is immediately in my view line. I finish my repast before I pace the short distance to it. Protected by circular railings, it is decorated with many brightly coloured prayer flags. I offer a blessing, and place on the earth underneath the Holy Tree a white quartz crystal and a lovely white and black magpie's feather. The site of the original thorn which is believed to have been cut down during the English Civil War, is marked by a solitary broken stone slab adjacent to the tree. It is this slab, according to Hamish Miller that the St Michael Line runs through.

I continue my climb to the top of the hill, passing a tame rabbit, obviously a pet by its colouring, nibbling away at the fresh grass - I do hope he finds his way home. The views from up here are far reaching. My eyes are particularly drawn across the valley to Glastonbury Tor - the St Michael Tower set against a blue-sky backdrop, is lit up by the early afternoon sunshine. The lowlands of Somerset spread out all around with knolls rising out of the flat landscape, give a clear picture of how it must have been for the lake dwellers of past times. In my imagination, I can see Mary and Naomi, with Jesus and Joseph, making their way to Glastonbury in their dug-out canoes.

The Sacred Glastonbury Thorn on Wearyall Hill with Glastonbuty Tor beyond

This is my final visit on my amazing pilgrimage to Glastonbury. It is now, as I make my way back to Devon through Somerset, that I take a look at Dundon Hill Fort and the local St Andrew Church, followed by the St Michael Church at Othery. For Mary and Naomi, their journey from Glastonbury took them to the coast at Burnham-on-Sea and on to Wales, to meet with their Druid family at Aconbury settlement, which is documented in the Epilogue.

MY REFLECTIONS ON GLASTONBURY

I have left the Isle of Avalon with all my treasured memories close to my heart. I have been able to explore the ancient area and see places of my past, renewing connections on many levels. Uppermost in my mind is my pilgrimage to Chalice Well, my sacred Hyperborean Ceremony at Glastonbury Tor, followed by my discovery of the ancient Druidic Temple settlement, with Gog and Magog.

As I ponder my Glastonbury experience and re-read my notes, the very human frailty of self-doubt creeps in. Had I played my part as was required of me? Was what I received from a pure source? Perhaps these unusually negative feelings are now entering my frontal mind because on re-tracking I find it all so amazing. Further, this is my final Mission with Mary and I am in a foreign and rather strange personal space. I sit before my altar and light a candle for an attunement. Divine Mary offers comforting and wise words alleviating all my doubts. In turn I am moved almost to tears by the wonder of it all. I offer

Mary a blessed thank you. So here endeth my pilgrimage with the Lady Mary in the mystic South West of Britain. Next time I meet with her will be at Aconbury. I leave the final word for my beloved Mary:

BELOVED MARY

"My dear child. You have done all we have asked of you. Your Mission is complete. Rest assured that all is well. We would wish to say that further revelations will happen at Glastonbury, but these are for others to discover and share with your World. Much work has been undertaken on all levels by many in the past, and will be in the future. Your role dearest one, is as Bringer of the Ancient Light and it is good. Foundations have been laid - perhaps we might say - another layer is in place - and so it will continue through the Ages. The Temple is in place. The Ancient Wisdom will gradually filter through the ethers and penetrate into human minds and hearts. As time goes by much will be revealed in ancient Glaston.

Our journey there 2,000 years ago, was but one level of truth which was laid down and impregnated within the landscape. From this day onwards, the Light will expand to fill human hearts and understanding. The New Jerusalem IS here. In time many will hear its call and respond to it. The Light in Britain is pure and strong, and its power will be felt by many.

The seed is planted - the Star Seed of ancient times is planted in the hearts of humankind - it is planted in the landscape, and deep within the Earth's crust. The Crystal is pulsating with new energy and vigour - it is alive with Cosmic Energy. It is ready to be used by a new generation of Light Workers for the upliftment of your Planet and its people. The Crystal Energy has been since time began. It was implanted deep within the earth as your Planet was being formed How wondrous is that my dearest child.

There is much more to learn. This is the beginning of what is to be a quite miraculous New Age - the Age of the Water Bearer - and how beautifully is that represented by Chalice Well and its pure energies. The Christ Light has been regenerated - the seed planted and growth on all levels will surely happen at Glastonbury - the heart of the New Jerusalem. Amen."

CONCLUSION TO SOMERSET

I give you a review of Mary's pilgrimage in Somerset. On leaving Devonshire, the Lady Mary with Naomi, Jesus and Joseph, arrived at the foothills of Exmoor. Travelling across the high moors they reached the ancient Druidic Temple settlement of Cow Castle dedicated to the Goddess, where Mary's first Mission in Somerset was to conduct a sacred Ceremony of Light. Their next settlement was K'SH'B'H. Once again Mary's role was to enhance the Cosmic Light at the Culbone Hill settlement and prepare the Atlantean Temple in the Etheric for a future age. It was at K'SH'B'H that the Sumerian Master arrived 4,000 BC to set up a School of Learning. It was to K'SH'B'H that the boy Jesus made his first visit with his mother - Mary. He would return in adulthood to put into action the 'Flame of Caring' thus implanting His Divine Essence for the future of our planet. The Holy Family left this area by boat for Kilve on the North Somerset coast, making an inland detour to Hungerford settlement. The next section of their journey took them up to The Quantock Hills for the Trendle Ring Druidic settlement, then saw them traversing the Quantock ridge along the ancient pilgrim route to Broomfield settlement. To conclude Mary's pilgrimage in this area, she and her family crossed the watery landscape of the Somerset Levels to take rest at Dundon Hill Fort settlement before proceeding to Glastonbury. Her sacred Ceremony at Glastonbury Tor to reactivate the ancient Hyperborean Temple in the Etheric, was her final Mission in Somerset and brought to a conclusion her pilgrimage in the mystic South West of Britain.

During this section of my pilgrimage, I have tracked Mary's journey as closely as I could, bearing in mind the changing landscape since her day. I have conducted three sacred Ceremonies of Light as requested by Mary. The first was a Ceremony for the Goddess at Cow Castle. I then earthed an ancient Atlantean Temple at Culbone Hill. Finally at Glastonbury Tor, I once again earthed a Temple, this one of Hyperborian origin. Each of these Temple sites have awakened memories for me of past visits in this lifetime and remembrances of that previous incarnation, when as Naomi I travelled with Beloved Mary, Jesus and Joseph through ancient Dummonia. I have taken the opportunity to investigate historical and legendary aspects of K'SH'B'H and Glastonbury and thus these ancient places have been brought to life for me. This is the completion of my journeying with Mary in Somerset and indeed in this region of the mystic Isles of Britain.

This has been for me a wondrous pilgrimage through Somerset. I have received so much from the Lady Mary and the Divine Beings of the Light - guidance, protection, inspiration, encouragement, profound insights and the most sacred words. I close this final part of my journey with humble gratitude to all the Beloved Ones in the Land of Light.

MISSION ACCOMPLISHED

My Mission with the Lady Mary has come to an end - my pilgrimage in the South West of Britain completed. Seasons have come and gone since my first contact with my beloved Mary in the spring of 2008 - it is now the autumn of 2010 as I write these final words. I feel like a band should play or trumpets sound! Maybe this IS happening in the Heavenly World!

My journey began and ended in Wales. Our Lady initially made herself known to me at the ruined St Michael Church, Trefenty in Carmarthenshire where I first heard that sweet song, and when she spoke with me (see Prologue). It concluded with her precious words at the Aconbury Druidic settlement after I had followed her journey along the River Wye (see Epilogue). From those early beginnings, I was to gradually realize through personal insight and sacred messages, what was being asked of me. My Mission for the Light in the South West of these ancient mystic Isles of Britain was to begin. A pilgrimage which started for me at Place in the Roseland

Peninsula, where Mary, Naomi, Jesus and Joseph landed from the Holy Land, has taken me through much of ancient Cornwall, Devon and Somerset, to complete my Mission at Glastonbury - the Isle of Avalon.

And - WHAT A JOURNEY - what an remarkable voyage of discovery and wonderment - a truly magical mystery tour. I have walked the pilgrim path and the whole of my travelling has been a sacred odyssey - a Pilgrimage of Light - and for me a very personal one. I have moved through the seasons in tune with and enjoying the beauties of the natural world, respecting Mother Earth as a living breathing entity. I have had times of exhaustion and my fair share of mishaps of varying degrees! I have been through a gambit of emotions - times of self-doubt and moments of elation and pure joy - all of which you the reader, have had the 'dubious pleasure' of sharing! But this is part of any journey of significance. Whatever the circumstances I have never strayed from my path. My journeying with our blessed Lady, I have faithfully undertaken with dedication and total trust in The Divine. My mantra for this pilgrimage has been '*Not my Will but Thine Oh Lord*'. As this Mission draws to its conclusion, my cardinal expression is that of humbleness at what has come to pass. I feel privileged and blessed to have been an instrument for this beautiful soul to release her story to the World.

And so, the Mission, directed by the Masters of Light and guided by the Lady Mary, is at its end. Druidic Light Centres have been reactivated - ancient Star Temples from the Etheric Realm earthed, and Crystals laid in place. The great Cosmic Light and energetic forces have been focused at some of the major sacred centres in the South West and pierced through the Earth's crust, stimulating the Earth Star Crystal at its core. We have learnt that the Crystalline Grid is being perfected. ALL these things in preparation for the Aquarian Age.

I have played my part, though of course I am but one instrument - one link in the Chain of Light. Down the ages there have been many dedicated Servers of the Light, who have acted out their role for the advancement of the New Jerusalem within Albion - these mystic British Isles. And it will continue - there will be others who will take up the Baton of Cosmic Consciousness and walk their pilgrim journey into the Light. The sacred Rose of Love is awakening in the heart of each pilgrim of spiritual conscience and the Chalice is being filled with the purest Light Energies. The ancient Brotherhood - the Silent Watchers - are guiding each and every one of us. Our precious Planet Earth WILL move into the new Golden Age - it is decreed from the very highest point of Cosmic Life.

This book is a precious testament to my faith and belief in the presence of Beloved Mary and the Divine Beings. I honour you all. I have 'fallen-in-love' with those Beings of Light and am in humble adoration. I thank each and every one of the Masters of Light and those from the Angelic Realms, who have been my guides and protectors during my pilgrimage. I especially thank and bless my Lady of the Light - my constant companion on this sacred journey. My heart is full of the deepest purist love. You are the Rose in my Heart.

Finally, I realize that I cannot prove anything which I have offered to you in this work. What I can say is that these are MY insights - this is MY truth - this is MY journey - and this is MY story, offered from a place of Love and Divine Trust. My story has been Mary's story. I honour you beloved one - the Lady Mary - the *'Rose in the Heart'*.

EPILOGUE
Somerset to Wales - Final Journey

LEAVING SOMERSET FOR WALES

Following their pilgrimage in the South West of Britain, the Lady Mary and her daughter Naomi, went to Wales in order to meet with their Druidic family, as preparation for their return as refugees from their homeland after the crucifixion. Joseph and Jesus stayed in Glastonbury to make preparations for their own future journeying in the South West. On leaving Glastonbury Mary and Naomi travelled by boat with their Celtic guides, through the Somerset Levels to the coast of North Somerset at Burnham-on-Sea. From here they entered the mouth of the River Severn to reach the River Wye, which they followed almost all the way to Aconbury Hill settlement, their destination. All the Druidic settlements where they stayed while travelling up-river except one, were on its west bank, thereby were in Wales, as 2,000 years ago the River Wye was the natural border between Wales and England. Inland from the river and now in Herefordshire, Aconbury Hill was also once in Wales. Further - the flow of the River Wye in that era would in many places have been substantially wider. As we follow Mary's journey along the River Wye and overland to Aconbury, looking at the map we see a multitude of place names which have association with Mary and the Holy Land. In addition Druid names such as grove, ash, yew, alder, oak, raven etc. are scattered over the landscape. Now follows a brief documentation of Mary and Naomi's journey along the River Wye to Aconbury.

DRUIDIC SETTLEMENTS
Position and Place Name Associations.

1. MATHERN. Close to the mouth of the River Wye. Names: *Lady Bench, Apostles Rock, St Mary's Church - Penterry (marked on the map with a '+') and the ruined Church of St Mary at Tintern.*
2. TRELLECH. North-west of Llandogo. Names: *Hart Hill, St Ann's Well and Mary Land.*

3.   BIBLINS. North of Staunton. Names: *Jordon's Pond, Lord's Grove, May Hill, Marion Enclosure, Berry Hill, Merryweather Farm, Lady Grove, Lady Park Wood, Lord's Wood.*

4.   LORD'S GROVE. North of English Bicknor. Names: *Lord's Grove, Worrell Hill (Wearyall), Hollow Bank. Rose-mary Topping and St Mary's Church - English Bicknor.*

5.   ACONBURY HILL. North of Llanwarne. Names on the journey: *Geddes (Goddess), Rose Farm, Ross-on-Wye, Merrivale, Bridstow, Hollington, Hollymount, St Mary's Church - Hentland and Harewood End.* Names around Llanwarne: *Ark Cottages, Lady Wood, Merryvale Wood, Merryvale Farm, Star Acre Farm, The Stars and Blewhenstone (Prescilli's Blue-stone),* Names around Aconbury: *Merryvale Farm, Lady's Coppice, Apostle Wood, St Ann's Well, Kings Thorn (Joseph of Arimathea), Hollywell Farm, Ark Wood, Blue Bowl (J of A), Lady's Coppice, Merry Hill, Merryhill Farm and Apostle Wood.*

A-maz-ing!

In 2009 I made two visits to Aconbury Hill with a dear friend from Carmarthenshire on two separate weeks, one in May the other in September and what I was to discover was astonishing. In brief, I was to learn that my Welsh friend of today, was a Druidic Priestess 2,000 years ago and further more, that she was the companion and mentor of Naomi, the Priestess from the Holy Land with whom she travelled through Wales preaching! As space is at a premium, I will give you the salient sections from my original copious notes.

MY JOURNEY TO WALES SPRING 2009

As you will see Mary's story gradually unfolds. But when did I learn of Mary and Naomi's travelling to Wales? It was one evening in the cottage near Abergavenny, where my Welsh friend and I were staying on holiday in the spring of 2009. The opportunity for this break had arisen but due to my being right in the midst of my Mission with Mary in the South West, I was rather reluctant to take time out. However, I found myself involuntarily saying: *"yes"* followed by the thought that there must be a reason for this. I left it at that for the time being.   `

Now at the cottage we are pouring over maps spread out on the floor deciding on our plan for the next day, when Aconbury Hill just south of Hereford with a St Ann's Well close-by, jumps out at me. It is in this moment I know that Mary and Naomi would have met with their Druid family in Wales rather than Somerset as I had previously considered. I scrutinize the map more thoroughly and see that the River Wye goes inland all the way to Hereford and beyond, which would have made it a convenient mode of transport. Now I am looking for a possible alighting point from the river, but could come to no conclusion at the time. At a later date I discover this was at a place called Holly(Holy)mount a mile to the south of Peterstowe.

That evening in the quiet of my own bedroom Mary is with me:

MARY

"Well done little daughter. You now know why you have been allowed this little break in your journeying in Cornwall. You now know why it is here we wished you to visit. When you as Naomi travelled this way, your friend was your mentor. You will learn more of this soon. Yes - it is true - that as Naomi you travelled with me to this part of Wales, this sacred land which has always been. Time before the great upheaval which destroyed Atlantis, this land WAS. You have much to learn on your subsequent days in this area of Wales. I will guide you - I will walk with you. Hold my hand dear daughter. I will lead the way. Follow the rose and you will discern much. Bless you my child."

I thank Mary for this insight. So - the purpose for my visit and a past life link with my present day friend is revealed. This, the first of many revelations.

THE CHURCH OF ST JOHN THE BAPTIST, LLANWARNE.

On route to Aconbury the following day, we feel drawn to visit this nearby ancient ruined church, which name translates as *'The church by the alder trees'*.

The old Church of St John, Llanwerne

I am a little behind my friend as we approach the church and I can hear her saying: *"it's like walking into paradise'.* With these words expressed, somehow I know we have been together at Llanwarne in that previous life. We both, only she was unaware of her intuitive ability at the time, were conscious of the powerful energies emanating from this sacred place.

In its time St John the Baptist Church was one of the oldest seats of Christianity in Wales. It was once owned by the now ruined Llanthony Priory, which is on the old pilgrim route through the Vale of Ewyas in the Black

Mountains, which went from Hay-on-Wye to Llanfihangel Crucorney and beyond. Worship took place here at St John's from the thirteenth to the nineteenth centuries, when flooding from the nearby Gamber Brook forced its eventual abandonment in 1864 and the new Christ Church to be built on higher ground close-by. Still in evidence within the framework of the ruined church are old monuments and the carved stone entrance porch depicting ancient symbols, including a skull and cross bones, a strange head and lettering difficult to decipher. I am picking up a link with the Knights Templar who were well established in this area. Sitting on a seat within the ruins I am conscious of Mary:

MARY

"My dear child we bring you here for a purpose and that is to remember the past - to relive the past. Seek and you will find. You will always search diligently. We my child, that is you and I, walked this ancient land 2,000 years before. It was close to here we rested before the long climb to Aconbury Hill Druidic settlement. I know you and your friend will be aware of past times here. But you Naomi and she, walked this land without me at a later date. You travelled much in your adopted country dearest one, long after I was gone. Of this, also in time you will learn more. This day for you and your friend is precious, enjoy each minute and you will re-live each second. I will guide you as ever my child. Bless you."

I thank Mary for her words about the past. Another little bit of the Welsh jigsaw slots into place.

ACONBURY HILL DRUIDIC SETTLEMENT

From Llanwerne we drive north to King's Thorn, which according to legend has a tree growing in its midst from a piece of the Sacred Thorn of Glastonbury. It is said that in the early fifth century, a saint had taken a piece of the original thorn from Wearyall Hill and planted it here, hence the name of the hamlet. We begin the walk to Aconbury Hill. There is a 'W' for a well marked on the map just below the settlement, which on perusing an old map we learn is a Holy Well. After some searching we believe we discovered it in the garden of a cottage.

We enter Aconbury Woods. It is a quite magical day, with clear blue skies - the stillness hanging on the warm air. All our senses are being opened. The trees seem to be sighing with the joy of a new spring. The woodland floor is carpeted with bluebells, white stitchwort and yellow archangel. A chiffchaff is serenading us. The scent of the flowers and the sounds of the natural world combine with an awareness of the soft gentle energies abroad. The fairy folk must be working exceedingly diligently to produce such enchantment. Walking the little path up through the trees, we are whispering. At the top we enter a large circular glade surrounded by great oak trees. This is an ancient Druidic Tree Temple. This is the sacred hilltop where Mary and Naomi stayed. I have a need to be within the circle in the silence for a little while.

Unfortunately there is a group of walkers sitting on logs having their lunch right in the middle. I move to the outer edge away from the group and sit down on a large log under an oak tree. I can hear their voices coming across in low murmurings, but it is not disturbing. My friend has wondered off looking at flora and fauna - she always knows when I have a need for solitude and is very happy doing her own thing. My beloved Mary's precious words:

MARY

"My dearest child you have found our settlement on the hill at Aconbury. Rest awhile dear Naomi and tune in to your past. Bring your friend with you into your heartland. Welcome the little people."

Just a few words from Mary as I believe she realizes that these are not the ideal conditions to offer a long message. When I return to Devon I shall have a further attunement and make a conscious link with Aconbury Hill. I leave a small offering under 'my' oak tree, then rise and meet with my friend for a picnic amongst the bluebells. After this we walk to the trig point, then to the outer embankment of this old fort. From this elevation we have the most magnificent views across to the Merbach Hills, the Clee Hills and even further to Ludlow. We pass a group of woods-folk working on 'The Wye Woods Project'. They have quite a little community set up in yurts and huts, all very much in keeping with the landscape. Some are sculpting wood into beautiful objects - others cooking over an open fire.

TO ACONBURY CHURCH AND ST ANN'S WELL.

On leaving Aconbury Hill my companion and I walk the woodland paths to Aconbury Church. We go via the Violett Szabo - G.C. Trail, which leads us to a lane offering a spectacle of spring flowers; early purple orchids, red campion, vetch, bugle and celandine. We are rather disappointed to find the church is closed but we have a browse around. The Aconbury Church is all that remains of the Priory of Aconbury, which is believed to have been a place of sanctuary for a group of Carmelite nuns. We could easily picture the nuns walking to the nearby St Ann's Well for water. If we accept that Mary visited Aconbury, it becomes quite feasible that a well might have been named in honour of her mother Anna.

Going in search of the well we come to a little brook and follow it to its head several hundred yards upstream. Here there is a huge yellow tank with a blue pipe siphoning off water. There is no water within the half moon area of scrub where it would have originally emerged from the hillside. St Ann's Well is looking rather sad and forlorn. It is impossible for us to reach it because the whole area is overgrown with high brambles and the bank drops away too steeply, but at least we have found it. I leave a small posy of wild flowers before we go on our way.

ON RETURNING FROM WALES

My dearest Mary has pre-empted my planned attunement for Aconbury and decided that 1.00 am immediately on my return from Wales, is a good time for a link!:

MARY

"My beloved child. I would wish to speak to you about Naomi. Naomi travelled far and wide in her new country to bring the Gospel of Love to the people. Her companion on her journeying was the Priestess Mair - my namesake. Mair was versed in the way of Druidic worship, which had at its base the way of truth, love and perfect understanding. In those days life in Britain was dangerous. In Wales the Roman insurgence lasted to well after my passing, and any travelling and teaching had to be undertaken within the confines of such a domination. Life for these travelling Priestesses in their world was fraught with danger, and yet they were at all times protected by the great Archangel Michael and the Masters of the Light.

One thing we would wish you to know is the dedication and pure love which these two women and many other Priests and Priestess, and later the saints, gave to their calling. They were born of the spirit and as such passed their way in loving gratitude always and in thankfulness of each day. Mair and Naomi met with many learned ones on their journey as they would spend time in Druidic settlements where the teaching was profound.

There was the time when Mair and Naomi travelled to the ancient Isle of Avalon and were enfolded in the magic and sacredness of this ancient place. (Mary now talks at length of Jesus, the Christ Consciousness and the New Jerusalem of which we've heard much). She continues...*As Naomi you were one of the pure ones who spread this Gospel of the Heart and brought the way to Eternal Life, not through any outside saviour but through the saviour of the heart - of pure love. The way was hard, the pathway rocky, but dearest one you persevered against all odds. One day you will learn more of your travelling in your adopted country. I bless you my beloved child."*

These sacred words from Mary are graciously and gratefully received as a little more of the story comes to light.

MY JOURNEY TO WALES AUTUMN 2009

It is later in the year and I am enjoying another week's holiday with my Welsh companion, this time based in the Wye Valley. My intention is to visit some of the Druidic settlements where Mary and Naomi stayed as they travelled the River Wye to Aconbury Hill.

1. MATHERN SETTLEMENT.

Situated at the mouth of the River Wye - this first settlement on their journey I was unable to visit.

2. TRELLECH SETTLEMENT.

From Mathern Mary and Naomi with their guides, journeyed north along the wide winding river through present day Chepstow and Tintern to the settlement at Trellech.

On the most beautiful of autumn days, my friend and I arrive in the village of Trellech. We take a public footpath across a field to THE HAROLD STONES. As I stop before them, I know that we are at the ancient Druidic settlement where Mary and Naomi stayed. The Harold Stones are three gigantic granite menhirs in a row - what an impressive sight. They are reputed to be 3,500 years old. Resting my hands on one of the great monoliths, I am feeling strong vibrations emanating from it. Intuitively I know these ancient stones to be on a direct alignment, south to Chepstow (later finding it was Mathern settlement) and on across the Severn Estuary to Glastonbury Tor. Its northern route went through Llanwerne to Aconbury Hill. Before leaving I offer a blessing and leave a small white quartz crystal for the Druids.

The Harold Stones, Trellech

While in the area we decide to explore Trellech and its surrounds. First we follow a country lane out of the village which leads us to ST ANN'S WELL better known as The Virtuous Well. We enter a field through a little gate to find this delight. There are brightly coloured ribbons in the overhanging trees. The old well is surrounded by a low stone wall and is most beautifully preserved. I walk down the couple of steps and kneel reverently on a stone slab before the well. Peering into the gloom I see a deep round pool of crystal clear water with moss and ferns growing around its edge. Offerings are resting in tiny stone niches. I lay my own gift of a rose-pink crystal for St Ann and the

Lady Mary. We continue out explorations and come to an on-going archeological dig for the thirteenth century LOST CITY OF TRELLECH. Stuart Wilson the Excavation Director, was on site and showed us what had been unearthed - low walls and fireplaces of the old houses, plus artifacts such as medieval jugs, cooking pots and glass bottles. Further down the lane we reach the remains of the TRELLECH CROSS situated within the shelter of an enormous sycamore tree. We return to Trellech via a high track, which offers us fine views of the Offas Dyke ridge and Holy Mountain (Ysgyryd Fawr) in the Abergavenny area. Back at the village centre, we take a look at TUMP TERRET - the Castle Mound, which is a man made motte built at a time when Trellech was ruled by a Norman Lord. Our last call of the day is the ancient ST NICHOLAS CHURCH which began its life in the thirteenth century replacing a wooden structure. Entering through the massive oak door, we step into a surprisingly large Gothic-arched church, its size indicative of the importance of Trellech in Norman times. At the west end is a square granite-stone plinth topped with a sun dial, depicting the Harold Stones, St Ann's Well and Tump Terret. There are quite stunning stained glass windows including a most beautiful one of the Virgin Mary and the Christ Child. This visit brings to an end a wonderful day in Trellech.

St Ann's Well, Trellech

3. BIBLINS SETTLEMENT.

Biblins is the next place of rest for Mary and Naomi. From Llandogo near Trellech, the River Wye goes through a deep wooded gorge before it opens out around Monmouth. It now curves right through Lady Park Wood, to pass below Seven Sisters Rocks and flow under Biblins Bridge for the settlement. The Seven Sisters are the principal stars of the Pleiades in the constellation of Taurus which is ruled by Venus, Mary's planet of harmony and love. How befitting.

The next day sees us walking the river path along this route. The sun shines once more and lights up the river, which runs slow and easy along this stretch, and is enjoyed by swans and ducks, the bank offering up a display of bright pink Indian balsam. We are walking quietly in the hope that we might see a kingfisher. We reach Biblins Bridge, a structure of rope and metal hanging high-up over the water, which was built by the Forestry Commission. On a notice board it is advised that only six persons at a time cross, and no running or jumping. On the bridge now, we tread rather gingerly until we reach the safety of the far bank. In search of the settlement we enter Lord's Wood by way of a tiny path almost hidden in the undergrowth. We have just stepped into another world - a tranquil haven - we are here. Can the whispering woodland tell us of past times? Dotted amongst the trees are some huge stone formations - pale in colour. Although they do not look blue, I find myself saying to my companion that I believe there is a connection here with the Blue Stones of the Prescilli Hills in Pembrokeshire. My dedicated friend goes foraging and returns with the most beautiful piece of Blue-stone. It is wonderful how so often she is guided to discover something of importance. I am sitting quietly amongst the trees attuning to my dearest Mary:

MARY

"My beloved child. Thank you for making the pilgrimage to our ancient settlement where you and I stayed on our travelling to Aconbury. We are so happy that you Naomi, and Mair, are spending this sacred time together. I can confirm that the piece you picked up and much of what you see around you is Blue-stone from the Prescilli Hills in Pembrokeshire. The stone would be transported along the coast and up the River Wye to this settlement. It was brought in to balance the energies in this sacred place. The feminine essence was needed on this site. Bless you my Children of Light - go forth on your journeying with joy and much happiness. You have found your companion of the past dear Naomi. Welcome it. (I mentally ask if I can tell Mair any of these things and hear…) You may share if you wish beloved one."

From me: *"Bless you Mary."* I leave two small pieces of quartz crystal - white and pink to maintain the balance of the ancient energies in this sacred place. I accept Mary's words as confirmation of my intuitive thoughts regarding the Blue-stone, but something still mystifies me - that is the lack of blue in the rest of the stones in the woodland. Overtime the problem is solved, as a year later, the one piece I have, has lost its blue colour, leading me to realize that open to the elements the colour fades. Am I glad I took a photograph when on site. So where did the piece come from which was found? I suspect it was materialized from the Etheric Realm for my friend to discover, which possibility I did consider at the time.

As we continue through the wood, we both hear a commotion in the thicket and my friend sees the greyish top of an animal's back and recognizes it is a boar. It disappears rather quickly and I missed it! Back at the river we enjoy a pot of tea and piece of cake in the garden of a little cottage which doubles as a tea-room. We return to Biblins Bridge and make our way back to our car by scrambling up through the very steep Highmeadow Woods. We reflect on another quite special day.

4. LORD'S GROVE SETTLEMENT.

From Biblins the River Wye takes a circuitous route as it winds its way round the base of Symonds Yat, until it reaches a place called Lord's Grove where at a Druidic settlement a rest is taken by the two travellers from the Holy Land.

Our plan for today not even being aware of the ancient site is to take a circular walk along the River Wye to Symonds Yat. Parking at English Bicknor, we follow a path below Rosemary (Rose-Mary) Topping, which leads us to a field opening on to the river. From here we have splendid views of Coldwell Rocks, a well-known haunt for peregrines. Strolling alongside the gently flowing river is very peaceful - we are two very contented pilgrims without a care in the world, when all of a sudden: *"where are my sunglasses?"* I search bag and pockets - nothing - but KNEW I was wearing them because the sun was bright! Okay, we decide to go back and see if we can find them though I did have my doubts. We only retrace our steps a few hundred yards to a little clearing by the river, when my friend spies them in the grass under an oak tree. I stand stock still, because there is no way they could have come off! Then I voice the thought: *"okay so we've been brought back here for something - what is it?'* My intuitive friend says: *"perhaps this is where you came off the river."* She was absolutely right. I dowsed and got answers. This spot was an ancient settlement and during the journey up-river Mary and Naomi had taken rest here. For me a wake-up call, because I had gone breezily by not picking up on the ancient energies - Mary made certain I returned. A more intent look at the map tells us that we are in Lord's Grove!

The return journey sees us climbing up through the ancient Eliot Wood, which is coloured with late purple knapweed, various species of fungi and where heart-tongue ferns grace our path. We eventually reach the look-out point of Symonds Yat. A touch of vertigo prevents me hanging over the edge staring into the abyss as some folk are doing! The views from my safe distance are magnificent with much of our walk in both directions laid out within the landscape far below.

Arriving back at English Bicknor we take a look at its ST MARY CHURCH. This is a very ancient church which stands in the bailey of a Norman Castle. Inside, Norman arches run its length and one is decorated with stone sculptures of animal heads from the Herefordshire School, similar to those at the St Mary and St John Church at Kilpeck in Mommouthshire. Having explored this wonderful building, I sit quietly in a pew and receive some welcoming words from Beloved Mary. This concludes another extraordinary day, the *'piece de resistance'* being the discovery of Lord's Grove settlement of my past.

5. ACONBURY SETTLEMENT.

Mary and Naomi left the River Wye at Hollymount, to the west of Ross-on-Wye. They went by way of a little inlet off the main river, now called Crow Brook, to Peterstowe. From here they mounted horses which took them through Hentland and Llanwerne for Aconbury.

Aconbury Settlement

Our pilgrimage to Aconbury this second time around is undertaken with new knowledge and fresh insights. We begin at the large old house called HOLLYMOUNT. There is nothing else here, so I just spend a little time tuning in and visualizing us alighting from the River Wye in the vicinity. Next we drive the country lanes to Peterstow for ST PETER'S CHURCH, which is a lovely little church with a spired bell tower. In the churchyard is a very ancient hollowed yew tree. We don't stay very long here because we are eager to reach Llanwarne Church and Aconbury Settlement.

However after travelling approximately three miles along the A49, we find ourselves taking a little detour down a narrow no-through road for the

HENTLAND CHURCH OF ST DUBRICIUS. On arrival I realize we a**
destined to be here - it is later I learn that Mary and Naomi rode this wa*
What a place. The entrance to the churchyard through the lych gate is frame
by two most beautiful well established yew trees. I walk through the gate *
another very large yew and offer a blessing and small gift. I hear:

YEW TREE DEVA

"My dear pilgrim. Thank you for recognizing my presence. I have guarded th
churchyard for many a long year and have seen many changes. This day for you and yo
friend is a special day - a sacred day. You will learn much and you will be filled with gre
joy. I bless you. You may take one of my twigs for Aconbury pilgrim."

I thank the deva as I carefully break off a small piece of twig which com*
away in the shape of a Celtic cross.

This region has a fascinating history. There is evidence to suggest th*
Hentland was a thriving community as far back as the fourth and fift
centuries. The Anglo-Saxon name for this area was Archenfield, which th
Celts called 'Ergyng' meaning 'Land of the Hedgehog.' St Dubricius who w*
a legendary figure in those days took this symbol as his own. He founded
monastery at Llanfrother a couple of miles to the north of Hentland, calle
'The Church of the Brethren' to which Hentland Church was linke*
Hentland is rich in treasures. In a beautiful stained glass window, St Dubriciu
is depicted robed in blue and white, holding a staff and religious book with
hedgehog at his feet. There is Victorian stencil art, medieval wall paintings,
1920s wheeled funeral bier, a seventeenth century chest and a carved Jacobea*
chair - and so it goes on. Meticulous searching brings us to the HOLY WEL
on the east side of the church set in a little dell, alongside which is a mo*
modern stone well. I gently place a bright yellow flower head on the surface *
the water.

We now pay a return visit to the ruined ST JOHN THE BAPTIS*
CHURCH, LLANWARNE. It was in Llanwarne where Mair the Druid
Priestess met Mary and Naomi to accompany them to Aconbury. I a*
wandering once again within the sacred walls and hear: *"You are so welcome de*
pilgrims. Let the peace of this sacred place enfold you."

Finally we reach the ACONBURY SETTLEMENT. The little pat
through the woods today offers a quite a different environment with autum*
leaves falling. We become silent as we make our way to the settlement on th
hill. The grassy clearing is lit with sunshine and this time all is quiet - there a*
no people. In the centre is a young tall ash tree. I immediately walk over to
tuning into the ancient ones. In the soft earth at its base, I bury a pink and
white quartz crystal and lay a few wild flowers with my Celtic cross yew tw*
from Hentland. I pour over it all a little of the precious water from St Neot
Holy Well in Cornwall. I offer a prayer and blessing remembering my pa*
time here as Naomi: *" Beloved ones I honour you. I bless you ALL. My beloved Ma*

I'm here. I've waited a long time to return." My friend has left me for my quiet time. I sit on a log and hear:

MARY

"WE'VE waited a long time to welcome you once more to this ancient settlement. Your friend and companion Mair met with us at Llanwarne and we journeyed together to this sacred place. It was Mair who guided us to Aconbury. On your return to Wales many years later after we 'lost' our beloved Jesus, she - Mair, was to be your constant companion in your new land - your adopted country. I've told you before dear one, that you travelled far and wide throughout this ancient land and had many adventures and a few what you would today call 'scrapes'. For the going for you both was not always easy. As Druidic Priestesses teaching the ancient ways of love, peace and harmony, was not always easily accepted by the people, whose lives were simple and yet fraught with danger. The Romans were never far behind you as you travelled throughout the land, and the threat of attack was never very far away - it was REAL. BUT, you dear ones were protected from on high, and guided and protected by your Druid clanspeople. There were times when you slept under the stars and other times when shelter was made available for you. You embraced the natural landscape and were in tune with the elements of the natural world. YOU EMBRACED IT ALL.

My dearest daughter there will be more I shall tell you in due course, but for now this is enough information. Thank you - thank you dearest child for your gifts - for your offerings. The energies in this sacred place are still strong and still in tact, even following Roman occupation at later times. It is time for you to walk now. I would wish that you perambulate the ancient circle. Bless you dear one. I bless you."

I acknowledge Mary's words with a blessing. I feel that a goodly time was spent at this Druidic Temple settlement by Mary and Naomi, becoming acquainted with Mair and their Celtic family, whom I've learnt were not blood relations, all in preparation for the time some twenty years hence when they would return. I make a perambulation around the circle as requested by Mary. My companion returns from her own wanderings and together we explore the ancient site once more, finally passing the tented camp of the woods-folk. Relaxing in our cottage that evening we are very contented with our day.

FINALLY

Before I bring to a close my journeying in Wales, there are just a few final mentions.

The first - following permission by Mary at Biblins settlement that I may share with my friend a little of our past life together, the right moment arose on our final day. We were undertaking a walk from the Higher Wyndcliffe car park to Eagle Rock viewpoint, going through the surrounding countryside. We took the little field-path to the ancient St Mary's Church, Penterry and were sitting in the sun on a seat outside the church. I tell her of a time - 2,000 years ago when we were Priestesses and that our names were Naomi and Mair. I was a Priestess of the Egyptian Temples and a refugee from the Holy Land. She was a Druid Priestess from Wales. She was my companion and mentor, and we travelled Wales together teaching Celtic Christianity. This is all for now. She seemed to be quite overwhelmed with these revelations even though I had been dropping little snippets to her throughout the holiday. However, it gave explanation to her love of the countryside, lifetime wanderings along the highways and byways, and her feeling of oneness with the Welsh landscape. We sat together in silence for a long long while. My beloved Mary:

MARY

"My child. You two precious people are well blessed. Enjoy each moment - savour every experience. There will be more dear ones for you and Mair. This time together has cemented the past times indelibly - you will never part this lifetime or any - the bond is too great. You are both truly blessed. You will meet again very soon dear ones. Bless you."

I thank and bless Mary. These few words epitomize what I have been feeling.

Further - following my excursions to Wales and the revelations received, I have remembered that after my Light Ceremony for Veryan Castle, Taibu when talking of himself, said that: *'I was an Elder in Druidic Society at the time when you were in Wales as Naomi. I was your mentor and you could come to me in times of need.'* To date I have received no further information in this regard. I am therefore going to assume that he was a mentor for both Naomi and Mair - perhaps a Druid Priest of high degree.

One last thing - I am curious as to the many place names in the area linked to both Joseph of Arimathea and the Master Jesus. By way of example, for Joseph there is Worrell Hill, Kings Thorn, Blue Bowl and for Jesus, Lord's Wood, Lord's Grove, Apostles Rock, Apostle Wood. I did wonder if either had visited this area. I attuned, dowsed and received the answer 'No'. So the link has come came through the Lady Mary and possibly the saints who travelled this land centuries after her time.

LEAVING WALES FOR THE HOLY LAND

After Aconbury Mary and Naomi retraced their journey down the River Wye, out into the Severn Estuary and across to Burnham-on-Sea. Joseph with Jesus had travelled from Glastonbury to meet with them there.

I am looking at my map and wondering where they would have sailed from for their voyage home. Of course - it's obvious - they would have taken the quickest route across land to the south coast. Their pilgrimage was at an end and they would have been eager to return to their homeland. So together once more, the Lady Mary and her family travelled through Somerset by way of canoes and trackways to Lyme Bay on the Dorset coast, where I am led to believe there was an ancient trading port. A boat was waiting for them. They crossed the English Channel to Gaul, went overland to the port of Marseilles on the Mediterranean, from where they set sail for the Holy Land.

What a profound sacred pilgrimage for the Lady Mary, who on reaching the Holy Land, would have felt such joy and elation at reuniting with her family. She must now prepare for future events surrounding her beloved son. What an adventure for the two young people Jesus and Naomi, who were to continue with their Temple training. Joseph their guide must have felt a sense of quiet satisfaction at the successful completion of their pilgrimage and Mary's Mission. He would return to Britain on more than one occasion with Jesus in the future time. The Holy Family had been away from their home country for approximately eighteen months.

This amazing jigsaw is complete - well for this sacred pilgrimage anyway. But what about Naomi and Mair. Where did they travel in Wales so long ago? Where did the Lady Mary join them? Another story - another time?

Bibliography

Ashbee, Paul, *Ancient Scilly - From the first Farmers to the early Christians,* David Charles, Newton Abbot, 1974

Baigent, Michael and Leigh, Richard and Lincoln, Henry, *The Holy Blood and the Holy Grail,* Book Club Associates by arrangement with Jonathon Cape Ltd, London, 1982

Blake, William, *Jerusalem*

Caine, Mary, *The Glastonbury Zodiac,* Mary Caine, Kingston, Surrey, 1978

Celtic Prayer from The Celtic Morning Worship, St Illogan Church, The Archbishop's Council, 2000

Cooke, Grace and Ivan, *The Light in Britain,* The White Eagle Lodge Publishing Trust, Liss, Hampshire, 1983

Cooper, Diana, *The Wonder of Unicorns,* Findhorn Press, Forres, Scotland, 2009

Cooper, Diana, and Crosswell, Kathy, *Ascension through Orbs,* Findhorn Press, Forres, Scotland, 2008

Cooper, Joan D'Arcy, *Culbone - a Spiritual History,* from *Joan D'Arcy Cooper's Collected Works, Electronic World Wide Web Internet Edition,* The Neith Network Library, Exeter, 1999

Coulbeck, A.E., *Granite Stones in St Just-in-Roseland Churchyard,* J.H.Lake, Falmouth

Dowling, Jeremy, *Church Trails in Cornwall - The Padstow Area,* The North Cornwall Heritage Coast and Countryside Service

Eeles, Dr. F.C., *Culbone Church,* Williton Printers, Williton

Fox, Aileen, *Prehistoric Hill Forts in Devon,* Devon Books, Tiverton, Devon, 1996

Hammond, Vavasor, *St Just Church Leaflet,* J.H. Lake, Falmouth

Harte, Edwards, *The Story of Place. St Anthony-in-Roseland,* Oscar Blackford, London and Truro

Hayman, J.J.A, *A Brief History of Holford,* 1973

Holy Bible, The, British and Foreign Bible Society, London, 1906

Maltwood, Katherine, E, *Glastonbury's Temple of the Stars,* James Clarke and Co Ltd, Cambridge, 1982

Mayhew, Kevin, *The Prayer of St Francis,* A Devotional Card

Michell, John, *Prehistory Sites in Cornwall,* Wessex Books, Salisbury, 2003

Mildren, James, *Saints of the South West,* Bossiney Books, Bodmin, Cornwall, 1989

Miller, Gerald, *A description of The Parish Church of St Mary the Virgin, Down St. Mary',* Down St Mary PCC, 1992

Miller, Hamish and Broadhurst, Paul, *The Sun and the Serpent,* Pendragon Press, Cornwall, 1998

Pennick, Nigel, *Lost Lands and Sunken Cities,* Fortean Tomes, London, 1956

Phillips, Graham, *The Marian Conspiracy,* Pan Macmillan Ltd, London, 2000

Raphael's Astronomical Ephemeris of the Planets' Places for 2008, W. Fowlsham, Slough, Berks

Rothovius, Andrew, *Asteroid Impact,* Kitra's Krystal Kave, Google, 2004

Stella Polaris, The Journal of the White Eagle Lodge December-January 2005/6, The White Eagle Publishing Trust, Liss, Hampshire

Straffon, Cheryl, *The Earth Mysteries Guide to Bodmin Moor and North Cornwall,* Meyn Mamvro Publications, Penzance, 2000

There is Something you can do Now...Leaflet, The White Eagle Publishing Trust, Liss, Hampshire

Thomas, Charles, *Explorations of a Drowned Landscape, Archaeology and History of the Isles of Scilly,* Batsford, a division of Anova Books, London, 1985

Tudor Pole, Wellesley, *The Silent Road,* Neville Spearman, Suffolk, 1978

Watkins, Alfred, *The Old Straight Track,* Sphere Books Ltd, London, 1974

White Eagle, *White Eagle on Divine Mother - The Feminine and the Mysteries,* The White Eagle Lodge Publishing Trust, Liss, Hampshire, 2004

White Eagle, *The Way of the Sun,* The White Eagle Publishing Trust, Liss, Hampshire, 1993

White Eagle, *On Living in Harmony with the Spirit,* The White Eagle Publishing Trust, Liss, Hampshire, 2005

Williamson, George Hunt, *The Secret Places of the Lion,* Neville Spearman, London 1966

Wilson, Stuart and Prentis, Joanna, *The Essenes Children of the Light,* Ozark Mountain Publishers, Huntsville, AR 72740, USA, 2005

Wingfield, Megan, *The Grail Journey Through Wales,* Athena Press, London, 2007

Your Guide to Padstow, Padstow and District Chamber of Commerce, 2007

Visitors Guide - The Church of St Petroc, Padstow, The Parochial Church Council of Padstow, 2003

MUSIC - CDs

Edwards, Lyn and Robinson, Gay, *Cellular Alchemy,* The White Eagle Lodge, Wilomee Audio, Australia, 2003

Goldman, Jonathan *Ultimate Om,* M.M.I. Spirit Music Inc., - Ethrean Music Inc.., Boulder, CO80306, USA

O'Donnell, Daniel, *Faith and Inspiration,* Ritz Productions Ltd, Dublin and Middlesex, 2000

About the Author

Caroline Harris is a native of South Wales. She has lived in Devon for over forty years, returning to her homeland regularly, to walk in the mountains and explore the countryside. She was brought up in the Spiritualist tradition, which school of thought gave her the foundation for the future. For the greater part of her life she has been a member of the White Eagle Lodge, welcoming the gentle heart-centred philosophies of meditation, healing and attunement. She acknowledges her gift of intuitive insight, portrayed in her writing, with reverence.

Caroline honours her mother, a concert pianist and her father, an academic, both now deceased, for playing inspirational and supportive roles in her life. Today, her children and their respective spouses, with her grandchildren, are the most precious part of her life.

Among her academic achievements, Caroline has a BA (Hon), a Diploma in Applied Social Sciences and a Post Graduate Certificate in Education. She also has qualifications in Stress Management and Therapeutic Counselling, and as a contact healer with the White Eagle Lodge, is a member of the Confederation of Healing Organizations. Now retired, during her lifetime she has worked as a Secretary and has been a Familial and Professional Carer. She went on to devise her own Positive Lifestyle Programme, offering Courses and Workshops within Adult Education and for Social Services.

Life's chosen (before coming into incarnation) pathway for Caroline, has thrown up a number of challenging circumstances, testing her resolve. However, she has travelled on, embracing each part of the journey, maintaining her link with The Light and trust in The Divine